ICC A117.1-2009 STANDARD AND COMMENTARY

ACCESSIBLE AND USABLE BUILDINGS AND FACILITIES

Accessible and Usable Buildings and Facilities Commentary
(ICC A117.1-2009)

First Printing: October 2012

ISBN: 978-1-60983-408-1

T024454

PRINTED IN THE USA

AMERICAN NATIONAL STANDARD

Approval of an American National Standard requires verification by ANSI that the requirements for due process, consensus, and other criteria for approval have been met by the standards developer.

Consensus is established when, in the judgement of the ANSI Board of Standards Review, substantial agreement has been reached by directly and materially affected interests. Substantial agreement means much more than a simple majority, but not necessarily unanimity. Consensus requires that all views and objections be considered, and that a concerted effort be made toward their resolution.

The use of American National Standards is completely voluntary; their existence does not in any respect preclude anyone, whether he or she has approved the standards or not, from manufacturing, marketing, purchasing, or using products, processes, or procedures not conforming to the standards.

The American National Standards Institute does not develop standards and will in no circumstances give an interpretation of any American National Standard. Moreover, no person shall have the right or authority to issue an interpretation of an American National Standard in the name of the American National Standards Institute. Requests for interpretations should be addressed to the secretariat or sponsor whose name appears on the title page of this standard.

CAUTION NOTICE: This American National Standard may be revised or withdrawn at any time. The procedures of the American National Standards Institute require that action be taken periodically to reaffirm, revise, or withdraw this standard. Purchasers of American National Standards may receive current information on all standards by calling or writing the American National Standards Institute.

FOREWORD

[The information contained in this foreword is not part of this American National Standard (ANS) and has not been processed in accordance with ANSI's requirements for an ANS. As such, this foreword may contain material that has not been subjected to public review or a consensus process. In addition, it does not contain requirements necessary for conformance to the standard.]

Development

The 1961 edition of ANSI Standard A117.1 presented the first criteria for accessibility to be approved as an American National Standard and was the result of research conducted by the University of Illinois under a grant from the Easter Seal Research Foundation. The National Easter Seal Society and the President's Committee on Employment of People with Disabilities became members of the Secretariat, and the 1961 edition was reaffirmed in 1971.

In 1974, the U.S. Department of Housing and Urban Development joined the Secretariat and sponsored needed research, which resulted in the 1980 edition. After further revision that included a special effort to remove application criteria (scoping requirements), the 1986 edition was published and, when requested in 1987, the Council of American Building Officials (CABO) assumed the Secretariat. Central to the intent of the change in the Secretariat was the development of a standard that, when adopted as part of a building code, would be compatible with the building code and its enforcement. The 1998 edition largely achieved that goal. The 2009 edition of the standard is the latest example of the A117.1 committee's effort to continue developing a standard that is compatible with the building code. [When CABO was consolidated into the International Code Council (ICC) in 1998, the Secretariat duties were assumed by ICC.]

2009 Edition

New to the 2009 edition are coordinated criteria for the various types of dwelling units that provide a step-down between the unit types; technical requirements for Type C (Visitable) Units; Variable Message Signs (i.e., signs that change the information they show such as gate information in train stations and airports); better consistency of sign requirements regarding when raised characters and braille are required; location of toilet paper dispensers (more design options, recessed fixtures addressed, single point of measurement, etc.); a new chapter for a variety of types of recreational facilities; an index and margin markings that will help users find requirements and identify changes from the 2003 edition. In addition, the new standard continued to provide a level of coordination between the accessible provisions of this standard and the federal government accessibility requirements in the Fair Housing Accessibility Guidelines (FHAG) and the 2010 Americans with Disabilities Act (ADA) Standard for Accessible Design.

ANSI Approval

This Standard was processed and approved for submittal to ANSI by the Accredited Standards Committee A117 on Architectural Features and Site Design of Public Buildings and Residential Structures for Persons with Disabilities. ANSI approved the 2009 edition on October 20, 2010. Committee approval of the Standard does not necessarily imply that all Committee members voted for its approval.

Adoption

ICC A117.1–2009 is available for adoption and use by jurisdictions internationally. Its use within a governmental jurisdiction is intended to be accomplished through adoption by reference in accordance with proceedings establishing the jurisdiction's laws.

Formal Interpretations

Requests for Formal Interpretations on the provisions of ICC A117.1–2009 should be addressed to: ICC, Chicago District Office, 4051 W. Flossmoor Road, Country Club Hills, IL 60478–5795.

Maintenance—Submittal of Proposals

All ICC standards are revised as required by ANSI. Proposals for revising this edition are welcome. Please visit the ICC web site at www.iccsafe.org for the official "Call for proposals" announcement. A proposal form and instructions can also be downloaded from www.iccsafe.org.

ICC, its members and those participating in the development of ICC A117.1-2009 do not accept any liability resulting from compliance or noncompliance with the provisions of ICC A117.1-2009. ICC does not have the power or authority to police or enforce compliance with the contents of this standard. Only the governmental body that enacts this standard into law has such authority.

Marginal Markings

In the ICC A117.1 Standard (but not in this commentary) solid vertical lines in the margins within the body of the code indicate a technical change from the requirements of the 2003 edition. Deletion indicators in the form of an arrow (➡) are provided in the margin where an entire section, paragraph, exception or table has been deleted or an item in a list of items or a table has been deleted.

Accredited Standards Committee A117 on Architectural Features and Site Design of Public Buildings and Residential Structures for Persons with Disabilities

At the time of ANSI approval, the A117.1 Committee consisted of the following members:

Chair	Kenneth M. Schoonover, PE
Vice Chair	Vacant
A117 Committee Secretary	Jay Woodward

Organizational Member	**Representative**
Accessibility Equipment Manufacturers Association (AEMA) (**PD**)	Kevin Brinkman Robert Murphy (Alt)
American Bankers Association (ABA) (**BO**)	Virginia E. O'Neil Nessa Feddis (Alt)
American Council of the Blind (ACB) (**CU**)	Patricia Beattie Eric Bridges (Alt)
American Hotel and Lodging Association (AHLA) (**BO**)	Gerald Gross, AIA, FARA Kevin Maher (Alt)
American Institute of Architects (AIA) (**P**)	David C. Collins, FAIA Larry M. Schneider, AIA (Alt)
American Occupational Therapy Association (AOTA) (**P**)	S. Shoshana Shamberg
American Society of Interior Designers (ASID) (**P**)	Samantha McAskill, ASID Barbara J. Huelat, ASID, IIDA (Alt)
American Society of Plumbing Engineers (ASPE) (**P**)	Robert H. Evans, Jr., CIPE/CPD Julius A. Ballanco, P.E. (Alt)
American Society of Safety Engineers (ASSE) (**P**)	Dr. William Marletta John B. Schroering, P.E. C.S.P. (Alt) Mary Winkler, CSP (Alt)
American Society of Theatre Consultants (ASTC) (**P**)	Scott Crossfield, ASTC William Conner, ASTC (Alt) R. Duane Wilson, ASTC (Alt)
Association for Education & Rehabilitation of the Blind & Visually Impaired (AERBVI) (**P**)	Billie Louise "Beezy" Bentzen, PhD Helen Elias (Alt)
Brain Injury Association of America (BIAA) (**CU**)	Robert Dale Lynch, FAIA Greg Ayotte (Alt)
Builders Hardware Manufacturers Association, Inc. (BHMA) (**PD**)	Michael Tierney Richard Hudnut (Alt)
Building Owners and Managers Association International (BOMA) (**BO**)	Lawrence G. Perry, AIA Ron Burton (Alt)
Disability Rights Education and Defense Fund (DREDF) (**CU**)	Marilyn Golden Logan Hopper (Alt)
Hearing Loss Association of America (HLAA) (**CU**)	Sharon Toji Brenda Battat (Alt)
International Association of Amusement Parks and Attractions (IAAPA) (**BO**)	John Paul Scott, AIA, NCARB Stephanine See (Alt)
International Code Council (ICC) (**R**)	Kimberly Paarlberg, RA Phil Hahn, (Alt)

Organization	Representative
International Sign Association (ISA) (**PD**)	Teresa Cox Bill Dundas (Alt) Mike Santos (Alt) John Souter, PhD. (Alt)
Little People of America, Inc. (LPA) (**CU**)	Tricia Mason
Montgomery County Department of Permitting Services (MCDPS) (**R**)	Thomas Heiderer
National Association of Home Builders (NAHB) (**BO**)	Steve Orlowski Larry Brown (Alt) Don Surrena, CBO (Alt)
National Association of the Deaf (NAD) (**CU**)	Neil McDevitt Rosaline Crawford (Alt)
National Conference of States on Building Codes and Standards (NCSBCS) (**R**)	Curt Wiehle
National Electrical Manufacturers Association (NEMA) (**PD**)	Rodger Reiswig, SET Jack McNamara (Alt)
National Elevator Industry, Inc. (NEII) (**PD**)	Brian D. Black Barry Blackaby (Alt) George A. Kappenhagen (Alt)
National Fire Protection Association (NFPA) (**R**)	Allan B. Fraser Ron Coté, PE (Alt)
National Multi Housing Council (NMHC) (**BO**)	Ronald G. Nickson
New Mexico Governor's Commission on Disability (NMGCD) (**CU**)	Hope Reed Anthony H. Alarid (Alt)
Paralyzed Veterans of America (PVA) (**CU**)	Mark H. Lichter, AIA (Alt) Frank Menendez (Alt)
Plumbing Manufacturers Institute (PMI) (**PD**)	Charles Hernandez David Hagopian (Alt)
Society for Environmental Graphic Design (SEGD) (**P**)	Kenneth A. Ethridge, AIA, RIBA Craig Berger (Alt) Ann Makowski (Alt) Dave Miller (Alt)
Stairway Manufacturers Association (SMA) (**PD**)	David Cooper Paul Wishnoff (Alt)
United Cerebral Palsy Association, Inc. (UCPA) (**CU**)	Gina Hilberry Maureen Fitzgerald (Alt) Janna Starr (Alt)
United Spinal Association (**CU**)	Dominic Marinelli John Rooney (Alt)
U.S. Architectural & Transportation Barriers Compliance (Access) Board (ATBCB) (**R**)	Marsha K. Mazz Jim Pecht (Alt)
U.S. Department of Agriculture (USDA) (**R**)	William Downs Meghan Walsh (Alt)
U.S. Department of Housing and Urban Development (HUD) (**R**)	Cheryl D. Kent Louis F. Borray (Alt)
World Institute on Disability (WID) (**CU**)	Hale Zukas

Individual Members

Shahriar Amiri, CBO (**P**)
Todd Andersen, AIA (**P**)
George P. McAllister, Jr. (**P**)
Jake L. Pauls, CPE (**P**)
Ed Roether (**P**)
John P. S. Salmen, AIA (**P**)
Kenneth M. Schoonover, P.E. (**P**)

Acknowledgment

The updating of this standard over the past 6 years could only be accomplished by the hard work of not only the current committee members listed at the time of approval but also the many committee members who participated and contributed to the process over the course of development. ICC recognizes their contributions as well as those of the participants who, although not on the committee, provided valuable input during this update cycle.

INTEREST CATEGORIES

Builder/Owner/Operator (BO) – Members in this category include those in the private sector involved in the development, construction, ownership and operation of buildings or facilities; and their respective associations.

Consumer/User (CU) – Members in this category include those with disabilities, or others who require accessibility features in the built environment for access to buildings, facilities and sites; and their respective associations.

Producer/Distributor (PD) – Members in this category include those involved in manufacturing, distributing, or sales of products; and their respective associations.

Professional (P) – Members in this category include those qualified to engage in the development of the body of knowledge and policy relevant to their area of practice, such as research, testing, consulting, education, engineering or design; and their respective associations.

Regulatory (R) – Members in this category include federal agencies, representatives of regulatory agencies or organizations that promulgate or enforce codes or standards; and their respective associations.

Individual Expert (IE) (Nonvoting) – Members in this category are individual experts selected to assist the consensus body. Individual experts shall serve for a renewable term of one year and shall be subject to approval by vote of the consensus body. Individual experts shall have no vote.

Category	Number
Builder/Owner/Operator – (**BO**)	6
Consumer/User – (**CU**)	11
Professional – (**P**)	15
Producer/Distributor – (**PD**)	7
Regulatory – (**R**)	7
TOTAL	**46**

PREFACE

Purpose and Application

This standard contains technical specifications (i.e., how to) for elements that are used in creating accessible functional spaces. For example, it specifies technical requirements for making doors, routes, seating and other elements accessible. These accessible elements are used for designing accessible functional spaces such as classrooms, hotel rooms, lobbies or offices.

This standard does not include scoping criteria (i.e., what, where and how many). Scoping provisions are contained in laws, ordinances or model building codes that reference this standard. This standard is for adoption by government agencies and by organizations setting model codes to achieve uniformity in the technical design criteria in building codes and other regulations. This standard is also used by nongovernmental entities as technical design guidelines or requirements to make buildings and facilities accessible to and usable by persons with physical disabilities.

Provisions of this standard are suitable for:

– the design and construction of new buildings and facilities, including both spaces and elements, site improvements and public walks.

– remodeling, alteration and rehabilitation of existing construction.

– permanent, temporary and emergency conditions.

Criteria are established for individual building spaces and elements. The intention is that these accessible spaces and elements combine to provide accessibility throughout a building and related site facilities. General criteria, such as the minimum width of an accessible route, can apply to different building or site elements, including sidewalks, corridors and aisles between library stacks. Other criteria are for specific elements such as drinking fountains, water closets, sinks and lavatories.

The principal purpose of the commentary is to provide a basic volume of knowledge and facts relating to building construction as it pertains to the regulations set forth in the ICC A117.1.

In the chapters that follow, discussions focus on the full meaning and implications of the text. Guildelines suggest the most effective method of application, and the consequences of not adhering to the text. Illustrations are provided to aid understanding; they do not necessarily illustrate the only methods of achieving compliance.

The format of the commentary includes the full text of each section, table and figure in the standard, followed immediately by the commentary applicable to that text. At the time of printing, the commentary reflects the most up-to-date text of the 2009 ICC A117.1. Each section's narrative includes a statement of its objective and intent and usually includes a discussion about why the requirement commands the conditions set forth. Standard text and commentary text are easily distinguished from each other. All standard text is shown as it appears in the ICC A117.1 and all commentary is indented below the code text with the symbol ❖.

Readers should note that the commentary is to be used in conjunction with the ICC A117.1 and not as a substitute for the standard. The commentary is advisory only; the code official alone possesses the authority and responsibility for interpreting the code and referenced standards.

Comments and recommendations are encouraged, for through your input, we can improve future editions. Please direct your comments to the Codes and Standards Development Department at the Chicago District Office.

Recommendations to Adopting Authorities

Administration

This standard does not establish which occupancy or building types are covered and the extent to which each type is covered. Such requirements for application of this standard must be specified by the adopting authority, including which and how many functional spaces and elements are to be made accessible within each building type.

The standard does not establish which or how many buildings, facilities and spaces or elements within these spaces must be made accessible. This standard correlates with the adoption of scoping provisions by the administrative authority. This is typically accomplished through the adoption of a model building code which references this standard. The adopted scoping provisions will establish where accessibility is required, and this standard will establish how those required elements and spaces are to be made accessible. A set of recommended scoping provisions was developed by the Board for the Coordination of the Model Codes of the Council of American Building Officials, and is reflected in the current editions of the model building codes. The International Code Council (ICC) continues developing requirements through their public hearings and code development process.

By adopting this standard through the building code, enforcement can be accomplished at the state or local level. In contrast, the requirements of Titles II and III of the Americans with Disabilities Act (ADA) can be enforced only as a civil rights statute by the United States Department of Justice. Although many provisions in this standard are comparable to parallel requirements contained in the 2010 Americans with Disabilities Act (ADA) Standard for Accessible Design, compliance with the ADA should be verified independently.

The ICC A117.1 1998 and 2003 editions have been designated by the department of Housing and Urban Development (HUD) as 'safe harbor' documents for compliance with the technical provisions of the Fair Housing Act (FHA). However, scoping provisions for how many units must comply are contained in the FHA or the *International Building Code* (IBC®) 2003 or 2006 editions. The 2009 ICC A117.1 and the 2009 and 2012 IBC are currently under review by HUD.

Number of Spaces and Elements

The administrative authority adopting this standard must specify the actual number of spaces and elements—or establish procedures for determining them—based on, but not limited to:

- population to be served.
- availability to occupants, employees, customers and visitors.
- distances and time required to use the accessible elements.
- provision of equal opportunity and treatment under the law.

The need for accessible spaces and elements can vary widely. For example, the number of parking spaces for some medical facilities may be significantly greater than for most commercial office buildings.

Remodeling

The specifications in this standard are based on the functional requirements of persons with physical disabilities. The administrative authority adopting this standard must specify the extent to which it is to cover remodeling, alteration or rehabilitation within its jurisdiction.

The administrative authority specifies the extent to which this standard applies to existing buildings, including buildings of historic significance. Accessibility in historic buildings and facilities that must be made accessible and usable by persons with disabilities should be accomplished in a manner that maintains the significant historic fabric and historic aspects of such buildings and facilities.

Historic aspects are the particular features of the historic site, building or facility that give it its historic significance. These may include historic background, noteworthy architecture, unique design, works of art, memorabilia and artifacts. Historic fabric consists of the original materials and portions of the building intact when exposed, or as they appeared and were used in the past. Historic buildings are buildings and facilities that are eligible for listing or are listed in the National Register of Historic Places, or such properties designated as historic under a statute of the appropriate state or local government body.

If the historic fabric or historic aspects are threatened or destroyed by strict compliance with the provisions of this standard, reasonably equivalent access and use may be accomplished by using these concepts. Reasonably equivalent access and use means that the entry to, and use of, a building or facility by persons with disabilities is achieved with standards or measures which are individually tailored to the historic building or facility.

Should the above still be deemed to destroy the historic fabric or historic aspect, additional consideration may be given to the following:

1. Deviations should be on an item-by-item or case-by-case basis.
2. Interpretive exhibits and/or equal services of significant historic aspects which do not comply with this standard are provided for the public in a location fully accessible to and usable by persons with disabilities, including people with hearing and sight impairments.
3. Services are provided in an accessible location equal to those services provided in the locations that do not comply with this standard.
4. The owner/designer has submitted written documentation stating the reasons for the consequent exemption. Such statements should include the opinions and/or comments of a representative local group of persons with disabilities and should be submitted to the administrative authority for approval.

Review Procedures

To promote effective compliance with the requirements of this standard, the administrative authority adopting it should establish a review and approval procedure for construction projects that come under its jurisdiction.

Where this standard is adopted by the administrative authority, a construction project that must comply with these provisions should be reviewed for compliance in the same manner the project is reviewed to determine compliance with other provisions of the building code.

Contents

List of Figures

Chapter 1. Application and Administration

❖ Chapter 1 provides for the general application of this document.

- Section 101 establishes the purpose of the standard.
- Section 102 establishes the basis for the technical requirements.
- Section 103 allows for alternative compliance.
- Section 104 establishes conventions used for the requirements.
- Section 105 provides a list of referenced standards.
- Section 106 includes definitions for the purpose of this document.

101 Purpose

The technical criteria in Chapters 3 through 9, Sections 1002, 1003 and 1006 and Chapter 11 of this standard make sites, facilities, buildings and elements accessible to and usable by people with such physical disabilities as the inability to walk, difficulty walking, reliance on walking aids, blindness and visual impairment, deafness and hearing impairment, incoordination, reaching and manipulation disabilities, lack of stamina, difficulty interpreting and reacting to sensory information, and extremes of physical size. The intent of these sections is to allow a person with a physical disability to independently get to, enter, and use a site, facility, building, or element.

Section 1004 of this standard provides criteria for Type B units. These criteria are intended to be consistent with the intent of the criteria of the U.S. Department of Housing and Urban Development (HUD) *Fair Housing Accessibility Guidelines*. The Type B units are intended to supplement, not replace, Accessible units or Type A units as specified in this standard.

Section 1005 of this standard provides criteria for minimal accessibility features for one and two family dwelling units and townhouses which are not covered by the U.S. Department of Housing and Urban Development (HUD) *Fair Housing Accessibility Guidelines*.

This standard is intended for adoption by government agencies and by organizations setting model codes to achieve uniformity in the technical design criteria in building codes and other regulations.

❖ Independence for persons with physical and sensory disabilities is a primary goal of this standard. It is essential that accessibility into and throughout buildings and facilities be part of the initial design process. ICC A117.1 provides details, dimensions and specifications to help building designers develop their plans so that the facility will offer unobstructed entry and ease of use to all users with disabilities.

The technical specifications in this standard are intended to create elements and spaces that can be used independently by persons with disabilities. The requirements are based on anthropometrics for an average adult male, and may not be appropriate for all applications (see commentary, Section 102).

The intent is to serve as wide a spectrum of persons with disabilities as possible, based on currently available knowledge and experience. Because needs and capabilities vary from individual to individual, it is not possible to set technical criteria that would permit independent use by all persons with disabilities. For example, not everyone is able to transfer from a wheelchair to a water closet, even though the clearances necessary for such a transfer satisfy this standard. Criteria contained in the standard are based on the best information and research available to the A117.1 Standard Review Committee during the process of review and update. The committee welcomes results of recent research from all interested and affected parties.

For dwelling units and sleeping units, the Standard provides four distinct sets of criteria: Accessible units, Type A units, Type B units and Type C units. The requirements in Section 1004 for Type B dwelling units and sleeping units are technical criteria that are consistent with the requirements of the Fair Housing Act. For additional information, see the commentary to Chapter 10.

Understanding and consistency in the application of the criteria throughout the country would be of immeasurable value to the person with a disability, as well as building regulators, designers and owners, and the community in general. Consistency would result in a greater level of comfort for a person with a disability in his or her daily activities. A person with a disability would know what to expect within a facility instead of finding new obstacles to overcome in each situation. There are many accessibility features that benefit not only people with disabilities, but also are a tangible benefit to people without disabilities.

101.1 Applicability. Sites, facilities, buildings, and elements required to be accessible shall comply with the applicable provisions of Chapters 3 through 9 and Chapter 11. Dwelling units and sleeping units shall comply with the applicable provisions of Chapter 10.

❖ Criteria are established for individual building spaces and elements. These accessible spaces and elements are intended to combine to provide accessibility throughout a building and related site facilities. General criteria, such as the minimum width of an accessible route, can apply to different building or site elements, including sidewalks, corridors and aisles. Other criteria are provided for specific elements such as drinking fountains, water closets, sinks and lavatories.

Specifics are provided for Accessible, Type A, Type B and Type C dwelling units and sleeping units in Chapter 10.

102 Anthropometric Provisions

The technical criteria in this standard are based on adult dimensions and anthropometrics. This standard also contains technical criteria based on children's dimensions and anthropometrics for drinking fountains, water closets, toilet compartments, lavatories and sinks, dining surfaces, work surfaces and benches.

❖ Anthropometrics for an adult male who uses a wheelchair provided the technical basis for many of the requirements. For example, the 27-inch (686 mm) height for knees is used for the building block for the knee clearances, which in turn is referenced for the heights for drinking fountains, working surfaces and dining surfaces [see Commentary Figure C102(a)]. At this time, criteria for scooters have not been incorporated into the standard. The A117.1 Standard Review Committee is reviewing research on this subject for possible inclusion in the future.

Adult dimensions do not always work for children. Unique criteria for children have been provided for the listed elements. Designing for children is a choice, but once that choice has been made, the requirements for the element must be followed. For example, if a child-sized bathroom is desired, all criteria for the child-sized toilet, sink and grab bar must be followed. (See the commentary for the specific items listed for additional child-sized information.)

There are three basic types of devices that typically use the "wheelchair" spaces:

Manual chair: The manual chair category considers all wheelchair devices not powered by a motor. Attendant-driven devices (those wheelchairs that do not have a hand-held drive wheel) are also included in this category because they do not have a motor. The manual chair category spans the gamut from standard hospital chairs to lightweight sports chairs [see Commentary Figure C102(b)].

Power chair: This category includes motor-driven chairs that do not fall into the category of scooters. Power chairs are controlled primarily by a joystick and can use front, mid or rear drive wheels. Many power chairs come with therapeutic features such as the tilt-in-space feature that allows the owner to relieve pressure. Additionally, chairs in this category also use body positioning technology (such as head rests, pummels, and adductor/abductor pads) that help keep one's body aligned [see Commentary Figure C102(b)].

Scooter: This category is also motor-driven. The controls are typically on a tiller placed anterior to the individual. Overall, scooters tend to be the largest and take up the most space. Maneuvering a scooter can be difficult because of the tiller steering system (which allows for generally larger turning radii) [see Commentary Figure C102(b)].

103 Compliance Alternatives

Nothing in this standard is intended to prevent the use of designs, products, or technologies as alternatives to those prescribed by this standard, provided they result in equivalent or greater accessibility and such equivalency is approved by the administrative authority adopting this standard.

❖ The requirements in this standard are not intended to inhibit innovative ideas or technological advances. A comprehensive regulatory document cannot envision and then address all future innovations in the industry. The fact that a material, product or method of construction is not addressed is not an indication that prohibition of the material, product or method is intended. The building official is expected to apply sound technical judgment in accepting materials, systems or methods that, although not anticipated by the drafters of the current text, can be demonstrated to offer equivalent performance. The responsibility for providing information for demonstrating equivalent facilitation lies with the designer or contractor who is working with the code official.

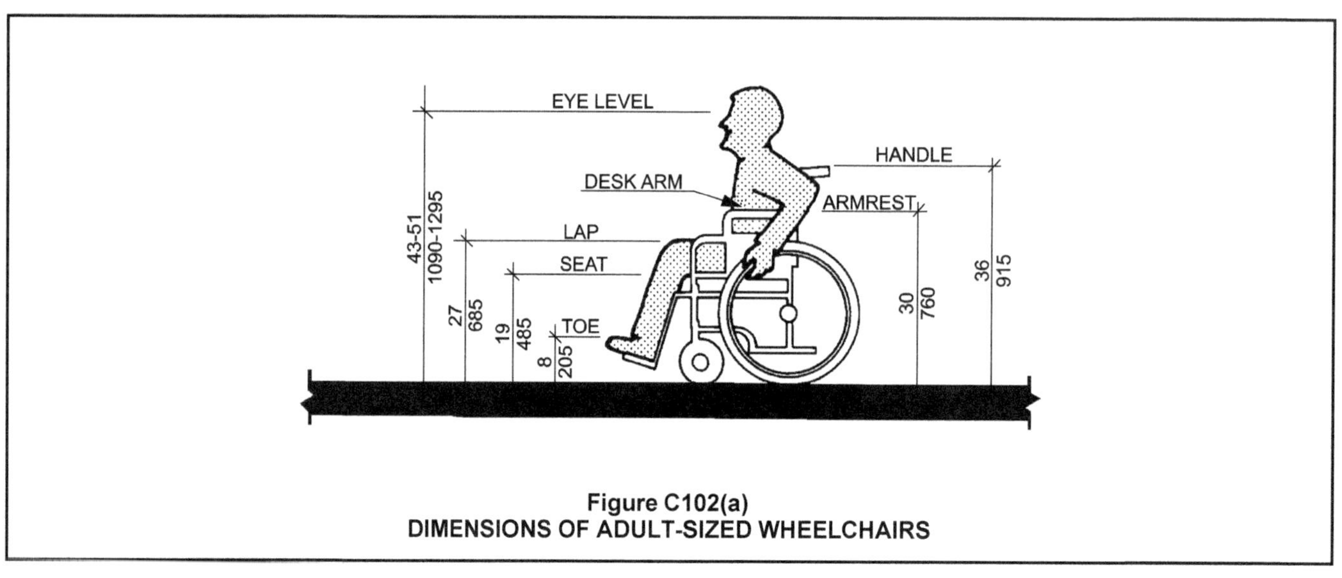

Figure C102(a)
DIMENSIONS OF ADULT-SIZED WHEELCHAIRS

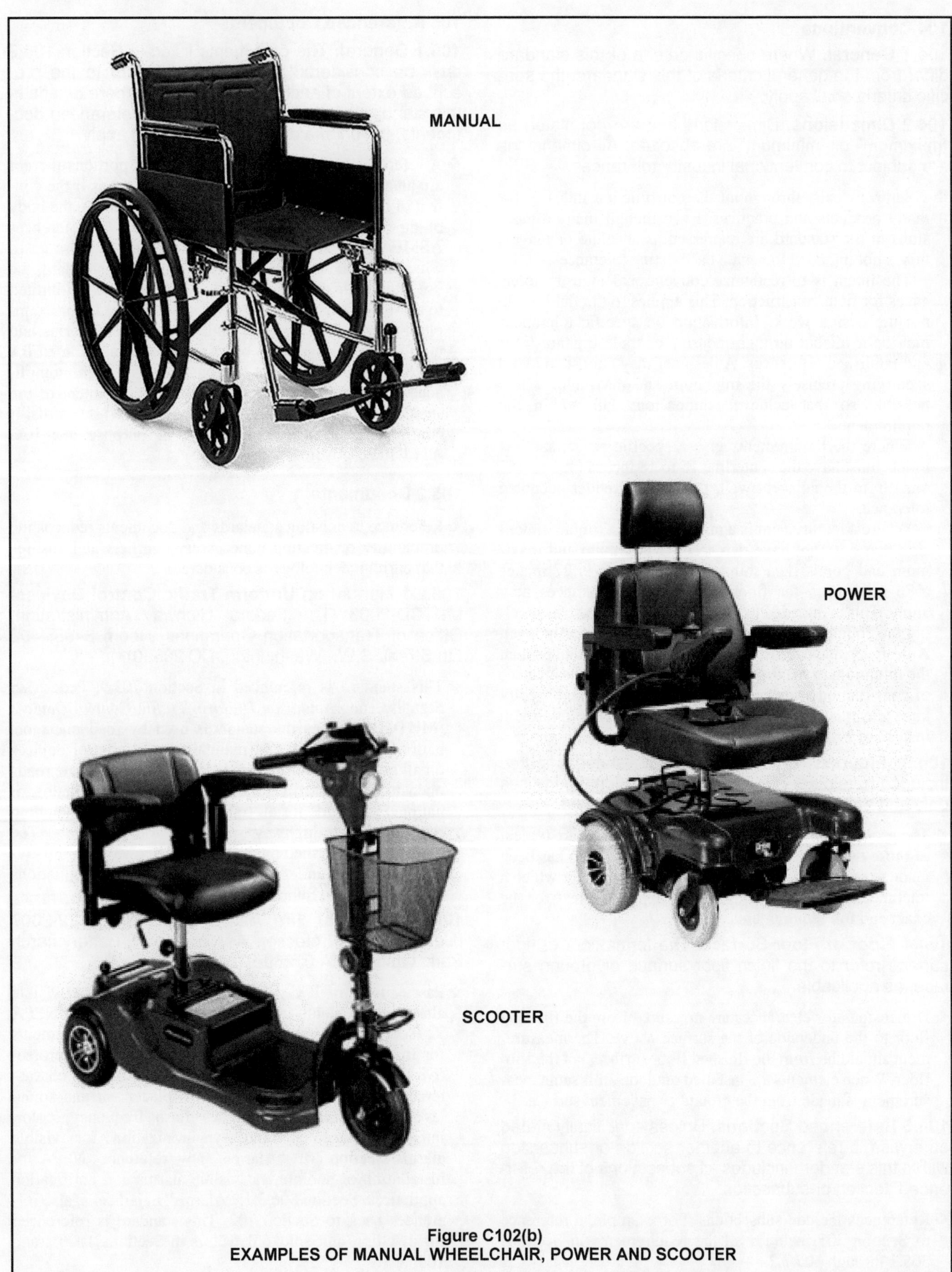

Figure C102(b)
EXAMPLES OF MANUAL WHEELCHAIR, POWER AND SCOOTER

104 Conventions

104.1 General. Where specific criteria of this standard differ from the general criteria of this standard, the specific criteria shall apply.

104.2 Dimensions. Dimensions that are not stated as "maximum" or "minimum" are absolute. All dimensions are subject to conventional industry tolerances.

❖ Tolerances exist throughout the construction industry for many products and practices. Even though many dimensions in the standard are expressed as absolute or ranges, this is not intended to negate the existing tolerances.

The intent is to recognize conventional industry tolerances for field construction. This applies to the field work, not the design work. Information on specific tolerances may be available through industry or trade organizations and published references. A designer may choose to avoid specifying precisely the minimum and maximum where possible so that achieved dimensions fall within the requirements.

Where the requirements give a specific range, such as toilets must have the centerline 16 to 18 inches (406 to 457 mm) from the adjacent wall, the range provides adequate tolerance.

Where a requirement is a minimum or maximum dimension that does not have two specific minimum and maximum end points [i.e., minimum knee space is 27 inches (686 mm) from the floor], construction tolerances may apply. This is intended to allow for situations such as leveling the counter where the floor may not be perfectly level. A designer may choose to specify a different number than the minimum or maximum in order to decrease the chances of construction tolerances becoming an issue [i.e., specify knee clearance under a counter at 28 inches minimum instead of 27 inches (686 mm)].

104.3 Figures. Unless specifically stated, figures included herein are provided for informational purposes only and are not considered part of the standard.

❖ The graphic conventions shown in Figure 104.3 are typical of those used in construction drawings. An effort has been made to consistently set forth those dimensions for which a tolerance has been set. Review the applicable text for the exact and full requirements.

104.4 Floor or Floor Surface. The terms floor or floor surface refer to the finish floor surface or ground surface, as applicable.

❖ Dimensions for clearances are measured from the finished floor to the underside of the surface above. The measurement should be from the finished floor surface, not the subfloor. When elements are installed outdoors, this same measurement is made from the ground or pavement surface.

104.5 Referenced Sections. Unless specifically stated otherwise, a reference to another section or subsection within this standard includes all subsections of the referenced section or subsection.

❖ References include subsections. For example, a reference to Section 305 includes all the requirements in Sections 305.1 through 305.7.2.

105 Referenced Documents

105.1 General. The documents listed in Section 105.2 shall be considered part of this standard to the prescribed extent of each such reference. Where criteria in this standard differ from those of these referenced documents, the criteria of this standard shall apply.

❖ A referenced standard and documents or portions thereof are an enforceable extension of this standard as if the content of the standard or document were included in the body of this standard. For example, Section 407.1 references ASME A17.1 in its entirety for elevators. In those cases where the code references only portions of a standard, the use and application of the referenced standard are limited to those portions that are specifically identified. For example, Section 702.1 requires audible and visual alarms and notification appliances to be installed as required in NFPA 72. Section 702.1 cannot be construed to require compliance with NFPA 72 in its entirety. It is the intent of the standard to be in harmony with the referenced standards. If conflicts occur because of scope or purpose, the ICC A117.1 text governs.

105.2 Documents.

❖ Reference to existing standards and documents reduces the probability of creating unnecessary conflicts and ensures that current technology is considered.

105.2.1 Manual on Uniform Traffic Control Devices. MUTCD-2003 (The Federal Highway Administration, Office of Transportation Operations, Room 3408, 400 7th Street, S.W., Washington, DC 20590).

❖ This standard is referenced in Section 703.9, Pedestrian Signals. The *Manual on Uniform Traffic Control Devices* (MUTCD) defines the standards used by road managers nationwide to install and maintain traffic control devices on all public streets, highways, bikeways and private roads open to public traffic. The MUTCD is a compilation of national standards for all traffic control devices, including road markings, highway signs and traffic signals. The MUTCD is published by the Federal Highway Administration (FHWA) under 23 Code of Federal Regulations (CFR), Part 655, Subpart F.

105.2.2 National Fire Alarm Code. NFPA 72-2007 (National Fire Protection Association, 1 Batterymarch Park, Quincy, MA 02269-9101).

❖ Past editions of ICC A117.1 included audible and visible alarm requirements intended to be consistent with NFPA 72 (see Section 702). This standard includes requirements for installation, performance and maintenance of protective signaling systems. The standard specifies the characteristics of audible alarms, such as placement and sound levels. The standard addresses flash frequency, color, intensity, placement and synchronization for visible alarms. Section 702, "Alarms," now references NFPA for installation of audible and visible alarms and notification appliances. Section 806.3.1, "Alarms" in jail cells, also references back to Section 702. This standard is referenced for dwelling unit smoke detectors in Sections 1006.2 and 1006.4.1.

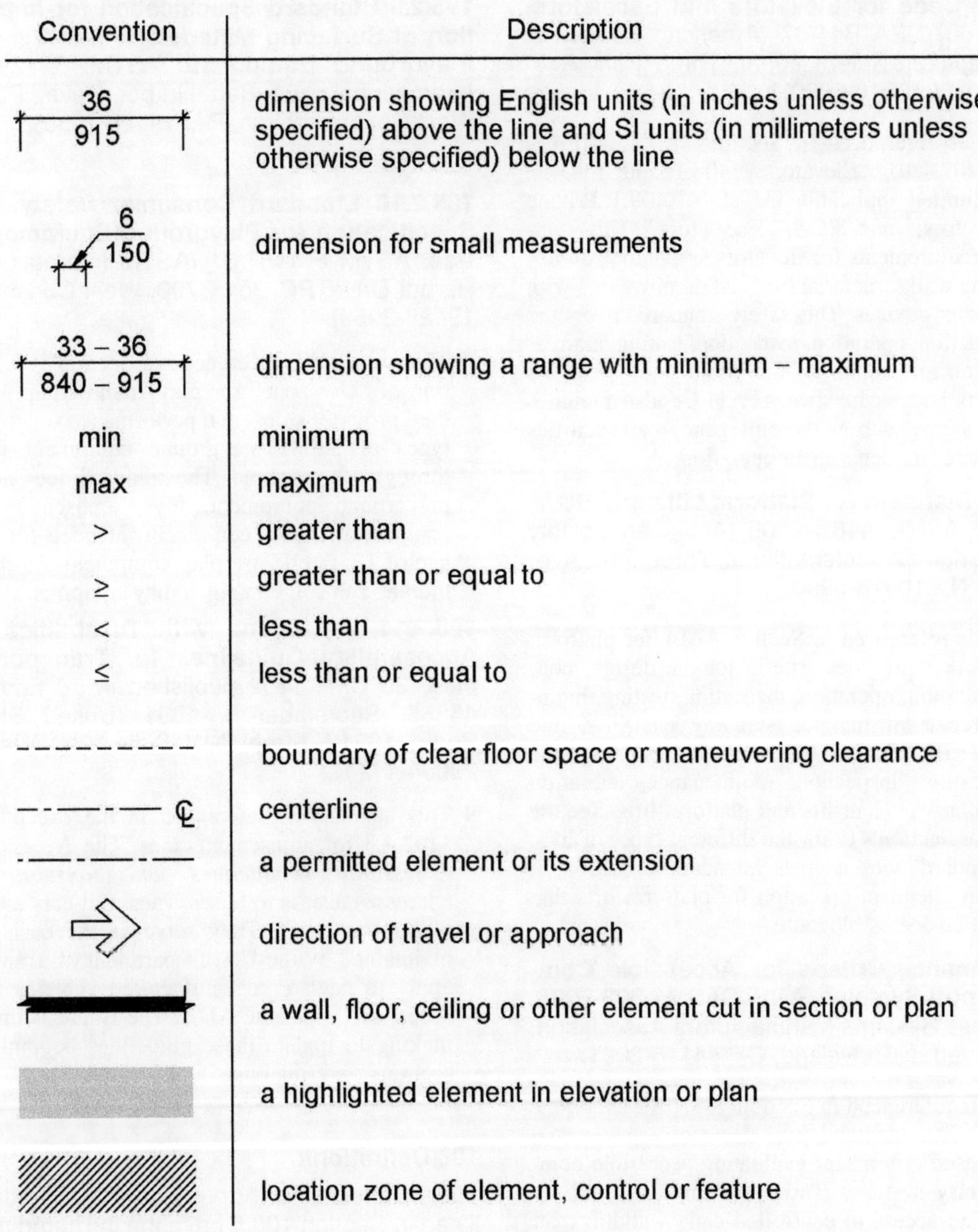

FIGURE 104.3
GRAPHIC CONVENTION FOR FIGURES

105.2.3 Power Assist and Low Energy Power Operated Doors. ANSI/BHMA A156.19-2007. (Builders Hardware Manufacturers' Association, 355 Lexington Avenue, 15th Floor, New York, NY 10017).

❖ This standard is referenced in Sections 404.3 for automatic doors, 408.3.2.1 for doors on limited-use/limited-application elevators and 409.3.1 for doors on private residence elevators. The scope of this standard is for power assist doors, low energy power-operated doors or low energy power open doors for pedestrian use and some small vehicular use. Provisions intended to reduce the chance of user injury or entrapment are included.

105.2.4 Power Operated Pedestrian Doors. ANSI/BHMA A156.10-2005 (Builders Hardware Manufacturers' Association, 355 Lexington Avenue, 15th Floor, New York, NY 10017).

❖ This standard is referenced in Section 404.3, "Automatic doors." Requirements in this standard apply to power-operated doors for pedestrian use, which open automatically when approached by pedestrians or by a knowing act (i.e., such as push panel operation). Provisions to reduce the chance of user injury or entrapment are included. Power-operated doors for industrial or trained traffic are not covered in this standard.

105.2.5 Safety Code for Elevators and Escalators. ASME A17.1-2007/CSA B44-07 (American Society of Mechanical Engineers International, Three Park Avenue, New York, NY 10016-5990).

❖ This standard is referenced in Sections 407.1, 407.4.3, 407.4.5 and 407.4.10, "Elevators;" 408.1 and 408.4.3, "Limited-use/limited-application elevators;" 409.1, Private residence elevators;" and 805.9, "Escalators." This standard includes requirements for elevators, escalators, dumbwaiters, moving walks, material lifts and dumbwaiters with automatic transfer devices. This safety standard covers the design, construction, operation, inspection, testing, maintenance, alteration and repair of the listed equipment, its associated parts and its hoistways. A117.1 also includes provisions for items such as the emergency call facilities for occupants and fire department operation.

105.2.6 Safety Standard for Platform Lifts and Stairway Chairlifts. ASME A18.1-2005 (American Society of Mechanical Engineers International, Three Park Avenue, New York, NY 10016-5990).

❖ This standard is referenced in Section 410.1 for platform lifts. ASME A18.1 provides criteria for the design, construction, installation, operation, inspection, testing, maintenance and repair of inclined stairway chairlifts, and inclined and vertical platform lifts. Regulations govern the installation, testing, inspection, maintenance, alteration and repair of stairway chairlifts and platform lifts. See the commentary for Section 410 for the different types of lifts. While the standard does address attendant operation, it does not permit attendant operation for platform lifts that serve as part of an accessible route.

105.2.7 Performance Criteria for Accessible Communications Entry Systems. ANSI/DASMA 303-2006. (Door and Access Systems Manufacturers Association, 1300 Sumner Avenue, Cleveland, OH 44115-2851).

❖ This standard is referenced in Section 708.4 for telephone entry systems. This standard provides requirements and performance-based criteria for evaluating accessible communications entry systems. These systems are used for public pedestrian access to controlled entry buildings for intercom or assistance purposes. This standard is not intended to cover communications entry systems generally used for emergency access.

105.2.8 Standard Specification for Impact Attenuation of Surface Systems Under and Around Playground Equipment. ASTM F 1292-99. (ASTM International, 100 Barr Harbor Drive, PO Box C700, West Conshohocken, PA, 19428-2959).

❖ This standard is referenced in Section 1108.4.1.6.2 for ground surfaces under playground equipment. This standard specifies impact performance requirements for surfaces and provides a means of determining impact performance. This standard is referenced inside a play area use zone where a fall attenuation surcease is required in the same areas where an accessible route is required. Either the 1999 or 2004 edition of the standard can be used.

105.2.9 Standard Specification for Impact Attenuation of Surfacing Materials Within the Use Zone of Playground Equipment. ASTM F 1292-04 (ASTM International, 100 Barr Harbor Drive, PO Box C700, West Conshohocken, PA, 19428-2959).

❖ See Section 105.2.8.

105.2.10 Standard Consumer Safety Performance Specification for Playground Equipment for Public Use. ASTM F 1487-01 (ASTM International, 100 Barr Harbor Drive, PO Box C700, West Conshohocken, PA, 19428-2959).

❖ This standard is referenced in Section 106.5 in the definition of "Use zone" for playground equipment. This standard provides safety and performance standards for various types of public playground equipment for children 2 through 12 years old. The standard does not cover home playground equipment, toys, amusement rides, sports equipment, fitness equipment intended for users over the age of 12, public use play equipment for children 6 to 24 months and soft contained play equipment.

105.2.11 Americans with Disabilities Act (ADA) Accessibility Guidelines for Transportation Vehicles. 36 CFR 1192 published in 56 Federal Register 45558, September 6, 1991 (United States Access Board, 1331 F Street, NW, Suite 1000, Washington, DC 20004-1111).

❖ This standard is referenced in the exception to Section 1102.4.3 for amusement rides. The Access Board's *ADA Accessibility Guidelines for Transportation Vehicles* addresses access to buses, vans, rail cars and other modes of public transit. They serve as the basis for standards maintained by the U.S. Department of Transportation that apply to new or remanufactured vehicles required to be accessible under the ADA. The Board is undertaking rule making to update these guidelines beginning with those sections covering buses and vans.

106 Definitions

106.1 General. For the purpose of this standard, the terms listed in Section 106.5 have the indicated meaning.

❖ Terms that may have a specific meaning when used in the context of this standard are defined in Section 106.5.

106.2 Terms Defined in Referenced Documents. Terms specifically defined in a referenced document, and not defined in this section, shall have the specified meaning from the referenced document.

❖ Words and terms defined in the referenced documents in Section 105.2 are applicable for this standard unless defined otherwise in Section 106.5.

106.3 Undefined Terms. The meaning of terms not specifically defined in this standard or in a referenced document shall be as defined by collegiate dictionaries in the sense that the context implies.

❖ Words or terms not defined in ICC A117.1 are intended to be applied based on their "ordinarily accepted meanings."

The intent is that a dictionary definition may suffice if it is in context. Oftentimes, terms used throughout the standard are not specifically defined in the standard or even in a dictionary. In such a case, the definitions contained in the referenced standards (see Section 105.2) and published textbooks on the subject in question are good resources.

106.4 Interchangeability. Words, terms, and phrases used in the singular include the plural, and those used in the plural include the singular.

❖ Although the definitions contained or referenced in Section 106 are to be taken literally, gender and tense are interchangeable.

106.5 Defined Terms.

❖ Terms defined in the standard are listed alphabetically in Section 106.5. Standards, by their very nature, are technical documents. Literally every word, term and punctuation mark can add to or change the meaning or the intended result. These terms often have multiple meanings depending on the context or discipline being used at the time. For these reasons, a consensus on the specific meaning of terms contained in the standard must be maintained. Section 106.5 performs this function by stating clearly what specific terms mean for the purpose of this standard.

accessible: Describes a site, building, facility, or portion thereof that complies with this standard.

❖ This general definition states that compliance with this standard will result in accessibility for the built environment. The definition does not attempt to prescribe any criteria for an accessible element. This is accomplished through the various requirements within the standard. (Refer to Section 1002 for requirements for Accessible dwelling and sleeping units.)

administrative authority: A jurisdictional body that adopts or enforces regulations and standards for the design, construction, or operation of buildings and facilities.

❖ Building codes are typically adopted at the state or local level. A city or county building department or a state building commission are examples of an administrative authority with code enforcement responsibility.

amusement attraction: Any facility, or portion of a facility, located within an amusement park or theme park which provides amusement without the use of an amusement device. Amusement attractions include, but are not limited to, fun houses, barrels, and other attractions without seats.

❖ Amusement attractions are facilities in amusement parks that do not include some type of cab, car or other type of seat. Examples of attractions with amusement devices would be ferris wheels, merry-go-rounds or go-carts. An amusement attraction can be a portion of an attraction, such as the preshow area before a ride (see Section 1102).

amusement ride: A system that moves persons through a fixed course within a defined area for the purpose of amusement.

❖ An amusement ride has some type of seat or device that moves a person, typically by pairs or groups, through a set course, most typically along some type of track system. Examples of amusement rides would be ferris wheels, roller coasters, boat/tube rides or rides on rails. The definition does not include rides that do not have a fixed course, such as a bumper car. The amusement ride can either have a riding position that allows the person using a wheelchair onto the ride while in the wheelchair, or the person can transfer into an amusement ride seat (see Section 1102).

amusement ride seat: A seat that is built-in or mechanically fastened to an amusement ride intended to be occupied by one or more passengers.

❖ Amusement rides have a variety of riding positions, from nearly prone to full standing. Where seats are used, they may be for an individual (like a bucket seat) or for a group (like a bench seat) (see Section 1102).

area of sport activity: That portion of a room or space where the play or practice of a sport occurs.

❖ Examples of sport activity areas are: playing fields, gymnasiums, swimming pools, ice/roller rinks, bowling alleys, racket courts, running/biking/vehicle tracks, teeing/shooting positions, ski slopes, riding arenas, exercise/training areas, climbing walls, etc. While the area of sports activity typically includes the playing surface, it can include surrounding areas that may still be in the field of play. An example would be the sidelines area and end zones of a football field (see Commentary Figure C1101.2.2).

boarding pier: A portion of a pier where a boat is temporarily secured for the purpose of embarking or disembarking.

❖ A boarding pier is a boat boarding location that does not require a person to enter the water. Piers are typically constructed over water, thus allowing someone to move along the pier to access their boat (see Section 1103).

boat launch ramp: A sloped surface designed for launching and retrieving trailered boats and other water craft to and from a body of water.

❖ These ramps are intended primarily for vehicles that allow a person to take their boat into and out of the water [see Section 1103 and Commentary Figure C106(a)].

boat slip: That portion of a pier, main pier, finger pier, or float where a boat is moored for the purpose of berthing, embarking, or disembarking.

❖ Boat slips are typically bordered with piers or posts on one, two or three sides to passively restrain a vessel. Boat slips are effectively parking spaces for boats [see Commentary Figures C106(b) and C1103].

FIGURE C106(a)
BOAT LAUNCH RAMP

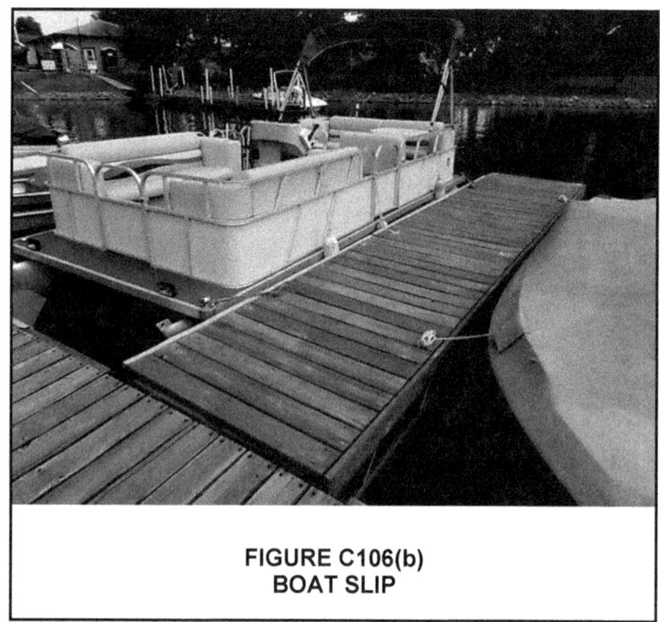

FIGURE C106(b)
BOAT SLIP

catch pool: A pool or designated section of a pool used as a terminus for water slide flumes.

❖ Catch pools are the pools at the bottom of water slides. For safety reasons, the pools are not used for regular swimming activities (see Section 1109.1.1).

characters: Letters, numbers, punctuation marks, and typographic symbols.

❖ Character size, stroke width and contrast are important for the readability of signs (see commentary, Section 703),

children's use: Spaces and elements specifically designed for use primarily by people 12 years old and younger.

❖ Specific provisions allowing for children's smaller size are stated for drinking fountains, water closets, toilet compartments, lavatories, sinks, dining surfaces and work surfaces (see Section 102).

circulation path: An exterior or interior way of passage from one place to another for pedestrians.

❖ A circulation path differs from an accessible route in that it can be used by most pedestrians, but not necessarily by those who use wheelchairs. Accessible stairs complying with Section 504 may be part of a circulation path, but not of an accessible route.

counter slope: Any slope opposing the running slope of a curb ramp.

❖ Slopes intersecting and opposite a running slope may create difficulty for persons using wheelchairs and persons with an ambulatory impairment. For example, the slope of a street from the center to the side creates a counter slope to the running slope of a curb ramp. Another example is the slope of a street gutter, which opposes the running slope of a curb ramp (see commentary Section 406.2 and Figure 406.2).

cross slope: The slope that is perpendicular to the direction of travel (see running slope).

❖ Cross slopes are a concern for persons with mobility impairments when they have to deal with a slope in two directions at the same time. Cross slope is the slope of the walking surface perpendicular to the direction of travel (see commentary, Section 405.3).

curb ramp: A short ramp cutting through a curb or built up to it.

❖ Curb ramps provide a means of access from a sidewalk to a street, parking lot or other vehicular way for a person using a wheelchair. The slope of a curb ramp also provides a cue to long-cane users that they have arrived at an intersection (see Section 406).

destination-oriented elevator system: An elevator system that provides lobby controls for the selection of destination floors, lobby indicators designating which elevator to board, and a car indicator designating the floors at which the car will stop.

❖ This type of elevator system has a unique call system. The intent is to allow for an efficient system of determining elevator car assignments and is an alternative to a zoned elevator system. Requirements are offered as exceptions to general elevator requirements in Section 407.

detectable warning: A standardized surface feature built in or applied to floor surfaces to warn of hazards on a circulation path.

❖ Detectable warnings are required only in very limited areas (see commentary, Sections 406.12, 406.13, 406.14 and 705).

dwelling unit: A single unit providing complete, independent living facilities for one or more persons including permanent provisions for living, sleeping, eating, cooking and sanitation.

❖ A dwelling unit contains elements necessary for independent living, including provisions for living spaces (family rooms, living rooms, dens, etc.); sleeping quarters; food preparation and eating spaces; and personal hygiene, cleanliness and sanitation facilities. A dwelling unit is occupied in one of two ways, either through renting or by ownership. The standard requirements are applied consistently to all dwellings, regardless of the type of ownership. Both owner-occupied and rented or leased dwellings must comply with the requirements of the standard.

A dwelling unit can exist singularly as a one-family dwelling or in combination with other dwelling units. When two dwelling units are grouped together in the same structure, the structure is considered a two-family dwelling or duplex. Three or more dwelling units in the same structure are considered as a multiple-family dwelling or multiple single-family dwellings, such as an apartment building, condominiums or townhouses (for technical criteria, see Chapter 10).

element: An architectural or mechanical component of a building, facility, space, or site.

❖ Examples of elements are telephones, curb ramps, doors, drinking fountains, seating and water closets.

elevated play component: A play component that is approached above or below grade and that is part of a composite play structure consisting of two or more play components attached or functionally linked to create an integrated unit providing more than one play activity.

❖ Play structures often have multiple activity levels that can each be accessed by more than one route. Elevated play components are typically accessed from platforms or ramps rather than the ground. Slides are an example of an elevated play area (see Commentary Figure 1108.3.2.2).

elevator car call sequential step scanning: A technology used to enter a car call by means of an up or down floor selection button.

❖ This type of system for indicating a floor choice is used typically where there are more than 16 floors in a building and the controls cannot all fit within reach ranges (see commentary, Section 407.4.8).

facility: All or any portion of a building, structure, site improvements, elements, and pedestrian routes or vehicular ways located on a site.

❖ Facilities include all occupiable interior rooms and spaces, occupiable exterior spaces, interior and exterior elements intended for human use and interior and exterior routes developed for pedestrians or vehicles.

gangway: A variable-sloped pedestrian walkway that links a fixed structure or land with a floating structure. Gangways that connect to vessels are not addressed by this document.

❖ A gangway allows a pedestrian route between a fixed structure and a floating, anchored structure to remain intact with water level fluctuations (see Sections 1103 and 1105).

golf car passage: A continuous passage on which a motorized golf car can operate.

❖ Golf courses have dedicated paths, often paved, intended to handle the light vehicle traffic of golf cars (i.e., golf carts) and maintenance vehicles. They are typically referred to as "cart paths" and are intended to minimize vehicle traffic on groomed fairways, especially during periods of wet weather. Golf car passages follow the course terrain and may have portions steeper than permitted for pedestrian ramps. A golfer with a mobility disability would be expected to utilize a golf car to negotiate golf car passages and fairways (see Section 1106).

ground level play component: A play component that is approached and exited at the ground level.

❖ A ground level play component does not require a vertical travel route for access. Swings are an example of ground level play components (see Commentary Figure C1108.3.2.1).

habitable: A space in a building for living, sleeping, eating or cooking. Bathrooms, toilet rooms, closets, halls, storage or utility spaces and similar areas are not considered habitable spaces.

❖ These spaces are normally considered inhabited in the course of residential living and provide the four basic characteristics associated with it: living, sleeping, eating and cooking. Other spaces may be usable and occupiable (bathrooms, closets, halls, utility rooms) but are not considered habitable.

key surface: The surface or plane of any key or button that must be touched to activate or deactivate an operable part or a machine function or enter data.

❖ Key surface requirements for automatic teller machines and fare machines are discussed in Sections 707.6.1, 707.6.2 and 707.9. Requirements for elevator call buttons and car controls do not use this term.

marked crossing: A crosswalk or other identified path intended for pedestrian use in crossing a vehicular way.

❖ Markings may be on the floor or ground, or signage may be used to mark a crossing. Regulations for color or pattern are often specified by state Departments of Transportation [see Commentary Figure C106(c)].

**FIGURE C106(c)
MARKED CROSSING**

operable part: A component of an element used to insert or withdraw objects, or to activate, deactivate, or adjust the element.

❖ This term is used extensively, typically with reference to Section 309. Examples of operable parts are telephone coin slots, push buttons, switches and handles (see Sections 309, 606.7, 1002.9, 1003.9 and 1004.9). While door hardware is also an operable part, Section 404.2.6 specifically limits the application of the requirement in Section 309.

pictogram: A pictorial symbol that represents activities, facilities, or concepts.

❖ A pictogram is a picture representing words. This graphic symbol or picture represents a word or idea in some writing systems, as opposed to a symbol such as a letter of the alphabet representing an individual sound. The wheelchair symbol used to indicate accessible features is an example of a pictogram (see commentary, Section 703.5).

play area: A portion of a site containing play components designed and constructed for children.

❖ Play areas may be indoors or outdoors. They are areas specifically intended for children's play. Natural features, such as large trees or boulders, may be in or near play areas but not be intended as play components. A playing field without play components is not regulated as a play area. A baseball field laid out with baselines, backstop, infield and outfield areas is considered a play area (see Section 1108).

play component: An element intended to generate specific opportunities for play, socialization or learning. Play components are manufactured or natural; and are stand-alone or part of a composite play structure.

❖ Elements designed and/or intended for children's play including built structures (play equipment, climbing walls, skateboard parks, zip lines), sport field markings (field sports) and assemblages of natural materials (dirt bike trails, ski slopes) (see Section 1108).

ramp: A walking surface that has a running slope steeper than 1:20.

❖ On an accessible route, ramps provide a means for independently going from one elevation to another by persons who cannot use stairs. If a floor or walk slopes 1:20 or less, it is not considered a ramp, but rather a sloped walking surface (see Section 405 for ramp requirements).

running slope: The slope that is parallel to the direction of travel (see cross slope).

❖ The running slope for a ramp is measured from landing to landing in the direction of the run of the sloped portion (see Sections 405.2 and 406.1).

sign: An architectural element composed of displayed textual, symbolic, tactile, or pictorial information.

❖ Uniformity of signage design and location at a facility provides for independent use by a person who is blind or visually impaired (see Section 703). Signs can contain words, braille or pictograms.

Accessible elements can be identified using the International Symbols of Accessibility (see Figure 703.6.3.1).

site: A parcel of land bounded by a property line or a designated portion of a public right-of-way.

❖ This term is typically defined in model building codes. Accessibility requirements include the site, as well as the buildings within the site.

A site for purposes of accessibility requirements is the same as that considered in the application of other code requirements. The property within the boundaries of the site is under the control of the owner. The owner can be held responsible for code compliance of the site and all facilities on it.

sleeping unit: A room or space in which people sleep that can also include permanent provisions for living, sleeping, eating, and either sanitation or kitchen facilities but not both. Such rooms and spaces that are also part of a dwelling unit are not sleeping units.

❖ This definition is included to coordinate the *Fair Housing Act Guidelines* with the code. The definition for "sleeping unit" is needed to clarify the differences between sleeping units and dwelling units. Some examples would be a hotel guestroom, a dormitory, a boarding house, congregate residences, assisted living facilities, nursing homes, etc. Another example would be a studio apartment with a kitchenette (i.e., microwave, sink, refrigerator). Because the cooking arrangements are not permanent, this configuration would be considered a sleeping unit, not a dwelling unit. As already defined in this standard, a dwelling unit must contain permanent independent facilities for living, sleeping, eating, cooking and sanitation (see Chapter 10).

soft contained play structure: A play structure made up of one or more play components where the user enters a fully enclosed play environment that utilizes pliable materials, such as plastic, netting, or fabric.

❖ These types of play structures are usually indoors and scaled for smaller/younger children (see Commentary Figure 1108.2.2).

teeing ground: In golf, the starting place for the hole to be played.

❖ On a golf course the teeing ground or "tee" is the flat, slightly raised, highly manicured starting position from which play is initiated for each "hole." In miniature golf, the tee is again the starting point but all surfaces are artificial and all play is with a putter (see Section 1106).

transfer device: Equipment designed to facilitate the transfer of a person from a wheelchair or other mobility aide to and from an amusement ride seat.

❖ Transfer devices are often custom designed for a specific ride or type of ride. They are intended to be used with staff assistance (see Section 1102).

TTY: An abbreviation for teletypewriter. Equipment that employs interactive, text-based communications through the transmission of coded signals across the standard telephone network. The term TTY also refers to devices known as text telephones and TDDs.

❖ TTYs include telecommunications display devices, telecommunication devices for deaf persons, text telephones and computers (see Sections 704.4 through 704.7).

use zone: The ground level area beneath and immediately adjacent to a play structure or play equipment that is designated by ASTM F 1487 listed in Section 105.2.10, for unrestricted circulation around the play equipment and where it is predicted that a user would land when falling from or exiting the play equipment.

❖ The use zone is a designated use and impact area under and around a play structure. The physical qualities of the ground surface in the use zone are required to be improved in accordance with ASTM F 1487-01 (*Standard Consumer Safety Performance Specification for Playground Equipment for Public Use*). The improved ground surface in a given installation is typically extended beyond the minimum required use zone (see Section 1108).

variable message signs (VMS): Electronic signs that have a message with the capacity to change by means of scrolling, streaming, or paging across a background.

❖ Variable message signs have been in use for decades in transportation facilities such as airports, train stations and bus terminals. Newer technologies have made them less costly, easier to read, immediately responsive and nearly maintenance free. They are able to complement audible communication systems in many environments. They can be as simple as arrays of lights, or a display on a monitor (see Section 703.7).

variable message sign (VMS) characters: Characters of an electronic sign are composed of pixels in an array. High resolution VMS characters have vertical pixel counts of 16 rows or greater. Low resolution VMS characters have vertical pixel counts of 7 to 15 rows.

❖ A character is a letter, number or other symbol (i.e., question mark). Character resolution affects the readability and rate of communication possible with variable message signs. The more pixels used to make up individual letters, the higher the resolution of the characters (see Section 703.7).

vehicular way: A route provided for vehicular traffic.

❖ Vehicular ways are public streets and alleys. While cars also move through parking lots, drivers anticipate a large number of pedestrians in these locations, so parking lots are typically not considered vehicular ways. However, in large parking lots, there is a level of interpretation required where there are main drives without immediately adjacent parking.

walk: An exterior pathway with a prepared surface for pedestrian use.

❖ Walks are exterior circulation routes. This includes general pedestrian areas such as sidewalks, plazas and courts.

wheelchair space: A space for a single wheelchair and its occupant.

❖ "Wheelchair space" dimensions (Sections 802.3, 802.4 and 1102.4) are not to be confused with the "clear floor space" dimensions in Section 305. Both are based on the size of a standard wheelchair, but wheelchair space dimensions vary depending on occupancy and arrangement. A wheelchair space is typically a destination position that a person will occupy for an extended period of time, such as in the audience of a theater. A "clear floor space" is generally associated with maneuvering positions along an accessible route or as a minimum required floor area at an accessible element.

wheelchair space locations: A space for a minimum of a single wheelchair and the associated companion seating. Wheelchair space locations can contain multiple wheelchair spaces and associated companion seating.

❖ A "wheelchair space location" is a specifically designated seating area configured for a person in a wheelchair with his/her companion. Each such designated seating area may include more than one wheelchair space with companion seating.

Chapter 2. Scoping

❖ Chapter 2 is a general overview of the provisions within this technical standard.

- Section 201 covers the general principle for what makes something accessible.
- Section 202 introduces the special provisions for Accessible, Type A, Type B and Type C dwelling and sleeping units.
- Section 203 states that the administrative authority will administer this standard as an extension of their scoping requirements.

201 General

This standard provides technical criteria for making sites, facilities, buildings, and elements accessible. The administrative authority shall provide scoping provisions to specify the extent to which these technical criteria apply. These scoping provisions shall address the application of this standard to: each building and occupancy type; new construction, alterations, temporary facilities, and existing buildings; specific site and building elements; and to multiple elements or spaces provided within a site or building.

❖ The standard does not establish which or how many buildings, facilities and spaces or elements within these spaces must be made accessible. This standard correlates with the adoption of scoping provisions by the administrative authority. This is typically accomplished through the adoption of a model building code, which references this standard. The adopted scoping provisions will establish what, how many and where accessibility is required, and this standard will establish how those required elements and spaces are to be made accessible. A set of recommended scoping provisions was developed by the Board for the Coordination of the Model Codes of the Council of American Building Officials, and is reflected in the current editions of the model building codes published by the International Code Council® (ICC®).

By adopting this standard through the building code, enforcement can be accomplished at the state or local level. In contrast, the requirements of Title II of the Americans with Disabilities Act (ADA) can be enforced only as a civil rights statute by the U.S. Department of Justice (DOJ). Although many provisions in this standard are comparable to parallel requirements contained in the ADA's *Accessibility Guidelines* (ADAAG-1991), compliance with the ADA should be verified independently. ICC continues to work with the federal government to coordinate requirements. Note that on September 15, 2010, the DOJ published updates to its ADA regulations and adopted new design standards. The 2010 ADA *Standards for Accessible Design* is the 2004 ADA/ABA *Accessibility Guidelines*. The 2010 ADA standard, along with the additional requirements in the DOJ regulations, must be complied with for any new construction or alterations begun after March 15, 2012.

It is not the intent for either the building requirements in the 2010 ADA Standards or the *International Building Code*® (IBC®) to control, but rather for the designer to comply with the standard that requires the higher level of accessibility. The Access Board and ICC have worked together extensively to coordinate the requirements.

Scoping documents sometimes require elements, such as toilet facilities, and then specify which of those elements must be accessible. Scoping documents may require accessible elements only when those elements are provided, such as passenger drop offs. Certain elements covered in ICC A117.1 may not be scoped at all. For example, ICC A117.1 contains technical provisions for telephones in Section 704. If the scoping document does not specify accessible phones, the accessibility requirements in ICC A117.1 for phones are not a requirement, but a choice.

Certain items may be limited by the standard. For example, the scoping document may require accessible lavatories in accordance with Section 606. The enhanced reach ranges in Section 606.5, starting with "where... required" must be specifically scoped in order to be applicable. Section 606.5 is not generally applicable to all accessible lavatories.

202 Dwelling and Sleeping Units

Chapter 10 of this standard contains dwelling unit and sleeping unit criteria for Accessible units, Type A units, Type B units, Type C (Visitable) dwelling units and units with accessible communication features. The administrative authority shall specify, in separate scoping provisions, the extent to which these technical criteria apply. These scoping provisions shall address the types and numbers of units required to comply with each set of unit criteria.

❖ Chapter 10 covers technical provisions for dwelling and sleeping units. See the commentary for these defined terms in Section 106.5. The provisions for Accessible units and Type A units exceed Fair Housing Act requirements. The provisions for Type B units are intended to be consistent with the provisions in the Fair Housing Act. Accessible units are considered more accessible than Type A units. Type A units are considered more accessible than Type B units. Scoping provisions for all three types of units can be found in the model building code.

The Type C dwelling unit is new to this edition of the standard. Type C units provide a low level of accessibility that is not intended to match any federal requirement. Type C dwelling units are considered visitable units, meaning that mobility-impaired guests or residents who are temporarily disabled or aging in place will have an accessible route to and within the entrance level of the unit (see Section 1005 for additional information). The provisions for Type C dwelling units are intended to be scoped for residential facilities that fall below the threshold of FHA requirements, such as townhouses and single-family homes. Scoping for Type C units would be through local ordinances. Many jurisdictions have already developed visitable criteria; especially those jurisdictions that have large percentages of residents over 65 years of age.

203 Administration

The administrative authority shall provide an appropriate review and approval process to ensure compliance with this standard.

❖ Where this standard is adopted by the administrative authority, a construction project that must comply with these provisions should be reviewed for compliance in the same manner the project is reviewed to determine compliance with other provisions of the applicable building code.

Chapter 3. Building Blocks

❖ Chapter 3 describes the core requirements that are referenced by other sections of this standard. The intent is to reduce duplication of requirements through the use of "building blocks." For example, knee and toe clearances are referenced for drinking fountains, working surfaces, dining surfaces and lavatories.

- Section 301 is a general statement indicating the "building blocks" may be referenced directly from scoping provisions, or as part of requirements elsewhere in this standard.
- Section 302 contains requirements for floor and ground surfaces.
- Section 303 sets out criteria for changes in level, typically when floor surfaces change or at door thresholds.
- Section 304 provides technical criteria for turning.
- Section 305 contains criteria for a clear floor space for a wheelchair, including moving into a restricted area such as an alcove.
- Section 306 establishes the three-dimensional space needed for clearances for knees and toes of a person using a wheelchair when they move under an element or counter.
- Section 307 contains criteria for objects that may protrude over a walking surface so the chances for injury to a person with visual impairments are reduced.
- Section 308 provides guidance for the height of items so they can be reached by someone using a wheelchair. This includes reaching over obstructions such as a counter.
- Section 309 provides technical criteria for any operable parts, such as light switches, heating/air-conditioning controls or controls on plumbing fixtures.

301 General

❖ This chapter is appropriately named "building blocks." The chapter provides the core requirements that are used to establish accessible items. These technical provisions and the limitations within them are used in later chapters for the full range of elements and spaces that are included within the scope of the standard and eliminate the need for duplicating the provisions in numerous sections.

301.1 Scope. The provisions of Chapter 3 shall apply where required by the scoping provisions adopted by the administrative authority or by Chapters 4 through 11.

❖ Although the provisions of this chapter may, in general, improve the design and usability of all buildings, it is important to note that the section is qualified by the phrase "where required." This is intended to be consistent with the fact that scoping provisions are not included in this standard (see commentary, Chapter 2).

301.2 Overlap. Unless otherwise specified, clear floor spaces, clearances at fixtures, maneuvering clearances at doors, and turning spaces shall be permitted to overlap.

❖ Overlap of clearances is common in confined spaces. See Commentary Figure C301.2 for an example of two doors in a corner. See Commentary Figure C603.2 for examples of clearance overlap at wheelchair turning spaces, plumbing fixtures and doors. This section had previously been repeated in several sections of the code. By placing this allowance for overlap in the building block chapter of the standard, overlap is universally permitted unless another section specifically states otherwise.

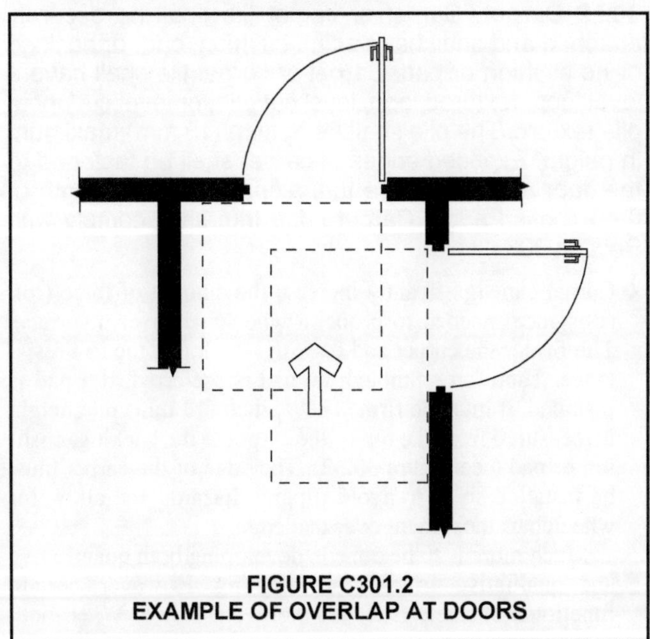

FIGURE C301.2
EXAMPLE OF OVERLAP AT DOORS

302 Floor Surfaces

❖ Note that Section 104.4 states that the term "floor surface" refers as applicable to the finished floor or ground surface.

302.1 General. Floor surfaces shall be stable, firm, and slip resistant, and shall comply with Section 302. Changes in level in floor surfaces shall comply with Section 303.

❖ Ambulatory and semi-ambulatory people who have difficulty maintaining balance and those with restricted gaits are particularly sensitive to slipping and tripping hazards. For those people, a stable and regular surface is necessary to walk safely. Wheelchairs are propelled most easily on surfaces that are hard, stable and regular. Soft, loose surfaces such as shag carpet, loose sand, gravel, crushed stone or wet clay, and irregular surfaces such as cobblestone, significantly impede movement of a wheelchair.

A stable surface is one that remains unchanged by contaminants or applied force, so that when the contaminant or force is removed, the surface returns to its original condition. A firm surface resists deformation by either indentation or particles moving on its surface. It is not the intent of the standard to require only paved surfaces; however, any other types (e.g., wood chips, gravel) would need to be evaluated.

Slip resistance is based on the frictional force necessary to keep a shoe or crutch tip from slipping on a walking surface under the conditions of use likely for that surface. For example, outside surfaces or entryways may be wet from rain or snow, or bathroom floors may be wet and should be evaluated under those conditions; however, the tile on the upstairs hallway would typically not be influenced by outside weather and should be evaluated in a dry condition. Although it is known that the static coefficient of friction is one basis of slip resistance, there is not as yet a generally accepted method to evaluate the slip resistance of walking surfaces for all use conditions.

302.2 Carpet. Carpet or carpet tile shall be securely attached and shall have a firm cushion, pad, or backing or no cushion or pad. Carpet or carpet tile shall have a level loop, textured loop, level cut pile, or level cut/uncut pile texture. The pile shall be $^1/_2$ inch (13 mm) maximum in height. Exposed edges of carpet shall be fastened to the floor and shall have trim along the entire length of the exposed edge. Carpet edge trim shall comply with Section 303.

❖ Carpet can significantly increase the amount of force (roll resistance) needed to propel a wheelchair over a surface. The firmer the carpet and backing, the lower the roll resistance. Therefore, although no pad is preferred, if a pad is installed, it must be firm. The $^1/_2$-inch (13 mm) pile height is measured from the top of the carpet to the backing, cushion or pad (see Figure 302.2). The edge of the carpet must be installed so as to avoid tripping hazards and allow for wheelchair movement over that edge.

Much more is to be done in developing both quantitative and qualitative criteria for carpeting. However, certain functional characteristics are well established. When both carpet and padding are used, it is desirable to have minimum movement (preferably none) between the floor and the pad and the pad and the carpet, which would allow the carpet to hump or warp. In heavily trafficked areas, a thick, soft (plush) pad or cushion, particularly in combination with long pile, makes it difficult for individuals in wheelchairs and those with other ambulatory disabilities to get about. Firm carpeting is achieved through proper selection and combination of pad and carpet, sometimes with the elimination of the pad or cushion, and with proper installation.

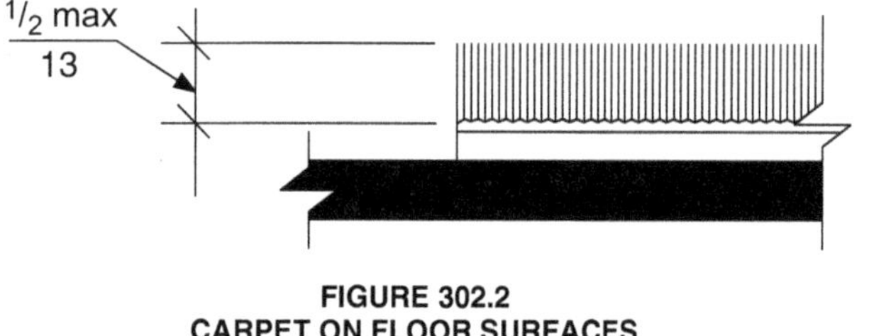

FIGURE 302.2
CARPET ON FLOOR SURFACES

302.3 Openings. Openings in floor surfaces shall be of a size that does not permit the passage of a $^1/_2$ inch (13 mm) diameter sphere, except as allowed in Sections 407.4.3, 408.4.3, 409.4.3, 410.4, and 805.10. Elongated openings shall be placed so that the long dimension is perpendicular to the predominant direction of travel.

❖ These limitations are intended to eliminate openings of a size or orientation into which a crutch tip or the wheels of a chair could drop [see Commentary Figure C302.3(a)]. If elongated openings are oriented perpendicular to the expected direction of travel, the casters of a wheelchair will roll over them without great difficulty because the openings will be no wider than $^1/_2$ inch (13 mm) in the direction of travel [see Figure 302.3 and Commentary Figure C302.3(b)].

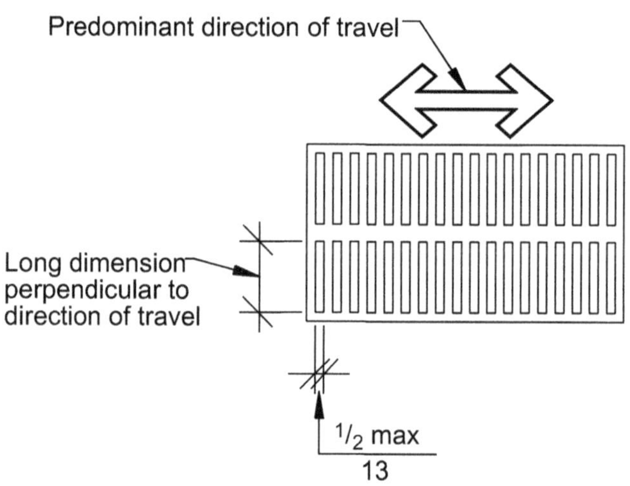

FIGURE 302.3
OPENINGS IN FLOOR SURFACES

FIGURE C302.3(a)
GRATE OPENINGS CREATE PROBLEMS FOR WHEELCHAIRS

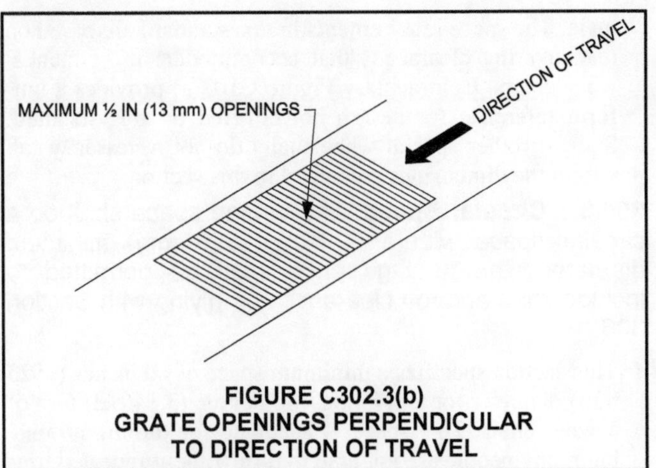

FIGURE C302.3(b)
GRATE OPENINGS PERPENDICULAR TO DIRECTION OF TRAVEL

303 Changes in Level

303.1 General. Changes in level in floor surfaces shall comply with Section 303.

❖ As used in the standard, a change in level is a change in the elevation of a walking surface. Typical examples would be a change in floor surface from tile to carpet or door thresholds.

303.2 Vertical. Changes in level of $^1/_4$ inch (6.4 mm) maximum in height shall be permitted to be vertical.

❖ Abrupt changes in elevation can create a significant barrier for a person using a wheelchair because of the small caster wheels on the wheelchair. Changes in elevation up to $^1/_4$ inch (6 mm) can be negotiated by a person using a wheelchair with minimal difficulty and do not present an unreasonable tripping hazard. The standard permits a vertical edge at the level change and does not require a beveled or special edge treatment (see Figure 303.2).

FIGURE 303.2
VERTICAL CHANGE IN LEVEL

303.3 Beveled. Changes in level greater than $^1/_4$ inch (6.4 mm) in height and not more than $^1/_2$ inch (13 mm) maximum in height shall be beveled with a slope not steeper than 1:2.

❖ Changes in elevation between $^1/_4$ inch and $^1/_2$ inch (6.4 mm and 13 mm) cannot be as easily negotiated by a wheelchair. They create edges on the accessible route surface that can "catch" the small caster wheels on a wheelchair. Additionally, they present a greater potential tripping hazard because of the increased likelihood of a crutch tip or toe of a shoe catching the edge. For changes in elevation in this range, it is preferable that the entire edge be beveled as shown in Figure 303.3(b) of the standard. However, by combining the provisions of Sections 303.2 and 303.3, it could be acceptable to bevel only the portion that is over $^1/_4$ inch (6.4 mm) in height [see Figure 303.3(a)]. This permits the bottom $^1/_4$ inch (6.4 mm) of the edge created by the elevation change to be an abrupt vertical change and requires the remainder of the edge between $^1/_4$ inch (6.4 mm) and $^1/_2$ inch (13 mm) to be sloped or beveled at a slope no steeper than 1 unit vertical to 2 units horizontal (50-percent slope). This is significantly steeper than is allowed for a ramp but is adequate for the limited rise. However, in no case may the combined changes in level exceed $^1/_2$ inch (13 mm).

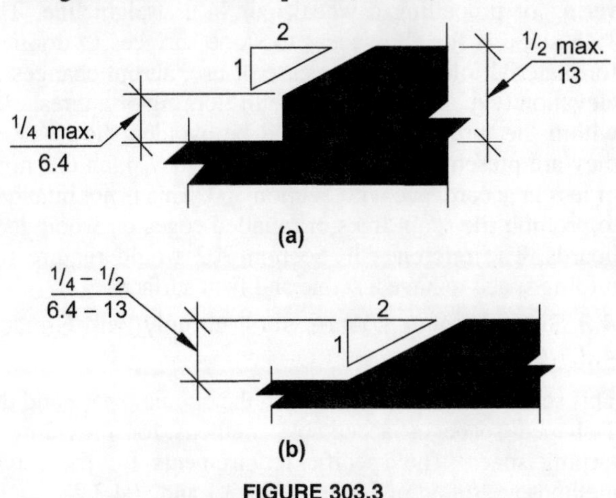

FIGURE 303.3
BEVELED CHANGES IN LEVEL

303.4 Ramps. Changes in level greater than $^1/_2$ inch (13 mm) in height shall be ramped and shall comply with Section 405 or 406.

❖ Changes in level exceeding $^1/_2$ inch (13 mm) must comply with ramps, curb ramps or sloped walks.

304 Turning Space

304.1 General. A turning space shall comply with Section 304.

❖ This section provides the requirements for a space that will permit a person using a wheelchair, scooter or other walking aid to turn and change directions along their route of travel. The standard specifies where the turning space is actually required (see Sections 603.2.1, 612.3, 803.2, 807.2, 1002.3.2, 1003.3.2, 1102.3, 1105.5, 1108.4.3.1 and 1110.1 and see Commentary Figure C304.1).

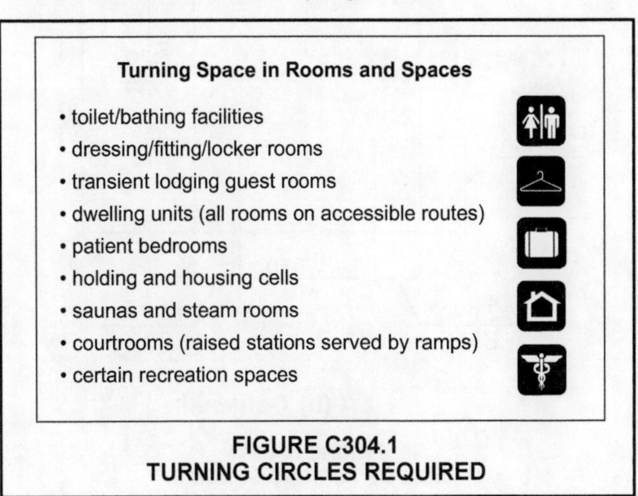

FIGURE C304.1
TURNING CIRCLES REQUIRED

304.2 Floor Surface. Floor surfaces of a turning space shall comply with Section 302. Changes in level are not permitted within the turning space.

EXCEPTION: Slopes not steeper than 1:48 shall be permitted.

❖ Any type of cross slope steeper than 1:48 on the surface of a turning space can cause considerable difficulty in maneuvering or propelling a wheelchair in a straight line. The 1:48 slope is for allowances to slope surfaces to drain or for material tolerances. For ease of use, abrupt changes in elevation (e.g., such as a change in flooring or a threshold) within the turning space should be avoided; however, if they are present, they must be limited to $^1/_2$ inch (13 mm) or less in accordance with Section 303. This is not intended to prohibit tile grout lines or rounded edges on wood deck boards. The reference to Section 302 would require the turning space to have a stable and firm surface.

304.3 Size. Turning spaces shall comply with Section 304.3.1 or 304.3.2.

❖ This section simply refers to both the circular space and the T-shaped space as acceptable methods for providing a turning space. The specific requirements for these two methods are found in Sections 304.3.1 and 304.3.2.

The user and wheelchair shown in Commentary Figure C102(a) represent typical dimensions for a large adult male. The space requirements in this standard are based on maneuvering clearances that accommodate most manual wheelchairs. Commentary Figure C102(a) provides a uniform reference for design not covered by this standard. Sport or other special wheelchairs do not necessarily fall within the dimensions contained in this section.

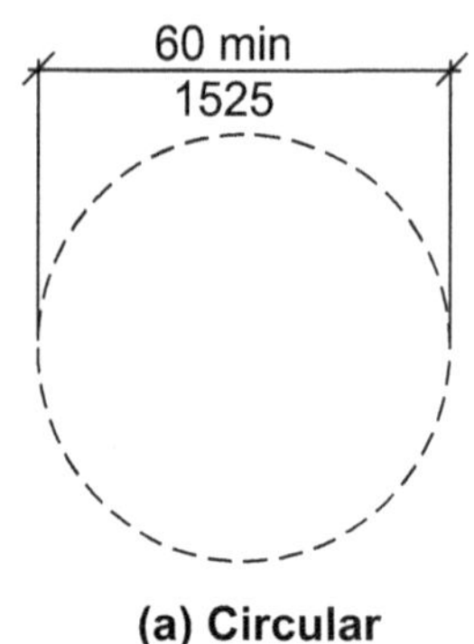

(a) Circular

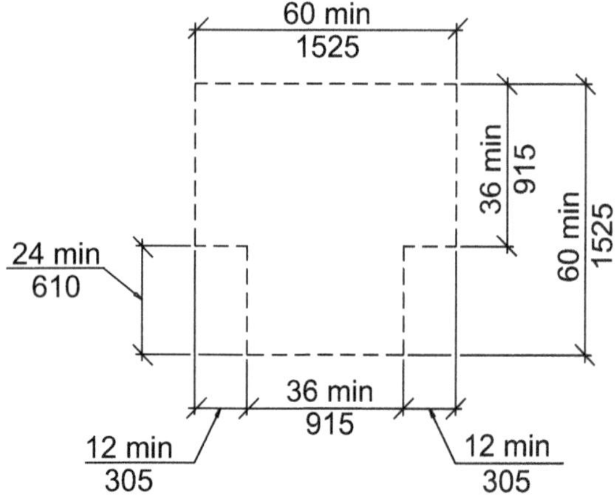

(b) T-shaped

**FIGURE 304.3
SIZE OF TURNING SPACE**

304.3.1 Circular Space. The turning space shall be a circular space with a 60-inch (1525 mm) minimum diameter. The turning space shall be permitted to include knee and toe clearance complying with Section 306.

❖ This section specifies a minimum space of 60 inches (1525 mm) diameter for a pivoting 180-degree (3.14 rad) turn of a wheelchair. This space is adequate for turning around, but many people are not able to turn without repeated tries and bumping into surrounding objects [see Commentary Figure C304.3.1(a)].

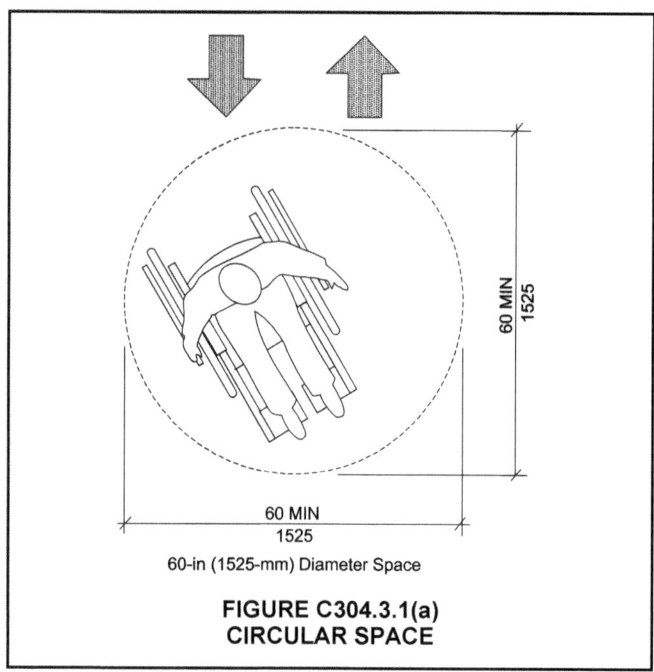

**FIGURE C304.3.1(a)
CIRCULAR SPACE**

To make a turn, both wheels are simultaneously turned in opposing directions within a 60-inch (1525 mm) diameter. For electrically powered wheelchairs, coordination of this opposing wheel rotation, coupled with the longer wheel base typical of powered chairs, makes the full turning space even more critical compared to a smaller, manually operated wheelchair.

The standard does permit objects such as lavatories, drinking fountains or any other item to encroach into the 60-inch-diameter (1525 mm) circle provided the knee and toe clearances beneath such objects comply with Section 306 of the standard. See Section 306 for additional details and discussion. This will mean that when properly located, the space under an element may be usable when making a turn. While not specified, good design would have the circular turning space only rely on knee and/or toe clearance on one side of the circle, similar to the T-turn. Obstructions on more than one side would make turning more difficult, if not impossible [see Commentary Figure C304.3.1(b)].

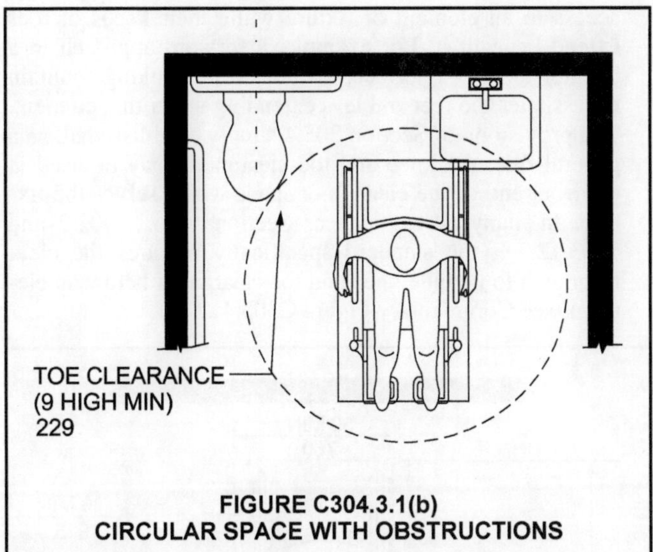

FIGURE C304.3.1(b)
CIRCULAR SPACE WITH OBSTRUCTIONS

304.3.2 T-Shaped Space. The turning space shall be a T-shaped space within a 60-inch (1525 mm) minimum square, with arms and base 36 inches (915 mm) minimum in width. Each arm of the T shall be clear of obstructions 12 inches (305 mm) minimum in each direction, and the base shall be clear of obstructions 24 inches (610 mm) minimum. The turning space shall be permitted to include knee and toe clearance complying with Section 306 only at the end of either the base or one arm.

❖ The T-shaped space permits the user to approach and turn within the space. The T-shaped space is every bit as acceptable as the circular space listed in Section 304.3.1.

60 MIN 1525; 12 MIN 305; 36 MIN 915; 12 MIN 305; 60 MIN 1525; 36 MIN 915

NOTE: Dashed lines indicate minimum length of clear space required on each arm of the T-shaped space in order to complete the turn.

FIGURE C304.3.2(a)
T-SHAPED SPACE

The layout of the T and the approach to it may be made from either direction on the arm or from the base. This type of turning space is commonly used at intersections of accessible routes or within rooms or areas where cabinets or counters may be located in the spaces adjacent to the T [see Commentary Figure C304.3.2(a)]. As discussed in the commentary to Section 304.3.1, the T-shaped space may include knee and toe clearances beneath an object on one leg of the T as long as the knee and toe clearances are in compliance with Section 306. See Section 306 for additional details and discussion [see Commentary Figure C304.3.2(b)].

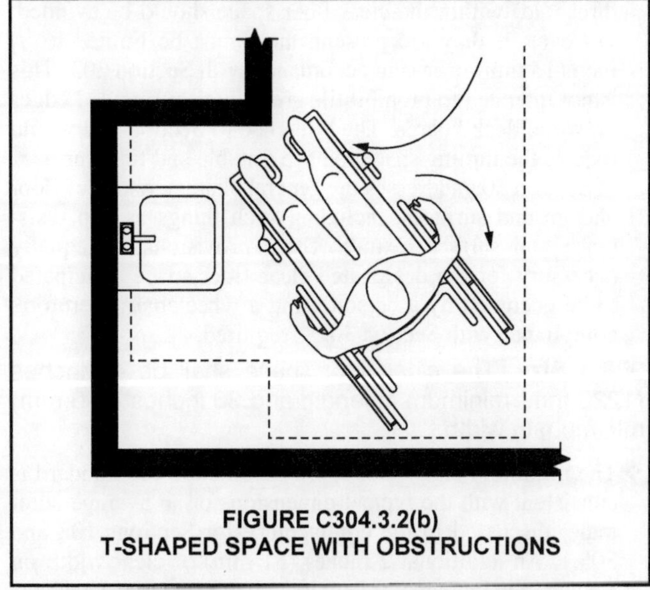

FIGURE C304.3.2(b)
T-SHAPED SPACE WITH OBSTRUCTIONS

304.4 Door Swing. Unless otherwise specified, doors shall be permitted to swing into turning spaces.

❖ A door swinging through the turning circle will generally not create a problem because Section 404.2.4 requires maneuvering clearances around the door. This permits users to operate the door and then, once it is closed or out of the turning space, they are able to make their turn.

305 Clear Floor Space

❖ Note that Section 104.4 states that the term "floor surface" refers to the finished floor or ground surface as applicable.

305.1 General. A clear floor space shall comply with Section 305.

❖ This section ensures that a properly sized space is available for people to be able to position themselves for the use of accessible fixtures and facilities. The user and wheelchair shown in Commentary Figure C102(a) represent typical dimensions for a large adult male. The space requirements in this standard are based on maneuvering clearances that accommodate most manual wheelchairs. Commentary Figure C102(a) provides a uniform reference for design not covered by this standard. Sport or other special wheelchairs do not necessarily fall within the dimensions contained in this section.

305.2 Floor Surfaces. Floor surfaces of a clear floor space shall comply with Section 302. Changes in level are not permitted within the clear floor space.

EXCEPTION: Slopes not steeper than 1:48 shall be permitted.

❖ Cross slopes steeper than 1:48 on walks and ground or floor surfaces cause considerable difficulty in propelling a wheelchair in a straight line or when moving into a position to use an accessible item. Steeper slopes can also create an unstable situation where users may be more likely to tip or simply feel off balance. For ease of use, abrupt changes in elevation (e.g., such as a change in flooring or a threshold) within the clear floor space should be avoided; however, if they are present, they must be limited to $^{1}/_{2}$ inch (13 mm) or less in accordance with Section 303. This is not intended to prohibit tile grout lines or rounded edges on wood deck boards. The reference to Section 302 would require the turning space to have a stable and firm surface.

Section 302 addresses the general characteristics of floor and ground surfaces, including such things as slip resistance and surface texture. These provisions are equally necessary for the designated clear floor space anticipated to be occupied by a person using a wheelchair; therefore, compliance with Section 302 is required.

305.3 Size. The clear floor space shall be 48 inches (1220 mm) minimum in length and 30 inches (760 mm) minimum in width.

❖ The minimum clear floor space specified in the standard is consistent with the typical dimensions of an average adult male, discussed in the commentary for Sections 102 and 305.1. An additional 2 inches (51 mm) of clear width on each side is included to anticipate hand and forearm clearance beyond the chair. This fundamental dimension is the basis for many of the provisions throughout this standard for maneuvering clearances and spaces anticipated to be occupied by a wheelchair.

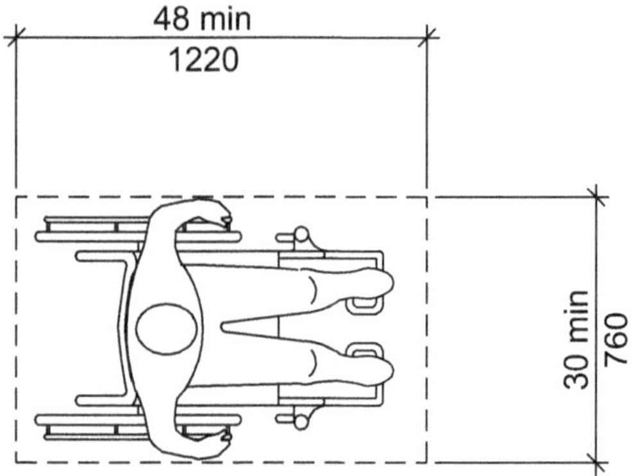

FIGURE 305.3
SIZE OF CLEAR FLOOR SPACE

305.4 Knee and Toe Clearance. Unless otherwise specified, clear floor space shall be permitted to include knee and toe clearance complying with Section 306.

❖ Section 306 contains the dimensional criteria for knee and toe clearances that permit a person using a wheelchair access to an element or fixture while their knees or toes extend beneath it. For example, a forward approach to a counter top work surface, lavatory or a drinking fountain necessitates the feet and legs extending under that element. The provisions of Section 305.4 simply establish that, as a general rule, the knee and toe clearances may be used at the front end of the clear floor space which serves the fixture. In many cases, such as Sections 606.2, 902.2 and 1003.12.3.1, the standard specifically requires the clear floor area to include knee and toe clearances below an element (see Commentary Figure C305.4).

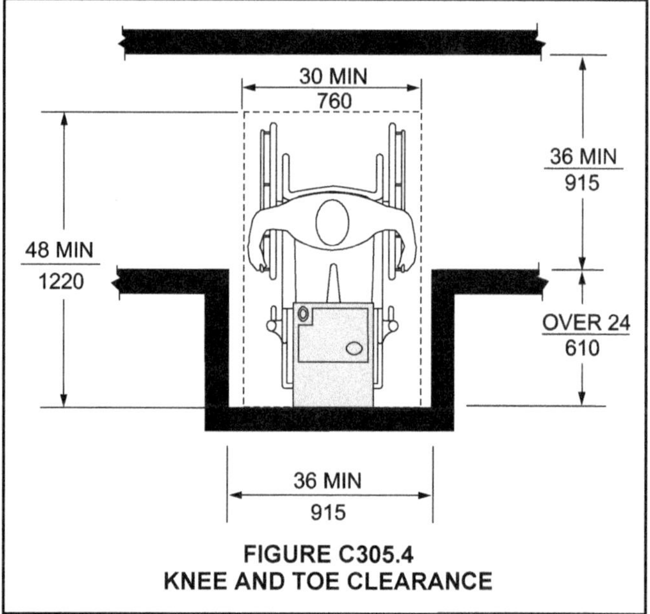

FIGURE C305.4
KNEE AND TOE CLEARANCE

305.5 Position. Unless otherwise specified, the clear floor space shall be positioned for either forward or parallel approach to an element.

❖ To use an element or device such as a plumbing fixture, telephone or light switch, or to occupy a space such as a viewing location in an assembly occupancy or the access aisle adjacent to a parking space, a person using a wheelchair must approach the element and subsequently position the chair in preparation for use of the element (see Figure 305.5). Assuming an unlimited amount of space around a given point, a person in a wheelchair could approach that point from an infinite number of angles. Where an accessible element or fixture is located on or at a wall surface, the person using a wheelchair could approach the element from any one of 180 degrees of angle, assuming there are no obstructions to the clear floor space.

This provision would result in the greatest degree of accessibility by affording the full range of possible approach angles. However, this also requires a larger clear floor space around accessible elements, which could place unnecessary constraints on floor layout and design, spacing of a battery of accessible elements, corridor and passageway widths, and similar building features. To balance such design impacts with an acceptable degree of accessibility, the standard requires that the approach to accessible elements need be provided based on either (not both) a parallel approach or a forward approach to the element.

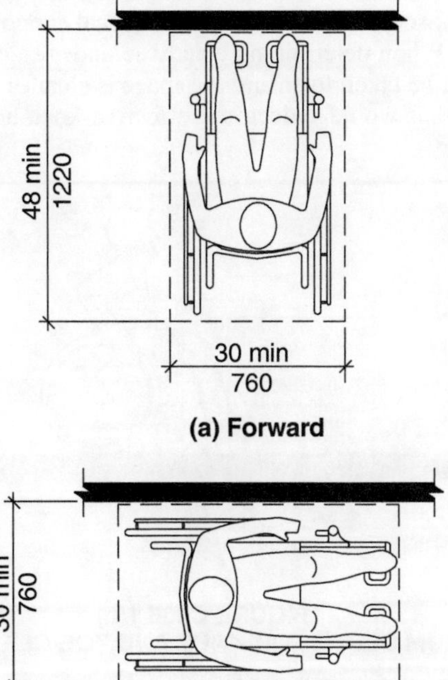

FIGURE 305.5
POSITION OF CLEAR FLOOR SPACE

305.6 Approach. One full, unobstructed side of the clear floor space shall adjoin or overlap an accessible route or adjoin another clear floor space.

❖ The requirement that one full side of the wheelchair clear floor space adjoin an accessible route ensures that the element is reachable from the accessible route. This can be the either the 30-inch (760 mm) side or the 48-inch (1220 mm) side. Clearly, any clear floor space at an element or fixture is of no value if it cannot be reached from an accessible route.

305.7 Alcoves. If a clear floor space is in an alcove or otherwise confined on all or part of three sides, additional maneuvering clearances complying with Sections 305.7.1 and 305.7.2 shall be provided, as applicable.

❖ The provisions for alcoves require additional width for a forward approach or additional length for a parallel approach when the alcove or other obstruction exceeds the depths specified in Section 305.7.1 or 305.7.2. This additional size is intended to ensure that sufficient space is provided to maneuver the wheelchair into position for using the element located within the alcove (see Figure 305.7).

305.7.1 Parallel Approach. Where the clear floor space is positioned for a parallel approach, the alcove shall be 60 inches (1525 mm) minimum in width where the depth exceeds 15 inches (380 mm).

❖ Similar to the parallel parking of a car, maneuvering clearances are needed to permit a person using a wheelchair to perform a parallel approach and then transition into the

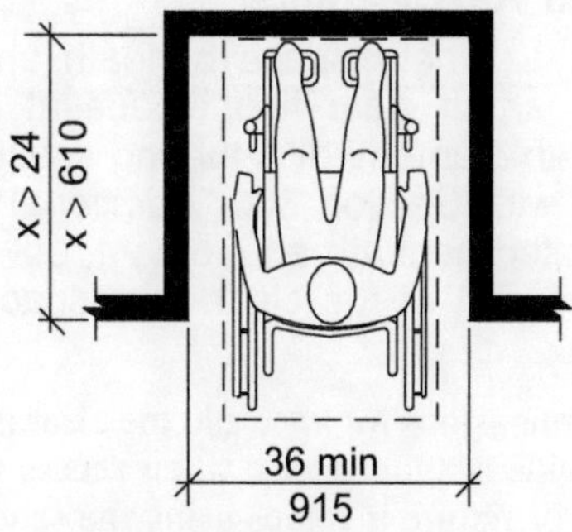

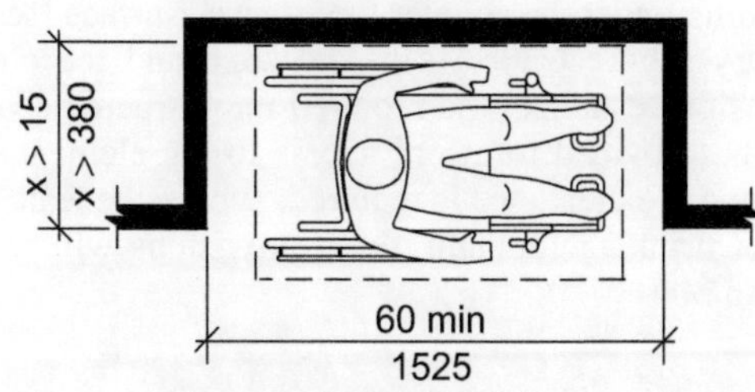

FIGURE 305.7
MANEUVERING CLEARANCE IN ALCOVE

clear floor space that is located within an area where three sides are confined. Looking at Commentary Figure C102(a), the length of the chair and the user's feet are at the 48-inch (1220 mm) limit, which is normally required for the clear floor space. Therefore, the increased length of 60 inches (1525 mm) is needed when the clear floor space is located within an alcove.

305.7.2 Forward Approach. Where the clear floor space is positioned for a forward approach, the alcove shall be 36 inches (915 mm) minimum in width where the depth exceeds 24 inches (610 mm).

❖ The normal 30-inch (760 mm) width of a clear floor space must be increased to 36 inches (915 mm) when any type of obstruction occurs on all or part of three sides and the clear floor space extends more than 24 inches (610 mm) into the confined area. A drinking fountain located within a deep alcove or a counter top work area with adjacent base cabinets below would be examples where this provision could be applicable. It is important to consider how far the required clear floor space extends into the alcove, not just the actual depth of the alcove (see Commentary, Figure C305.4).

As an example, if a counter top work area had 31 inches (790 mm) of clear floor space located in a circulation aisle and had the remaining 17 inches (430 mm) of length as the minimum size knee and toe clearance beneath the counter, it would not matter that the actual depth of the area beneath the counter where the knee and toe clearance was located extended to a greater depth of 28 inches (710 mm). In such a situation, the width would remain as a minimum of 30 inches (760 mm) for the clear floor space.

306 Knee and Toe Clearance

306.1 General. Where space beneath an element is included as part of clear floor space at an element, clearance at an element, or a turning space, the space shall comply with Section 306. Additional space shall not be prohibited beneath an element, but shall not be considered as part of the clear floor space or turning space.

❖ Minimum dimensions for knee and toe clearances are specified to provide design criteria when access to an accessible element or fixture involves using the space underneath an element or fixture. For example, a forward approach to a counter top or work surface necessitates the feet and legs extending under the counter top or work surface [see Commentary Figure C306.1(a)]. The knee and toe clearance dimensions establish the required unobstructed space that must be provided to afford access to the element. Where knee and toe clearance is required, such as beneath a lavatory or drinking fountain, those provisions will reference Section 306.

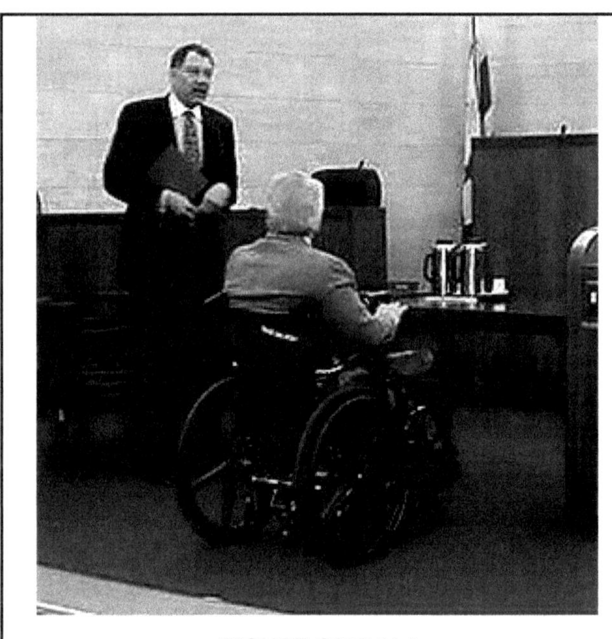

FIGURE C306.1(a)
KNEE AND TOE CLEARANCE UNDER WORK SURFACES

Knee and toe clearances are often a "package deal." Provisions for minimums and maximums for both knee and toe clearances must be addressed when looking for adequate clearance under an object [see Commentary Figures C306.1(b) and C306.1(c) and Sections 306.2 and 306.3]. Providing additional vertical or horizontal clearance beneath an element is permitted; however, the extra space is limited by the maximum extent that a person can fit under the counter or other obstruction. For example, a work surface can be 36 inches (915 mm) deep, but a person cannot move more than 25 inches (635 mm) under the work surface because their chest will come in contact with the edge of the table.

Clearances are measured in relation to the usable clear floor space, not necessarily the vertical support for an element. When determining clearance under an element, care should be taken to ensure the space is clear of any obstructions that would reduce the effective knee and toe clearances.

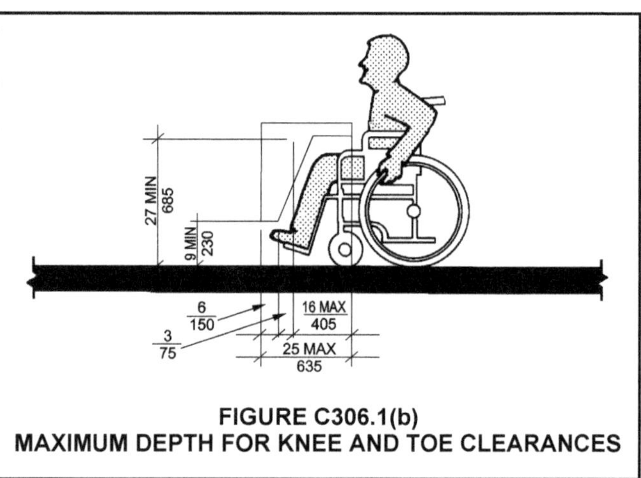

FIGURE C306.1(b)
MAXIMUM DEPTH FOR KNEE AND TOE CLEARANCES

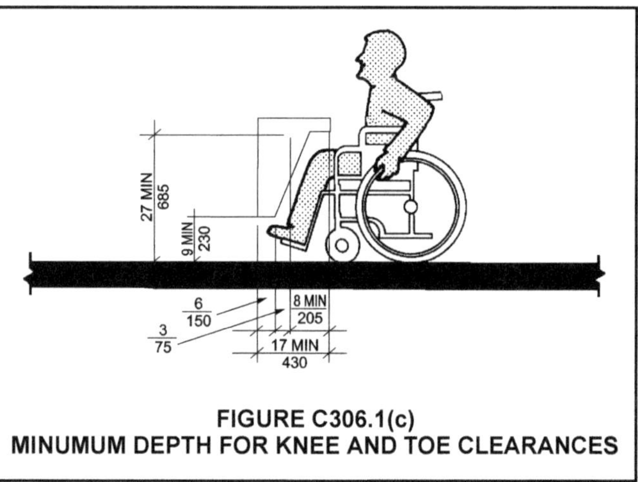

FIGURE C306.1(c)
MINUMUM DEPTH FOR KNEE AND TOE CLEARANCES

306.2 Toe Clearance.

❖ The subsections of Section 306.2 contain all the technical provisions for toe clearance. Figure 306.2 shows some of the requirements for toe space. While knee and toe clearances have separate technical requirements, they are often required as a package (see commentary, Section 306.1).

306.2.1 General. Space beneath an element between the floor and 9 inches (230 mm) above the floor shall be considered toe clearance and shall comply with Section 306.2.

❖ The 9 inches (230 mm) for toe clearance is based on the typical height of the kick plates on the front of a wheelchair. For example, although not required, the kickplates on cabinets may be raised to over 9 inches (230 mm) to facilitate moving closer to a counter over a cabinet when a front approach is provided. Another example would be the allowances for tighter toilet stalls when the partitions are raised 9 inches (230 mm) or more so that the footplates can extend underneath during maneuvering (Section 604.9.5).

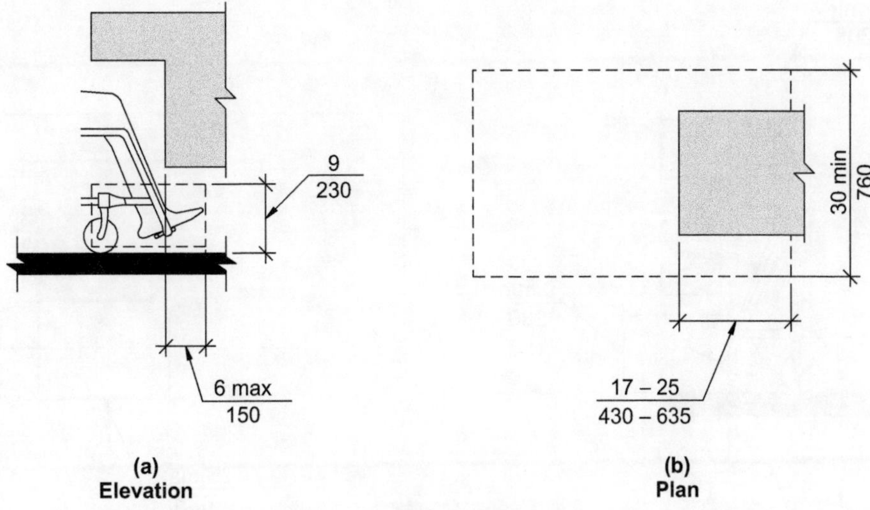

FIGURE 306.2
TOE CLEARANCES

306.2.2 Maximum Depth. Toe clearance shall be permitted to extend 25 inches (635 mm) maximum under an element.

❖ This depth limit is based on the size of the typical user and wheelchair. The 25-inch (635 mm) maximum depth includes both the knee and toe clearances and limits how much of the required clear floor space may extend underneath an element. The location of the upper body and/or arms of the wheelchair would not allow a person to slide farther under the counter or fixture [see Commentary Figure C306.1(b)]. The actual area beneath the element may extend beyond the 25-inch (635 mm) limit, but that space is not considered part of the toe or knee space or the area designated as being the clear floor space. The maximum dimension does not require any area beyond the 25-inch (635 mm) length to be blocked off even though the space extends beyond that depth (see commentary, Section 306.3.2).

306.2.3 Minimum Depth. Where toe clearance is required at an element as part of a clear floor space complying with Section 305, the toe clearance shall extend 17 inches (430 mm) minimum beneath the element.

❖ This minimum depth is established to ensure that a user may get positioned under the element and have items within their reach range. See Figures 308.2.1 and 308.2.2 of the standard for examples of how the position of the clear floor space, and therefore, where the person using a wheelchair is located affects the use of a fixture or element. Note that this is when toe space is required under an element [see Commentary Figure C306.1(c) and commentary, Section 306.3.3].

306.2.4 Additional Clearance. Space extending greater than 6 inches (150 mm) beyond the available knee clearance at 9 inches (230 mm) above the floor shall not be considered toe clearance.

❖ If there is a barrier or wall blocking the knee clearance under a counter or fixture (e.g., pipe protection under a lavatory), the toe clearance cannot extend more than 6 inches (150 mm) past the provided knee clearance [see Commentary Figure C306.1(b)]. Space may be available beyond this required limit, but because it would not be useable as toe clearance, the additional space cannot be considered as being a part of the required knee and toe space or the area designated as being the clear floor space. As discussed in the commentary to Section 306.2.2, the additional space need not be blocked off in any manner.

306.2.5 Width. Toe clearance shall be 30 inches (760 mm) minimum in width.

❖ This requirement coordinates with the minimum required width for a clear floor space and permits persons using wheelchairs to fit their toes and the chair beneath the obstruction. If this space is under a counter and is used as part of a T-turn, the width would have to be 36 inches (915 mm) in accordance with Section 304.3.2 [see Figure 304.3(b), Figure 305.3 and Commentary Figure C305.4].

306.3 Knee Clearance.

❖ The subsections of Section 306.3 contain all the technical provisions for knee clearance. Figure 306.3 shows some of the requirements for knee space. Even though knee and toe clearances have separate technical requirements, they are often required as a package. See the commentary for Section 306.1 for related discussion.

306.3.1 General. Space beneath an element between 9 inches (230 mm) and 27 inches (685 mm) above the floor shall be considered knee clearance and shall comply with Section 306.3.

❖ Space below 9 inches (230 mm) is considered toe clearance. Space between 9 inches and 27 inches (685 mm) is considered knee clearance (see commentary, Section 306.2).

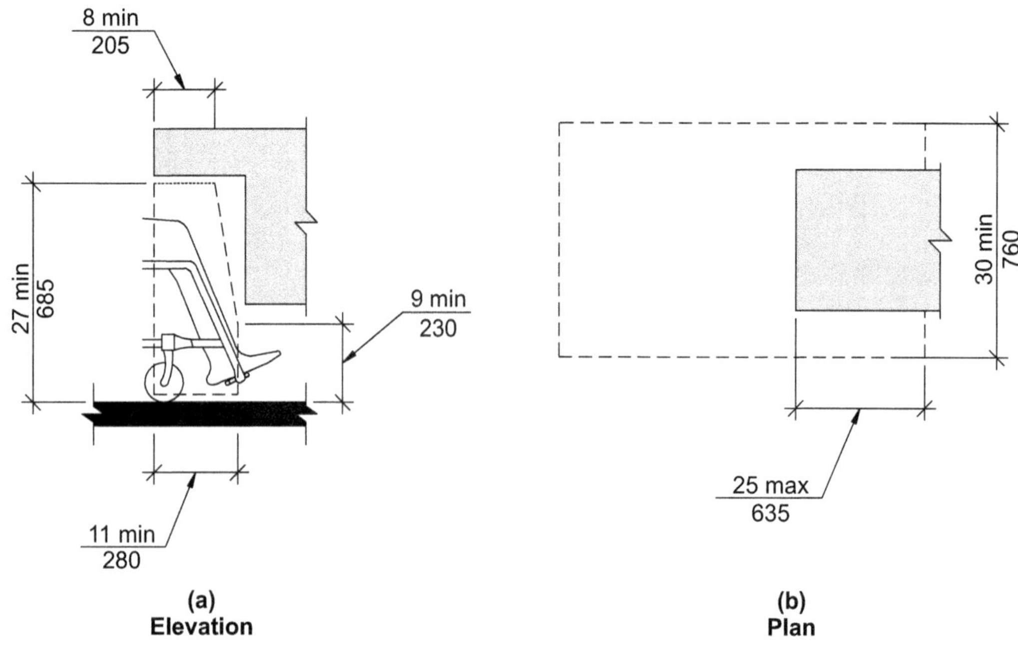

FIGURE 306.3
KNEE CLEARANCE

306.3.2 Maximum Depth. Knee clearance shall be permitted to extend 25 inches (635 mm) maximum under an element at 9 inches (230 mm) above the floor.

❖ This depth limit is based on the size of the typical user and wheelchair. The 25-inch (635 mm) maximum depth includes both the knee and toe clearances and limits how much of the required clear floor space may extend underneath an element. The location of the upper body and/or arms of the wheelchair would not allow a person to slide farther under the counter or fixture [see Commentary Figure C306.1(b)]. The actual area beneath the element may extend beyond the 25-inch (635 mm) limit, but that space is not considered part of the toe or knee space or the area designated as being the clear floor space. The maximum dimension does not require any area beyond the 25-inch (635 mm) length to be blocked off even though the space extends beyond that depth.

Combined with the requirements of Section 306.2.2, the actual maximum depth of the knee clearance is 19 inches (480 mm) maximum (i.e., 25-inch depth - 6-inch toe clearance = 19 inches) at the bottom of the knee space, and 16-inches (i.e., 25-inch depth - 6-inch toe clearance - 3-inch slope allowance = 16 inches) at the top of the knee space [see Commentary Figure C306.1(b)].

306.3.3 Minimum Depth. Where knee clearance is required beneath an element as part of a clear floor space complying with Section 305, the knee clearance shall be 11 inches (280 mm) minimum in depth at 9 inches (230 mm) above the floor, and 8 inches (205 mm) minimum in depth at 27 inches (685 mm) above the floor.

❖ Minimum dimensions for knee and toe clearances are specified to provide design criteria when access to an accessible element or fixture involves using the space underneath an element or fixture. For example, a forward approach to a counter top or work surface necessitates the feet and legs extending under the counter top or work surface as shown in Commentary Figure C306.1(c). The knee and toe clearance dimensions establish the required unobstructed space that must be provided to afford access to the element. Where knee and toe clearance is required, such as beneath a lavatory or drinking fountain as specified in Section 602.2 or 606.2, these minimum dimensions are required.

As shown in Figure 306.3 the area represented by the dashed lines shows how the knee clearance may be less deep at the top and then increased as it approaches the toe clearance level. The increase of the depth of the knee clearance, starting at 8 inches (205 mm) at the top and increasing to 11 inches (280 mm) at the bottom, is in recognition of the alignment of the legs of a person sitting in a wheelchair.

Combined with the requirements of Section 306.2.3, the actual minimum depth of the knee clearance results in a total of 17 inches (430 mm) for knee and toe clearances under a counter or fixture [see Commentary Figure C306.1(c)].

306.3.4 Clearance Reduction. Between 9 inches (230 mm) and 27 inches (685 mm) above the floor, the knee clearance shall be permitted to be reduced at a rate of 1 inch (25 mm) in depth for each 6 inches (150 mm) in height.

❖ The minimum depth requirements for knee clearance are established in Section 306.3.3. If additional knee space is provided, the clearance reduction is intended to be consistent with the allowance for the alignment of a person's legs for all knee clearances [see Commentary Figures C306.1(b) and C306.1(c)].

306.3.5 Width. Knee clearance shall be 30 inches (760 mm) minimum in width.

❖ This requirement coordinates with the minimum required width for a clear floor space and will permit a person using a wheelchair to fit his or her legs and the chair beneath the obstruction. If this space is under a counter and is used as part of a T-turn, the width would be required to be 36 inches (915 mm) in accordance with Section 304.3.2 [see Figures 304.3(b), 305.3 and 306.3(b) and Commentary Figure C305.4].

307 Protruding Objects

❖ Many items along the path of travel can be protruding objects for persons with visual impairments, or persons who may be momentarily distracted. There are additional concerns during emergency events where smoke may obscure objects and people are hurrying to escape. The following section addresses criteria for a variety of protruding objects (see Commentary Figure C307).

FIGURE C307
EXAMPLES OF PROTRUDING OBJECTS

307.1 General. Protruding objects on circulation paths shall comply with Section 307.

❖ This section addresses items that extend into the circulation path that people may bump into. Guide dogs are trained to recognize and assist their handlers to avoid hazards. However, people with severe vision impairments may use the long cane as an aid to mobility. With the customary cane technique, the cane is moved in arcs from side to side to touch points outside both shoulders of the user [see Commentary Figures C307.1(a) and C307.1(b)].

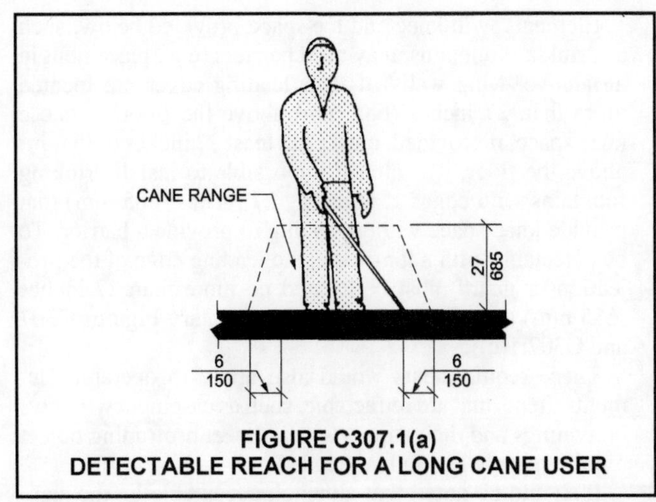

FIGURE C307.1(a)
DETECTABLE REACH FOR A LONG CANE USER

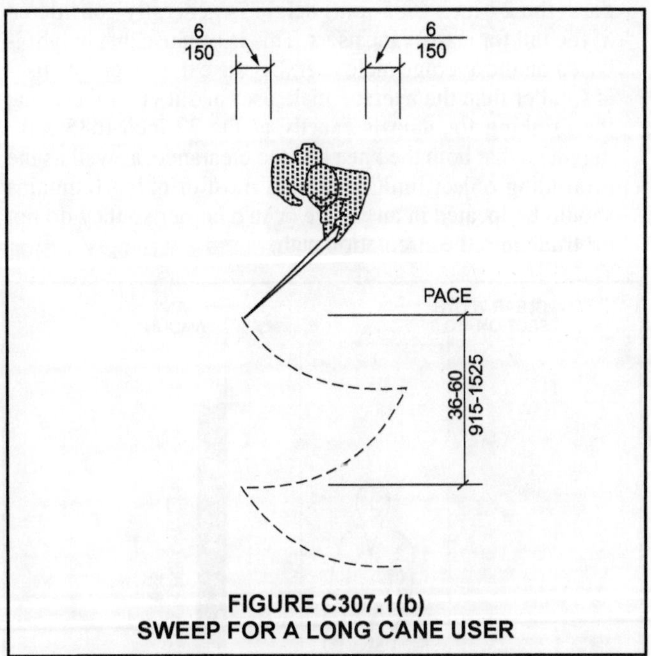

FIGURE C307.1(b)
SWEEP FOR A LONG CANE USER

Potentially hazardous objects may be detected by long-cane users if they fall within the detection range of canes. This gives a person sufficient time to detect the element with the cane before there is body contact. People with visual impairments walking toward an object can detect an overhang if its lowest surface is no higher than 27 inches (685 mm) [see Commentary Figure C307.1(c)]. Because of imperfect forward protection provided by the long cane and individual variations in how people use their canes, detection of protruding objects is not assured. Individuals with low vision may have poor acuity or depth perception and cannot reliably see low-lying protruding objects.

It is also important to check all portions of the projection and not just the lowest part. For example, a bowl-type drinking fountain may be mounted on an arm or pedestal which is at the 27-inch (685 mm) height, but because the bowl above it sticks out farther and is at a higher level, the projection must also be considered. Therefore, check both the height and the overall projection of all elements that protrude into the circulation path.

Elements with knee and toe space provided below, such as drinking fountains, may need barriers (e.g., placement in an alcove, wing walls) if their leading edges are located more than 27 inches (685 mm) above the floor. Because knee space, if provided, must be at least 27 inches (685 mm) above the floor, it is almost impossible to install drinking fountains with edges at precisely 27 inches (685 mm) that provide knee space without having to provide a barrier. To be detectable with a long cane, the leading edge of the projection or guard must be located no more than 27 inches (685 mm) above the floor [see Commentary Figures C307 and C307.1(c)].

These requirements would also apply to operable elements. Items that are retractable, such as casement windows or awnings and their supports, must meet protruding object requirements when fully extended.

It should be noted that although acceptable by the standard, the 27-inch (685 mm) height is generally considered as too tall for many cane users. This is because that height is based on the average male user. Because the "average" user is smaller than the average male user and it is unlikely that the drinking fountain is exactly at the 27-inch (685 mm) height so that both the knee and toe clearance, as well as the protruding object limits, are met, most drinking fountains should be located in an alcove or in a corner so they do not protrude into the circulation path.

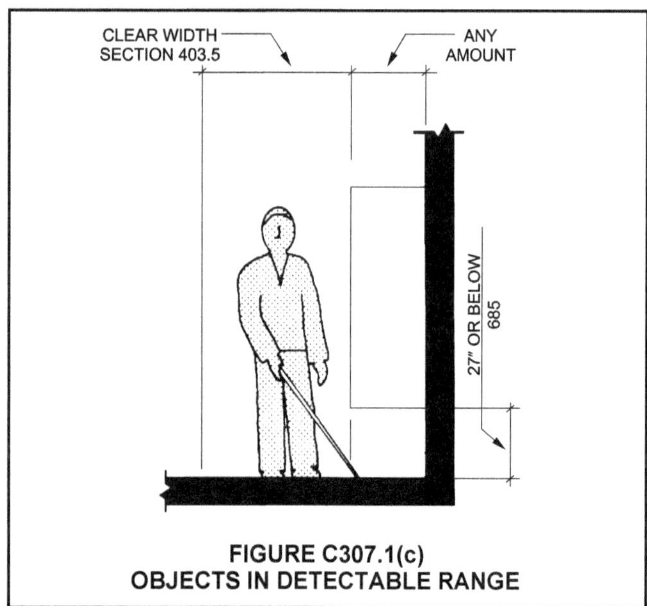

FIGURE C307.1(c)
OBJECTS IN DETECTABLE RANGE

307.2 Protrusion Limits. Objects with leading edges more than 27 inches (685 mm) and not more than 80 inches (2030 mm) above the floor shall protrude 4 inches (100 mm) maximum horizontally into the circulation path.

> **EXCEPTION:** Handrails shall be permitted to protrude $4^1/_2$ inches (115 mm) maximum.

❖ The overall height limitation of 80 inches (2030 mm) is important. One of the more common injuries for persons with sight impairments is striking their heads on overhanging objects, such as overhead signage or sconces.

Objects such as drinking fountains with leading edges that are 27 inches (685 mm) above a surface allow a person using a wheelchair to make a forward approach and use the space below as knee and toe space. It is also the highest point at which a long-cane user can detect the object [see Commentary Figure C307.1(a)]. As such, any protrusion above 27 inches (685 mm) will not be readily detectable. The user could unexpectedly impact the protrusion and sustain an injury. An object with the leading edge at or below 27 inches (685 mm) above the floor can protrude any amount because the protrusion is considered detectable and avoidable.

The allowable protrusion of 4 inches (100 mm) recognizes that avoidance of all protrusions is unrealistic, and limits them to an extent that minimizes the likelihood of inadvertent contact. Protrusions higher than 80 inches (2030 mm) above the floor are not limited because they are assumed to be overhead and not subject to accidental impact (see Figure 307.2). Eighty inches (2030 mm) is consistent with the required headroom clearances specified in the model building codes. These limitations on protruding objects serve to protect all people, not just those with a vision impairment, from unintended contact and potential injury.

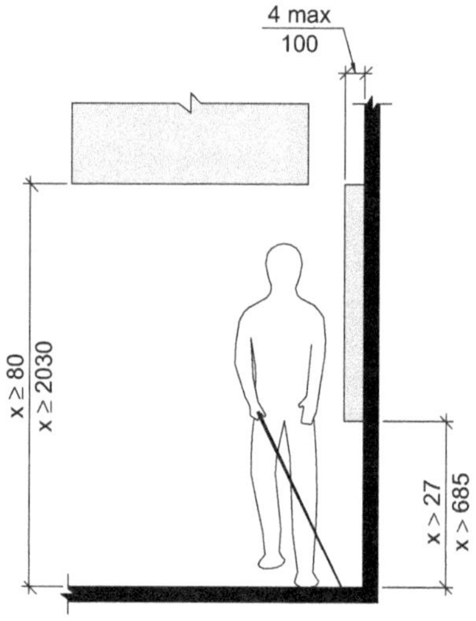

FIGURE 307.2
LIMITS OF PROTRUDING OBJECTS

It is important to look at the entire object that is protruding and determine what the appropriate requirements would be. For example, part of the object may be located so that it is below the 27-inch (685 mm) limitation even though other portions may be located at a higher level or extend beyond the lower projection. In these circumstances it is important to determine the lowest, the highest and the farthest projections of that object to determine exactly how the protrusion must be protected and how far it may extend.

The exception for handrails is based on the fact that they are typically installed on stairs and ramps and the level changes would help to provide the user with an awareness of the handrail. The $4^1/_2$-inch (115 mm) dimension coordinates with the projection depth for handrails in the *International Building Code*® (IBC®). Although this exceeds the normal depth permitted for a protruding object, the limited location and the fact that handrails must be mounted within a height of 34 to 38 inches (864 to 965 mm) above the walking surfaces help to make this situation acceptable (see Section 505.4). This exception is limited to the run of the stair or ramp. Handrail end projections must be detectable.

307.3 Post-Mounted Objects. Objects on posts or pylons shall be permitted to overhang 4 inches (100 mm) maximum where more than 27 inches (685 mm) and not more than 80 inches (2030 mm) above the floor. Objects on multiple posts or pylons where the clear distance between the posts or pylons is greater than 12 inches (305 mm) shall have the lowest edge of such object either 27 inches (685 mm) maximum or 80 inches (2030 mm) minimum above the floor.

EXCEPTION: Sloping portions of handrails between the top and bottom riser of stairs and above the ramp run shall not be required to comply with Section 307.3.

❖ Similar to wall- and ceiling-mounted protrusions discussed in the commentary for Section 307.2, the intent of these provisions is to specify dimensional criteria that limit protrusions within various ranges that may not be readily detectable and avoidable. These limitations benefit all people, not just those with a visual impairment.

The criteria for objects mounted between posts or pylons apply when the pylons are more than 12 inches (305 mm) apart (see Figure 307.3). In this circumstance, it is possible that a person using a long cane could directly approach the pylons but not detect them with the sweep pattern of the cane. Therefore, the standard requires that the bottom edge of the obstruction between the pylons be either 27 inches (685 mm) maximum above the floor, so that the cane will detect the object before the person bumps into it, or it must be at least 80 inches (2030 mm) above the floor.

To be consistent with the protruding object provisions in Section 307.2, the outside edge of the sign on multiple posts, or items mounted on single posts (e.g., accessible parking signs, outdoor telephones) may not protrude more than 4 inches (100 mm) from the support.

These provisions are for objects along flat walking surfaces and are not intended to be applied to the sloped portion of handrails along a stair or ramp (other than end projections) or signs located over grass areas.

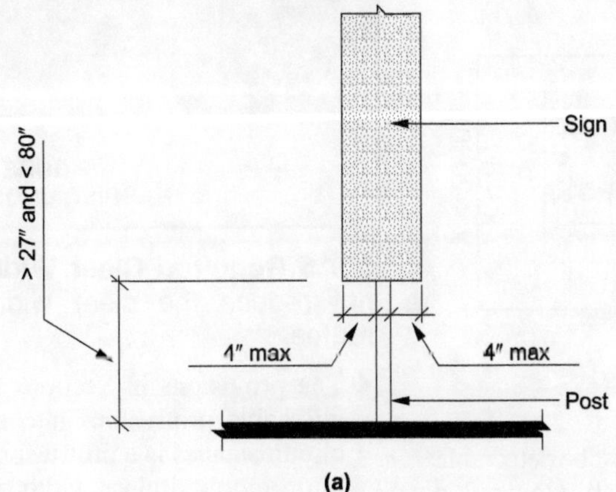

(a)

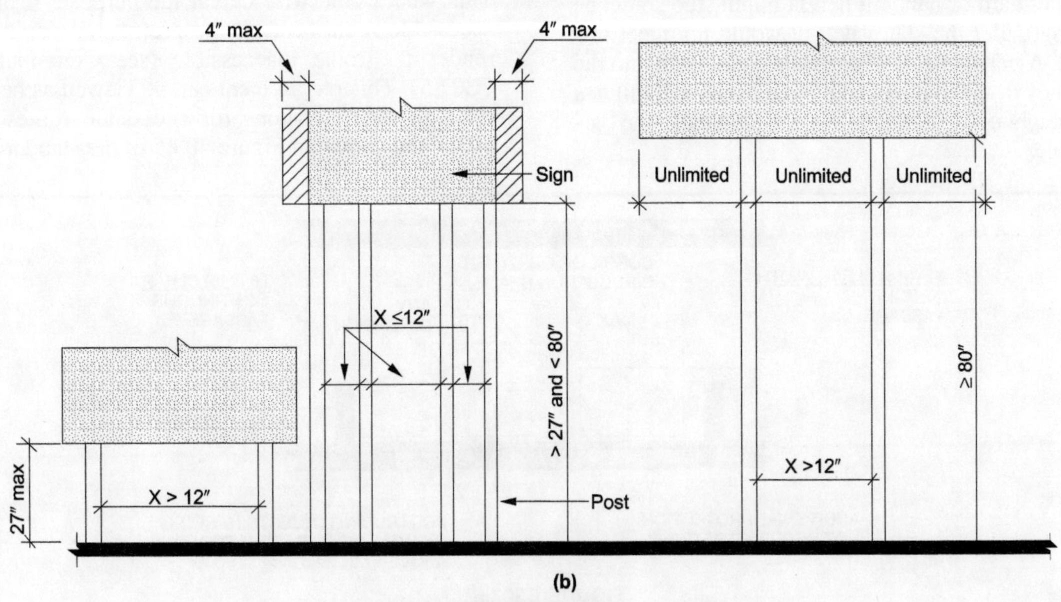

(b)

FIGURE 307.3
POST-MOUNTED PROTRUDING OBJECTS

307.4 Vertical Clearance. Vertical clearance shall be 80 inches (2030 mm) minimum. Rails or other barriers shall be provided where the vertical clearance is less than 80 inches (2030 mm). The leading edge of such rails or barrier shall be located 27 inches (685 mm) maximum above the floor.

EXCEPTION: Door closers and door stops shall be permitted to be 78 inches (1980 mm) minimum above the floor.

❖ For safety reasons, generally the means of egress requirements in model building codes do not permit headroom clearances of less than 80 inches (2030 mm) above a walking surface. However, there are circumstances, such as the space beneath a stairway, where it is possible for a person with a visual impairment to approach that area and bump into the portion that occurs below the headroom clearance height of 80 inches (2030 mm). The purpose of this provision is to require that a guard or other type of barrier be installed so that it can be detected before a person bumps into the overhead protrusion. Figure 307.4 illustrates this requirement.

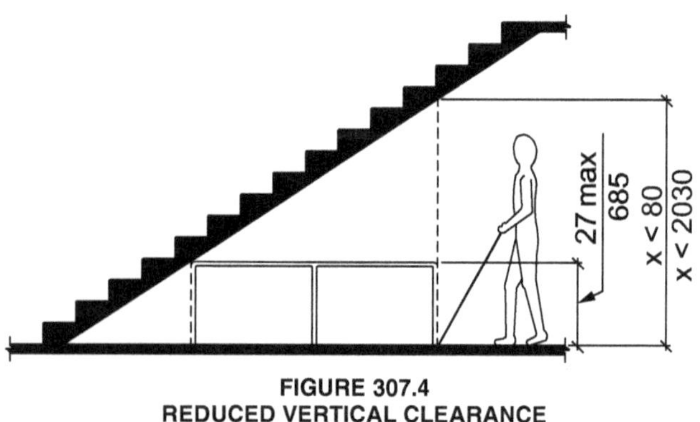

FIGURE 307.4
REDUCED VERTICAL CLEARANCE

Note that whatever barrier is chosen, it must be detectable by a long cane. This could be a full-height wall, a low rail, a planter, etc. (see Commentary Figure C307.4). A single horizontal rail at guard or handrail height might stop someone from walking under the stairway, but would not meet this requirement. A person using a long cane could walk into the rail before they detected it. An additional horizontal rail at a maximum height of 27 inches or lower would make the barrier detectable.

The use of a platform or curb under a protruding stair would be detectable, but if it could be perceived by a person with low vision as a step up, rather than a barrier, it would not meet the intent of this provision.

The exception is to allow for a minimal reduction in clearance for door closers. With an 80-inch (2030 mm) minimum height required for door openings, the door closer must protrude below the frame to attach to and retract the door.

FIGURE C307.4
BARRIER UNDER STAIRWAY

307.5 Required Clear Width. Protruding objects shall not reduce the clear width required for accessible routes.

❖ The provisions in Sections 307.2 through 307.4 establish allowable protrusions into an accessible route. Under no circumstances is a protrusion permitted to reduce the minimum required clear width of an accessible route, even if the protrusion complies with one of the previous sections. This would otherwise defeat the purpose of providing an accessible route because the protrusion would effectively render the route inaccessible (see Commentary Figure C307.5). This requirement can be viewed as being comparable to the provisions for accessible routes in Section 403.5 and shown in Figure 403.5 of the standard.

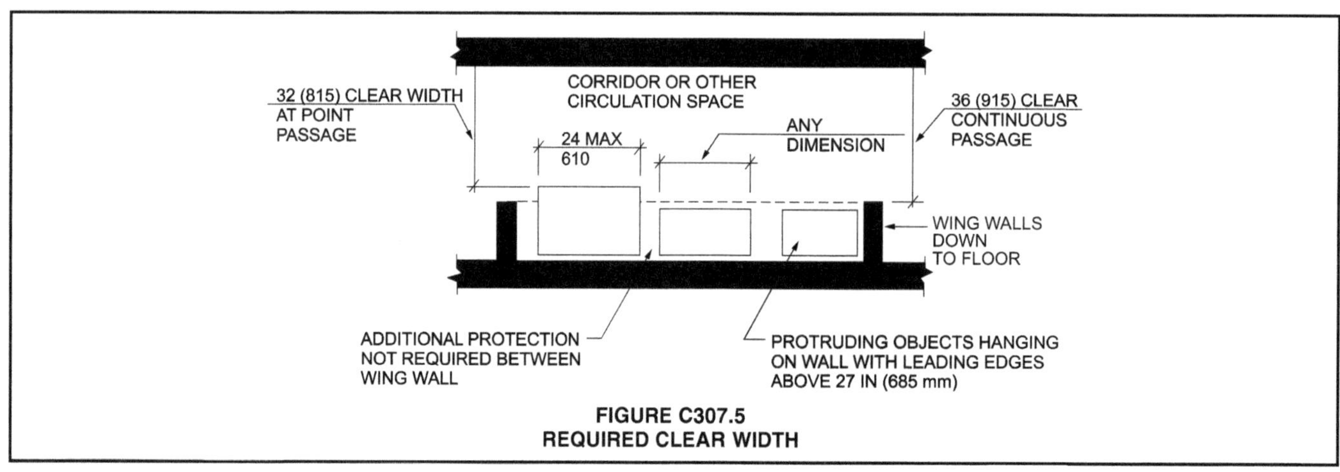

FIGURE C307.5
REQUIRED CLEAR WIDTH

308 Reach Ranges

308.1 General. Reach ranges shall comply with Section 308.

❖ These provisions identify the reach range that is understood to be achievable by the person using a wheelchair. From a sitting position, one can reach up or down, to either the front or the side only to a limited point. These dimensions determine the vertical dimensions within which an element must be located to be accessible. Anything located outside these ranges may not be reachable, and therefore, not accessible. These ranges also benefit persons who are short of stature (see commentary, Section 308.3).

It should also be noted that the standard currently addresses to a limited extent the reach restrictions for depth for adults with dwarfism and others of short stature in Sections 606.5 and 606.7.

The U.S. Access Board has reviewed provisions for children. Commentary Table C308.1 is based on that research and provides guidance on unobstructed reach ranges for children according to age where building elements such as coat hooks, lockers, or operable parts are designed for use primarily by children. This table is for information only and is not intended to provide requirements. The dimensions apply to either forward or side reaches. Accessible elements and operable parts designed for adult use or children over age 12 are addressed by Section 308.

308.2 Forward Reach.

❖ This section provides technical requirements for a forward reach when persons using a wheelchair can locate themselves directly in front of an object (unobstructed) or when they must reach over a counter, table or other object (obstructed). It is difficult for persons using a wheelchair to reach past their toes. Reach ranges are typically referenced for access to controls (e.g., lights, heating/air conditioning, appliance controls, plumbing controls).

308.2.1 Unobstructed. Where a forward reach is unobstructed, the high forward reach shall be 48 inches (1220 mm) maximum and the low forward reach shall be 15 inches (380 mm) minimum above the floor.

❖ The forward reach to an element is considered unobstructed when the wheelchair can be moved as close as possible to the element, typically a switch or control on a wall as shown in Figure 308.2.1. This position allows the greatest possible forward reach from a sitting position.

It is not the intent of this section to consider types of wall finishes or standard trim, such as baseboards or chair rails, as obstructions. Although a specific limit for the depth is not indicated, the concern is whether the wall finish or trim stopped the person using the wheelchair from moving forward to the maximum extent possible. A common error is the 40 inches (1015 mm) being measured to the center of the electrical box instead of the control, for example, on some styles of thermostats.

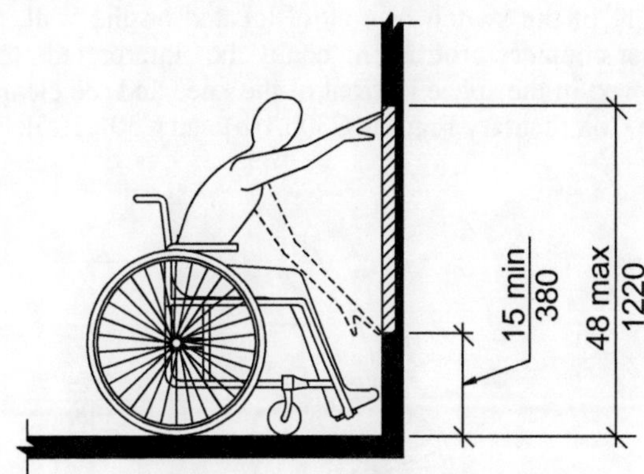

FIGURE 308.2.1
UNOBSTRUCTED FORWARD REACH

308.2.2 Obstructed High Reach. Where a high forward reach is over an obstruction, the clear floor space complying with Section 305 shall extend beneath the element for a distance not less than the required reach depth over the obstruction. The high forward reach shall be 48 inches (1220 mm) maximum above the floor where the reach depth is 20 inches (510mm) maximum. Where the reach depth exceeds 20 inches (510 mm), the high forward reach shall be 44 inches (1120 mm) maximum above the floor, and the reach depth shall be 25 inches (635 mm) maximum.

❖ This section establishes the reach height limitation based on the horizontal reach depth over an obstruction, such as a counter. The forward reach to an element is considered obstructed when an architectural feature such as a countertop prevents the person using a wheelchair from moving as close as possible to the element. In such cases, the effective reach height is reduced. The effective reach height is a function of the depth of the obstruction and how close the obstruction allows the user to go to the element. The farther from the element, the lower the reachable distance above the element. The closer to the element, the higher the reachable distance.

In a lot of situations, the knee and toe clearances available under the counter are the same depth as the counter. If there is something under the counter that would stop someone from moving fully under the counter (e.g., pipe protection, privacy shield, cable tray), the obstruction under the counter could effectively control the possible reach over

Table C308.1
UNOBSTRUCTED CHILDREN'S REACH RANGES

UNOBSTRUCTED CHILDREN'S REACH RANGES			
Forward or Side Reach	**Ages 3 and 4**	**Ages 5 through 8**	**Ages 9 Through 12**
High (maximum)	36 in. (915 mm)	40 in. (1015 mm)	44 in. (1120)
Low (minimum)	20 in. (510 mm)	15 in. (455 mm)	16 in. (405 mm)

the counter. Therefore, the requirement for "shall extend beneath the element for a distance not less than the required reach depth" would require a designer to look at the depth someone could move under a counter, as well as the reach over the counter, to determine the appropriate height of the switch or control located on the wall. Such under-counter protrusion could be interpreted to be allowed in the space in front of the knee and toe clearance [see Commentary Figures C306.1(b) and C306.1(c)].

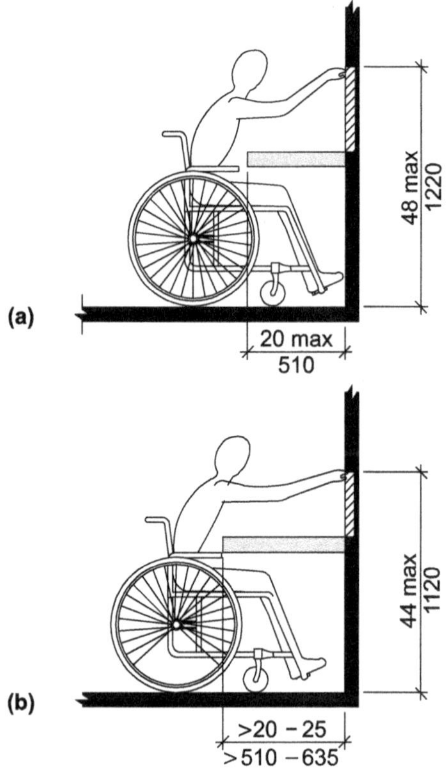

FIGURE 308.2.2
OBSTRUCTED HIGH FORWARD REACH

308.3 Side Reach.

❖ Research with persons using wheelchairs has shown that the reach height from the side of a wheelchair (parallel approach –9 inches to 54 inches) varies from that for a forward reach (forward approach –15 inches to 48 inches). This occurs because the parallel approach brings the person closer to the element and also because of the body's range of motion. Any obstructions that limit the proximity of the wheelchair to the element will reduce the reach range.

The A117.1 Standard Review Committee revised the side reach ranges in the 1998 edition of the standard. This revision was based on information provided by an organization called Little People of America. They were able to provide statistical information based on the limited reach of some of their members that demonstrated the need for the 48-inch (1220 mm) maximum reach.

308.3.1 Unobstructed. Where a clear floor space complying with Section 305 allows a parallel approach to an element and the edge of the clear floor space is 10 inches (255 mm) maximum from the element, the high side reach shall be 48 inches (1220 mm) maximum and the low side reach shall be 15 inches (380 mm) minimum above the floor.

EXCEPTION: Existing elements that are not altered shall be permitted at 54 inches (1370 mm) maximum above the floor.

❖ This section includes the effective reach range assumed to be achievable by a person using a wheelchair when there are no obstructions that limit how close the chair can be positioned relative to the element. Side reach is considered unobstructed when something below an operable part is less than 10 inches (255 mm) deep. This allowance would permit side approaches to be considered unobstructed when a person would need to reach over projections, such as heating controls over baseboard heaters, or a light switch on the side wall over a counter.

Although many persons using wheelchairs can reach lower, the 15-inch (380 mm) criterion serves persons with arthritis, back problems, severely limited reach and limited finger dexterity.

The exception recognizes that earlier editions of the standard permitted a high side reach range of 54 inches (1370 mm). Therefore, in facilities constructed using the earlier standard, such elements may remain at this higher level as long as that element is not altered.

While the side reach requirements literally would allow for the element anywhere along the side of the clear floor space, it is difficult, if not impossible, to reach in the far corners. See Commentary Figure C308.3.1 for a graphic representation. Good design would take the reach into consideration when placing the clear floor space.

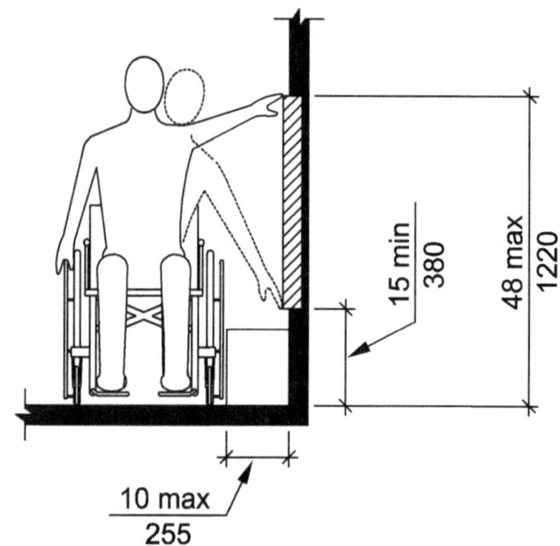

FIGURE 308.3.1
UNOBSTRUCTED SIDE REACH

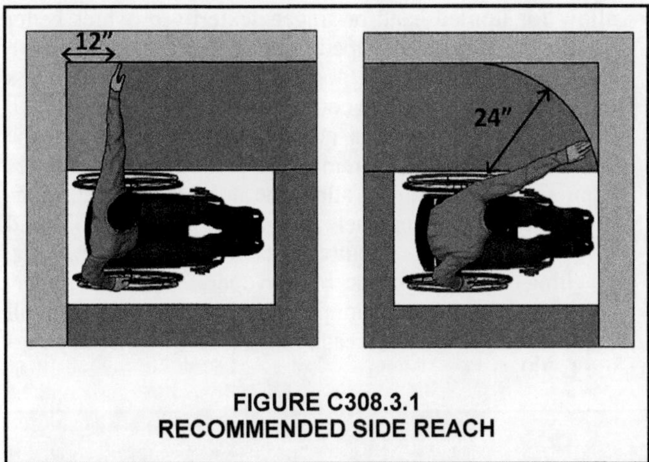

FIGURE C308.3.1
RECOMMENDED SIDE REACH

308.3.2 Obstructed High Reach. Where a clear floor space complying with Section 305 allows a parallel approach to an element and the high side reach is over an obstruction, the height of the obstruction shall be 34 inches (865 mm) maximum above the floor and the depth of the obstruction shall be 24 inches (610 mm) maximum. The high side reach shall be 48 inches (1220 mm) maximum above the floor for a reach depth of 10 inches (255 mm) maximum. Where the reach depth exceeds 10 inches (255 mm), the high side reach shall be 46 inches (1170 mm) maximum above the floor for a reach depth of 24 inches (610 mm) maximum.

EXCEPTION: At washing machines and clothes dryers, the height of the obstruction shall be permitted to be 36 inches (915 mm) maximum above the floor.

❖ The maximum reach range is reduced when an obstruction prevents the person using a wheelchair from moving within 10 inches (255 mm) of the element. Note that the maximum projection of the obstruction is indicated as 24 inches (610 mm). This means that if the wheelchair cannot move to within at least 24 inches (610 mm) of the element, the element would not be considered reachable, and therefore, not accessible. See Figure 308.3.2 of the standard for details of this requirement.

The height of the obstruction is also limited. An obstruction that is higher would not permit the user to reach beyond that obstruction with his or her arm fully extended to the side. Because of this height limitation, most electrical receptacles and switches located on the wall behind and above kitchen counters [which are typically higher than 34 inches (865 mm)] would not be accessible. Options would be to locate the outlets or switches on the front surface of the cabinets, locate the outlets and switches over the accessible work surface or accessible sink location, or locate the switches on a side wall so that the reach over the counter is less than 10 inches (see Section 309 for additional discussions).

Washing machines and clothes dryers with rear panel controls typically have a deck height of 36 inches (915 mm). These standard machine heights are acknowledged and given an exception.

309 Operable Parts

❖ For buildings and spaces to be usable by all people, all of the components possible are required to be accessible. This includes the controls and operable parts of equipment and appliances intended for operation by the occupants in a space. If a standard control would be out of the reach range (e.g., exhaust hood over a cooktop, ceiling fan), a solution would be redundant controls at an accessible location.

309.1 General. Operable parts required to be accessible shall comply with Section 309.

❖ To make sure that the elements truly are accessible, other sections of the standard such as those for drinking fountains (Section 602.3), water closet flush controls (Section 604.6), lavatories and sinks (Section 606.4), and kitchen appliances (Section 804.6.2) will direct the user back to and required compliance with this section. Other examples of operable parts that are within the scope of this provision include light switches, dispenser controls, electrical appliance controls, electrical receptacles and communications system receptacles. While door hardware is considered an operable part, Section 404.2.6 does not reference Section 309. Door hardware requirements use a lot of the same lan-

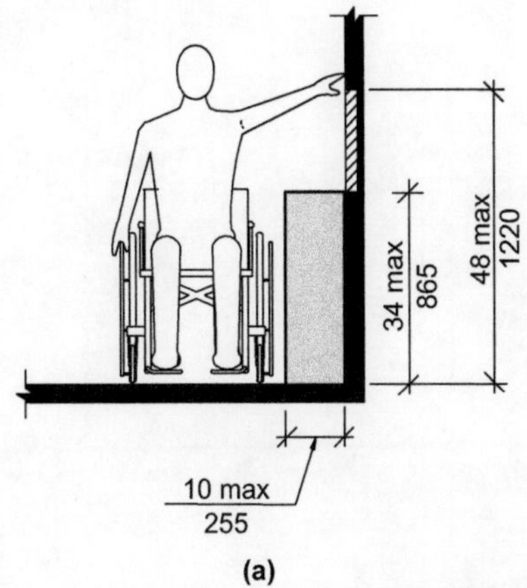

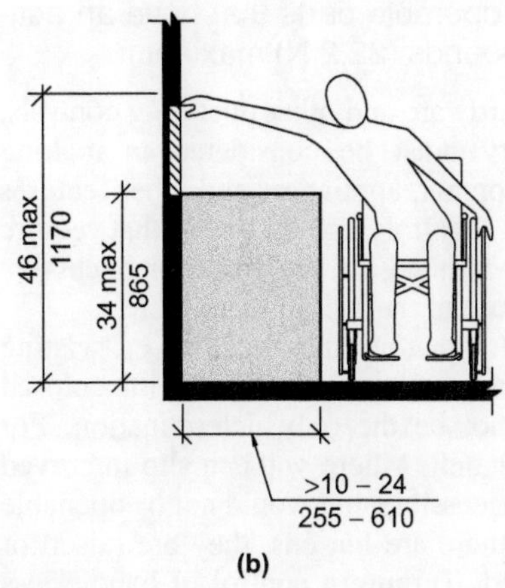

FIGURE 308.3.2
OBSTRUCTED HIGH SIDE REACH

guage for clear floor space, height and manipulation (i.e., not tight pinching, grasping, twisting of the wrist), but do not require 5 pounds (2.22 N) for hardware operation. Hardware force requirements are set in the IBC for some types of hardware (i.e., panic hardware) (see Section 404.2.8 for door opening force).

309.2 Clear Floor Space. A clear floor space complying with Section 305 shall be provided.

❖ Providing a place for persons using a wheelchair to position their chair in close proximity to controls is especially important for operable parts of equipment and appliances. Wall fixtures or equipment located in an alcove situation must also be considered.

309.3 Height. Operable parts shall be placed within one or more of the reach ranges specified in Section 308.

❖ All of a control, receptacle or other operable parts are to be within the specified reach ranges. Electrical and communications receptacles on walls are required by Sections 308.2 and 308.3 to be at least 15 inches (380 mm) above the floor.

Specific requirements and/or exceptions in other parts of the standard, or scoping requirements from the model codes, may limit this requirement. For example, model codes exempt spaces that are accessed only by maintenance and service personnel; therefore, special equipment with operational needs that preclude installation within reach ranges may be exempted. One example is the controls on a furnace or boiler located in a basement furnace room for an office building.

A second example would be applicable to a dedicated outlet, such as the one for a refrigerator, that is located behind the appliance. Requirements in kitchens are for access to appliance controls. The refrigerator would have to be moved to have access to that outlet; therefore, the outlet for the refrigerator would not need to be within the normal reach ranges.

309.4 Operation. Operable parts shall be operable with one hand and shall not require tight grasping, pinching, or twisting of the wrist. The force required to activate operable parts shall be 5.0 pounds (22.2 N) maximum.

EXCEPTION: Gas pump nozzles shall not be required to provide operable parts that have an activating force of 5.0 pounds (22.2 N) maximum.

❖ As with all types of hardware and other operating controls, limited hand dexterity must be considered in making spaces, facilities, equipment, appliances and other features accessible and usable. Controls and hardware that require grasping, pinching or twisting of the wrist, or excessive force, can make a feature of the building unusable.

One way to determine that no tight pinching or twisting would be needed is if something was useable with a closed fist, but this should not be the only determination. For example, a U-shaped handle where you can slip in curved fingers is considered accessible, but would not be openable with a closed fist. If there are buttons, they are raised or flush, and not recessed. Turning a control of handle less than 90 degrees (1.6 rad) is not typically considered "twisting of the wrist." Any shape of controls that turns that allow for limited hand or finger dexterity provides better access, such as an x-shaped control rather than a smooth round control. Nonfixed portions, such as keys or access cards, are not required to comply with this section.

The exception for gas pump nozzles results from the concern that safety requirements to prevent the gas nozzles from spilling would not allow the nozzles to meet the 5-pounds-force requirements. The gas nozzle could still need to comply with the requirements for no tight grasping, pinching or twisting of the wrist to operate. The other operable parts for a gas pump must still comply with all requirements, including reach range (see Commentary Figure C309.4).

FIGURE C309.4
GAS PUMPS

Chapter 4. Accessible Routes

❖ Chapter 4 provides the technical requirements for accessible routes, both outside and inside of a building. Accessible routes connect accessible elements.

- Section 401 is a general statement about the Chapter 4 criteria being applicable for accessible routes where required by the authority having jurisdiction.
- Section 402 lists what elements are considered part of an accessible route, as well as stating that revolving doors, gates and turnstiles cannot be part of an accessible route.
- Section 403 deals with walking surface requirements.
- Section 404 contains criteria for all types of doors—manual swinging and sliding doors, door openings and automatic doors, including power-assisted, low-energy and fully powered.
- Sections 405 and 406 overlap with criteria for ramps and curb ramps.
- Sections 407, 408 and 409 address requirements for different types of passenger elevators—passenger, limited-use/limited access and private residence. Unique criteria for destination-oriented and existing elevators are dispersed throughout where applicable. Where each type of passenger elevator can be used is limited by the referenced standard, ASME A17.1.
- Section 410 is concerned with platform lift criteria.

401 General

401.1 Scope. Accessible routes required by the scoping provisions adopted by the administrative authority shall comply with the applicable provisions of Chapter 4.

❖ A route must comply with all of the applicable provisions of Chapter 4 to be considered as an acceptable accessible route. This section further clarifies that all of the individual components of an accessible route, such as width, passing space, surface texture, slope and the other features, must comply with the applicable provisions. The sum total of all components of an accessible route is that which accomplishes the intent of this standard to provide access to required elements of buildings and facilities.

Note that these provisions apply to the accessible routes required by the scoping provisions, not all routes (see Section 201).

402 Accessible Routes

❖ The accessible route allows a person with a disability to approach, enter and use a building or facility. Interior accessible routes may include doors, floors, ramps, elevators, platform lifts and clear floor space at fixtures. Exterior accessible routes may include parking, access aisles, walks, ramps and curb ramps. The extent to which accessible elements and spaces must be connected by an accessible route is established in the scoping provisions. Please note that while there are criteria for stairways in Section 504 of this standard, stairways are never considered part of an accessible route.

402.1 General. Accessible routes shall comply with Section 402.

❖ Accessible routes must comply with all of the provisions of Section 402 to provide an acceptable degree of accessibility to the elements they serve. See the requirements in Section 402.2 for components that make up accessible routes.

402.2 Components. Accessible routes shall consist of one or more of the following components: walking surfaces with a slope not steeper than 1:20, doors and doorways, ramps, curb ramps excluding the flared sides, elevators, and platform lifts. All components of an accessible route shall comply with the applicable portions of this standard.

❖ This section identifies the various types of architectural elements that contribute to an accessible route. In effect, any surface that a person can travel using a wheelchair to reach an accessible element can be a part of an accessible route if it complies with the provisions of Chapter 4. Chapter 4 includes provisions for the elements listed as part of the accessible route (see Commentary Figure C402.2).

By the definition for ramps in Section 106.5, any walking surface that slopes at 1:20 (1 inch rise to 20 inches of run) or less is considered a sloped walkway. Walking surfaces that slope from 1:20 up to 1:12 (1 inch rise to 12 inches of run) are considered to be accessible ramps (Section 405) or curb ramps (Section 406).

Although stairways may have elements that could be a concern for persons with mobility impairments, they are not considered part of an accessible route.

(a) Walks

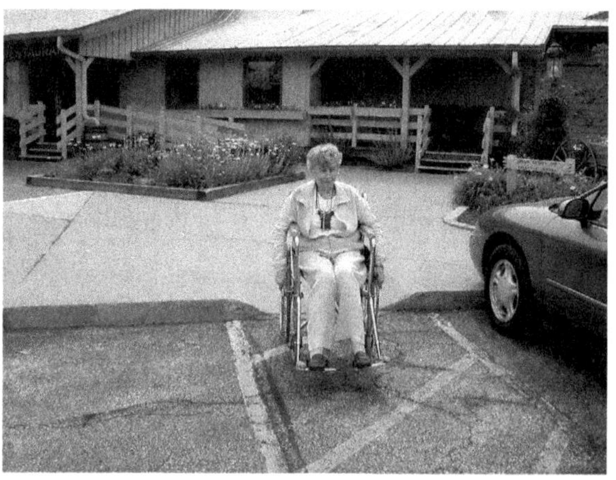

(d) Curb ramps

(b) Entrances

(e) Elevators

(c) Ramps

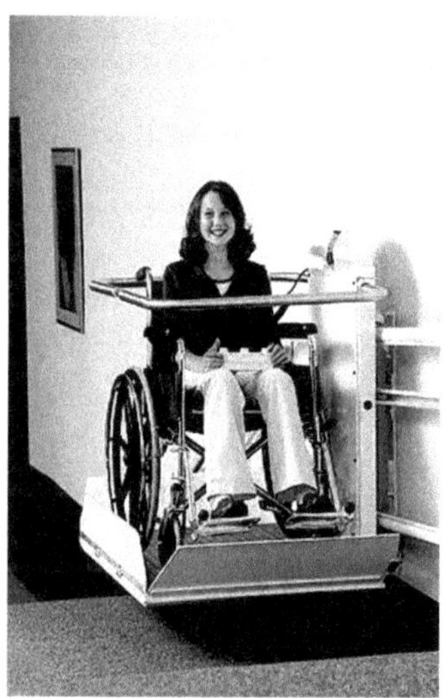

(f) Platform Lifts

FIGURE C402.2
ACCESSIBLE ROUTE COMPONENTS

402.3 Revolving Doors, Revolving Gates, and Turnstiles. Revolving doors, revolving gates, and turnstiles shall not be part of an accessible route.

❖ This section states that manually operated revolving doors, revolving gates and turnstiles are not to be used within an accessible route for ingress or egress; however, under certain circumstances the model building codes allow the use of revolving doors, revolving gates and turnstiles as part of a means of egress.

Even when allowed in a means of egress, there must be a side swinging door adjacent to the revolving door or gate.

A route through a hinged or sliding door differs remarkably from that provided through a revolving door. For a revolving door, the route includes a turn into the doorway, an arcing path of travel as the door revolves, followed by a change of direction when leaving the door. Items that may cause difficulty for anyone with mobility impairments could involve the overall doorway diameter, the number of leaves and their relative angle, and the configuration of the return walls surrounding the revolving door. Additionally, the speed of the door movement if motorized, or the force required for movement if not motorized, would be a concern for anyone who needed to keep both hands on their device to move forward (e.g., walker or wheelchair).

Automatic revolving doors, if large enough, may be usable by many people who use wheelchairs. However, the intent of this section is that these types of doors not be the only means of passage at an entrance or exit. An alternate door in full compliance with this section is considered necessary because some people with disabilities may be uncertain of the usability, or may not have enough strength or speed to use them. Although manufacturers have developed safety criteria, certain questions remain, such as the appropriate maximum and minimum speeds.

It is important to remember that application of this section is limited because it is part of Section 404.2 rather than Section 404.3, and it applies only to revolving doors, revolving gates and turnstiles. Therefore, it is possible that automatic items such as fare gates, which may be considered being included in the generic phrase "turnstiles" by some people, could be found on an accessible route. An appropriate fare gate would be permitted because they are not included in the prohibition of this section and because they are permitted by other sections of the standard.

403 Walking Surfaces

403.1 General. Walking surfaces that are a part of an accessible route shall comply with Section 403.

❖ This section regulates the various characteristics of the floor surface to ensure that the route is stable, usable and does not contain obstructions that would prevent its use in reaching an accessible element.

403.2 Floor Surface. Floor surfaces shall comply with Section 302.

❖ The suitability of an accessible route depends on certain characteristics of the surface itself. This section requires compliance with the general provisions of Section 302, which addresses characteristics that relate to both safety (slip resistance) and usability (stable and firm).

Section 104.4 states that the term "floor surface" refers to the finished floor or ground surface as applicable.

Ambulatory and semi-ambulatory people who have difficulty maintaining balance and those with restricted gaits are particularly sensitive to slipping and tripping hazards. For those people, a stable and regular surface is necessary to walk safely. Wheelchairs are propelled most easily on surfaces that are hard, stable and regular. Soft, loose surfaces such as shag carpet, loose sand, gravel, crushed stone or wet clay, and irregular surfaces such as cobblestone, significantly impede movement of a wheelchair.

A stable surface is one that remains unchanged by contaminants or applied force, so that when the contaminant or force is removed, the surface returns to its original condition. A firm surface resists deformation by either indentation or particles moving on its surface. It is not the intent of the standard to require only paved surfaces; however, any other types (e.g., wood chips, gravel) would need to be evaluated.

Slip resistance is based on the frictional force necessary to keep a shoe or crutch tip from slipping on a walking surface under the conditions of use likely to be found on the surface. For example, outside surfaces or entryways may be wet from rain or snow, or bathroom floors may be wet and should be evaluated under those conditions. The tile on the upstairs hallway would typically not be influenced by outside weather and should be evaluated in a dry condition. Although it is known that the static coefficient of friction is one basis of slip resistance, there is not as yet a generally accepted method to evaluate the slip resistance of walking surfaces for all uses.

403.3 Slope. The running slope of walking surfaces shall not be steeper than 1:20. The cross slope of a walking surface shall not be steeper than 1:48.

❖ The slope of an accessible route is an important factor that affects the usability of such routes by people with mobility impairments. This section correlates with Section 405 by limiting the slope of a "walking surface" to a maximum slope of 1:20. Therefore, any portion of an accessible route with a slope steeper than 1:20 is considered a ramp that must comply with the provisions of Section 405.

Controlling the cross slope of an accessible route is important to provide a reasonably level surface across one's direction of travel. Excessive cross slope could affect the balance of a person who uses a walking aid while traveling on the accessible route and also cause considerable difficulty in a straight line motion. In worst cases, extreme cross slopes are hazardous and unsafe. They can cause the person using a wheelchair to lose control and veer to the side.

403.4 Changes in Level. Changes in level shall comply with Section 303.

❖ Change in level means a change in elevation between horizontal planes in the direction of travel along an accessible route. These provisions are covered in Section 303, which is generally applicable to all floor surfaces of accessible routes (see commentary, Section 303).

403.5 Clear Width. The clear width of an accessible route shall be 36 inches (915 mm) minimum.

EXCEPTION: The clear width shall be permitted to be reduced to 32 inches (815 mm) minimum for a length of 24 inches (610 mm) maximum provided the reduced width segments are separated by segments that are 48 inches (1220 mm) minimum in length and 36 inches (915 mm) minimum in width.

❖ Most persons using a wheelchair need a minimum 30-inch (765 mm) clear opening width for doorways, gates and other openings when the passage through the opening is straight on. Greater clear widths are needed if the person using a wheelchair is making a turn or is unfamiliar with a building; if competing traffic is heavy; if sudden or frequent movements are needed; if a difficult threshold is encountered; etc. For most situations, the addition of an inch (25 mm) of leeway on either side is sufficient to address these difficulties. Thus, a minimum clear width of 32 inches (815 mm) provides adequate clearance. However, if an opening or another type of restriction in a passageway is more than 24 inches (610 mm) in depth, it is essentially a passageway and must be a minimum of 36 inches (915 mm) in width (see Figure 403.5 and Commentary Figure C403.5). This allows for doors, framed openings, pilasters or other minimal restrictions along the accessible route.

Although people who use walking aids do maneuver through clear width openings of 32 inches (815 mm), they need passageways and walks that are 36 inches (915 mm) wide. Crutch tips, often extending down at a wide angle, are a hazard in narrow passageways where they are not seen by other pedestrians.

Able-bodied people in winter clothing, walking straight ahead with arms swinging, need 32 inches (815 mm) of width, which includes 2 inches (51 mm) on either side for sway, and another 1-inch (25 mm) tolerance on either side for clearing nearby objects or other pedestrians. Almost all persons using a wheelchair and those who use walking aids also manage within this 32-inch (815 mm) width for short distances.

403.5.1 Clear Width at 180 Degree Turn. Where an accessible route makes a 180 degree turn around an object that is less than 48 inches (1220 mm) in width, clear widths shall be 42 inches (1065 mm) minimum approaching the turn, 48 inches (1220 mm) minimum during the turn, and 42 inches (1065 mm) minimum leaving the turn.

EXCEPTION: Section 403.5.1 shall not apply where the clear width during the turn is 60 inches (1525 mm) minimum.

❖ The requirements for clear width at turns are for level surfaces, not ramps. For ramp landing requirements, see Section 405.7.

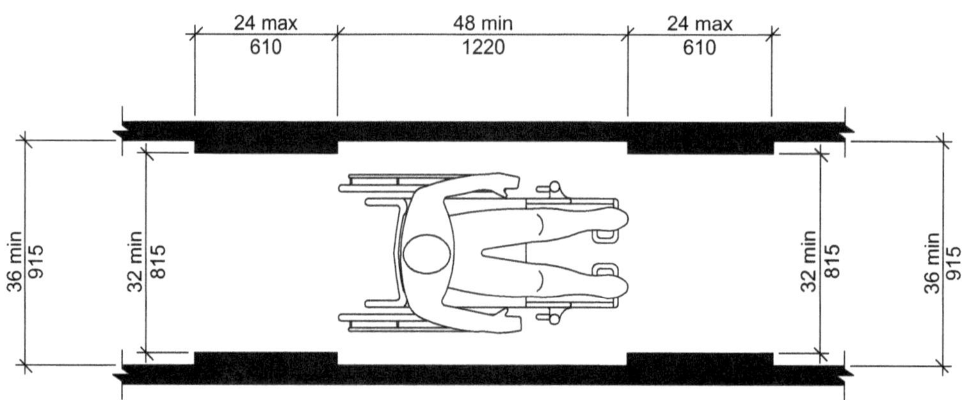

FIGURE 403.5
CLEAR WIDTH OF AN ACCESSIBLE ROUTE

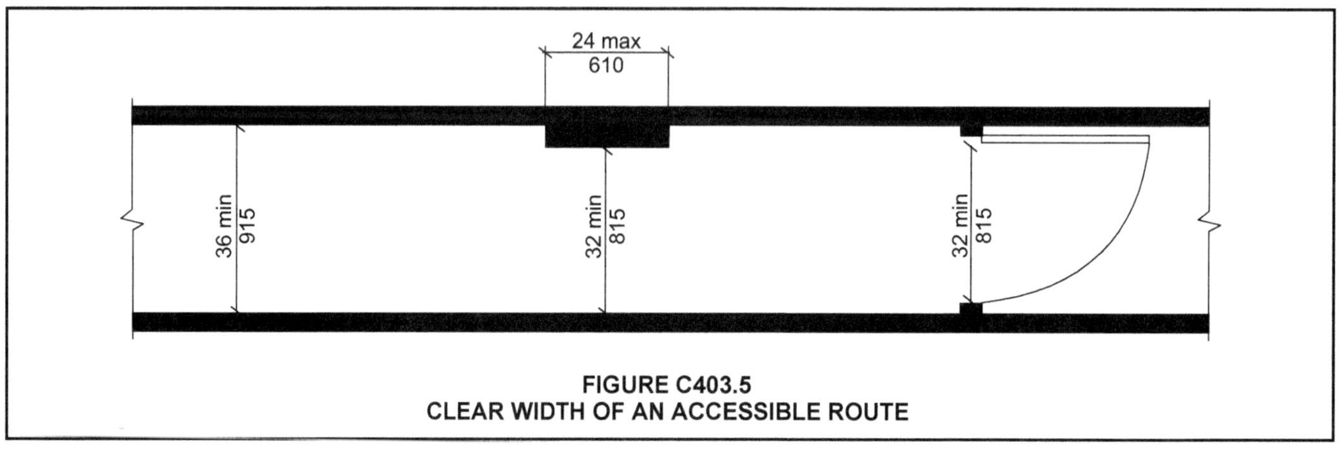

FIGURE C403.5
CLEAR WIDTH OF AN ACCESSIBLE ROUTE

It is much more difficult for a person using a wheelchair to negotiate a U-turn (half-circle turn) around a narrow obstacle than to make two right-angle turns separated by a distance of 48 inches (1220 mm) minimum. The accessible route, therefore, must be wider if the person using a wheelchair has to negotiate a turn around a narrow obstacle. Figure 403.5.1(a) of the standard illustrates this requirement. The standard does not specify how far back into the approaching path the 42-inch (1065 mm) increased width must extend. Therefore the administrative authority adopting this standard would need to make such a determination if the approaching path was being widened to the 42-inch (1065 mm) width only as it neared the turn.

Another alternative would be to maintain the 36-inch-wide (915 mm) path but then provide a 60-inch (1525 mm) turning space in accordance with the exception at the turn where the obstruction is less than 48 inches (1220 mm) wide. See Figure 403.5.1(b) for an illustration of this option.

When the obstruction is 48 inches (1220 mm) or more, it will essentially result in the person using a wheelchair making two right-angle turns and therefore the route may remain at 36 inches (915 mm) minimum width through the entire path. Commentary Figure C403.5.1 illustrates this provision.

403.5.2 Passing Space. An accessible route with a clear width less than 60 inches (1525 mm) shall provide passing spaces at intervals of 200 feet (61 m) maximum. Passing spaces shall be either a 60-inch (1525 mm) minimum by 60-inch (1525 mm) minimum space, or an intersection of two walking surfaces that provide a T-shaped turning space complying with Section 304.3.2, provided the base and arms of the T-shaped space extend 48 inches (1220 mm) minimum beyond the intersection.

❖ This provision ensures that passing spaces are available at reasonable intervals along a long, narrow accessible route, anticipating the possibility of wheelchair traffic approaching from opposite directions along such a path. A person using a wheelchair and another adult walking together take up a width of about 48 inches (1220 mm). Two persons using wheelchairs need a minimum of 60 inches (1525 mm) in width [see Commentary Figure 403.5.2(a)].

Passing spaces at the specified interval minimize the need for either person to have to back up excessive distances to reach a point at which they can pass one another. One person can also see the other approaching and wait at a passing space until the other user passes. This concept is a compromise that minimizes the impact on space design and layout. It would be unduly restrictive to require that the full length of all accessible routes be 60 inches (1525 mm) wide to allow passage of two wheelchairs at all points. The intersections of two walks, paths or corridors are considered passing spaces. When the accessible route is widened to provide the 60-inch by 60-inch (1525 by 1525 mm) space as shown in Commentary Figure C403.5.2(b), it essentially is creating a parallel approach maneuvering clearance in an alcove similar to that shown in Figure 305.7(b) of the standard. A T-turn at an intersection of corridors is another option for providing a passing space. For this option to work effectively, both parties must be able to maneuver out of the path of the other [see Commentary Figure C403.5.2(c)].

The nature of building design would make for passing spaces in a number of locations (including doors into rooms), but a path outside may require a wider area at intervals [see Commentary Figure C403.5.2(d)].

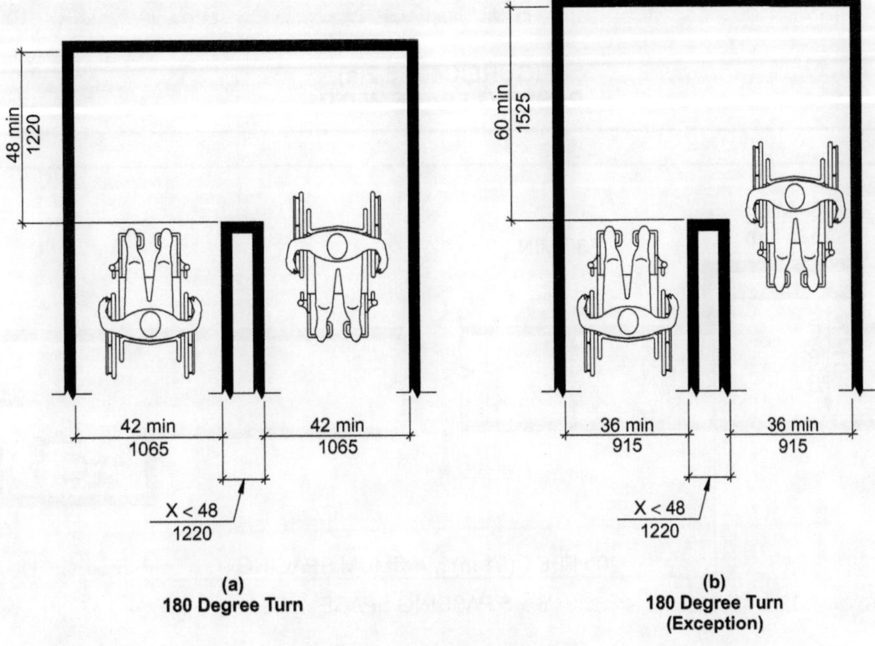

(a)
180 Degree Turn

(b)
180 Degree Turn
(Exception)

FIGURE 403.5.1
CLEAR WIDTH AT 180 DEGREE TURN

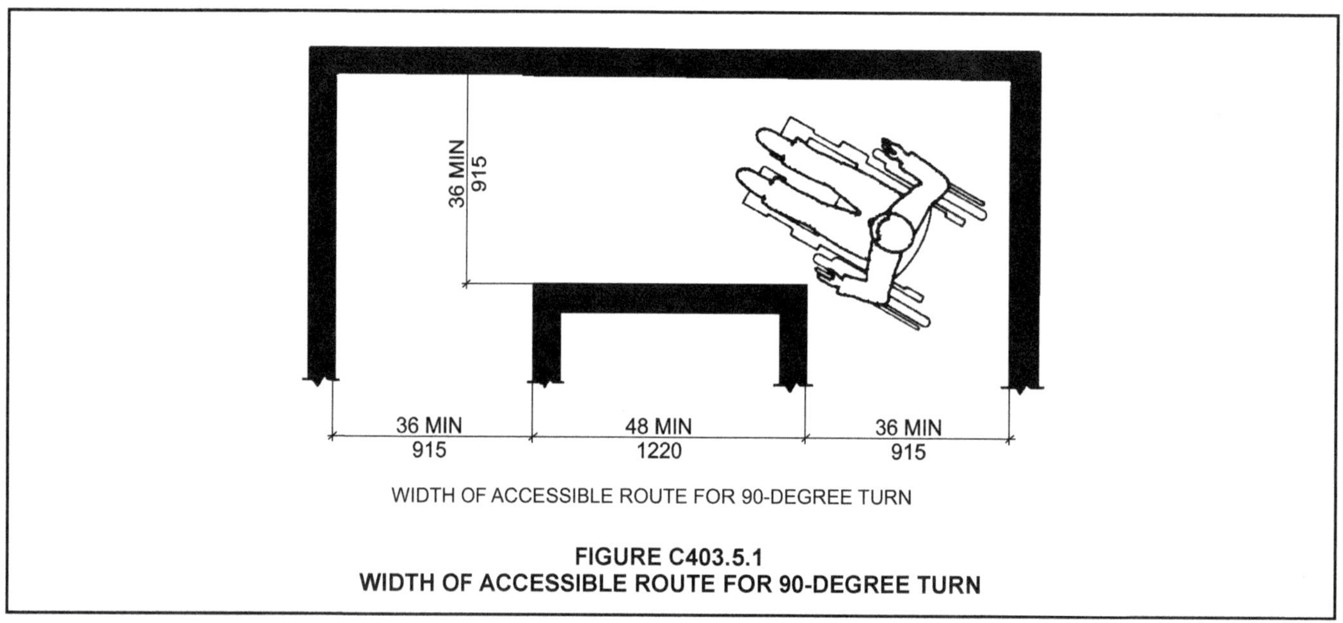

FIGURE C403.5.1
WIDTH OF ACCESSIBLE ROUTE FOR 90-DEGREE TURN

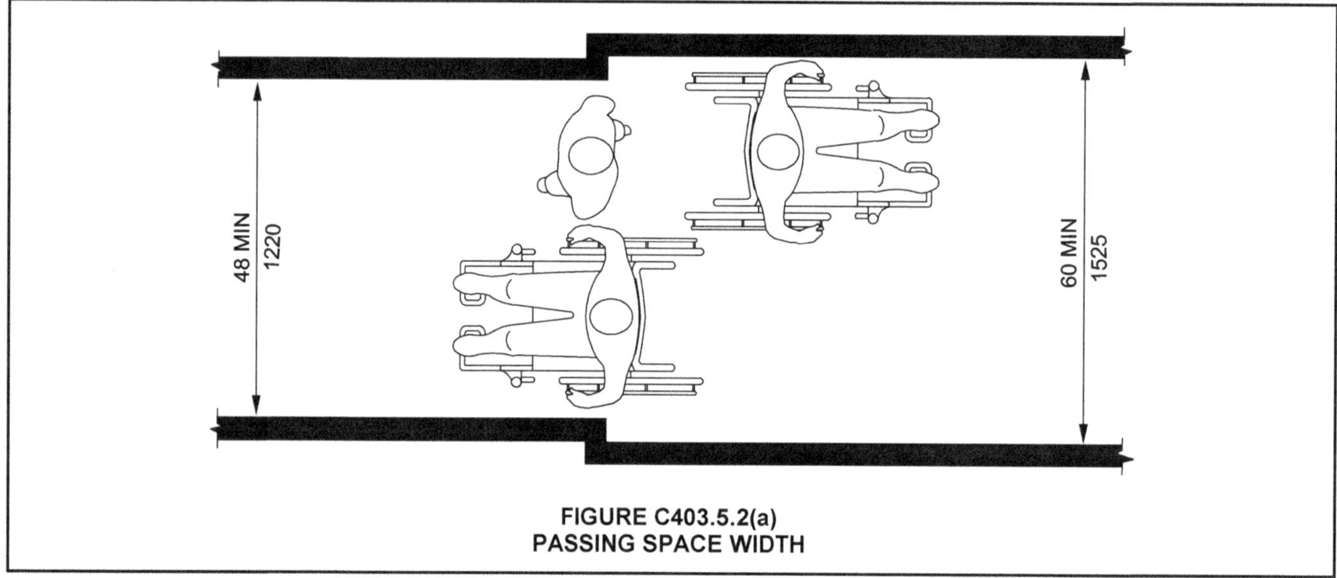

FIGURE C403.5.2(a)
PASSING SPACE WIDTH

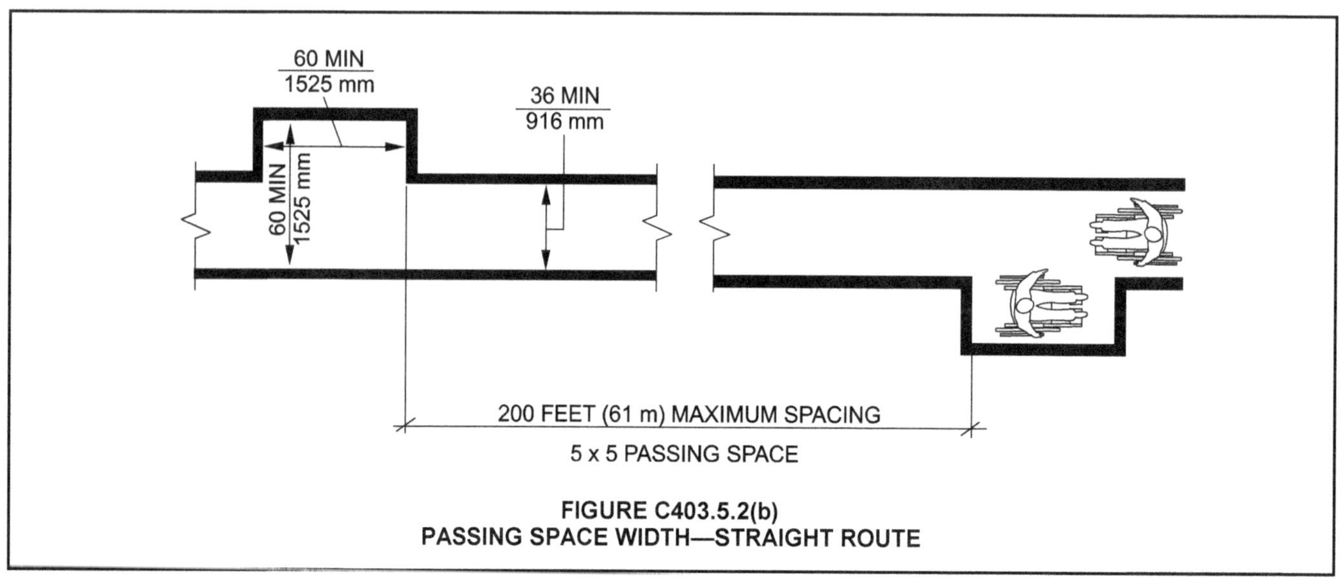

FIGURE C403.5.2(b)
PASSING SPACE WIDTH—STRAIGHT ROUTE

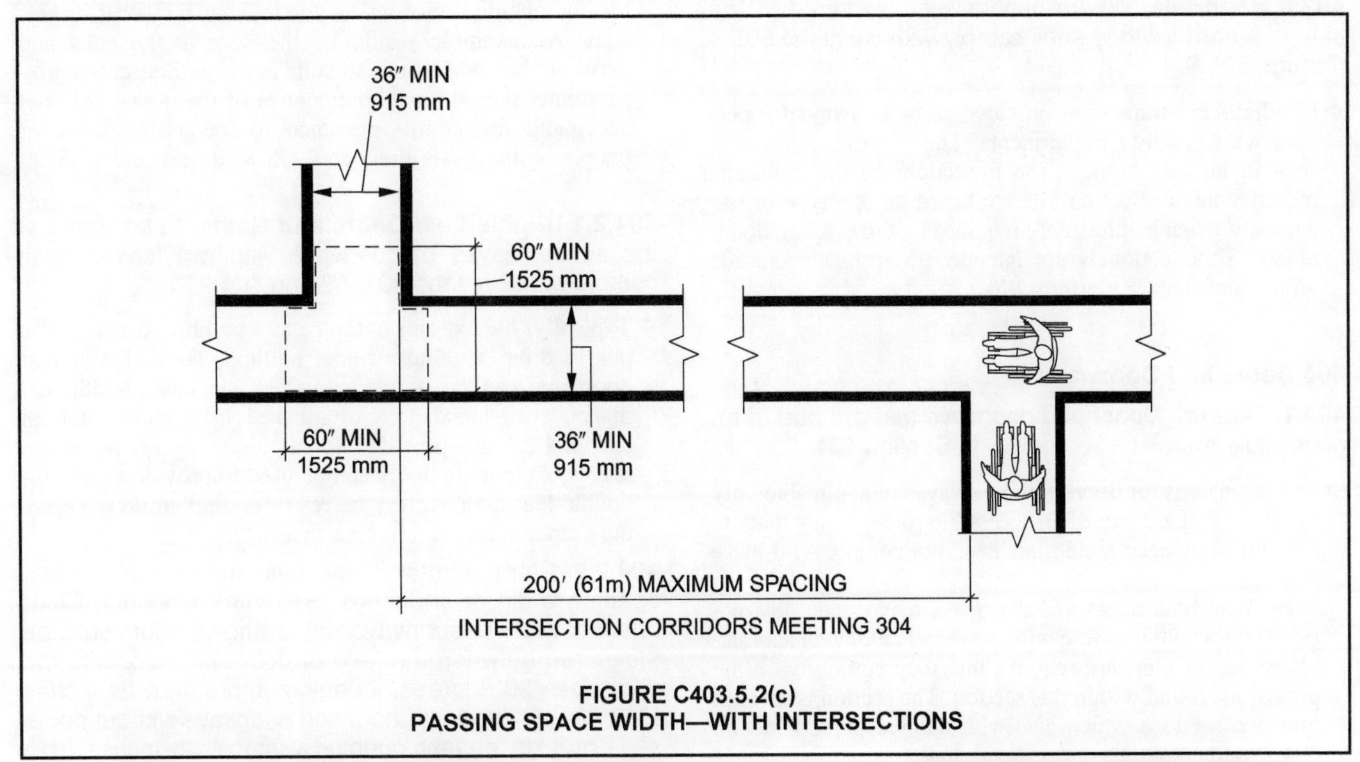

FIGURE C403.5.2(c)
PASSING SPACE WIDTH—WITH INTERSECTIONS

FIGURE C403.5.2(d)
EXAMPLE OF EXTERIOR PASSING SPACE

403.6 Handrails. Where handrails are required at the side of a corridor they shall comply with Sections 505.4 through 505.9.

❖ Handrails are sometimes provided along hallways for persons with mobility impairments. This is most commonly seen in nursing homes. The limitations to the handrails requirements in Section 505 are based on this type of use and only when handrails are required by the scoping documents. This section is not intended to include handrails within elevators or platform lifts.

404 Doors and Doorways

404.1 General. Doors and doorways that are part of an accessible route shall comply with Section 404.

❖ The provisions for doors and doorways are applicable only for doors that are part of an accessible route. Doors that are not part of an accessible route need not comply with these provisions.

Because both doors and doorways may create obstructions that would interfere with movement along an accessible route, the standard requires that they comply with the provisions found within this section. The section is divided into two sections which deal with manual doors (Section 404.2) and automatic doors (Section 404.3).

Requirements for approaches, thresholds, hardware, closers and opening force are stated in this section. Care should be exercised in considering any or all doors, and the maneuvering space necessary to make them accessible. When using a combination of forward reach and side reach and the minimum approach clearances, an inadvertent reversal of the latch side to the hinge side may render the door inaccessible to an individual in a wheelchair. Therefore, each door should be reviewed not only during the design stage of a project but also once the installation is completed to ensure that the installation complies with the standard.

404.2 Manual Doors. Manual doors and doorways, and manual gates, including ticket gates, shall comply with Section 404.2.

EXCEPTION: Doors, doorways, and gates designed to be operated only by security personnel shall not be required to comply with Sections 404.2.6, 404.2.7 and 404.2.8.

❖ When a door must be manually operated by the user, it must comply with all of the applicable provisions of this section. This includes the width, maneuvering clearances, arrangement, hardware and other items that affect the usability of the door. This section simply provides a reminder to users of the standard of all of the potential requirements.

Doors that are operated only by security personnel should meet accessible door requirements with the exception of door hardware, closing speed and door opening force. Examples of security personnel are guards in jails, bailiffs in courthouses and guards at security gates. The intent is not to exempt all the doors that these people access, but to exempt doors that these people are responsible for opening, closing and/or locking for security reasons. An example would be the door at the cells and between the courtroom and cells in a courthouse. Security personnel should have sole control of the doors. It is not acceptable for security personnel to operate the doors for people with disabilities and allow others independent access.

404.2.1 Double-Leaf Doors and Gates. At least one of the active leaves of doorways with two leaves shall comply with Sections 404.2.2 and 404.2.3.

❖ Typically, the exterior entrance to a building consists of a pair of doors without a center mullion. These double-leaf doorways can be a barrier unless the clear width and maneuvering clearances established in Sections 404.2.3 and 404.2.4 are provided for at least one of the active leaves. Automatic doors can be used to provide access for double-leaf door narrow leaves or doors that do not have the proper maneuvering clearances.

404.2.2 Clear Width. Doorways shall have a clear opening width of 32 inches (815 mm) minimum. Clear opening width of doorways with swinging doors shall be measured between the face of door and stop, with the door open 90 degrees. Openings more than 24 inches (610 mm) in depth at doors and doorways without doors shall provide a clear opening width of 36 inches (915 mm) minimum. There shall be no projections into the clear opening width lower than 34 inches (865 mm) above the floor. Projections into the clear opening width between 34 inches (865 mm) and 80 inches (2030 mm) above the floor shall not exceed 4 inches (100 mm).

EXCEPTIONS:

1. Door closers and door stops shall be permitted to be 78 inches (1980 mm) minimum above the floor.
2. In alterations, a projection of $^{5}/_{8}$ inch (16 mm) maximum into the required clear opening width shall be permitted for the latch side stop.

❖ A person using a wheelchair must, in many cases, approach a doorway at an angle rather than perpendicular to the opening. Thresholds, angled approaches and some surfaces create a condition that necessitates a doorway having a clear opening of at least 32 inches (815 mm). A 34-inch (865 mm) wide, $1^{3}/_{4}$ inch-thick (46 mm) door does not generally provide the required clear opening after the door thickness and the door stop have been subtracted. It is also important to note that the standard requires that this measurement be made when the door is opened 90 degrees (1.6 rad). Some building codes have permitted the clear width at doors to be measured when the door is "fully opened." However, when the issue is accessibility, the 90-degree (1.6 rad) requirement from the standard must be used for determining the clear width.

If the wall in which the doorway is installed or the jambs of the doorway itself are more than 24 inches (610 mm) deep, the clear width of the opening must be increased from 32 inches (815 mm) to 36 inches (915 mm). This increased width coincides with the accessible route requirements of Section 403.5 for segments over 24 inches (610 mm) long.

Although the standard does not specifically mention door hardware, that is the intent of the requirements related to projections. If a cylinder that is the size of the height and width requirements could be maneuvered through the doorway without coming into contact with the door hardware, accessibility is achieved [see Commentary Figure C404.2.2(a)]. This would be of most concern when a door is equipped with panic hardware that extends the full width of the door. Commentary Figure C404.2.2(b) Illustrates this requirement. Door hardware that is located above the 34-inch (865 mm) height is regulated as a protruding object and is consistent with the maximum projection found in Section 307.2. Based on the projections, it is important to realize that the "clear width" at the door may be different for accessibility purposes than what it is for general egress purposes.

Some of the rationale used in establishing minimum widths for persons using wheelchairs and persons using walking aids is found in the commentary to Section 403.5.

ALLOW PASSAGE FOR CYLINDER OF 32 IN. DIAMETER AND 78 IN. HEIGHT
DOOR OPENINGS
CLEAR WIDTH - 32/815
DOOR FRAME
WALL
DOOR

FIGURE C404.2.2(a)
TYPICAL DOOR OPENING CLEARANCE

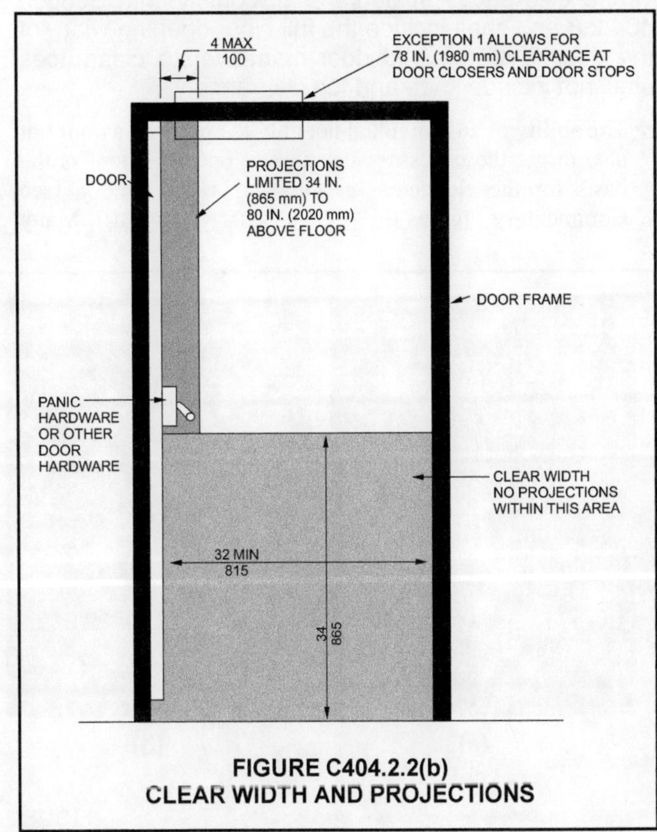

FIGURE C404.2.2(b)
CLEAR WIDTH AND PROJECTIONS

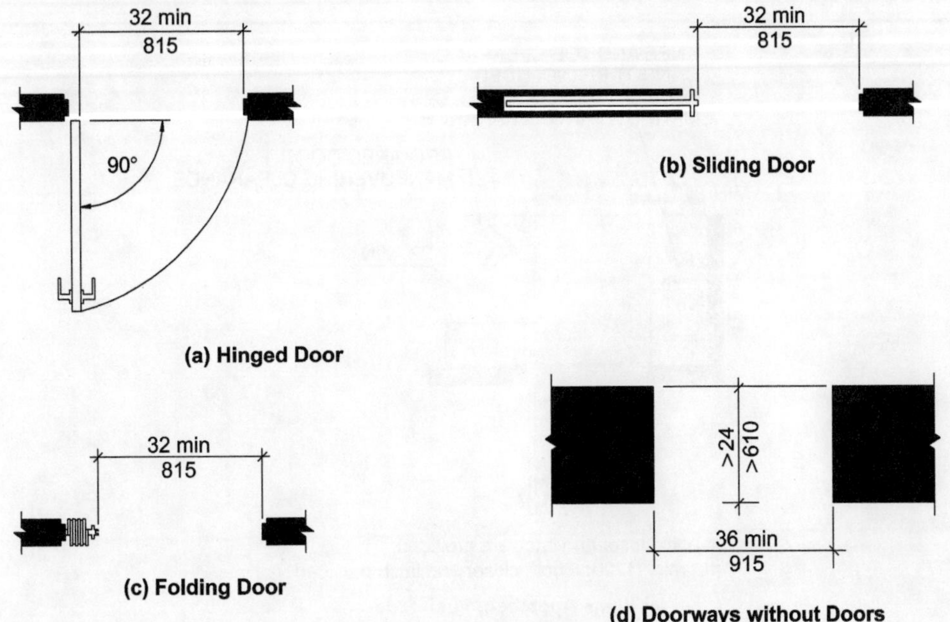

FIGURE 404.2.2
CLEAR WIDTH OF DOORWAYS

A reduction of the minimum height requirement is provided for door closers and stops. For the door closer to operate, the operator must extend below the door frame. The second exception is an allowance for the latch side stop on existing doors.

404.2.3 Maneuvering Clearances. Minimum maneuvering clearances at doors shall comply with Section 404.2.3 and shall include the full clear opening width of the doorway. Required door maneuvering clearances shall not include knee and toe clearance.

❖ The ability of an individual not only to approach a door but also to get the necessary leverage to open the door is the basis for the clearances established in this section [see Commentary Figures C404.2.3(a), (b), (c) and (d)]. Many combinations of conditions may confront a person who is disabled: approaching from the pull, push, hinge or latch side; whether the door is equipped with a closer; a parallel or perpendicular approach; and so forth. The front approach is similar to the forward reach (see Section 308.2.1) and the hinge or latch side approach is similar to the side reach (see Section 308.3.1).

Although doors are listed as part of the accessible route components in Section 402.2, the scoping provisions may not require every possible route to be accessible. When doors may be approached from more than one direction (e.g., a door along a hallway), even though providing for more than one clearance at the doors along the normal routes of travel may be the better design, the literal requirement is only to provide one maneuvering clearance at each

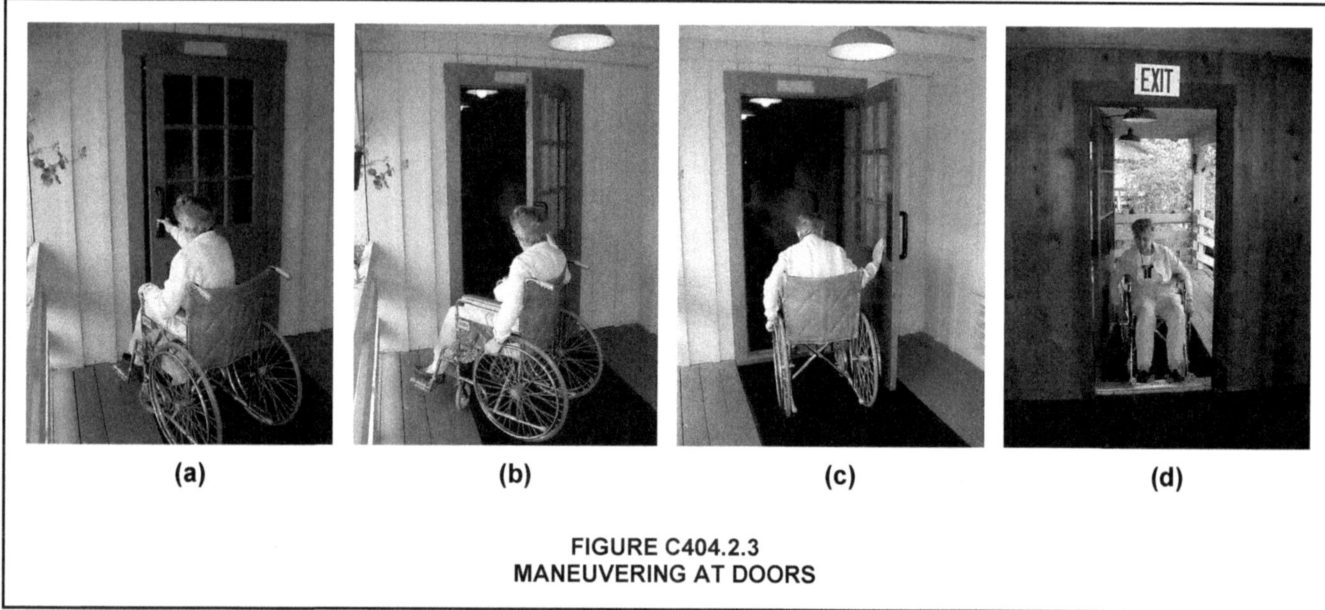

FIGURE C404.2.3
MANEUVERING AT DOORS

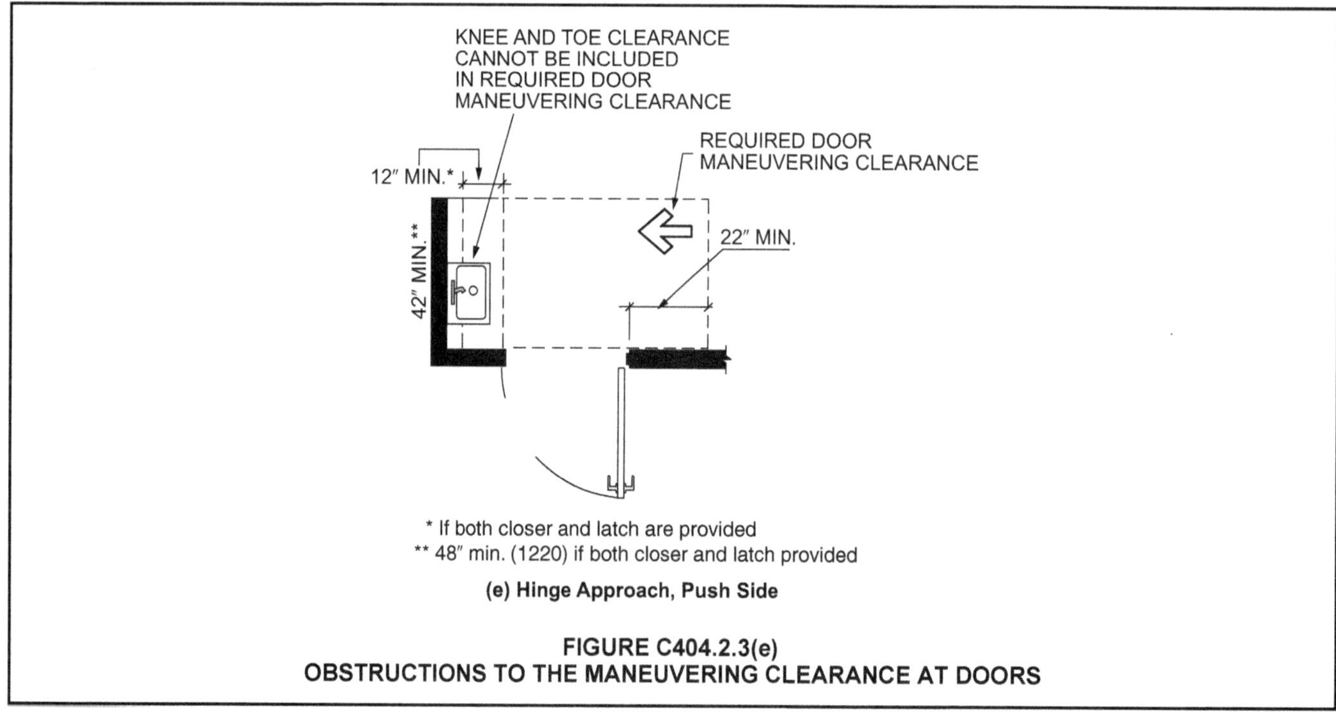

FIGURE C404.2.3(e)
OBSTRUCTIONS TO THE MANEUVERING CLEARANCE AT DOORS

door. Some configurations may require a person to move past the door, turn around and come back from another direction to have maneuvering clearance to open the door. At the same time, there is no prohibition from having maneuvering clearances overlap for adjacent doors or doors across the hall. A person is expected to move through a door opening, as opposed to occupying a floor space at a work surface or lavatory. Door maneuvering clearances encompass all of the vertical space above the required clearance area. Protruding objects in the maneuvering clearance area, such as a counter or lavatory, could prevent a standing person with a walker or a person using a wheelchair from fully utilizing the clearance area. Therefore, provisions for knee and toe clearances under elements cannot overlap the door maneuvering clearances [see Commentary Figure C404.2.3(e)].

Maneuvering clearances at doors permit the user approach and passage. The standard does not require maneuvering clearances that would permit the user to make a turn and pull or push the door closed after passing through the doorway. If such maneuvering space is provided near, but not adjacent to, the door, then the user must make a 180-degree (3 rad) turn where space is provided, retrace the path, close the door and move away from the door backward. Consideration should be given to providing sufficient maneuvering space for the closing and opening of, as well as approach to and retreat from, doors.

404.2.3.1 Floor Surface. Floor surface within the maneuvering clearances shall have a slope not steeper than 1:48 and shall comply with Section 302.

❖ A sloped surface would make it difficult for a person using a wheelchair or a walking aid to remain stationary while at the same time trying to unlatch and open a door. Thus, thc slope of these floor surfaces is limited to the same slope allowed for the cross slope of accessible routes in general. The slope in any direction shall not be steeper than 1:48. This should be adequate for drainage for door landings exposed to weather.

404.2.3.2 Swinging Doors. Swinging doors shall have maneuvering clearances complying with Table 404.2.3.2.

❖ This section provides the reference to Table 404.2.3.2, which establishes the minimum clearances for maneuvering adjacent to manual swinging doors. The table establishes the actual requirements that are then illustrated in Figures 404.2.3.2(a) through (g). Figure C404.2.3.2 helps to illustrate how a person using a wheelchair would need to operate a door and therefore how and why the maneuvering clearances are established (see commentary Section 404.2.3).

FIGURE 404.2.3.2(a). See page 4-13.

❖ The front approach to the pull side of a door requires an 18-inch (455 mm) clear space adjacent to the latch side of the door. This space may be used to position a wheelchair, crutches or other walking aid to gain the leverage necessary to open the door. This space also enables the user to be outside the swing of the door as it begins to open. By pulling at an angle to the axis of the wheelchair without the required clearances, there is a possibility of interference between the edge of the door and the footrest on the wheelchair, which would render the door inaccessible to the person using a wheelchair.

The dimension of 60 inches (1525 mm) perpendicular to the door accommodates the wheelchair in the clear floor space dimension of 48 inches (1220 mm) at an angle [see Figure 404.2.3.2(a)].

FIGURE 404.2.3.2 (b). See page 4-13.

❖ The front approach to the push side of a door that has a latch and closer requires a smaller clear space to the side because it is easier to push and follow than to pull and maneuver through the opening. For the same reason, the dimension perpendicular needs to be only 48 inches (1220 mm) instead of 60 inches (1525 mm) because the smaller dimension is the same as found in Section 305.

TABLE 404.2.3.2—MANEUVERING CLEARANCES AT MANUAL SWINGING DOORS

TYPE OF USE		MINIMUM MANEUVERING	
Approach	Door Side	Perpendicularr	Parallel to Doorway (beyond latch unless noted)
From front	Pull	60 inches (1525 mm)	18 inches (455 mm)
From front	Push	48 inches (1220 mm)	0 inches (0 mm)[3]
From hinge side	Pull	60 inches (1525 mm)	36 inches (915 mm)
From hinge side	Pull	54 inches (1370 mm)	42 inches (1065 mm)
From hinge side	Push	42 inches (1065 mm)[1]	22 inches (560 mm)[3, 4]
From latch side	Pull	48 inches (1220 mm)[2]	24 inches (610 mm)
From latch side	Push	42 inches (1065 mm)[2]	24 inches (610 mm)

[1]Add 6 inches (150 mm) if closer and latch provided.
[2]Add 6 inches (150 mm) if closer provided.
[3]Add 12 inches (305 mm) beyond latch if closer and latch provided.
[4]Beyond hinge side.

❖ Figures 404.2.3.2(a) through (g) are diagrams for the information in Table 404.2.3.2. The direction of the arrow is the anticipated approach toward the door. It is important to pay attention to notes for the table (indicated as asterisks in the figures). When closers and/or latches are installed, the doors may be more difficult to operate; therefore, additional clearances will be required. Overall sizes are not indicated because door sizes may vary.

Doors equipped with only a closer or a latch (but not both) are not required to have the 12-inch (305 mm) maneuvering space. The additional maneuvering space requirement is based on the fact that the user needs to exert more force and perform a combination of movements to open doors that have both a latch and a closer. A door that has a latch but no closer can be opened by disengaging the latching mechanism and pushing with the hand, with the door remaining open during passage. A door that has a closer but no latch can be pushed open by the momentum of the user without requiring additional hand or arm movement. Typically, this is accomplished by pushing the door open with the feet or wheelchair footrest. For a door that has both a latch and a closer, the user must perform all of these movements simultaneously, which requires additional maneuvering space. Figure 404.2.3.2(b) illustrates the requirements for this type of door use.

The front approach to the push side of a door that does not have both a latch and a closer requires less maneuvering and effort to open; therefore, less space is required. Clear space is not required on the side adjacent to the door opening because the approach would be directly in line with the 32-inch (1815 mm) minimum required doorway. The dimension, perpendicular, is the same as found in Section 305 and is required in most cases when a front approach is used and no additional maneuvers, such as to drinking fountains in an alcove, are needed.

FIGURE 404.2.3.2 (c and d). See page 4-13.

❖ Of the various configurations and approaches, this is probably the most difficult and requires the largest clear floor space. A space of approximately 15 square feet (1.4 m^2) is required to the side of the door because of the need to unlatch, reverse direction while opening the door, maneuvering around the door, and then turning and passing through. These dimensions are required regardless of the existence of a latch or a closer on the door.

The dimensions of the maneuvering space depend on the configuration of the walls surrounding the door. If the dimension adjacent to the latch is between 36 inches (915 mm) and 42 inches (1065 mm), the dimension perpendicular to the door in the closed position must be no less than 60 inches (1525 mm). When the length of the adjacent wall is 42 inches (1065 mm) or more, the other dimension need be only 54 inches (1370 mm). Figures 404.2.3.2(c) and (d) show these two situations.

The designer has a number of options available to reduce the space required. Changing from a left-hand to a right-hand door, reversing the swing or placing a sliding or folding door in the opening can often reduce the required clearance.

FIGURE 404.2.3.2(e). See page 4-13.

❖ Without both a latch and a closer, a parallel approach to the hinge side of a door that swings in the direction of travel requires a maneuvering clear space width of 22 inches (560 mm) measured from the hinge side of the door and a perpendicular distance of 42 inches (1065 mm). This requirement is shown in Figure 404.2.3.2(e). When the door is equipped with both a latch and a closer, this arrangement requires a perpendicular dimension of 48 inches (1220 mm) instead of the previously stated 42 inches (1065 mm) and an additional 12 inches (305 mm) measured from the latch side. Assuming a 32-inch (845 mm) clear width door, the total width would be 66 inches (1675 mm). This additional maneuvering space is required to allow the user enough room to get the pushing power to overcome the closer resistance.

FIGURE 404.2.3.2(f). See page 4-13.

❖ When approaching the latch side of a door without a closer that swings against the direction of travel, maneuvering space must be provided along the wall adjacent to the latch side. This dimension shall be at least 24 inches (610 mm). The dimension perpendicular to this wall must be at least 48 inches (1220 mm). Figure 404.2.3.2(f) provides the detail of this provision. Because this condition assumes a parallel approach, these dimensions differ from the front approach shown in Figure 404.2.3.2(a).

If the door has a closer, an additional 6 inches (150 mm) [for a total of 54 inches (1370 mm)] is needed perpendicular to the doorway. This additional 6 inches (150 mm) is required to allow the user enough maneuvering space to overcome the resistance of the closer.

FIGURE 404.2.3.2(g). See page 4-13.

❖ When approaching the latch side of a door that swings in the direction of travel and the door is not equipped with a closer, 24 inches (610 mm) of maneuvering space must be provided along the wall adjacent to the latch side. This is the same dimension that is required for the same approach, but from the pull side of the door [see Figure 404.2.3.2(f)]. The dimension perpendicular to the doorway must be not less than 42 inches (1065 mm). The resulting space, at least 56 inches (1420 mm) [24 inches plus 32 inches] by 42 inches (1065 mm), is required to complete the turn.

Similar to the latch approach from the pull side [Figure 404.2.3.2(f)], an additional space of 6 inches (150 mm) is needed perpendicular to the doorway if the door has a closer. This 6-inch (150 mm) increase in both Figures 404.2.3.2(f) and (g) is based solely on the installation of a closer and is not like the requirements shown in Figures 404.2.3.2(b) and (e) that require an increase when both a closer and a latch are installed.

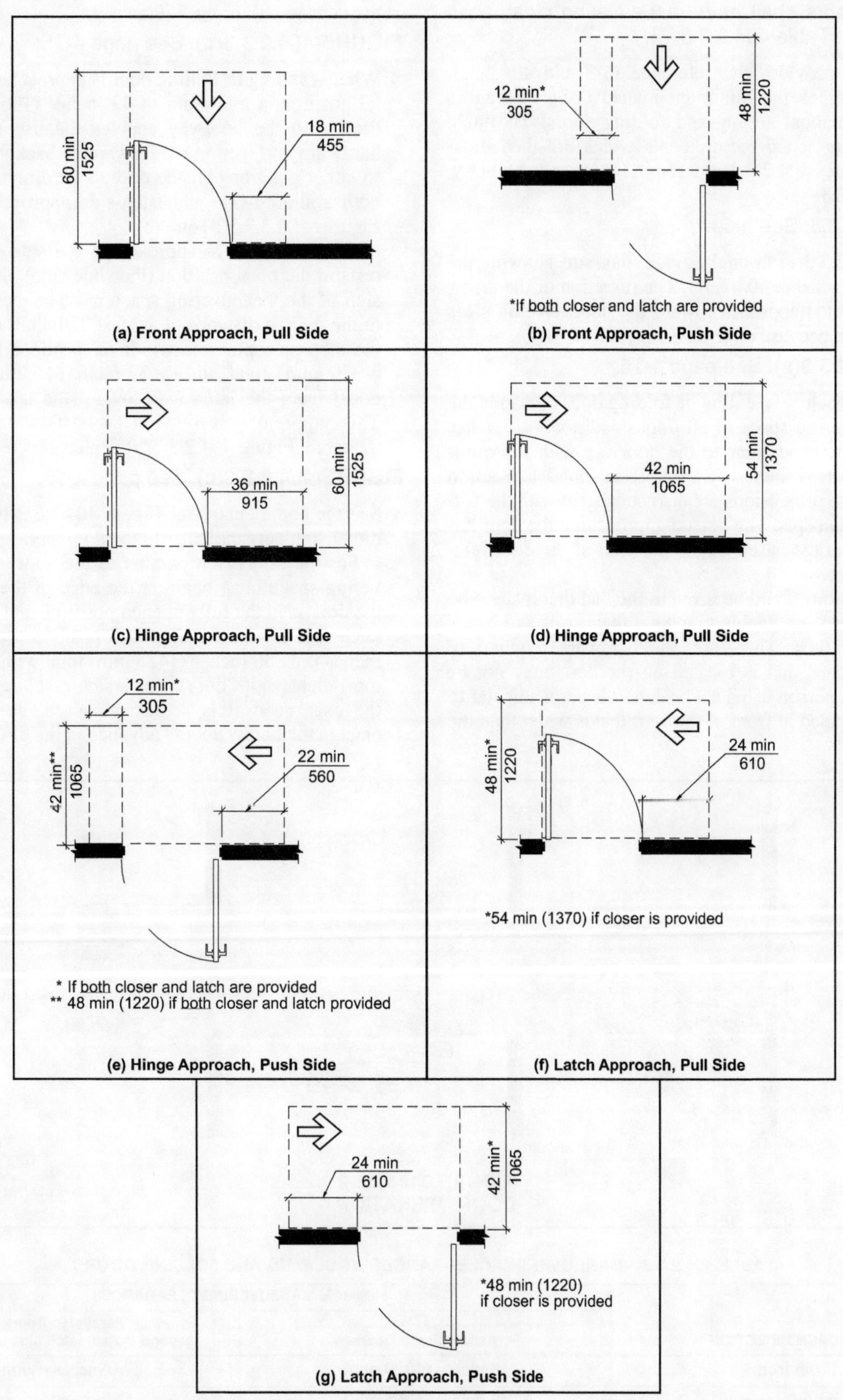

FIGURE 404.2.3.2
MANEUVERING CLEARANCES AT MANUAL SWINGING DOORS

404.2.3.3 Sliding and Folding Doors. Sliding doors and folding doors shall have maneuvering clearances complying with Table 404.2.3.3.

❖ This section provides the reference to Table 404.2.3.3, which establishes the minimum maneuvering clearances adjacent to manual sliding and folding doors. The table establishes the actual requirements which are then illustrated in Figures 404.2.3.3(a) through (c) (see commentary, Section 404.2.3).

TABLE 404.2.3.3. See below.

❖ Figures 404.2.3.3(a) through (c) are diagrams showing the information in Table 404.2.3.3. The direction of the arrow is the anticipated approach toward the door. Overall sizes are not shown because door sizes may vary.

FIGURE 404.2.3.3(a). See page 4-15.

❖ A front approach to a sliding or folding door demands the least maneuvering space of all door conditions–48 inches (1220 mm) perpendicular to the doorway with the minimum width of 32 inches (815 mm) as found in Section 404.2.2. These dimensions are also consistent with the forward reach concepts. The person approaching the door has sufficient leverage based on the position of the door relative to the user.

Consideration should be given to the fact that many who use wheelchairs are unable to extend their arms and hands beyond their toes. Therefore, the hardware required to operate the door that is located on the door may not be reachable if a person using a wheelchair is perpendicular to it. Space provided in front of the door that is wider than the door opening would allow the user to become parallel with the door to pull or push it open.

FIGURE 404.2.3.3(b). See page 4-15.

❖ When a sliding or folding door is approached from a parallel position, a minimum of 42 inches (1065 mm) perpendicular to the doorway enables the user to operate the hardware and then move forward or backward as required to either push or pull the door. This dimension applies to both a sliding-side and latch-side approach, as shown in Figures 404.2.3.3(b) and (c).

When the user is approaching the side where the door rests in the open position (the slide side), the other dimension of the maneuvering space must be measured, parallel to the door, a distance of at least 22 inches (560 mm) from the stop side plus the width of the door [i.e., 54 inches (1370 mm) total with a 32-inch (815 mm) clear width door] from the latch side toward the approach position. This requirement is found in Table 404.2.3.3 and Note 1 to the table. Figure 404.2.3.3(b) depicts this requirement.

FIGURE 404.2.3.3(c). See page 4-15.

❖ See the commentary for Figure 404.2.3.3(b) regarding the dimension perpendicular to the doorway.

For the dimension parallel to the doorway, the maneuvering space must begin at the edge of the opening when the door is in the fully opened position, and extend past the latch side toward the approach position a minimum of 24 inches [i.e., 56 inches (1425 mm) total with a 32-inch (815 mm) clear width door]. For a side reach to be completed, the user needs this additional space along the wall to engage the hardware and advance in the direction of travel.

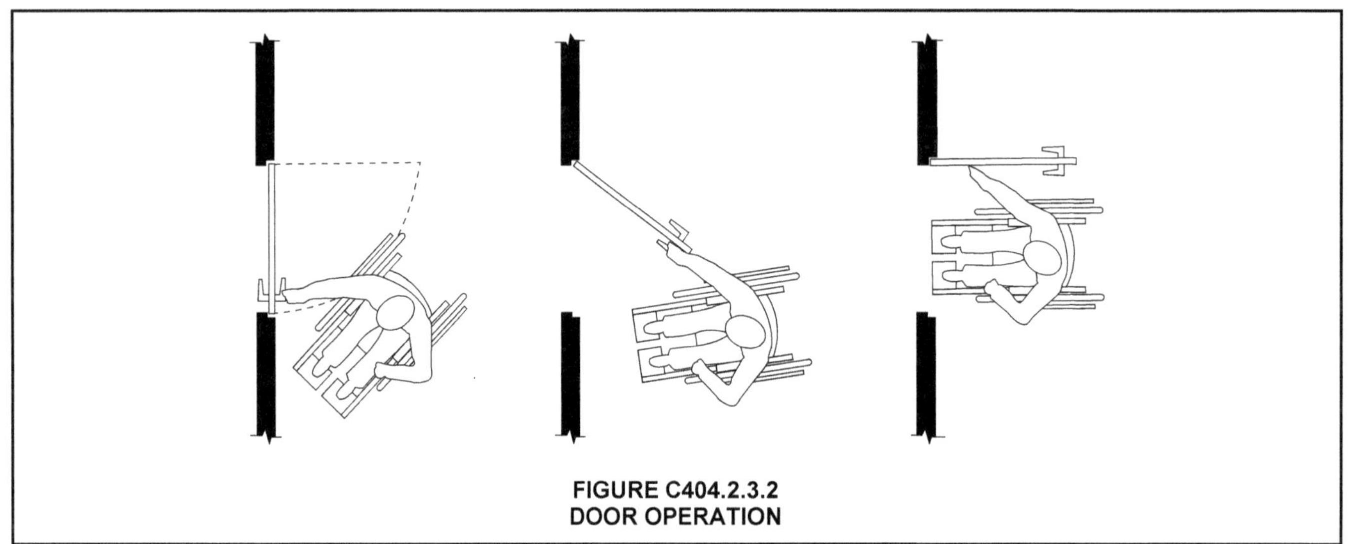

FIGURE C404.2.3.2
DOOR OPERATION

TABLE 404.2.3.3—MANEUVERING CLEARANCES AT SLIDING AND FOLDING DOORS

APPROACH DIRECTION	MINIMUM MANEUVERING CLEARANCES	
	Perpendicular to Doorway	Parallel to Doorway (beyond stop or latch side unless noted)
From front	48 inches (1220 mm)	0 inches (0 mm)
From nonlatch side	42 inches (1065 mm)	22 inches (560 mm)[1]
From latch side	42 inches (1065 mm)	24 inches (610 mm)

[1]Beyond pocket or hinge side.

404.2.3.4 Doorways without Doors. Doorways without doors that are less than 36 inches (915 mm) in width shall have maneuvering clearances complying with Table 404.2.3.4

❖ This section refers to Table 404.2.3.4, which establishes the minimum maneuvering clearances adjacent to doorways which do not have a door leaf installed in them. This is essentially dealing with cased openings. The table establishes the actual requirements, which are fairly simple to comply with (see commentary, Section 404.2.3).

TABLE 404.2.3.4. See below

❖ Figures 404.2.3.3(a) and (b) are diagrams showing the information in Table 404.2.3.4. The direction of the arrow is the anticipated approach toward the door. Overall sizes are not shown because door sizes may vary.

FIGURE 404.2.3.4(a). See page 4-16.

❖ When the approach is from the front (forward approach), a clear space of 48 inches (1220 mm) is required perpendicular to the doorway. This essentially creates a space very similar to the clear floor space shown in Figure 305.5(a) of the standard. The only difference is that the space must be slightly wider. The clear floor space must be the full width of the doorway and would be a minimum of 32 inches (815 mm) wide to comply with Sections 403.5 and 404.2.2.

FIGURE 404.2.3.4(b). See page 4-16.

❖ When the approach is from the side, a 42-inch (1065 mm) distance perpendicular to the doorway is required. This is similar to the dimension required and shown in Figures 404.2.3.3(b) and (c) for sliding and folding doors. However, this section does not specify any additional dimension beyond the full width of the door. The general accessible route requirements will adequately provide any additionally needed maneuvering space near the doorway, and because the user does not have to operate any door hardware or push and pull a door, a turn is the only maneuver that the user may need to make.

404.2.3.5 Recessed Doors. Where any obstruction within 18 inches (455 mm) of the latch side of a doorway projects more than 8 inches (205 mm) beyond the face of the door, measured perpendicular to the face of the door, maneuvering clearances for a forward approach shall be provided.

❖ A door can be recessed because of wall thickness or the placement of the trim or other fixed elements adjacent to the door opening. Doors may also be recessed in an alcove to meet means of egress requirements for minimum clearances in exit access corridors. This section addresses situations in which a door is recessed for any of these reasons. The provisions are intended to address configurations similar to those shown in Figures 404.2.3.2(a) and (b). Because these doors are recessed from the general circulation route, the standard requires an arrangement that permits a front approach. Depending on the type of door involved, manual swinging or sliding and folding doors, Sections 404.2.3.2 and 404.2.3.3 would specify the required clearances. These spaces must be provided so that the door is approachable and usable. Consideration also must be given to the maneuvering space on the other side of the door.

The provisions of this section apply when the door is recessed more than 8 inches (200 mm) from the plane of the wall adjacent to the general accessible route. The clear width requirements of Section 403.5 should also be considered for these doors. When the alcove is over 24 inches (610 mm) deep, the minimum required clear width of the alcove will be increased from 32 inches to 36 inches (815 to 915 mm). The clear width of the doorway may still be 32 inches (815 mm) even when the alcove depth is over 24 inches (610 mm) (see commentary, Section 404.2.3).

FIGURE 404.2.3.5(a). See page 4-16.

❖ See commentary, Figure 404.2.3.2(a).

FIGURE 404.2.3.5 (b and c). See page 4-16.

❖ See the commentary for Figure 404.2.3.2(b) and (c). Note the difference in maneuvering clearances when a closer and latch are provided.

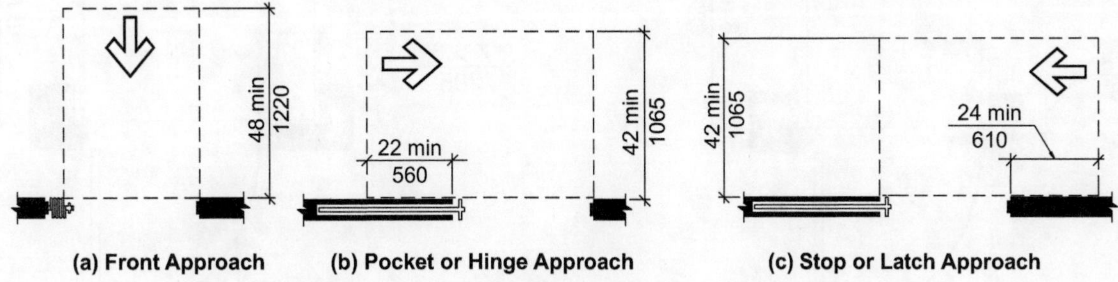

FIGURE 404.2.3.3
MANEUVERING CLEARANCES AT SLIDING AND FOLDING DOORS

TABLE 404.2.3.4—MANEUVERING CLEARANCES FOR DOORWAYS WITHOUT DOORS

APPROACH DIRECTION	MINIMUM MANEUVERING CLEARANCES PERPENDICULAR TO DOORWAY
From front	48 inches (1220 mm)
From side	42 inches (1065 mm)

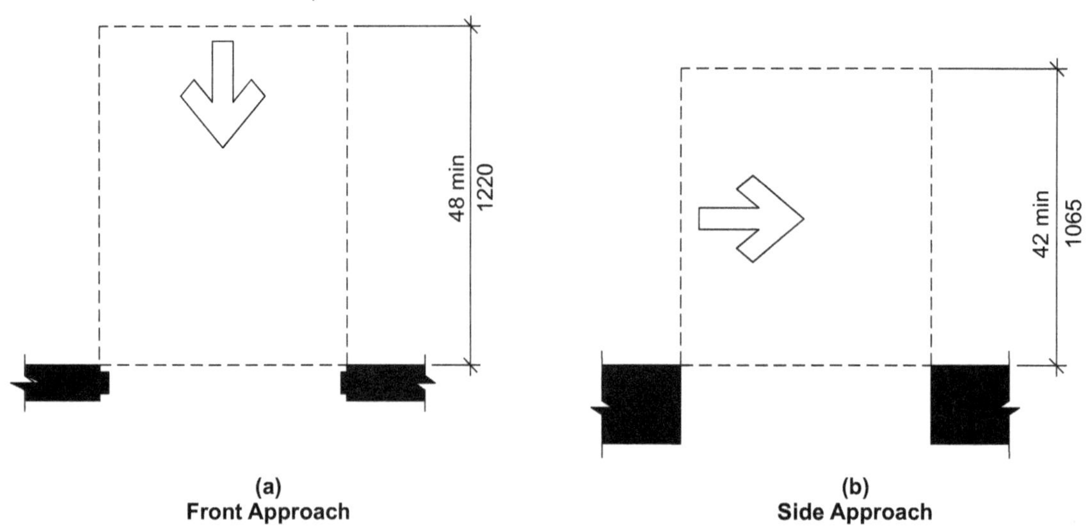

FIGURE 404.2.3.4
MANEUVERING CLEARANCE AT DOORWAYS WITHOUT DOORS

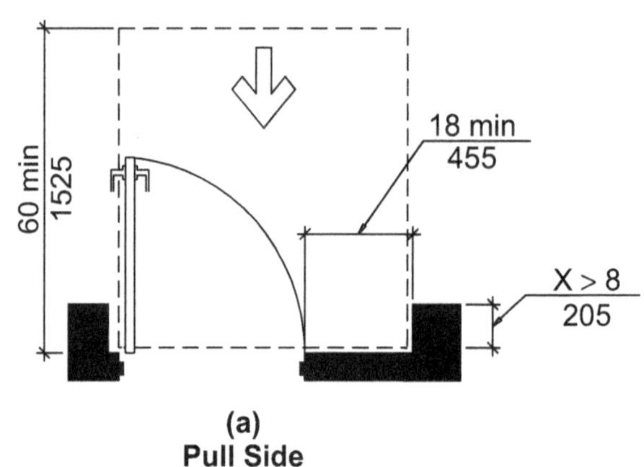

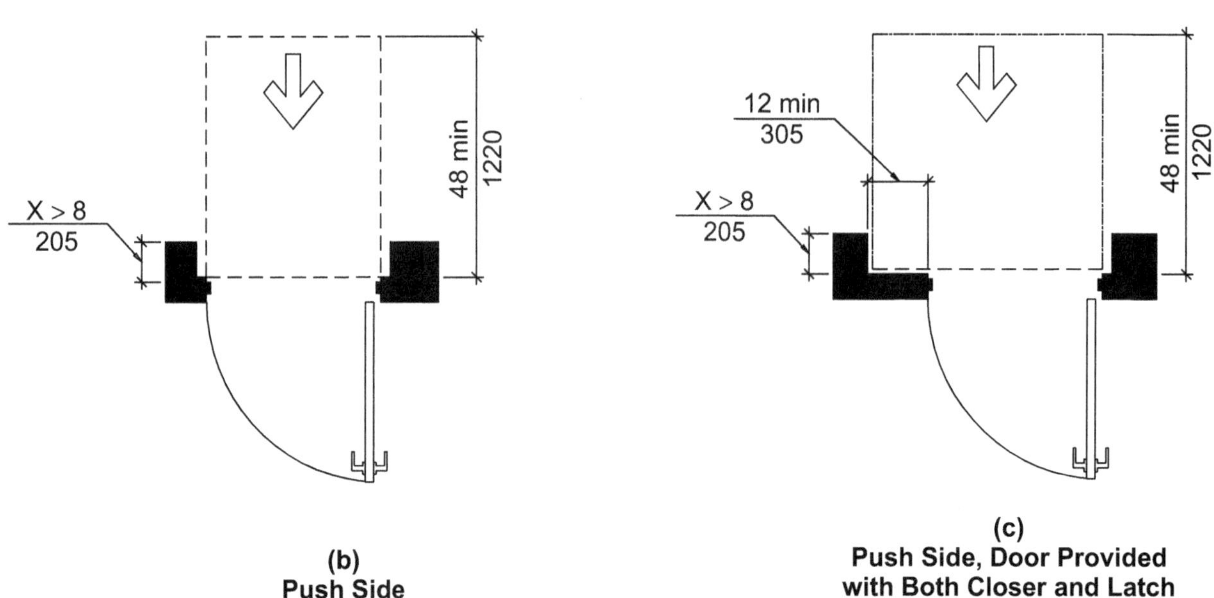

FIGURE 404.2.3.5
MANEUVERING CLEARANCE AT RECESSED DOORS

404.2.4 Thresholds. If provided, thresholds at doorways shall be $^1/_2$ inch (13 mm) maximum in height. Raised thresholds and changes in level at doorways shall comply with Sections 302 and 303.

EXCEPTION: An existing or altered threshold shall be permitted to be $^3/_4$ inch (19 mm) maximum in height provided that the threshold has a beveled edge on each side with a maximum slope of 1:2 for the height exceeding $^1/_4$ inch (6.4 mm).

❖ Thresholds and changes in the surface height at doorways are particularly inconvenient for a person using a wheelchair because complex maneuvering is required to address the level change while operating the door. A person using a wheelchair may have multiple physical conditions including low stamina or restrictions in arm movement.

The model building codes typically establish $^1/_2$ inch (13 mm) as the maximum change in elevation at a doorway where access for a person with a disability is required and a different amount at other doorways. Section 303 requires that where a threshold is over $^1/_4$ inch (6 mm) high, at least half of the height of the threshold should be beveled (see Commentary Figure C404.2.4).

The exception is in recognition of the difficulties with existing buildings and changes in flooring materials and elevations at doors and doorways.

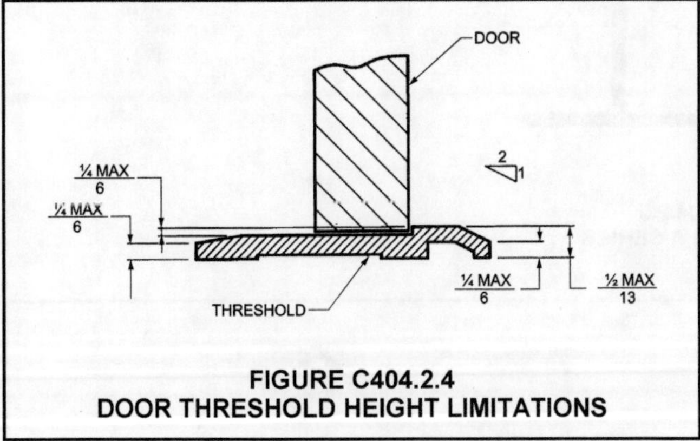

FIGURE C404.2.4
DOOR THRESHOLD HEIGHT LIMITATIONS

404.2.5 Two Doors in Series. Distance between two hinged or pivoted doors in series shall be 48 inches (1220 mm) minimum plus the width of any door swinging into the space. The space between the doors shall provide a turning space complying with Section 304.

❖ Typically, the doors-in-series condition occurs in entry vestibules that are used to reduce the infiltration of outside air. It is important to realize that this requirement applies only when the user must pass through two doors in succession. The requirement would not be applicable if, instead of a vestibule, the situation was a corridor and the two doors were into offices located on opposite sides of the corridor. A storm or screen door immediately in front of an entrance door or communicating doors between two hotel rooms are not considered doors in a series.

Swinging doors in series when placed too closely together can create a condition where a person using a wheelchair may pass through one door, and still have to hold that door open while trying to open the second door. To resolve this condition, a minimum distance of 48 inches (1220 mm) is required between the doors if the doors swing away from each other or 48 inches (1220 mm) plus the width of any door swinging into the space is required [see Figure 404.2.5 and Commentary Figure C404.2.5(a)].

Doors in a series are not always in a straight line. Doors may be offset, or located on adjacent walls rather than opposite walls. The intent is that a clear floor space for a wheelchair [i.e., 30 inches by 48 inches (765 by 1220 mm)] is available past the swing of the first door so the person entering can let one door close before they start to open the second door [see Commentary Figure C404.2.5 (b)].

The requirement for 5 pounds (22 N) maximum opening force in Section 404.2.8 is not applicable to outside doors; thus, sometimes outside doors are difficult for persons with limited mobility to open. In addition, the second door in a series could be locked. A turning space is required between the doors to avoid entrapment in this area. The turning space can overlap the swing of the doors and the door maneuvering clearances.

404.2.6 Door Hardware. Handles, pulls, latches, locks, and other operable parts on accessible doors shall have a shape that is easy to grasp with one hand and does not require tight grasping, pinching, or twisting of the wrist to operate. Operable parts of such hardware shall be 34 inches (865 mm) minimum and 48 inches (1220 mm) maximum above the floor. Where sliding doors are in the fully open position, operating hardware shall be exposed and usable from both sides.

EXCEPTION: Locks used only for security purposes and not used for normal operation shall not be required to comply with Section 404.2.6.

❖ Some people with disabilities are unable to grasp objects with their hands or twist their wrists. Such people are unable to operate, or have great difficulty in operating, door hardware other than lever-operated mechanisms, push-type mechanisms and U-shaped handles. Door hardware that can be operated with a closed fist or a loose grip accommodates the greatest range of users. Hardware that requires simultaneous hand and finger movement requires greater dexterity and coordination and should be avoided for doors along an accessible route (see Commentary Figure C404.2.6).

This section also ensures that the hardware falls within the reach ranges specified in Section 308. The exception would accept a situation such as an unframed glass door at the entry to a building where the door lock is located at the very bottom of the door. Note that the security lock must not conflict with the door surface on the push side, in accordance with Section 404.2.9.

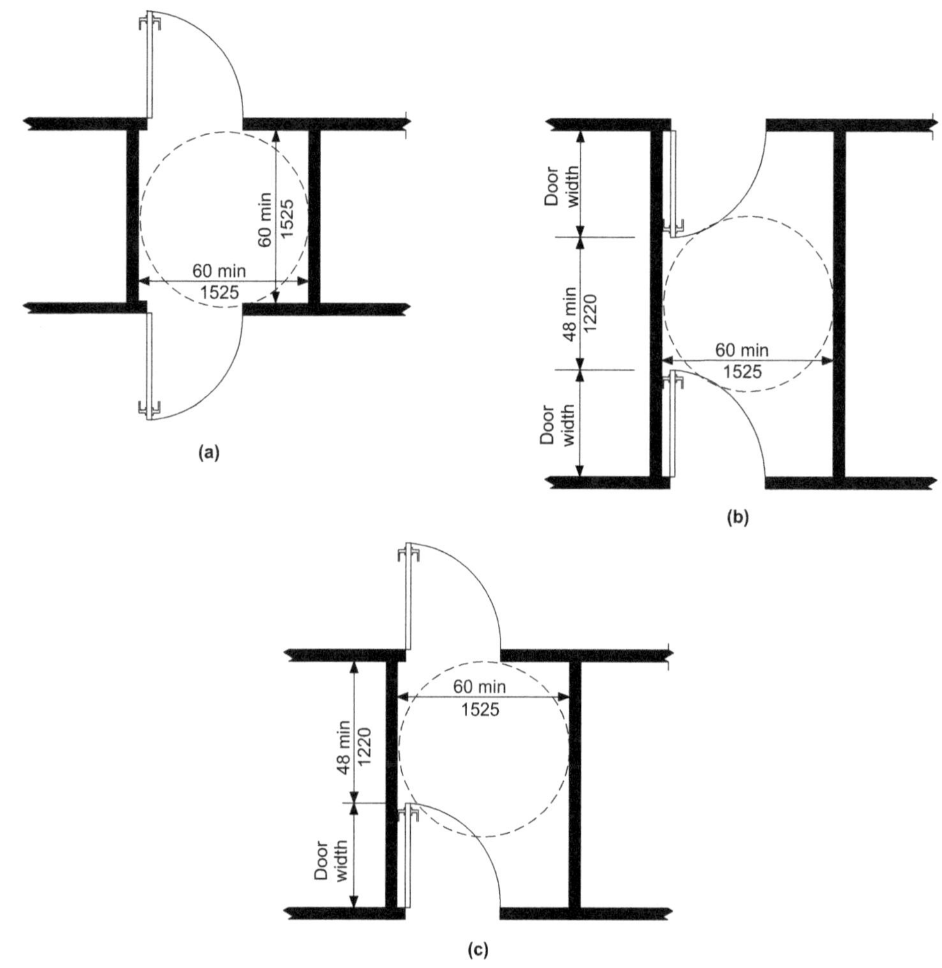

FIGURE 404.2.5
TWO DOORS IN A SERIES

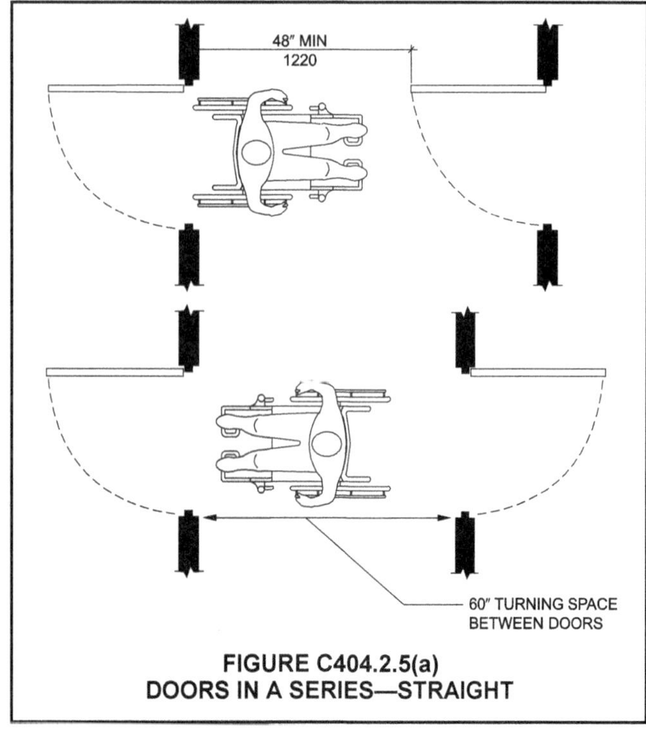

FIGURE C404.2.5(a)
DOORS IN A SERIES—STRAIGHT

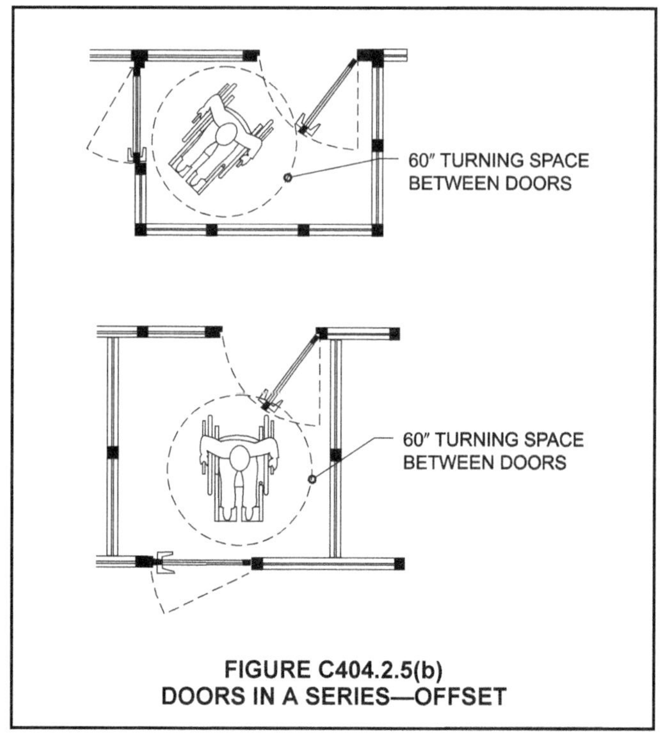

FIGURE C404.2.5(b)
DOORS IN A SERIES—OFFSET

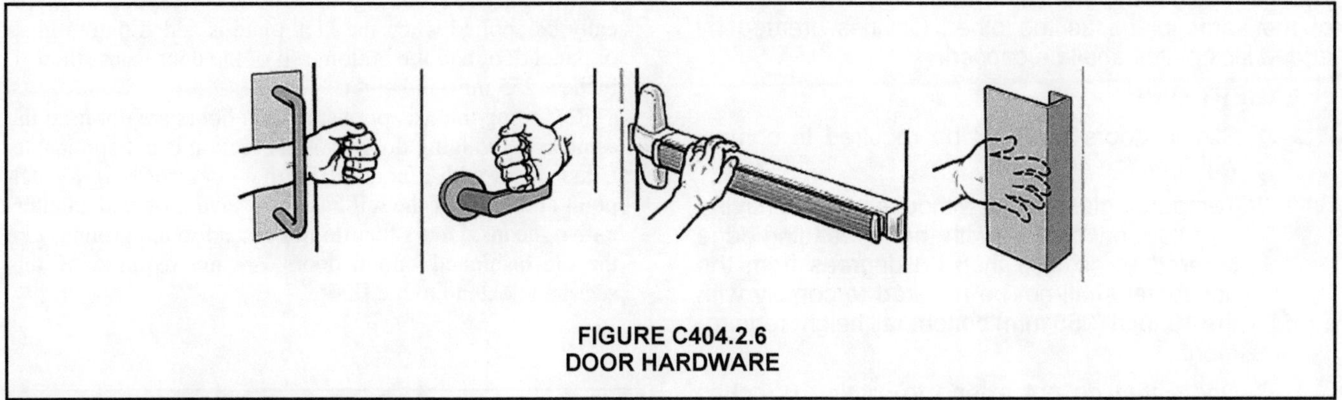

FIGURE C404.2.6
DOOR HARDWARE

404.2.7 Closing Speed.

404.2.7.1 Door Closers. Door closers shall be adjusted so that from an open position of 90 degrees, the time required to move the door to an open position of 12 degrees shall be 5 seconds minimum.

❖ Closers with delayed action features give a person more time to maneuver through doorways. They are particularly useful on frequently used interior doors. When used on fire doors, the closer should be adjusted so that the delay does not exceed requirements established by the administrative authority. This requirement also provides sufficient time for persons using walking aids, such as walkers and crutches, to maneuver through the door without the added burden of working against the door and closer.

404.2.7.2 Spring Hinges. Door spring hinges shall be adjusted so that from an open position of 70 degrees, the door shall move to the closed position in 1.5 seconds minimum.

❖ Although not considered as a "door closer" in the general sense, spring hinges create the same difficulty for people trying to open and then maneuver through the door. Therefore, for the same reasons that are mentioned in the commentary for Section 404.2.7.1, the standard establishes a minimum length of time for the door to close.

404.2.8 Door-Opening Force. Fire doors shall have the minimum opening force allowable by the appropriate administrative authority. The force for pushing or pulling open doors other than fire doors shall be as follows:

1. Interior hinged door: 5.0 pounds (22.2 N) maximum
2. Sliding or folding door: 5.0 pounds (22.2 N) maximum

These forces do not apply to the force required to retract latch bolts or disengage other devices that hold the door in a closed position.

❖ The maximum force pertains to the continuous application of force necessary to fully open a door, not the initial force needed to overcome the inertia of the door. It does not apply to the force required to retract bolts or to disengage other devices used to keep the door in a closed position.

Although some people with disabilities are unable to exert the maximum allowable force to open the door as given in this subsection, these forces are the minimum practical to permit the door closers to function. Door closers have certain minimum closing forces to close (and/or latch) doors satisfactorily. Opening forces are measured with a spring scale as follows:

1. Hinged Doors. Apply force perpendicular to the door at the actuating device or 30 inches (765 mm) from the hinged side, whichever is the farthest from the hinge.
2. Sliding or Folding Doors. Apply force parallel to the door at the door pull or latch.
3. Application of Force. Apply force gradually so that the applied force does not exceed the resistance of the door. Air-pressure differentials, especially in high-rise buildings, have an adverse effect on door-opening force. Accessible openings located in these areas sometimes require modification or possibly the use of automatic or power-assisted doors to comply with the allowable forces given.

Forces to operate a door involve more than a simple, single operation. For example, doors that are latched are unlatched by a force that consists of depressing a lever or applying a direct force. The initial force to overcome the inertia of a door exceeds that required to maintain movement of the door. In general, only a momentary auxiliary force is needed to exceed the force given in Section 404.2.8. It is important to notice that this section does not apply to "fire doors." This exclusion should not be considered as allowing an unlimited amount of force but is instead simply recognizing that for the door to be able to close against the force (pressures) generated by a fire, the door closer may need to exceed the 5.0 pound (22 N) limitation. The administrative authority should make sure that the closer on a fire door has the capacity to close against the forces generated by the fire, but the actual force should be kept as low as possible. Doing this will help to assure that the fire door can perform as intended but also still permit use of the door by people who may have strength and mobility limitations.

404.2.9 Door Surface. Door surfaces within 10 inches (255 mm) of the floor, measured vertically, shall be a smooth surface on the push side extending the full width of the door. Parts creating horizontal or vertical joints in such surface shall be within $^1/_{16}$ inch (1.6 mm) of the same plane as the other. Cavities created by added kick plates shall be capped.

EXCEPTIONS:

1. Sliding doors shall not be required to comply with Section 404.2.9.
2. Tempered glass doors without stiles and having a bottom rail or shoe with the top leading edge tapered at no less than 60 degrees from the horizontal shall not be required to comply with the 10-inch (255 mm) bottom rail height requirement.
3. Doors that do not extend to within 10 inches (255 mm) of the floor shall not be required to comply with Section 404.2.9.

❖ This provision is intended to assist people who will be attempting to open a door from the "push" side of the door. Some persons with disabilities push against doors with their chairs or walkers to open them. Applied kickplates on doors with closers reduce the required maintenance by withstanding abuse from wheelchairs and canes. By providing a smooth surface [one with no more than $^1/_{16}$ inch (1.6 mm) variation], a user can be assured that the door will slide along the user's foot, the leg rest of a wheelchair or the bottom of a walker or crutch that is being pushed against the door without catching. A vertical bar or rod on the latch side of a door is likely to interfere with the opening of a door when the feet or footrest are pressed against a door to open it [see Commentary Figure C404.2.9(a)]. To be effective, a kickplate must cover the door width, less approximately 2 inches (50 mm), up to a height of 10 inches (255 mm) from the floor [see Commentary Figure C404.2.9(b)]. This range will allow for the most common height settings for wheelchair footplates.

The sentence requiring that cavities be capped will typically be applied when the kick plate is added onto a glass or panel door and the bottom rail of the door is less than 10 inches (255 mm) in height.

Regarding the exceptions: sliding doors are not used the same as a swinging doors, so this section is not applicable. Glass doors with a bottom rail that does not have a catch point at the top of the rail basically have provided an alternative means. Doors that do not extend to the ground, like the old-fashioned saloon doors, are not required by this section to extend to the floor.

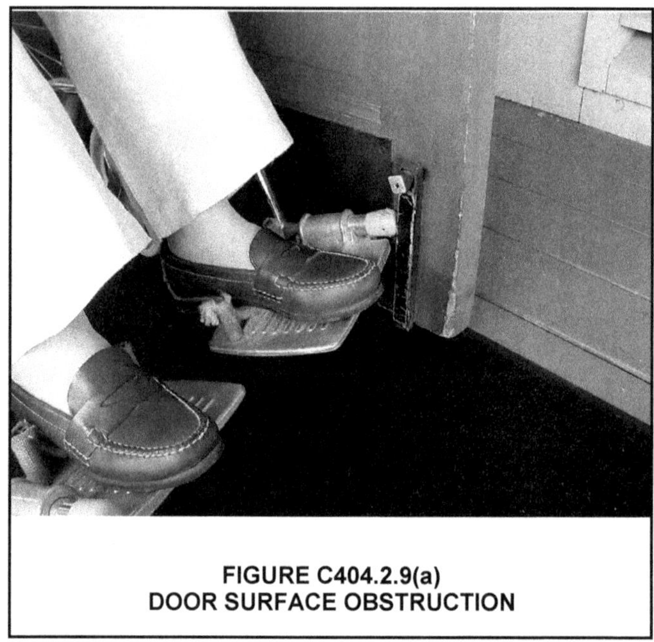

FIGURE C404.2.9(a)
DOOR SURFACE OBSTRUCTION

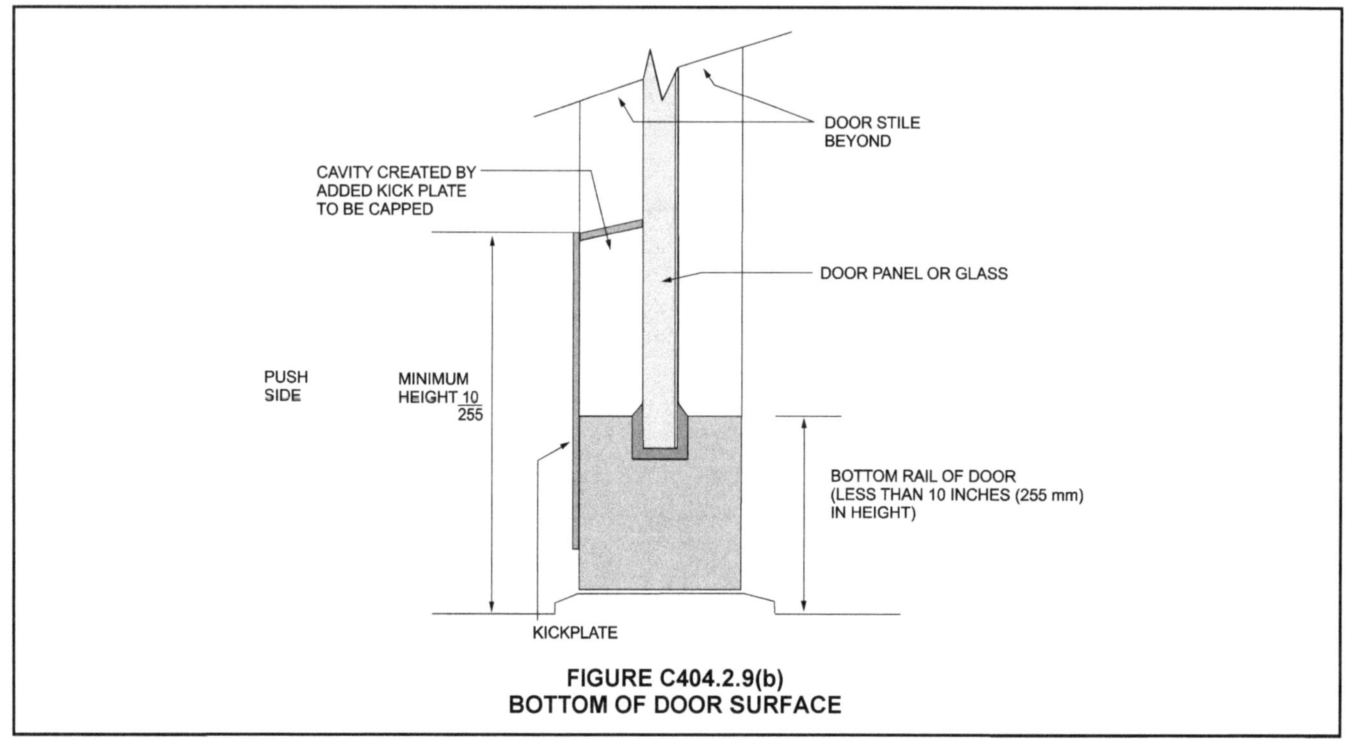

FIGURE C404.2.9(b)
BOTTOM OF DOOR SURFACE

404.2.10 Vision Lites. Doors and sidelites adjacent to doors containing one or more glazing panels that permit viewing through the panels shall have the bottom of at least one panel on either the door or an adjacent sidelite 43 inches (1090 mm) maximum above the floor.

EXCEPTION: Vision lites with the lowest part more than 66 inches (1675 mm) above the floor shall not be required to comply with Section 404.2.10.

❖ If either a door with glazing or a sidelite located adjacent to the door would permit viewing from one side of the door to the other, at least one portion of the glazing must be located at a maximum height of 43 inches (1090 mm) above the floor. There are two important aspects of this requirement. The first is that the provision does not require a vision panel. It simply states that when one is installed that permits viewing, the bottom edge of viewable glazing must be no higher than 43 inches (1090 mm) above the floor (see Commentary Figure C404.2.10). Secondly, it is important to note that only one glazed panel is required to meet this height limitation. Therefore, if a door has a glazed portion located with the bottom edge 60 inches (1525 mm) above the floor and a sidelite is also installed, having the sidelite meet the 43-inch (1090 mm) maximum height limitation and not require a lower glazing height on the door itself would be acceptable. This 43-inch (1090 mm) height was established to provide a person using a wheelchair a view through the glazing at a height that is as low as possible without interfering with the typical door hardware installation height. See Figure C102(a) to see how this height coordinates with the view of the typical person using a wheelchair.

The intent of the exemption is only to regulate vision lites that are located at a height where the typical standing person could see through. If glazing such as a transom window above a door is installed, this section should not be viewed as requiring the low-level viewing panel. The exception allows glazing that has a bottom edge 66 inches (1675 mm) or higher above the floor. This is typically a fire door. The size of windows in fire doors is very limited, and the windows are needed by fire fighters to check the floor before leaving the stairway.

404.3 Automatic Doors. Automatic doors and automatic gates shall comply with Section 404.3. Full powered automatic doors shall comply with ANSI/BHMA A156.10 listed in Section 105.2.4. Power-assist and low-energy doors shall comply with ANSI/BHMA A156.19 listed in Section 105.2.3.

EXCEPTION: Doors, doorways, and gates designed to be operated only by security personnel shall not be required to comply with Sections 404.3.2, 404.3.4, and 404.3.5.

❖ Besides requiring compliance with the applicable standard, this section provides a reference to the requirements found within the subsections, which address the clear opening width and other issues related to these doors. The building hardware industry has developed two consensus standards for automatic and power-assisted doors. Issues such as safety, durability, usability, operation and installation are covered. The standards are available from the American National Standards Institute, 25 West 43rd Street, Fourth Floor, New York, New York 10036.

The model building codes also have requirements with which power-operated and power-assisted doors must comply to ensure the usability of these doors when they are part of a required means of egress. The term "automatic doors" is actually more of a generic term that includes both "full-powered" automatic doors that open on their own and "low-energy"/"automatic" doors that do not open by sensor but

FIGURE C404.2.10
VISION LITES

will instead open fully upon application of an initial minimum force to a button or an operator. The key distinction between "low-energy" and "power-assisted" doors is the difference in the method of initiating the opening of the door. A power-assist door requires a force to the door to start the mechanism that helps open the door.

Automatic doors, in general, are favored by people with disabilities because of the ease of use. These doors can be used by individuals with disabilities who are unable to use manually operated doors.

Doors that are operated only by security personnel should meet accessible requirements for automatic doors with the exception of maneuvering clearance, doors-in-series and control switches. Examples of security personnel are guards in jails, bailiffs in courthouses and guards at security gates. The intent is not to exempt all the doors that these people access, but to exempt doors that these people are responsible for opening, closing and/or locking for security reasons. An example would be cell doors and doors in the route between the courtroom and cells in a courthouse. Security personnel should have sole control of these doors. It is not acceptable for security personnel to operate the doors only for people with disabilities and allow others to have independent access.

404.3.1 Clear Width. Doorways shall have a clear opening width of 32 inches (815 mm) in power-on and power-off mode. The minimum clear opening width for automatic door systems shall be based on the clear opening width provided with all leafs in the open position.

❖ This provision ensures that the 32-inch (815 mm) clear width required by the accessible route provisions of Section 403.5 is maintained at the door. This also matches the width found in Section 404.2.2 for manual doors. This clear width is required whether the door power is on and operating or is not turned on. The second portion of this section is an important distinction between automatic doors and manual doors. Under this provision, if an automatic door uses two leaves to meet the 32-inch (815 mm) clear width, that is acceptable. Manual doors are limited by Section 404.2.1 to having at least one leaf that meets this clear width requirement. Because of this, an automatic door having two 30-inch (765 mm) leaves that both open together would be acceptable in meeting the clear width requirement. Typically the "power off" mode is in play when the door has a "break-away" feature for emergency evacuation with a loss of power to the building.

404.3.2 Maneuvering Clearances. Maneuvering clearances at power-assisted doors shall comply with Section 404.2.3.

❖ Instead of duplicating the requirements, a reference to the provisions for manual doors is used (see commentary, Section 404.2.3). Maneuvering clearances at doors permit the user passage and approach whether the door is manual or power-assisted.

Automatic doors only need maneuvering clearance for a straight-on approach. The door opens for the user without any application of force (except at a button/switch when used). One of the advantages of using automatic doors is that they work where the maneuvering space is not available. This is especially true for rehabilitation of existing buildings.

404.3.3 Thresholds. Thresholds and changes in level at doorways shall comply with Section 404.2.4.

❖ Instead of duplicating the requirements, a reference to the provisions for manual doors is used (see commentary, Section 404.2.4). Thresholds and other changes in level at doors could affect access whether the door is manual or automatic.

404.3.4 Two Doors in Series. Doors in series shall comply with Section 404.2.5.

❖ Instead of duplicating the requirements, a reference to the provisions for manual doors is used (see commentary, Section 404.2.5). Doors placed too close together can affect access whether the door is manual or automatic.

404.3.5 Control Switches. Manually operated control switches shall comply with Section 309. The clear floor space adjacent to the control switch shall be located beyond the arc of the door swing.

❖ By referring to Section 309, any control switches that must be operated by the user must be: 1) provided with a clear floor space near the device, 2) located at a height that is within the reach ranges and 3) easily operated. An example of items affected by this provision would be the push button that is sometimes used with low-energy automatic doors. The button to initiate the opening of the low-energy automatic door must be located so that when the door opens, it will not bump into the person using the button (see Commentary Figure C404.3.5).

Power-operated doors have a switch located near the top of the door that can be used to either turn off power to the door or to an occupant-sensing device. These switches are not used in the normal door operation by the building occupants and are not required to be accessible.

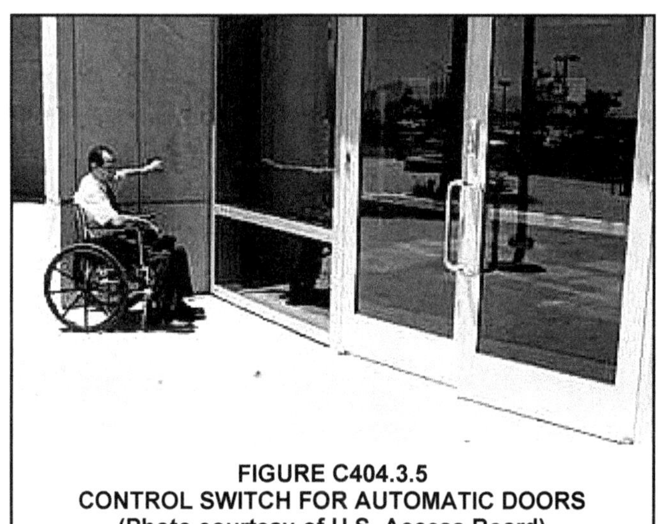

FIGURE C404.3.5
CONTROL SWITCH FOR AUTOMATIC DOORS
(Photo courtesy of U.S. Access Board)

405 Ramps

❖ The intent of this section is to address ramps that are part of an accessible route. Ramps that are not part of an accessible route, such as those in portions of assembly seating that are not required to be accessible, may have steeper slopes. Specific use ramps (vehicle, utility, service access, etc.) may not be required to comply with the provisions for accessible ramps when specifically addressed by the model codes adopted by the authority having jurisdiction,

The model codes also include provisions for guards at drop-offs as an issue of safety. These would be applicable to all ramps, including accessible ramps. Although this section does include requirements for edge protection and handrails, it does not include information on guards. See Commentary Figure C405 for an example of a ramp with a required guard.

405.1 General. Ramps along accessible routes shall comply with Section 405.

EXCEPTION: In assembly areas, aisle ramps adjacent to seating and not serving elements required to be on an accessible route shall not be required to comply with Section 405.

❖ According to the definition for "Ramps" in Section 106.5, a sloped walking surface with a rise of more than 1 inch per 20 inches (1:20) of run is considered a ramp. If elevators or platform lifts are not available to connect different levels, ramps are essential for a person using a wheelchair or scooter.

A gradual slope of 1:20 or less is treated as essentially level. However, many persons who use manual wheelchairs cannot travel long distances on such a slope. Therefore, even if the sloped walking surface does not qualify as a ramp, level areas should be provided in a path of travel at intervals of not more than 200 feet (61 mm) to provide rest areas (see Section 403.5.2, Passing space).

Sloped aisles in assembly seating areas that are not intended or not required to provide an accessible route are not regulated by Section 405.

405.2 Slope. Ramp runs shall have a running slope greater than 1:20 and not steeper than 1:12.

EXCEPTION: In existing buildings or facilities, ramps shall be permitted to have slopes steeper than 1:12 complying with Table 405.2 where such slopes are necessary due to space limitations.

❖ The ability to manage an incline is related to both its slope and its length. Persons using wheelchairs with disabilities affecting arms or with low stamina have serious difficulty using inclines. Most ambulatory people and people who use wheelchairs can more easily manage a slope of 1:16 and runs of 20 feet (6100 mm). Many people have difficulty managing a slope of 1:12 for 30 feet (9150 mm). A

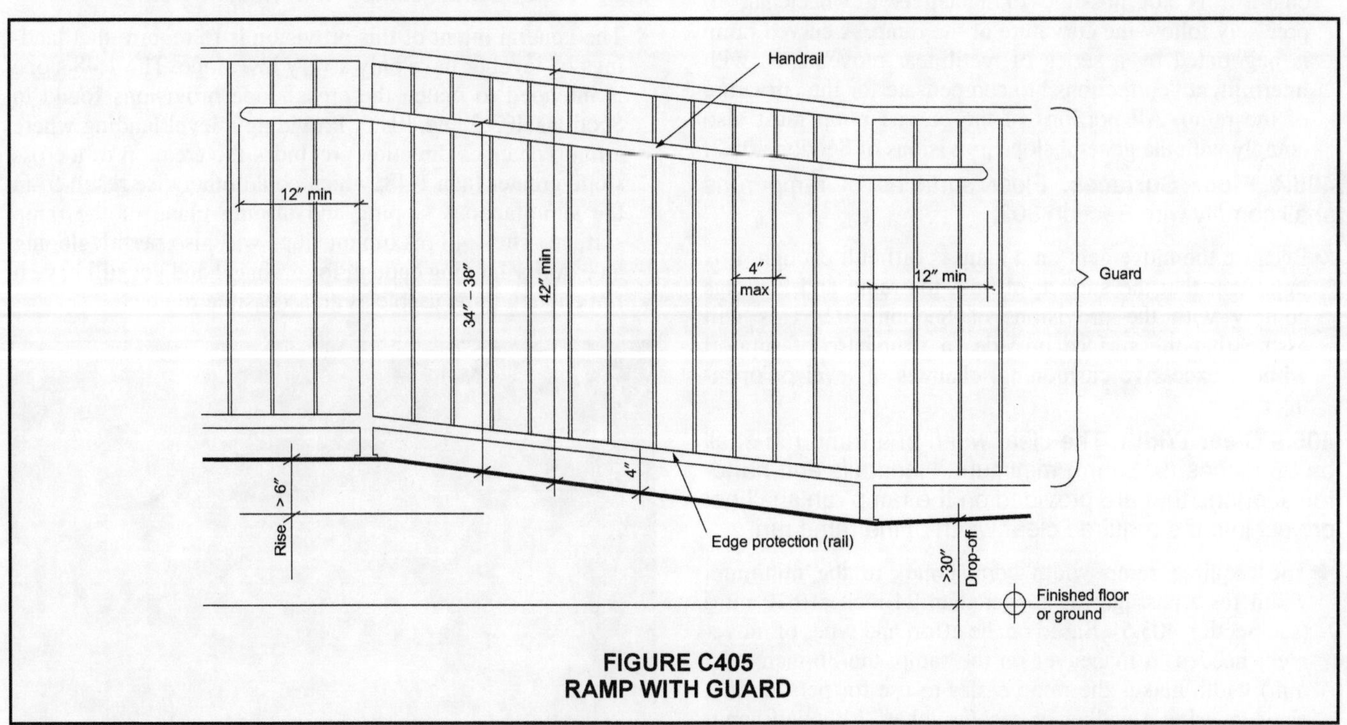

FIGURE C405
RAMP WITH GUARD

TABLE 405.2—ALLOWABLE RAMP DIMENSIONS FOR CONSTRUCTION IN EXISTING SITES, BUILDINGS AND FACILITIES

Slope[1]	Maximum Rise
Steeper than 1:10 but not steeper than 1:8	3 inches (75 mm)
Steeper than 1:12 but not steeper than 1:10	6 inches (150 mm)

[1]A slope steeper than 1:8 shall not be permitted.

walking surface having a slope of 1:20 or less is not regulated as a ramp. Ramps should be straight, not curved, unless engineering analysis has been performed to ensure that the slope of the curved ramp is not steeper than 1:12 anywhere along the line of travel and the maximum cross slope in Section 405.3 is not exceeded. All four wheels of a wheelchair must remain in contact with the ramp surface at all times.

405.3 Cross Slope. Cross slope of ramp runs shall not be steeper than 1:48.

❖ The slope of a ramp in the direction perpendicular to the path of travel can greatly affect the use of a ramp. Where the "cross slope" of the ramp is too great, it can make moving on the ramp in a straight direction very difficult. If severe enough, it may create situations in which persons using a wheelchair are concerned with tipping or could prevent them or persons using a walker from being adequately supported. A larger cross slope can also affect any pedestrian by causing their feet and ankles to tip to unstable angles.

The cross slope of a curved ramp should be carefully designed and checked. A curved ramp is likely to have a difference in elevation from the inside to the outside of the curve, which creates a cross slope steeper than 1:48 and a curved surface on which only three of the four wheels of a wheelchair rest at any one time. Dangerous handling problems are therefore created for the person using a wheelchair. It is not possible to maneuver a wheelchair to precisely follow the curvature of the ramp. A curved ramp is negotiated by a series of rectilinear movements, with intermittent "corrections" to compensate for the curvature of the ramp. All portions of the curved ramp must also comply with the general slope provisions of Section 405.2.

405.4 Floor Surfaces. Floor surfaces of ramp runs shall comply with Section 302.

❖ Because the movement on a ramp is difficult enough, it is important that the surface of both the ramp and landings comply with the provisions of Section 302. This will assure that the surface provides a firm base of support without excessive cushioning, changes of level or openings.

405.5 Clear Width. The clear width of a ramp run shall be 36 inches (915 mm) minimum. Handrails and handrail supports that are provided on the ramp run shall not project into the required clear width of the ramp run.

❖ The required ramp width corresponds to the minimum width for a passageway longer than 24 inches (610 mm) (see Section 403.5). Based on the effort and types of movement needed to maneuver on the ramp, the 36-inch (915 mm) width makes the ramp easier to use for persons in a chair or using a walker or cane/crutches. Although handrails are permitted to protrude from the walls along an accessible route (see Section 307.2, Exception 1), in order for the handrails to not be an obstruction, the clear width of a ramp is determined by the clear horizontal space between opposing handrails and/or between any posts, fittings or supports for the handrail, whichever results in the lesser width (see Commentary Figure C405.5).

405.6 Rise. The rise for any ramp run shall be 30 inches (760 mm) maximum.

❖ The ability to manage an incline is related to both its slope and its length. A person using a wheelchair with disabilities affecting arms or with low stamina has serious difficulty using inclines. Therefore, the code establishes a maximum rise of 30 inches (765 mm) for any ramp between landings or floor levels. Though accepted by the standard, some people may have difficulty managing a slope of 1:12 for 30 feet (9 m). Therefore, a smaller rise and lower slope would generally improve access. Most ambulatory people and most people who use wheelchairs can more easily manage a slope of 1:16 and runs of 20 feet (6 m) versus the permitted 1:12 slope and a 30-inch (765 mm) rise that would be obtained over a 30-foot (9 m) run.

405.7 Landings. Ramps shall have landings at the bottom and top of each ramp run. Landings shall comply with Section 405.7.

❖ Landings provide an area for resting, turning or passing another wheelchair. They are, therefore, an important part of creating accessible ramps that permit the transition from one level to another along an accessible route. The individual features of slope, width, length, change in direction and doorways are addressed by the referenced subsections (see Figure 405.7 and Commentary Figure C405.7.4).

405.7.1 Slope. Landings shall have a slope not steeper than 1:48 and shall comply with Section 302.

❖ The general intent of this provision is to require that landings be level or have only a very low slope. The 1:48 slope is intended to match the cross slope provisions found in Sections 403.3 and 405.3. Providing a level landing where a ramp changes direction precludes the creation of a cross slope greater than 1:48, which could otherwise result from the simultaneous sloping and turning plane of the ramp surface. The 1:48 maximum slope will also permit sloping an exterior landing enough for drainage and yet still have it flat enough to be usable as an accessible route.

FIGURE C405.5
MINIMUM CLEAR WIDTH

405.7.2 Width. Clear width of landings shall be at least as wide as the widest ramp run leading to the landing.

❖ This provision simply ensures that the landing is at least as wide as any ramp that it serves and therefore does not narrow or reduce the available route of travel. If the ramp is wider than the minimum width required by Section 405.5, the landing width must also be increased even though the ramp is in excess of the minimum required width. This provision does not deal with the "required" width but is instead tied to the actual width of the ramp that the landing serves. The width of the landing may need to be increased from that specified by this section if the landing is being used to change the direction of travel (see Section 405.7.4).

405.7.3 Length. Landings shall have a clear length of 60 inches (1525 mm) minimum.

❖ A length of 60 inches (1525 mm) provides a stopping distance, which is greater than the length of the wheelchair. This will also provide additional space to allow a chair user to maneuver before approaching another ramp, door or other object because the landing is longer than the wheelchair.

405.7.4 Change in Direction. Ramps that change direction at ramp landings shall be sized to provide a turning space complying with Section 304.3.

❖ The minimum landing where a ramp changes direction provides maneuvering space for the person using a wheelchair (see Commentary Figure C405.7.4). The 60-inch (1525 mm) turning space may result in a landing that is larger than the width that is required by Section 405.7.2. This size landing can provide for a turning space in compliance with Section 304.3 or can allow passage of two chair users at the landing similar to the requirements of Section 403.5.2.

Providing a landing where a ramp changes direction precludes the creation of a cross slope greater than 1:48, which could otherwise result from the simultaneous sloping and turning plane of the ramp surface (see Sections 405.3 and 405.7.1).

405.7.5 Doorways. Where doorways are adjacent to a ramp landing, maneuvering clearances required by Sections 404.2.3 and 404.3.2 shall be permitted to overlap the landing area. Where a door that is subject to

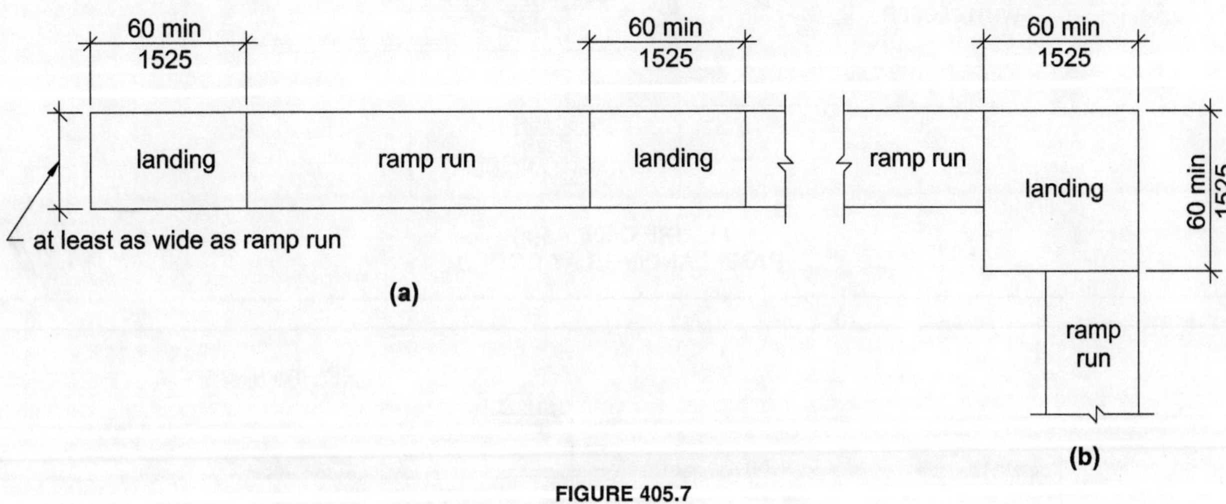

FIGURE 405.7
RAMP LANDINGS

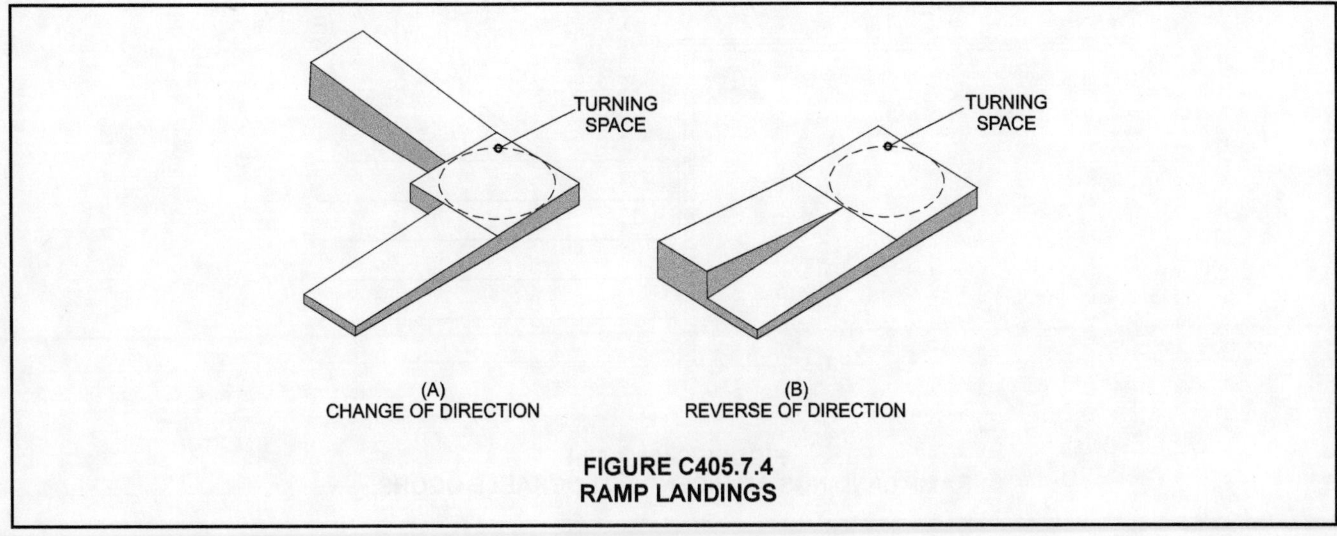

FIGURE C405.7.4
RAMP LANDINGS

locking is located adjacent to a ramp landing, the landing shall be sized to provide a turning space complying with Section 304.3.

❖ This section serves to remind designers that the landing may be used for the dual purpose of also providing the maneuvering space adjacent to a doorway [see Commentary Figure C405.7.5(a)]. One aspect of this section that is important to note, but is very subtle, is the fact that the doors are permitted only adjacent to the ramp landing and not adjacent or on the ramp itself. This wording about "adjacent to a ramp landing" can also be considered as supporting or reinforcing the provision of Section 404.2.4.5 that requires a level landing.

It is not possible for a person in a wheelchair to travel backwards down a ramp and maintain adequate control. If the door at the top or bottom landing of a ramp could be locked, a turning space must be provided at that top or bottom landing to allow the person to turn around and go back along the ramp when necessary [see Commentary Figure C405.7.5(b)].

405.8 Handrails. Ramp runs with a rise greater than 6 inches (150 mm) shall have handrails complying with Section 505.

❖ Handrails on ramps provide a graspable object for guidance and support while negotiating a ramp. Although handrails on ramps serve many of the same functions as

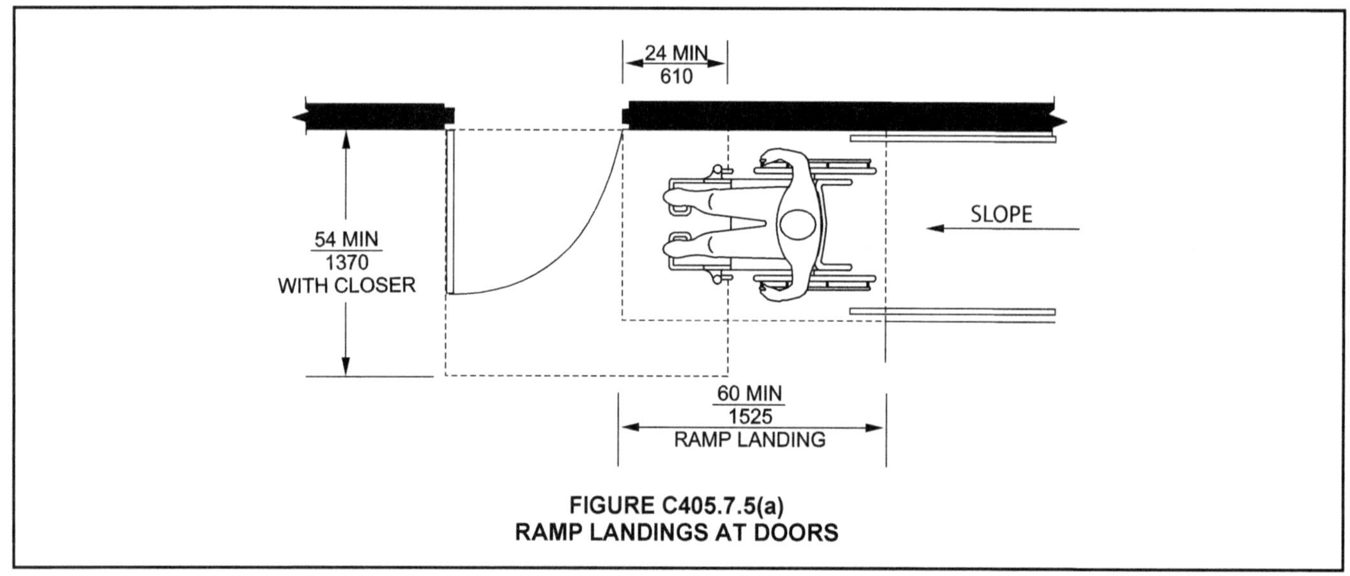

FIGURE C405.7.5(a)
RAMP LANDINGS AT DOORS

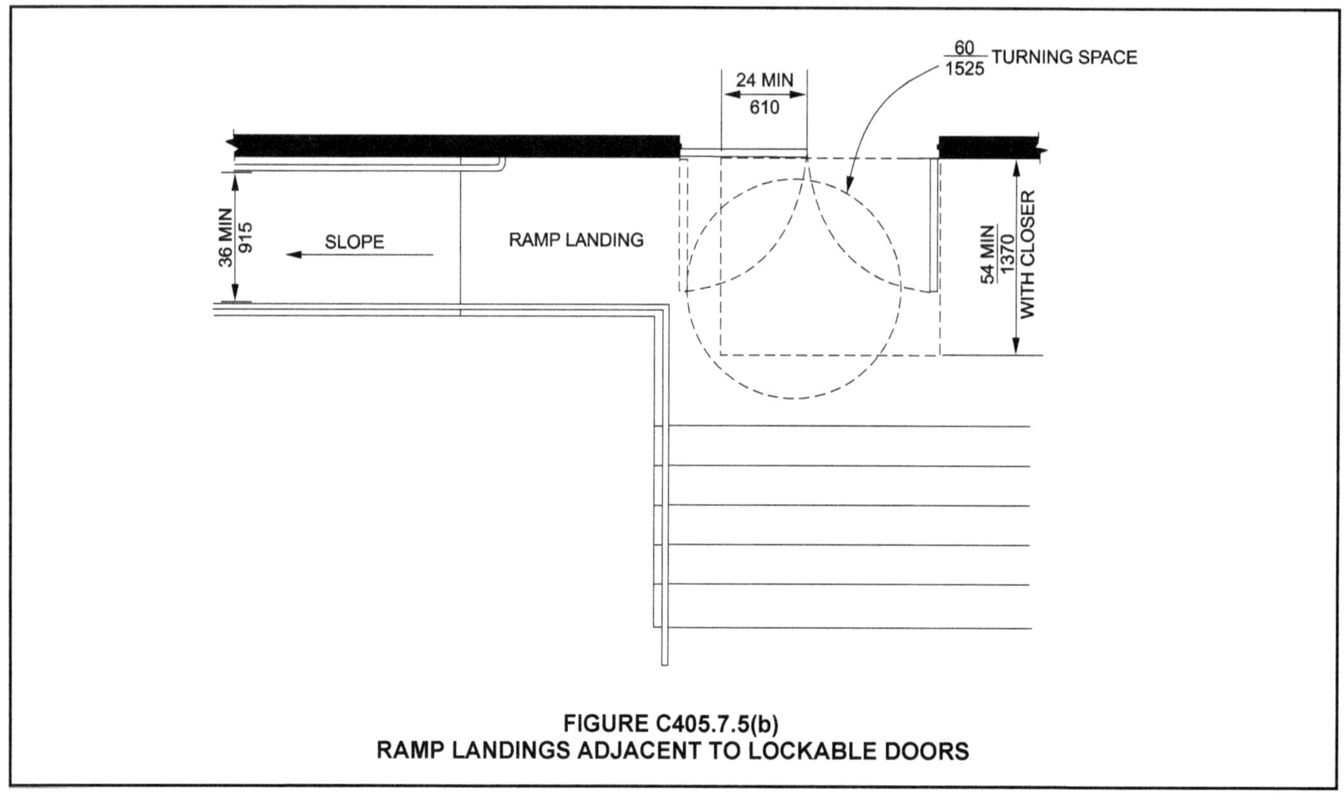

FIGURE C405.7.5(b)
RAMP LANDINGS ADJACENT TO LOCKABLE DOORS

those on stairs, the need for a handrail on a stairway is recognizably more critical because of the greater degree of difficulty involved in traversing a stairway as compared to a ramp. Handrails are nonetheless necessary for ramps because the ramp is not a flat, level surface and the user must exercise caution to avoid a slip or fall. The handrail provides a solid, stable element to grasp that can help arrest a fall. This is especially important for individuals with varying degrees of mobility impairments. A handrail can also be used to propel a wheelchair forward, to control forward descent and to control backward descent. The exclusion for ramps with a rise of 6 inches (150 mm) or less recognizes that most users would be able to easily manage a climb or descent of such heights and lengths.

Handrails may protrude over an accessible route, but along a ramp they must not reduce the clear width of the ramp to less than 36 inches (915 mm) between the handrails (see Section 405.5).

Commentary Figures C405, C405.9.2.1 and C405.9.2.2(a) and (b) also illustrate how the handrail and edge protection options work together.

405.9 Edge Protection. Edge protection complying with Section 405.9.1 or 405.9.2 shall be provided on each side of ramp runs and at each side of ramp landings.

EXCEPTIONS:

1. Edge protection shall not be required on ramps not required to have handrails and that have flared sides complying with Section 406.3.
2. Edge protection shall not be required on the sides of ramp landings serving an adjoining ramp run or stairway.
3. Edge protection shall not be required on the sides of ramp landings having a vertical drop-off of $^1/_2$ inch (13 mm) maximum within 10 inches (255 mm) horizontally of the minimum landing area specified in Section 405.7.
4. Edge protection shall not be required on the sides of ramped aisles where the ramps provide access to the adjacent seats and aisle access ways.

❖ Handrails, curbs, walls and extended edges serve to prevent wheels of wheelchairs from dropping off the edge of a ramp and stranding or injuring the user. They also serve a similar purpose for persons using other walking aids. Handrails and walls are also used by some persons using wheelchairs to slow their rate of descent if necessary. This section provides the reference to the two sections that provide the specific details of how edge protection is to be obtained. Commentary Figure C405.9 provides examples of alternate options and different views.

The four exceptions address situations where either the ramp or landings are not required to have edge protection. Exception 1 allows the use of flared sides adjacent to the ramp similar to those used for curb ramps. Literally, if a ramp has a rise of 6 inches (150 mm) or less (i.e., no handrails required by Section 405.8), there is an option of using flared sides similar to a curb ramp. Exception 2 addresses a case that should be self-evident, but will ensure that a curb or other type of edge protection is not placed between the ramp and the landing and at the location where a stairway may be using the same landing as the ramp. Exception 3, illustrated in Figure 405.9, acknowledges that ramps and landings essentially following adjacent ground or floor levels do not pose a drop-off hazard. Exception 4 exempts edge protection where sloped or ramped aisles adjoin aisle accessways (i.e., the aisles between rows of seats).

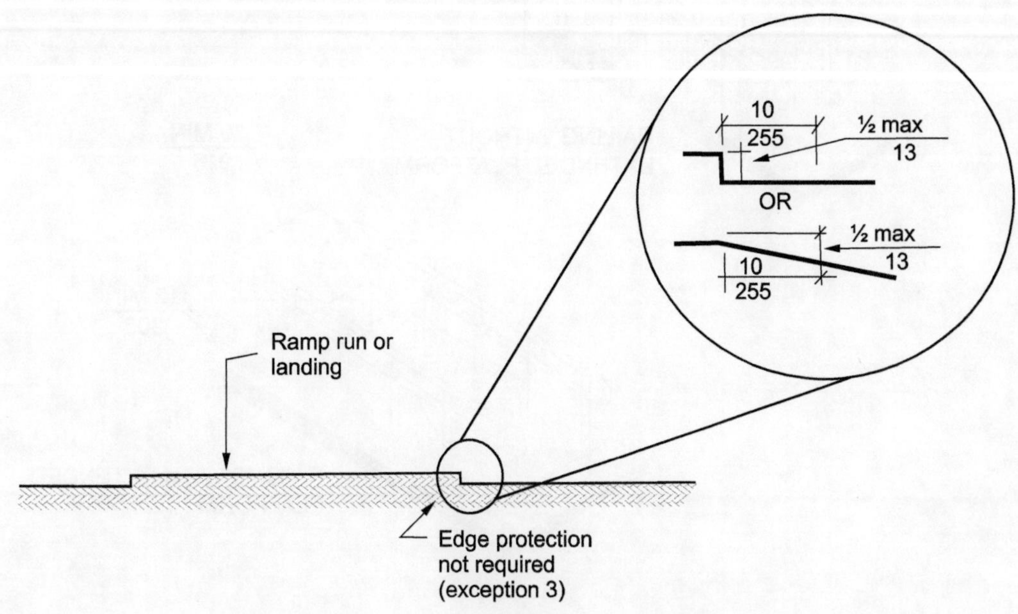

FIGURE 405.9
EDGE PROTECTION—LIMITED DROP OFF

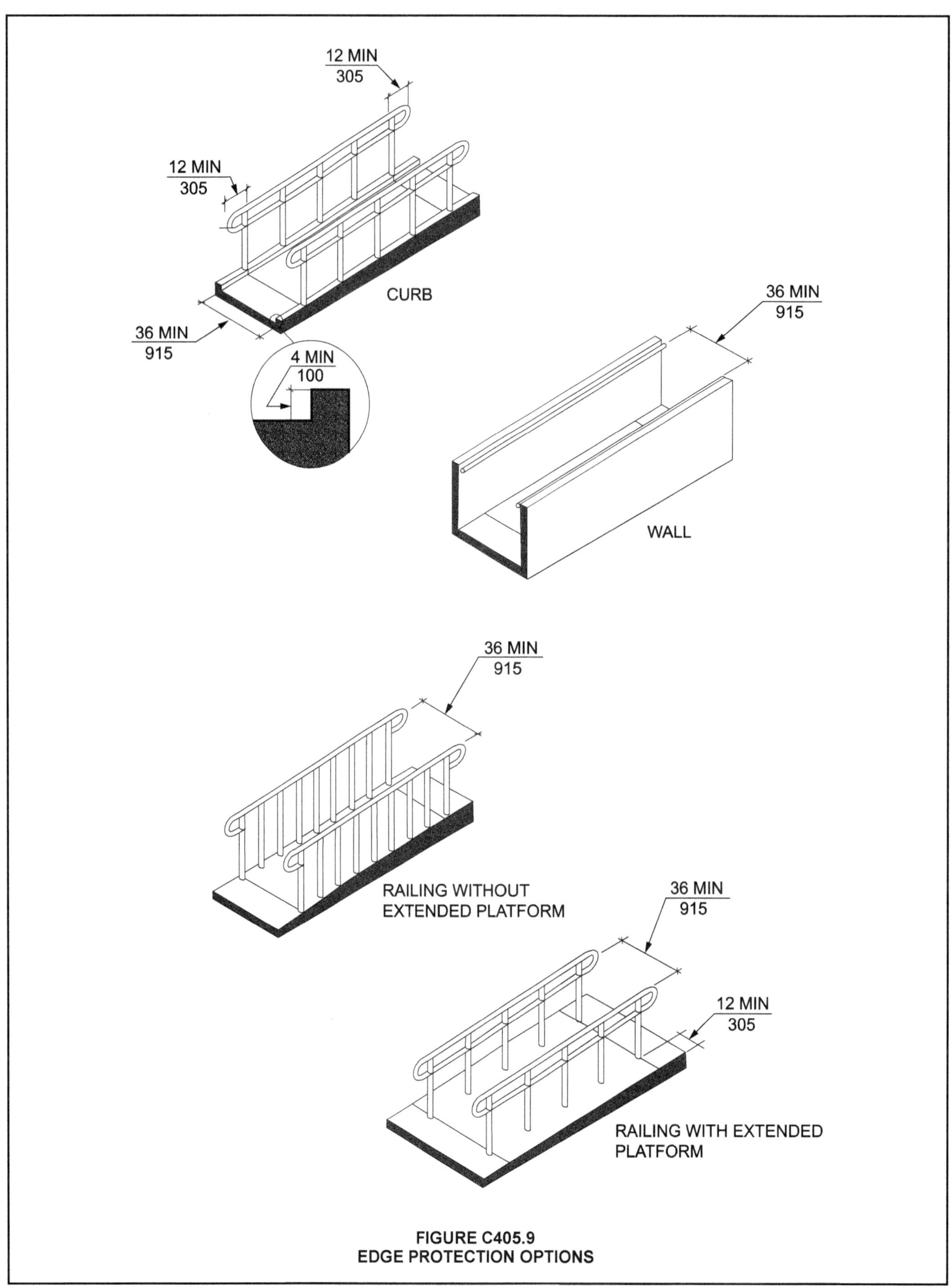

FIGURE C405.9
EDGE PROTECTION OPTIONS

405.9.1 Extended Floor Surface. The floor surface of the ramp run or ramp landing shall extend 12 inches (305 mm) minimum beyond the inside face of a railing complying with Section 505.

❖ By extending the surface of the ramp or landing beyond the railing or by being at the same level as the floor or ground surface, a person using a wheelchair will be less likely to get near any edge where a wheel could drop over. This is also beneficial for persons using walkers, canes or crutches (see Figure 405.9.1 or the "extended platform" shown in Commentary Figure C405.9).

405.9.2 Curb or Barrier. A curb complying with Section 405.9.2.1 or a barrier complying with Section 405.9.2.2 shall be provided.

❖ Where edge protection is required, there are two basic options for edge protection on ramps: curbs or barriers. Any type of curb or barrier that can prevent the passage of a 4-inch-diameter (100 mm) sphere at this low height will be adequate to keep the wheels of a chair or the tip of a crutch from getting to the edge of the ramp or landing (see Commentary Figure C405.9.2).

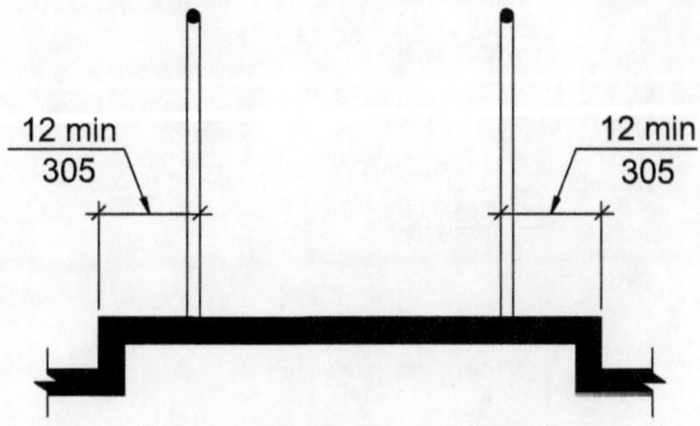

FIGURE 405.9.1
EXTENDED FLOOR SURFACE

405.9.2.1 Curb. A curb shall be a minimum of 4 inches (100 mm) in height.

❖ Figure 405.9.2(a) and Commentary Figure C405.9.2 illustrate a solid curb-type barrier. The 4-inch (100 mm) height is considered equivalent to the language "prevents the passage of a 4-inch (100 mm) diameter sphere," but is specific to curb configurations. Commentary Figures C405, C405.9.2.1 and C405.9.2.2(a) and (b) also illustrate how the handrail and edge protection options work together.

405.9.2.2 Barrier. Barriers shall be constructed so that the barrier prevents the passage of a 4-inch (100 mm) diameter sphere where any portion of the sphere is within 4 inches (100 mm) of the floor.

❖ A wall can serve as the barrier on the side of a ramp. Alternatively, the barrier can be a part of a guard or ornamental feature. If a guard or ornamental feature is used, the bottom edge must be no more than 4 inches (100 mm) above the floor of the ramp surface. Figure 405.9.2(b) shows how bars or rails elevated above the ramp or landing surface can provide equivalent protection to that provided by a curb. Another alternative would be pickets spaced so that the openings between pickets are less than 4 inches (100 mm). Commentary Figures C405, C405.9.2.1 and C405.9.2.2(a) and (b) also illustrate how the handrail and edge protection options work together.

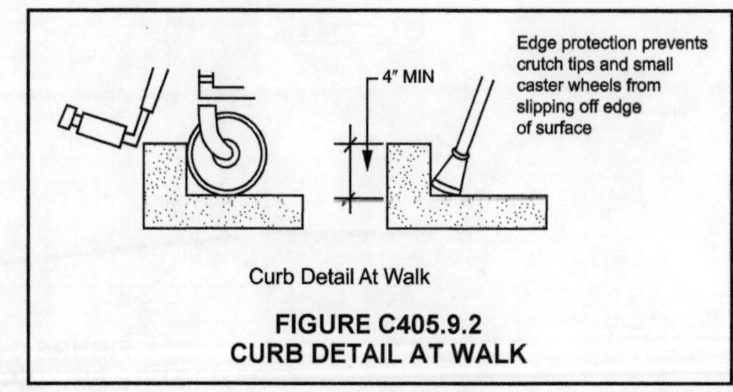

FIGURE C405.9.2
CURB DETAIL AT WALK

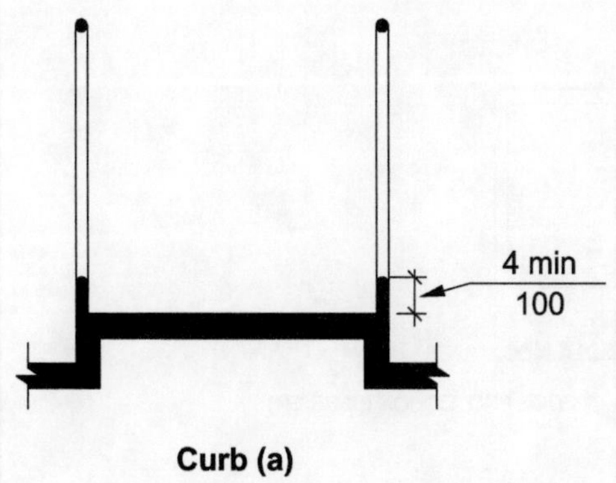

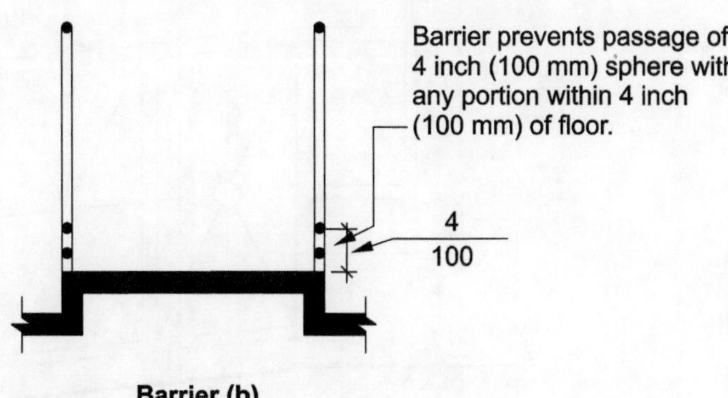

FIGURE 405.9.2
RAMP EDGE PROTECTION

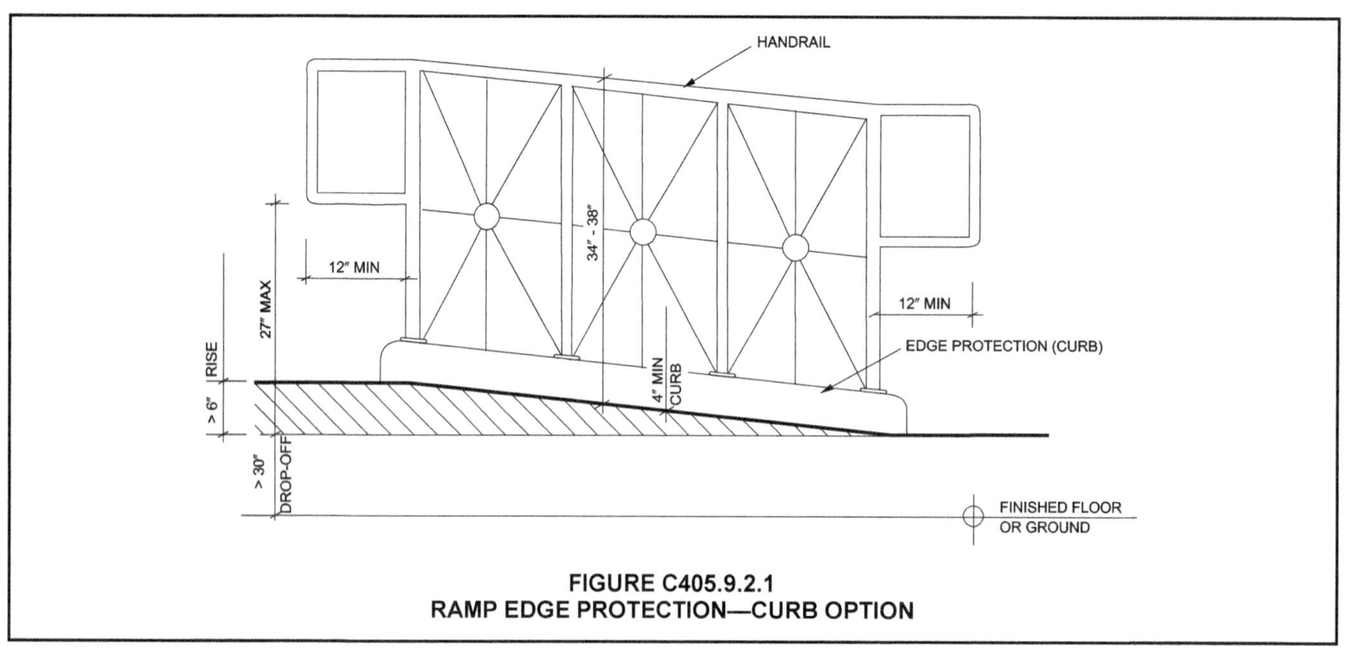

FIGURE C405.9.2.1
RAMP EDGE PROTECTION—CURB OPTION

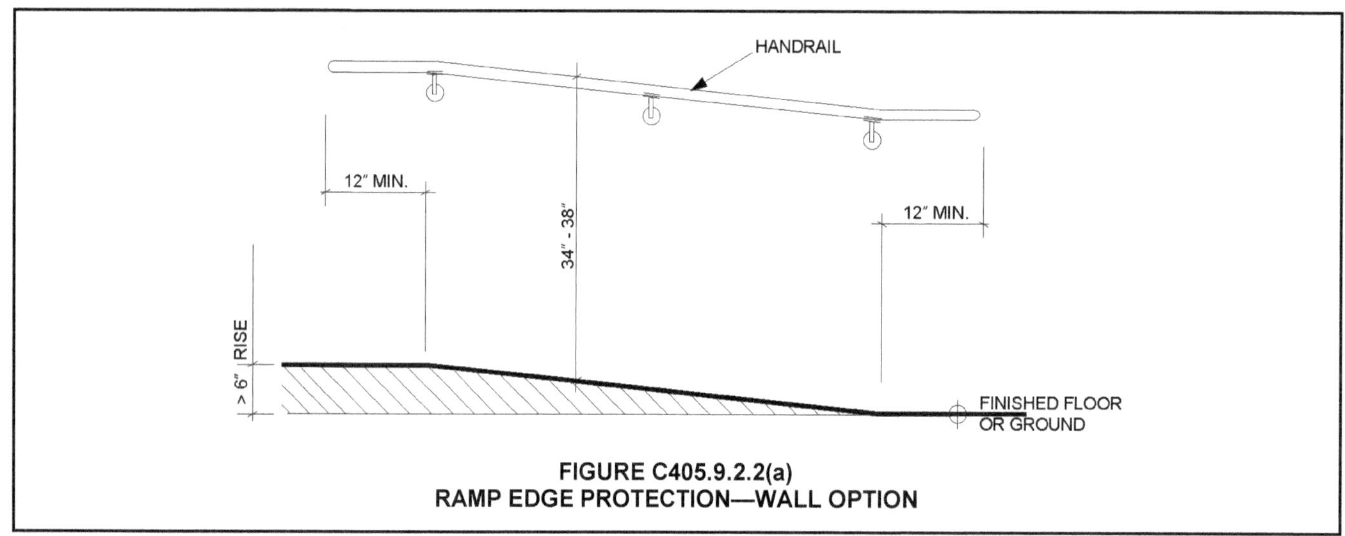

FIGURE C405.9.2.2(a)
RAMP EDGE PROTECTION—WALL OPTION

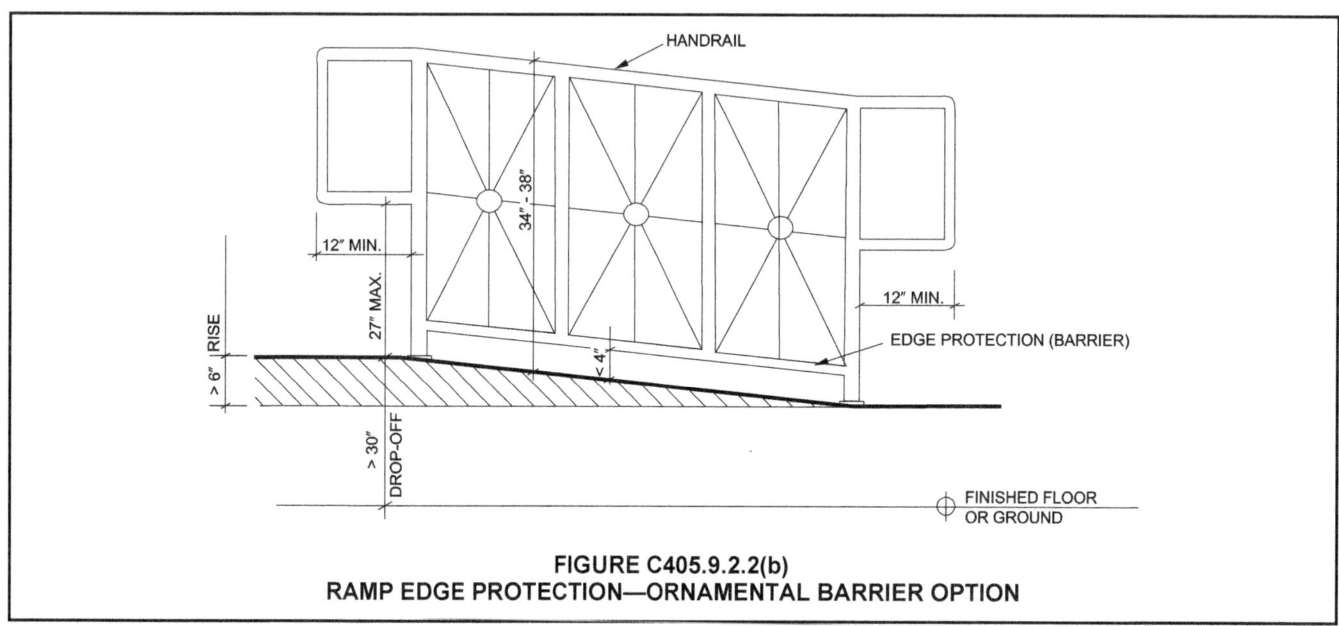

FIGURE C405.9.2.2(b)
RAMP EDGE PROTECTION—ORNAMENTAL BARRIER OPTION

405.10 Wet Conditions. Landings subject to wet conditions shall be designed to prevent the accumulation of water.

❖ This is a universally sound design principle that has many benefits beyond the accessibility perspective. The concern of this standard is the potential safety hazard that would exist. Standing water can render a ground surface significantly more slippery for both foot traffic and crutch tips. In freezing climates, water that accumulates can freeze, creating an extremely dangerous condition for all pedestrians, including people in wheelchairs. Standing water at building entrances can be tracked inside the building, increasing the slipperiness of interior floor surfaces such as tile and terrazzo. Under most circumstances, the allowable slope of 1:48 will be sufficient for drainage. Care should also be taken to avoid drainage from overhead surfaces discharging onto ramp surfaces and approaches. In situations where gutters may freeze and overflow, it may be prudent to locate ramps so that they are not under gutters so that ice will not accumulate on the ramped surface. Wet conditions may also be found in some indoor spaces, such as adjacent to pool areas.

406 Curb Ramps

406.1 General. Curb ramps on accessible routes shall comply with Sections 406, 405.2, 405.3, and 405.10.

❖ Curb ramps are a unique type of ramp construction suited for use at curbs between sidewalks and vehicular ways or any other similar location wherein a change in level occurs along an accessible path. Curb ramp construction can comply with minimal provisions in Section 405 for ramps and yet be fully functional. For example, it would be impractical to require handrails (Section 405.8) or guards or other edge protection (Section 405.9) because of the obstructions such features would present to the surrounding areas, which are typically a circulation path or public way. The attributes that are unique to curb ramps make them suitable for their purpose primarily because of the limited rise (curb height) that they serve.

By the references to Sections 405.2 and 405.3, the primary sloped segment of a curb ramp is required to have a running slope of 1:12 maximum and a cross slope of 1:48 maximum, the same as for all other pedestrian ramps. It is appropriate to provide a slope that can be negotiated by a wheelchair without great difficulty and is also consistent with Section 303.4, which effectively establishes that the slope of the transition between changes in level greater than $^1/_2$ inch (13 mm) is a critical consideration.

Because curb ramps are most often located outside, they should be constructed so water does not accumulate at the approach to or along the curb ramp. Water on approach surfaces could cause slick conditions, so these surfaces should be minimally sloped to drain (see Section 405.10).

406.2 Counter Slope. Counter slopes of adjoining gutters and road surfaces immediately adjacent to the curb ramp shall not be steeper than 1:20. The adjacent surfaces at transitions at curb ramps to walks, gutters and streets shall be at the same level.

❖ In general, this provision results in a transition across a curb that is reasonably and smoothly usable by a wheelchair while minimizing the impact of its presence on other pedestrian traffic. Counter slopes typically occur at the bottom of curb ramps because of the beveling of gutter sides or the crown of the road surface. Counter slopes steeper than 1:20 pose a risk that the footrest of the wheelchair could catch on the ascending slope of the gutter or road crown, ultimately tipping the person out of the wheelchair (see Figure 406.2).

406.3 Sides of Curb Ramps. Where provided, curb ramp flares shall comply with Section 406.3.

❖ Careful consideration should be given to the location of curb ramp placement in relation to cross-pedestrian traffic. It would be preferable to locate curb ramps so that they do not extend perpendicular into a primary path of pedestrian travel. If they are not located out of the main circulation path, pedestrians are then faced with traveling perpendicular across a portion of the curb ramp and stepping onto the flared side or onto the sloped portion of the curb ramp.

406.3.1 Slope. Flares shall not be steeper than 1:10.

❖ The standard does not require a curb ramp to have flared sides if the expected traffic pattern would not involve pedestrians crossing the curb ramp (i.e., 36 inches past the top of the ramp). In alterations, where there is not space for an adequate landing, Section 406.7 provides specific provisions to account for that condition. Commentary Figure C406.3.1(a) illustrates when flared sides are provided. If flared sides are not provided, and if the pedestrian routes would cross the curb ramp, this might be considered a tripping hazard. One option to avoid this situation is for a curb ramp to cut through a parkway, as in Commentary Figure C406.3.1(b)].

Whether or not they are required, where flared sides are used, they are limited to a maximum slope of 1:10 to minimize the hazard to perpendicular traffic. Locating curb

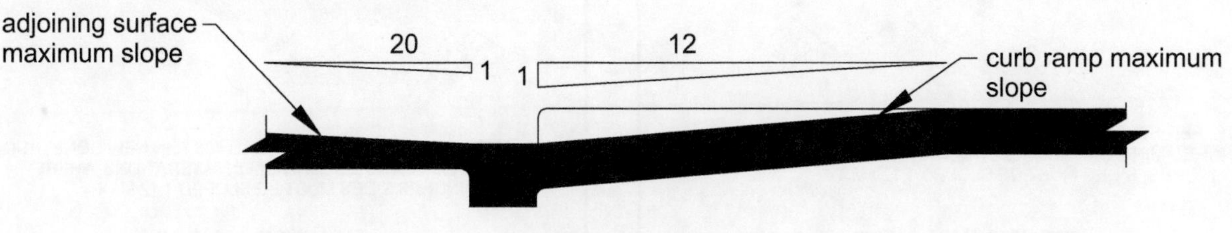

FIGURE 406.2
COUNTER SLOPE OF SURFACES ADJACENT TO CURB RAMPS

ramps where they will not extend into expected pedestrian cross-traffic paths is preferable, but this is not always feasible. Rather than leaving the transition from the sides of curb ramps to adjoining surfaces abrupt, flared sides are provided as a safety feature for all pedestrians.

406.3.2 Marking. If curbs adjacent to the ramp flares are painted, the painted surface shall extend along the flared portion of the curb.

❖ Curbs are painted for various reasons including for designation of fire lanes and passenger loading areas. When curbs encompassing curb ramps are painted (for any reason), the painting shall extend along the portion of the curb at the flared sides. This improves visibility of the curb ramp for all pedestrians and particularly for those with low vision. For the locations and examples, see Figures 406.3 and Commentary Figure C406.3.2. The flared sides or ramp surface itself should not be painted. This will become a slipping hazard during wet conditions.

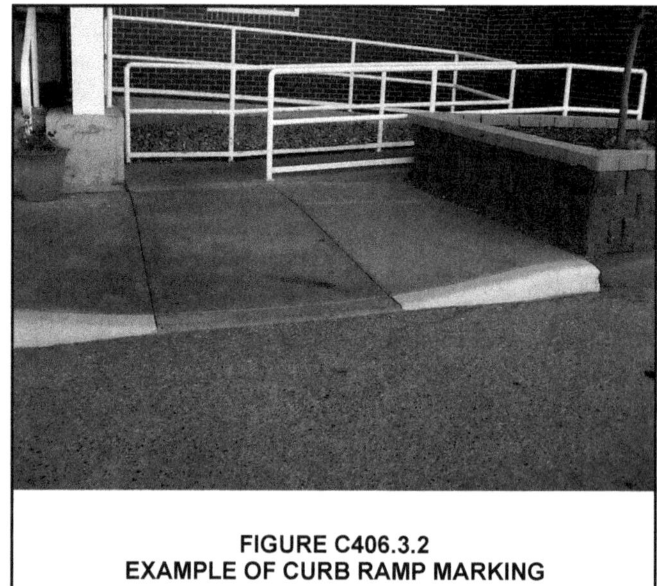

FIGURE C406.3.2
EXAMPLE OF CURB RAMP MARKING

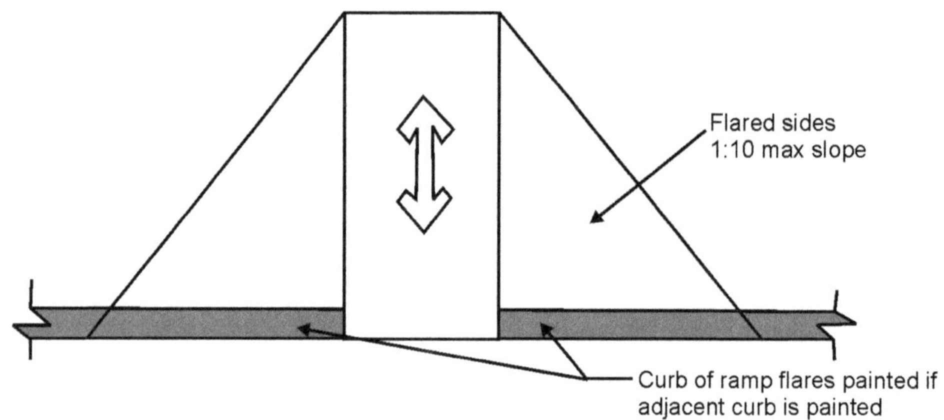

FIGURE 406.3
SIDES OF CURB RAMP

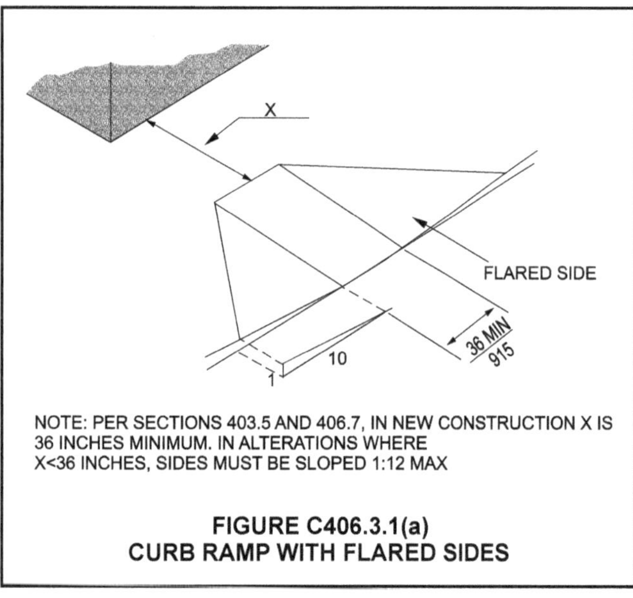

FIGURE C406.3.1(a)
CURB RAMP WITH FLARED SIDES

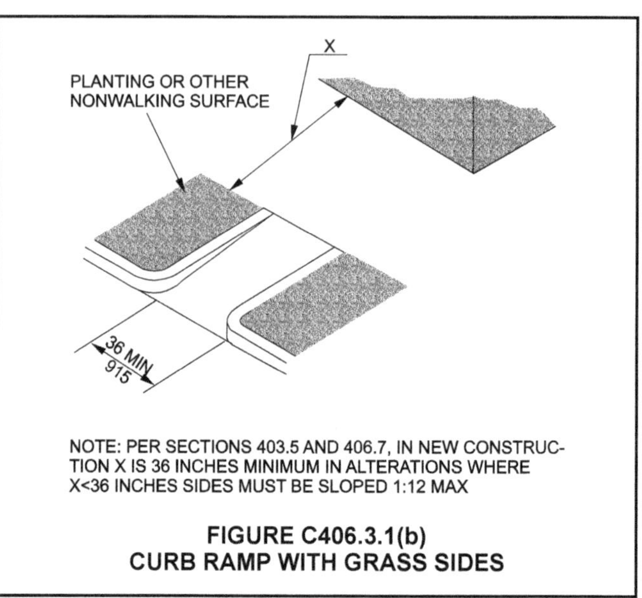

FIGURE C406.3.1(b)
CURB RAMP WITH GRASS SIDES

406.4 Width. Curb ramps shall be 36 inches (915 mm) minimum in width, exclusive of flared sides.

❖ The required width of the curb ramp corresponds to the standard wheelchair passage width for a passageway longer than 24 inches (610 mm) (see Section 403.5). While the sides of a curb ramp are seldom enclosed by construction such as walls, the required 36-inch (915 mm) width represents an appropriate, functional minimum for the construction of curb ramps [see Commentary Figures C406.3.1(a), C406.3.1(b), C406.7(a) and C406.7(b)].

406.5 Floor Surface. Floor surfaces of curb ramps shall comply with Section 302.

❖ The surface features of curb ramps are just as critical as other floor or ramp surfaces required to comply with Section 302.

As noted in Section 406.13, the standard does not require detectable warnings on the curb ramps.

406.6 Location. Curb ramps and the flared sides of curb ramps shall be located so they do not project into vehicular traffic lanes, parking spaces, or parking access aisles. Curb ramps at marked crossings shall be wholly contained within the markings, excluding any flared sides.

❖ This provision ensures the curb ramps remain usable and are not blocked or damaged by vehicles, as well as protecting persons using wheelchairs from moving vehicles (also see Section 406.8).

Previously these provisions applied only to "built-up" curb ramps. Depending on the specific design, the problems addressed by this section could affect either a depressed or built-up curb ramp. Built-up curb ramps can be an effective solution where space limitations, such as narrow sidewalks, preclude the use of a depressed curb ramp. Flares of built-up curb ramps that extend to front doors of cars and adjacent to side-mounted wheelchair lifts create uneven, dangerous sloping surfaces that make maneuvering for boarding vehicles difficult, if not impossible, for many persons using wheelchairs and persons with mobility impairments. Further, the extreme hazard to the user that would be created if the ramp extended into vehicular lanes makes it clearly unacceptable and an arrangement to be avoided. Commentary Figure C406.7(b) helps to show how a built-up curb ramp may create problems if it does protrude into the listed locations.

This provision ensures that the designed traffic pattern for persons using wheelchairs occurs within the same designed traffic pattern for all pedestrians. There is a certain degree of protection from vehicular traffic that is afforded by the marking of pedestrian crosswalks. It would be inappropriate to locate the curb ramp where the person using a wheelchair would have to leave the marked crossing while still in the vehicular way, and thus be exposed to a greater level of danger than other pedestrians. The exclusion for the flared sides is important because they can occur either partially or wholly outside of the marked crossing (see Commentary Figure C406.6).

406.7 Landings. Landings shall be provided at the tops of curb ramps. The clear length of the landing shall be 36 inches (915 mm) minimum. The clear width of the landing shall be at least as wide as the curb ramp, excluding flared sides, leading to the landing.

EXCEPTION: In alterations, where there is no landing at the top of curb ramps, curb ramp flares shall be provided and shall not be steeper than 1:12.

❖ Persons using the sidewalk perpendicular to the curb ramp have a difficult time with the changes in slopes if they have to move across the curb ramp. Therefore, in new construction, a minimum of a 36-inch-wide (915 mm) path must be available across the top of the curb ramp to allow for a flat perpendicular route [see Figure 406.7 and Commentary Figures C406.3.1(a) and C406.3.1(b)]. If there is not enough space to allow for this configuration, an alternative would be to lower a portion of the sidewalk to be level with the parking or road surface, with a straight curb ramp at both ends. For an illustration of this option, see Commentary Figure C406.7(a).

Built-up curb ramps are another alternative [see Commentary Figure C406.7(b)]. However, if built-up ramps are chosen they must not protrude into the aisle accessway for parking spaces or passenger loading zones. Those areas are required to be level.

In alterations, when it is necessary to locate a curb ramp where the width of the walking surface adjacent to the top of the curb ramp is less than 36 inches (915 mm), the flared sides become part of the accessible route that the person using a wheelchair must traverse. The slope of the flared sides is then limited to 1:12 to provide a gentler slope. Technically, 1:12 is correlated with the maximum permitted ramp slope (Section 405.2). This benefits all pedestrians, including wheelchair and other mobility aid users [see Commentary Figure C406.3.1(a)].

406.8 Obstructions. Curb ramps shall be located or protected to prevent their obstruction by parked vehicles.

❖ Clearly, a curb ramp is unusable when it is obstructed by a parked vehicle. Many times, curb ramps will occur at corners and at pedestrian crossings where parking is typically prohibited and policed by local authorities. However, at any location where a parked vehicle blocks a curb ramp, some type of design modification such as moving the ramp location, installing a vehicle barrier or posting of signs is required.

406.9 Handrails. Handrails shall not be required on curb ramps.

❖ Handrails are not necessary at curb ramps because of the limited rise and run of the curb ramp. They present an unnecessary and undesirable obstruction to pedestrian cross traffic. Unlike ramps (Section 405.8), this is true even when the curb ramp has a rise of more than 6 inches (150 mm).

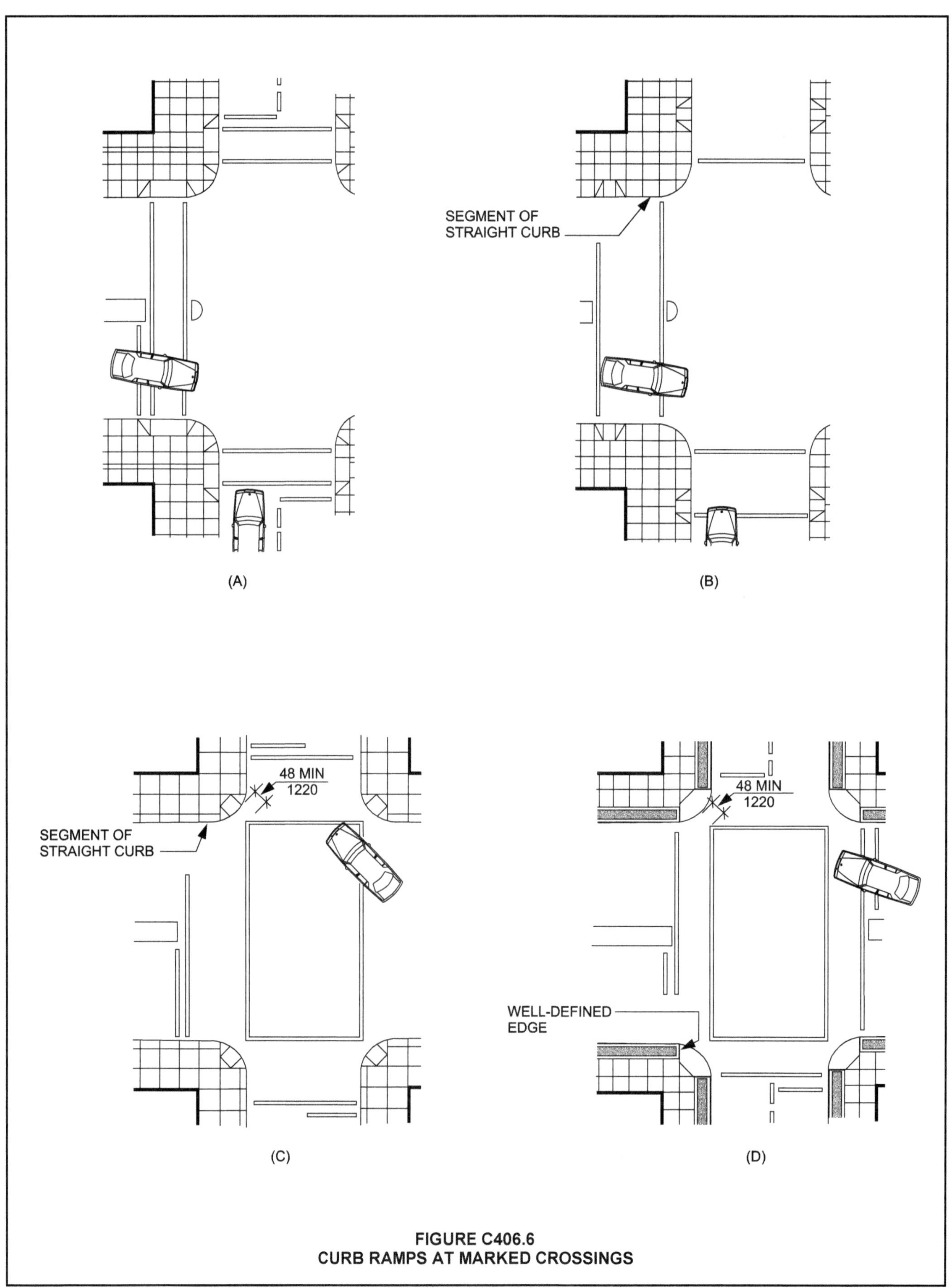

FIGURE C406.6
CURB RAMPS AT MARKED CROSSINGS

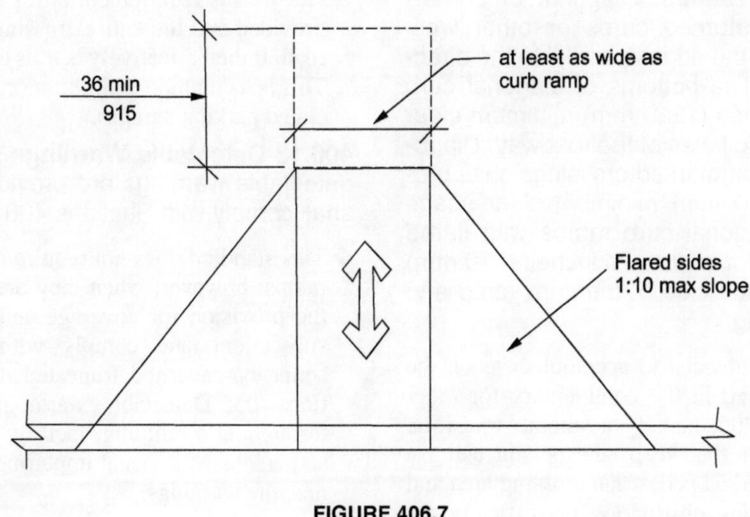

FIGURE 406.7
LANDINGS

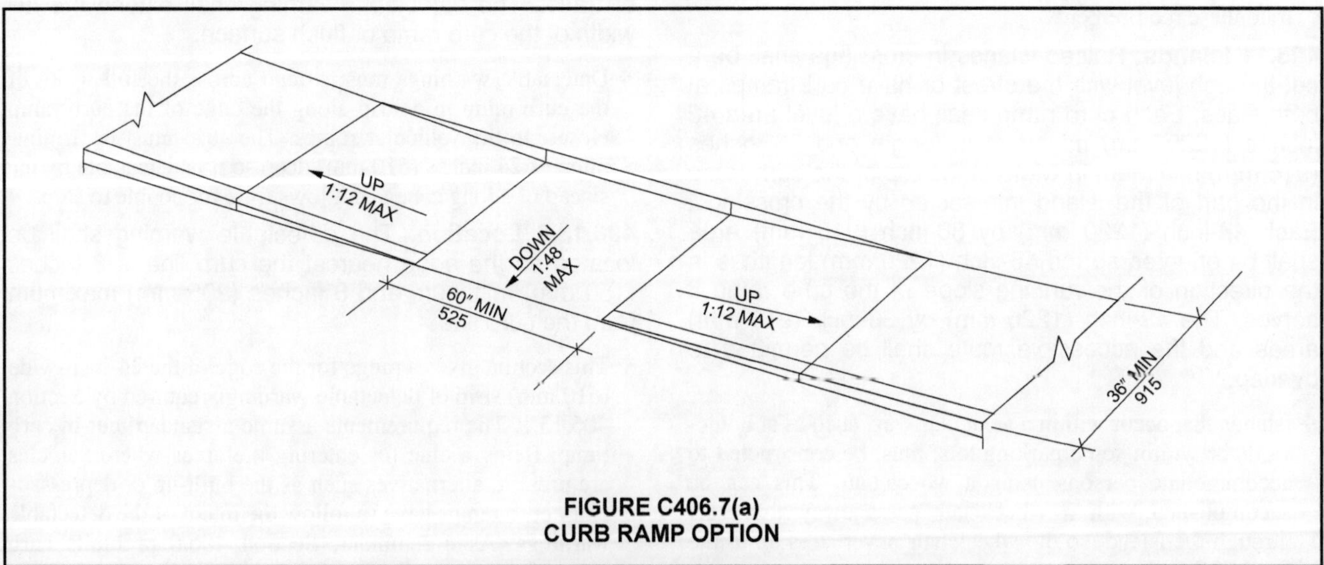

FIGURE C406.7(a)
CURB RAMP OPTION

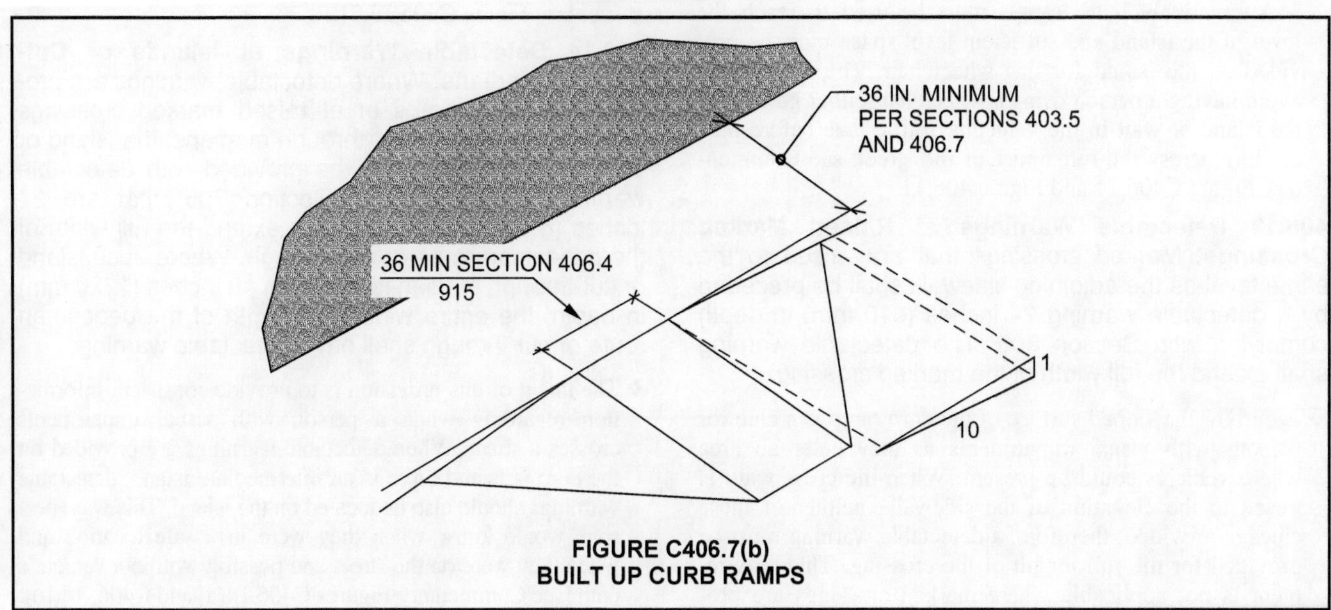

FIGURE C406.7(b)
BUILT UP CURB RAMPS

406.10 Diagonal Curb Ramps. Diagonal or corner-type curb ramps with returned curbs or other well-defined edges shall have the edges parallel to the direction of pedestrian flow. The bottoms of diagonal curb ramps shall have 48 inches (1220 mm) minimum clear space outside active traffic lanes of the roadway. Diagonal curb ramps provided at marked crossings shall provide the 48 inches (1220 mm) minimum clear space within the markings. Diagonal curb ramps with flared sides shall have a segment of curb 24 inches (610 mm) minimum in length on each side of the curb ramp and within the marked crossing.

❖ These requirements are intended to accomplish much the same purpose as described in the commentary for other sections under Section 406, namely a smooth transition over a curb in a manner that keeps the person using a wheelchair within the marked pedestrian crossing area and does not present an undue obstruction or difficulty for other pedestrian traffic. Commentary Figures C406.6(c) and (d) as well as Figure 406.10 from the standard illustrate these requirements.

406.11 Islands. Raised islands in crossings shall be a cut-through level with the street or have curb ramps at both sides. Each curb ramp shall have a level area 48 inches (1220 mm) minimum in length and 36 inches (915 mm) minimum in width at the top of the curb ramp in the part of the island intersected by the crossings. Each 48-inch (1220 mm) by 36-inch (915 mm) area shall be oriented so the 48-inch (1220 mm) length is in the direction of the running slope of the curb ramp it serves. The 48-inch (1220 mm) by 36-inch (915 mm) areas and the accessible route shall be permitted to overlap.

❖ Islands that occur within a vehicular way, such as at boulevards or within some parking lots, must be constructed to accommodate persons using a wheelchair. This can be accomplished with a wheelchair passageway that cuts through the island, so the wheelchair never rises up to the level of the island.

Alternatively, curb ramps must be used to reach the level of the island and sufficient level space must be provided on the island for one wheelchair. The intent is to avoid having a person using a wheelchair either go around the island or wait in the vehicular traffic lane before proceeding across the remainder of the street. see Commentary Figure C406.11 and Figure 406.11.

406.12 Detectable Warnings at Raised Marked Crossings. Marked crossings that are raised to the same level as the adjoining sidewalk shall be preceded by a detectable warning 24 inches (610 mm) in depth complying with Section 705. The detectable warning shall extend the full width of the marked crossing.

❖ A curb or the sloped surface of the curb ramp is a clue for persons with visual impairments as they enter an area where vehicles could be present. When the cross walk is raised to the elevation of the sidewalk, neither of these clues is provided; therefore, a detectable warning must be provided for the full length of the crossing. This requirement is not applicable where marked crossings are provided. This requirement is for when a marked crossing is provided and the entire crossing is raised as it crosses the road. It then effectively acts as a giant speed bump for cars. This is a common configuration between airports and associated parking garages.

406.13 Detectable Warnings at Curb Ramps. Where detectable warnings are provided on curb ramps, they shall comply with Sections 406.13 and 705.

❖ This standard does not require detectable warnings at curb ramps; however, when they are provided they must meet the provision for coverage and location in the following subsections and comply with the contrast, resilience/sound-on-cane and truncated dome requirements in Section 705. Detectable warnings should be standardized throughout a building, facility, site or group of buildings, so persons with visual impairments can more easily recognize the warnings.

406.13.1 Area Covered. Detectable warnings shall be 24 inches (610 mm) minimum in depth in the direction of travel. The detectable warning shall extend the full width of the curb ramp or flush surface.

❖ Detectable warnings must extend across the full width of the curb ramp in a strip along the edge of the curb ramp closest to the vehicular routes. The strip must be a minimum of 24 inches (610 mm) deep so it is detectable by the sweep of a long cane and allows time for people to stop.

406.13.2 Location. The detectable warning shall be located so the edge nearest the curb line is 6 inches (150 mm) minimum and 8 inches (205 mm) maximum from the curb line.

❖ This section gives a range for the edge of the 24-inch-wide (610 mm) strip of detectable warnings required by Section 406.13.1. The requirements assume a standard cut-in curb ramp. Being a clue for entering the areas where vehicles are present, alternatives such as the built-up or depressed-entry curb ramps have to follow the intent of the detectable warnings. As a reminder, Section 406.6 prohibits curb ramps from protruding into the vehicular way (see Commentary Figure C406.13.2).

406.14 Detectable Warnings at Islands or Cut-through Medians. Where detectable warnings are provided on curb ramps or at raised marked crossings leading to islands or cut-through medians, the island or cut-through median shall be provided with detectable warnings complying with Section 705, that are 24 inches (610 mm) in depth, and extend the full width of the pedestrian route or cut-through. Where such island or cut-through median is less than 48 inches (1220 mm) in depth, the entire width and depth of the pedestrian route or cut-through shall have detectable warnings.

❖ The intent of this provision is to provide consistent information regarding when a person with visual impairments crosses a street. When detectable warnings are provided on the curb cuts and there is an intermediate island, detectable warnings should also be located on the island. This way, persons would know when they were in a safe location and when they were on the street and possibly within a vehicle's path [see Commentary Figures C406.14(a) and C406. 14(b)].

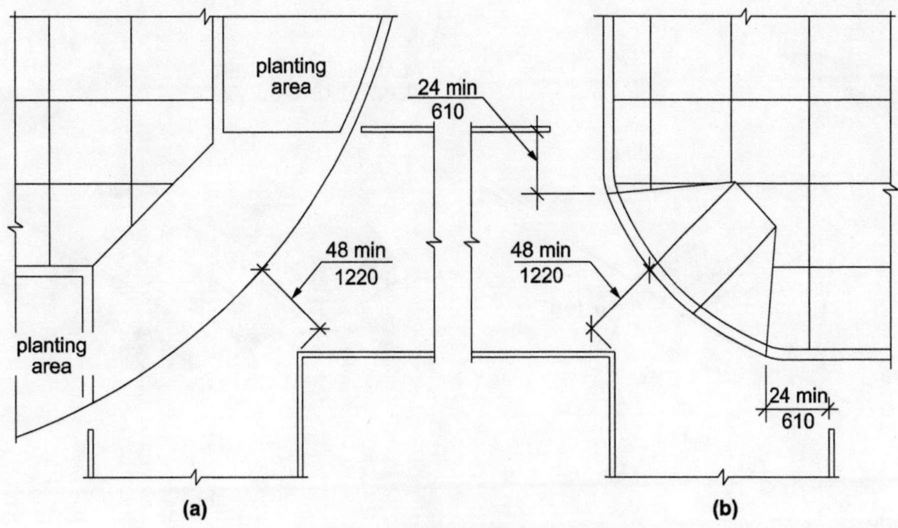

FIGURE 406.10
DIAGONAL CURB RAMP

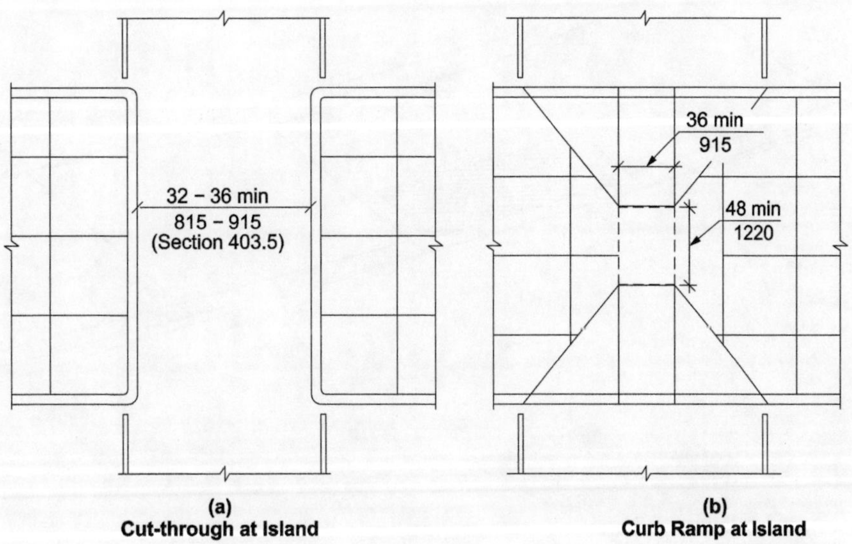

FIGURE 406.11
ISLANDS

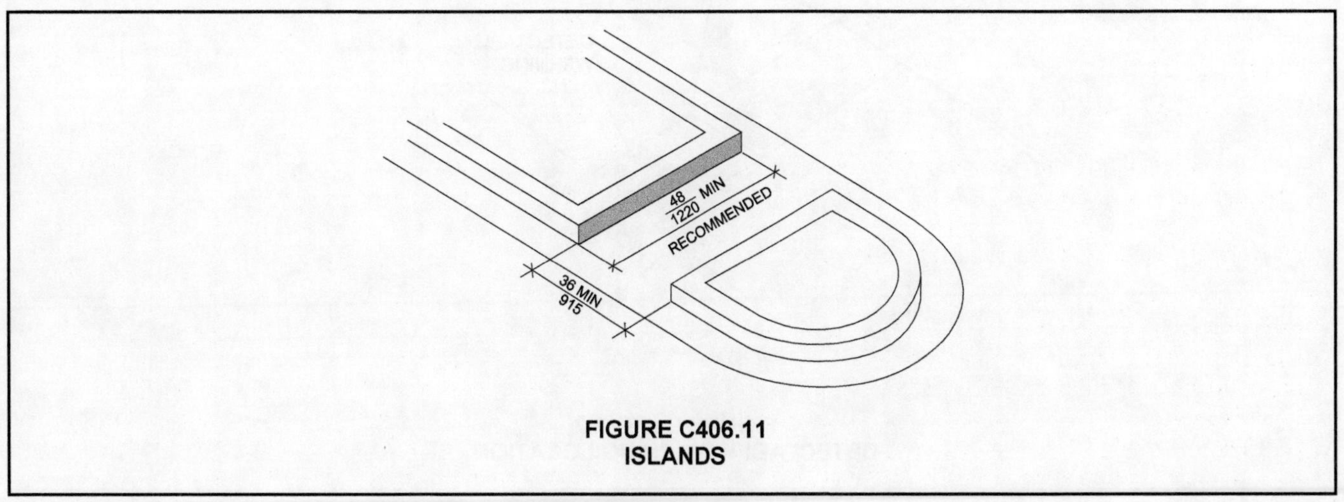

FIGURE C406.11
ISLANDS

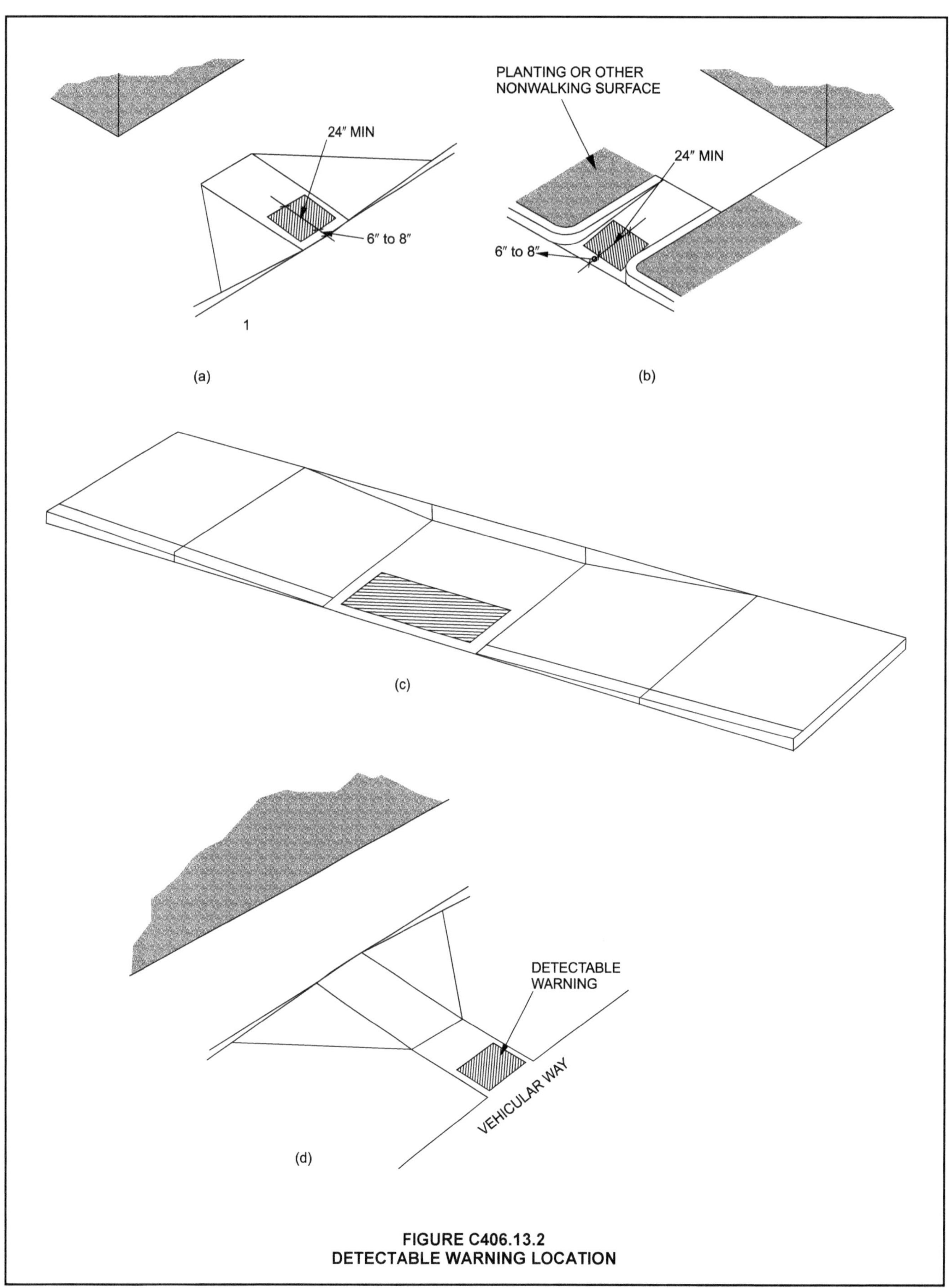

FIGURE C406.13.2
DETECTABLE WARNING LOCATION

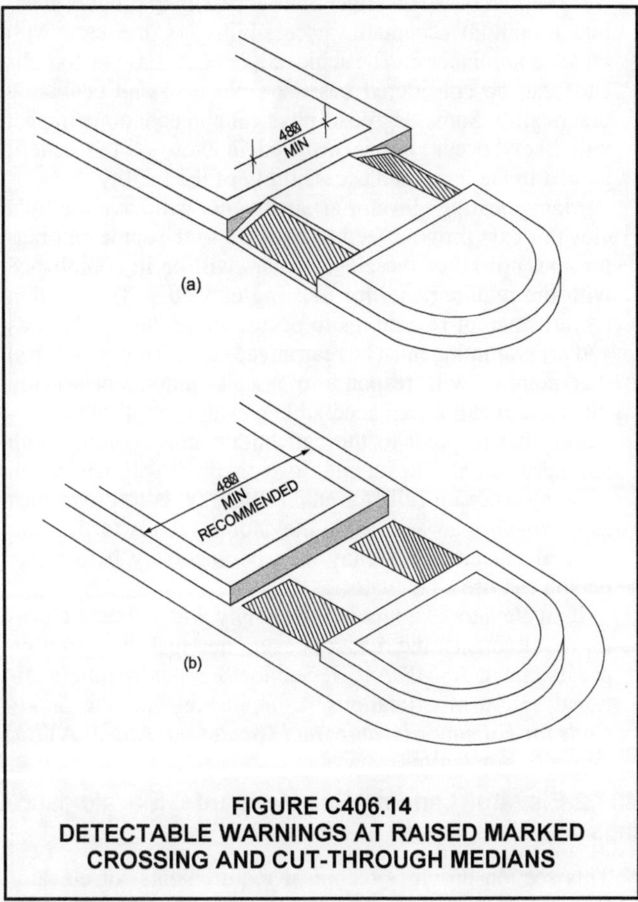

FIGURE C406.14
DETECTABLE WARNINGS AT RAISED MARKED CROSSING AND CUT-THROUGH MEDIANS

407 Elevators

❖ The origin of many of the elevator provisions in Section 407 are described in the book by Edward A. Donoghue, *ADA and Building Transportation*, available from Elevator World, P. O. Box 6507, Mobile, AL 36660 or http://www.elevator-world.com. *ADA and Building Transportation* served as the basis for much of the commentary in Section 407.

407.1 General. Elevators shall comply with Section 407 and ASME A17.1/CSA B44 listed in Section 105.2.5. Elevators shall be passenger elevators as classified by ASME A17.1/CSA B44. Elevator operation shall be automatic.

❖ During the development of the 2003 edition of ICC A117.1, the elevator requirements were editorially reformatted to harmonize with the April 2002 draft of the *ADA/ABA Accessibility Guidelines*. Provisions for destination-oriented elevators and existing elevators have been incorporated into the relevant sections in Section 407. Limited-access/limited-use elevator technical provisions are in Section 408. Private residence elevator requirements were moved from Chapter 10 to Section 409. All types of elevators listed in these sections are considered passenger elevators and are permitted to serve as part of an accessible route. Where each type can be used is limited by the referenced standard, ASME A17.1. For example, ASME A17.1 limits the use of private residence elevators to installations either within individual dwelling units or to serve single dwelling units (ASME A17.1, Sections 5.3 and 5.4) provided the elevator is not accessible to the general public. Private residence elevators are small and cannot conform to Section 407.4.1. Provisions for passenger elevators in this section are divided into elevator landing requirements (Section 407.2), elevator door requirements (Section 407.3) and elevator car requirements (Section 407.4) (see Commentary Figure C407.1).

Elevators are used as the primary means to provide wheelchair access to upper and lower floors in multistory buildings. Typically, the scoping provisions in the model building codes do not specifically mandate that an elevator be provided for access from the ground floor. The designer is given the option of providing access to other floors by any approved means, such as a ramp. Elevators remain the most commonly used method.

For accessibility, elevators that are attendant operated are not considered acceptable because of the potential for the attendant to not be readily available. Also, elevator controls that require continuous pressure for operation are not acceptable because they are not suitable for people who have limited use of their hands.

ASME A17.1 does not recognize "combination passenger and freight elevators." Rather, it allows passenger elevators to carry freight, and under very strict limitations, freight elevators to carry passengers. In the latter instance, the elevator must not be accessible to the general public, the elevator capacity must meet the minimum rated load for passenger use and be capable of withstanding a passenger overload, and the elevator entrance must be approved for

FIGURE C407.1
ELEVATORS

passenger use (ASME A17.1, Sections 2.11 and 2.16.4). Typical passenger elevator entrances are the horizontally sliding type. However, some vertically sliding type entrances, normally associated with freight elevators, are also approved for passenger elevator applications. In short, most elevators installed and used exclusively for carrying freight will not be classified as a passenger elevator and cannot be considered accessible.

Destination-oriented elevators—Destination-oriented elevators are an alternative to conventional elevators where floor selection is made by passengers after they enter the elevator car. This system provides lobby controls enabling passengers to select floor stops when they enter the elevator lobby instead of inside the elevator car itself. Responding cars are programmed for maximum efficiency by reducing the number of stops to deliver passengers that the elevator will be making on each trip. Lobby indicators let the passengers know which elevator is responding to their floor request. Indicators inside the car let passengers know which floors that particular car will be stopping at.

Existing Elevators—Scoping provisions in the model building codes can require that accessibility be upgraded in existing buildings that undergo renovations, alterations and changes of occupancy. It would be overly restrictive and impractical to mandate that existing elevators be retrofitted to fully comply with all of the requirements for accessibility that are applicable to new elevators. However, certain upgrades are reasonable and appropriate to improve accessibility, particularly where a building is not currently accessible. The applicable provisions in Section 407 represent the baseline minimum expectations for an existing elevator to be considered as providing a reasonable degree of accessibility—watch the exceptions for allowances. Certain provisions for new elevators in this standard are intended to be retroactively applicable to existing elevators.

Determining the extent that existing elements are required to conform to the requirements for new elements cannot be done arbitrarily and without consideration of the impact. A general principle in construction code enforcement holds that existing construction, which complies with the codes and standards applicable at the time of original construction has a right to exist without change unless one of the three following situations occurs:

1. The existing construction, in this case an elevator, is unsafe;
2. Retroactive provisions are established requiring upgrading of the existing elevator, or
3. The owner, on his or her own initiative, decides to upgrade his or her elevator.

There is precedent in code enforcement law that supports the validity of applying reasonable and justified regulations retroactively. The model building codes and *Safety Code for Existing Elevators and Escalators*, ASME A17.3, adequately address retroactive safety provisions. This standard deals with retrospective provisions that are deemed reasonable and justified for accessibility.

The specific provisions for new construction identified in this subsection as applicable to existing accessible elevators were chosen based on either their necessity to provide absolute minimum acceptable accessibility, or the ease with which compliance can be achieved, or both. Ease of compliance can be considered based on physical and economic practicality. Some degree of physical and economic impact will likely occur, but is justified in view of the benefit gained in the increased accessibility of the facility.

Many existing elevator arrangements will have multiple elevator cars programmed to respond to the same call button, but not all of the elevator cars will be in compliance with the requirements for existing elevators. This section requires one of two things to occur: either the call buttons and programming must be rearranged so only the elevator(s) that comply will respond to a call button specifically intended to call for an accessible elevator, or all of the elevators that respond to the call button must comply with these provisions. The intent is to avoid the situation in which a disabled person calls for an elevator, but is left to chance as to whether an accessible elevator responds to the call. Several repeated calls may then be necessary before that person can use an elevator.

If an elevator is upgraded to comply with existing elevator requirements, the reader is cautioned that the alteration provisions in ASME A17.1, Section 8.7 may require additional safety modifications. Compliance with the *Safety Code for Existing Elevators and Escalators*, ASME A17.3, may also be required.

407.2 Elevator Landing Requirements. Elevator landings shall comply with Section 407.2.

❖ This section provides technical requirements for elevator landings including call controls, hall signals, hoistway signs and destination signs.

407.2.1 Call Controls. Where elevator call buttons or keypads are provided, they shall comply with Sections 407.2.1 and 309.4. Call buttons shall be raised or flush. Objects beneath hall call buttons shall protrude 1 inch (25 mm) maximum.

EXCEPTIONS:

1. Existing elevators shall be permitted to have recessed call buttons.
2. The restriction on objects beneath call buttons shall not apply to existing call buttons.

❖ Several locations are usually provided in the lobby or approach to the lobby to call the elevator. All locations must be accessible. The reference to Section 407.2.1 picks up subsections 407.2.1.1 through 407.2.1.7; the reference to Section 309.4 picks up the operational requirements under operable parts.

For standard call buttons, the requirement for the buttons to be raised or flush (not recessed) ensures that the buttons are suitable for people who have limited use of their hands. With destination-oriented elevators, a keypad is used in place of elevator call buttons. The desired floor is selected prior to boarding the elevator. Projections beneath the buttons are restricted to eliminate hazards for the visually impaired who may need to feel for the buttons and to allow unrestricted access for persons with short stature and persons using wheelchairs and scooters.

407.2.1.1 Height. Call buttons and keypads shall be located within one of the reach ranges specified in Section 308, measured to the centerline of the highest operable part.

> **EXCEPTION:** Existing call buttons and existing keypads shall be permitted to be located 54 inches (1370 mm) maximum above the floor, measured to the centerline of the highest operable part.

❖ The maximum button or keypad height is equal to the maximum high forward and side reach range specified in Sections 308.2 and 308.3 (see Figure 407.2.1.1). This height requirement was new to the 1998 edition of ICC A117.1. Prior editions specified that call buttons in elevator lobbies be centered at 42 inches (1065 mm). This was based on a continued use of the former industry standards established by National Elevator Industry, Inc. (NEII) in the mid-1970s. Although a lower end dimension different from the reach ranges [(i.e., 15 inches (386 mm)] is not specified, call buttons and keypads below 35 inches (890 mm) may be too low for proper access for taller persons.

The exception for existing elevators is based on the earlier editions of ICC A117.1 and the 1994 ADAAG allowing 54 inches (1370 mm) maximum height for a side reach range.

407.2.1.2 Size. Call buttons shall be $^3/_4$ inch (19 mm) minimum in the smallest dimension.

> **EXCEPTION:** Existing elevator call buttons shall not be required to comply with Section 407.2.1.2.

❖ Minimum dimensions for the buttons ensure that the buttons are suitable for people who have limited use of their hands (see also Section 407.2.1.6).

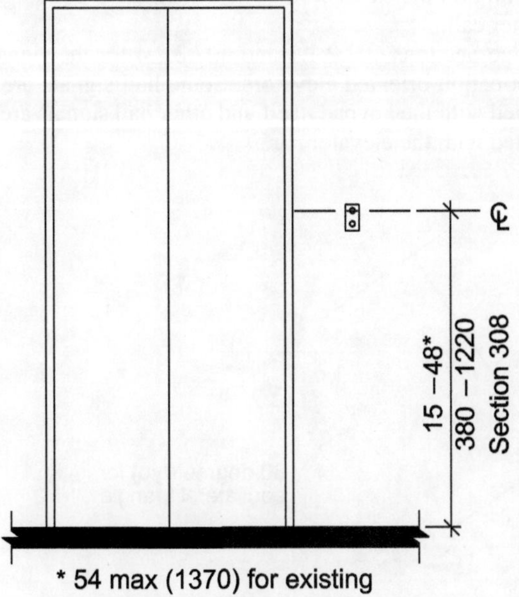

FIGURE 407.2.1.1
HEIGHT OF ELEVATOR CALL BUTTONS

407.2.1.3 Clear Floor Space. A clear floor space complying with Section 305 shall be provided at call controls.

❖ Requirements for the 30-inch by 48-inch (765 by 1220 mm) wheelchair space in front of the call controls allow for easy access. Although either a side or front approach is permitted, note that the specific protrusion limits under Section 407.2.1 would not allow for reaches over an obstruction greater than 1 inch (25 mm). If the location of the call buttons is confined on three sides in some manner, the alcove provisions in Section 305.7 must also be observed.

407.2.1.4 Location. The call button that designates the up direction shall be located above the call button that designates the down direction.

> **EXCEPTION:** Destination-oriented elevators shall not be required to comply with Section 407.2.1.4.

❖ Consistency in the location of the up and down buttons rather than the centerline of the fixture is important to people with visual impairments who may not be able to distinguish the marking on the buttons. Destination-oriented elevators are not required to comply with this provision because the call buttons operate differently (see Sections 407.2.1.6 and 407.2.1.7).

407.2.1.5 Signals. Call buttons shall have visible signals to indicate when each call is registered and when each call is answered. Call buttons shall provide an audible signal or mechanical motion of the button to indicate when each call is registered.

> **EXCEPTIONS:**
>
> 1. Destination-oriented elevators shall not be required to comply with Section 407.2.1.5, provided a visible signal and audible tones and verbal announcements complying with Section 407.2.1.7 are provided.
> 2. Existing elevators shall not be required to comply with Section 407.2.1.5.

❖ Visual indications are required to let the user know that a call has been registered and when it is answered, to aid users with hearing impairments. For persons with vision impairments, the buttons must also provide either an audible tone or have a way to allow a person to "feel" that the call has registered. The different approach for notification for destination-oriented elevators is recognized in Exception 1.

407.2.1.6 Keypads. Where keypads are provided, keypads shall be in a standard telephone keypad arrangement and shall comply with Section 407.4.7.2.

❖ For destination-oriented elevators, call buttons in the lobby and halls approaching the lobby are generally in the form of a large keypad. The keypad assembly has several associated items; a visual display located above the keypad, a bar key located below the keypad and a speaker located within the keypad enclosure. Keypads are in standard telephone format and have $^3/_4$-inch (20 mm) minimum buttons with $^5/_8$-inch (16 mm) visual numbers. For tactile information there is a tactile dot on the number "5" key. For consistency the star appearing on the lower left key will be visually the same as the five-pointed star in Table 407.4.7.1.3 and when pushed will enter a call to the "Main" floor designated for the elevator. Entering the "Main" floor number will do the same. The "Pound" key position in the lower right hand position is used to enter minus "-" floors (floors below the "Main" floor) such as levels or parking. The "Pound" key position and then a number in succession will enter the appropriate calls to these floors. To enter floor calls above the "Main" floor such as floor 15, it is only necessary to push "1" and then "5" in succession.

407.2.1.7 Destination-oriented Elevator Signals. Destination-oriented elevators shall be provided with a visible signal and audible tones and verbal announcements to indicate which car is responding to a call. The audible tone and verbal announcement shall be activated by pressing a function button. The function button shall be identified by the International Symbol for Accessibility and a raised indication. The International Symbol for Accessibility, complying with Section 703.6.3.1, shall be $^5/_8$ inch (16 mm) in height and be a visual character complying with Section 703.2. The indication shall be three raised dots, spaced $^1/_4$ inch (6.4 mm) at base diameter, in the form of an equilateral triangle. The function button shall be located immediately below the keypad arrangement or floor buttons.

❖ For destination-oriented elevators, the visual display above the keypad provides two pieces of information: 1) the car's designation (e.g., "A," "B") and 2) the direction of the car (e.g., left, right).

The audible hall signals are normally inactive unless turned on at the control keypad. Usually a bar key located just below the keypad serves this purpose. The format is similar to a button used to activate the in-car audible floor signal. The bar key also turns on several other accessibility features not required but usually provided; such as more time to push successive keypad numbers, more time to reach the car, a larger allocation of car space where possible, (e.g., fewer passengers assigned to use designated car) and optional visual and audible enhancements (see also the commentary to Section 407.2.2.1).

407.2.2 Hall Signals. Hall signals, including in-car signals, shall comply with Section 407.2.2.

❖ Signals that indicate what elevator is arriving at the elevator lobby may be provided outside or inside the elevator cab. Hall signals must comply with the provisions for audible and visual notification. Distinct requirements are provided for destination-oriented elevators based on each element's unique form of operation.

407.2.2.1 Visible and Audible Signals. A visible and audible signal shall be provided at each hoistway entrance to indicate which car is answering a call and the car's direction of travel. Where in-car signals are provided they shall be visible from the floor area adjacent to the hall call buttons.

EXCEPTIONS:

1. Destination-oriented elevators shall not be required to comply with Section 407.2.2.1, provided a visible signal and audible tones and verbal announcements complying with Section 407.2.1.7 are provided.
2. In existing elevators, a signal indicating the direction of car travel shall not be required.

❖ Typically, the arriving elevator is announced to the passengers waiting in the elevator lobby by a visible and audible signal located on the wall to the side of the elevator door (see Section 407.2.2.2), so it can be seen above the heads of the other passengers waiting in the lobby. The use of in-car lanterns is acceptable, but they will affect door open time, slowing elevator service in the building. Door open time is calculated from the sounding of the audible signal and illumination of the directional lantern, so the person waiting for the car is notified which car is responding to his or her call.

See Sections 407.2.1.7 and 407.2.2.4 for the signals for destination-oriented elevators. Some hall signals are associated with the keypad itself and other hall signals are associated with the elevator car.

Visual and tactile information

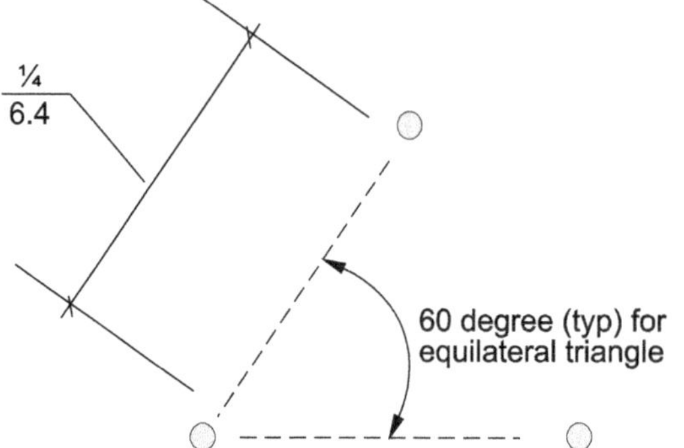

Tactile information

FIGURE 407.2.1.7
DESTINATION-ORIENTED ELEVATOR INDICATION

407.2.2.2 Visible Signals. Visible signal fixtures shall be centered at 72 inches (1830 mm) minimum above the floor. The visible signal elements shall be $2^1/_2$ inches (64 mm) minimum between the uppermost and lowest edges of the illuminated shape measured vertically. Signals shall be visible from the floor area adjacent to the hall call button.

EXCEPTIONS:

1. Destination-oriented elevators shall be permitted to have signals visible from the floor area adjacent to the hoistway entrance.
2. Existing elevators shall not be required to comply with Section 407.2.2.2.

❖ The visible signals can be in a vertical or a horizontal arrangement with two signal elements such as arrows or triangles if the signal elements serve to indicate direction. Color distinctions are not acceptable because some people are color blind.

The specified minimum height and size allows the visible signal to be seen when persons in the elevator lobby are standing at the call button (see Figure 407.2.2.2).

If in-car lanterns are used, the door would have to be opened before minimum door timing (see Section 407.3.4) would start. Floor lanterns and audible signals, on the other hand, can announce the car before it reaches a floor and the door opens, to allow people to gather near the car before the door opens.

Because the call controls have indicated which car will be responding to a particular call, the user knows at what elevator to wait; therefore, the visible signals for arrival must be seen only from immediately in front of the elevator entrance. In-car signals are not permitted.

407.2.2.3 Audible Signals. Audible signals shall sound once for the up direction and twice for the down direction, or shall have verbal annunciators that indicate the direction of elevator car travel. Audible signals shall have a frequency of 1500 Hz maximum. Verbal annunciators shall have a frequency of 300 Hz minimum and 3,000 Hz maximum. The audible signal or verbal annunciator shall be 10 dBA minimum above ambient, but shall not exceed 80 dBA, measured at the hall call button.

EXCEPTIONS:

1. Destination-oriented elevators shall not be required to comply with Section 407.2.2.3, provided the audible tone and verbal announcement is the same as those given at the call button or call button keypad.
2. The requirement for the frequency and range of audible signals shall not apply in existing elevators.

❖ The sound level specified is intended to make sure the signal can be heard above ambient noise but not cause damage to a person's hearing.

See Sections 407.2.1.7 and 407.2.2.4 for the signals for destination-oriented elevators. Some hall signals are associated with the keypad itself and other hall signals are associated with the elevator car.

407.2.2.4 Differentiation. Each destination-oriented elevator in a bank of elevators shall have audible and visible means for differentiation.

❖ Destination-oriented elevators provide a unique approach for visual and audible differentiation. Visible designations follow the same form as standard elevators; however, the lights typically also have a letter or number for car identification.

For verbal differentiation, following bar key activation and entry of a floor destination, a verbal announcement confirming the floor number and designation of what car (e.g., car "A," "B," etc.) to take will occur. The keypad speaker will then emit a unique audible tone, assigned to the specific car. A speaker at the car will emit the same tone at intervals for the duration of the notification time. The duration will correspond to the distance from the particular keypad in question to a point directly in front of the

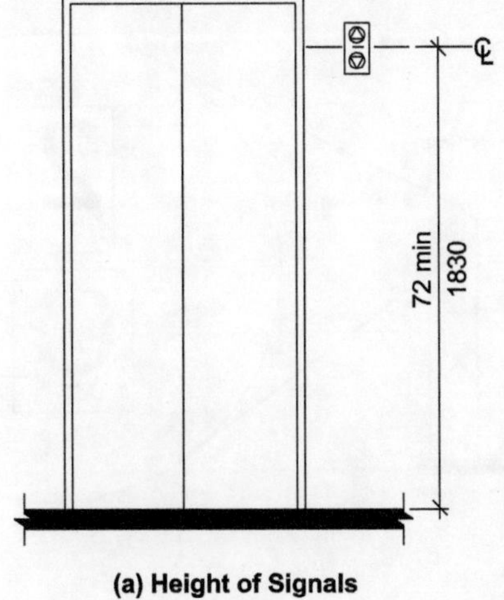

(a) Height of Signals

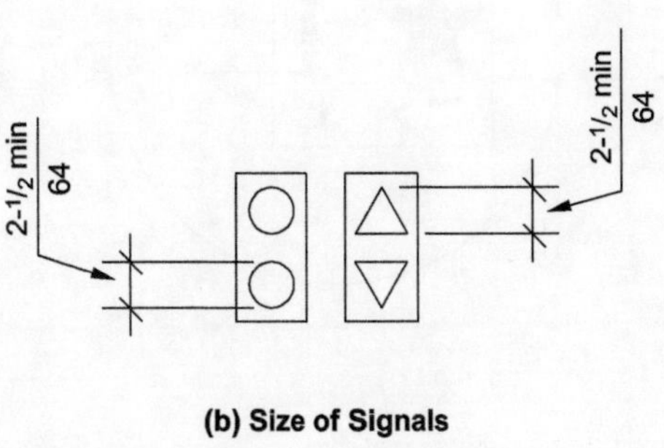

(b) Size of Signals

FIGURE 407.2.2.2
ELEVATOR VISIBLE SIGNALS

specified car (see the commentary to Section 407.3.4). Supplementary verbal announcements are often provided, but not required, example: "there is no floor 13."

407.2.3 Hoistway Signs. Signs at elevator hoistways shall comply with Section 407.2.3.

❖ Tactile signage communicates vital information to people with vision impairments. It is also useful information for those with hearing impairments, as well as the general public. Plates that have the appropriate raised characters are acceptable if the plates are permanently fixed to the hoistway entrance jambs.

407.2.3.1 Floor Designation. Floor designations shall be provided in raised characters and braille complying with Sections 703.3 and 703.4. Raised characters shall be 2 inches (51 mm) minimum in height. Floor designations shall be located on both jambs of elevator hoistway entrances. A raised star shall be provided on both jambs at the main entry level.

❖ Information regarding the floor level that the elevator has arrived at must be provided on both jambs of the elevator hoistway entrance. Tactile information must include both raised numbers and Braille. The main entry floor is always the first floor per Section 407.4.6.2.2. The main entrance level must be identified with a star in addition to the number (see Figure 407.2.3.1). This is coordinated with the requirement for a "star" symbol on the control panel.

407.2.3.2 Car Identification. Destination-oriented elevators shall provide car identification in raised characters and braille complying with Sections 703.3 and 703.4. Raised characters shall be 2 inches (51 mm) minimum in height. Car identifications shall be located on both jambs of the hoistway immediately below the floor designation.

❖ As further correlation, the specified car identification (e.g., car "A," "B," etc.) is placed on both jambs immediately below the floor designation. The floor designation is always numeric to match the keypad and the car designation is always alphabetic. The five-pointed raised star to indicate the main entry is next to the main floor designation. In most cases the "Main" entry will be floor 1; however, some new buildings are adopting the convention used in most other countries and calling it floor "0." The next floor is identified as 1 and one floor below is identified as 1. (See Figure 407.2.3.2).

407.2.4 Destination Signs. Where signs indicate that elevators do not serve all landings, signs in raised characters and braille complying with Sections 703.3 and 703.4 shall be provided above the hall call button or keypad.

> **EXCEPTION:** Destination oriented elevator systems shall not be required to comply with Section 407.2.4.

❖ When the elevator system is zoned (i.e., elevators serve only certain floors), signs are typically located at the entrance to each bank indicating what floor levels are served. This information must be repeated on a tactile sign (i.e., raised letters/numbers and Braille) above the hall call buttons. Because destination-oriented elevators do not limit their operation to only certain floors, this type of system is not considered a zoned system, and signage is not required.

407.3 Elevator Door Requirements. Hoistway and elevator car doors shall comply with Section 407.3.

❖ Elevator doors are both the doors to the elevator shaft and the doors on the cabs themselves. These doors must meet the provisions for type, width, operation, reopening devices and timing specified in Sections 407.3.1 through 407.3.6.

407.3.1 Type. Elevator doors shall be horizontal sliding type. Car gates shall be prohibited.

❖ Typical passenger elevator entrances are the horizontal sliding type. The upper or lower section of a vertically sliding door could become a bump or a trip hazard for the visually impaired. The lower section of a vertically sliding door is difficult for wheelchairs to cross.

Separate car gates that are operated manually once a person is inside of the elevator (e.g., construction elevators) are not permitted in accessible elevators.

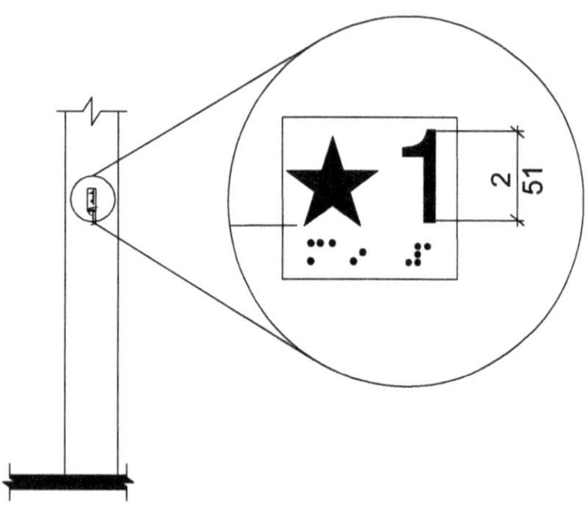

FIGURE 407.2.3.1
FLOOR DESIGNATION

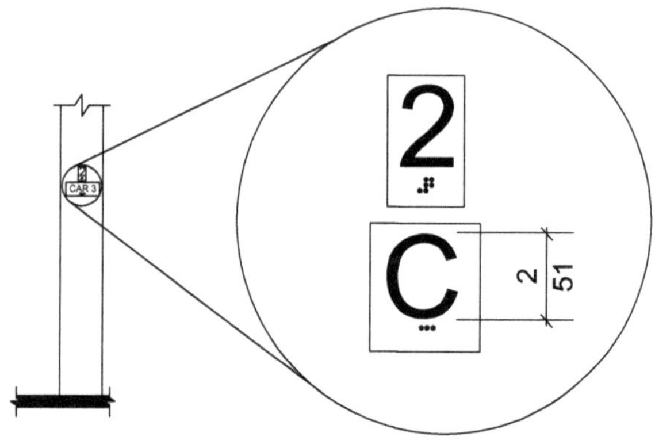

FIGURE 407.2.3.2
DESIGNATION-ORIENTED ELEVATOR CAR IDENTIFICATION

407.3.2 Operation. Elevator hoistway and car doors shall open and close automatically.

EXCEPTION: Existing manually operated hoistway swing doors shall be permitted, provided the following criteria are met:

a) The hoistway doors comply with Sections 404.2.2 and 404.2.8;

b) The car door closing is not initiated until the hoistway door is closed.

❖ With automatic doors, a person with limited mobility can enter the car, access controls and exit the car without turning around in the car or requiring assistance.

Some existing elevators have manual swing doors on the hoistway with automatic doors on the car. These are permitted when doors provide a clear width of 32 inches (815 mm) (Section 404.2.2), meet the door opening forces (Section 404.2.8) and the automatic car (interior) door is not activated until the manual hoistway door is closed.

407.3.3 Reopening Device. Elevator doors shall be provided with a reopening device complying with Section 407.3.3 that shall stop and reopen a car door and hoistway door automatically if the door becomes obstructed by an object or person.

EXCEPTION: In existing elevators, manually operated doors shall not be required to comply with Section 407.3.3.

❖ A noncontact door-reopening device will stop the door and reopen it if the doorway opening becomes obstructed. The noncontact device remains effective for 20 seconds, i.e., it will stop and reopen the door if a person passes the device. Once the next person intercepts the noncontact device, the door will stop and reopen. This requirement does not mandate that the door remain open for 20 seconds, only that the reopening device be alert for people passing through the door for 20 seconds or until the door has fully closed.

The required door-reopening device holds the door open for 20 seconds if the doorway remains continuously obstructed. After 20 seconds, the door is permitted to begin closing. However, if designed in accordance with ASME A17.1, the door closing movement is still stopped if a person or object exerts sufficient force at any point on the door edge. Sufficient force is defined by ASME A17.1 as 30 pounds-force (134 N). If all door-reopening devices are rendered inoperative, ASME A17.1 also requires the average kinetic energy of the door system be reduced from 7 ft-lbf to $2^1/_2$ ft-lbf (9.5 to 3.4 J).

Because the kinetic nature of the motion, reversal of the closing door is not instantaneous. Until the continued movement of the door is arrested, it is possible that limited movement of the door may cause it to come in contact with a person or object in its path.

407.3.3.1 Height. The reopening device shall be activated by sensing an obstruction passing through the opening at 5 inches (125 mm) nominal and 29 inches (735 mm) nominal above the floor.

❖ See commentary, Section 407.3.3.

407.3.3.2 Contact. The reopening device shall not require physical contact to be activated, although contact shall be permitted before the door reverses.

❖ See commentary, Section 407.3.3.

407.3.3.3 Duration. The reopening device shall remain effective for 20 seconds minimum.

❖ See commentary, Section 407.3.3.

407.3.4 Door and Signal Timing. The minimum acceptable time from notification that a car is answering a call until the doors of that car start to close shall be calculated from the following equation:

T = D/(1.5 ft/s) or T = D/(455 mm/s) = 5 seconds minimum, where T equals the total time in seconds and D equals the distance (in feet or millimeters) from the point in the lobby or corridor 60 inches (1525 mm) directly in front of the farthest call button controlling that car to the centerline of its hoistway door.

EXCEPTIONS:

1. For cars with in-car lanterns, T shall be permitted to begin when the signal is visible from the point 60 inches (1525 mm) directly in front of the farthest hall call button and the audible signal is sounded.
2. Destination-oriented elevators shall not be required to comply with Section 407.3.4.

❖ This provision allows variation in the location of call buttons, advance time for warning signals and the door-holding period used to meet the time requirement. Examples of the application of this provision are shown in Commentary Figure C407.3.4.

This requirement gives sufficient time for a person outside the car to gain access to an elevator based on studies completed at Syracuse University in the mid-1970s, which indicated that the disabled needed $1^1/_2$ seconds for each 1 foot (305 mm) of travel. This requirement gives the disabled time to move into the path of the car door. The provision for door reopening (Section 407.3.3) allows sufficient time to move through the open door.

On a destination elevator, the passenger is immediately advised what car to take and can go directly to it. Thus the timing starts at the keypad, calculates the time to reach the hoistway entrance, adds door opening time and time to move into the path of the open door.

407.3.5 Door Delay. Elevator doors shall remain fully open in response to a car call for 3 seconds minimum.

❖ The length of time that elevator doors remain open typically can be adjusted, but this standard requires the doors to remain open for not less than 3 seconds after reaching the fully opened position. This is the least amount of time deemed necessary to enable a person within the car to fully enter the path of the elevator doors and activate the noncontact door-reopening device.

407.3.6 Width. Elevator door clear opening width shall comply with Table 407.4.1.

> **EXCEPTION:** In existing elevators, a power-operated car door complying with Section 404.2.2 shall be permitted.

❖ The tolerance in car door widths in Table 407.4.1 is to allow for hard metric door sizes (see commentary Section 407.4.1).

407.4 Elevator Car Requirements. Elevator cars shall comply with Section 407.4.

❖ The elevator car has specific requirements for items such as dimensions, floor surfaces, platform to hoistway clearances, leveling, illumination, car controls, car position indicators and emergency communication.

Accessibility is a function of the inside car dimension, door location and size, and access to controls, especially in smaller cars. Because of automatic operation of the doors, a turning space within the elevator car itself is not required.

407.4.1 Inside Dimensions. Inside dimensions of elevator cars shall comply with Table 407.4.1.

> **EXCEPTION:** Existing elevator car configurations that provide a clear floor area of 16 square feet (1.5 m²) minimum, and provide a clear inside dimension of 36 inches (915 mm) minimum in width and 54 inches (1370 mm) minimum in depth, shall be permitted.

❖ The specified dimensions are based on industry standard car arrangements that can be found in the *Building Transportation Standards and Guidelines*, NEII-1, available free at www.neii.org. Both imperial and hard metric elevator configurations are included in NEII-1. The industry standards are based on studies performed at Syracuse University in the mid-1970s. Accessibility in smaller-sized cars is dependent on the inside floor area and location of the car door. This was taken into account when Table 407.4.1 was developed. Note 2 states that any elevator car that provides a clear door width of at least 36 inches (915 mm) and a turning space (i.e., circular or T-turn) within the cab would be considered accessible (see Figure 407.4.1).

The exception recognizes that the size of an existing elevator is fixed. As an example, the industry standard 2000-

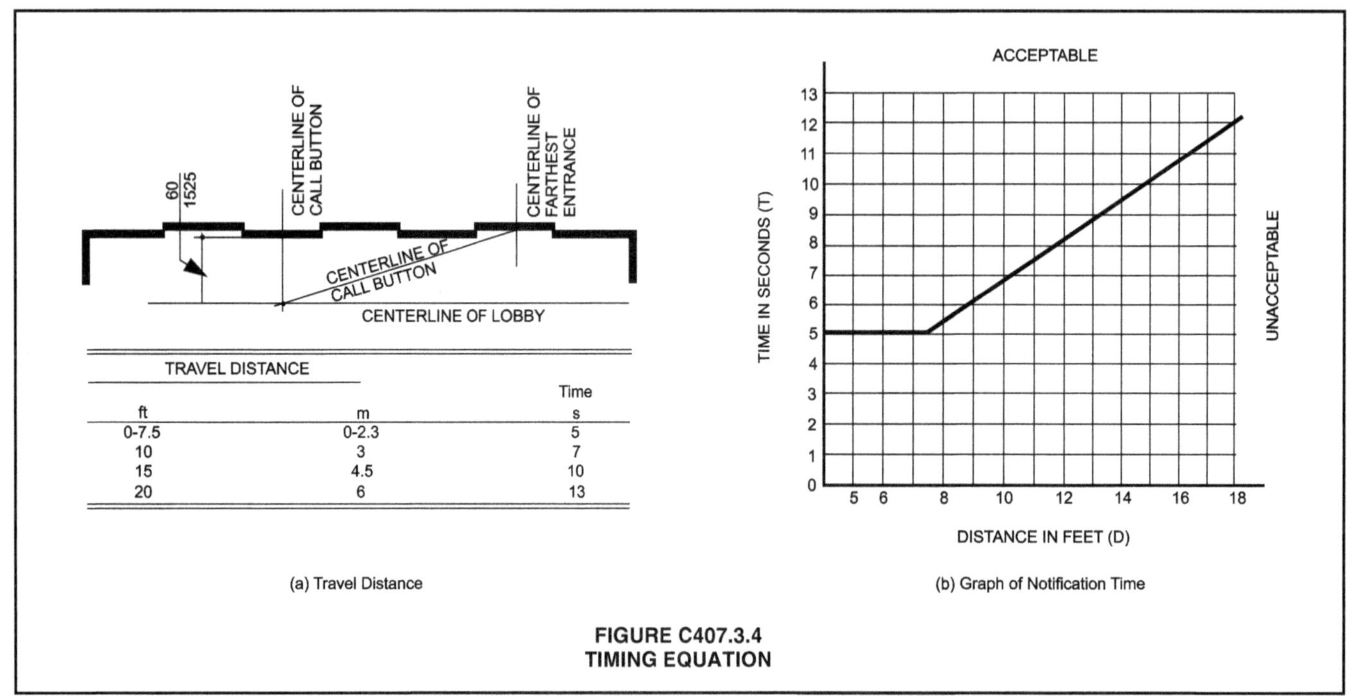

(a) Travel Distance

(b) Graph of Notification Time

**FIGURE C407.3.4
TIMING EQUATION**

TABLE 407.4.1—MINIMUM DIMENSIONS OF ELEVATOR CARS

Door Location	Door Clear Opening Width	Inside Car, Side to Side	Inside Car, Back Wall to Front Return	Inside Car, Back Wall to Inside Face
Centered	42 inches (1065 mm)	80 inches (2030 mm)	51 inches (1295 mm)	54 inches (1370 mm)
Side (Off Center)	36 inches (915 mm)[1]	68 inches (1725 mm)	51 inches (1295 mm)	54 inches (1370 mm)
Any	36 inches (915 mm)[1]	54 inches (1370 mm)	80 inches (2030 mm)	80 inches (2030 mm)
Any	36 inches (915 mm)[1]	60 inches (1525 mm)[2]	60 inches (1525 mm)[2]	60 inches (1525 mm)[2]

[1] A tolerance of minus $^5/_8$ inch (16 mm) is permitted.

[2] Other car configurations that provide a 36-inch (915 mm) door clear opening width and a turning space complying with Section 304 with the door closed are permitted.

pound (907 kg) elevator was reconfigured in the mid-1970s to permit the turning of a wheelchair. Elevators of this capacity and others that predate that change cannot be reconfigured. If full compliance with Table 407.4.1 was mandated, the existing elevator would need to be completely replaced and a new hoistway constructed to allow for the reconfigured platform size.

407.4.2 Floor Surfaces. Floor surfaces in elevator cars shall comply with Section 302.

❖ The surface features of elevator car floors are just as critical as other floor or ramp surfaces used by people with disabilities, and are required to comply with Section 303.

407.4.3 Platform to Hoistway Clearance. The clearance between the car platform sill and the edge of any hoistway landing shall comply with ASME A17.1/CSA B44 listed in Section 105.2.5.

❖ The vertical and horizontal clearance between the car platform sill and the edge of any hoistway landing is a required running clearance for movement of the elevator. This clearance received much attention in the early 1970s. Persons using wheelchairs wanted the clearance to be close to zero. A large gap can be cumbersome to traverse with a wheelchair, especially for the front wheels. It wasn't until the industry explained and demonstrated that a running clearance was required that the tolerance was agreed upon. The requirement in ASME A17.1 for the horizontal clearance between the platform sill and the edge of the landing sill is $1^1/_4$ inches (32 mm) maximum.

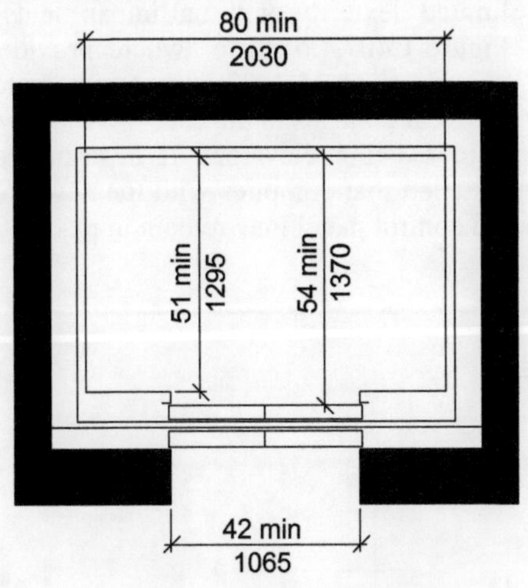

(a) Centered Door Location

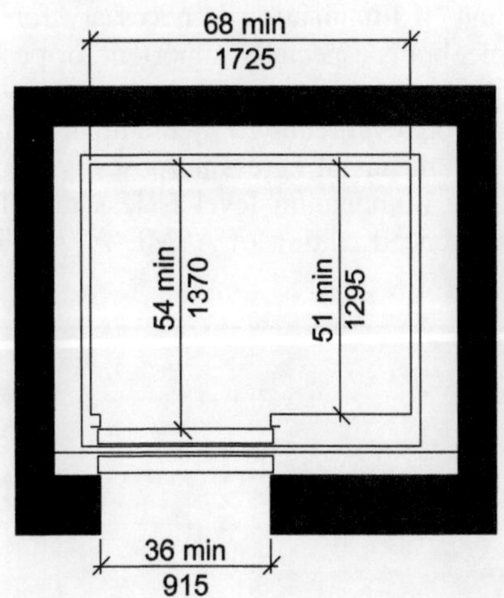

(b) Side (Off-Centered Door) Location

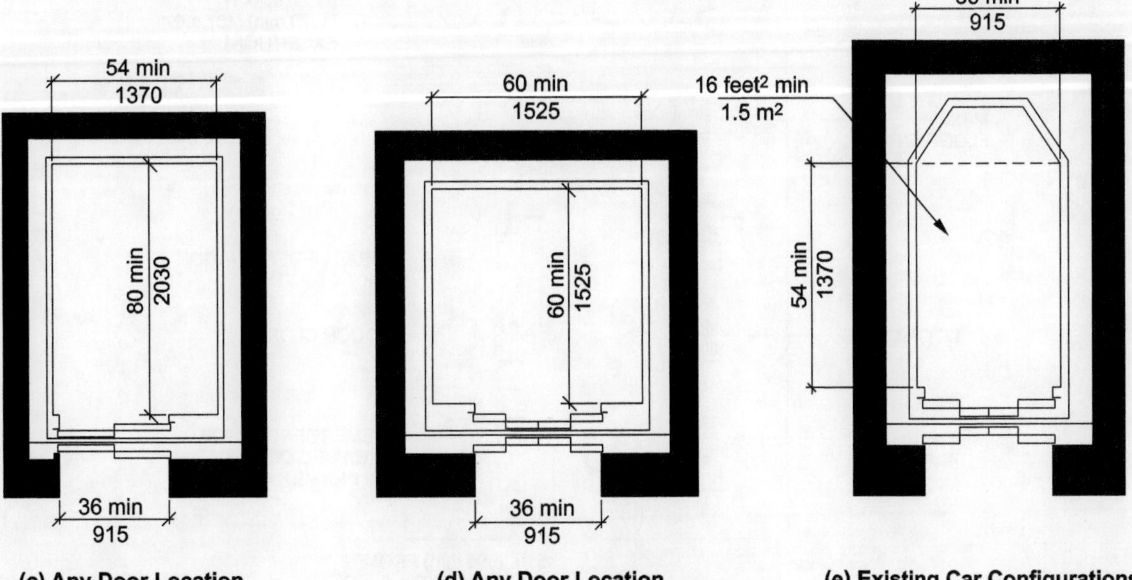

(c) Any Door Location

(d) Any Door Location

(e) Existing Car Configurations

FIGURE 407.4.1
INSIDE DIMENSIONS OF ELEVATOR CARS

407.4.4 Leveling. Each car shall automatically stop and maintain position at floor landings within a tolerance of $^1/_2$ inch (13 mm) under rated loading to zero loading conditions.

❖ A full elevator car may stop within $^1/_2$ inch (13 mm) of a floor landing only to creep to greater distance as people get on and off and the load increases or decreases on the elevator. This change in loading will cause the elevator to move away or toward the landing. Without releveling to the $^1/_2$ inch (13 mm) of the landing, the resulting vertical level change may make the car inaccessible to many persons with disabilities.

407.4.5 Illumination. The level of illumination at the car controls, platform, car threshold and car landing sill shall comply with ASME A17.1/CSA B44 listed in Section 105.2.5.

❖ A minimum amount of illumination is necessary for the benefit of all people, but is especially important for people with limited mobility who must use greater care in moving about. The illumination level required by the model building codes for general means of egress purposes is 1 footcandle (11 lux). The illumination level is less than that required by the referenced edition of ASME A17.1. The 2000 edition of ASME A17.1 raised the illumination level to 10 footcandles (108 lux).

407.4.6 Elevator Car Controls. Where provided, elevator car controls shall comply with Sections 407.4.6 and 309.

EXCEPTION: In existing elevators, where a new car operating panel complying with Section 407.4.6 is provided, existing car operating panels shall not be required to comply with Section 407.4.6.

❖ Car controls are the buttons inside the car that allow users to indicate the desired floor they wish to travel to with the associated designation immediately adjacent (see Section 407.4.7). In addition to the controls being in an accessible location (e.g., a clear floor space in front of the controls and controls within reach ranges), there are concerns for button size, arrangement and designation for persons with limited dexterity or visual impairments (see Commentary Figure C407.4.6). The "where provided" language is in consideration of destination-oriented elevators that do not have car controls in the cab.

In existing elevators, if a second operating panel is installed that complies with the new provisions, the original control panel may remain in place.

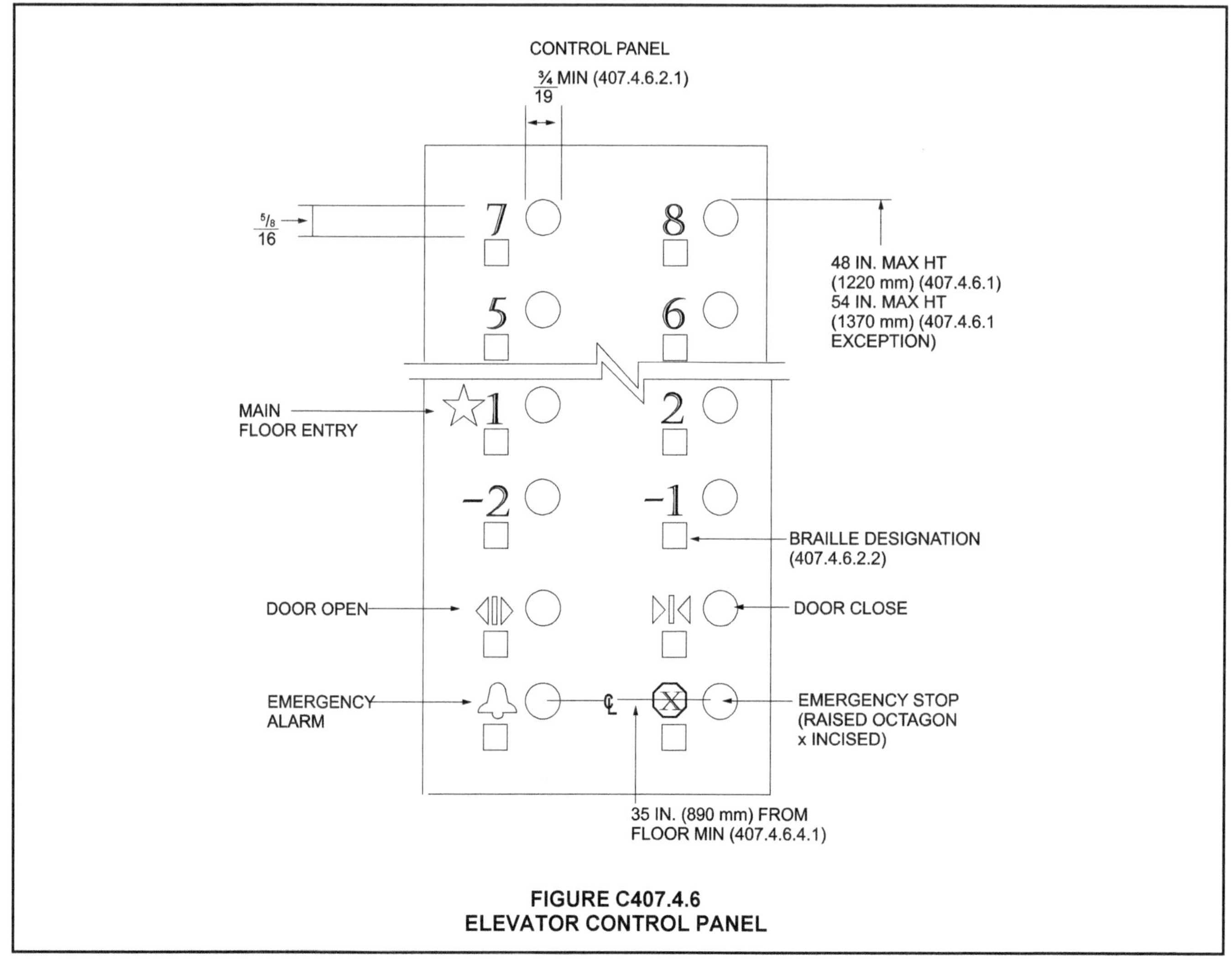

FIGURE C407.4.6
ELEVATOR CONTROL PANEL

407.4.6.1 Location. Controls shall be located within one of the reach ranges specified in Section 308.

EXCEPTIONS:

1. Where the elevator panel complies with Section 407.4.8.
2. In existing elevators, where a parallel approach is provided to the controls, car control buttons with floor designations shall be permitted to be located 54 inches (1370 mm) maximum above the floor. Where the panel is changed, it shall comply with Section 407.4.6.1.

❖ These provisions are intended to ensure that controls are located within reach of a person in a wheelchair. In most cases, it is possible to locate the highest control on elevator panels within 48 inches (1220 mm) of the floor (see Commentary Figure C407.4.6 and Section 407.4.6.4).

When the elevator serves more than 16 openings (regulated by "openings" rather than "landings" to accommodate cars with front and rear openings) there may not be sufficient space in the front return panel to fit all the buttons within 48 inches (1220 mm) of the floor. Research using industry standard 2000-pound and 2500-pound (907 and 1134 kg) capacity elevators indicates that side reach from a facing position is not possible unless flush-mounted car controls are located 23.5 inches (595 mm) or more from a corner. This is not possible in these cars.

When Exception 1 is used, the elevator must have sequential step scanning in accordance with Section 407.4.8.

In existing elevators, existing control panels may remain at the higher reach. When a panel is replaced, it must comply with the new provisions for panels.

407.4.6.2 Buttons. Car control buttons with floor designations shall be raised or flush, and shall comply with Section 407.4.6.2.

EXCEPTION: In existing elevators, buttons shall be permitted to be recessed.

❖ Car controls are the buttons inside the car that allow users to indicate the desired floor they wish to travel to. In addition to the controls being in an accessible location (e.g., a clear floor space in front of the controls and controls within reach ranges), there are concerns for button size and designation for person with limited dexterity or visual impairments. Buttons must be raised from or flush with the faceplate or trim ring if provided (see Figure 407.4.6.2).

The exception establishes that for existing elevators, compliance with the provisions for arrangement of the control buttons within the operating panel is not required unless the operating panel is changed. It is considered impractical, and in many cases impossible, to rearrange the buttons within an existing operating panel in full compliance with Section 407.4.6.2. These constraints do not exist when the entire operating panel is replaced.

407.4.6.2.1 Size. Buttons shall be $^{3}/_{4}$ inch (19 mm) minimum in their smallest dimension.

❖ See commentary, Section 407.4.6.2 and Commentary Figure C407.4.6.

407.4.6.2.2 Arrangement. Buttons shall be arranged with numbers in ascending order. Floors shall be designated . . . -4, -3, -2, -1, 0, 1, 2, 3, 4, etcetera, with floors below the main entry floor designated with minus numbers. Numbers shall be permitted to be omitted, provided the remaining numbers are in sequence. Where a telephone keypad arrangement is used, the number key ("#") shall be utilized to enter the minus symbol ("-"). When two or more columns of buttons are provided they shall read from left to right.

❖ Because of the confusion for persons unfamiliar with the building, a standard designation in the elevator for the different floors up and down from the entry level is required. This avoids unique designations such as "M" for mezzanine or "B2" for the basement levels. Even though the "0" designation may be popular in Europe, most buildings in the United States designate the entry level as Floor 1. Note the allowance to omit numbers. When there are enough floor levels that columns of buttons must be used, the buttons should first read from left to right and then move up a row (see Commentary Figure C407.4.6).

An alternative arrangement for multiple buttons would be a scrolling option, when persons hold down a button until their floor designation lights up and then they release to register that call. See commentary under Section 407.4.6.3 if a keypad is chosen to enter floor calls.

407.4.6.3 Keypads. Where provided, car control keypads shall be in a standard telephone keypad arrangement and shall comply with Section 407.4.7.2.

❖ An alternative to rows of buttons is a keypad entry system. If this option is chosen, the keypad should follow the telephone arrangement in Section 707.5. The number 5 must have a raised dot. The # key is used to enter negative numbers for level below the entry floor (see Sections 407.4.7.2 and 707.5).

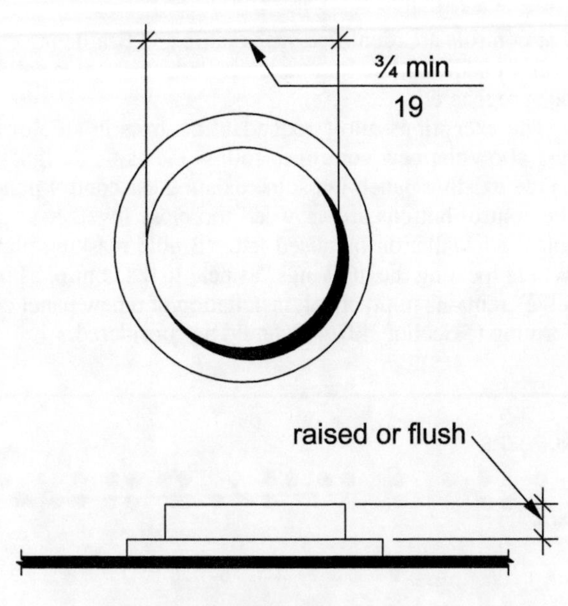

FIGURE 407.4.6.2
ELEVATOR CAR CONTROL BUTTONS

407.4.6.4 Emergency Controls. Emergency controls shall comply with Section 407.4.6.4.

❖ Emergency controls are typically the "HELP" button used to summon assistance if the elevator malfunctions or becomes stuck for some reason and "DOOR OPEN" button to stop an automatic closing door. It is important that these pieces of equipment be accessible for everyone when needed. The 35-inch (890 mm) value was chosen because the lower end of the reach ranges [i.e., 15 inches (380 mm)] was considered too low for proper access for taller persons. For consistency in elevators, they should always be located below the car controls.

In-car switches not intended for passenger use (e.g., fireman's operation) do not have to be accessible.

407.4.6.4.1 Height. Emergency control buttons shall have their centerlines 35 inches (890 mm) minimum above the floor.

❖ See the commentary for Section 407.4.6.4.

407.4.6.4.2 Location. Emergency controls, including the emergency alarm, shall be grouped at the bottom of the panel.

❖ See the commentary for Section 407.4.6.4.

407.4.7 Designations and Indicators of Car Controls. Designations and indicators of car controls shall comply with Section 407.4.7.

EXCEPTIONS:

1. In existing elevators, where a new car operating panel complying with Section 407.4.7 is provided, existing car operating panels shall not be required to comply with Section 407.4.7.
2. Where existing building floor designations differ from the arrangement required by Section 407.4.6.2.2, or are alphanumeric, a new operating panel shall be permitted to use such existing building floor designations.

❖ Car controls are identified with tactile and Braille information. In addition, the buttons must indicate when a call has been registered.

The exceptions allow redundant controls in an elevator and allow the new control to follow the same designation as the existing panel. On some existing car control panels, the control buttons are crowded too close together to permit the installation of raised letter/Braille marking plates. Where locating the markings "as near to the control as possible" remains impractical, installation of a new panel conforming to Section 407.4.6 should be considered.

407.4.7.1 Buttons. Car control buttons shall comply with Section 407.4.7.1.

❖ Buttons shall comply with the requirements for identification, location, symbols and visible indicators in Sections 407.4.7.1.1 through 407.4.7.1.4.

407.4.7.1.1 Type. Control buttons shall be identified by raised characters and braille complying with Sections 703.3 and 703.4.

❖ Permanently applied plates that have the appropriate raised characters/symbols and Braille are an acceptable means of providing raised control designations when nontelephone-type key pads are provided.

407.4.7.1.2 Location. Raised character and braille designations shall be placed immediately to the left of the control button to which the designations apply. Where a negative number is used to indicate a negative floor, the braille designation shall be a cell with the dots 3 and 6 followed by the ordinal number.

EXCEPTION: Where space on an existing car operating panel precludes raised characters and braille to the left of the control button, markings shall be placed as near to the control button as possible.

❖ Raised numbers and Braille designations must be placed immediately to the left of each control button (see Commentary Figure C407.4.6). For Braille numbers, see Commentary Figure C407.4.7.1.2(a). The main floor must also have the star symbol. The Braille symbol for the negative number is the bottom two dots in the Braille cell [see Commentary Figure C407.4.7.1.2(b) and Section 407.4.6.2.2].

407.4.7.1.3 Symbols. The control button for the emergency stop, alarm, door open, door close, main entry floor, and phone, shall be identified with raised symbols and braille as shown in Table 407.4.7.1.3.

❖ Common controls found inside elevator cabs must be identified with both raised symbols and Braille designations as indicated in Table 407.4.7.1.3.

407.4.7.1.4 Visible Indicators. Buttons with floor designations shall be provided with visible indicators to show that a call has been registered. The visible indication shall extinguish when the car arrives at the designated floor.

❖ Visible indicators do not have to be proved by the button itself. Lights beside buttons are permitted but cannot interfere with the placement of the raised and Braille characters.

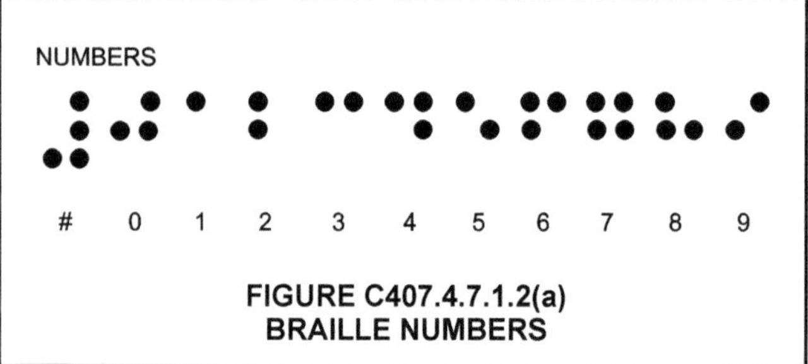

FIGURE C407.4.7.1.2(a)
BRAILLE NUMBERS

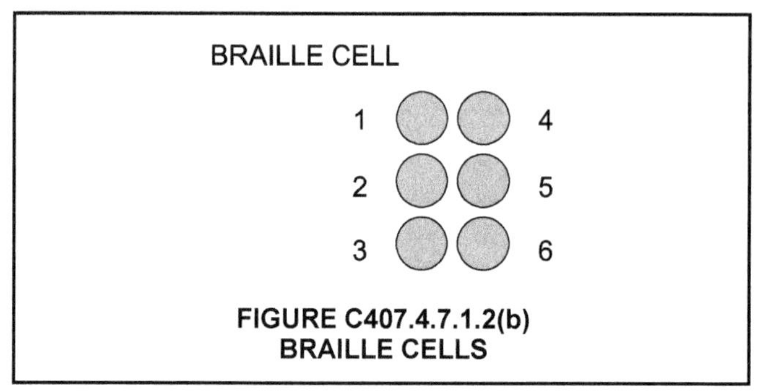

FIGURE C407.4.7.1.2(b)
BRAILLE CELLS

TABLE 407.4.7.1.3—CONTROL BUTTON IDENTIFICATION

Control Button Type	Raised Symbol	Braille Message	Proportions (Open circles indicate unused dots within each braille cell)
3.0 mm TYP. BETWEEN ELEMENTS; 16.0 mm; 4.8 mm; DOOR OPEN		op"en"	2.0 mm; 2.0 mm
REAR/SIDE DOOR OPEN		op"en"	
DOOR CLOSE		close	
REAR/SIDE DOOR CLOSE		close	
MAIN		ma"in"	
ALARM		al"ar"m	
PHONE		ph"one"	
EMERGENCY STOP (WHEN PROVIDED) X on face of octagon is not required to be tactile		"st"op	

407.4.7.2 Keypads. Keypad keys shall be identified by visual characters complying with Section 703.2 centered on the corresponding keypad button. The number five key shall have a single raised dot. The dot shall have a base diameter of 0.118 inch (3 mm) minimum and 0.120 inch (3.05 mm) maximum, and a height of 0.025 inch (0.6 mm) minimum and 0.037 inch (0.9 mm) maximum.

❖ Telephone type key pad arrangements were addressed in the 1998 standard for the first time. For tactile information where the standard telephone arrangement is used [see Figure 707.5(a)], there is a tactile dot on the number "5" key. The remainder of the keys are identified visually. For consistency the star appearing on the lower left key will be visually the same as the five-pointed star in Table 407.4.7.1.3 and when pushed will enter a call to the "Main" floor designated for the elevator. Entering the "Main" floor number will do the same. The "Pound" key position in the lower righthand position is used to enter minus "-" floors such as below-grade levels or parking. The "Pound" key position and then a number in succession will enter the appropriate calls to these below-grade floors. To enter floor calls above the "Main" floor such as floor 15, it is only necessary to push "1" and then "5" in succession.

407.4.8 Elevator Car Call Sequential Step Scanning. Elevator car call sequential step scanning shall be provided where car control buttons are provided more than 48 inches (1220 mm) above the floor. Floor selection shall be accomplished by applying momentary or constant pressure to the up or down scan button. The up scan button shall sequentially select floors above the current floor. The down scan button shall sequentially select floors below the current floor. When pressure is removed from the up or down scan button for more than 2 seconds, the last floor selected shall be registered as a car call. The up and down scan button shall be located adjacent to or immediately above the emergency control buttons.

❖ Persons who are short of stature and some people who use wheelchairs may not be able to reach the upper buttons when Exception 1 to Section 407.4.6.1 is permitted. The sequential step scanner provides an alternative means that would allow a person to choose a floor. Sequential step scanning works like the up/down button on a TV. When the "up" button is pressed, floor selection proceeds in a sequential order (car floor buttons light up) until the "up" button is released. The last floor selected is registered as a car call.

407.4.9 Car Position Indicators. Audible and visible car position indicators shall be provided in elevator cars.

❖ During the ascent or descent of an elevator car, information must be provided inside the car that indicates the car's location. This information must be provided visibly and audibly as indicated in Sections 407.4.9.1 through 407.4.9.2.3.

407.4.9.1 Visible Indicators. Visible indicators shall comply with Section 407.4.9.1.

❖ The location and size of the visible indicator must be readily seen by everyone in the car, but most importantly, it must be in a standardized location so people will become accustomed to it being in the same location in all accessible elevators.

407.4.9.1.1 Size. Characters shall be $^{1}/_{2}$ inch (13 mm) minimum in height.

❖ See the commentary for Section 407.4.9.1.

407.4.9.1.2 Location. Indicators shall be located above the car control panel or above the door.

❖ See the commentary for Section 407.4.9.1.

407.4.9.1.3 Floor Arrival. As the car passes a floor and when a car stops at a floor served by the elevator, the corresponding character shall illuminate.

EXCEPTION: Destination-oriented elevators shall not be required to comply with Section 407.4.9.1.3, provided the visible indicators extinguish when the call has been answered.

❖ The indicators above the car control or above the door are location indicators that indicate progress up and down the hoistway. They can be on a strip where the floor number illuminates at approximately the time the car passes each floor; or they can be a changing number display.

For destination-oriented elevators, the indicators are the same size and in the same location, but the information is displayed slightly differently (see the commentary for Section 407.4.9.1.4).

407.4.9.1.4 Destination Indicator. In destination-oriented elevators, a display shall be provided in the car with visible indicators to show car destinations.

❖ In destination-oriented elevators, the in-car display provides information regarding what floor the car is traveling to next. The visible indicators on the in-car display will remain lit until the floor designated has been reached. The visible indication is extinguished after the call has been answered. Other enhancements such as having the next designated stop begin to flash are used, but are not required.

407.4.9.2 Audible Indicators. Audible indicators shall comply with Section 407.4.9.2.

❖ A verbal announcement is preferred by persons with visual impairments and the general public. A nonverbal, audible signal is difficult to use in high-rise buildings and when nonstandard floor arrangements (e.g., basement, lobby, mezzanine, 2nd floor, 12th floor, 14th floor, etc.) are used.

407.4.9.2.1 Signal Type. The signal shall be an automatic verbal annunciator that announces the floor at which the car is about to stop. The verbal announcement indicating the floor shall be completed prior to the initiation of the door opening.

EXCEPTION: For elevators other than destination-oriented elevators that have a rated speed of 200 feet per minute (1 m/s) maximum, a non-verbal audible signal with a frequency of 1500 Hz maximum that sounds as the car passes or is about to stop at a floor served by the elevator shall be permitted.

❖ See the commentary for Section 407.4.9.2.

407.4.9.2.2 Signal Level. The verbal annunciator shall be 10 dBA minimum above ambient, but shall not exceed 80 dBA, measured at the annunciator.

❖ A minimum sound pressure level is necessary to ensure that the audible signal can be reasonably heard over and above ambient noise levels in the elevator car. The sound level specified is intended to make sure the signal can be heard above ambient noise but not cause damage to a person's hearing.

407.4.9.2.3 Frequency. The verbal annunciator shall have a frequency of 300 Hz minimum and 3,000 Hz maximum.

❖ See the commentary for Section 407.4.9.2.2.

407.4.10 Emergency Communications. Emergency two-way communication systems between the elevator car and a point outside the hoistway shall comply with Section 407.4.10 and ASME A17.1/CSA B44 listed in Section 105.2.5.

❖ The referenced edition of ASME A17.1, Rule 2.27.1, requires that a means to activate two-way communication "HELP" button be provided in elevators. These provisions address the details that are necessary to ensure that the emergency communications devices are accessible to and usable by people who are unable to use voice communication (e.g., people with speech/hearing impairments). A telephone symbol with Braille is generally used to identify the two-way communications means, which may be an intercom or a telephone. A device that requires no handset is required by A117.1 and is easier to use by people who have difficulty reaching.

It is not the intent of this section to apply to any two-way communication equipment for use only by the fire department.

407.4.10.1 Height. The highest operable part of a two-way communication system shall comply with Section 308.

❖ All operable parts of the emergency communication equipment must be within the reach ranges of Section 308.

407.4.10.2 Identification. Raised characters and braille complying with Sections 703.3 and 703.4 and raised symbols complying with Section 407.4.7.1.3 shall be provided adjacent to the device.

❖ The raised phone symbol and Braille information must be provided in accordance with Table 407.4.1.3.

408 Limited-use/Limited-application Elevators

408.1 General. Limited-use/limited-application elevators shall comply with Section 408 and ASME A17.1/CSA B44 listed in Section 105.2.5. Elevator operation shall be automatic.

❖ The organization of this section is similar to that of the elevator section; elevator landing (Section 408.2), elevator doors (Section 408.3), and elevator cars (Section 408.4).

A limited-use/limited-application (LULA) elevator is defined by ASME A17.1 as "a power passenger elevator where the use and application is limited by size, capacity, speed and rise." LULA elevators are generally used where installation of a full passenger elevator is not practical or economically feasible. LULA elevators provide many of the same features as full passenger elevators and provide accessibility in situations where access may otherwise not be provided.

ASME A17.1 provides comprehensive safety requirements for the installation of LULA elevators. For example, LULA elevators are restricted to 25 feet (7620 mm) of travel, a speed of 30 feet per minute (9145 mm/min), an 18-square-foot (1.7 m^2) car size and 1400-pound (635 kg) capacity. Because of their limited travel and smaller size, fire fighter emergency operation is not required on LULA elevators (see Commentary Figure C408.1).

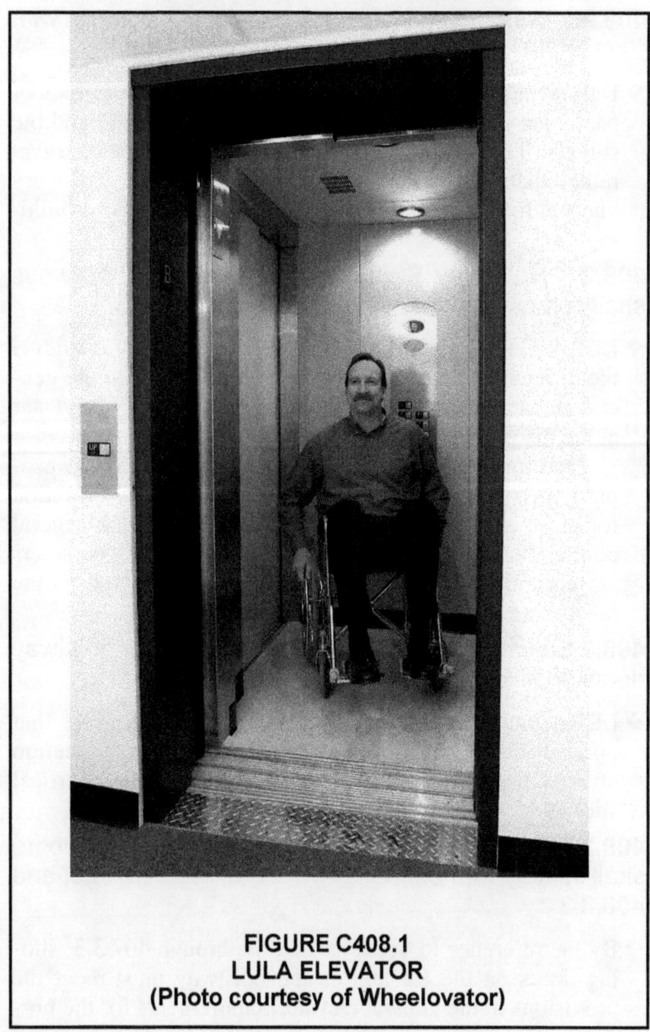

FIGURE C408.1
LULA ELEVATOR
(Photo courtesy of Wheelovator)

For purposes of accessibility, elevators that are attendant operated are not considered acceptable because of the potential for the attendant not being readily available. Also, elevator controls that require continuous pressure for operation are not allowed, because they may not be suitable for people who have limited use of their hands.

408.2 Elevator Landing Requirements. Landings serving limited-use/limited application elevators shall comply with Section 408.2.

❖ Similar to other types of passenger elevators, at each floor level that is served by the LULA elevator, there are provisions for controls to call the car, the signals for car arrival at the floor level and floor level information on the elevator door jambs.

408.2.1 Call Controls. Elevator call buttons and keypads shall comply with Section 407.2.1.

❖ Car controls in LULA elevators must comply with the same provisions as other types of passenger elevators. This would include access to the controls, car button requirements, visual and audible indicators, etc. There should never be a problem with meeting the reach ranges because of the limited levels served (see Section 407.2.1).

408.2.2 Hall Signals. Hall signals shall comply with Section 407.2.2.

❖ Hall signals for LULAs are the same as for other types of passenger elevators. This includes both visual and audible signals. This is mostly to address the direction of travel rather than which elevator is arriving because it is very unusual for more than one LULA to be installed in a building.

408.2.3 Hoistway Signs. Signs at elevator hoistways shall comply with Section 407.2.3.

❖ LULA elevators must have raised and Braille floor-level identification at each hoistway entrance similar to the general elevator requirements. This would include a raised star at the main level.

Tactile signage communicates vital information to people with vision impairments. It is also useful information for those with hearing impairments, as well as the general public. Plates that have the appropriate raised characters are acceptable if the plates are permanently fixed to the hoistway entrance jambs.

408.3 Elevator Door Requirements. Elevator hoistway doors shall comply with Section 408.3.

❖ LULA elevators may use swinging or sliding doors that operate automatically. The car door width and location affects the accessibility of the LULA elevator. Vertical sliding doors are not allowed.

408.3.1 Sliding Doors. Sliding hoistway and car doors shall comply with Sections 407.3.1 through 407.3.3, and 408.3.3.

❖ By the reference to Sections 407.3.1 through 407.3.3, sliding doors on the car and on the hoistway must meet the provisions in the general elevator requirements for the horizontal sliding type, operate automatically and be equipped with a reopening device. The reference to Section 408.3.3 stipulates minimum width and location relative to the car shape.

408.3.2 Swinging Doors. Swinging hoistway doors shall open and close automatically and shall comply with Sections 408.3.2, 404, and 407.3.2.

❖ Some LULA elevators have a swinging door at the hoistway openings. These doors must be automatic (Section 407.3.2) and meet the power operation and duration requirement in the subsections of Section 408.3.2. In addition, the door must meet the provisions in Section 404.3 for automatic doors. Because the car door is horizontal sliding and automatic, the car and hoistway doors are not considered doors in a series (see Section 404.3.4).

408.3.2.1 Power Operation. Swinging doors shall be power-operated and shall comply with ANSI/BHMA A156.19 listed in Section 105.2.3.

❖ The building hardware industry has developed consensus standards for automatic doors. Issues such as safety, durability, usability, operation and installation are covered. The standard is available from the American National Standards Institute, 25 West 43rd Street, Fourth Floor, New York, New York 10036.

408.3.2.2 Duration. Power-operated swinging doors shall remain open for 20 seconds minimum when activated.

❖ The intent of the 20 seconds is to allow sufficient time for passengers to enter the elevator without the door closing on them.

408.3.3 Door Location and Width. Car doors shall comply with Section 408.3.3.

❖ LULA elevator cars can have a variety of door configurations. Section 408.3.3.1 deals with cars with a door on one end, or doors on both ends. Section 408.3.3.2 deals with cars with doors on adjacent sides.

408.3.3.1 Cars with Single Door or Doors on Opposite Ends. Car doors shall be positioned at the narrow end of cars with a single door and on cars with doors on opposite ends. Doors shall provide a clear opening width of 32 inches (815 mm) minimum.

❖ In a standard LULA elevator with one door, minimally, the door must have a clear width of 32 inches (815 mm) and be located at the narrow end of the car (see Figure 408.4.1).

LULA elevators may sometimes have two doors. If doors are at opposite ends, the requirements are the same as for a single car door [see Figures 408.3.3(a) and (b)]. Car size, per Section 408.4.1, is at least 42 inches (1065 mm) wide and 15.75 square feet (1.46 square meters) minimum in area.

408.3.3.2 Cars with Doors on Adjacent Sides. Car doors shall be permitted to be located on adjacent sides of cars that provide an 18 square foot (1.67 m^2) platform. Doors located on the narrow end of cars shall provide a clear opening width of 36 inches (915 mm) minimum. Doors located on the long side shall provide a clear opening width of 42 inches (1065 mm) minimum and be located as far as practicable from the door on the narrow end.

EXCEPTION: Car doors that provide a clear opening width of 36 inches (915 mm) minimum shall be permitted to be located on adjacent sides of cars that provide a clear floor area of 51 inches (1295 mm) in width and 51 inches (1295 mm) in depth.

❖ Where doors are on adjacent sides of the LULA car, the door widths and car size have additional requirements. If doors are on adjacent walls, the minimum clear width is increased to 36 inches (915 mm) for the door at the narrow end and 42 inches (1065 mm) at the wide end. In addition, the minimum car size is increased to 18 square feet (1.67 m^2) [see Figure 408.3.3(c)]. There is an option that allows for two 36-inch-wide (915 mm) doors if the minimum dimensions are 51 inches by 51 inches (1295 by 1295 mm) minimum, which also happens to be 18 square feet (1.67 m^2) in size. The square layout offers better maneuverability.

408.4 Elevator Car Requirements. Elevator cars shall comply with Section 408.4.

❖ LULA cars must comply with provisions for minimum dimensions, floor surface, platform to hoistway clearances, leveling of the car, illumination, in-car controls, floor designations and car location information and emergency communication. Many of these requirements are the same as those for general passenger elevators.

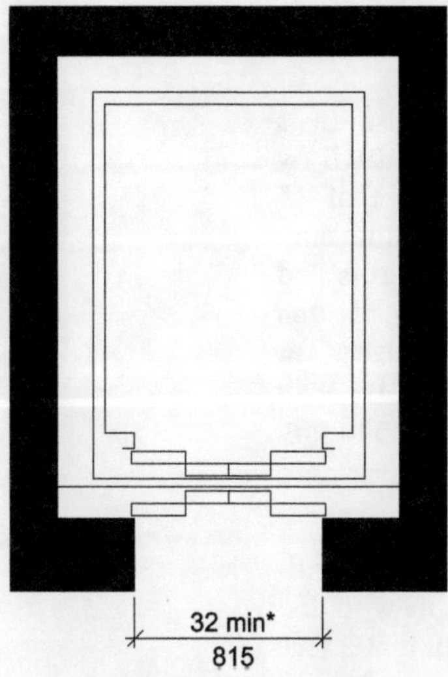

(a) Car with Single Door
*Door opening size from Section 408.3.3

(b) Doors on Opposite Sides

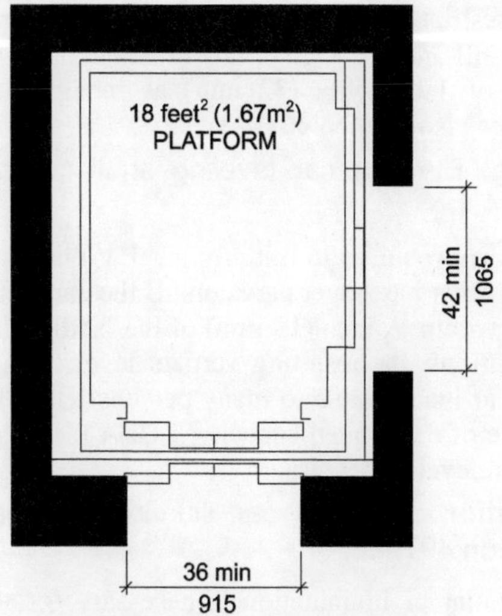

(c) Doors on Adjacent Sides

FIGURE 408.3.3
DOOR LOCATIONS FOR LIMITED USE/LIMITED APPLICATION (LULA) ELEVATORS

408.4.1 Inside Dimensions. Elevator cars shall provide a clear floor width of 42 inches (1065 mm) minimum. The clear floor area shall not be less than 15.75 square feet (1.46 m^2).

EXCEPTION: For installations in existing buildings, elevator cars that provide a clear floor area of 15 square feet (1.4 m^2) minimum, and provide a clear inside dimension of 36 inches (915 mm) minimum in width and 54 inches (1370 mm) minimum in depth, shall be permitted. This exception shall not apply to cars with doors on adjacent sides.

❖ The inside dimensions of the elevator car provide adequate space for a person using a wheelchair to enter the car, operate the controls and exit the car. Per Section 408.3.3, doors are positioned on the narrow ends of the platform to allow the user to go in and out of the elevator car without turning. The car doors are required to meet the same 32-inch (815 mm) clear width as other accessible doors.

Existing conditions sometimes require the use of a smaller car. The dimensions of 36 inches by 54 (915 by 1370 mm) inches minimum and a minimum size of 15 square feet (1.4 m^2) allow for this, while still providing adequate room for the user to enter, operate the controls and exit the lift. The *Building Transportation Standards and Guidelines*, NEII-1, also provides standard industry car dimensions and door arrangements that comply with A117.1. NEII-1 is available free of charge at www.neii.org.

408.4.2 Floor Surfaces. Floor surfaces in elevator cars shall comply with Section 302.

❖ The surface features of elevator car floors are just as critical as other floor or ramp surfaces used by people with disabilities, and are required to comply with Section 302 (see also Section 407.4.2).

408.4.3 Platform to Hoistway Clearance. The clearance between the car platform sill and the edge of any hoistway landing shall comply with ASME A17.1/CSA B44 listed in Section 105.2.5.

❖ This provision restricts the horizontal clearance between the car platform sill and the edge of any hoistway landing to a maximum of $1^1/_4$ inches (32 mm) as required by ASME A17.1 (see also Section 407.4.3).

408.4.4 Leveling. Elevator car leveling shall comply with Section 407.4.4.

❖ LULA elevators are required to initially level at the landings the same as other passenger elevators. If the car is not required to stop within $^1/_2$ inch (13 mm) of the landing for all loading conditions, the resulting vertical level change may make this car inaccessible to many persons with disabilities. Because of the limited capacity, LULA elevators do not require a releveling feature.

408.4.5 Illumination. Elevator car illumination shall comply with Section 407.4.5.

❖ A minimum amount of illumination is necessary for the benefit of all people, but is especially important for people with limited mobility who must use greater care in moving about. The illumination level required by the model building codes for general means of egress is 1 footcandle (11 lux). The illumination level of 5 footcandles (54 lux) at the car controls, platform and car threshold is less than that required by the referenced edition of ASME A17.1. The 2000 edition of ASME A17.1 raised the requirement to 10 footcandles (108 lux).

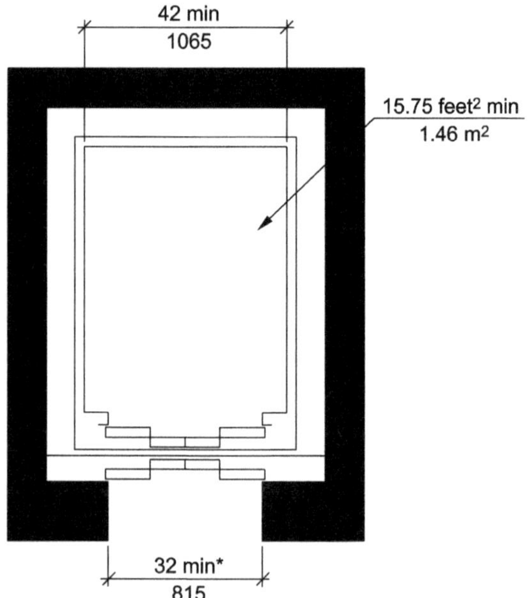

(a) New Construction

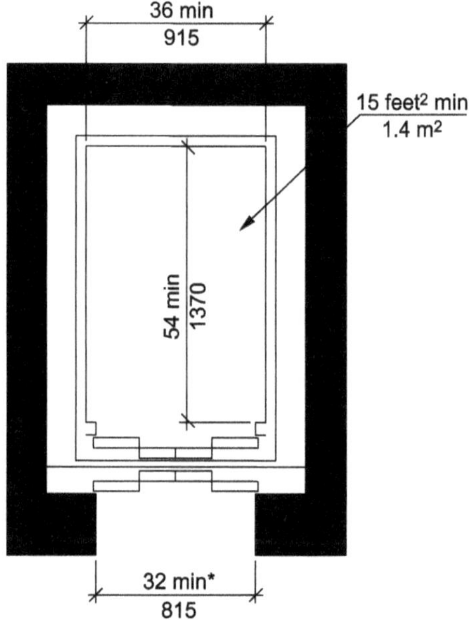

(b) Existing Building Exception

*Door opening size from Section 408.3.3

FIGURE 408.4.1
INDSIDE DIMENSIONS OF LIMITED USE/LIMITED APPLICATION (LULA) ELEVATOR CARS

408.4.6 Elevator Car Controls. Elevator car controls shall comply with Section 407.4.6. Control panels shall be centered on a side wall.

❖ In LULA elevators, the car controls within the cab must meet the same provisions as for typical passenger elevators in Section 407.4.6. This includes provisions for control height, button style and emergency controls (see Section 407.4.6).

In LULA elevators, for easy access, controls should be centered on a side wall. The controls in the elevator car are most conveniently located for the person using a wheelchair from a side reach. The size and configuration of the elevator car does not allow for the user to complete a turn, and, therefore, the controls cannot be on the end walls. If the controls are moved toward a corner, they may end up behind the shoulder of the person entering the cab and the result could be that they were not reachable given the tight space of the cab floor.

408.4.7 Designations and Indicators of Car Controls. Designations and indicators of car controls shall comply with Section 407.4.7.

❖ Car controls are identified with raised numbers and Braille information, including a star at the main floor. Permanently applied plates that have the appropriately raised characters and symbols are an acceptable means of providing raised control designations. In addition, the buttons must indicate what calls have been registered (see Sections 407.4.7 through 407.4.7.2).

408.4.8 Emergency Communications. Car emergency signaling devices complying with Section 407.4.10 shall be provided.

❖ The referenced edition of ASME A17.1, Rule 2.27.1, requires that a means to activate two-way communication "HELP" button be provided in elevators. These provisions address the details that are necessary to ensure that the emergency communications devices are accessible to and usable by people who are unable to use voice communication (e.g., people with speech/hearing impairments). A telephone symbol with Braille is generally used to identify the two-way communications means, which may be an intercom or a telephone. A device that requires no handset is required by A117.1 and is easier for people who have difficulty reaching to use.

409 Private Residence Elevators

409.1 General. Private residence elevators shall comply with Section 409 and ASME A17.1/CSA B44 listed in Section 105.2.5. Elevator operation shall be automatic.

> **EXCEPTION:** Elevators complying with Section 407 or 408 shall not be required to comply with Section 409.

❖ Private residence elevators must comply with Section 5.3 of ASME A17.1. Operation of the elevator must be automatic. The only elevator landing requirement is call buttons (Section 409.2). For car and hoistway door requirements, see Section 409.3. Car requirements are in Section 409.4.

Private residence elevators are limited by the standard to a maximum of 50 feet (15 240 mm) vertical travel distance, and a maximum speed of 40 feet per minute (12 190 mm/min). The standard also limits the application of these types of elevators to within an individual unit or private access to an individual unit (see Commentary Figure C409.1).

The requirements for private residence elevators are not as restrictive as the provisions for passenger elevators or LULAs because of the familiarity of the users. The majority of private residence elevators are connected within a vertical shaft. Most have a pit with a depth of about 6 inches (150 mm).

Private residence elevators can be used as part of the required accessible route in Accessible or Type A units. When private residence elevators are installed within individual townhouse style units with four or more units in a structure, Type B unit requirements are applicable to units with elevators.

The exception allows for elevators installed within a single dwelling unit or providing private access to a single dwelling unit to be passenger elevators, LULAs or private residence elevators.

FIGURE C409.1
PRIVATE RESIDENCE ELEVATORS
(Photo courtesy of Wheelovator)

409.2 Call Controls. Call buttons at elevator landings shall comply with Section 309. Call buttons shall be $^3/_4$ inch (19 mm) minimum in their smallest dimension.

❖ Call buttons must meet all the provisions for operable parts: clear floor space, height and operation. Typically, buttons are located between 35 and 48 inches (890 and 1220 mm) above the floor (see Section 407.2.1.1). Minimum dimensions for the buttons ensure that the buttons are suitable for people who have limited use of their hands.

When a private residence elevator is accessed from a public area, the call is required by ASME A17.1 to be via key operation for security, similar to locking your front door.

409.3 Doors and Gates. Elevator car and hoistway doors and gates shall comply with Sections 409.3 and 404.

EXCEPTION: The maneuvering clearances required by Section 404.2.3 shall not apply for approaches to the push side of swinging doors.

❖ Two doors are installed at each elevator opening, one for the car and one for the hoistway. Typically, the car door slides sideways, and the hoistway door is a swinging door. Both doors must comply with this section specific to elevator doors, and the general provisions for doors in Section 404. These doors would not be considered doors in a series. Because of the small size of the elevator cab, the maneuvering clearances for doors are not required on the elevator side for the hoistway door.

409.3.1 Power Operation. Elevator car doors and gates shall be power operated and shall comply with ANSI/BHMA A156.19 listed in Section 105.2.3. Elevator cars with a single opening shall have low energy power operated hoistway doors and gates.

EXCEPTION: Hoistway doors or gates shall be permitted to be of the self-closing, manual type, where that door or gate provides access to a narrow end of the car that serves only one landing.

❖ When the elevator cab has only one door, both the door to the cab and the door to the hoistway must be power operated because the person using a wheelchair in this elevator would be dealing with a pull in-back out situation. The exception allows the doors to the hoistway to be manual if the elevator has a door on each end of the cab and the elevator only moves between two levels (see Commentary Figure C409.3.1). In this situation, the person using the wheelchair would be dealing with a pull in-pull out situation. Doors must be self-closing to allow the elevator to operate effectively. If the door is not closed, the elevator cannot be called. This exception is similar to what is permitted for platform lifts under Section 410.2.1.

409.3.2 Duration. Power operated doors and gates shall remain open for 20 seconds minimum when activated.

❖ The power operated door device holds the doors open for 20 seconds if the doorway remains continuously obstructed. After 20 seconds, the door is permitted to begin closing. However, if designed in accordance with ASME A17.1, the door closing movement is still stopped if a person or object exerts sufficient force at any point on the door edge. Sufficient force is defined by ASME A17.1 as 30 pounds-force (134 N). If all door reopening devices are rendered inoperative, ASME A17.1 also requires the average kinetic energy of the door system be reduced from 7 ft-lbf to $2^1/_2$ ft-lbf (9.5 J to 3.4 J).

409.3.3 Door or Gate Location and Width. Car gates or doors positioned at a narrow end of the clear floor area required by Section 409.4.1 shall provide a clear opening width of 32 inches (815 mm) minimum. Car gates or doors positioned on adjacent sides shall provide a clear opening width of 42 inches (1065 mm) minimum.

❖ Given the size of the cab in Section 409.4, cab doors and hoistway doors must provide a 32-inch (815 mm) clear width (Sections 404.2.2 and 409.3) and be located at the narrow end of the cab. Doors on the long side of a platform that have a 90-degree (1.6 rad) turn, need to be wider [42 inches (1065 mm) clear] to allow the user to complete the turn as they are entering or exiting the lift.

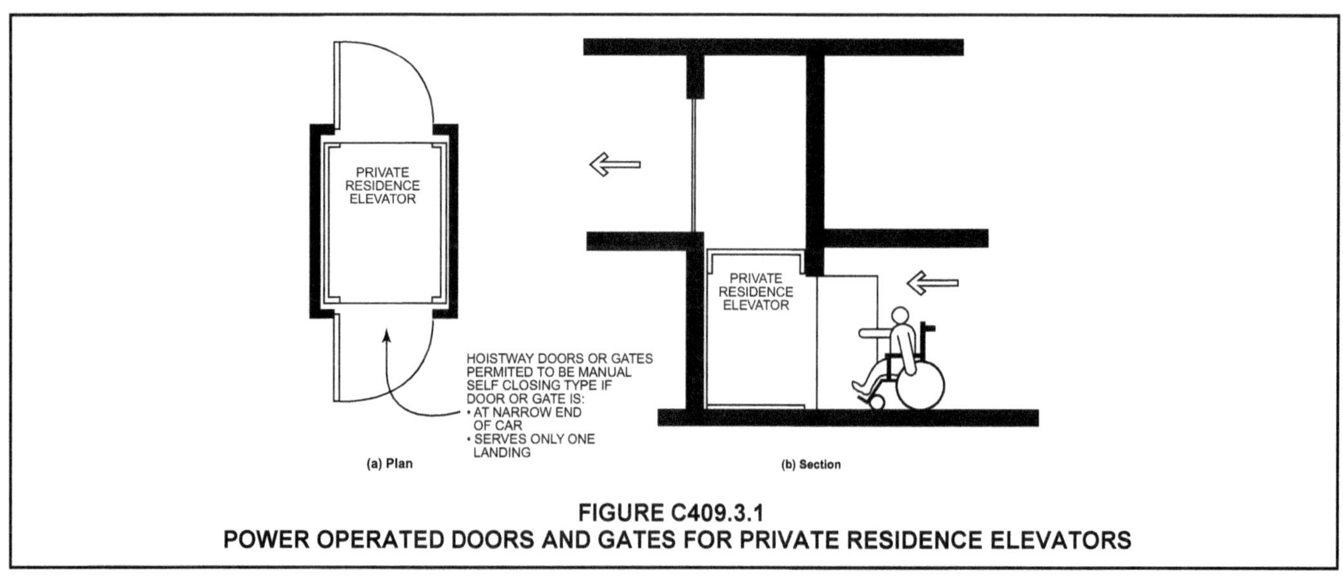

FIGURE C409.3.1
POWER OPERATED DOORS AND GATES FOR PRIVATE RESIDENCE ELEVATORS

409.4 Elevator Car Requirements. Elevator cars shall comply with Section 409.4.

❖ The elevator car must comply with the car size, floor surface, clearance between hoistway and cab, illumination, car controls and emergency communication requirements in this section.

409.4.1 Inside Dimensions. Elevator cars shall provide a clear floor area 36 inches (915 mm) minimum in width and 48 inches (1220 mm) minimum in depth.

❖ The minimum cab size is consistent with the alcove provisions in Section 305.7.2. The car size must be a minimum of 36 inches (915 mm) wide and 48 inches (1220 mm) deep, which computes as a minimum area of 12 square feet (1.1 m^2). ASME A17.1 limits the maximum cab size in a private residence elevator to 15 square feet (1.4 m^2).

409.4.2 Floor Surfaces. Floor surfaces in elevator cars shall comply with Section 302.

❖ The floor surface in the elevator cab must be stable, firm and slip resistant. If carpet is installed, the carpet must meet the requirements in Section 302.2. By reference in Section 302, any changes in elevation along the floor of the cab must be limited to the change in level provisions in Section 303.

409.4.3 Platform to Hoistway Clearance. The clearance between the car platform sill and the edge of any hoistway landing shall be $1^1/_4$ inches (32 mm) maximum.

❖ The vertical and horizontal clearance between the car platform sill and the edge of any hoistway landing is a required running clearance for movement of the elevator. This clearance received much attention in the early 1970s. Persons using wheelchairs wanted the clearance to be close to zero. A large gap can be cumbersome to traverse with a wheelchair, especially for the front wheels. It wasn't until the industry explained and demonstrated that a running clearance was required that the tolerance was agreed upon.

The referenced edition of ASME A17.1 allows for a $1^1/_2$-inch (38 mm) clearance for private residence elevators. ICC A117.1 is more restrictive, but is consistent with the hoistway clearance for passenger elevators and LULAs.

409.4.4 Leveling. Each car shall automatically stop at a floor landing within a tolerance of $^1/_2$ inch (13 mm) under rated loading to zero loading conditions.

❖ When the car is at rest, the floor of the car must be within $^1/_2$ inch (13 mm) up or down from the floor of the level served.

409.4.5 Illumination. The level of illumination at the car controls, platform, and car threshold and landing sill shall be 5 foot-candles (54 lux) minimum.

❖ A minimum amount of illumination is necessary for the benefit of all people, but is especially important for people with limited mobility who must use greater care in moving about. The illumination level required by the model building codes for general means of egress purposes is 1 foot-candle (11 lux). The illumination level is the same as required by the referenced edition of ASME A17.1-1996.

409.4.6 Elevator Car Controls. Elevator car controls shall comply with Sections 409.4.6 and 309.4.

❖ Basically car controls must be located so that they are reachable by a person using a wheelchair. Controls must also meet operation requirements found in the operable parts provisions in Section 309.4.

409.4.6.1 Buttons. Control buttons shall be $^3/_4$ inch (19 mm) minimum in their smallest dimension. Control buttons shall be raised or flush.

❖ Minimum dimensions for the buttons ensure that the buttons are suitable for people who have limited use of their hands.

409.4.6.2 Height. Buttons with floor designations shall comply with Section 309.3.

❖ Car control buttons must be located within the reach ranges. Typically, buttons are located between 35 and 48 inches (890 and 1220 mm) above the floor (see Section 407.4.6.1). Controls located lower may be blocked by a wheelchair in the elevator.

409.4.6.3 Location. Controls shall be on a sidewall, 12 inches (305 mm) minimum from any adjacent wall.

❖ The location of controls within the cab will result in controls that are at the shoulder location or forward for a person using a wheelchair (see Figure 409.4.6.3). Locating the controls closer to the end walls could result in controls that were effectively behind the user and would be unreachable.

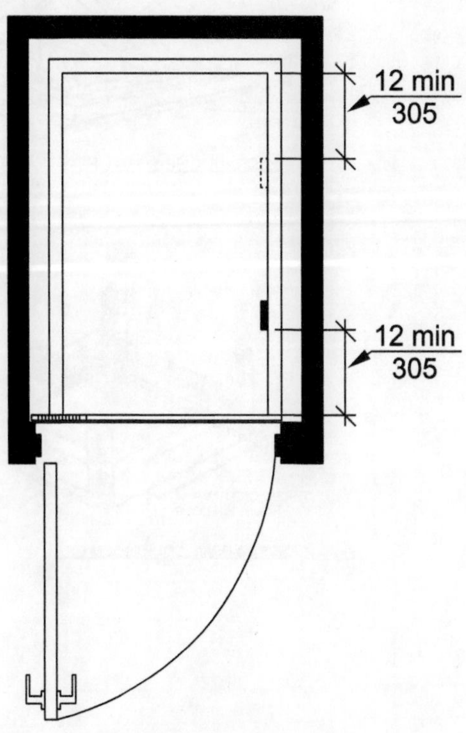

FIGURE 409.4.6.3
LOCATION OF CONTROLS IN PRIVATE RESIDENCE ELEVATORS

409.4.7 Emergency Communications. Emergency communications systems shall comply with Section 409.4.7.

❖ Private residence elevators must have emergency communication devices in case of an elevator malfunction or power outage.

409.4.7.1 Type. A telephone and emergency signal device shall be provided in the car.

❖ A phone that is connected to a central telephone exchange must be located within the cab. The phone line is typically located in the cab traveling cable. A cell phone is not acceptable because of concerns over batteries in the phones possibly running out, signal strength and power outages making the phones inoperable.

An emergency signaling device is also required in the elevator. This alarm is intended for internal notification and need not be connected to an outside alarm. If no one is in the house to assist, help can be summoned with the phone.

409.4.7.2 Operable Parts. The telephone and emergency signaling device shall comply with Section 309.3 and 309.4.

❖ The phone and the emergency signaling device must be located within reach ranges. Typically these devices are located adjacent to or under car controls. A consideration should be that a wheelchair in the cab would not block access to the phone and the emergency signaling system.

409.4.7.3 Compartment. If the device is in a closed compartment, the compartment door hardware shall comply with Section 309.

❖ If either the phone or the alarm is located in a closed compartment, the door hardware must meet the operable parts provisions including clear floor space, height and operation.

409.4.7.4 Cord. The telephone cord shall be 29 inches (735 mm) minimum in length.

❖ So that the phone cord will extend far enough for easy use, the cord must be a minimum of 29 inches (735 mm) long.

410 Platform Lifts

❖ During the development of the 2003 edition of ICC A117.1, platform lift requirements were editorially reformatted to harmonize with the April 2002 draft of the ADA/ABA Accessibility Guidelines. The authority having jurisdiction provides scoping for when platform lifts may be used as part of an accessible route for ingress and/or egress.

Platform lifts may move vertically or inclined. There are many different types of lifts. Some types require pits or floor depressions. Space for operational equipment is typically required immediately adjacent to the lift. See Commentary Figure C410 for examples of different types.

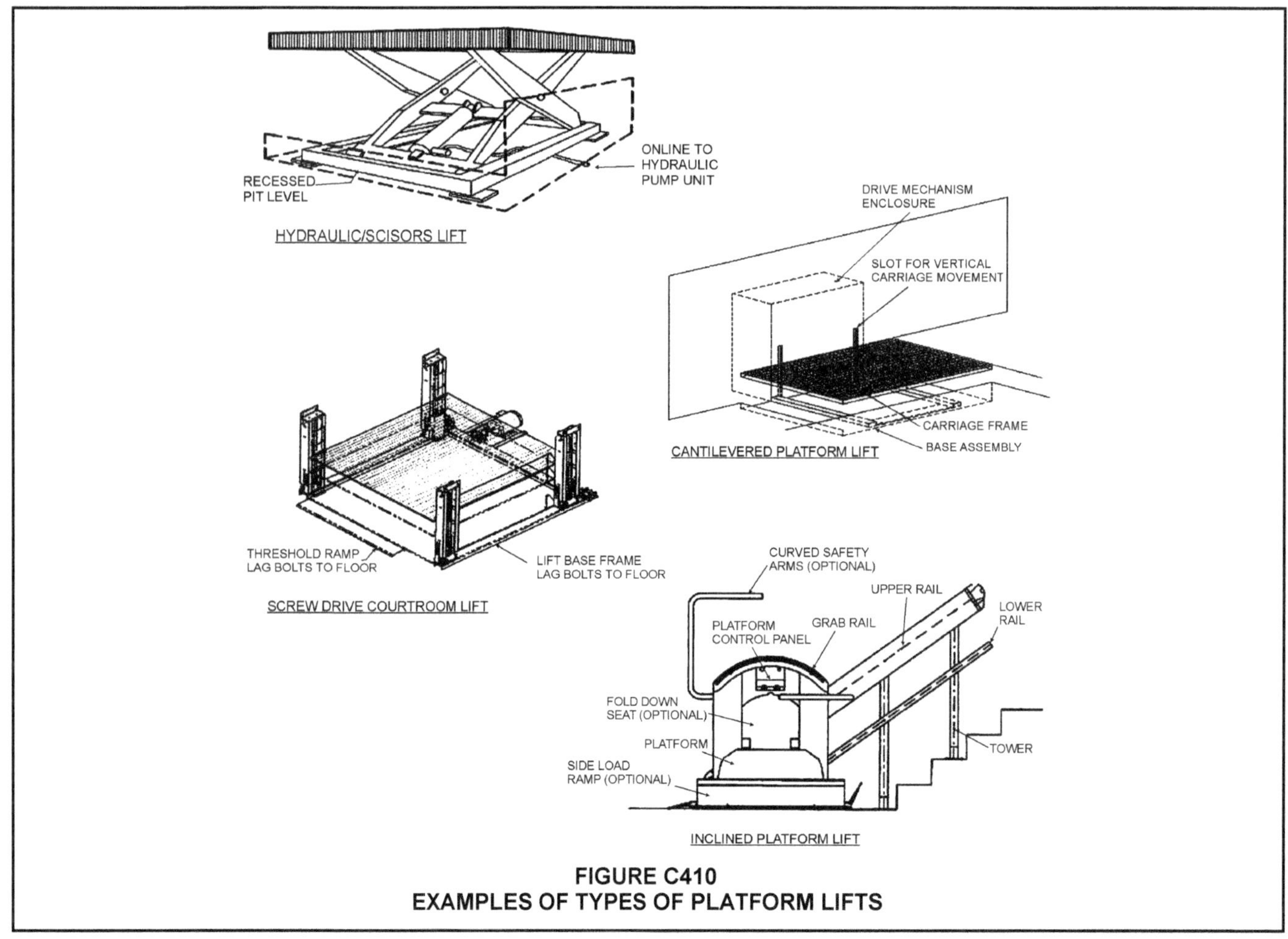

FIGURE C410
EXAMPLES OF TYPES OF PLATFORM LIFTS

410.1 General. Platform lifts shall comply with Section 410 and ASME A18.1 listed in Section 105.2.6. Platform lifts shall not be attendant operated and shall provide unassisted entry and exit from the lift.

❖ A platform lift consists of a platform designed to carry a user, traveling on an incline [see Commentary Figure C410.1(a)], such as along stairways, or vertically [see Commentary Figure C410.1(b)] to accomplish movement from one floor level to another. Typical building code scoping provisions permit these mechanisms to serve as part of an accessible route in new construction into limited applications, such as performing areas, wheelchair viewing areas, small areas not open to the general public, raised areas in courtrooms, amusement rides, play components, team or player seating, and within dwelling units. Platform lifts can also be part of the accessible means of egress when supplied with standby power. In existing buildings lifts can be used for any application requiring access if they are installed in compliance with the requirements of the referenced edition of ASME A18.1. Please see the building codes for specific scoping provisions.

The referenced edition of ASME A18.1 contains comprehensive requirements for the installation of platform lifts. For example, lifts are limited to penetrating one floor, and vertical platform lifts may not travel more than 12 feet (3660 mm). ASME A18.1 is currently being modified to allow for a maximum travel distance of 14 feet (4265 mm).

Platform lifts are not permitted to be of the attendant-operated type. To provide an appropriate degree of accessibility, the lift must be arranged to allow unassisted entry, operation and egress from the lift. Unassisted access is one of the reasons ASME A18.1 requires push button controls. The requirements for inclined lifts were changed in ASME 1a-2001. The new requirements eliminated the requirement for attendant operation by adding barrier arms around the perimeter of the platform to enclose the user. This change allows the incline lifts to be in compliance with this standard.

ASME A18.1 has a requirement that permits a fold-down seat on inclined platform lifts for use by ambulatory persons. Further, it does not prohibit a similar fold-down seat to accommodate ambulatory persons on vertical lifts. Persons with other types of mobility aids may also use these lifts [see Commentary Figure C410.1(c)]. For this reason and to coordinate with ASME A18.1, the term "platform" has replaced the term "wheelchair" to help clarify that ambulatory disabled persons can also use these lifts.

410.2 Lift Entry. Lifts with doors or gates shall comply with Section 410.2.1. Lifts with ramps shall comply with Section 410.2.2.

❖ Many lifts have doors or gates. Some lifts may include ramps to provided access onto the platform. This section does not require these items, but if they are installed, they must comply with the applicable section.

410.2.1 Doors and Gates. Doors and gates shall be low energy power operated doors or gates complying with Section 404.3. Doors shall remain open for 20 seconds minimum. On lifts with one door or with doors on opposite ends, the end door clear opening width shall be 32 inches (815 mm) minimum. On lifts with one door on a narrow end and one door on a long side, the end door clear opening width shall be 36 inches (915 mm) minimum. Side door clear opening width shall be 42 inches (1065 mm) minimum. Where a door is provided on a long side and on a narrow end of a lift, the side door shall be located with either the strike side or the

FIGURE C410.1(a)
INCLINED PLATFORM LIFT
(Photo courtesy of Wheelovator)

FIGURE C410.1(b)
VERTICAL LIFT
(Photo courtesy of Wheelovator)

hinge side in the corner furthest from the door on the narrow end.

EXCEPTIONS:

1. Doors or gates shall be permitted to be of the self-closing, manual type, where that door or gate provides access to a narrow end of the platform that serves only one landing. This exception shall not apply to doors or gates with ramps.
2. Lifts serving two landings maximum and having doors or gates on adjacent sides shall be permitted to have self closing manual doors or gates provided that the side door or gate is located with the strike side furthest from the end door. This exception shall not apply to door or gates with ramps.

❖ Lifts are required to have power operated doors or gates to make them more accessible. The power doors or gates are required to meet the same guidelines as other power operated doors (Section 404.3). Doors or gates should remain open for 20 seconds minimum to allow the user ample time to enter or exit the lift. Doors positioned on the narrow end of the platform are required to meet the same 32-inch (815 mm) minimum clear opening as other doors on an accessible route. Doors on the long side of a platform that have a 90-degree (1.6 rad) turn, need to be wider [42 inches (1065 mm) clear] to allow the user to complete the turn as he or she is entering or exiting the lift. Per Exception 1, lifts that both serve only two landings and that use doors or gates on opposite ends of the platform are not required to have power gates because the configuration allows the user to move straightforward when entering and exiting the lift in all entry and exit scenarios. Exception 2 provides the same option for platform lifts with doors on adjacent sides if the platform lift only serves two levels total. See Commentary Figure C410.2.1 for configurations where the exceptions would and would not be applicable. In addition, if there is a ramp to access the platform lift, the doors must be automatic.

FIGURE C410.1(c)
PERSON USING A SCOOTER ON A PLATFORM LIFT
(Photo courtesy of Wheelovator)

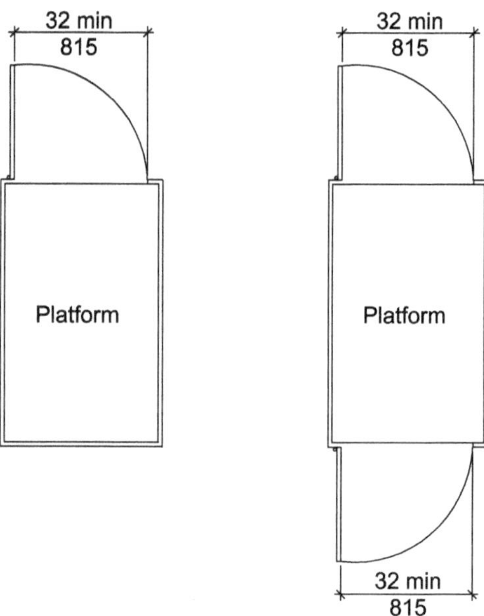

(a) Platform lift with door at one end or opposite ends

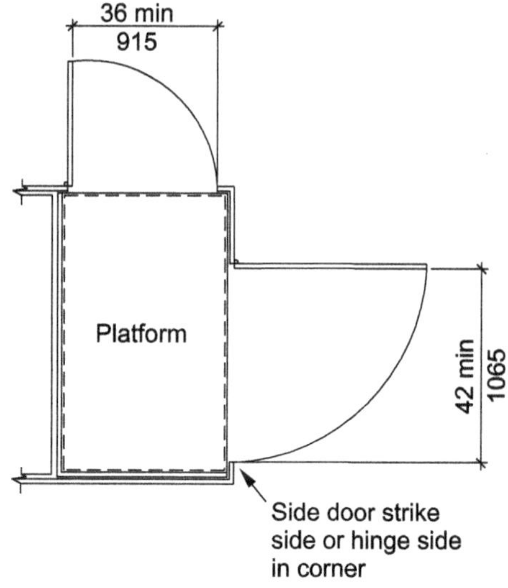

(b) Platform with doors on adjacent sides

FIGURE 410.2.1
PLATFORM LIFT DOORS AND GATES

410.2.2 Ramps. Ramp widths shall not be less than the platform opening they serve.

❖ When ramps provide access to the floor of the platform lift, ramps must be the same width as the platform door served. Ramps must also meet the slope, cross slope and edge protection restrictions found in Section 405.

410.3 Floor Surfaces. Floor surfaces of platform lifts shall comply with Section 302.

❖ The floor surface in the platform must be stable, firm and slip resistant. If carpet is installed, the carpet must meet the requirements in Section 302.2. By the reference in Section 302, any changes in elevation along the floor of the cab must be limited to the change inlevel provisions in Section 303. The criterion in Section 410.4 is more specific to this particular situation; therefore, Section 302.3 would not be applicable to the platform-to-runway clearance.

410.4 Platform to Runway Clearance. The clearance between the platform sill and the edge of any runway landing shall be $1^1/_4$ inch (32 mm) maximum.

❖ The vertical and horizontal clearance between the car platform sill and the edge of any runway landing is a required running clearance for movement of the lift. This clearance received much attention in the early 1970s. Persons using wheelchairs wanted the clearance to be close to zero. A large gap can be cumbersome to traverse with a wheelchair, especially for the front wheels. It wasn't until the industry explained and demonstrated that a running clearance was required that the tolerance was agreed upon.

410.5 Clear Floor Space. Clear floor space of platform lifts shall comply with Section 410.5.

❖ The size of the base for the platform lift depends on the configuration of the doors

410.5.1 Lifts with Single Door or Doors on Opposite Ends. Platform lifts with a single door or with doors on opposite ends shall provide a clear floor width of 36 inches (915 mm) minimum and a clear floor depth of 48 inches (1220 mm) minimum.

❖ The space available on the floor of the platform lift must provide a clear floor space consistent with the alcove provisions in Section 305.7.

410.5.2 Lifts with Doors on Adjacent Sides. Platform lifts with doors on adjacent sides shall provide a clear floor width of 42 inches (1065 mm) minimum and a clear floor depth of 60 inches (1525 mm) minimum.

EXCEPTION: In existing buildings, platform lifts with doors on adjacent sides shall be permitted to provide a clear floor width of 36 inches (915 mm) and a clear floor depth of 60 inches (1525 mm).

❖ The space available on the floor of the platform lift must provide a clear floor space consistent with the alcove provisions in Section 305.7. The exception for a narrower platform in existing buildings is based on the limitations that might occur because of the width of the existing stairway.

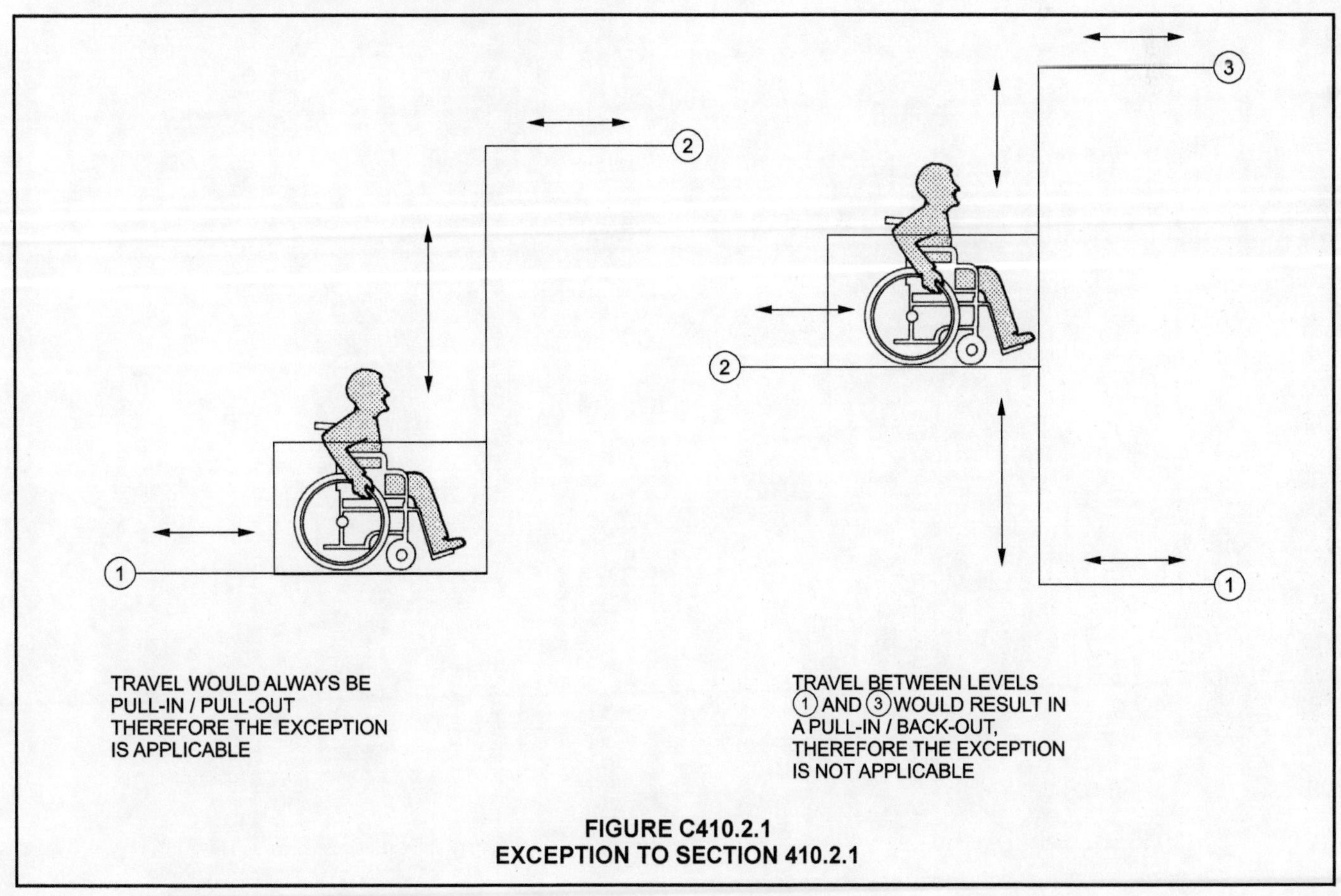

FIGURE C410.2.1
EXCEPTION TO SECTION 410.2.1

410.6 Operable Parts. Controls for platform lifts shall comply with Section 309.

❖ Basically platform lift controls, both inside and outside the lift, must be located so that the controls are reachable by a person using a wheelchair. Consideration should be given to the physical location of a wheelchair on the lift so the wheelchair will not block access to the controls. Controls must also meet operation requirements found in the operable parts provisions in Section 309.4. As indicated in ASME A18.1, key operation for normal operation of the platform lifts is not permitted.

Chapter 5. General Site and Building Elements

❖ Chapter 5 contains technical criteria for elements that are typically found outside a building, but on the site (e.g., parking spaces and passenger loading zones). This chapter also includes some specific building elements that may be specifically scoped by the authority having jurisdiction to be accessible (e.g., stairways and windows).

- Section 501 is a general statement about the Chapter 5 criteria being applicable for site and building elements that are referenced to this standard by the authority having jurisdiction.
- Section 502 contains criteria for car-accessible and van-accessible parking spaces and their associated signage.
- Section 503 provides criteria for passenger loading and drop-off zones.
- When stairways must be accessible, Section 504 provides provisions for stairway construction as well as the lighting and striping of stairways.
- The provisions in Section 505 are handrail requirements that are referenced from stairways (Section 504.6), ramps (Section 405.8) and when handrails are required along level walking surfaces (see Section 403.6).
- Section 506 provides a reference to operable parts requirements for windows that are required to be accessible.

501 General

501.1 Scope. General site and building elements required to be accessible by the scoping provisions adopted by the administrative authority shall comply with the applicable provisions of Chapter 5.

❖ This chapter mainly deals with general site elements such as parking and passenger loading zones and general building elements such as stairways, handrails, and windows. Note that these provisions apply to site and building elements as required by the scoping provisions (e.g., model codes) of the administrative authority (see Section 201).

502 Parking Spaces

502.1 General. Accessible car and van parking spaces shall comply with Section 502.

❖ This section provides the technical requirements for accessible parking spaces for both cars and vans. Typically zoning ordinances establish the number of parking spaces required and the scoping documents (e.g., model codes) specify the number of accessible spaces required. Parking spaces designated for persons with physical disabilities are required by the model codes to be located on the shortest accessible circulation route to an accessible entrance of the building. In separate parking structures or lots that do not serve a particular building, a parking space for a person with a physical disability must be located on the shortest accessible circulation route to an accessible pedestrian entrance of the parking facility (see Commentary Figure C502.1).

FIGURE C502.1
ACCESSIBLE PARKING SPACE

502.2 Vehicle Space Size. Car parking spaces shall be 96 inches (2440 mm) minimum in width. Van parking spaces shall be 132 inches (3350 mm) minimum in width.

> **EXCEPTION:** Van parking spaces shall be permitted to be 96 inches (2440 mm) minimum in width where the adjacent access aisle is 96 inches (2440 mm) minimum in width.

❖ The minimum width of the accessible car parking space is required to be 96 inches (2440 mm), while the accessible van space can be either 132 inches (3350 mm) or 96 inches (2440 mm), depending on the width of the associated access aisle [see Figure 502.2, Commentary Figure C502.4.1(a) and Section 502.4.2]. The combination of the parking space and the associated access aisle is what makes the total accessible parking space. The length of the space is left up to the designer of the parking lot or the administrative authority because the length is dependent on the types of vehicles the lot will serve. The length of an average car is 19 feet (5795 mm).

502.3 Vehicle Space Marking. Car and van parking spaces shall be marked to define the width. Where parking spaces are marked with lines, the width measurements of parking spaces and adjacent access aisles shall be made from the centerline of the markings.

EXCEPTION: Where parking spaces or access aisles are not adjacent to another parking space or access aisle, measurements shall be permitted to include the full width of the line defining the parking space or access aisle.

❖ The width of parking spaces must be designated in some manner. The most common way is painting stripes on the paved surface, but it could be some other alternative. This section provides guidance for the specific points used to measure the width of the accessible parking space. For access aisles, see Section 502.4.4. Where accessible parking spaces are part of a row of parking spaces or on the side adjacent to the access aisle, the width is measured to the center of the dividing/marking lines. An exception is allowed if the accessible space is adjacent to a curb or drive. Then the width can be measured to the edge of the space or to the outside edge of a painted line.

502.4 Access Aisle. Car and van parking spaces shall have an adjacent access aisle complying with Section 502.4.

❖ Each accessible space must have an associated access aisle where persons may transfer from their vehicle. The access aisle must meet the location, width, length and marking requirements in the following subsection (see Figure 502.4).

502.4.1 Location. Access aisles shall adjoin an accessible route. Two parking spaces shall be permitted to share a common access aisle. Access aisles shall not overlap with the vehicular way. Parking spaces shall be permitted to have access aisles placed on either side of the car or van parking space. Van parking spaces that are angled shall have access aisles located on the passenger side of the parking space.

❖ The access aisle is often the start or end of the accessible route between the accessible parking space and an accessible building entrance. As such, the access aisle must meet

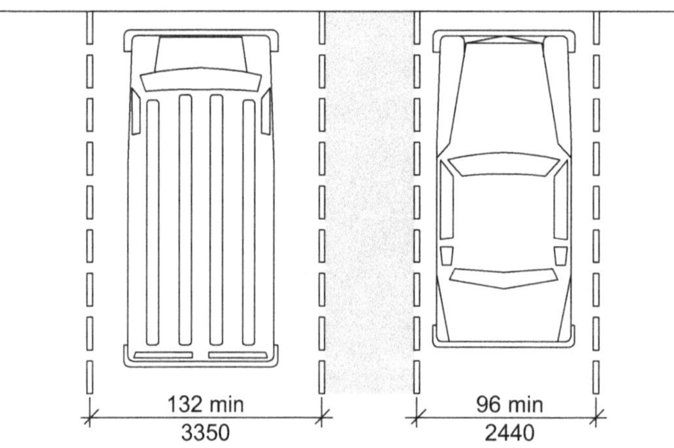

FIGURE 502.2
VEHICLE PARKING SPACE SIZE

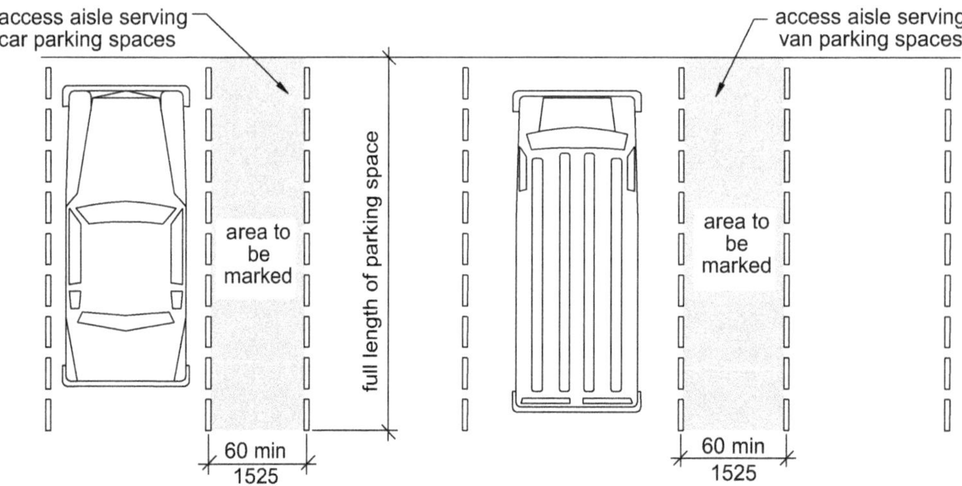

FIGURE 502.4
PARKING SPACE ACCESS AISLE

accessible route requirements, including the 1:48 maximum slope and a specified minimum width. The accessible route from other parking spaces or site arrival points may overlap the access aisle; however, if a built up curb ramp is used, it must not intrude into the access aisle. It is important that the slope in the access aisle be minimal to facilitate transfers. Often, the pedestrian circulation route to and from parking spaces is located immediately adjacent to and across the front of the parking spaces. In this event, the front (or rear) of the vehicles could possibly overhang the curb and extend into the circulation path. The accessible route requirements prohibit such vehicle overhangs from reducing the required clear width of the circulation route. This can be accomplished by providing curb stops that limit the distance a vehicle can extend into the circulation path or by providing a circulation path width sufficient to accommodate the vehicle overhang [see Commentary Figure C502.4.1(a)].

To minimize the amount of space committed to parking, the standard allows two adjacent accessible parking spaces to share a common access aisle. This is considered reasonable based on the unlikelihood of vehicles arriving simultaneously at both spaces and the occupants using the access aisle at the same time. If that does occur, one can wait while the other loads or unloads. In most situations it is anticipated that a driver would choose forward or backward parking as necessary to orient the access aisle to the transfer side of the vehicle. However, because van access is almost always from the passenger side, when angled parking is provided for the van space, the access aisle must be on the passenger side. Since most converted vans provide access through the passenger side, it would be beneficial to locate the van access aisle on the passenger side, even in straight-in parking.

For safety reasons, it is important that the access aisle not overlap the road or driveway where vehicles could possibly strike the person emerging from their vehicle. This is especially important when the option of parallel parking is provided [see Commentary Figure C502.4.1(b)]. The configuration for accessible parallel parking allows for either the driver or a passenger to transfer out of the vehicle.

The U.S. Access Board is developing requirements for the public right-of-way, which includes street parking. While this document does provide similar requirements for areas where there are enough easements, often existing sidewalks and buildings may create situations where alternatives must be considered. This proposed rule making is a good resource for practical alternatives for street parking configurations. The Department of Transportation has already started using this document as a means to provide equivalent facilitation.

502.4.2 Width. Access aisles serving car and van parking spaces shall be 60 inches (1525 mm) minimum in width.

❖ The required width of the parking space and adjacent access aisle is necessary to provide sufficient space for a person in a wheelchair to enter and exit a vehicle and to do so without being in the vehicular way.

The "universal space" for vans is a 132-inch-wide (3350 mm) parking space with a 60-inch-wide (1525 mm) access aisle. The exception to Section 502.2 would still permit the 96-inch-wide (2440 mm) van parking space adjacent to the 96-inch-wide (2440 mm) access aisle. Both spaces result in a total width of 182 inches (4880 mm). Using the 60-inch (1025 mm) aisle for both van and car spaces may help discourage parking in the access aisle.

A side lift mechanism that operates perpendicular to the van requires an aisle that is 96 inches (2440 mm) wide. The required 96 inches (2440 mm) is based on the distance

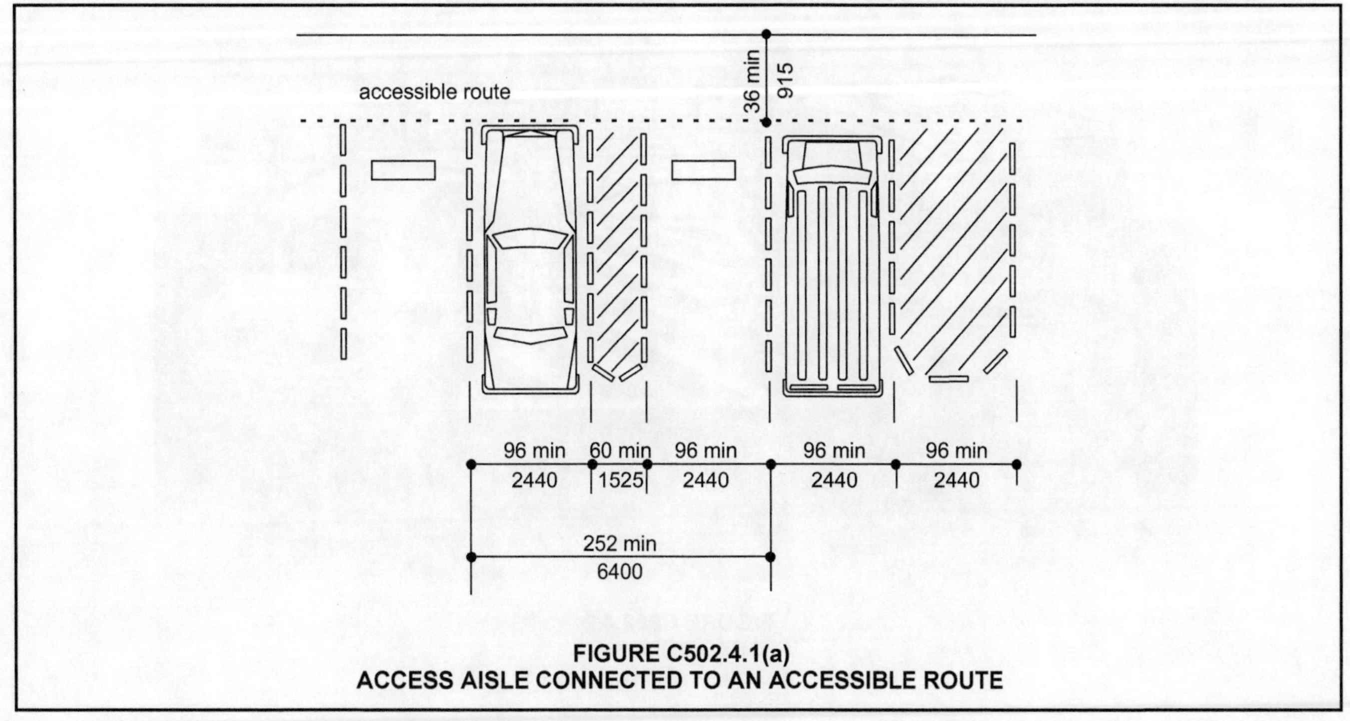

FIGURE C502.4.1(a)
ACCESS AISLE CONNECTED TO AN ACCESSIBLE ROUTE

the lift extends out from the side of the vehicle, i.e., 48 inches (1220 mm) for the lift and 48 inches (1220 mm) for the wheelchair that exits the lift perpendicular to the side of the vehicle (see Commentary Figure C502.4.2).

502.4.3 Length. Access aisles shall extend the full length of the parking spaces they serve.

❖ Vehicles vary in length. The access aisle must be the same length as the parking space it serves, be it compact car, van or bus. The average length for a parking space is 19 feet (5795 mm). The length of parking spaces is typically mandated by zoning laws or local ordinances.

502.4.4 Marking. Access aisles shall be marked so as to discourage parking in them. Where access aisles are marked with lines, the width measurements of access aisles and adjacent parking spaces shall be made from the centerline of the markings.

EXCEPTION: Where access aisles or parking spaces are not adjacent to another access aisle or parking space, measurements shall be permitted to include the full width of the line defining the access aisle or parking space.

❖ The access aisle should be marked or surfaced in a manner that makes it clear the access aisle is not a parking space.

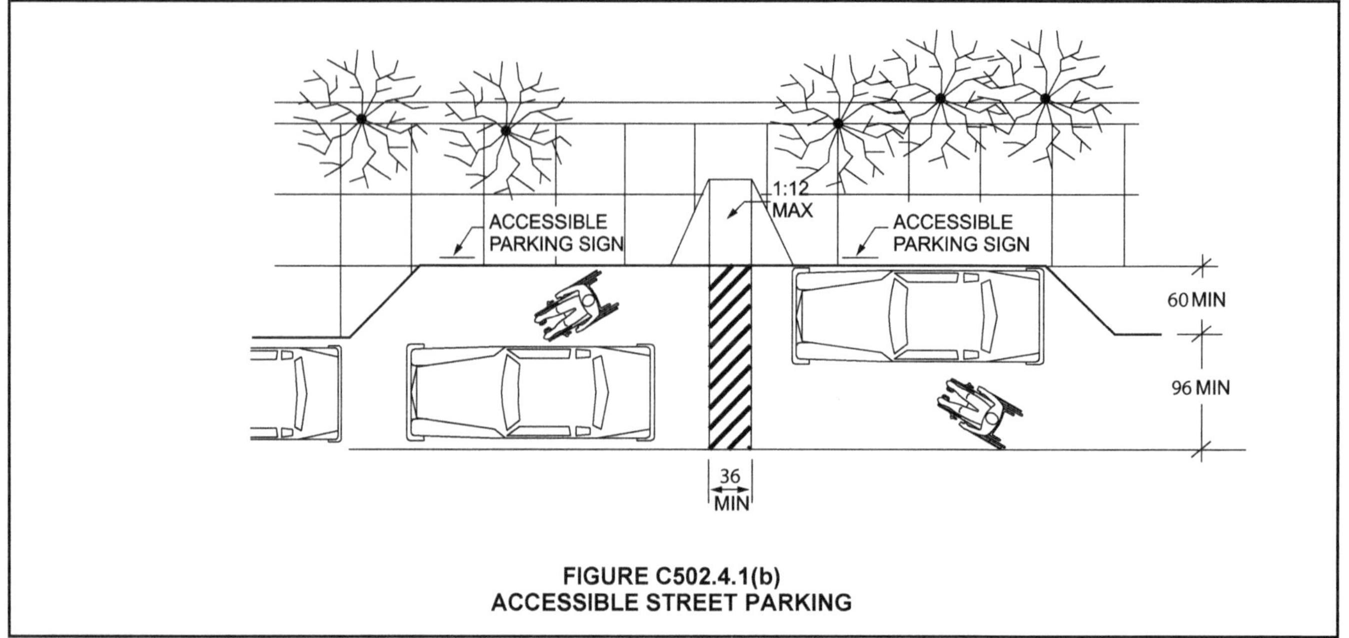

FIGURE C502.4.1(b)
ACCESSIBLE STREET PARKING

FIGURE C502.4.2
ACCESSIBLE VAN
(Drawing courtesy of U.S. Acess Board)

The access aisle must remain clear to allow for a person to approach the vehicle in a wheelchair and transfer into the car. The most common method of marking is striping on the paved surface. It is recommended that the access aisle should not be painted a different color over the entire surface. The types of paints typically used on parking lots are exceptionally slippery when wet and could cause problems during the approach and transfer to the vehicle in wet weather.

The width of the access aisle must be designated in some manner. The most common way is painting stripes on the paved surface, but it could be some other alternative. This section provides guidance for specific points to measure the width of the access aisle (See Section 502.3 for vehicle space marking). Where accessible parking spaces and access aisles are within a row of standard parking spaces, the width of the access aisle is measured to the center of the dividing/marking lines. The exception addresses access aisles adjacent to a curb or drive. The aisle width can then be measured to the outside edge of the line or whatever marks the edge of the space, such as a raised curb.

502.5 Floor Surfaces. Parking spaces and access aisles shall comply with Section 302 and have surface slopes not steeper than 1:48. Access aisles shall be at the same level as the parking spaces they serve.

❖ The accessible parking space and access aisles must be at the same elevation to facilitate entering and exiting a vehicle by a person in a wheelchair. It is unreasonably difficult to make the transition when the parking space and its access aisle are not level (with a slope of 1:48 maximum) or do not have a stable surface. Built-up curb ramps must be located so that they do not overlap the access aisle.

The suitability of an accessible route depends on certain characteristics of the surface itself. This section requires compliance with the general provisions of Section 302, which addresses characteristics that relate to both safety (slip resistance) and usability (stable and firm). Note that Section 104.4 states that the term "floor surface" refers to the finished floor or ground surface, as applicable.

Ambulatory and semi-ambulatory people who have difficulty maintaining balance, as well as those with restricted gaits, are particularly sensitive to slipping and tripping hazards. For such people, a stable and regular surface is necessary to walk safely. Wheelchairs are propelled most easily on surfaces that are hard, stable and regular. Soft, loose surfaces such as sand, gravel, crushed stone or wet clay, and irregular surfaces such as cobblestone, significantly impede movement of a wheelchair.

A stable surface is one that remains unchanged by contaminants or applied force, so that when the contaminant or force is removed, the surface returns to its original condition. A firm surface resists deformation by either indentation or particles moving on its surface. It is not the intent of the standard to require only paved surfaces; however, any other types (e.g., wood chips, gravel) would need to be evaluated.

Slip resistance is based on the frictional force necessary to keep a shoe or crutch tip from slipping on a walking surface under the conditions of use likely to be found on a given surface. For example, outside surfaces or entryways may be wet from rain or snow and should be evaluated under those conditions. Although it is known that the static coefficient of friction is one basis of slip resistance, there is not as yet a generally accepted method to evaluate the slip resistance of walking surfaces for all use conditions.

502.6 Vertical Clearance. A vertical clearance of 98 inches (2490 mm) minimum shall be provided at the following locations:

1. Parking spaces for vans.
2. The access aisles serving parking spaces for vans.
3. The vehicular routes serving parking spaces for vans.

❖ A height of 98 inches (2490 mm) minimum will accommodate most high-top lift-equipped vans. Vans retrofitted with lifts may have a higher profile because the roof of the van is raised to provide headroom within the van for someone sitting in a wheelchair. This is typically a concern in parking garages. The clearance must be maintained for the entire route from the entrances to the garage, to the accessible space and back out of the garage (including garage doors).

Although not required, because parking garages typically do not have adequate clearance throughout the garage, signage indicating the route to the van accessible spaces and the route to exit from those spaces would be beneficial to the user of the space as well as to the garage owner/operator.

502.7 Identification. Where accessible parking spaces are required to be identified by signs, the signs shall include the International Symbol of Accessibility complying with Section 703.6.3.1. Signs identifying van parking spaces shall contain the designation "van accessible." Such signs shall be 60 inches (1525 mm) minimum above the floor of the parking space, measured to the bottom of the sign.

❖ The International Symbol of Accessibility identifies the space as reserved for authorized vehicles. Typically, state Department of Transportation regulations have an additional requirement for text on the accessible parking signage, including fines for illegal parking. The required "van accessible" designation is intended to be informative, not restrictive, in identifying those spaces that are better suited for van use (see Commentary Figure C502.7).

Signs designating parking spaces for a person with a physical disability are seen from a driver's seat if the signs are mounted high enough above the ground and located at the front of a parking space. This provision effectively means that painting a symbol on the surface of the parking space does not by itself comply with the standard because it will be obscured when a vehicle is parked in the space, or by weather conditions, wear and tear darkness. Vehicle and traffic laws in many jurisdictions require that the symbol be mounted on a post or wall in front of the space as well as painted on the ground surface within the parking space. The sign for the space must be located or configured so that it will not be a protruding object (see commentary, Section 307.3).

FIGURE C502.7
EXAMPLE OF ACCESSIBLE
PARKING SPACE SIGNAGE

502.8 Relationship to Accessible Routes. Parking spaces and access aisles shall be designed so that cars and vans, when parked, cannot obstruct the required clear width of adjacent accessible routes.

❖ The access aisle is often the start or end of the accessible route between the accessible parking space and the accessible entrance. Often, the circulation route to and from parking spaces is located immediately adjacent to and across the front of the parking spaces. In this event, the front (or rear) of the vehicles will overhang the curb and extend into the circulation path.

The accessible route requirements prohibit vehicle overhangs from reducing the required clear width of the circulation route. This can be accomplished by providing curb stops that limit the distance a vehicle can extend into the circulation path or by providing a wider circulation path width sufficient to accommodate the vehicle overhang [see Commentary Figure C502.4.1(a)].

503 Passenger Loading Zones

503.1 General. Accessible passenger loading zones shall comply with Section 503.

❖ Passenger loading zones are typically required at institutional facilities such as assisted living facilities, hospitals and nursing homes. Passenger loading zones, when voluntarily provided, should also comply with these provisions.

Passenger loading zones that serve a particular building entrance should be located on the shortest accessible circulation route to an accessible entrance of the building (see Commentary Figure C503.1).

Passenger loading zones are fairly common at hotels; assembly occupancies such as theaters, convention facili-

FIGURE C503.1
PASSENGER DROP-OFF
(Drawing courtesy of U.S. Access Board)

ties, places of worship and restaurants; and at larger office and mercantile buildings. Where a parking valet service is provided, a passenger loading zone will be present.

503.2 Vehicle Pull-up Space Size. Passenger loading zones shall provide a vehicular pull-up space 96 inches (2440 mm) minimum in width and 20 feet (6095 mm) minimum in length.

❖ Passenger loading zones function in much the same manner as the access aisle adjacent to an accessible parking space except that they are not located at a permanent parking space. Passenger loading zones serve areas at which a vehicle will temporarily stop to load and unload passengers, and then depart. The vehicle space must be at least as wide as an accessible parking space and be the same length as the associated access aisle (see Section 503.3.3).

503.3 Access Aisle. Passenger loading zones shall have an adjacent access aisle complying with Section 503.3.

❖ An access aisle that serves as the passenger drop-off must have a stable and firm surface and be connected to an accessible route. The accessible route is typically accomplished with either a curb cut or a passenger drop-off and access aisle being constructed at the same elevation as the adjacent sidewalk. The following subsections contain criteria for the adjacency of the access aisle, the size and the markings (see Figure 503.3).

503.3.1 Location. Access aisles shall adjoin an accessible route. Access aisles shall not overlap the vehicular way.

❖ There must be an accessible route between the passenger drop-off zone and the accessible entrance. For safety the access aisle must not overlap any portion where there may be other moving vehicles, such as a car aisle or driveway (see Commentary Figure C503.1).

503.3.2 Width. Access aisles serving vehicle pull-up spaces shall be 60 inches (1525 mm) minimum in width.

❖ The access aisle must be the same width as that required for an accessible parking space (see Section 502.4.2).

The width of the parking space and adjacent access aisle must provide sufficient space for a person in a wheel-chair to enter and exit a vehicle and to do so without being in the vehicular way.

503.3.3 Length. Access aisles shall be 20 feet (6095 mm) minimum in length.

❖ The required length of 20 feet (6095 mm) provides the necessary range in which a vehicle can maneuver into and out of the space with the passenger side doors of the vehicle remaining positioned within the loading zone.

503.3.4 Marking. Access aisles shall be marked so as to discourage parking in them.

❖ The access aisle should be marked or surfaced in a manner that makes it clear the access aisle is not a parking space (see Commentary Figure C503.1). The access aisle must remain clear to allow a person in a wheelchair to approach the vehicle and transfer into the car. The most common method is striping on the paved surface. The access aisle should not be painted a different color over the entire surface. The types of paint typically used on parking lots are exceptionally slippery when wet and could cause problems during the approach and transfer to the vehicle.

503.4 Floor Surfaces. Vehicle pull-up spaces and access aisles serving them shall comply with Section 302 and shall have slopes not steeper than 1:48. Access aisles shall be at the same level as the vehicle pull-up space they serve.

❖ The accessible passenger loading zone and access aisle must be at the same elevation to facilitate a person in a wheelchair entering and exiting a vehicle. It would be unreasonably difficult to do so if the access aisle adjacent to the vehicle is not level (with a slope of 1:48 maximum), and does not have a stable surface. Note that Section 104.4 states that the term "floor surface" refers to the finished floor or ground surface, as applicable.

Ambulatory and semi-ambulatory people who have difficulty maintaining balance and those with restricted gaits are particularly sensitive to slipping and tripping hazards. For those people, a stable and regular surface is necessary to walk safely. Wheelchairs are propelled most easily on surfaces that are hard, stable and regular. Soft, loose surfaces such as sand, gravel, crushed stone or wet clay, and irregular surfaces such as cobblestone, significantly impede movement of a wheelchair.

A stable surface is one that remains unchanged by contaminants or applied force, so that when the contaminant or force is removed, the surface returns to its original condi-

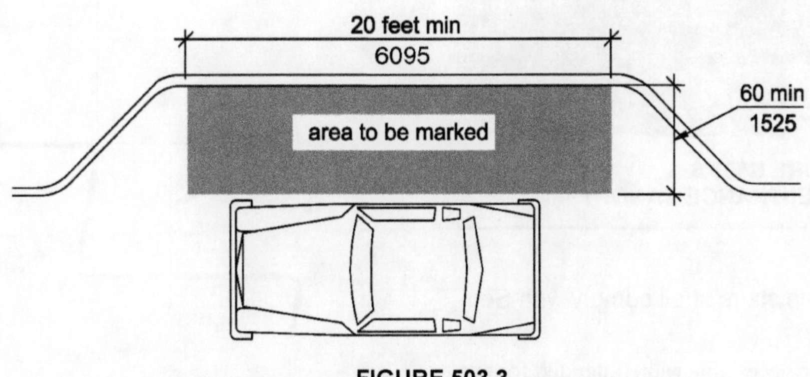

FIGURE 503.3
PASSENGER LOADING ZONE ACCESS AISLE

tion. A firm surface resists deformation by either indentation or particles moving on its surface. It is not the intent of the standard to require only paved surfaces; however, any other surface type (e.g., wood chips, gravel) would need to be evaluated.

Slip resistance is based on the frictional force necessary to keep a shoe or crutch tip from slipping on a walking surface under the conditions of use likely to be found on the surface. For example, outside surfaces or entryways may be wet from rain or snow and should be evaluated under those conditions. Although it is known that the static coefficient of friction is one basis of slip resistance, there is not as yet a generally accepted method to evaluate the slip resistance of walking surfaces for all uses.

503.5 Vertical Clearance. A vertical clearance of 114 inches (2895 mm) minimum shall be provided at the following locations:

1. Vehicle pull-up spaces;
2. The access aisles serving vehicle pull-up spaces;
3. A vehicular route from an entrance to the passenger loading zone, and;
4. A vehicular route from the passenger loading zone to a vehicular exit serving vehicle pull-up spaces.

❖ A height of 114 inches (9 ft.-6 in.) or (2895 mm) minimum will accommodate most high-top lift-equipped vans and small buses. A van retrofitted with a lift may have a higher profile because the roof of the van is raised to provide headroom within the van for someone sitting in a wheelchair. This is typically a concern at entrance canopies (see Commentary Figure C503.5).

FIGURE C503.5
EXAMPLE OF ENTRANCE CANOPY

504 Stairways

504.1 General. Accessible stairs shall comply with Section 504.

❖ Stairs cannot be part of an accessible route intended for use by persons who use wheelchairs. Stairs are "accessible" only to the extent that they comply with Section 504. These criteria for stairs provide greater usability for persons who are ambulatory, but have a mobility disability; in this case, stairs may be usable as a means of ingress and egress. Use of these criteria throughout a building or complex of buildings will also provide consistency that persons with vision impairments can rely on in their travels.

The model codes contain provisions for stairways that are more extensive than the provisions in this section. For example, there are no provisions in this standard for guards at drop-offs adjacent to stairs or consistency/variation in the riser height along a stairway run. Additionally, this standard does not address specifics that are unique to spiral and curved stairways.

504.2 Treads and Risers. All steps on a flight of stairs shall have uniform riser height and uniform tread depth. Risers shall be 4 inches (100 mm) minimum and 7 inches (180 mm) maximum in height. Treads shall be 11 inches (280 mm) minimum in depth.

❖ A great deal of research has been conducted and much debate has occurred over appropriate tread and riser dimensions, much of it in the forums for development of the model building codes. The tread and riser dimensions specified in this standard are consistent with those in the model building codes, with the exception of those stairs that are within individual dwelling units. The tread depth is based on the largest shoe size found within 95 percent of the adult population. An 11-inch (280 mm) tread allows for an appropriate amount of overhang beyond the tread nosing in descent. The combination of an 11-inch (280 mm) tread and a 7-inch (180 mm) rise provides a favorable stairway geometry for user comfort, expenditure of energy and rate of misstep as measured in research. If a nosing is provided in accordance with Section 504.5, the minimum tread depth must be measured past the nosing to allow for proper foot placement when descending the stairs (see Figure 504.2 and Commentary Figure C504.2).

Dimensional uniformity in riser and tread dimensions greatly reduces the tripping hazard for all users. Minimum requirements for variation along a stair flight are addressed in the model codes.

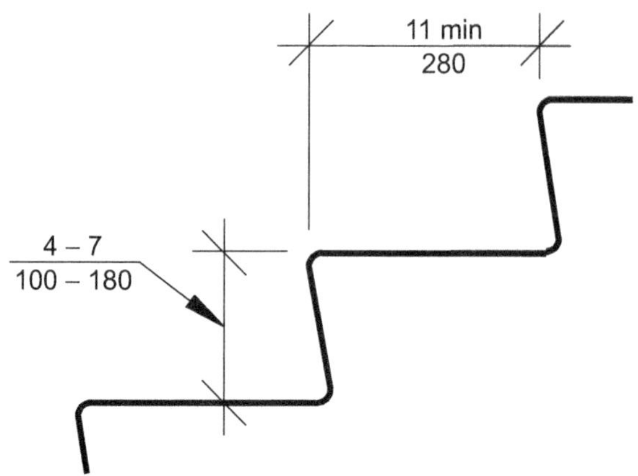

FIGURE 504.2
TREADS AND RISERS FOR ACCESSIBLE STAIRWAYS

504.3 Open Risers. Open risers shall not be permitted.

❖ Open risers present a detection problem for persons using long canes to sense the environment. Open risers also increase the potential for the toe of the foot to catch on the underside of the tread above when ascending, possibly resulting in a misstep or preventing further ascent.

504.4 Tread Surface. Stair treads shall comply with Section 302 and shall have a slope not steeper than 1:48.

❖ Stair treads must be a stable and firm surface. Openings in the tread surface are limited to $^1/_2$ inch (13 mm). Grating may be necessary so that the surfaces will not accumulate snow or water in outdoor locations. Treads must be level, but may be sloped to drain where needed.

Ambulatory and semi-ambulatory people who have difficulty maintaining balance and those with restricted gaits are particularly sensitive to slipping and tripping hazards. For those people, a stable and regular surface is necessary to walk safely.

A stable surface is one that remains unchanged by contaminants or applied force, so that when the contaminant or force is removed, the surface returns to its original condition. A firm surface resists deformation by either indentation or particles moving on its surface.

Slip resistance is based on the frictional force necessary to keep a shoe or crutch tip from slipping on a walking surface under the likely conditions of use. For example, outside steps or steps near entryways may be wet from rain or snow and should be evaluated under those conditions; surfaces on the inside stairway would typically not be influenced by outside weather and should be evaluated in a dry condition. Although it is known that the static coefficient of friction is one basis of slip resistance, there is not as yet a generally accepted method to evaluate the slip resistance of walking surfaces for all use conditions.

504.5 Nosings. The radius of curvature at the leading edge of the tread shall be $^1/_2$ inch (13 mm) maximum. Nosings that project beyond risers shall have the underside of the leading edge curved or beveled. Risers shall be permitted to slope under the tread at an angle of 30 degrees maximum from vertical. The permitted projection of the nosing shall be $1^1/_2$ inches (38 mm) maximum over the tread or floor below.

❖ Nosing dimensions are important to smooth, stable stairway usage. On descent, an excessively beveled nosing can reduce the available tread depth to the extent that this may cause the foot to pitch forward or slide off the tread. On stairway ascent, these criteria minimize the potential for the toe of a shoe to catch and be held by the underside of the tread above (see Figure 504.5 and Commentary Figure C504.5).

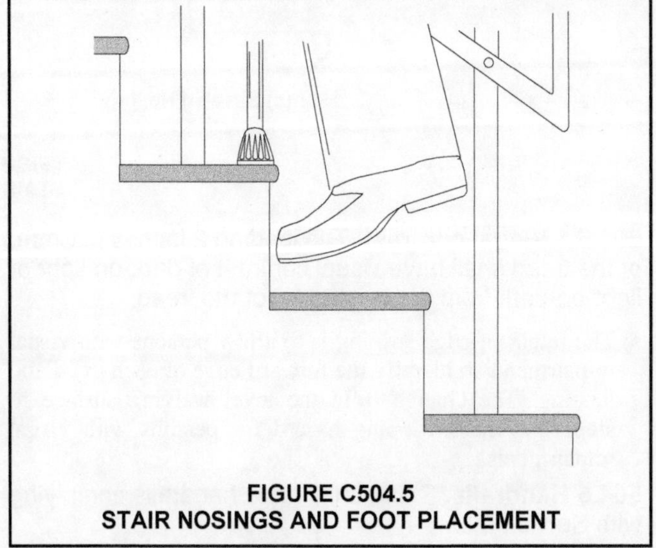

FIGURE C504.5
STAIR NOSINGS AND FOOT PLACEMENT

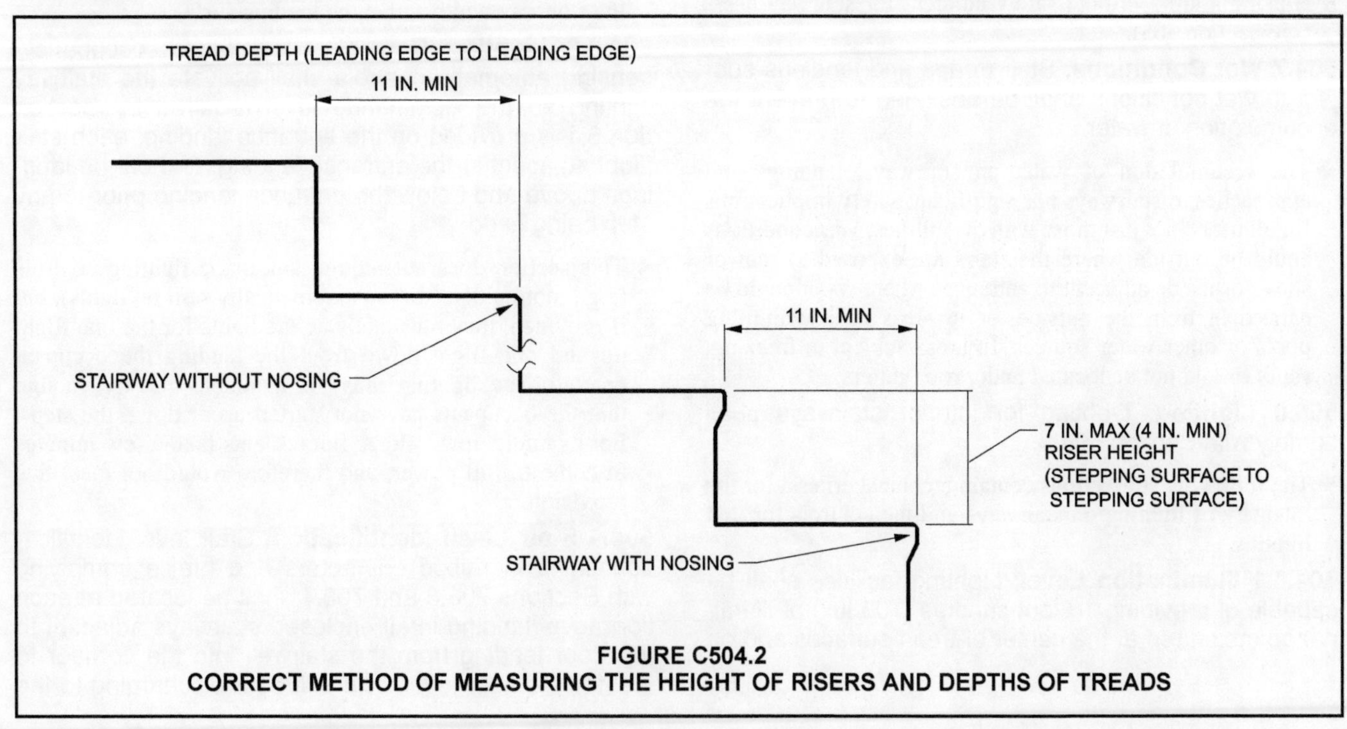

FIGURE C504.2
CORRECT METHOD OF MEASURING THE HEIGHT OF RISERS AND DEPTHS OF TREADS

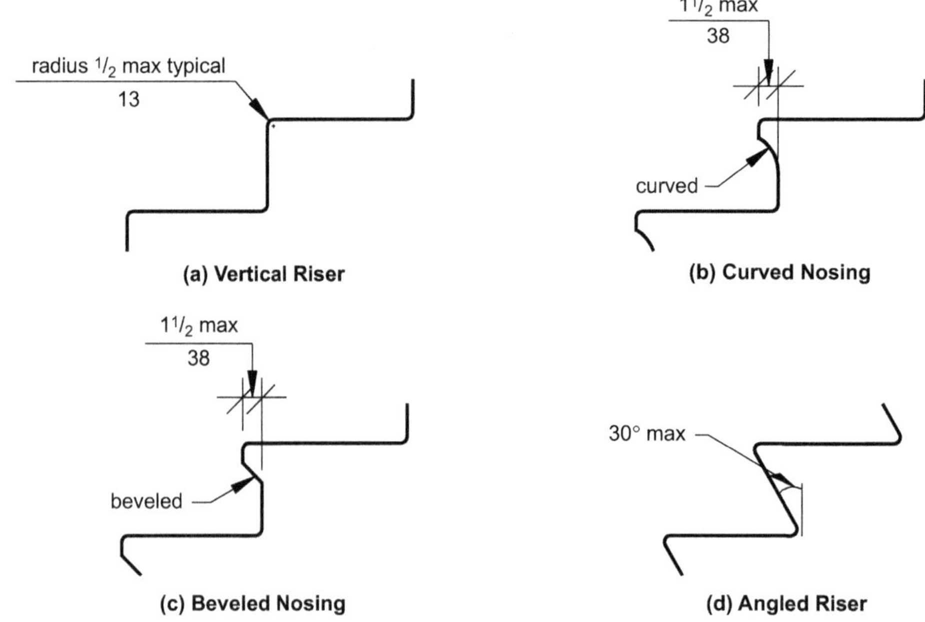

FIGURE 504.5
STAIR NOSINGS

504.5.1 Visual contrast. The leading 2 inches (51 mm) of the tread shall have visual contrast of dark-on-light or light-on-dark from the remainder of the tread.

❖ The intent of edge striping is to allow persons with visual impairments to identify the forward edge of each tread and landing. The change from the level walking surface to steps may be a tripping hazard for persons with visual impairments.

504.6 Handrails. Stairs shall have handrails complying with Section 505.

❖ Handrails are a critical safety element for stairway users (see Section 505).

504.7 Wet Conditions. Stair treads and landings subject to wet conditions shall be designed to prevent the accumulation of water.

❖ The accumulation of water on stairways, landings and approaches to stairways has significant safety implications for all users, not just those with disabilities. Wet conditions could be outside where the stairs are exposed to rain or snow, or inside adjacent to entrances where water could be carried in from the outside, or in areas near swimming pools or other water sources. In areas subject to freezing, stairs should not be located under roof gutters.

504.8 Lighting. Lighting for interior stairways shall comply with Section 504.8.

❖ The following subsections contain technical criteria for the intensity of lighting on stairways and the controls for that lighting.

504.8.1 Illumination Level. Lighting facilities shall be capable of providing 10 foot-candles (108 lux) of illuminance measured at the center of tread surfaces and on landing surfaces within 24 inches (610 mm) of step nosings.

❖ Model codes typically require a minimum of 1 foot-candle (11 lux) for the path for means of egress from a building. This section specifies that the light fixtures for the stairways must be capable of providing a minimum of 10 footcandles (108 lux). For treads, the lighting level should be measured at the center of stairway width and tread depth at the surface of the tread. For a landing, the light level should be measured within 24 inches (610 mm) from the edge of the landing on the side adjacent to the stairway run, in the center of the stairway width and at the landing surface.

504.8.2 Lighting Controls. If provided, occupancy-sensing automatic controls shall activate the stairway lighting so the illuminance level required by Section 504.8.1 is provided on the entrance landing, each stair flight adjacent to the entrance landing, and on the landings above and below the entrance landing prior to any step being used.

❖ This section does not require automatic lighting controls (e.g., motion detectors to automatically turn on lights), but if provided, they must activate the lights for the one flight up and one flight down from the landing the occupant entered. The lighting must be available quickly enough that the occupants have not started up or down the steps. For example, low-voltage fluorescents take a few minutes to come to full power, and therefore would not meet this provision.

504.9 Stair Level Identification. Stair level identification signs in raised characters and braille complying with Sections 703.3 and 703.4 shall be located at each floor level landing in all enclosed stairways adjacent to the door leading from the stairwell into the corridor to identify the floor level. The exit door discharging to the outside or to the level of exit discharge shall have a sign with raised characters and braille stating "EXIT."

❖ Raised numerals and braille signage must be provided adjacent to each door in a stairway indicating the floor level. This is in addition to the signage required by the model codes where floor levels must be identified on the wall across from the door so that occupants or emergency responders in the stairway can identify the level they are on.

At the door that leads to the outside, there should be additional raised and braille signage indicating "Exit." This requirement should still be followed when the stairway discharges to a lobby or exit passageway instead of directly to the exterior.

505 Handrails

505.1 General. Handrails required by Section 405.8 for ramps, or Section 504.6 for stairs, shall comply with Section 505.

❖ This standard generally is consistent with the requirements in the model building codes for handrail requirements. In the event of a conflict, the building code typically will supersede the standard. Structural requirements for handrails also are contained in the model building codes.

Handrails are required on ramp runs with a rise of more than 6 inches (150 mm) (see Section 405.8) and accessible stairways (see Section 504.6). Handrails are not required on curb ramps even when a curb is greater than 6 inches (150 mm) in height (see Section 406.9). Handrails are not required on walking surfaces with running slopes less than 1:20 (see the definition for "Ramp" in Section 106.5). However, handrails must comply with Sections 505.4 through 505.9 (see Section 403.6) when they are required in corridors (e.g., nursing homes or hospitals).

505.2 Location. Handrails shall be provided on both sides of stairs and ramps.

EXCEPTIONS:

1. In assembly seating areas, handrails shall not be required on both sides along aisle stairs, provided with a handrail either at the side or within the aisle.
2. In assembly seating areas, handrails shall not be required on the sides of ramped aisles serving seats.

❖ Handrails are an important safety consideration in the use of stairways and ramps for all people, not just people with disabilities. Because people can travel on either side of a stairway or a ramp, it is appropriate to require handrails on both sides to ensure that a handrail is available. This also enables persons with a mobility impairment to use the side of the ramp or stairway that corresponds to their strength, which may be significantly greater on their left or right.

Additional intermediate handrails can be provided if desired on ramps [see Commentary Figure C505.2(b)]. The building codes require additional handrails based on capacity requirements for stairways.

In the case of aisle stairs and aisle ramps, typically occurring in assembly occupancies, requiring handrails on both sides generally is unnecessary and may unduly impede access to and egress from assembly seating. The standard, therefore, within assembly seating areas, allows a single handrail either at one side or in the center of the aisle stairways [see Commentary Figure C505.2(a)] and no handrails along ramped aisles.

FIGURE C505.2(a)
AISLE STAIR HANDRAILS

FIGURE C505.2(b)
INTERMEDIATE HANDRAILS ON A RAMP

505.3 Continuity. Handrails shall be continuous within the full length of each stair flight or ramp run. Inside handrails on switchback or dogleg stairs or ramps shall be continuous between flights or runs. Other handrails shall comply with Sections 505.10 and 307.

> **EXCEPTION:** Handrails shall not be required to be continuous in aisles serving seating where handrails are discontinuous to provide access to seating and to permit crossovers within the aisles.

❖ Continuity of handrails is important so that gaps do not occur that would require people to release their grip and thus no longer be able to arrest their fall or steady themselves should they slip or misstep at that point. The exception recognizes the practical necessity of breaking handrail continuity at aisle seating to allow full access to seats [see Commentary Figure C505.2(a)].

It is reasonable to require the inside handrail of a stairway or ramp that turns or reverses direction (i.e., U-turn) to be continuous around the turn. This also provides the user with a continuous gripping surface while the turn is being negotiated and restaging for the next set of steps or ramp slope. Additionally, the continuous handrail may act as an indicator to users who are blind or have low vision that a stair run has not terminated and allows the user to anticipate additional steps.

The references to Sections 307 and 505.10 indicate that the handrail ends must comply with the applicable extensions and return in a manner that will make the ends readily detectable and not acting as protruding objects.

505.4 Height. Top of gripping surfaces of handrails shall be 34 inches (865 mm) minimum and 38 inches (965 mm) maximum vertically above stair nosings, ramp surfaces and walking surfaces. Handrails shall be at a consistent height above stair nosings, ramp surfaces and walking surfaces.

❖ The specified range for handrail heights corresponds to that determined appropriate for effectively arresting a fall on the stairway or ramp. Consistency of the handrail height is important so as not to affect the balance and cadence of the user (see Figure 505.4).

The heights for handrails are based on adults. When children are the principal user of a building (e.g., elementary school, children's museum), a second set of handrails at an appropriate height can assist them. A maximum height of 28 inches (715 mm) to the top of the gripping surface is recommended for handrails designed for children. Sufficient vertical clearance between upper and lower handrails, 9 inches (230 mm) minimum, should be provided to help prevent entrapment. Concerns for the climbability of the two handrail configuration should be considered as part of the design to help prevent children from attempting to climb the rails and end up falling over the guard along the side of the stair.

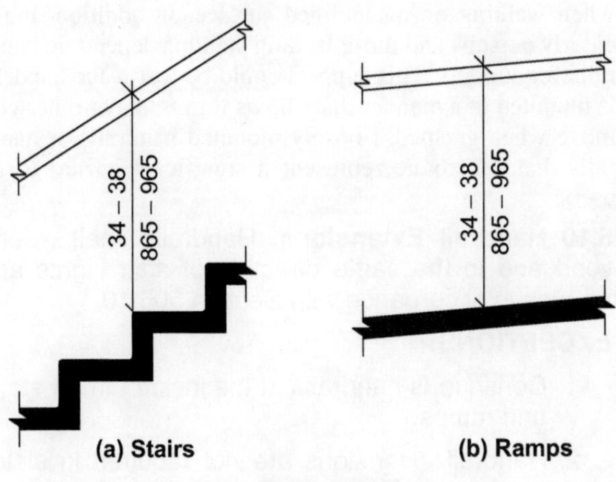

FIGURE 505.4
HANDRAIL HEIGHT

505.5 Clearance. Clearance between handrail gripping surface and adjacent surfaces shall be $1^1/_2$ inches (38 mm) minimum.

❖ The clearance required between a handrail and the adjacent wall surface is the minimum clearance necessary to allow the hand to fully grasp the handrail. The required clearance is a minimum dimension, unlike the absolute dimension required for grab bars. A clearance more than $1^1/_2$ inches (38 mm) is permitted for handrails because they are not used in the same manner as grab bars. At locations where gloved hands are likely, greater finger clearance is warranted (See Figure 505.5).

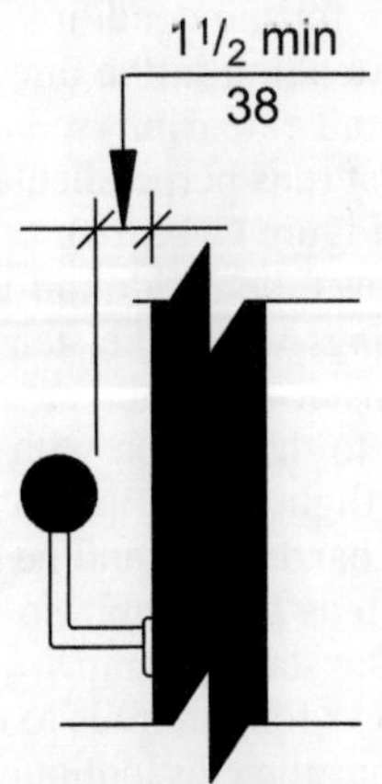

FIGURE 505.5
HANDRAIL CLEARANCE

505.6 Gripping Surface. Gripping surfaces shall be continuous, without interruption by newel posts, other construction elements, or obstructions.

EXCEPTIONS:

1. Handrail brackets or balusters attached to the bottom surface of the handrail shall not be considered obstructions, provided the brackets or balusters comply with the following criteria:
   a. Not more than 20 percent of the handrail length is obstructed,
   b. Horizontal projections beyond the sides of the handrail occur $1^1/_2$ inches (38 mm) minimum below the bottom of the handrail, and provided that for each $^1/_2$ inch (13 mm) of additional handrail perimeter dimension above 4 inches (100 mm), the vertical clearance dimension of $1^1/_2$ inch (38 mm) can be reduced by $^1/_8$ inch (3.2 mm), and
   c. Edges shall be rounded.
2. Where handrails are provided along walking surfaces with slopes not steeper than 1:20, the bottoms of handrail gripping surfaces shall be permitted to be obstructed along their entire length where they are integral to crash rails or bumper guards.

❖ Requiring continuity of the gripping surface affects specific details of the installation and mounting method for the handrail. As the hand slides along the handrail, no interruptions or obstructions can be encountered that will require users to release their grip to bypass the obstruction. For example, a handrail bracket that attaches to the side of the handrail will not allow the hand to slide past it without releasing the grip. Conversely, a bracket can be attached to the bottom surface of the handrail so that it will pass between the tips of the fingers as the hand slides past the bracket. The larger handrail size permits shorter brackets because geometrically the finger clearance is still maintained.

When combination crash rails and handrails are installed along the walls for balance assistance, the bottom of the handrail may be continually obstructed (see Commentary Figure C505.6).

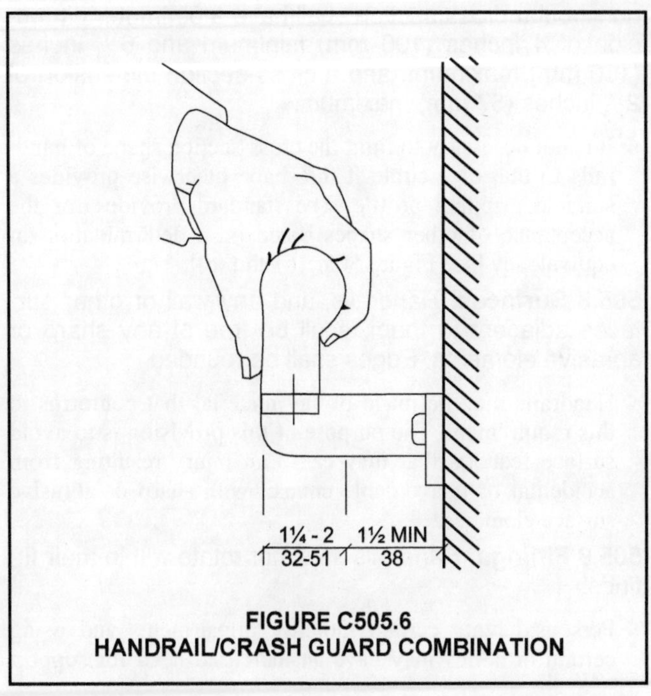

FIGURE C505.6
HANDRAIL/CRASH GUARD COMBINATION

505.7 Cross Section. Handrails shall have a cross section complying with Section 505.7.1 or 505.7.2.

❖ A handrail must be graspable with a power grip, not a pinching grip. Choices for either a circular cross section or shapes that provide equivalent graspability are indicated in the subsections that follow.

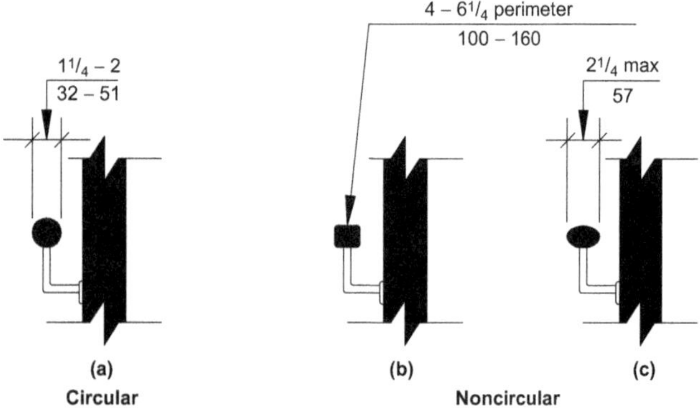

FIGURE 505.7
HANDRAIL CROSS SECTION

505.7.1 Circular Cross Section. Handrails with a circular cross section shall have an outside diameter of $1^1/_4$ inches (32 mm) minimum and 2 inches (51 mm) maximum.

❖ The shape of a handrail affects the ability to secure a power grip on the handrail. Shapes that are too narrow or too large in cross section will not allow a grip sufficient to enable the user to arrest a fall. These criteria are based on geometry that enables an average able-bodied person to securely grasp the handrail [see Figure 505.7(a)].

505.7.2 Noncircular Cross Sections. Handrails with a noncircular cross section shall have a perimeter dimension of 4 inches (100 mm) minimum and $6^1/_4$ inches (160 mm) maximum, and a cross-section dimension of $2^1/_4$ inches (57 mm) maximum.

❖ It is not necessary to limit the cross-section shape of handrails to that of a circle if the shape otherwise provides a suitable gripping profile. The standard provides for the acceptance of other shapes based on a determination of equivalency [see Figure 505.7(b) and (c)].

505.8 Surfaces. Handrails, and any wall or other surfaces adjacent to them, shall be free of any sharp or abrasive elements. Edges shall be rounded.

❖ Handrails may be made of any material that conforms to this requirement. The purpose of this provision is to avoid surface features that may cause an injury resulting from accidental or unavoidable contact with sharp or abrasive surface elements.

505.9 Fittings. Handrails shall not rotate within their fittings.

❖ Persons having certain mobility impairments and using certain orthotics may have an increased need for support when walking on an inclined surface. In addition, many elderly persons and those lacking stamina depend on handrails for support. This support could be lost if the handrail is mounted in a manner that allows it to rotate or otherwise move when grasped. Loosely mounted handrails or handrails that can rotate represent a significant hazard to all users.

505.10 Handrail Extensions. Handrails shall extend beyond and in the same direction of stair flights and ramp runs in accordance with Section 505.10.

EXCEPTIONS:

1. Continuous handrails at the inside turn of stairs and ramps.
2. Handrail extensions are not required in aisles serving seating where the handrails are discontinuous to provide access to seating and to permit crossovers within the aisle.
3. In alterations, full extensions of handrails shall not be required where such extensions would be hazardous due to plan configuration.

❖ Horizontal extensions and continuity at turns are beneficial for all users. Handrail extensions are especially needed by persons who wear leg braces or have similar disabilities. People with balance concerns use the handrail to balance themselves as they make the transition between the stepped or sloping surfaces and the landings. Bending the handrail extension at 90 degrees (1.6 rad) to the direction of travel puts the extension out of reach and defeats its purpose; therefore, the handrail top and bottom extension must extend in the same direction as the stair flight or ramp run. Exception 3 allows for the condition in existing buildings where handrails extending in the direction of the stairway may result in handrail extensions reducing the width of the means of egress that runs perpendicular to the stairway run (see Commentary Figure C505.10).

Exception 1 allows the inside rail to be continuous and not extend at landings where the stairway or ramp continues. Continuous, inside handrails on switchback or dogleg stairs can indicate to the person with a visual impairment that another stair flight or ramp run begins immediately after the turn. The handrail should be installed at a consistent height as much as practicable so that the handrail has the same slope as the stair or ramp.

Exception 2 allows for handrails to not have top and bottom extensions on the discontinuous handrails along stepped or sloped aisles that serve assembly seating areas. The handrail extension would block access to seats and possibly obstruct cross aisles, thus proving to be more of a hazard than a benefit [see Commentary Figure C505.2(a)].

505.10.1 Top and Bottom Extension at Ramps. Ramp handrails shall extend horizontally above the landing 12 inches (305 mm) minimum beyond the top and bottom of ramp runs. Extensions shall return to a wall, guard, or floor, or shall be continuous to the handrail of an adjacent ramp run.

❖ An extension of 12 inches (305 mm) will provide a sufficient length of handrail to enable users to complete the travel on the ramp and reach a stable, level floor area before having to release their grip. The requirement that the handrail return to the wall, guard or floor, or be continuous to the next segment, is intended to avoid a handrail end projecting out in mid-air and thus having the potential for unintended impact with the protruding end.

Handrails should return to the wall, guard, ground or support. Two concerns need to be addressed. The handrail extension must be formed so that clothing or carried items would not catch on the end and returns on handrail extensions must not become protruding objects for people crossing perpendicular to the ramp. Handrails that extend into circulation routes must be designed to be detectable by persons using a long cane (see Figure 505.10.1).

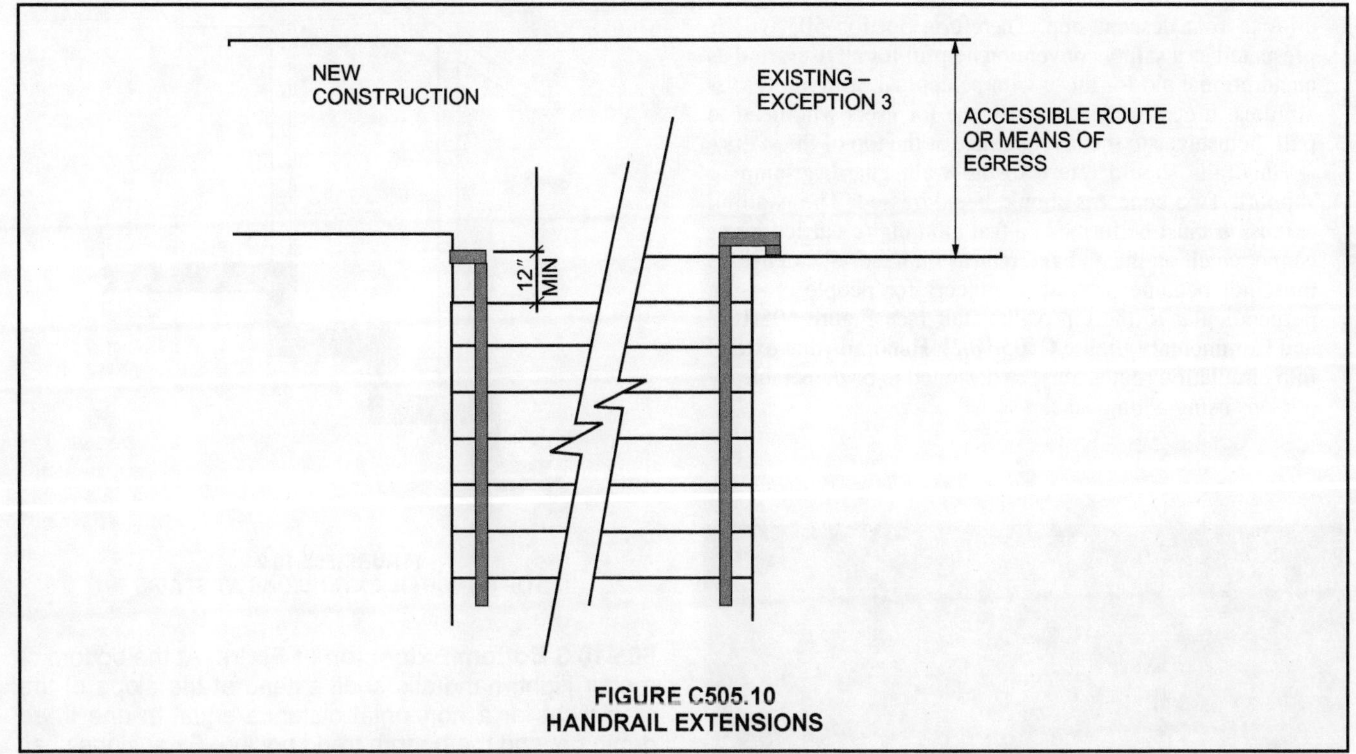

FIGURE C505.10
HANDRAIL EXTENSIONS

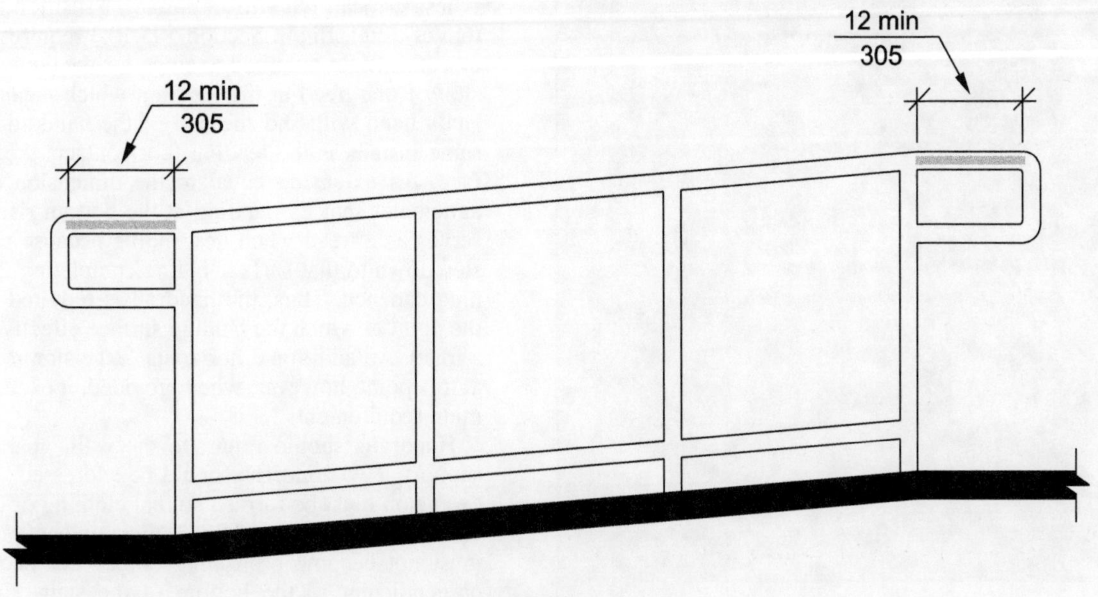

FIGURE 505.10.1
TOP AND BOTTOM HANDRAIL EXTENSIONS AT RAMP

505.10.2 Top Extension at Stairs. At the top of a stair flight, handrails shall extend horizontally above the landing for 12 inches (305 mm) minimum beginning directly above the landing nosing. Extensions shall return to a wall, guard, or the landing surface, or shall be continuous to the handrail of an adjacent stair flight.

❖ The most critical transition from level walking to stair use is at the top of a stair flight. One should be able to reach and grasp the handrail(s) in advance of attempting the very critical, first descent step. Therefore, Section 505.10.2 is presented as a safety convention helpful for all users and as an additional aid for those with perceptual or mobility disabilities. It also provides assistance for users who need to pull themselves to the level surface at the top of the stairs.

Handrails should return to the wall, guard, ground or support. Two concerns should be addressed. The handrail extension must be formed so that clothing or carried items cannot catch on the end and returns on handrail extensions must not become protruding objects for people crossing perpendicular to the top of the stair (see Figure 505.10.2 and Commentary Figure C505.10.2). Handrails that extend into circulation routes must be designed to be detectable by persons using a long cane.

FIGURE C505.10.2
EXAMPLE OF TOP EXTENSIONS AT STAIRS

12 min
305

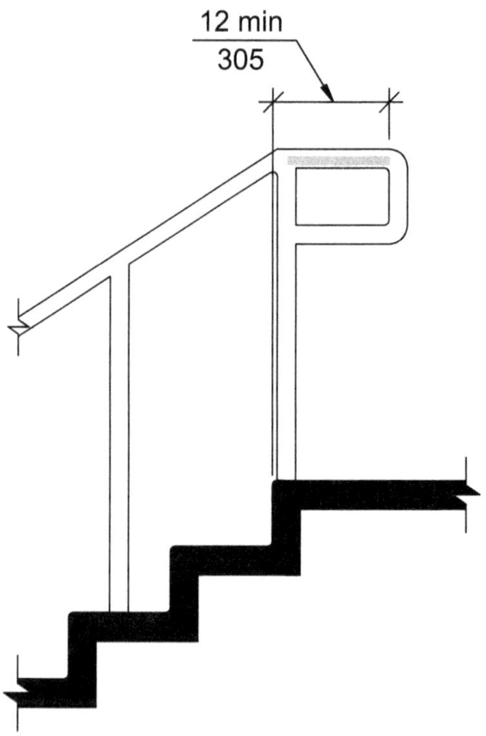

FIGURE 505.10.2
TOP HANDRAIL EXTENSIONS AT STAIRS

505.10.3 Bottom Extension at Stairs. At the bottom of a stair flight, handrails shall extend at the slope of the stair flight for a horizontal distance equal to one tread depth beyond the bottom tread nosing. Extensions shall return to a wall, guard, or the landing surface, or shall be continuous to the handrail of an adjacent stair flight.

❖ A less critical, but still important, transition is at the bottom of a stair flight. Section 505.10.3 requires the handrail at a stair flight continue to slope for the equivalent dimension of one tread at the landing, which means that a person's hand will find the end of the handrail at about the same instant as the leading foot contacts the landing surface. An extension equal to the dimension of one tread anticipates that the landing at the bottom riser effectively serves as a tread when descending because the user must step down to that surface before completing the stair-stepping cadence. Thus, the handrail is required to extend to the point at which the landing surface effectively serves as a tread. An additional horizontal extension is not required at this point, however, when provided, it exceeds the minimum requirements.

Handrails should return to the wall, guard, ground or support. Two concerns should be addressed. The handrail extension must be formed so that clothing or carried items cannot catch on the end and returns on handrail extensions must not become protruding objects for people crossing perpendicular to the bottom of the stair. Handrails that extend into space must be designed to be detectable by persons using a long cane (see Figure 505.10.3).

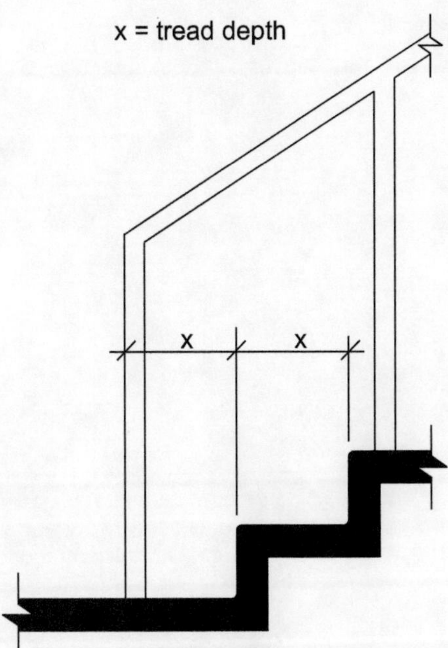

FIGURE 505.10.3
BOTTOM HANDRAIL EXTENSIONS AT STAIRS

506 Windows

506.1 General. Accessible windows shall have operable parts complying with Section 309.

❖ For those windows that must be accessible, it is logical to ensure that the mechanisms that lock and unlock or open and close must be positioned for accessibility, including clear floor space, reach ranges and graspability of the mechanisms. Examples of required operable windows would be egress windows in bedrooms and windows in spaces where natural ventilation is required. Examples of the types of operable windows include double-hung, sliding, casement and awning windows.

Chapter 6. Plumbing Elements and Facilities

❖ Chapter 6 deals with fixtures that would be connected to a building's water supply. This includes plumbing fixtures, as well as the requirements for other related items such as water closet stalls, laundry equipment, etc. Section 804 ("Kitchens and kitchenettes") references the sink requirements in Section 606.

Chapter 6 is also referenced from Chapter 10 for some of the criteria for toilet rooms or bathrooms located within or serving dwelling units or sleeping units (e.g., congregate residences, apartments, hotel rooms, assisted living, nursing homes, hospitals, etc.). However, users should first follow the provisions in Chapter 10 for the appropriate level of accessibility, and only look at Chapter 6 if it is referenced or if desiring to provide a higher level of access.

- Section 601 is a general scoping provision to indicate that the requirements in this chapter are applicable when referenced by the authority having jurisdiction.
- Section 602 deals with built-in drinking fountains.
- Section 603 contains the general requirements for the rooms that contain toilet and/or bathing facilities.
- Section 604 deals with the water closets (toilets) themselves. This includes the stall requirements for wheelchair-accessible and ambulatory stalls.
- Section 605 contains the technical requirements for accessible urinals.
- Section 606 contains criteria for both lavatories and sinks. Lavatories are typically used for hand washing. Sinks are typically used for other types of cleanup or work (lab sink, kitchen sink).
- Section 607 covers bathtub requirements. Bathtubs may include portable seats or built-in seats.
- Section 608 contains information for transfer, roll-in and an alternate roll-in shower compartment.
- Section 609 contains general grab bar information, which is referenced in the sections dealing with water closets, bathtubs and showers.
- Section 610 provides general information for the seats found in bathtubs and showers.
- Section 611 contains criteria for laundry equipment, both washers and dryers.
- Section 612 addresses the technical criteria for accessible saunas and steam rooms.

There are specific exemptions for toilet or bathing rooms accessed only through a private office. These can be found in Sections 603.2.2, 604.4, 604.5, 606.2, 606.3, 607.4, 608.2.1.3, 608.2.2.3, 608.2.3.2 and 608.3. The exceptions allow for adaptable features in this portion of an individual's work space, which includes reversal of the door to the toilet room; any height for the water closet; blocking for future installation of grab bars at the water closet, bathtub or shower, or seats in the shower; and no clear floor space or height restrictions for the lavatory. The room and fixtures must also meet other provisions for accessibility.

There are specific requirements for drinking fountains and toilet rooms sized for children. The standard does not require a designer to use child sized provisions, but once the choice is made for the drinking fountain or toilet room, all the pieces of the package must be followed. For example, the water closet would not be as usable if the child-sized seat height was used with the adult height for grab bars (see Sections 602.2, 604.1, 604.9.2.2, 604.9.5.2, 604.11 through 604.11.8, 606.2 and 609.4.2). Section 602.2 contains technical criteria for children's accessible drinking fountains. Provisions for child sized toilet rooms call for water closets closer to the wall with the grab bar, lower water closet seat height, lower flush controls, a lower reach range for the toilet paper dispenser, lower lavatories (including a possible side approach) and lower grab bars. Provisions for child sized toilet compartments also include higher toe clearance requirements for stall partitions, as well as larger compartment sizes for stalls with wall-hung water closets.

601 General

601.1 Scope. Plumbing elements and facilities required to be accessible by scoping provisions adopted by the administrative authority shall comply with the applicable provisions of Chapter 6.

❖ The provisions in this chapter are intended to cover the requirements for plumbing fixtures found in general use toilet rooms and bathrooms. Toilet rooms and bathrooms associated with Accessible, Type A and Type B dwelling and sleeping units are more specifically addressed in Chapter 10. Chapter 10 references Chapter 6 when applicable. Note that these provisions apply to plumbing elements required by the scoping documents (see Section 201).

602 Drinking Fountains

❖ This standard does not require drinking fountains, but once they are provided, the percentages specified by the scoping document must meet the requirements in this section. Typically, the locally adopted plumbing code specifies the number of required drinking fountains based on the number of occupants and use of the space. This section includes provisions for drinking fountains for standing persons, as well as accessible drinking fountains for adults and children who use wheelchairs.

602.1 General. Accessible drinking fountains shall comply with Sections 602 and 307.

❖ This section is not intended to cover bottle-type water coolers, which generally rely on paper cups and are not permanently piped. This section is intended to address the clear floor space and access to the controls and water for built-in drinking fountains. Please be aware that accessible drinking fountains by their clearance requirements are not within the detectable range for a cane user; therefore, provisions for protruding objects and alcoves are additional concerns. This is may be even more of a concern for the drinking fountains raised for standing persons. Drinking fountains may be located in an alcove or provide adjacent barriers that are detectable by a person with a long cane (see Commentary Figure C602.1 and Section 307).

FIGURE C602.1
DRINKING FOUNTAINS IN ALCOVE

602.2 Clear Floor Space. A clear floor space complying with Section 305, positioned for a forward approach to the drinking fountain, shall be provided. Knee and toe space complying with Section 306 shall be provided. The clear floor space shall be centered on the drinking fountain.

EXCEPTIONS:

1. Drinking fountains for standing persons.
2. Drinking fountains primarily for children's use shall be permitted where the spout outlet is 30 inches (760 mm) maximum above the floor, a parallel approach complying with Section 305 is provided and the clear floor space is centered on the drinking fountain.

❖ In addition to having accessible spout design and controls, a water fountain must be located on an accessible route, have appropriate knee and toe clearance and have clear floor space. The space required in Section 305 must be provided to ensure that the person can maneuver from the accessible route directly to the water fountain or into an alcove to get into position to drink [see Commentary Figure C602.2(a) and (b)].

The height and shape of the drinking fountain must permit an individual in a wheelchair to access the fixture. A cantilevered unit at least 17 inches (430 mm) deep allows the legs and feet of the user to be positioned under the unit. The knee and toe clearances required in Sections 306.2 and 306.3 are consistently required throughout the standard for a forward approach.

Drinking fountains for standing persons are not required to meet the clear floor space and knee and toe clearance requirements in this section (Exception 1).

Accessible drinking fountains with the spout at 36 inches (915 mm) (Section 602.4) have been found to be outside of the reach of children using wheelchairs. However, if the spout outlet height is installed at 30 inches (760 mm) maximum, the knee and toe clearances typically are not available. Therefore, a parallel side approach, centered on the drinking fountain, is required (Exception 2) (see Figure 602.2).

There are some existing drinking fountains having a parallel approach. Where a parallel approach drinking fountain is replaced, either due to renovation or as part of improvements to the accessible route, the new drinking fountain should be a front approach drinking fountain unless there is difficulty with the placement. For example, if the front approach drinking fountain would block the route or means of egress past the drinking fountain, a par-

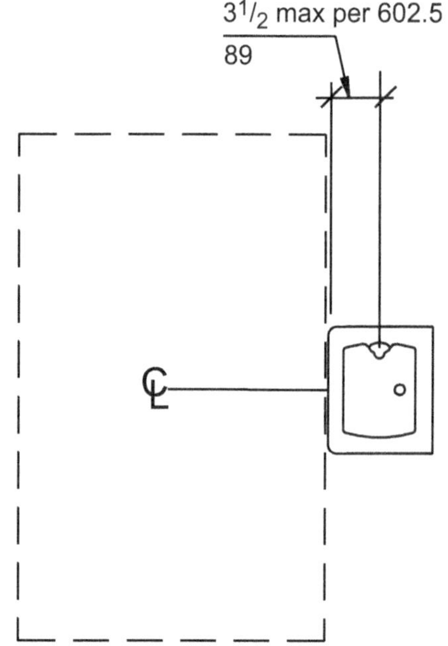

FIGURE 602.2
PARALLEL APPROACH AT DRINKING FOUNTAINS PRIMARILY FOR CHILDREN'S USE—(EXCEPTION 2)

allel approach drinking fountain may be approved by the local building official (see Commentary Figure C602.2(c)].

602.3 Operable Parts. Operable parts shall comply with Section 309.

❖ Operable parts of the drinking fountain include controls to activate the water flow. These controls must comply with Section 309 for height and operation. The clear floor space can be the same as that provided for the drinking fountain itself.

Although it is the intent for drinking fountains for standing persons to meet the height and operation requirements in Sections 309.3 and 309.4, the clear floor spaces required in Section 309.2 are not literally needed by standing persons. The specific exemption from Section 602.2, Exception 1, should be used to eliminate the clear floor space requirement instead of imposing the requirement from Section 309.2. The operable parts requirements are beneficial for persons with limited use of their hands.

Although not specifically required, it may be desirable when designing for children to use the reach ranges indicated in Table C308.1.

602.4 Spout Outlet Height. Spout outlets of wheelchair accessible drinking fountains shall be 36 inches (915 mm) maximum above the floor. Spout outlets of drinking fountains for standing persons shall be 38 inches (965 mm) minimum and 43 inches (1090 mm) maximum above the floor.

❖ The height of 36 inches (915 mm) has been established as the maximum for a person to be able to drink water from a spout from a seated position. For persons who have difficulty bending over, the 43-inch (1090 mm) maximum height results in a higher level of comfort.

This requirement is not intended to require two drinking fountains—there is a choice of providing separate drinking fountains or combined drinking fountains. There are commercially available drinking fountains that have two spouts at varying heights which are ideally suited both for people in wheelchairs and people who find it difficult or awkward to bend low. One spout is located at the 36-inch (915 mm) height and the higher spout at the 43-inch (1090 mm) height.

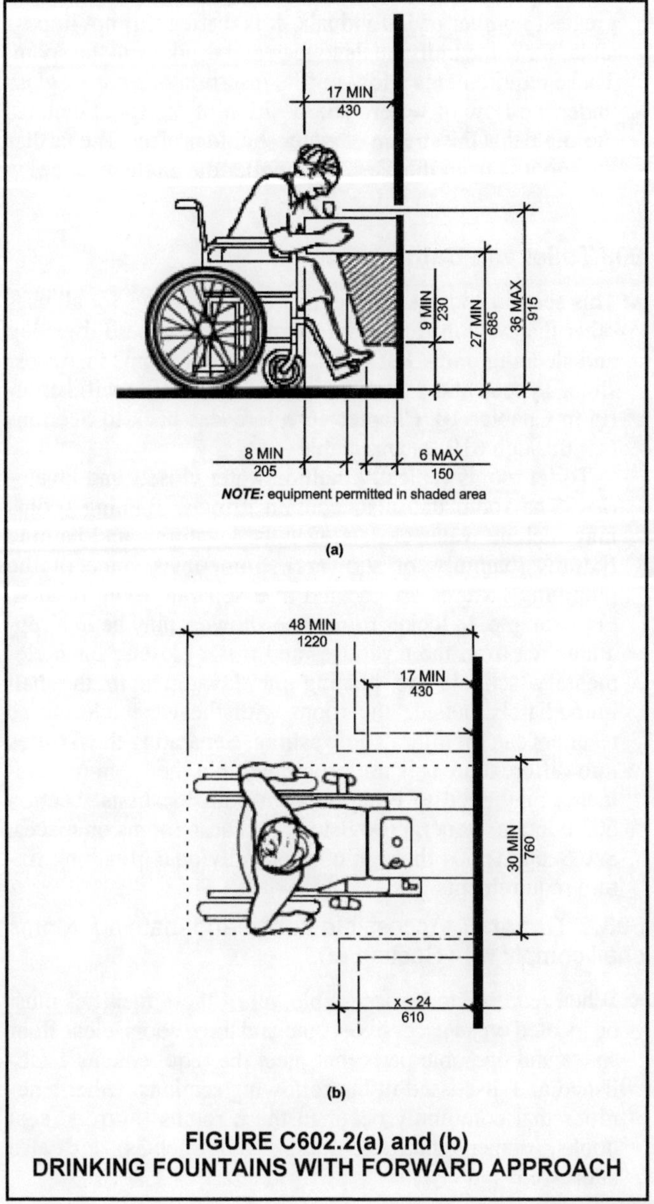

FIGURE C602.2(a) and (b)
DRINKING FOUNTAINS WITH FORWARD APPROACH

FIGURE C602.2(c)
EXISTING DRINKING FOUNTAINS
WITH PARALLEL SIDE APPROACH

If designing an accessible drinking fountain for children, the maximum spout outlet height is 30 inches (760 mm) as stated in Exception 2, Section 602.2.

602.5 Spout Location. The spout shall be located 15 inches (380 mm) minimum from the vertical support and 5 inches (125 mm) maximum from the front edge of the drinking fountain, including bumpers. Where only a parallel approach is provided, the spout shall be located $3^1/_2$ inches (90 mm) maximum from the front edge of the drinking fountain, including bumpers.

❖ Criteria are provided for both a parallel and a forward approach. See Section 602.2, Exception 2, regarding when a parallel approach is permitted. For a parallel approach, it is difficult to lean laterally over the wheelchair arms, and the spout must be located within $3^1/_2$ inches (89 mm) of the front edge of the unit. Because it is less difficult to lean forward than to twist and lean laterally, this dimension may be increased to 5 inches (125 mm) in a forward approach. If the spout is located lower or farther forward or both, the maximum distance from the front edge becomes less critical. The front edge is the unit edge, not the location of the controls.

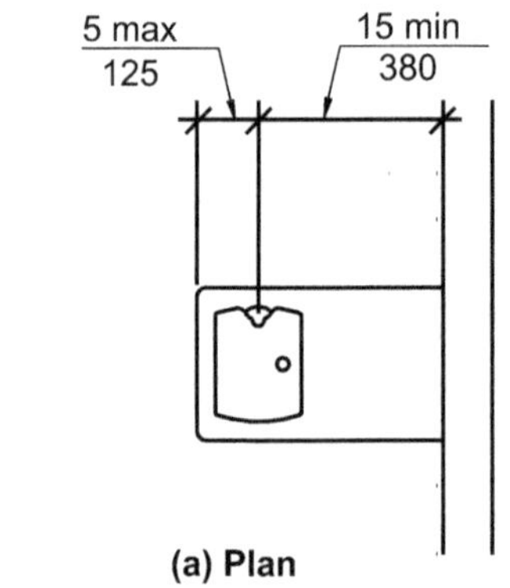

(a) Plan

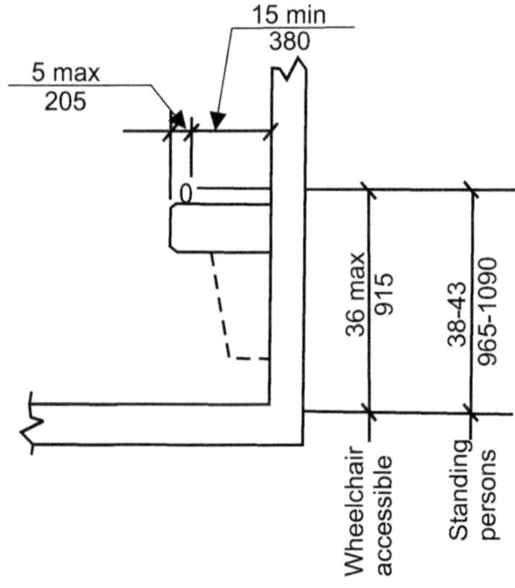

(b) Elevation

FIGURE 602.5
DRINKING FOUNTAIN SPOUT LOCATION

Knee and toe clearances are also needed for a forward approach. The 15-inch (380 mm) dimension from the vertical support locates the spout far enough away from the wall so the user's knees and toes may extend below the unit (see Figure 602.5).

While literally this would also apply to drinking fountains for standing persons, because no clearances are required for drinking fountains for standing persons, the spout location requirements may be considered more of a feature of ease of use.

602.6 Water Flow. The spout shall provide a flow of water 4 inches (100 mm) minimum in height. The angle of the water stream from spouts within 3 inches (75 mm) of the front of the drinking fountain shall be 30 degrees maximum, and from spouts between 3 inches (75 mm) and 5 inches (125 mm) from the front of the drinking fountain shall be 15 degrees maximum, measured horizontally relative to the front face of the drinking fountain.

❖ This requirement permits the drinking fountain to serve the greatest number of individuals. It is difficult, if not impossible, for some individuals to lean and drink from the spout. These requirements allow for the insertion of a cup or glass under the flow of water. The position of the spout dictates the angle that the stream of water should project. The farther the spout is from the user, the smaller the angle must be.

603 Toilet and Bathing Rooms

❖ This section addresses toilet and bathing rooms for all uses other than within Accessible, Type A and Type B dwelling and sleeping units. For toilet and bathing rooms in Accessible, Type A and Type B units, see the more specific criteria in Chapter 10. Chapter 10 references back to Sections 604 through 610, as applicable.

Toilet rooms typically include water closets and lavatories. The room can also contain urinals. Bathing rooms may include water closets, urinals, lavatories and bathing fixtures (bathtubs or showers). Sometimes some of the plumbing fixtures are located in a separate room or area. For example, in locker rooms the showers may be in a separate area from the lavatories and water closets; some elementary schools are placing the lavatories in the hall immediately outside the room with the water closets so teachers can monitor hand washing. Separating the fixtures into different areas is not prohibited, but the room requirements may need to be applied in both locations. Section 603 contains general provisions for these rooms or spaces. See Sections 604 through 608 for individual plumbing fixture requirements.

603.1 General. Accessible toilet and bathing rooms shall comply with Section 603.

❖ When required to be accessible, all of these facilities must be located on an accessible route and have doors, clear floor space and operable parts that meet the requirements established and discussed in the following sections. Other amenities that commonly occur in these rooms (mirrors, coat hooks, diaper changing tables and shelves) are also addressed.

603.2 Clearances.

❖ The intent of the clearance requirements is to assure that a person using a wheelchair can enter the room, close the door, access the fixtures and exit the room.

It is important to understand that the clear floor space, or location where a wheelchair would sit when using a fixture, is permitted to overlap. However, the fixture itself cannot overlap the clear floor space of another (Section 301.2, 603.2.2 and 604.3.3). The most common mistake in public single user toilet rooms is to locate the lavatory adjacent to the water closet and over the water closet clear floor space. With the lavatory at this location the clear floor space required for a side transfer to the water closet is not available. Because the clear floor space at fixtures and the turning space are permitted to overlap, portions of the turning space may extend underneath the lavatory (see commentary, Section 604.3.3 and Commentary Figure C603.2).

Floor drains located in front of accessible plumbing fixtures can create slopes that cause undesired movement of a wheelchair or walking aid when using plumbing fixtures (see Section 305.2). If a room floor drain is provided, when designers are choosing the location, they should consider clear floor spaces and circulation routes within the room.

603.2.1 Turning Space. A turning space complying with Section 304 shall be provided within the room. The required turning space shall not be provided within a toilet compartment.

❖ A 60-inch (1525 mm) turning circle or a 60-inch (1525 mm) T-turn space is required within the bathing room or toilet room. This ensures that persons using the room can turn to address each fixture or operable part they may need to access. These turning spaces can use knee and toe clearances under the lavatory or toe clearance at the water closet as indicated in Section 304.3.

In multistall bathrooms, the only turning space provided within the room should not be within the accessible stall. If someone enters the room and the accessible stall is occupied, they may need to turn around and leave. It is permitted for there to be a turning space both within the room and inside and outside the stall.

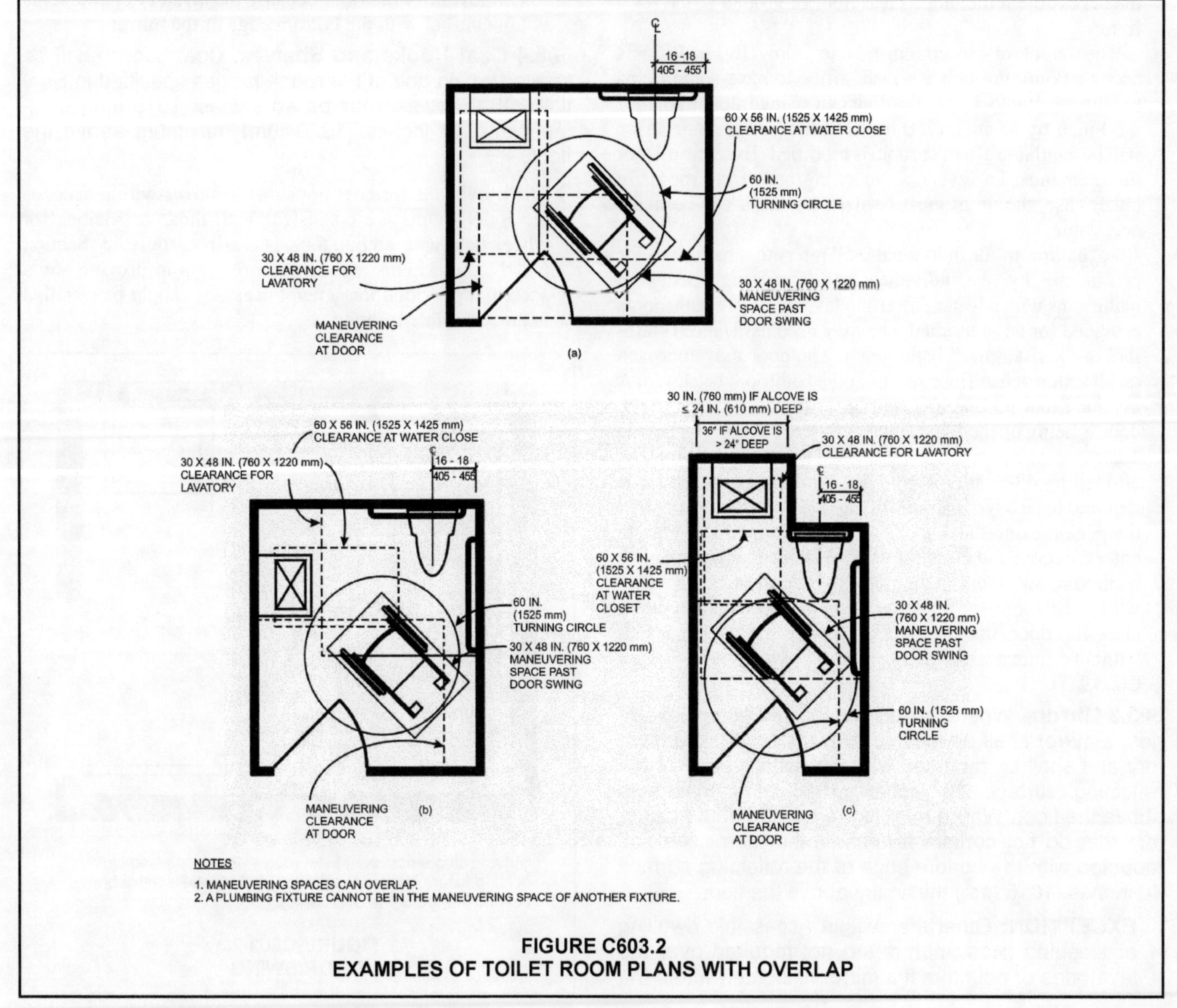

FIGURE C603.2
EXAMPLES OF TOILET ROOM PLANS WITH OVERLAP

603.2.2 Door Swing. Doors shall not swing into the clear floor space or clearance for any fixture.

EXCEPTIONS:

1. Doors to a toilet or bathing room for a single occupant, accessed only through a private office and not for common use or public use shall be permitted to swing into the clear floor space, provided the swing of the door can be reversed to comply with Section 603.2.2.
2. Where the room is for individual use and a clear floor space complying with Section 305.3 is provided within the room beyond the arc of the door swing, the door shall not be required to comply with Section 603.2.2.

❖ In a multiuser bathroom, the locations where a person in a wheelchair may be sitting to use a fixture must be out of the swing of the door. This is to prevent the wheelchair from being struck when others leave or enter the room. Although not the best design alternative, the door may swing over the turning space within the room. The turning space is part of the accessible route, not a clear floor or ground space for a fixture.

The intent of Exception 1 is to allow for bathrooms accessed only through a private office to have some items readily adaptable. Either the door can swing into the room if a 30-inch by 48-inch (760 by 1220 mm) clear floor space will be available after the room is modified (Exception 2), or the door must be reversible to swing out of the room. In either case, the room must be sized so that it can be made accessible.

A "bathroom for individual use" refers to a bathroom for private use by one individual at a time (single-occupant bathrooms with a water closet and lavatory) or in bathrooms provided for an individual who may need assistance ("family" or "assisted use" bathrooms). The door may encroach on all fixture-clear floor spaces in the bathroom because it is assumed that no one else will be using the fixtures as the door is being opened. However, a fixture cannot overlap the maneuvering space required for the door to the room. The 30-inch by 48-inch (760 by 1220 mm) clear floor space is required to be beyond the arc of the door swing to ensure that the person using the wheelchair is positioned to be able to enter the room and close the door. When a door opens into a bathroom, sufficient maneuvering space must be provided within the room for a person using a wheelchair to enter, close the door, use the fixtures, reopen the door and exit without undue difficulty (see Commentary Figure C603.2.3).

603.3 Mirrors. Where mirrors are located above lavatories, a mirror shall be located over the accessible lavatory and shall be mounted with the bottom edge of the reflecting surface 40 inches (1015 mm) maximum above the floor. Where mirrors are located above counters that do not contain lavatories, the mirror shall be mounted with the bottom edge of the reflecting surface 40 inches (1015 mm) maximum above the floor.

EXCEPTION: Other than within Accessible dwelling or sleeping units, mirrors are not required over the lavatories or counters if a mirror is located within the same toilet or bathing room and mounted with the bottom edge of the reflecting surface 35 inches (890 mm) maximum above the floor.

❖ The normal eye level of a person using a wheelchair, 43 inches to 51 inches (1090 to 1295 mm), provides an angle of incidence sufficient for reflection from a mirror with a maximum bottom edge of 40 inches (1015 mm) above the floor to have an adequate field of view to accomplish the desired activities while allowing for clearance over the backsplash on the lavatory or counter [see Commentary Figure C102(a)].

If mirrors are to be used by both ambulatory people and wheelchair users, design standards recommend that the top most edge be at a minimum 74-inch (1880 mm) height. It would typically be considered best design practice to make the mirror over the accessible lavatory the accessible mirror, but a mirror in another location within the room, maybe even a full length mirror, would accommodate all people, including children. If a mirror is not located over the accessible lavatory or a counter, but in another location in the space, the bottom edge can be at a minimum of 35 inches (890 mm) above the floor because the lavatory or counter is not in conflict with the bottom edge of the mirror.

603.4 Coat Hooks and Shelves. Coat hooks shall be located within one of the reach ranges specified in Section 308. Shelves shall be 40 inches (1015 mm) minimum and 48 inches (1220 mm) maximum above the floor.

❖ The provisions for coat hooks and shelves within accessible toilet rooms are consistent with those provisions for wheelchair and ambulatory accessible stalls in Section 604.8. These items are not required, but to provide equal access, if provided for general use, they should be installed in an accessible location.

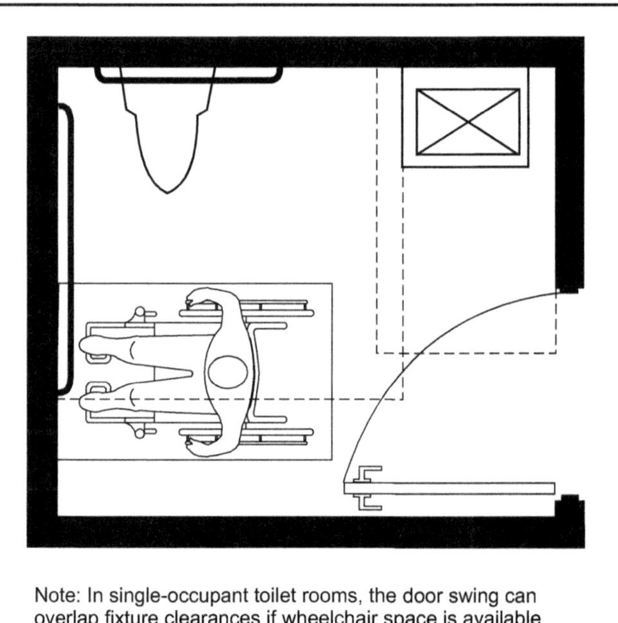

Note: In single-occupant toilet rooms, the door swing can overlap fixture clearances if wheelchair space is available beyond the arc of the door swing.

FIGURE C603.2.3 DOOR SWING

Coat hooks must be located within reach ranges. Measurements are to be taken to the top of the shelf or coat hook. If a shelf is provided, it should be located within reach ranges and also so that it won't interfere with maneuvering within the space. The shelf considered for this requirement of 40 inches (1015 mm) minimum and 48 inches (1220 mm) maximum was a purse shelf that was intended for users in the stall (see Commentary Figure C603.4). A supply storage shelf within the room was not considered. Some facilities provide a shelf on the wall on top of the toilet paper dispenser for someone to be able to set small items adjacent for when they are needed close to hand. There are no specific provisions for child sizes because the expected reach ranges (see Table C308.1) are lower than that permitted for adults.

FIGURE C603.4
EXAMPLE OF PURSE SHELF

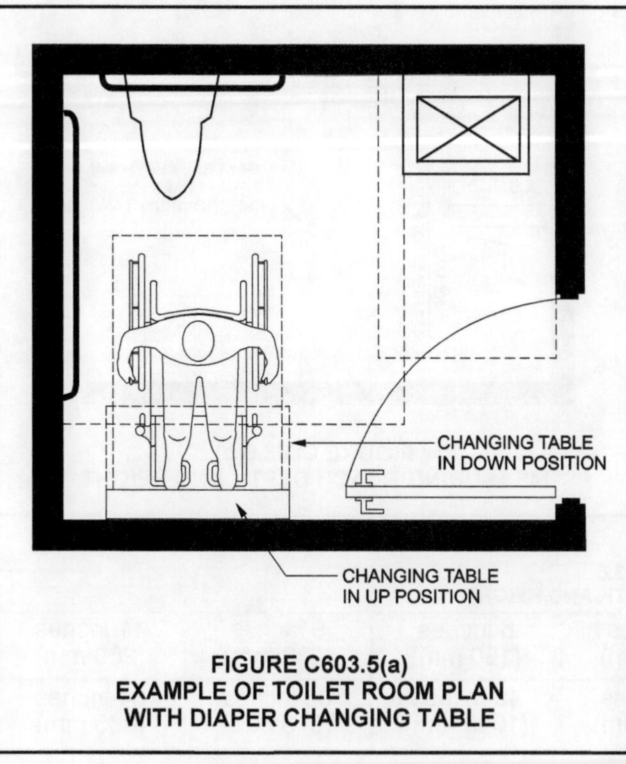

FIGURE C603.5(a)
EXAMPLE OF TOILET ROOM PLAN
WITH DIAPER CHANGING TABLE

603.5 Diaper Changing Tables. Diaper changing tables shall comply with Sections 309 and 902

❖ Diaper changing tables, when provided, must meet the criteria for reach range and work surfaces. Diaper changing tables can be fixed or the fold-up type [see Commentary Figure C603.5(b) and (c)]. The handle or strap to open the folded types must be within reach ranges. When the table is folded down or if the table is fixed, it must have knee and toe clearances and have the surface for changing the baby at 34 inches (865 mm) maximum above the floor.

When a folding diaper changing table is within an accessible single occupant bathroom or the accessible stall,

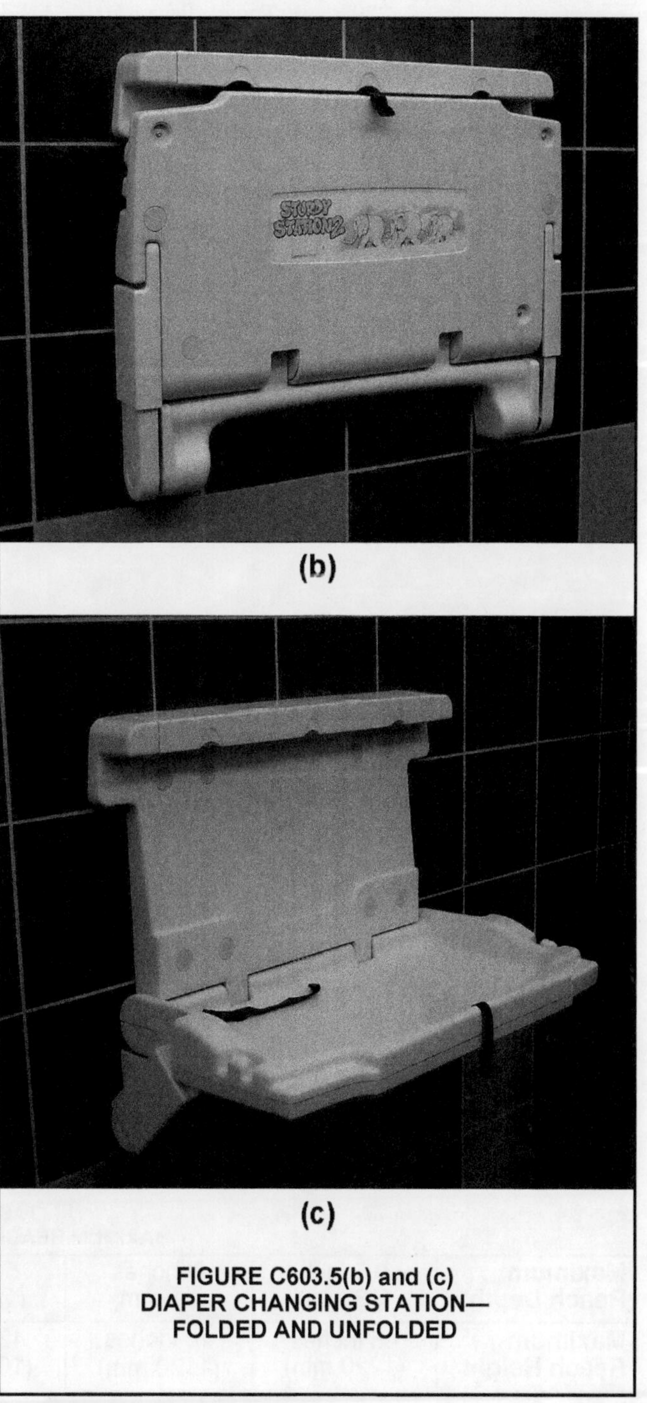

(b)

(c)

FIGURE C603.5(b) and (c)
DIAPER CHANGING STATION—
FOLDED AND UNFOLDED

when folded up, it should not overlap the clear floor space for any fixture (see Section 604.3.3). However, the diaper changing table can overlap the clearances when in the folded down position [see Commentary Figure C603.5(a)].

603.6 Operable Parts. Operable parts on towel dispensers and hand dryers serving accessible lavatories shall comply with Table 603.6.

❖ Towel dispensers or hand dryers associated with the accessible lavatory have requirements that are more restrictive than the typical obstructed reach range requirements in Sections 308.2.2 and 308.3.2. With the lavatory at 34 inches (865 mm) in height, the towel dispenser or hand dryer must be on a side wall where the maximum reach depth is 11 inches (280 mm). Towel dispensers or hand dryers in the room cannot be located on the back wall over the lavatory or counter unless there are others in the same room that are within reach, in accordance with Table 603.6. If the towel dispenser or hand dryer is located somewhere else in the room, the height can be higher, but the reach over an obstruction underneath is less. For example, a wall mounted towel dispenser can have the outlet at 48 inches (1220 mm), but the waste receptacle underneath cannot stick out more than $^{1}/_{2}$ inch (13 mm) [see Commentary Figure C603.6(a)]. This is an aid to persons who are short of stature as well as children.

FIGURE C603.6(a)
TOWEL DISPENSER

TABLE 603.6. See below.

❖ See Commentary Figure C603.6(b) for a graphic example of how to measure using the table requirements.

604 Water Closets and Toilet Compartments

❖ This section addresses water closets and toilet compartments.

- Sections 604.2 through 604.4 are the water closet requirements.
- Section 604.5 deals with grab bar orientation and length.
- Section 604.6 addresses flush controls.
- Section 604.7 contains technical criteria for toilet paper dispensers.
- The criteria for the coat hooks and shelves provided within stalls addressed in Section 604.8 are the same as required for within the toilet room specified in Section 603.4.
- Sections 604.9 and 604.10 have the technical criteria for accessible and ambulatory stalls. The criteria for these two types of stalls are different because they are intended for two different groups of mobility impairments.

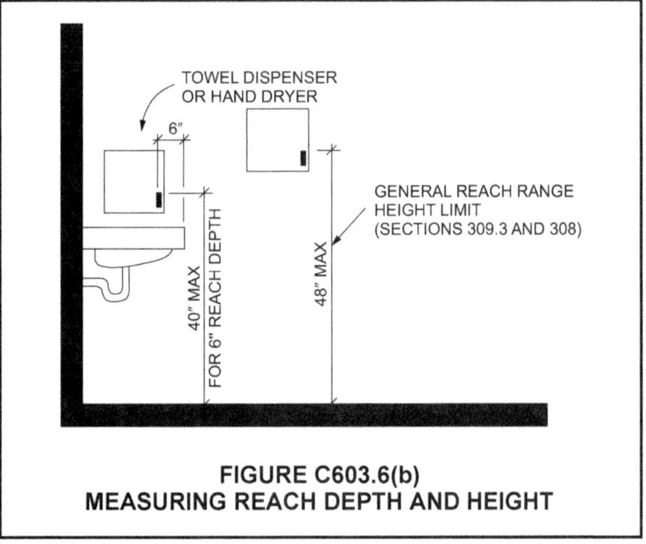

FIGURE C603.6(b)
MEASURING REACH DEPTH AND HEIGHT

TABLE 603.6
MAXIMUM REACH DEPTH AND HEIGHT

Maximum Reach Depth	0.5 inch (13 mm)	2 inches (51 mm)	5 inches (125 mm)	6 inches (150 mm)	9 inches (230 mm)	11 inches (280 mm)
Maximum Reach Height	48 inches (1220 mm)	46 inches (1170 mm)	42 inches (1065 mm)	40 inches (1015 mm)	36 inches (915 mm)	34 inches (865 mm)

- Children's requirements in Section 604.11 provide either specific criteria or appropriate reference for the water closet, grab bars, flush controls, toilet paper dispensers and compartments sized for children.

604.1 General. Accessible water closets and toilet compartments shall comply with Section 604. Compartments containing more than one plumbing fixture shall comply with Section 603. Wheelchair accessible compartments shall comply with Section 604.9. Ambulatory accessible compartments shall comply with Section 604.10.

EXCEPTION: Water closets and toilet compartments primarily for children's use shall be permitted to comply with Section 604.11 as applicable.

❖ The maneuvering space, seat height, grab bars, controls and dispensers must be located to permit use by a person with a disability. This section addresses water closets in uses other than dwellings and sleeping units. See Chapter 10 for water closets in dwellings and sleeping units.

If a toilet compartment contains a lavatory and a water closet, it must meet the same provisions as a single occupant toilet room. The criteria for wheelchair-accessible and ambulatory-accessible stalls are different because they are intended for two different groups of mobility impairments.

The exception allows for bathrooms or toilet compartments specifically designed for children to be appropriately sized for their different wheelchair sizes and reach ranges. If this option is chosen, the criteria must be followed for all applicable elements. The option does not allow picking and choosing between the different elements (e.g., grab bar height, water closet location, stall size). Children's requirements in Section 604.11 provide either specific criteria or appropriate reference for the water closet, grab bars, flush controls, toilet paper dispensers and compartments sized for children.

604.2 Location. The water closet shall be located with a wall or partition to the rear and to one side. The centerline of the water closet shall be 16 inches (405 mm) minimum and 18 inches (455 mm) maximum from the side wall or partition. Water closets located in ambulatory accessible compartments specified in Section 604.10 shall have the centerline of the water closet 17 inches (430 mm) minimum and 19 inches (485 mm) maximum from the side wall or partition.

❖ Sixteen inches (405 mm) to 18 inches (455 mm) has been established as the optimal dimension from a side wall or partition to the centerline of the water closet to allow optimum bearing and reach for the grab bar [see Figure 604.2(a)]. The 17-inch to 19-inch (430 to 485 mm) dimension for ambulatory stalls permits a similar 2-inch (55 mm) tolerance [see Figure 604.2(b)]. Once everything is installed, this 2-inch tolerance addresses differences that occur between the plumbing rough-in and the finished wall to water closet measurement.

See Section 604.11.2 for provisions for water closet location in toilet rooms or stalls designed specifically for children's use.

604.3 Clearance.

❖ This section addresses the clearances around the water closet in the single occupant toilet room and what is permissible to overlap that clearance. Section 604.11.3 references this provision for clearances in toilet rooms or stalls specifically designed for children.

604.3.1 Clearance width. Clearance around a water closet shall be 60 inches (1525 mm) minimum in width, measured perpendicular from the sidewall.

❖ The 60-inch (1525 mm) requirement provides approximately 30 inches (760 mm) between the water closet and the nearest wall or fixture (see Figure 604.3). This space allows the wheelchair user to back into the space and accomplish a side transfer from the wheelchair to the water closet [see Commentary Figure C604.3.1(a)]. This transfer requires less maneuvering than a diagonal or front transfer [see Commentary Figure C604.3.1(b)]. Diagonal or front transfers are difficult, if not impossible, for persons who have no use of their legs or need assistance to transfer. Another fixture (e.g., lavatory) is not permitted within this clear floor space (see Section 604.3.2).

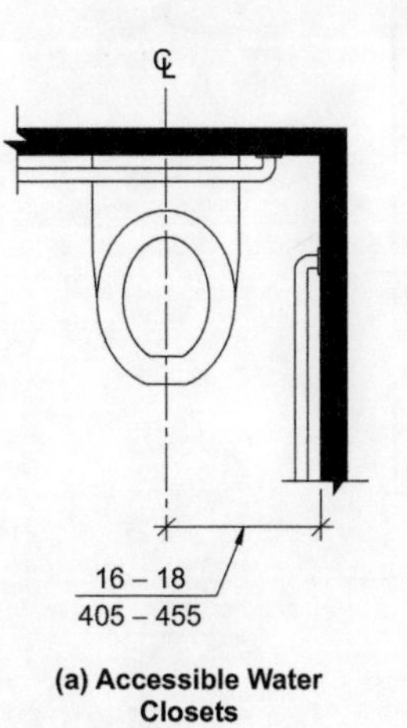

(a) Accessible Water Closets

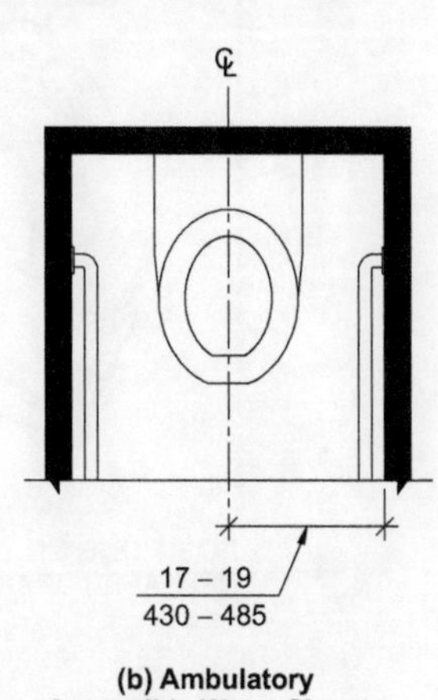

(b) Ambulatory Accessible Water Closets

FIGURE 604.2
WATER CLOSET LOCATION

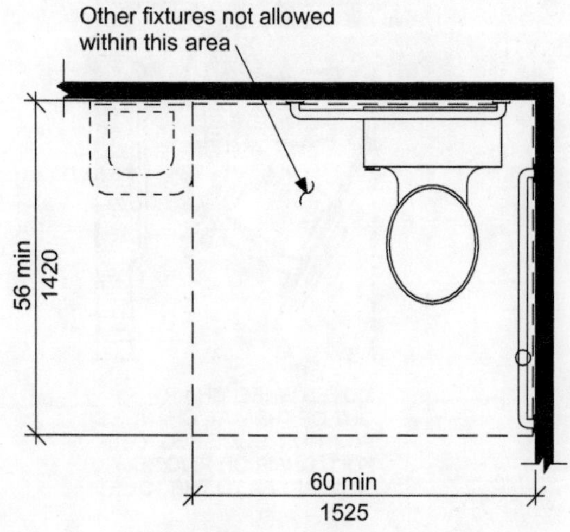

FIGURE 604.3
SIZE OF CLEARANCE FOR WATER CLOSET

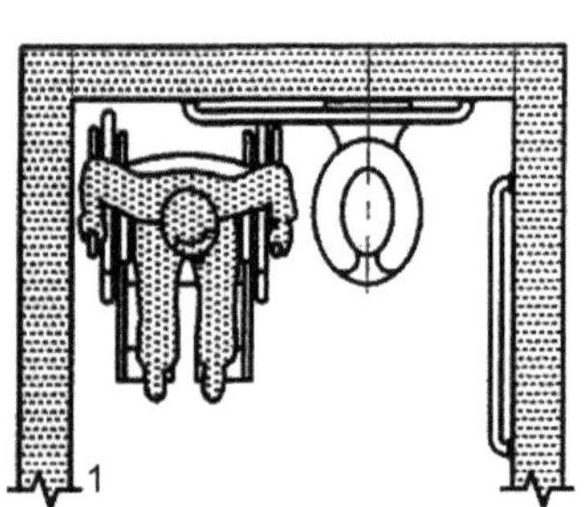

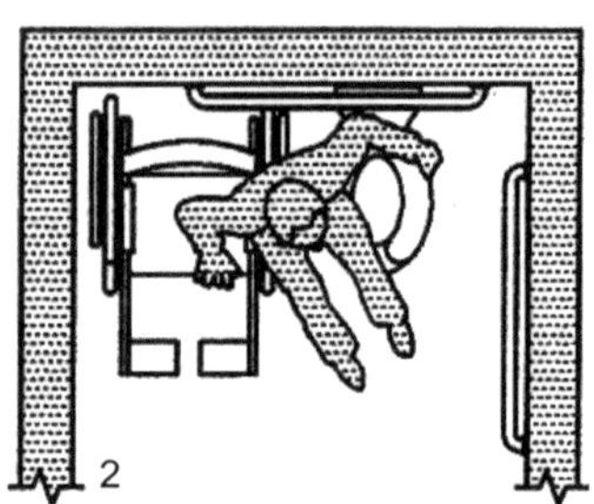

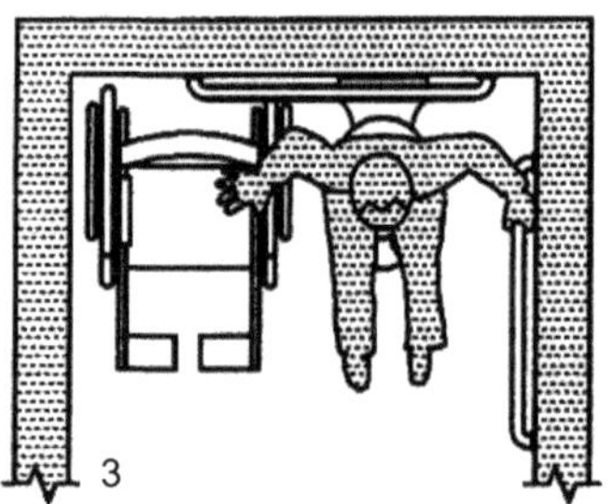

FIGURE C604.3.1(a)
SIDE TRANSFER

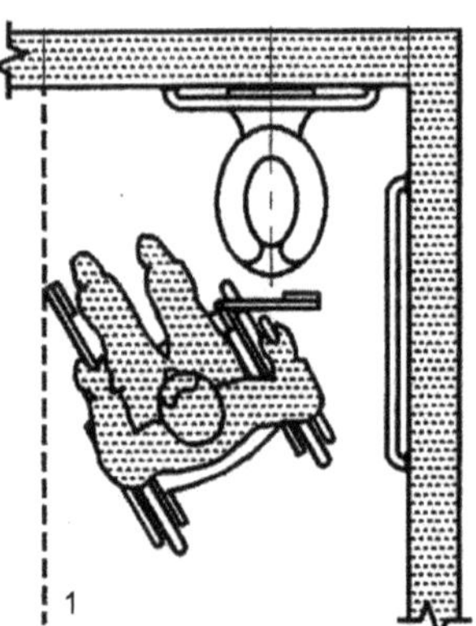

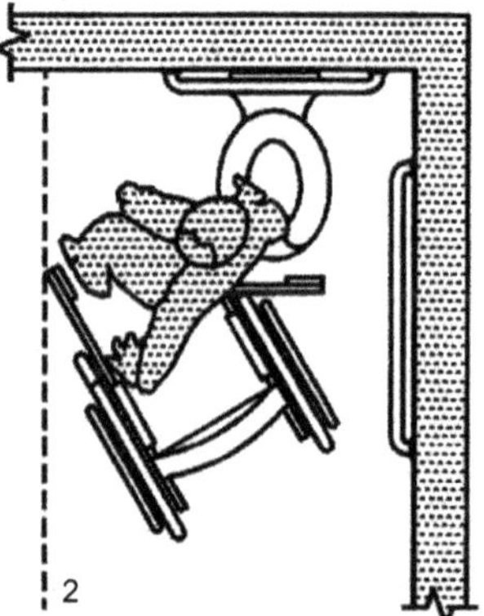

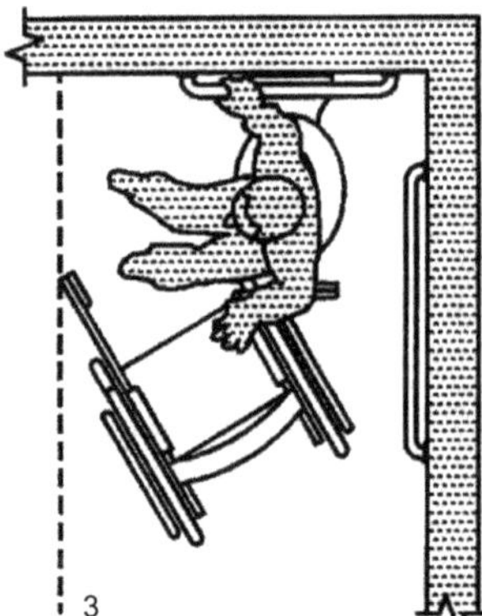

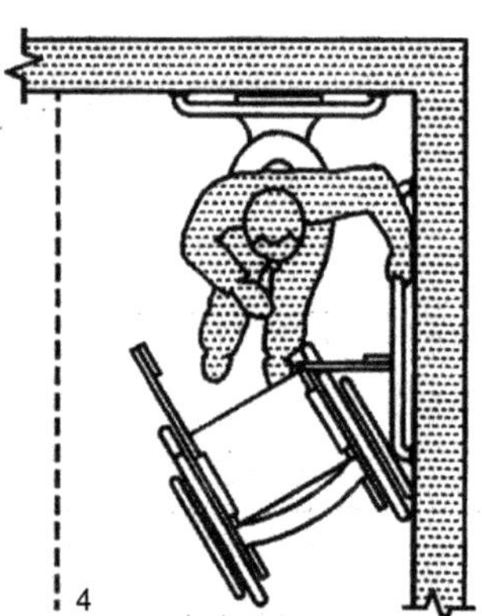

FIGURE C604.3.1(b)
FRONT OR DIAGONAL TRANSFER

604.3.2 Clearance Depth. Clearance around the water closet shall be 56 inches (1420 mm) minimum in depth, measured perpendicular from the rear wall.

❖ The 56-inch (1220 mm) minimum depth is intended to be consistent with the requirements in water closet compartments for clearances around the water closet. Since there are additional requirements for rooms versus stalls, the additional depth for floor mounted water closets is not required (see Figure 604.3).

604.3.3 Clearance Overlap. The required clearance around the water closet shall be permitted to overlap the water closet, associated grab bars, paper dispensers, sanitary napkin receptacles, coat hooks, shelves, accessible routes, clear floor space at other fixtures and the turning space. No other fixtures or obstructions shall be within the required water closet clearance.

❖ The water closet clearance can overlap elements of the accessible route (path of travel, door clearance) including the turning space required in the toilet room (see Section 301.2) [see Commentary Figures C604.3.3(a), C603.2(a), C603.2(b) and C603.2(c)].

Items that can overlap the clear floor space of the water closet without blocking access to the water closet include grab bars and the tissue dispenser. Items that cannot overlap the clear floor space for the water closet include counters or the accessible lavatory. Because there is an assumption that only one person will be using the toilet room facilities at a time, the spaces at other fixtures where the wheelchair user would sit to use those fixtures may overlap the clear floor space at the water closet [see Commentary Figures C604.3.3(b), C604.3.3(c), C603.2(a), C603.2(b) and C603.2(c)].

Other items listed, such as paper dispensers, sanitary napkin receptacles, coat hooks and shelves, are items commonly found in toilet rooms or toilet stalls. Other items that also are often found in the bathroom are seat cover dispensers and fold-up diaper changing tables. It is not the intent of this section to prohibit these items within the toilet room or stall, but rather to make sure that these items are located so that they do not block access to the water closet within the room or stall.

For diaper changing stations, see Section 603.5. The requirements would be the same regardless of whether the diaper changing station is in the accessible stall or in the room.

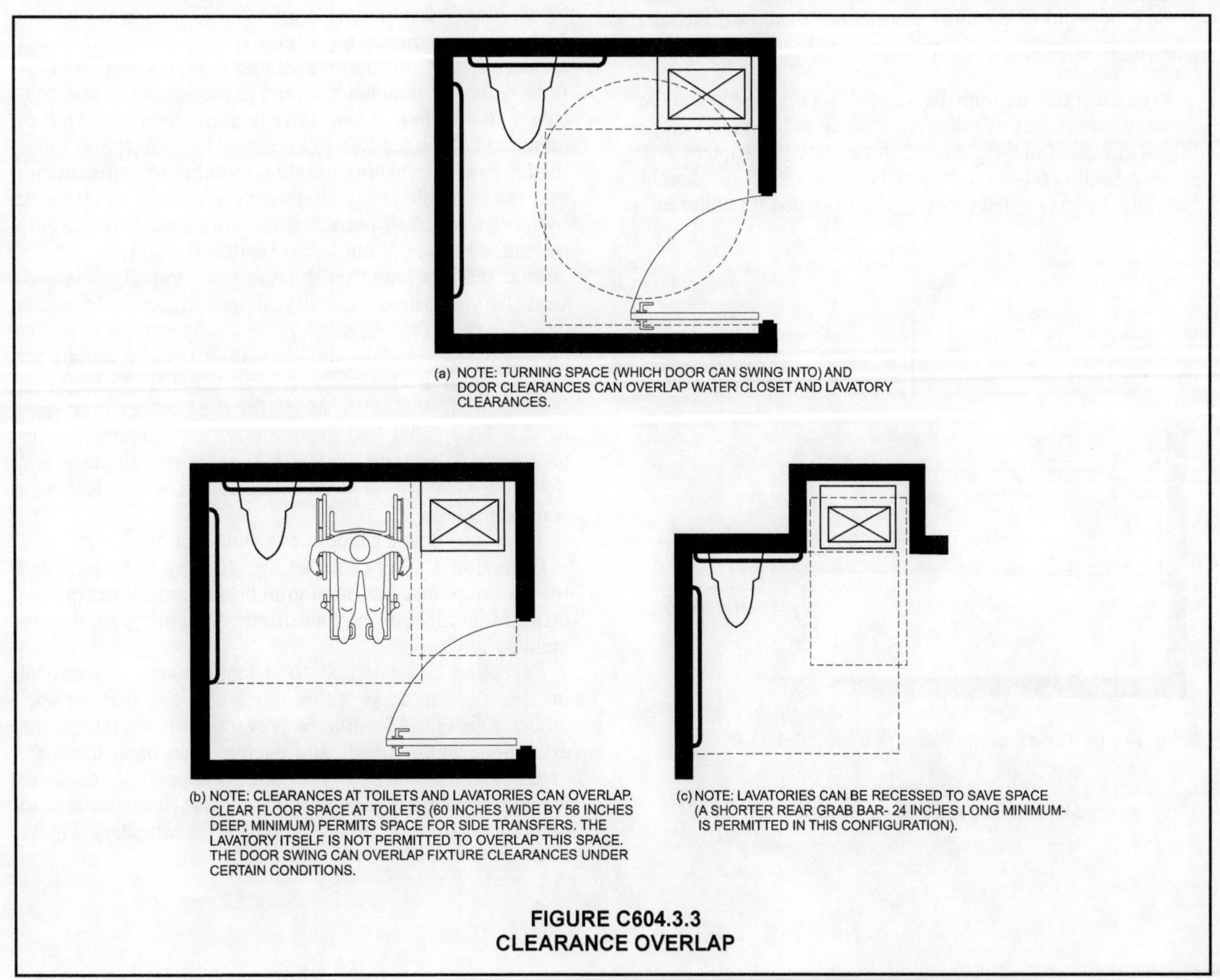

(a) NOTE: TURNING SPACE (WHICH DOOR CAN SWING INTO) AND DOOR CLEARANCES CAN OVERLAP WATER CLOSET AND LAVATORY CLEARANCES.

(b) NOTE: CLEARANCES AT TOILETS AND LAVATORIES CAN OVERLAP. CLEAR FLOOR SPACE AT TOILETS (60 INCHES WIDE BY 56 INCHES DEEP, MINIMUM) PERMITS SPACE FOR SIDE TRANSFERS. THE LAVATORY ITSELF IS NOT PERMITTED TO OVERLAP THIS SPACE. THE DOOR SWING CAN OVERLAP FIXTURE CLEARANCES UNDER CERTAIN CONDITIONS.

(c) NOTE: LAVATORIES CAN BE RECESSED TO SAVE SPACE (A SHORTER REAR GRAB BAR- 24 INCHES LONG MINIMUM- IS PERMITTED IN THIS CONFIGURATION).

FIGURE C604.3.3
CLEARANCE OVERLAP

604.4 Height. The height of water closet seats shall be 17 inches (430 mm) minimum and 19 inches (485 mm) maximum above the floor, measured to the top of the seat. Seats shall not be sprung to return to a lifted position.

EXCEPTION: A water closet in a toilet room for a single occupant, accessed only through a private office and not for common use or public use, shall not be required to comply with Section 604.4.

❖ Preferences for the heights of toilet seats vary considerably among persons with disabilities. Higher seat heights are an advantage to some ambulatory persons with disabilities, but a disadvantage for some persons who use wheelchairs. Toilet seats that are approximately 17 inches to 19 inches (430 to 485 mm) high are a reasonable compromise (see Figure 604.4). Seats and filler rings of various thicknesses are available to adapt china-fixture rims, which vary from 14 inches to 18 inches (355 to 455 mm) high.

A 17-inch to 19-inch (430 to 485 mm) water closet seat height is based on the assumption that a typical wheelchair seat height, with or without a cushion, would fall within that range. Both the seat of the wheelchair and the water closet must be as level as possible for ease of transfer. Although it would be easier to transfer "down" to a seat, more strength would be required to transfer back "up" to the wheelchair. An upward spring-loaded toilet seat will interfere with the user's transfer.

The exception for both the water closet seat height and the sprung seat is part of the private office toilet room exceptions discussed in the general commentary to Chapter 6.

See Section 604.11.4 for provisions for toilet seat height in toilet rooms or stalls specifically designed for children's use.

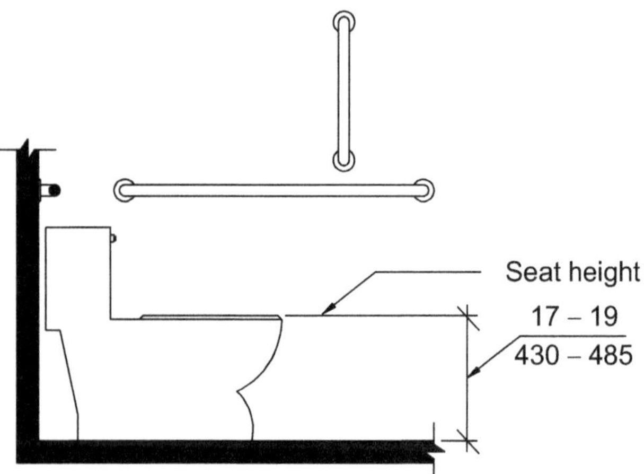

FIGURE 604.4
WATER CLOSET SEAT HEIGHT

604.5 Grab Bars. Grab bars for water closets shall comply with Section 609 and shall be provided in accordance with Sections 604.5.1 and 604.5.2. Grab bars shall be provided on the rear wall and on the side wall closest to the water closet.

EXCEPTIONS:

1. Grab bars are not required to be installed in a toilet room for a single occupant, accessed only through a private office and not for common use or public use, provided reinforcement has been installed in walls and located so as to permit the installation of grab bars complying with Section 604.5.
2. In detention or correction facilities, grab bars are not required to be installed in housing or holding cells or rooms that are specially designed without protrusions for purposes of suicide prevention.

❖ See Section 609 for specific requirements for grab bar size, wall clearance, height and installation requirements. Side and rear grab bars are required at all water closets. Section 604.11.5 references this provision for grab bar length and orientation in toilet rooms or stalls specifically designed for children's use.

A wall immediately adjacent to the water closet provides a solid support for grab bars. Grab bars mounted wall-to-floor without lateral bracing tend to become loose and contribute to a feeling of insecurity in users. Swing-down bars mounted behind the water closet may serve a person wearing leg braces or having a similar mobility impairment, but may not be stable enough to provide assistance in a transfer by most wheelchair users. Swing down grab bars are only permitted in Type B units (see Section 1004.11.1).

Side and rear grab bars should be horizontally mounted. Grab bars mounted vertically, diagonally or in locations other than on the walls behind and adjacent to the water closet do not provide equivalent stability or graspability for transfer from a wheelchair. A grab bar that is one piece, located along the entire range for the two separate grab bars, is acceptable (see Section 609.7). Commentary Figures C604.3.1(a) and C604.3.1(b) show the diagonal and side approaches used to transfer from a wheelchair to a water closet.

There are several exceptions to this section.

Exception 1 allows for just the blocking to be provided for the future installation of grab bars as part of the private office toilet room exceptions discussed in the general commentary to Chapter 6.

Exception 2 is limited to detention and correctional facilities and to areas within those facilities that are specifically designed for suicide prevention. Even though the exception would specifically exempt grab bars, there are grab bars made that have a continuous support so that there is no "bar" to allow someone to hook something through to potentially strangle themselves (see Commentary Figure C604.5).

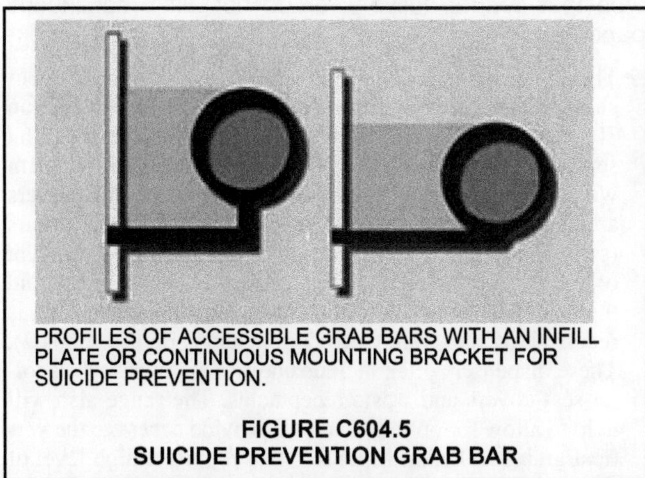

PROFILES OF ACCESSIBLE GRAB BARS WITH AN INFILL PLATE OR CONTINUOUS MOUNTING BRACKET FOR SUICIDE PREVENTION.

FIGURE C604.5
SUICIDE PREVENTION GRAB BAR

604.5.1 Fixed Side Wall Grab Bars. Fixed side-wall grab bars shall be 42 inches (1065 mm) minimum in length, located 12 inches (305 mm) maximum from the rear wall and extending 54 inches (1370 mm) minimum from the rear wall. In addition, a vertical grab bar 18 inches (455 mm) minimum in length shall be mounted with the bottom of the bar located 39 inches (990 mm) minimum and 41 inches (1040 mm) maximum above the floor, and with the center line of the bar located 39 inches (990 mm) minimum and 41 inches (1040 mm) maximum from the rear wall.

EXCEPTION: The vertical grab bar at water closets primarily for children's use shall comply with Section 609.4.2.

❖ The grab bar located on the side wall must be properly located and of sufficient length to allow the user to place an arm on the grab bar while transferring between the water closet and the wheelchair (see Figure 609.4.2).

The vertical bar on the side wall was added to aid a person who may use other types of mobility aids and needs assistance to rise or sit on the water closet. Grabbing the horizontal grab bar to rise would require twisting of the wrist and provide minimal leverage.

The exception allows for the vertical grab located at water closets designed for children to be lower and closer to the back wall so it is within the reach of children on the smaller water closets.

604.5.2 Rear Wall Grab Bars. The rear wall grab bar shall be 36 inches (915 mm) minimum in length, and extend from the centerline of the water closet 12 inches (305 mm) minimum on the side closest to the wall, and 24 inches (610 mm) minimum on the transfer side.

EXCEPTIONS:

1. The rear grab bar shall be permitted to be 24 inches (610 mm) minimum in length, centered on the water closet, where wall space does not permit a grab bar 36 inches (915 mm) minimum in length due to the location of a recessed fixture adjacent to the water closet.
2. Where an administrative authority requires flush controls for flush valves to be located in a position that conflicts with the location of the rear grab bar, that grab bar shall be permitted to be split or shifted to the open side of the toilet area.

❖ A 36-inch-long (915 mm) grab bar will provide 24 inches (610 mm) on the side of the water closet opposite the wall. This will aid the person who must reach across his or her body to reach the grab bar and make a transfer.

Exception 1 permits a 24-inch (610 mm) rear grab bar, centered on the water closet, in the configuration shown in Commentary Figure C603.2(c).

In some public bathrooms with heavy usage, a designer may choose to use a flush-o-meter system rather than a tank system (see Commentary Figure C604.5.2). The system has less maintenance and fewer chances for vandalism than the tank type. The flush-o-meter could possibly conflict with the rear grab bar. In such situations, per Exception 2, a split rear grab bar would be acceptable.

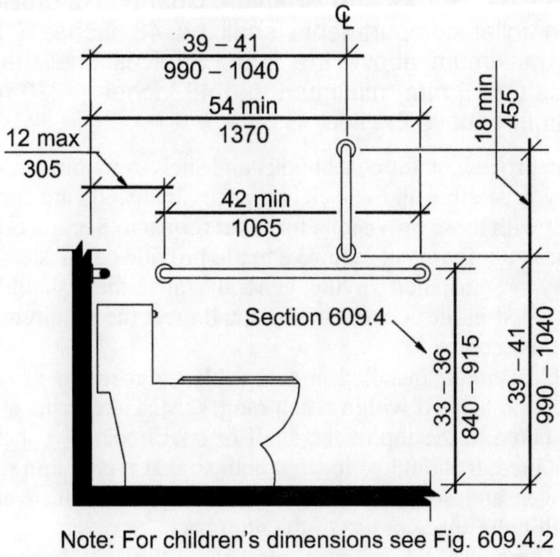

Note: For children's dimensions see Fig. 609.4.2

FIGURE 604.5.1
SIDE WALL GRAB BAR FOR WATER CLOSET

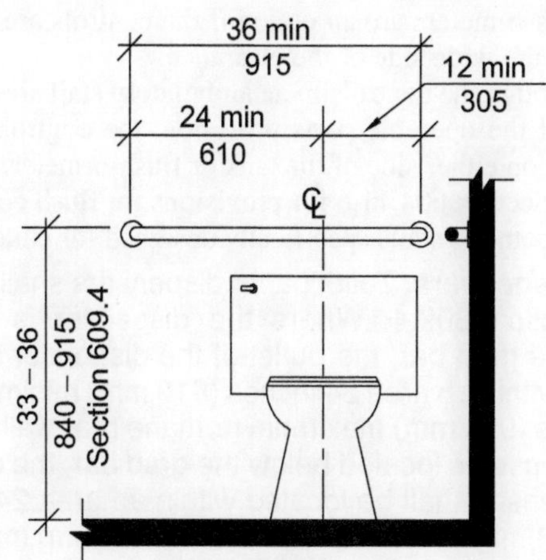

Note: For children's dimensions see Fig. 609.4.2

FIGURE 604.5.2
REAR WALL GRAB BAR FOR WATER CLOSET

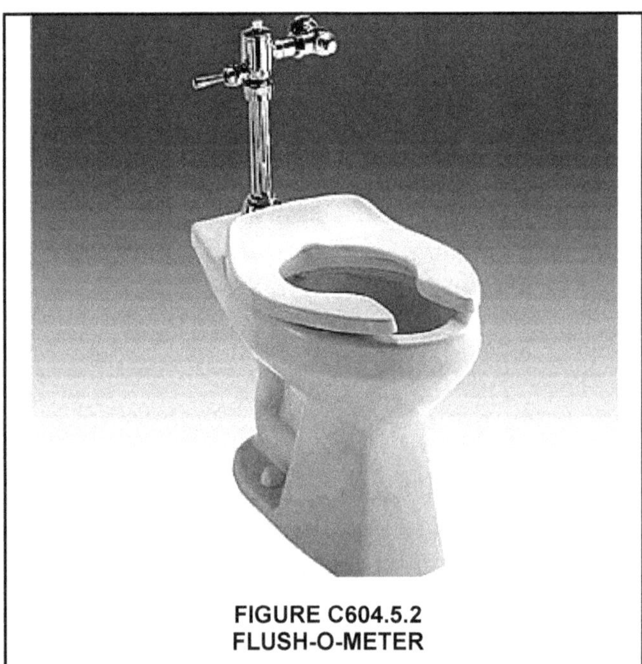

FIGURE C604.5.2
FLUSH-O-METER

604.6 Flush Controls. Flush controls shall be hand operated or automatic. Hand operated flush controls shall comply with Section 309. Flush controls shall be located on the open side of the water closet.

EXCEPTION: In ambulatory accessible compartments complying with Section 604.10, flush controls shall be permitted to be located on either side of the water closet.

❖ The reference to Section 309 assumes that the controls are operable. The controls must be within reach of a user sitting on the side from which the transfer is made. Automatic controls have no additional requirements.

Flush controls for tank-type toilets have a standardized mounting location on the left side of the tank (facing the tank). Tanks are available by special order with controls mounted on the right side. Tanks must not block access to the grab bar. See the commentary to Section 609.3 for clearances below the grab bar.

Flush-o-meters are an option if the controls are oriented toward the wide side of the clearance.

Although the controls in an ambulatory stall are required to meet the operable parts provision, the controls can be located on either side of the tank or flush-o-meter.

See Section 604.11.6 for provisions for flush controls in toilet rooms or stalls specifically designed for children.

604.7 Dispensers. Toilet paper dispensers shall comply with Section 309.4. Where the dispenser is located above the grab bar, the outlet of the dispenser shall be located within an area 24 inches (610 mm) minimum and 36 inches (915 mm) maximum from the rear wall. Where the dispenser is located below the grab bar, the outlet of the dispenser shall be located within an area 24 inches (610 mm) minimum and 42 inches (1065 mm) maximum from the rear wall. The outlet of the dispenser shall be located 18 inches (455 mm) minimum and 48 inches (1220 mm) maximum above the floor. Dispensers shall comply with Section 609.3. Dispensers shall not be of a type that control delivery, or do not allow continuous paper flow.

❖ The dispenser must be located within the prescribed dimensions, which fall within the reaches established in Section 308, but at the same time keep the dispenser over the toilet seat rim height (see Figure 604.7). A common problem within toilet rooms and compartments is that the dispensers are located so that they interfere with the use of the grab bars (see Section 609.3 for clearance requirements). The intent of the range allowing for the dispensers to be located behind the grab bars is to allow for the style of dispenser that is recessed in the wall (see Commentary Figure C604.7). These dispensers often include additional items such as toilet seat covers and waste receptacles. The range also will help to allow for options that will provide access to the vertical grab bar. Paper dispensers that require a high level of dexterity or effort are not acceptable.

See Section 604.11.7 for provisions for dispensers in toilet rooms or stalls specifically designed for children.

FIGURE C604.7
RECESSED DISPENSERS

604.8 Coat Hooks and Shelves. Coat hooks provided within toilet compartments shall be 48 inches (1220 mm) maximum above the floor. Shelves shall be 40 inches (1015 mm) minimum and 48 inches (1220 mm) maximum above the floor.

❖ The provisions for coats hooks and shelves within ambulatory accessible and wheelchair accessible stalls are consistent with those provisions for toilet rooms in Section 603.4. These items are not required, but to provide equal access, if they are installed in the general stalls, they should be installed in the accessible stalls and meet the requirements in this section.

Coat hooks installed in accessible toilet rooms or stalls must be located within reach ranges. Measurements are to be taken to the top of the shelf or coat hook. If a shelf is installed, it should be located both so that it is within reach ranges and so that it won't interfere with maneuvering within the space or use of the grab bars.

There are no specific provisions for children sizes because the expected reach ranges (see Commentary Table C308.1) are lower than that permitted for adults.

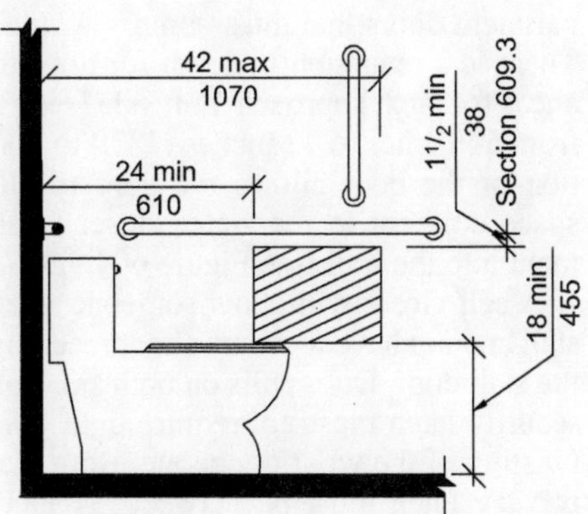

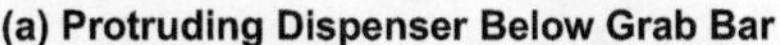

(a) Protruding Dispenser Below Grab Bar

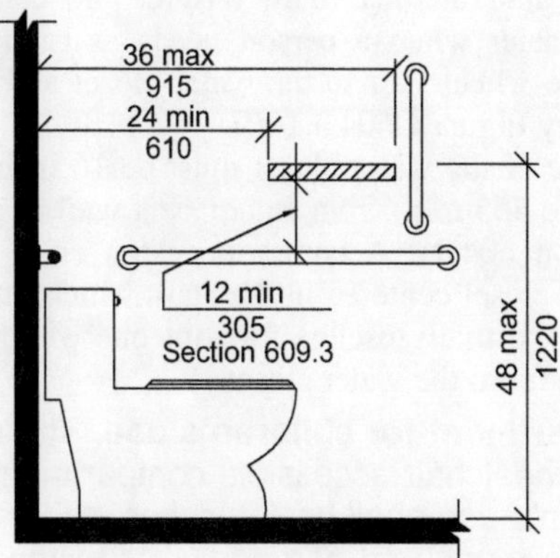

(b) Protruding Dispenser Above Grab Bar

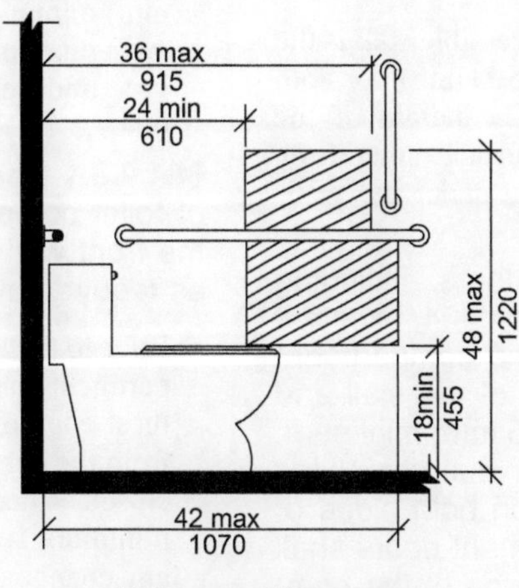

(c) Recessed Dispenser

Note: For children's dimensions see Fig. 604.11.7 dispenser outlet location

FIGURE 604.7
DISPENSER OUTLET LOCATION

604.9 Wheelchair Accessible Compartments.

❖ A wheelchair accessible compartment provides sufficient space for a person using a wheelchair to completely enter the water closet compartment and close the door.

Section 604.11.8 references this provision for toilet stalls specifically designed for children.

604.9.1 General. Wheelchair accessible compartments shall comply with Section 604.9.

❖ This standard recognizes two types of stalls: wheelchair accessible and ambulatory accessible. Scoping provisions adopted by the administrative authority will specify how many of each design are required.

Requirements for toilet fixture height, clear floor space, grab bars, flush controls and dispensers in Section 604 are the same for toilet stalls and separate toilet rooms. If a lavatory is also provided within the accessible toilet compartment, the compartment must comply with the same provisions as a single-occupant toilet room.

604.9.2 Size. Toilet compartments shall comply with Section 604.9.2.1 or 604.9.2.2 as applicable.

❖ Accessible toilet stalls are sized for adults (Section 604.9.2.1) or for children (Section 604.9.2.2).

604.9.2.1 Minimum area. The minimum area of a wheelchair accessible compartment shall be 60 inches (1525 mm) minimum in width measured perpendicular to the side wall, and 56 inches (1420 mm) minimum in depth for wall hung water closets, and 59 inches (1500 mm) minimum in depth for floor mounted water closets measured perpendicular to the rear wall.

❖ The compartment is sized to allow the person using the wheelchair to maneuver within so the occupant gains full and easy access to the water closet and its controls. The length is dependent on the type of water closet installed. Because floor-mounted water closets encroach on toe clearances, the compartment must be 3 inches (75 mm) longer than for the wall-mounted water closet (see Figure 604.9.2).

A 60-inch-wide (1525 mm) compartment would permit a wheelchair user to transfer to the water closet by pulling up parallel to the fixture and affecting a side transfer. More individuals are able to transfer from a position parallel to the water closet than diagonal to the fixture. This configuration is also easier when a person needs assistance to transfer from the wheelchair to the water closet and back [see Commentary Figure C604.3.1(a)].

The centerline of the water closet must be 16 inches to 18 inches (405 to 455 mm) from an adjacent wall or partition (see Section 604.2). A common design error is to locate the water closet centered in the stall, which renders the compartment virtually useless for someone who needs to do a side transfer to the water closet.

604.9.2.2 Compartment for children's use. The minimum area of a wheelchair accessible compartment primarily for children's use shall be 60 inches (1525 mm) minimum in width measured perpendicular to the side wall, and 59 inches (1500 mm) minimum in depth for wall hung and floor mounted water closets measured perpendicular to the rear wall.

❖ The size for the children's wheelchair accessible stall is the same, 60 inches by 59 inches (1525 by 1500 mm), for both wall-hung and floor-mounted toilets. The height of the children's footplates are higher than for an adult; therefore, they cannot take advantage of the space under the wall-hung toilet [see Figure 604.9.5(b)].

604.9.3 Doors. Toilet compartment doors, including door hardware, shall comply with Section 404, except if the approach is to the latch side of the compartment door clearance between the door side of the stall and any obstruction shall be 42 inches (1065 mm) minimum. The door shall be self-closing. A door pull complying with Section 404.2.6 shall be placed on both sides of the door near the latch. Toilet compartment doors shall not swing into the required minimum area of the compartment.

❖ The general reference to Section 404 results in toilet compartment doors that must comply with all door provisions. There is a reduction in depth for door maneuvering clearances for latch approach, pull side [see Figure 404.2.3.2(f)] from 54 inches to 42 inches (1370 to 1065 mm). The location of the door allows the door to align with the clear space adjacent to the water closet to allow easier movement into the stall [see Figure 604.9.3.1(a) and (b)].

A self closer will allow someone to enter the accessible stall and not have to worry about reaching back out to close the stall door. Door pulls on both sides of the doors and the security latch must not require tight grasping, pinching or twisting of the wrist to operate. Both the door pull and the privacy latch must be between 34 inches and 48 inches (865 and 1220 mm) above the floor.

There is an alternate wheelchair accessible stall that allows a narrower approach path. Thirty-six inches (915 mm) minimum of additional depth is needed to let the door swing into the stall and still allow the user to enter, maneuver and close the compartment door [see Figure 604.9.3.1(c)].

604.9.3.1 Door Opening Location. The farthest edge of toilet compartment door opening shall be located in the front wall or partition or in the side wall or partition as required by Table 604.9.3.1.

❖ Prior to the 2009 edition, regardless of how large the compartment was. the standard previously required that the farthest edge of the door be located a maximum of 4 inches from the corner of the compartment farthest from the water closet. Where water closet compartments are built to the minimum size required, Table 604.9.3.1 will not result in any change of the door location from what was required in the 2003 edition [see Figure 604.9.3.1(a) and (b)]. How-

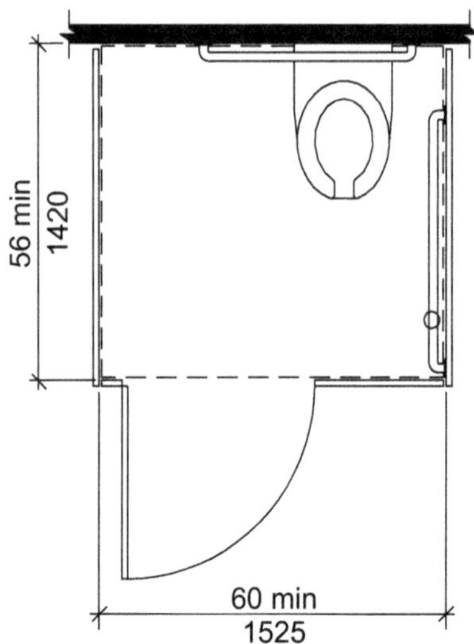

(a) Wall-Hung Water Closet – Adult

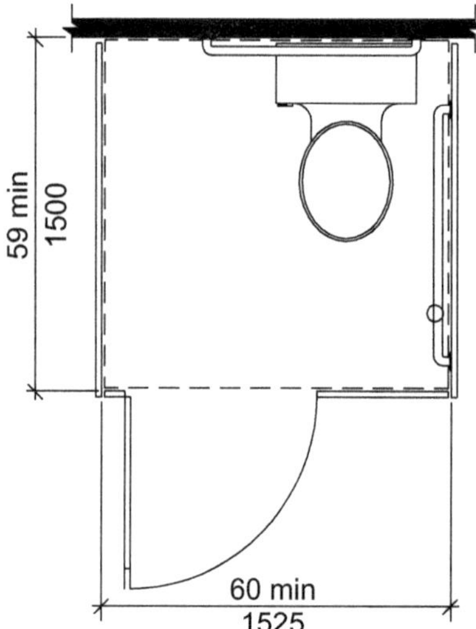

(b) Floor-Mounted Water Closet – Adult
Wall-Hung and
Floor-Mounted Water Closet – Children

FIGURE 604.9.2
WHEELCHAIR ACCESSIBLE TOILET COMPARTMENTS

ever, where the compartments are built larger than the required minimum size, the table and provisions will provide more design flexibility in establishing the location of the door. For larger compartments, the standard will permit the door to be located based on either of two separate requirements (see Commentary Figure C604.9.3.1.

The additional permitted dimensions for the opening location provide the same distance from the rear wall or side wall or partition as was previously required for either a floor-mounted or wall-hung water closet. For an opening located in the front partition, using the required minimum width of the compartment of 60 inches (1525 mm), the farthest edge of the door opening would be either 4 inches (100 mm) from the side wall or partition farthest from the water closet or 56 inches (1420 mm) from the side wall or partition that is closest to the water closet. If the width of the compartment was increased to 72 inches (1828 mm), Table 604.9.3.1 would provide a range of 12 inches (305 mm) in which the farthest edge of the door could be located. This additional range of location may assist in being able to design around some other fixture, allow a larger support member for the partition or provide some other benefit.

The 56-, 52-, and 55-inch (1420 by 1320 by 1395 mm) dimensions that are shown in the table were derived from subtracting the 4-inch (100 mm) requirement from the minimum size for a water closet compartment. For example, a floor-mounted water closet would require a 59-inch (1499 mm) minimum compartment depth based on the requirements of Section 604.9.2. Therefore, the standard will permit the door to be located in the side partition either a maximum of 4 inches from the front partition or 55 inches (1395 mm) (59 – 4 = 55) from the rear wall. Those two points will remain set regardless of the actual depth of the compartment.

Permitting the farthest edge of the opening to be located at a point equal to or greater than that required for a minimum sized compartment allows greater flexibility in design and use of building space without lessening the current minimum accessibility criteria for entering and exiting a wheelchair accessible compartment. In addition, a larger compartment will provide greater maneuvering space within the compartment and therefore make the compartment and access to the door easier for the users.

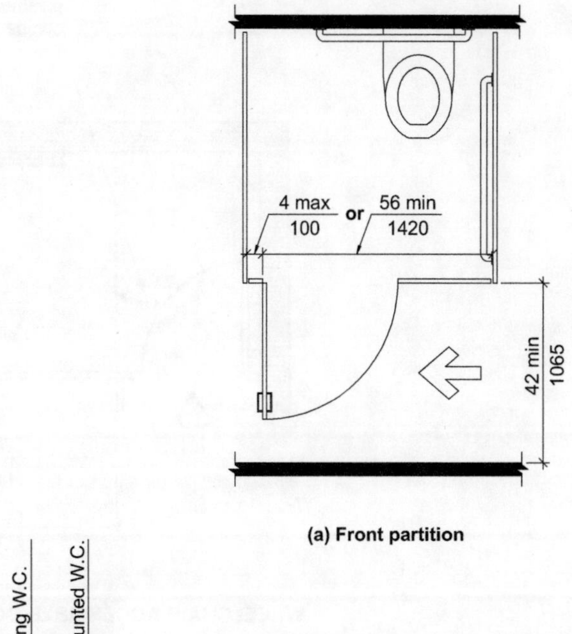

(a) Front partition

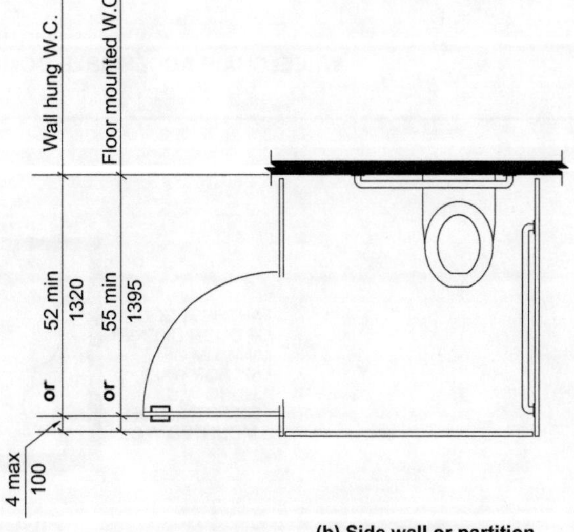

(b) Side wall or partition

FIGURE 604.9.3.1(a) and (b) WHEELCHAIR ACCESSIBLE COMPARTMENT DOOR OPENINGS

TABLE 604.9.3.1—DOOR OPENING LOCATION

Door Opening Location	Measured From	Dimension
Front Wall or Partition	From the side wall or partition closest to the water closet	56 inches (1420 mm) minimum
	or	
	From the side wall or partition farthest from the water closet	4 inches (100 mm) maximum
Side Wall or Partition Wall-Hung Water Closet	From the rear wall	52 inches (1320 mm) minimum
	or	
	From the front wall or partition	4 inches (100 mm) maximum
Side Wall or Partition Floor-Mounted Water Closet	From the rear wall	55 inches (1395 mm) minimum
	or	
	From the front wall or partition	4 inches (100 mm) maximum

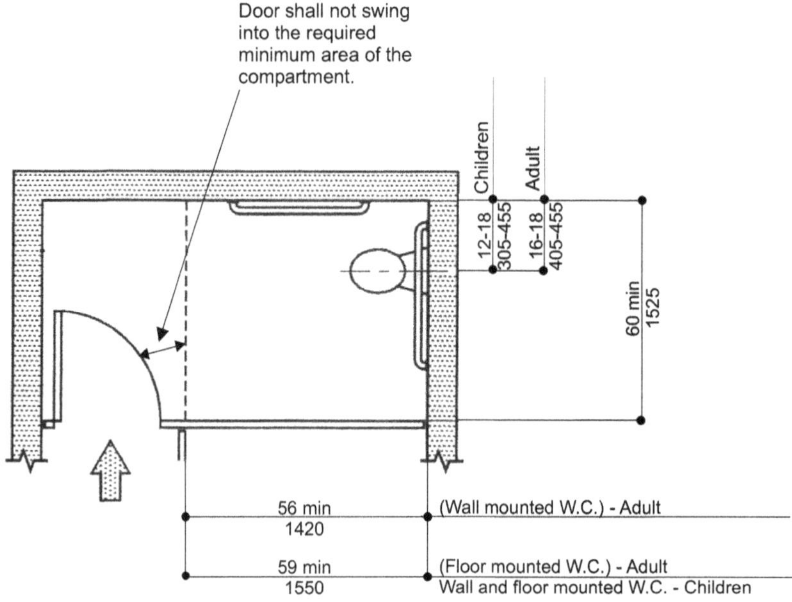

FIGURE 604.9.3.1(c)
WHEELCHAIR ACCESSIBLE COMPARTMENT DOOR OPENINGS-ALTERNATE

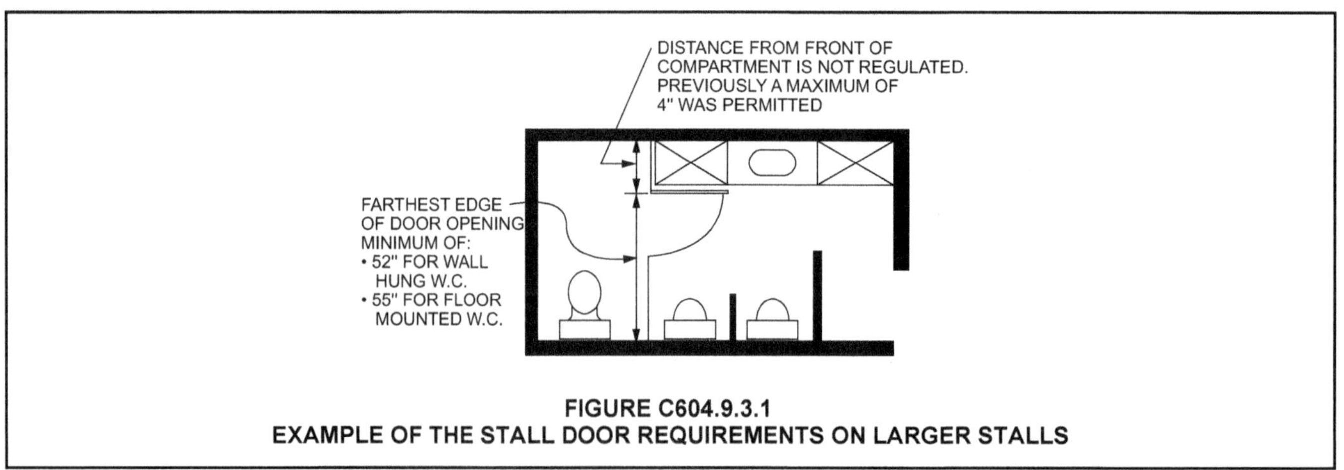

FIGURE C604.9.3.1
EXAMPLE OF THE STALL DOOR REQUIREMENTS ON LARGER STALLS

604.9.4 Approach. Wheelchair accessible compartments shall be arranged for left-hand or right-hand approach to the water closet.

❖ Both left-hand and right-hand approaches are acceptable as may be dictated by the proposed layout.

604.9.5 Toe Clearance. Toe clearance for compartments primarily for children's use shall comply with Section 604.9.5.2. Toe clearance for other wheelchair accessible compartments shall comply with Section 604.9.5.1.

❖ The toe clearance beneath the partition is used for maneuvering when the compartment is built to the minimum size. Partitions around stalls for children have a higher toe clearance requirement than for adults.

604.9.5.1 Toe Clearance at Compartments. The front partition and at least one side partition shall provide a toe clearance of 9 inches (230 mm) minimum above the floor and extending 6 inches (150 mm) beyond the compartment side face of the partition, exclusive of partition support members.

EXCEPTIONS:

1. Toe clearance at the front partition is not required in a compartment greater than 62 inches (1575 mm) in depth with a wall-hung water closet, or greater than 65 inches (1650 mm) in depth with a floor-mounted water closet.
2. Toe clearance at the side partition is not required in a compartment greater than 66 inches (1675 mm) in width.

❖ In the minimum sized stall, a person maneuvering will use some of the space under the stall walls on the front and at least one side of the stall. The average height of the toes of adults using a standard wheelchair requires the bottom of the stall walls to be at least 9 inches above the floor. The minimum depth needed for the toe clearance is 6 inches (150 mm), but additional space can be provided. If the size of the stall exceeds 65 inches (1650 mm) in depth and 66 inches (1675 mm) in width, a toe clearance is not required. If the stall exceeds the minimum dimension in only one direction, the toe clearance is not required on that side.

604.9.5.2 Toe Clearance at Compartments for Children's Use. The front partition and at least one side partition of compartments primarily for children's use shall provide a toe clearance of 12 inches (305 mm) minimum above the floor and extending 6 inches (150 mm) beyond the compartment side face of the partition, exclusive of partition support members.

EXCEPTIONS:

1. Toe clearance at the front partition is not required in a compartment greater than 65 inches (1650 mm) in depth.
2. Toe clearance at the side partition is not required in a compartment greater than 66 inches (1675 mm) in width.

❖ The logic for stalls serving children is the same as stalls serving adults (see Section 604.9.5.1), except that a child's footplates are located higher. This is because the seats of the wheelchairs are not substantially lower than adults, and the children's legs are shorter. Therefore, the clearance needed on a minimum sized stall serving children will need the bottom of the stall walls to be at least 12 inches (305 mm) above the floor. The minimum depth needed for the toe clearance is 6 inches (150 mm), but additional space can be provided. If the size of the stall exceeds 65 inches (1650 mm) in depth and 66 inches (1675 mm) in width, a toe clearance is not required. If the stall exceeds the minimum dimension in only one direction, the toe clearance is not required on that side.

604.9.6 Grab Bars. Grab bars shall comply with Section 609. Side wall grab bars complying with Section 604.5.1 located on the wall closest to the water closet, and a rear wall grab bar complying with Section 604.5.2, shall be provided.

❖ See Section 609 for specific requirements for size, wall clearance, height and installation requirements.

Requirements for grab bars within wheelchair accessible toilet stalls are the same as those for water closets in a room. Side grab bars include both the horizontal and vertical grab bars (see Sections 604.5.1 and 604.5.2). The use of swing-up grab bars is limited to Type B units found in Section 1004.11.1.1.

604.10 Ambulatory Accessible Compartments.

❖ An ambulatory accessible stall can be used by a person with a mobility impairment that may require additional support. Ambulatory stalls are typically scoped in the building codes so they occur when six or more water closets and urinals are provided within a single toilet room. This is in addition to the wheelchair accessible stall requirements, not an alternate or replacement for them.

Section 604.11.8 references this provision for ambulatory toilet stalls specifically designed for children.

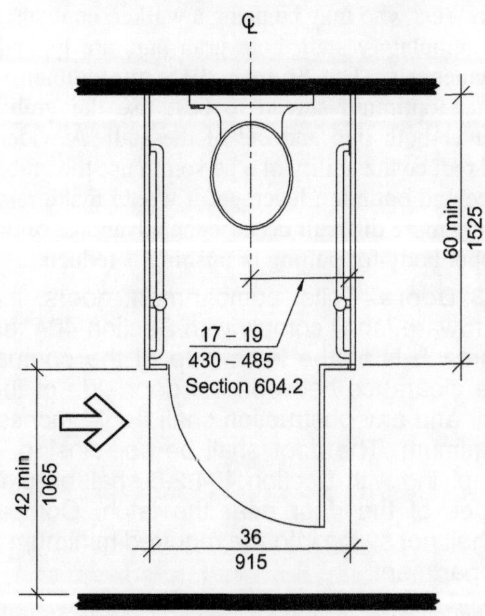

FIGURE 604.10
AMBULATORY ACCESSIBLE COMPARTMENT

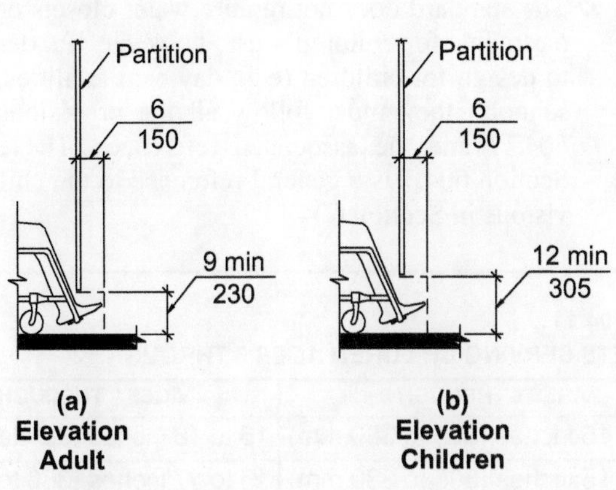

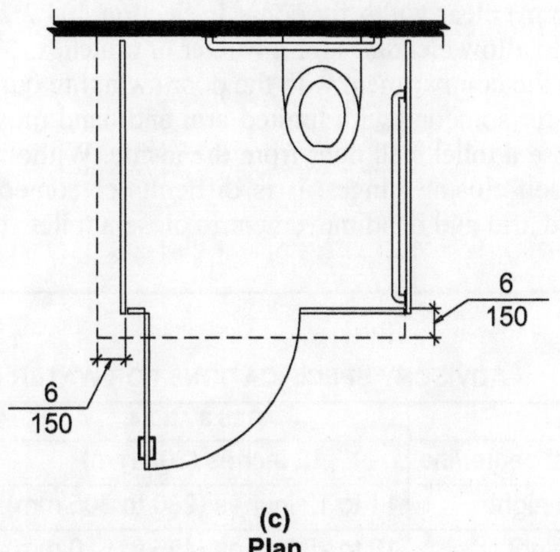

FIGURE 604.9.5
WHEELCHAIR ACCESSIBLE COMPARTMENT TOE CLEARANCE

604.10.1 General. Ambulatory accessible compartments shall comply with Section 604.10.

❖ This standard recognizes two types of stalls: wheelchair accessible and ambulatory accessible. Scoping provisions adopted by the administrative authority will specify the number of each design required.

Requirements for toilet fixture height, maneuvering space, grab bar technical criteria, flush controls and dispensers in Section 604 are the same for toilet stalls and separate toilet rooms (see Figure 604.10).

604.10.2 Size. The minimum area of an ambulatory accessible compartment shall be 60 inches (1525 mm) minimum in depth and 36 inches (915 mm) in width.

❖ The width dimension is absolute. A common mistake is to make the ambulatory stall wider, with the intent to better facilitate wheelchair access. However, the purpose of the ambulatory stall is more to serve persons with mobility impairments who may be using a walker, cane or crutches. In an ambulatory stall, both grab bars are typically used simultaneously. The 36-inch (915 mm) dimension provides an optimum spread to best use the grab bars to maneuver both into and out of the stall. A wider spread would reduce the ability of a person to use the grab bars for balance and optimum leverage. It would make raising and lowering more difficult because the advantage of the use of the upper body for pulling or pushing is reduced.

604.10.3 Doors. Toilet compartment doors, including door hardware, shall comply with Section 404, except if the approach is to the latch side of the compartment door the clearance between the door side of the compartment and any obstruction shall be 42 inches (1065 mm) minimum. The door shall be self-closing. A door pull complying with Section 404.2.6 shall be placed on both sides of the door near the latch. Compartment doors shall not swing into the required minimum area of the compartment.

❖ The general reference to Section 404 results in toilet compartment doors that must comply with all door provisions. There is a reduction in depth for door maneuvering clearances for latch approach, pull side [see Figure 404.2.3.2(f)] from 54 inches to 42 inches (1370 to 1065 mm). The 32-inch (815 mm) clear width for doors in Section 404.2.2 is applicable to allow clearance for a walker or crutches.

When in the compartment with the door swinging out, it is difficult for someone with limited arm and hand movement to close a toilet stall door from the inside. Without a handle or self-closing hinges, it is difficult for someone with limited arm and hand movement to close a toilet stall door from the inside. A self closer allows someone to enter the accessible stall and not have to worry about reaching back to close the stall door. Door pulls on both sides of the doors and the security latch must not require tight grasping, pinching or twisting of the wrist to operate. Both the door pull and the privacy latch must be between 34 inches (865 mm) and 48 inches (1220 mm) above the floor.

604.10.4 Grab Bars. Grab bars shall comply with Section 609. Side wall grab bars complying with Section 604.5.1 shall be provided on both sides of the compartment.

❖ See Section 609 for specific requirements for size, wall clearance, height and installation.

Side grab bars, both horizontal and vertical, are required on both sides of an ambulatory accessible stall. These bars provide balance and stability to a person while maneuvering in or out of the stall (see Section 604.5.1). Rear grab bars are not required in an ambulatory stall.

604.11 Water Closets and Toilet Compartments for Children's Use.

❖ These provisions are intended for water closets and toilet compartments specifically designed for children. The anticipated age is 3 to 12 years. The anthropometrics for children are different from those of the average adult male. The U.S. Access Board has reviewed provisions for children. Commentary Table C308.1 is based on that research and provides guidance on unobstructed reach ranges for children according to age when building elements such as coat hooks or operable parts are primarily designed for use by children. The dimensions apply to either forward or side reaches. In addition, Table C604.11 provides guidance in applying the specifications for water closets for children according to the age group served and reflects specifications that correspond to the age of the primary use group. The specifications of one age group should be consistently applied in the installation of water closets and related items. These tables are informational only and are not intended to present requirements.

604.11.1 General. Accessible water closets and toilet compartments primarily for children's use shall comply with Section 604.11.

❖ The standard does not require water closets or toilet compartments for children's use; however, if a designer wants to design for children (e.g., day care facilities, elementary schools) they must follow all the provisions in Section 604.11 and the associated references. The exception in Section 604.1 is a general reference to the child sized provisions in Section 604.11.

Table C604.11
ADVISORY SPECIFICATIONS FOR WATER CLOSETS SERVING CHILDREN AGES 3 THROUGH 12

	AGES 3 AND 4	AGES 5 THROUGH 8	AGES 9 THROUGH 12
Water closet centerline	12 inches (305 mm)	12 to 15 inches (305 to 380 mm)	15 to 18 inches (380 to 455 mm)
Toilet seat height	11 to 12 inches (280 to 305 mm)	12 to 15 inches (305 to 380 mm)	15 to 17 inches (380 to 430 mm)
Grab bar height	18 to 20 inches (455 to 510 mm)	20 to 25 inches (510 to 635 mm)	25 to 27 inches (635 to 685 mm)
Dispenser height	14 inches (355 mm)	14 to 17 inches (355 to 430 mm)	17 to 19 inches (430 to 485 mm)

604.11.2 Location. The water closet primarily for children's use shall be located with a wall or partition to the rear and to one side. The centerline of the water closet shall be 12 inches (305 mm) minimum and 18 inches (455 mm) maximum from the side wall or partition. Water closets located in ambulatory accessible toilet compartments specified in Section 604.10 shall be located as specified in Section 604.2.

❖ In single occupant rooms or wheelchair accessible stalls designed for children, the center of the water closet can be located closer to the wall than required for adults (see Section 604.2 and Figure 604.11.2). The center of the water closet in an ambulatory accessible stall is the same as for adults.

604.11.3 Clearance. A clearance around the water closet primarily for children's use complying with Section 604.3 shall be provided.

❖ The clearance around a water closet in an accessible toilet room designed for children is the same as for adults (see Section 604.3). The lavatory or any fixture other than the water closet must not overlap this clear floor space.

604.11.4 Height. The height of water closet seats primarily for children's use shall be 11 inches (280 mm) minimum and 17 inches (430 mm) maximum above the floor, measured to the top of the seat. Seats shall not be sprung to return to a lifted position.

❖ The height for the water closet in accessible single occupant rooms, wheelchair accessible stalls or ambulatory accessible stalls designed for children can have the height of the water closet lower than the 17-inch to 19-inch (430 to 485 mm) required for adults in Section 604.4 (see Figure 604.11.4).

604.11.5 Grab Bars. Grab bars for water closets primarily for children's use shall comply with Section 604.5.

❖ The length and relative orientation of the grab bars in single occupant toilet rooms, wheelchair accessible stalls and ambulatory accessible stalls designed for children is the same as those for adults (see Sections 604.5.1 and 604.5.2). However, the height of the grab bars for children is lowered (see Section 609.4.2). The location for vertical grab bars in Section 604.5.1 is based on the adult provisions for grab bar height in Section 609.4. The exception in 604.5.1 allows for the vertical grab bar to be located so that the orientation of the vertical and horizontal grab bars is appropriate for children and their shorter size and reach.

604.11.6 Flush Controls. Flush controls primarily for children's use shall be hand operated or automatic. Hand operated flush controls shall comply with Sections 309.2 and 309.4 and shall be installed 36 inches (915 mm) maximum above the floor. Flush controls shall be located on the open side of the water closet.

EXCEPTION: In ambulatory accessible compartments complying with Section 604.10, flush controls shall be permitted to be located on either side of the water closet.

❖ Provisions for flush controls for adults are addressed in Section 604.6. Although the provisions for children are basically the same, the difference is that the upper reach range for flush controls is 36 inches (915 mm) rather than 48 inches (1220 mm). This results from the specifics in this section rather than the direct reference to Section 309.3. This is consistent with the reach ranges for 3 and 4 year olds indicated in Commentary Table C308.1.

604.11.7 Dispensers. Toilet paper dispensers primarily for children's use shall comply with Section 309.4. The outlet of dispensers shall be located within an area 24 inches (610 mm) minimum and 42 inches (1065 mm) maximum from the rear wall. The outlet of the dispenser shall be 14 inches (355 mm) minimum and 19 inches (485 mm) maximum above the floor. There shall be a clearance of $1^1/_2$ inches (38 mm) minimum below the grab bar. Dispensers shall not be of a type that control delivery or do not allow continuous paper flow.

❖ The provisions for toilet paper dispensers for adults are located in Section 604.7. The main difference for children is that the outlet of the dispenser are at a height range that only permits the toilet paper dispenser below the grab bar. The general provisions for grab bars in Section 609.3 will require a minimum of $1^1/_2$-inch (38 mm) clearance below the grab bars for adults as well as for children.

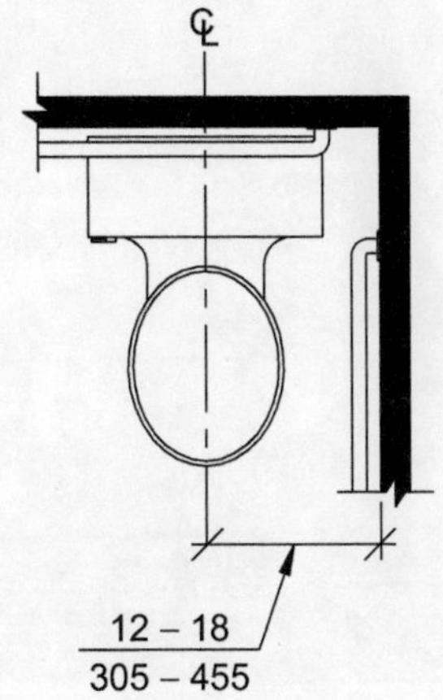

FIGURE 604.11.2
CHILDREN'S WATER CLOSET LOCATION

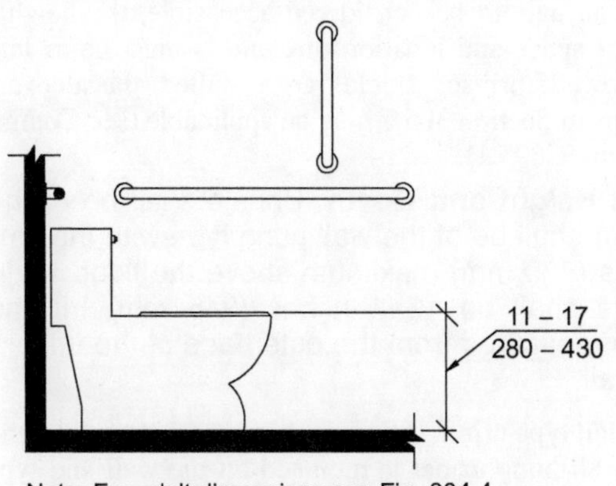

Note: For adult dimensions see Fig. 604.4

FIGURE 604.11.4
CHILDREN'S WATER CLOSET HEIGHT

It is not the intent to prohibit other types of dispensers from being provided, such as a toilet seat cover dispenser or a waste receptacle.

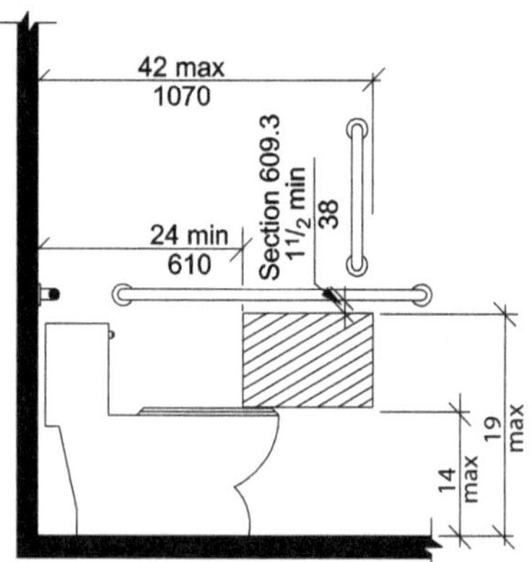

Note: For adult dimensions see Fig. 604.7

FIGURE 604.11.7
CHILDREN'S DISPENSER OUTLET LOCATION

604.11.8 Toilet Compartments. Toilet compartments primarily for children's use shall comply with Sections 604.9 and 604.10, as applicable.

❖ The general provisions for wheelchair accessible stalls and ambulatory accessible stalls are referenced for children. However, Section 604.9.2.2 contains child specific provisions for wheelchair accessible stall dimensions and Section 604.9.5.2 details child specific provisions for higher toe clearance requirements.

605 Urinals

❖ The intent of Section 605 is to address urinals for all uses other than within Accessible, Type A and Type B units. However, because urinals are not typically found in bathrooms in dwellings or sleeping units, requirements for urinals are not found in Chapter 10.

There are no specific provisions for urinals that are being designed for children.

605.1 General. Accessible urinals shall comply with Section 605.

❖ For urinals to be considered accessible, the height, clear floor space and location of controls must be as indicated below. If privacy shields are installed, the alcove provisions in Section 305.7 may be applicable (see Commentary Figure C605.1).

605.2 Height and Depth. Urinals shall be of the stall type or shall be of the wall hung type with the rim at 17 inches (430 mm) maximum above the floor. Wall hung urinals shall be $13^1/_2$ inches (345 mm) minimum in depth measured from the outer face of the urinal rim to the wall.

❖ A stall type urinal is floor mounted and extends up the wall. A wall hung urinal is mounted on the wall and typ-ically stops a few inches above the floor. The 17-inch (430 mm) maximum rim height is based on the assumption that 17 inches is a typical wheelchair seat height (see Figure 605.2).

Stall type urinals may be considered more accessible for a broader range of individuals, including people of short stature. A minimum depth of $13^1/_2$ inches (340 mm) from the outer face of the rim to the back surface of the fixture has been recommended as a usable depth for persons with disabilities.

605.3 Clear Floor Space. A clear floor space complying with Section 305, positioned for forward approach, shall be provided.

❖ The typical 30-inch by 48-inch (760 by 1220 mm) wheelchair space is required for a forward approach to urinals. The clear floor space should not extend under the urinal front rim. A person would need to stand up in front of a wheelchair to use the urinal.

To ensure a front approach, the urinal partition shall not extend past the front edge of the rim unless partitions are spaced at least 30 inches (760 mm) apart. If privacy partitions or adjacent walls extend more than 24 inches (610 mm) past the urinal rim, the clearances for alcoves in Section 305.7 would require a 36-inch (915 mm) minimum width.

605.4 Flush Controls. Flush controls shall be hand operated or automatic. Hand operated flush controls shall comply with Section 309.

❖ Manual flush controls must be located within reach ranges, and the controls themselves must meet the operable parts requirements. The best design practice would be that the clear floor space for the urinal is the same as the clear floor space required to access the flush controls, but that is not a requirement. Alternatively, automatic flush controls may be installed.

FIGURE C605.1
URINAL AND PARTITIONS

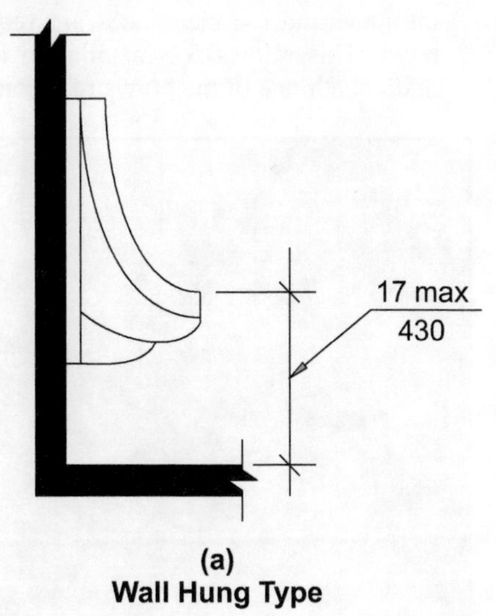

(a)
Wall Hung Type

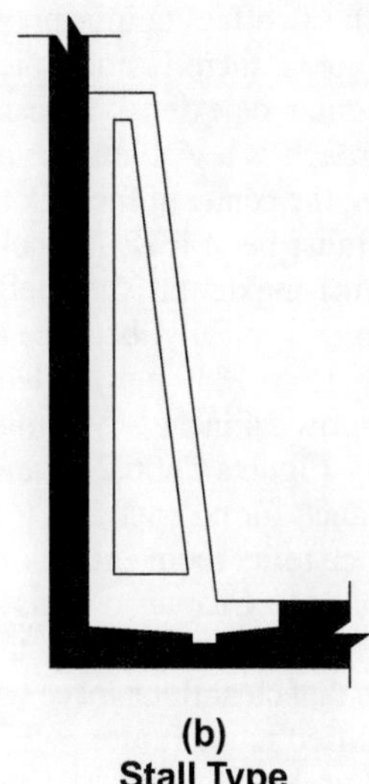

(b)
Stall Type

FIGURE 605.2
HEIGHT OF URINALS

606 Lavatories and Sinks

❖ This section addresses requirements for lavatories and sinks that must be accessible. Lavatories would typically be found in toilet and bathing rooms and used for bathing purposes such as washing hands. A sink is typically used for purposes other than bathing. Scoping provisions adopted by the administrative authority may exempt some types of sinks, such as service and mop sinks, from accessibility requirements. Special provisions for children are located in Section 606.2, Exceptions 3 and 4.

Accessible, Type A and Type B units will reference Chapter 6 for sinks and lavatories where applicable. See Chapter 10 for applicable requirements and references.

606.1 General. Accessible lavatories and sinks shall comply with Section 606.

❖ The clear floor space, knee and toe clearances, height and pipe protection for sinks and lavatories must be within the limitations in the standard to be accessible. The requirements for the faucets, soap dispensers, towel dispensers and hand dryers are to facilitate access to controls.

606.2 Clear Floor Space. A clear floor space complying with Section 305.3, positioned for forward approach, shall be provided. Knee and toe clearance complying with Section 306 shall be provided. The dip of the overflow shall not be considered in determining knee and toe clearances.

EXCEPTIONS:

1. A parallel approach complying with Section 305 and centered on the sink, shall be permitted to a kitchen sink in a space where a cook top or conventional range is not provided.
2. The requirement for knee and toe clearance shall not apply to a lavatory in a toilet or bathing facility for a single occupant, accessed only through a private office and not for common use or public use.
3. A knee clearance of 24 inches (610 mm) minimum above the floor shall be permitted at lavatories and sinks used primarily by children ages 6 through 12 where the rim or counter surface is 31 inches (785 mm) maximum above the floor.
4. A parallel approach complying with Section 305 and centered on the sink, shall be permitted at lavatories and sinks used primarily by children ages 5 and younger.
5. The requirement for knee and toe clearance shall not apply to more than one bowl of a multibowl sink.
6. A parallel approach complying with Section 305 and centered on the sink, shall be permitted at wet bars.

❖ For access to lavatories and sinks, knee and toe clearances and clear floor space must be considered. The 30-inch by 48-inch (760 by 1220 mm) dimensions in Section 305.3 are required in front of a sink or lavatory. This rectangular space may extend under the sink up to 25 inches (635 mm). An extension of not less than 17 inches (430 mm) is required for a forward approach [see Commentary Figures C306.1(b) and C306.1(c)].

The knee and toe clearances required in Sections 306.2 and 306.3 are consistently required throughout the standard. Pipes below the fixture must not restrict access to the lavatory or sink. The dip or overflow on a sink can result in a bump along the front and bottom edge of the bowl. Because this would typically be between a user's legs when they approached the sink, this should not be considered when determining whether adequate knee and toe clearances have been provided [see Commentary Figure C606.2(a)].

The first and sixth exceptions acknowledge that in kitchenette type areas, such as coffee stations in office buildings or wetbars in hotel rooms, there is not typically a need to wash dishes on a regular or extensive basis in this sink; therefore, a side approach is a viable alternative. With the centering requirement, the center of the sink to any adjacent side wall or cabinet must be at least 24 inches (610 mm). The 34-inch (865 mm) maximum sink height in Section 606.3 is still applicable. Typically, because these areas are only 3 feet to 6 feet (915 to 1830 mm) in length, the entire counter is installed below 34 inches (865 mm), not just the sink [see Commentary Figures C606.2(b) and C606.2(c)].

Exception 2 allowance for no knee and toe clearances is part of the private office toilet room exceptions discussed in the general commentary to Chapter 6. This is coordinated with the lavatory height exception in Section 606.3. The room must be sized so that clear floor space will be available if the lavatory is modified in the future.

Exceptions 3 and 4 provide for lower lavatories and sinks designed for use by children. For children age 5 and younger, a side approach is permitted [see Commentary, Figure C606.2(c)]. Even though the maximum height for the sink or lavatory is 34 inches (865 mm) (see Section 606.3), a lower height is permissible so the sink or lavatory can be used by all the children in the class. Exception 4 effectively allows any sink height at 34 inches (865 mm) or lower with no knee and toe clearances. For children 6 to 12 years old, the sink/counter maximum height is at the lower height of 31 inches (790 mm) with a minimum knee clearance of 24 inches (610 mm) instead of the 27 inches (685 mm) in Section 306.3.

Per Exception 5, when a double bowl sink is installed, the knee and toe clearances are required under only one bowl. This allows for installation of a garbage disposal underneath one of the bowls of a double bowl sink.

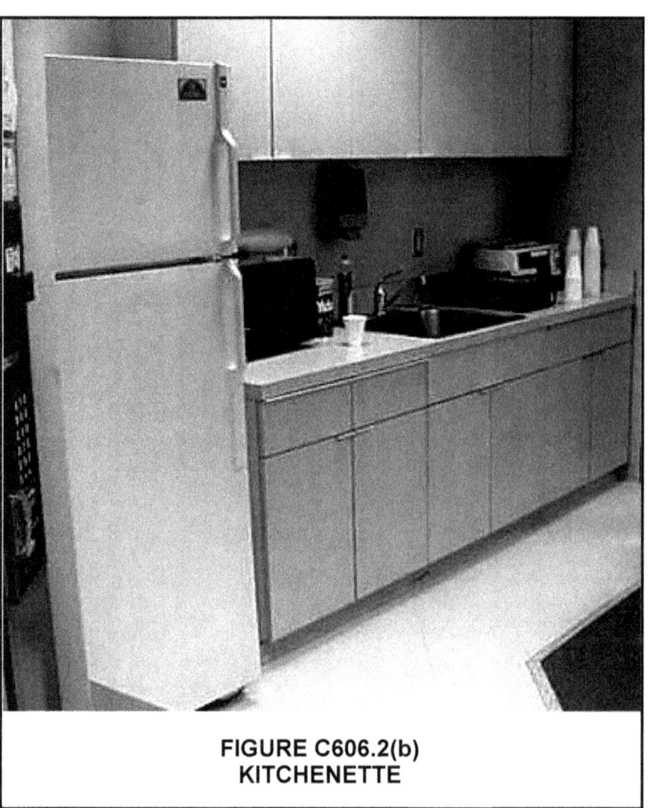

FIGURE C606.2(b)
KITCHENETTE

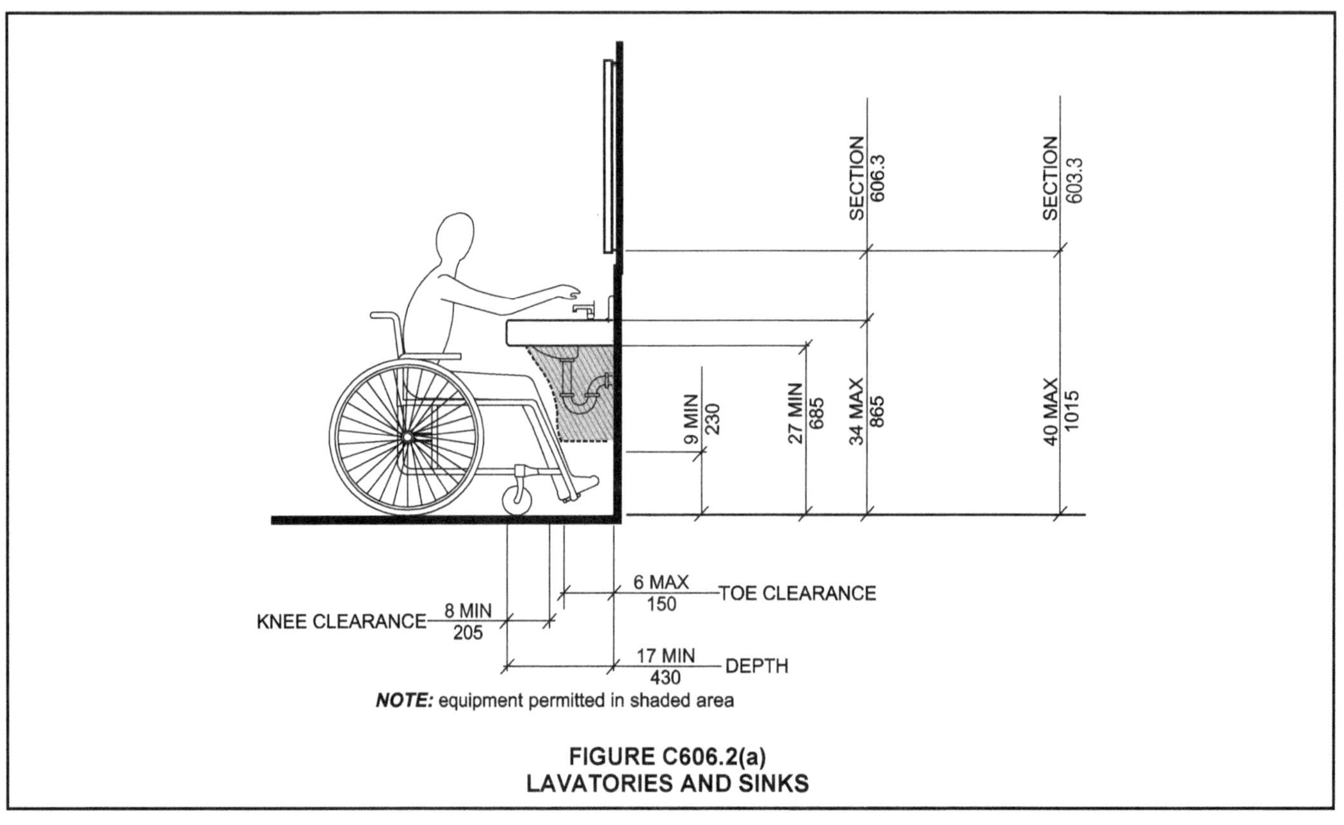

FIGURE C606.2(a)
LAVATORIES AND SINKS

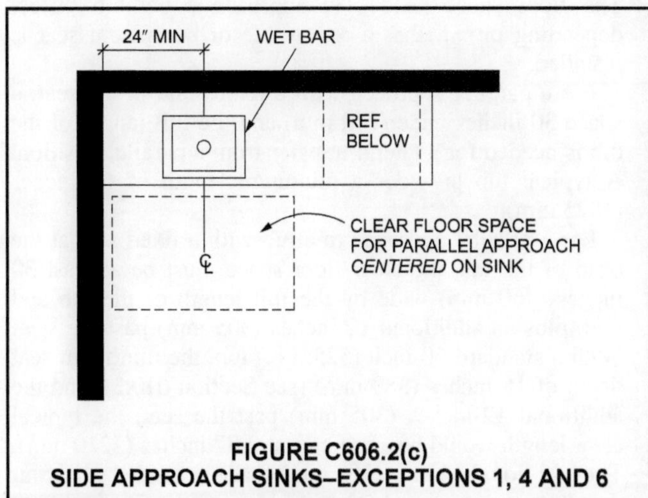

FIGURE C606.2(c)
SIDE APPROACH SINKS–EXCEPTIONS 1, 4 AND 6

606.3 Height. The front of lavatories and sinks shall be 34 inches (865 mm) maximum above the floor, measured to the higher of the rim or counter surface.

EXCEPTION: A lavatory in a toilet or bathing facility for a single occupant, accessed only through a private office and not for common use or public use, shall not be required to comply with Section 606.3.

❖ The 34-inch (865 mm) maximum height of lavatories and sinks ensures usability with an obstructed reach range. Built-in lavatories in counter tops should be placed as close as possible to the front edge of the counter top.

The exception allowance for no height restriction for the lavatory is part of the private office toilet room exceptions discussed in the general commentary to Chapter 6. This is coordinated with the knee and toe clearance exception in Section 606.2. A lavatory with removable cabinets would exceed code requirements (see Figure 606.3).

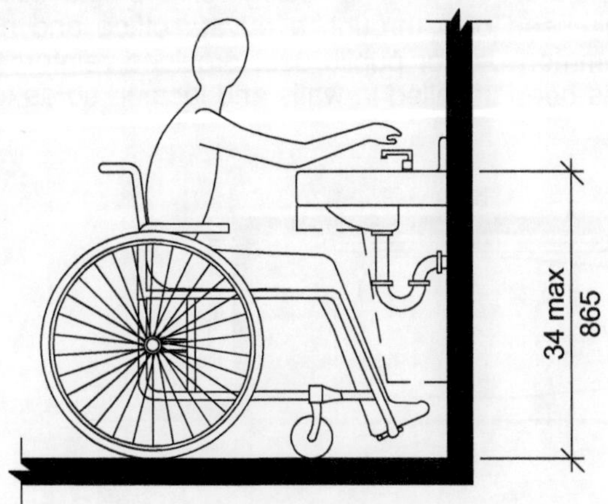

FIGURE 606.3
HEIGHT OF LAVATORIES AND SINKS

606.4 Faucets. Faucets shall comply with Section 309. Hand-operated metering faucets shall remain open for 10 seconds minimum.

❖ Conventional one-quarter-turn, lever-operated, push-type and automatically controlled mechanisms are examples of acceptable designs. See the commentary to Section 309 regarding the operable parts of the faucet. The 10-second time limit allows a person time to wash their hands once the faucet has been opened.

The model plumbing codes have "tempered" water requirements for some bathing fixtures—which limit the temperature at the fixture to less than 110°F (43°C).

606.5 Lavatories with Enhanced Reach Range. Where enhanced reach range is required at lavatories, faucets and soap dispenser controls shall have a reach depth of 11 inches (280 mm) maximum or, if automatic, shall be activated within a reach depth of 11 inches (280 mm) maximum. Water and soap flow shall be provided with a reach depth of 11 inches (280 mm) maximum.

❖ This standard requires enhanced reach range for lavatory faucets and soap dispensers when required by the authority having jurisdiction. Typically lavatories with enhanced reach range are required where there are six or more lavatories provided within a single toilet room or bathroom. When required, the faucets and soap dispenser must be located on the side of the lavatory [i.e., 11 inches (280 mm) maximum from the front edge of the counter] rather than at the back of the lavatory or on the back wall. This is beneficial for persons who are short in stature or have limited reach over the 34-inch (865 mm) lavatory or counter (see Commentary Figure C606.5). Alternatively, access could be provided from the side of the lavatory as well as from the front.

Where the accessible and enhanced reach range lavatories are separate fixtures, accessible lavatories (i.e., without enhanced reach range requirements) must have faucets and soap dispenser controls that meet the general operable parts requirements in Section 309.

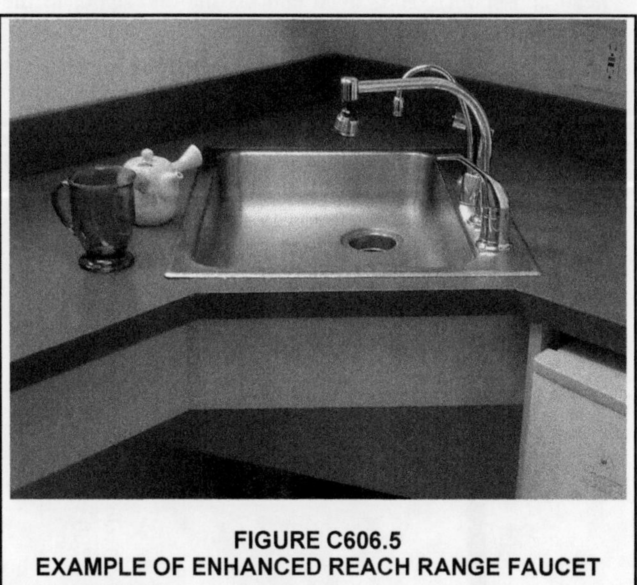

FIGURE C606.5
EXAMPLE OF ENHANCED REACH RANGE FAUCET

606.6 Exposed Pipes and Surfaces. Water supply and drainpipes under lavatories and sinks shall be insulated or otherwise configured to protect against contact. There shall be no sharp or abrasive surfaces under lavatories and sinks.

❖ Hot, cold and abrasive surfaces may cause harm to persons using a wheelchair because the ability to feel and react to such hazards may be diminished significantly as a result of paralysis or loss of sensation.

This protection can be provided by padding, apron walls, recessing the pipes, etc. This protection is not required to be the type of insulation required for steam pipes, hot water heating pipes or other types of extreme temperature system piping.

The model plumbing codes have "tempered" water requirement for most public lavatory fixtures—which limit the temperature dispensed at the fixture to less than 110°F (43°C).

607 Bathtubs

❖ Bathtubs and showers are both considered bathing facilities. This section addresses bathtubs. Technical criteria are stated for the situation where the tub is surrounded on three sides by walls. If a different configuration is constructed, Section 103 would allow for alternatives that provide the same or a higher level of accessibility.

Accessible, Type A and Type B units will reference Chapter 6 for bathtubs where applicable. See Chapter 10 for applicable requirements and references.

607.1 General. Accessible bathtubs shall comply with Section 607.

❖ For a bathtub to be accessible, the clear floor space, seat, grab bars and location of controls must comply with this section.

For purposes of this standard, the "control end" is the end of the bathtub with the controls (e.g., faucets, shower head and spout). The "head end" is the end opposite the controls.

607.2 Clearance. A clearance in front of bathtubs extending the length of the bathtub and 30 inches (760 mm) minimum in depth shall be provided. Where a permanent seat is provided at the head end of the bathtub, the clearance shall extend 12 inches (305 mm) minimum beyond the wall at the head end of the bathtub.

❖ The floor space needed to approach a bathtub differs depending on whether a removable or permanent seat is installed.

For a parallel approach with a removable in-tub seat, a space 30 inches wide (760 mm) and the full length of the tub is needed for a lateral transfer from a parallel position. A typical tub provides a minimum length of 60 inches (1525 mm).

For a parallel approach to a tub with a fixed seat at the head of the tub, the clear floor space must be at least 30 inches (760 mm) wide by the full length of the tub and seat, plus an additional 12 inches (305 mm) past the seat. With a standard 60-inch (525 mm) tub, the minimum seat depth of 15 inches (380 mm) (see Section 610.2), and the additional 12-inches (305 mm) past the seat, the typical clear length would be a minimum of 87 inches (2210 mm). The additional 12 inch (305 mm) space is needed to permit the alignment of the wheelchair seat with the fixed tub seat to complete the transfer.

No other fixture or counter may overlap any portion of this clear floor space (see Figure 607.2).

607.3 Seat. A permanent seat at the head end of the bathtub or a removable in-tub seat shall be provided. Seats shall comply with Section 610.

❖ Section 610 addresses the minimum size and structural strength for the seats found either in or at the head of the bathtubs. The depth must be a minimum of 15 inches (380 mm), and the height must be between 17 and 19 inches (430 and 485 mm). The seat serves as either a bathing platform or as a transfer location to move into the tub. This effectively sets the height for the tub rim.

607.4 Grab Bars. Grab bars shall comply with Section 609 and shall be provided in accordance with Section 607.4.1 or 607.4.2.

EXCEPTION: Grab bars shall not be required to be installed in a bathing facility for a single occupant accessed only through a private office and not for common use or public use, provided reinforcement has been installed in walls and located so as to per-

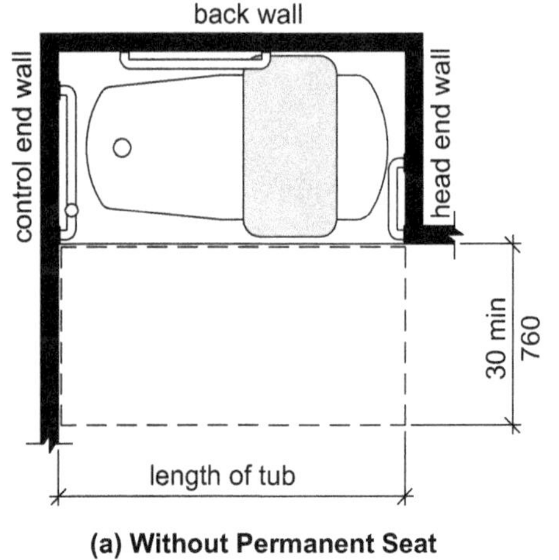

(a) Without Permanent Seat

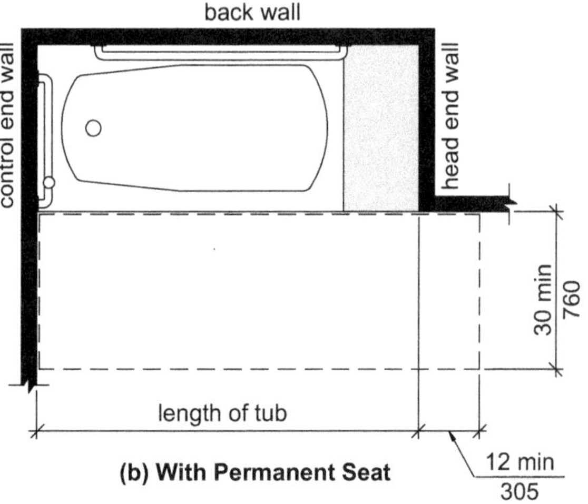

(b) With Permanent Seat

FIGURE 607.2
CLEARANCE FOR BATHTUBS

mit the installation of grab bars complying with Section 607.4.

❖ Properly located grab bars enable the user to transfer from a wheelchair to the tub, as well as the lowering or raising of oneself in and out of the tub. Specific criteria are provided for both bathtubs with permanent seats at the head end and bathtubs with removable seats. See Section 609 for specific requirements for size, wall clearance, height and installation requirements.

The exception allows for just the blocking to be provided for the future installation of grab bars as part of the private office toilet room exceptions discussed in the general commentary to Chapter 6.

607.4.1 Bathtubs with Permanent Seats. For bathtubs with permanent seats, grab bars complying with Section 607.4.1 shall be provided.

❖ When a permanent seat is installed at the head of the tub, one horizontal and one vertical grab bar are required at the control end and a double bar is required at the back wall. Any controls or built-in soap dishes should be located where they will not conflict with access to the grab bars. Grab bars are not required at the head end of the tub because the seat itself provides stability during transfer and the bar would conflict with leaning back on the seat. It is intended for the grab bars on the control wall to be consistent regardless of the type of seat chosen. The grab bars on the back wall vary in length relative to the seat choice.

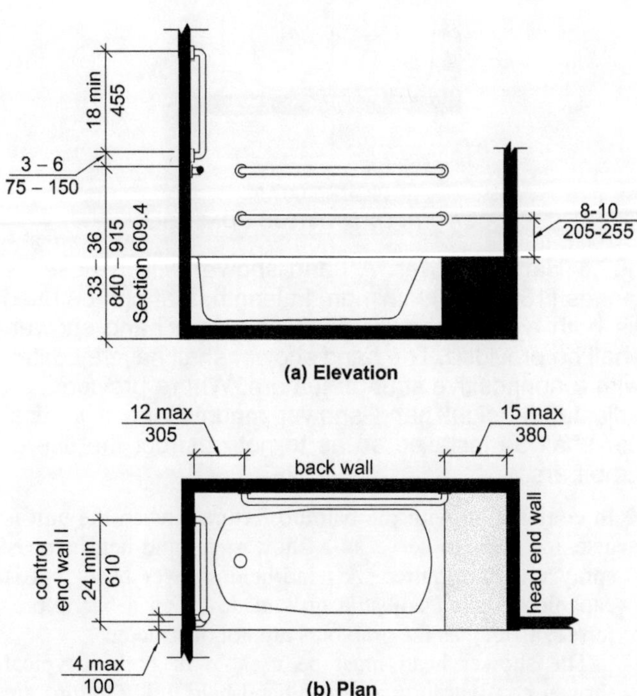

FIGURE 607.4.1
GRAB BARS FOR BATHRUBS WITH PERMANENT SEATS

607.4.1.1 Back Wall. Two horizontal grab bars shall be provided on the back wall, one complying with Section 609.4 and the other located 8 inches (205 mm) minimum and 10 inches (255 mm) maximum above the rim of the bathtub. Each grab bar shall be located 15 inches (380 mm) maximum from the head end wall and extend to 12 inches (305 mm) maximum from the control end wall.

❖ Two grab bars are required on the back wall. The top one is used during the transfer; the lower bar is used to move down into or up from the bottom of the tub. The placement of grab bars is essential to allow the person to transfer from the seat to the tub. Therefore, the end of the grab bar mounted on the back wall (opposite the open side) must be approximately even with the front edge of the seat at the head end of the bathtub.

607.4.1.2 Control End Wall. Control end wall grab bars shall comply with Section 607.4.1.2.

EXCEPTION: An L-shaped continuous grab bar of equivalent dimensions and positioning shall be permitted to serve the function of separate vertical and horizontal grab bars.

❖ The control wall grab bars are consistent regardless of the type of seat chosen. A horizontal and vertical bar are required on the control wall of the bathtub. These bars can be separate, or they can be one continuous bar. Alternatively, the horizontal bar along the control end and the top grab bar on the rear wall can be one continuous bar.

607.4.1.2.1 Horizontal Grab Bar. A horizontal grab bar 24 inches (610 mm) minimum in length shall be provided on the control end wall beginning near the front edge of the bathtub and extending toward the inside corner of the bathtub.

❖ This additional grab bar is used to move within the tub to gain access to the controls (see Figure 607.4.1). The language for the bar starting "near the front edge" is intended to allow for the bend at the end to be located far enough back so that the escutcheon plate and screws can be located where they have sufficient support and not so close to the front edge that the escutcheon plate hangs out or the screws rip out.

607.4.1.2.2 Vertical Grab Bar. A vertical grab bar 18 inches (455 mm) minimum in length shall be provided on the control end wall 3 inches (75 mm) minimum and 6 inches (150 mm) maximum above the horizontal grab bar, and 4 inches (100 mm) maximum inward from the front edge of the bathtub.

❖ This vertical grab bar is intended to be an aid for stability for persons with mobility impairments as they step into or out of the bathtub (see Figure 607.4.1).

607.4.2 Bathtubs without Permanent Seats. For bathtubs without permanent seats, grab bars complying with Section 607.4.2 shall be provided.

❖ When a removable seat is provided within the tub, one horizontal and one vertical grab bar are required at the control end, one bar is required at the head end and a double bar is required at the back wall. Any controls or built-in soap dishes should be located where they will not conflict with access to the grab bars. It is intended for the grab bars on the control wall to be consistent regardless of the type of seat chosen. The grab bars on the back wall vary in length relative to the seat choice. A grab bar at the head end of the tub is a stability aid for getting on and off the seat and is only required in bathtubs without permanent seats.

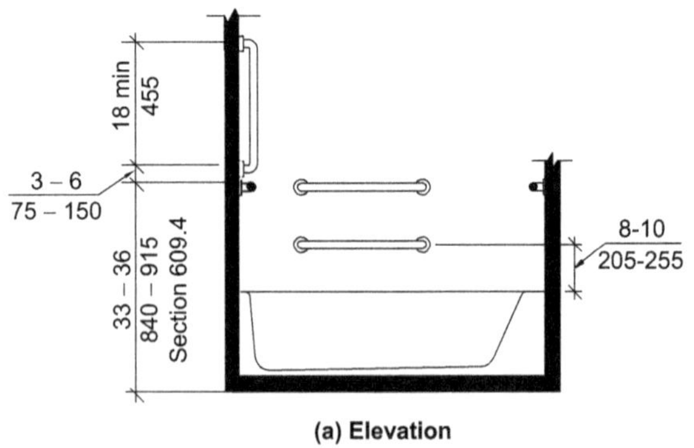

(a) Elevation

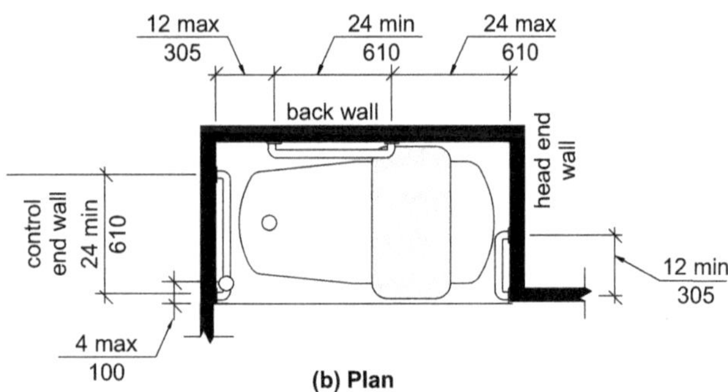

(b) Plan

FIGURE 607.4.2
GRAB BARS FOR BATHRUBS WITHOUT PERMANENT SEATS

607.4.2.1 Back Wall. Two horizontal grab bars shall be provided on the back wall, one complying with Section 609.4 and the other located 8 inches (205 mm) minimum and 10 inches (255 mm) maximum above the rim of the bathtub. Each grab bar shall be 24 inches (610 mm) minimum in length, located 24 inches (610 mm) maximum from the head end wall and extend to 12 inches (305 mm) maximum from the control end wall.

❖ Two grab bars are required on the back wall. The top one is used during transfer; the lower bar is used to move down into or up from the bottom of the tub. The placement of grab bars is essential to allow the person to transfer from the seat to the tub. With a removable seat, a grab bar shorter than the bars required for bathtubs with permanent seats is sufficient. Therefore, the grab bar mounted on the back wall (opposite the open side) must be within 24 inches (610 mm) of the wall at the head end (opposite the controls).

607.4.2.2 Control End Wall. Control end wall grab bars shall comply with Section 607.4.1.2.

❖ The control wall grab bars are consistent regardless of the type of seat chosen (see commentary, Section 607.4.1.2 and Figure 607.4.2).

607.4.2.3 Head End Wall. A horizontal grab bar 12 inches (305 mm) minimum in length shall be provided on the head end wall at the front edge of the bathtub.

❖ A grab bar at the end away from the controls is required to assist in the transfer. This bar is not required when a fixed seat is installed at the head end (see Section 607.4.1).

607.5 Controls. Controls, other than drain stoppers, shall be provided on an end wall, located between the bathtub rim and grab bar, and between the open side of the bathtub and the centerline of the width of the bathtub. Controls shall comply with Section 309.4.

❖ The controls must not be obstructed by the grab bars nor should the grab bars be obstructed by the controls. The controls are located toward the outside edge of the tub so they are more reachable by persons located in the adjacent clear floor space (see Figure 607.5). Controls must also meet the operation requirements in Section 309.4.

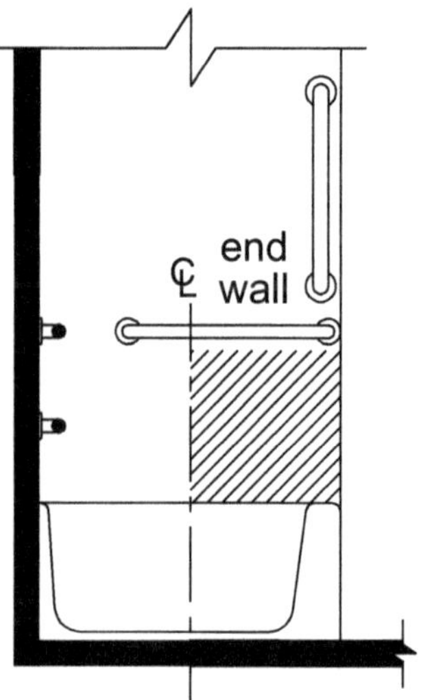

FIGURE 607.5
LOCATION OF BATHTUB CONTROLS

607.6 Hand Shower. A hand shower with a hose 59 inches (1500 mm) minimum in length, that can be used as both a fixed shower head and as a hand shower, shall be provided. The hand shower shall have a control with a nonpositive shut-off feature. Where provided, an adjustable-height hand shower mounted on a vertical bar shall be installed so as to not obstruct the use of grab bars.

❖ In conjunction with the bathtub fixtures, when the unit is also intended to serve as a shower, a hand-held shower spray unit is required. A hand-held shower head that is capable of being adjusted up and down on a bar is preferred, as long as the grab bars are not obstructed.

The shower head must be useable in both a typical shower configuration and as a hand-held unit. Options are a fixed wall mount that can hold the hand shower, or a bar with an adjustable mount. A shower head with a volume control mechanism (e.g., nonpositive shut-off feature) on the handset is a good design feature. This allows the shower occupant or attendant to reduce the flow of water to allow the handset to hang down while soaping or shampooing. Section 609.3, Exception 1, allows the vertical bar for the shower unit to extend within $1^1/_2$ inches (38 mm) above the grab bar.

607.7 Bathtub Enclosures. Enclosures for bathtubs shall not obstruct controls, faucets, shower and spray units or obstruct transfer from wheelchairs onto bathtub seats or into bathtubs. Enclosures on bathtubs shall not have tracks installed on the rim of the bathtub.

❖ Enclosures shall be mounted in a manner that allows the user full accessibility without defeating any of the design features required by the standard. Curtains on a standard rod would typically not block a transfer; however, shower doors would most likely be an obstruction. Tracks on the bathtub rim are very uncomfortable to traverse while making the transfer.

607.8 Water Temperature. Bathtubs shall deliver water that is 120°F (49°C) maximum.

❖ The temperature limitation for the water is to prevent accidental scalding. Options for controlling the temperature of the water at the tub are a balanced-pressure, thermostatic, or a combination balanced-pressure/thermostatic valve.

608 Shower Compartments

❖ Bathtubs and showers are both considered bathing facilities. This section addresses showers. Technical criteria are provided for the situation where the shower is surrounded on three sides by walls. If a different configuration is constructed, Section 103 allows for alternatives that result in the same or a higher level of accessibility.

Where applicable, Accessible, Type A and Type B units will reference Chapter 6 for showers where applicable. See Chapter 10 for applicable requirements and references.

608.1 General. Accessible shower compartments shall comply with Section 608.

❖ There are basically three types of showers addressed in this section—transfer, roll-in and alternate roll-in. Specific to each type of shower are the stall size, clear floor space, seat, grab bars and location of controls. There are also special criteria for hand showers, thresholds, enclosures and water temperature in showers.

608.2 Size, clearance and seat. Shower compartments shall have sizes, clearances and seats complying with Section 608.2.

❖ The size and clearances are different for transfer-type showers, roll-in-type showers and alternate roll-in shower compartments. Seats are required in all showers, Depending on the type of shower the seat may be a folding or non-folding seat but there are options in the larger stalls.

608.2.1 Transfer-type Shower Compartments. Transfer-type shower compartments shall comply with Section 608.2.1.

❖ A transfer-type stall is a shower fixture at which a person using a wheelchair can transfer from the chair to the required seat within the shower stall. The following three sections deal with the size, clearance and seat for a transfer-type shower (see Figure 608.2.1).

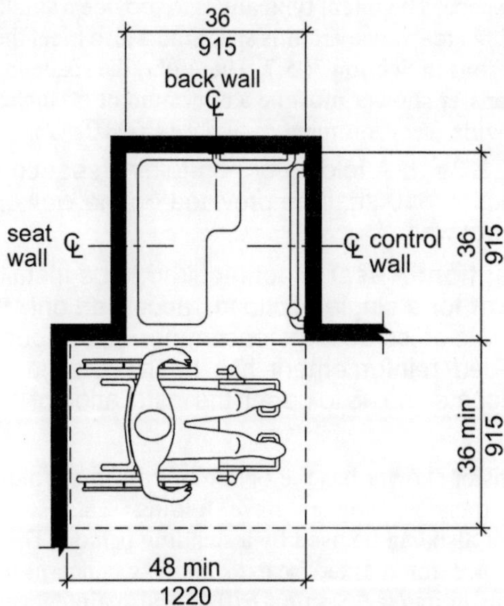

FIGURE 608.2.1
TRANSFER-TYPE SHOWER COMPARTMENT SIZE AND CLEARANCE

608.2.1.1 Size. Transfer-type shower compartments shall have a clear inside dimension of 36 inches (915 mm) in width and 36 inches (915 mm) in depth, measured at the center point of opposing sides. An entry 36 inches (915 mm) minimum in width shall be provided.

❖ For a transfer shower it is important to note that the 36-inch (915 mm) width and depth dimensions are an absolute requirement and are not a "minimum" or "maximum" dimension. Once a person transfers into the shower, the 36-inch by 36-inch (915 by 915 mm) inside finished dimensions allow a person of average size to reach and operate the controls without difficulty from the seat, while providing reasonable knee space for larger users. A transfer-type shower stall is also intended to serve persons without disabilities so a folding seat would provide more space for a standing person. Rounding of corners as necessitated in the manufacture of prefabricated shower stalls does not interfere with use. Therefore, the dimensions are measured at the center point of the walls rather than at the corners, and at a midpoint in the height (approximately shoulder height of a seated person), not at the base. The 36-inch (915 mm) minimum width entrance is required so that access to the transfer seat is not blocked.

608.2.1.2 Clearance. A clearance of 48 inches (1220 mm) minimum in length measured perpendicular from the control wall, and 36 inches (915 mm) minimum in depth shall be provided adjacent to the open face of the compartment.

❖ A 36-inch by 48-inch (915 by 1220 mm) clear floor space is required to allow a person in a wheelchair to work the controls and adjust the water flow and temperature while outside of the shower, before they transfer into the shower. A common mistake is to put a wall at both ends of this clear floor space. The intent typically is to provide a small private dressing area; however, this space must also meet the alcove provisions in Section 305.7. Therefore, the space in front of the transfer shower must be a minimum of 60 inches (1525 mm) wide (see Commentary Figure C608.2.1.2).

608.2.1.3 Seat. A folding or non-folding seat complying with Section 610 shall be provided on the wall opposite the control wall.

Exception: A seat is not required to be installed in a shower for a single occupant, accessed only through a private office and not for common use or public use, provided reinforcement has been installed in walls and located so as to permit the installation of a shower seat.

❖ A transfer shower has the option of a fixed or folding seat. Most transfer showers have folding seats so that the shower also can be used by a standing person. There is the allowance for a fixed seat to address concerns over the weight limits (see Section 610.4) and maintenance of the folding seats. See Section 608.4.1 for how the control locations relate to access from the seat.

The exception for eliminating the seat and only providing reinforcement for the seat's future installation is part of the private office toilet room exceptions discussed in the general commentary to Chapter 6. The intent of the exception is to allow for a shower in a private office to install a shower seat if the employee wants such a seat in the future. While not a common practice, some doctors do have private showers in their office bathrooms. This is consistent with other exceptions for bathrooms serving private offices found throughout this section. There is also a similar exception for the grab bars in this shower in Section 608.3.

608.2.2 Standard Roll-in-type Shower Compartments. Standard roll-in-type shower compartments shall comply with Section 608.2.2.

❖ A roll-in shower is sized to allow a person who uses a bathing wheelchair to move the wheelchair into the stall. Roll-in showers must also come equipped with seats so that they can also be used as transfer showers (see Section 608.2.2.3). Having a roll-in shower as a corner in a much larger room such as a gang shower in a locker room has also been addressed. The size in Section 608.2.2.1 is a minimum size, so there is no limit on the maximum size of the shower stall/room. The clearance in Section 608.2.2.2 may actually be inside the shower stall/room. The grab bars in Section 608.3.2 allow for only the bar adjacent to the seat

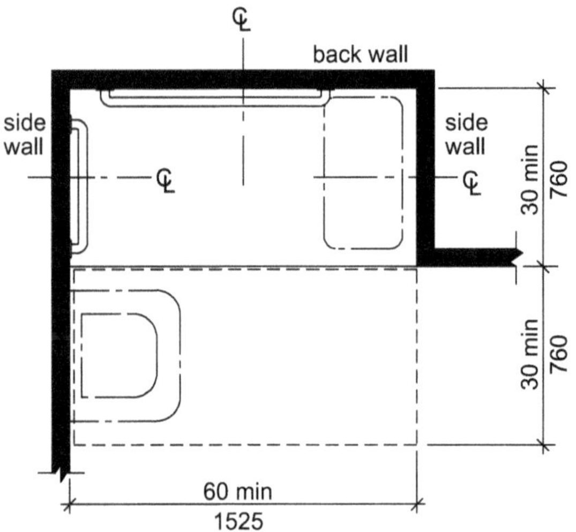

FIGURE 608.2.2
STANDARD ROLL-IN-TYPE SHOWER COMPARTMENT SIZE AND CLEARANCE

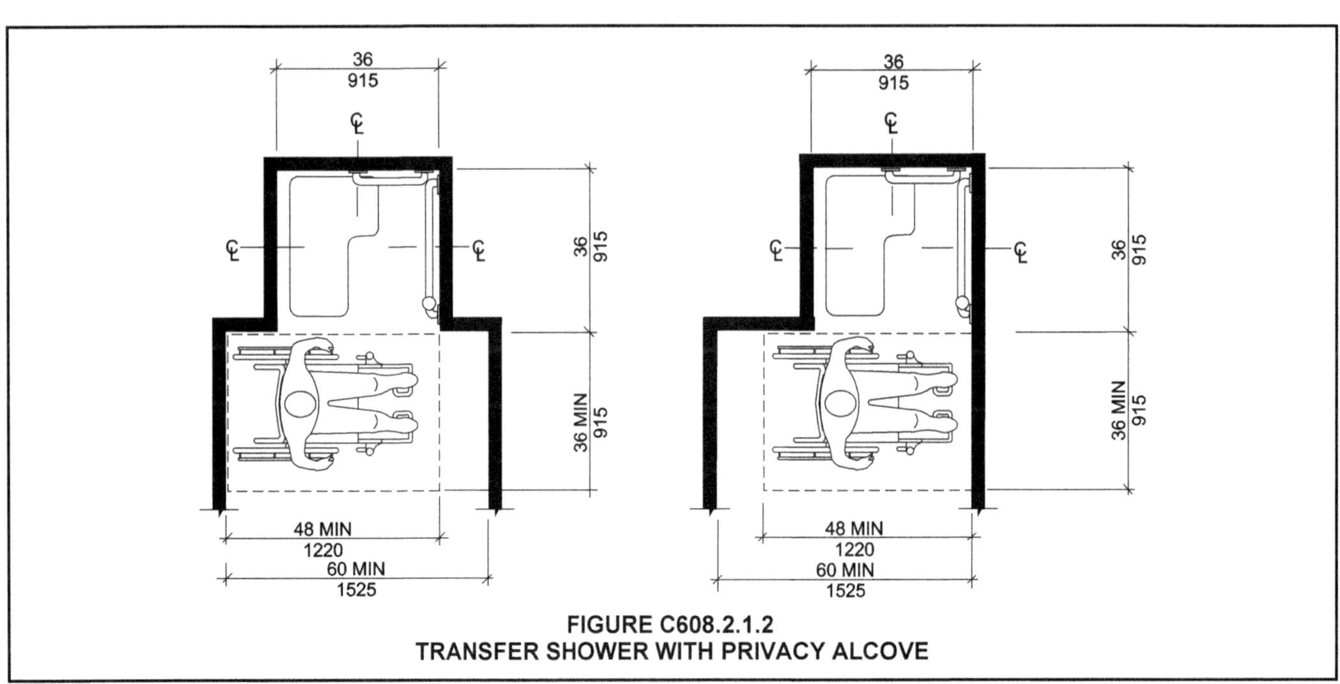

FIGURE C608.2.1.2
TRANSFER SHOWER WITH PRIVACY ALCOVE

in larger showers. Controls must also be within reach of the seat, in accordance with Section 608.5.

608.2.2.1 Size. Standard roll-in-type shower compartments shall have a clear inside dimension of 60 inches (1525 mm) minimum in width and 30 inches (760 mm) minimum in depth, measured at the center point of opposing sides. An entry 60 inches (1525 mm) minimum in width shall be provided.

❖ The roll-in-type shower stall in Figure 608.2.2 will fit into the space commonly provided for a bathtub. The 60-inch minimum width matches the size required for a parallel approach into an alcove (see Section 305.7) since the entry into the space is done in the same manner. Rounding of corners, as necessitated in the manufacture of prefabricated shower stalls or bases, does not interfere with use. Typically, the dimensions would be measured at the center point of the walls rather than at the corners, and at a midpoint in the height (approximately shoulder height of a seated person), not at the base.

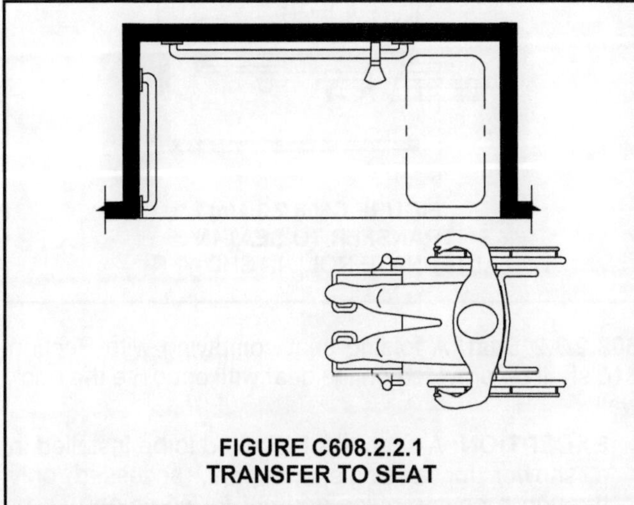

FIGURE C608.2.2.1
TRANSFER TO SEAT

608.2.2.2 Clearance. A clearance of 60 inches (1525 mm) minimum in length adjacent to the 60-inch (1525 mm) width of the open face of the shower compartment, and 30 inches (760 mm) minimum in depth, shall be provided.

EXCEPTION: A lavatory complying with Section 606 shall be permitted at the end of the clearance opposite the seat.

❖ A 30-inch by 60-inch (760 by 1525 mm) clear floor space is required to allow a person in a wheelchair to move into the space in front of the shower. The controls must be within reach of the person on the seat, so controls must be on the back wall (see Section 608.4.2). To facilitate transfer to a seat, an additional 12 inches (305 mm) may be desired past the wall behind the seat (see Commentary Figure C608.2.2.1).

A lavatory with knee and toe clearances may be located within the clear floor space outside of the shower if it does not block access to the controls or transfer to the seat (see Figure 608.2.2).

The concern about a dressing area/alcove in front of the roll-in shower is not the same as it is for a transfer shower. A roll-in shower plus its clear floor space should accommodate a 60-inch (1525 mm) turning space or a T-turn when there is knee space under the lavatory.

608.2.2.3 Seat. A folding seat complying with Section 610 shall be provided on an end wall.

EXCEPTIONS:

1. A seat is not required to be installed in a shower for a single occupant accessed only through a private office and not for common use or public use, provided reinforcement has been installed in walls and located so as to permit the installation of a shower seat.
2. A fixed seat shall be permitted where the seat does not overlap the minimum clear inside dimension required by Section 608.2.2.1.

❖ Providing a seat is required in a roll-in shower. In the minimum-sized shower, the seat must be folding so it can be raised out of the way of a person using a bathing chair. However, there is the option of a fixed seat if the 30-inch by 60-inch (760 by 1525 mm) space is available past the seat location (Exception 2). See Section 608.4.2 for how the control locations relate to access from the seat.

The intent of Exception 1 is to allow for a shower in a private office to install a shower seat if the employee wants such a seat in the future. While not a common practice, some doctors do have private showers in their office bathrooms. This is consistent with other exceptions for bathrooms serving private offices found throughout this section. There is also a similar exception for the grab bars in this shower in Section 608.3.

The locations of the grab bars and controls (see Sections 608.3.2 and 608.4.2) have been coordinated with the seat location. The controls must be located within reach of the seat, and the grab bars must not be located over the seat.

If there is a desire to make the stall deeper with the transfer space outside of the stall, it is important to keep the length of the seat consistent with the distance from the front edge and back wall (see Section 610). The seat wall should not exceed 36 inches (915 mm) because it would become difficult to slide into the corner if the user needed the wall for support. For much larger rooms or gang showers, see the commentary to Section 608.2.2.

608.2.3 Alternate Roll-in-type Shower Compartments. Alternate roll-in-type shower compartments shall comply with Section 608.2.3.

❖ The alternate roll-in shower is similar to the roll-in shower, in that it is intended to serve both persons who wish to transfer to a seat and those who wish to use a bathing chair (see Figure 608.2.3).

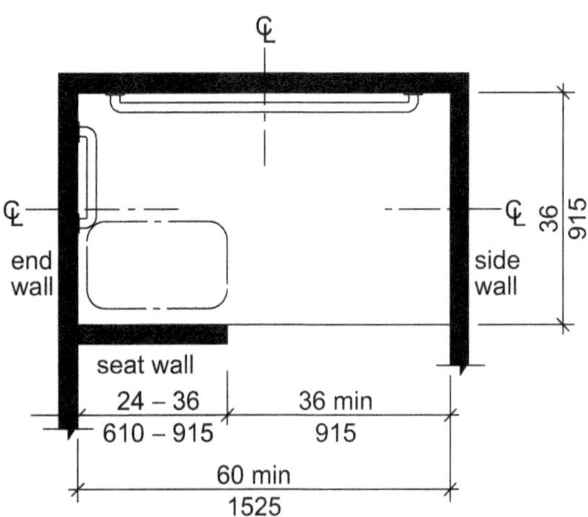

FIGURE 608.2.3
ALTERNATE ROLL-IN-TYPE SHOWER COMPARTMENT SIZE AND CLEARANCE

608.2.3.1 Size. Alternate roll-in shower compartments shall have a clear inside dimension of 60 inches (1525 mm) minimum in width, and 36 inches (915 mm) in depth, measured at the center point of opposing sides. An entry 36 inches (915 mm) minimum in width shall be provided at one end of the 60-inch (1525 mm) width of the compartment. A seat wall, 24 inches (610 mm) minimum and 36 inches (915 mm) maximum in length, shall be provided on the entry side of the compartment.

❖ As mentioned in the commentary for Section 608.2.3, the alternate roll-in shower can function as either a transfer shower or as a roll-in shower. Because of this dual function, the layout and the 36-inch depth (915 mm) 60-inch (1525 mm) minimum width and 24- to 36-inch (610 to 915 mm) seat wall dimensions are important. It is important to recognize that the 36-inch (915 mm) depth inside the shower is an absolute dimension and not a minimum or maximum. Much like the transfer shower requirements of Section 608.2.1, this ensures that a user can sit on the seat and reach the controls or hand shower which may be located opposite the seat on the back wall.

Although a clear floor space is not required in front of the shower unit, the entrance must be located on an accessible route [see Commentary Figure C608.2.3.1(a)], The opening is required to be 36 inches (915 mm) instead of 32 inches (813 mm) for a doorway because someone needs to turn 90 degrees to use the shower as a roll-in type.

When a person moves into the shower and/or transfers to the seat, the controls located on the back wall across from, or adjacent to, the seat will allow a person of average size to reach and operate the controls without difficulty [see Commentary Figure C608.2.3.1(b)] from either the seat or a bathing chair. To allow a viable transfer seat, the length of the seat wall is 24 inches to 36 inches (610 to 915 mm). This typically will result in the size of the shower stall being 36 inches (915 mm) deep and between 60 inches and 72 inches (1525 and 1830 mm) wide.

The shape of the seat provides support when the user's back is placed in the corner for support during the shower. The seat must be the full depth of the seat wall; it must be within 3 inches (75 mm) of the opening to minimize the distance between the seat and the wheelchair, and facilitate a transfer. See Sections 608.2.3.2 and 610 for seat type and size requirements.

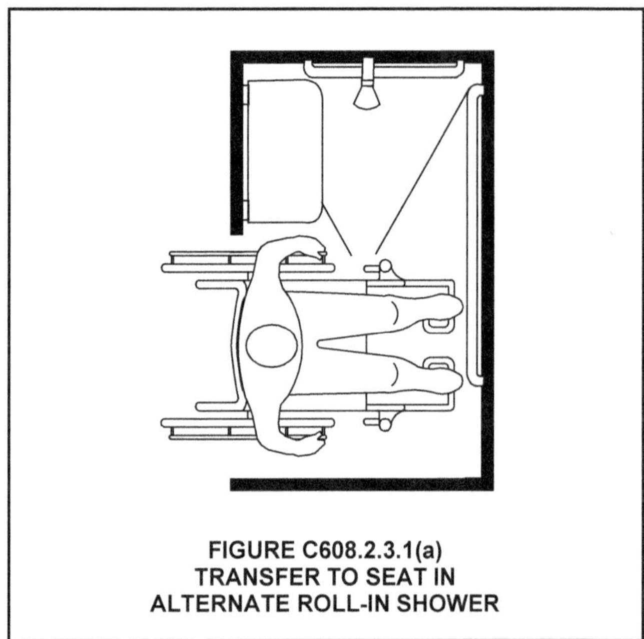

FIGURE C608.2.3.1(a)
TRANSFER TO SEAT IN ALTERNATE ROLL-IN SHOWER

608.2.3.2 Seat. A folding seat complying with Section 610 shall be provided on the seat wall opposite the back wall.

EXCEPTION: A seat is not required to be installed in a shower for a single occupant, accessed only through a private office and not for common use or public use, provided reinforcement has been installed in walls and located so as to permit the installation of a shower seat.

❖ The alternate roll-in shower is similar to the roll-in shower, in that it is intended to serve both persons who wish to transfer to a seat and those who wish to use a bathing chair. Unlike the roll-in or transfer showers, the alternate roll-in shower only allows for the option of a folding seat and not a fixed seat. See Commentary Figure C608.2.3.1(a) for where a person sits to transfer to the seat. See Commentary Figure C608.2.3.1(b) and Section 608.4.3 for how the control locations relate to access from the seat.

The intent of the exception is to allow for a shower in a private office to install a shower seat if the employee wants such a seat in the future. While not a common practice, some doctors do have private showers in their office bathrooms. This is consistent with other exceptions for bathrooms serving private offices found throughout this section. There is also a similar exception for the grab bars in the alternate roll-in shower in Section 608.3.

608.3 Grab Bars. Grab bars shall comply with Section 609 and shall be provided in accordance with Section 608.3. Where multiple grab bars are used, required horizontal grab bars shall be installed at the same height above the floor.

EXCEPTION: Grab bars are not required to be installed in a shower for a single occupant, accessed only through a private office and not for common use or public use, provided reinforcement has been installed in walls and located so as to permit the installation of grab bars complying with Section 608.3.

❖ Separate requirements for grab bars for transfer, roll-in and alternate roll-in showers are discussed in the following sections. The reference to Section 609 covers size, wall clearance, height and installation requirements. Fixture controls and other installed items, such as soap dishes, must be located so they do not interfere with access to the grab bars. Horizontal grab bars around the water closet, shower or tub should be at the same elevation. This provides a higher level of stability.

The exception allows for just the blocking to be provided for future installation of grab bars for a shower in a private office if the employee wants such grab bars in the future. There is a correlative change for blocking for the seat in the shower under each type of shower.

608.3.1 Transfer-Type Showers. Grab bars for transfer type showers shall comply with Section 608.3.1.

❖ Transfer showers are required to have horizontal bars and a vertical bar.

608.3.1.1 Horizontal Grab Bars. Horizontal grab bars shall be provided across the control wall and on the back wall to a point 18 inches (455 mm) from the control wall.

❖ Improperly located grab bars are likely to interfere with the transfer from a wheelchair to the seat or make the seat unusable if a grab bar is mounted over the seat.

A horizontal bar should be installed on the wall across from the seat and along the back wall in front of the seat. The seat in a transfer shower can be the fold-up type (see Section 608.2.1.3), so the grab bars may be used by a sitting or standing person. This can be one single bar or two separate bars. If two individual/separate horizontal bars are used, they should be installed at the same height. This bar will be used by persons with mobility impairments for transfer, rising, sitting or additional stability.

608.3.1.2 Vertical Grab Bar. A vertical grab bar 18 inches (455 mm) minimum in length shall be provided on the control end wall 3 inches (75 mm) minimum and 6 inches (150 mm) maximum above the horizontal grab bar, and 4 inches (100 mm) maximum inward from the front edge of the shower.

❖ This vertical grab bar is intended to be an aid for stability for persons with mobility impairments as they step into or out of the shower (see Figure 608.3.1).

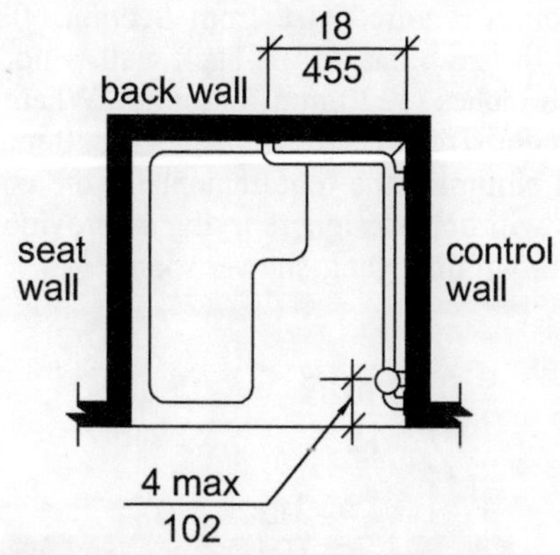

FIGURE 608.3.1
GRAB BARS IN TRANSFER-TYPE SHOWER

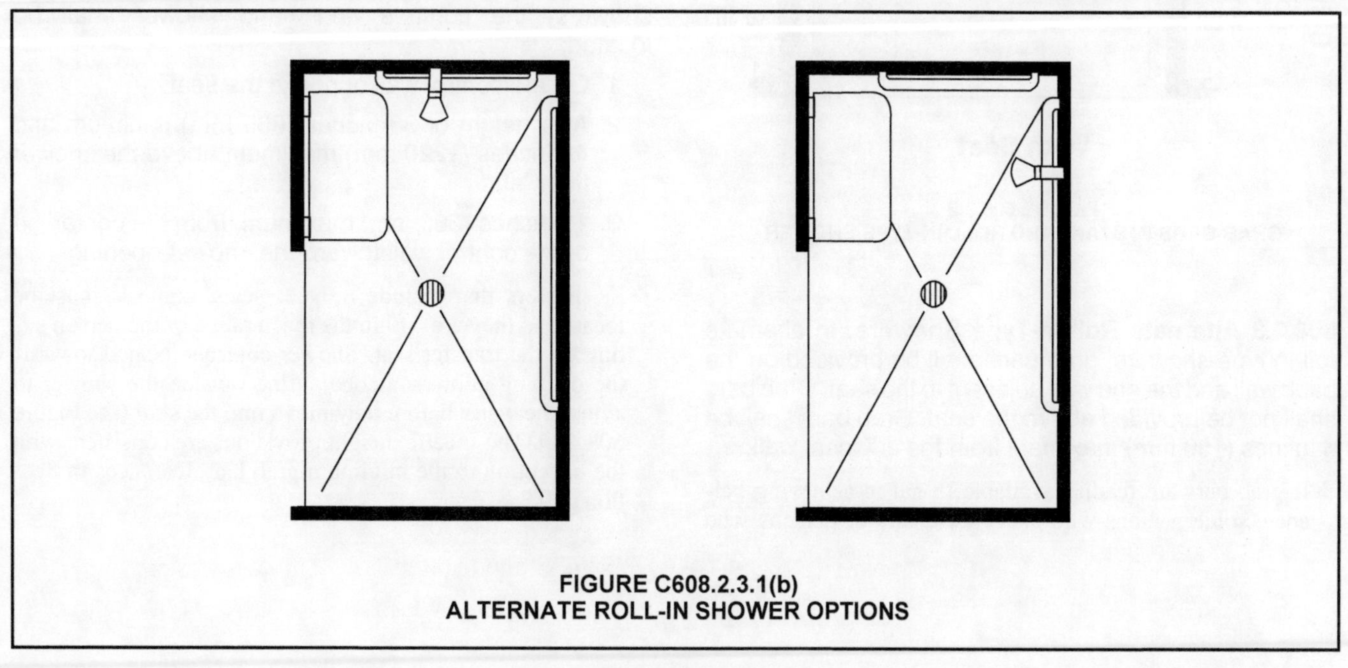

FIGURE C608.2.3.1(b)
ALTERNATE ROLL-IN SHOWER OPTIONS

608.3.2 Standard Roll-in-Type Showers. In standard roll-in type showers, a grab bar shall be provided on the back wall beginning at the edge of the seat. The grab bars shall not be provided above the seat. The back wall grab bar shall extend the length of the wall but shall not be required to exceed 48 inches (1220 mm) in length. Where a side wall is provided opposite the seat within 72 inches (1830 mm) of the seat wall, a grab bar shall be provided on the side wall opposite the seat. The side wall grab bar shall extend the length of the wall but shall not be required to exceed 30 inches (760 mm) in length. Grab bars shall be 6 inches (150 mm) maximum from the adjacent wall.

❖ Some persons who use wheelchairs or persons who use other types of mobility aid devices can stand to use a shower if grab bars are readily available to aid in achieving balance. In a standard roll-in-type shower, two separate grab bars or a single, L-shaped grab bar can be used. To provide the higher level of stability, if separate bars are used they should be installed at the same height. Grab bars should not be located over the seat (see Figure 608.3.2). There are allowances for where the shower size exceeds the minimum required size from Section 608.2.2.1. The length of the grab bar on the back wall is not required to exceed 48 inches (1220 mm) in length. Where the shower compartment size exceeds 72 inches (1830 mm), the standard will eliminate the requirement for the end wall grab bar. This will help designers trying to provide an accessible shower within a gang-shower room.

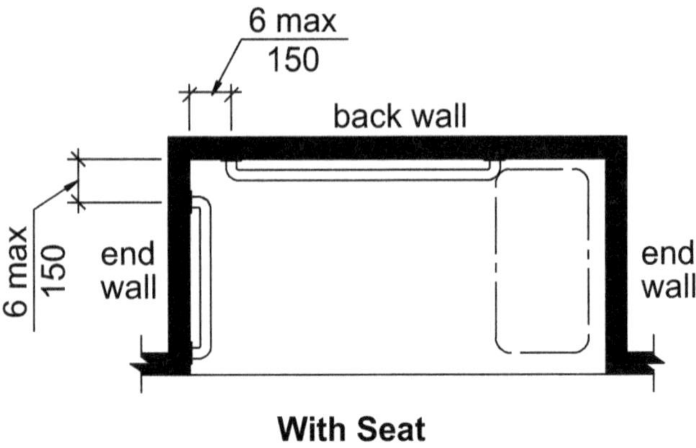

FIGURE 608.3.2
GRAB BARS IN STANDARD ROLL-IN-TYPE SHOWER

608.3.3 Alternate Roll-in-Type Showers. In alternate roll-in type showers, grab bars shall be provided on the back wall and the end wall adjacent to the seat. Grab bars shall not be provided above the seat. Grab bars shall be 6 inches (150 mm) maximum from the adjacent wall.

❖ If grab bars are readily available to aid in achieving balance, some persons who use wheelchairs or persons who use other types of mobility aid devices can stand to use a shower. The grab bars in alternate roll-in showers may be considered a hybrid of the transfer and standard roll-in-type grab bar configuration (see Figure 608.3.3). Two separate grab bars or a single, wraparound grab bar can be used. If separate horizontal bars are used they should be installed at the same height to provide a higher level of stability. Grab bars should not be located over the seat.

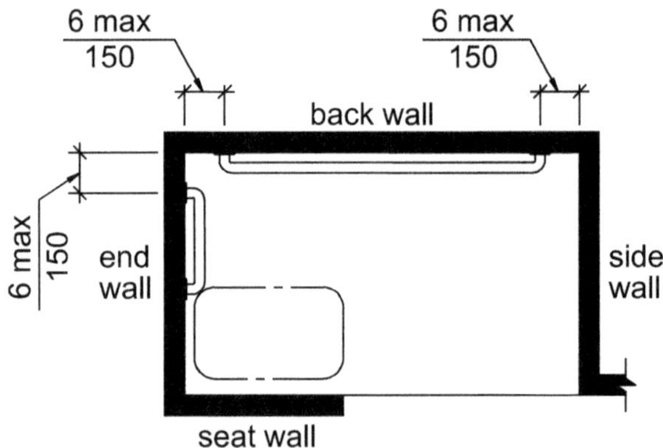

FIGURE 608.3.3
GRAB BARS IN ALTERNATE ROLL-IN-TYPE SHOWER

608.4 Controls and Hand Showers. Controls and hand showers shall comply with Sections 608.4 and 309.4.

❖ Controls for all types of accessible showers are addressed in the following subsections. Basically this section deals with the locations of the controls and the hand showers. For a discussion of options for the hand shower mounting heights, see commentary Section 608.5. All controls must meet the operation requirements in Section 309.4. In addition, hand showers must comply with Section 608.5.

608.4.1 Transfer-Type Showers. In transfer-type showers, the controls and hand shower shall be located:

1. On the control wall opposite the seat.
2. At a height of 38 inches (965 mm) minimum and 48 inches (1220 mm) maximum above the shower floor, and
3. 15 inches (380 mm) maximum, from the centerline of the control wall toward the shower opening.

❖ In showers that include transfer seats, controls must be located so they are within the reach range of the person sitting on the transfer seat. Shower controls located towards the opening allow someone sitting outside the shower to adjust the water before they move into the stall (see Figure 608.4.1). The specific height provisions are consistent with the exception to the minimum grab bar clearances in Section 609.3.

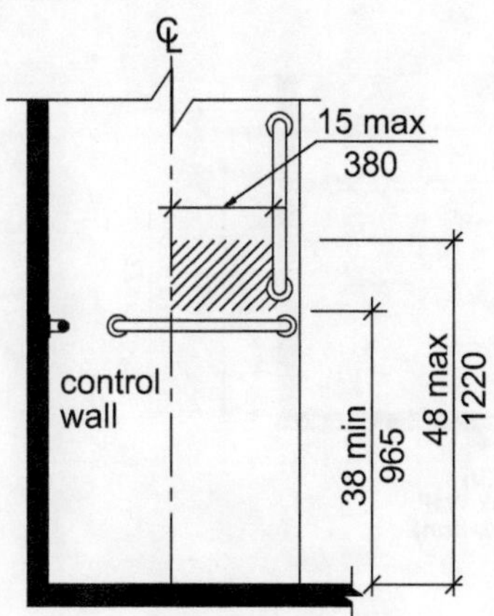

FIGURE 608.4.1
TRANSFER-TYPE SHOWER
CONTROLS AND HAND SHOWER LOCATION

608.4.2 Standard Roll-in Showers. In standard roll-in showers, the controls and hand shower shall be located on the back wall above the grab bar, 48 inches (1220 mm) maximum above the shower floor and 16 inches (405 mm) minimum and 27 inches (685 mm) maximum from the end wall behind the seat.

❖ In a roll-in shower, the control location is limited to the back wall so that controls can be adjusted from the seat. The range of 16 inches to 27 inches (405 to 685 mm) from the seat wall will locate the controls so that they are in front of the seat and not above the seat, and at the same time be within reach of a person using the seat. There is not a lower limit for the height of the controls, but since the grab bars are installed 33 inches to 36 inches (838 to 915 mm) above the floor, based on the clearance for grab bars (see Section 609.3, Exception 1), the range will be between approximately 38 and 48 inches (965 and 1220 mm). Where grab bars are located at a lower height, the controls could be slightly lower (see Figure 608.4.2).

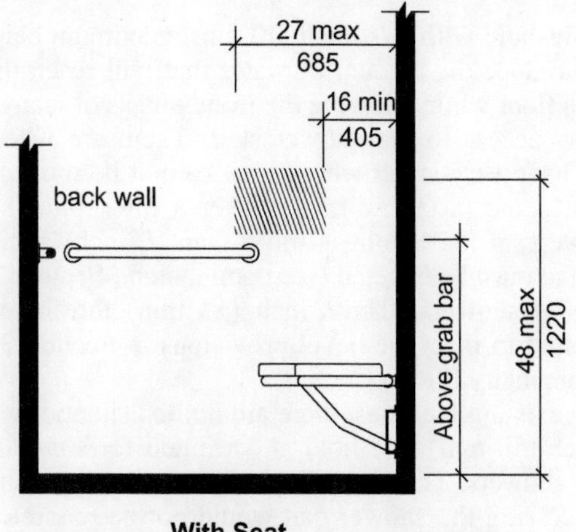

With Seat

FIGURE 608.4.2
STANDARD ROLL-IN-TYPE SHOWER
CONTROL AND HAND SHOWER LOCATION

608.4.3 Alternate Roll-in Showers. In alternate roll-in showers, the controls and hand shower shall be located 38 inches (965 mm) minimum and 48 inches (1220 mm) maximum above the shower floor. In alternate roll-in showers with controls and hand shower located on the end wall adjacent to the seat, the controls and hand shower shall be 27 inches (685 mm) maximum from the seat wall. In alternate roll-in showers with the controls and hand shower located on the back wall opposite the seat, the controls and hand shower shall be located within 15 inches (380 mm), left or right, of the centerline of the seat.

❖ Alternate roll-in showers are a hybrid of the roll-in and transfer situations. In an alternate roll-in shower, a transfer seat is required by Section 608.2.3.2. Controls must be located so that they are within the reach range of the person sitting on the transfer seat [see Commentary Figure C608.2.3.1(b) and Figure 608.4.3]. The specific height provisions are consistent with the exception to the minimum grab bar clearances in Section 609.3.

608.5 Hand Showers. A hand shower with a hose 59 inches (1500 mm) minimum in length, that can be used both as a fixed shower head and as a hand shower, shall be provided. The hand shower shall have a control with a nonpositive shut-off feature. Where provided, an adjustable-height hand shower mounted on a vertical bar shall be installed so as to not obstruct the use of grab bars.

EXCEPTION: In other than Accessible units and Type A units, a fixed shower head located 48 inches (1220 mm) maximum above the shower floor shall be permitted in lieu of a hand shower.

❖ Since the hand shower must be useable as both a fixed shower head and a hand shower, mounts for the shower heads can be adjustable to be within 48 inches (1220 mm) from the floor (see Commentary Figure C608.5), or fixed mounts may be provided at 48 inches (1220 mm). The hose of the hand shower must be at least 59 inches (1500 mm) long. A shower head with a volume control mechanism (e.g., nonpositive shut-off feature) on the handset is a good design feature. This allows the shower occupant or attendant to reduce the flow of water and allows the handset to hang down while soaping or shampooing. Section 609.3 allows for a minimum of $1^1/_2$ inches (38 mm) above the grab bar for the vertical bar supporting the hand shower.

A jurisdiction may determine that a fixed shower head is required instead of the hand-held type. For example, in facilities where vandalism causes a maintenance problem, such as in isolated or unmonitored areas, a fixed shower head could be used in lieu of a hand-held shower head. The fixed shower head should be mounted 48 inches (1220 mm) maximum above the shower floor so it is still within reach ranges. This exception cannot be used in Accessible units, such as in hotel rooms or nursing homes, or Type A units in apartment buildings.

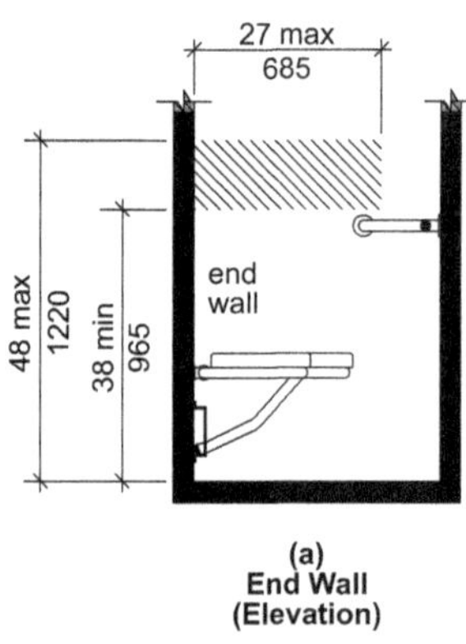

(a)
End Wall
(Elevation)

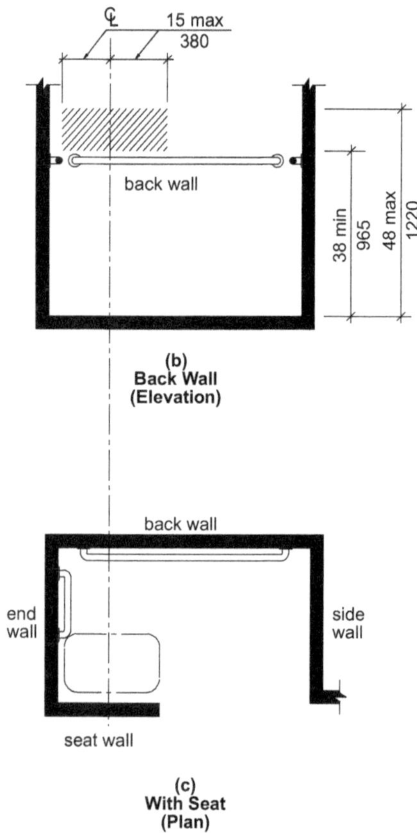

(b)
Back Wall
(Elevation)

(c)
With Seat
(Plan)

FIGURE 608.4.3
ALTERNATE ROLL-IN-TYPE SHOWER CONTROL AND HAND SHOWER LOCATION

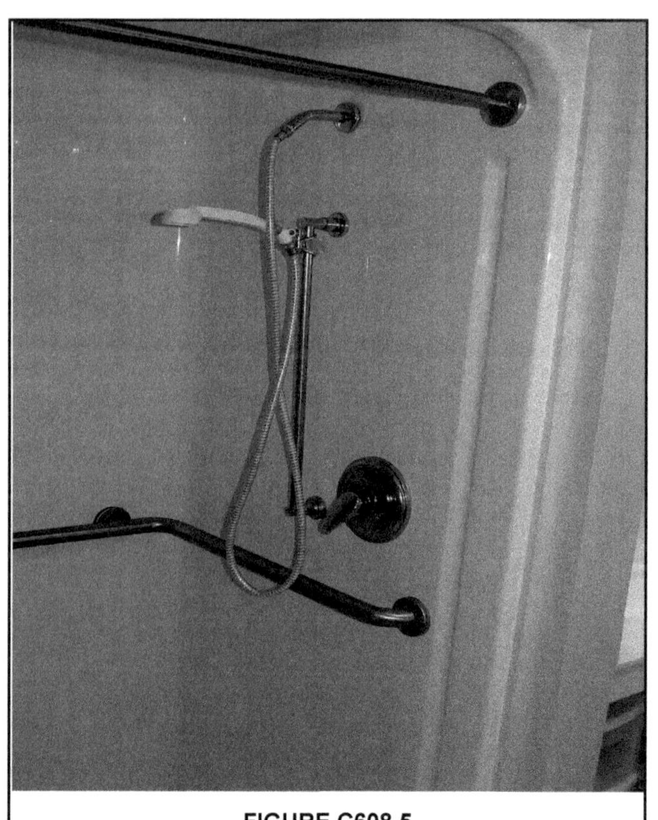

FIGURE C608.5
EXAMPLE OF ADJUSTABLE HAND SHOWER

608.6 Thresholds. Thresholds in roll-in-type shower compartments shall be $^1/_2$ inch (13 mm) maximum in height in accordance with Section 303. In transfer-type shower compartments, thresholds $^1/_2$ inch (13 mm) maximum in height shall be beveled, rounded, or vertical.

EXCEPTION: In existing facilities, in transfer-type shower compartments where provision of a threshold $^1/_2$ inch (13 mm) in height would disturb the structural reinforcement of the floor slab, a threshold 2 inches (51 mm) maximum in height shall be permitted.

❖ A threshold with a $^1/_2$-inch (13 mm) maximum height will help reduce the amount of water that will reach the bathroom floor while allowing the front wheels of many wheelchairs access to the shower stall. There are wheelchairs that have very small wheels that cannot be moved easily, or in some instances safely, over a threshold. In roll-in showers, if the height is more than $^1/_4$ inch (6 mm), the change must be beveled (see commentary, Section 303). In transfer showers, the $^1/_2$-inch (13 mm) threshold is not required to meet the bevel provisions in Section 303 (see Commentary Figure C608.6).

In existing facilities, there are limited situations where a 2 inch (50 mm) threshold is permitted for some transfer-type showers. The intent is to allow for a higher threshold if recessing the shower pan would not be possible due to the type of floor system. Examples of types of floor systems that could be adversely affected might be reinforced concrete, post-tensioned concrete, precast concrete, metal pan with metal studs or wired mesh.

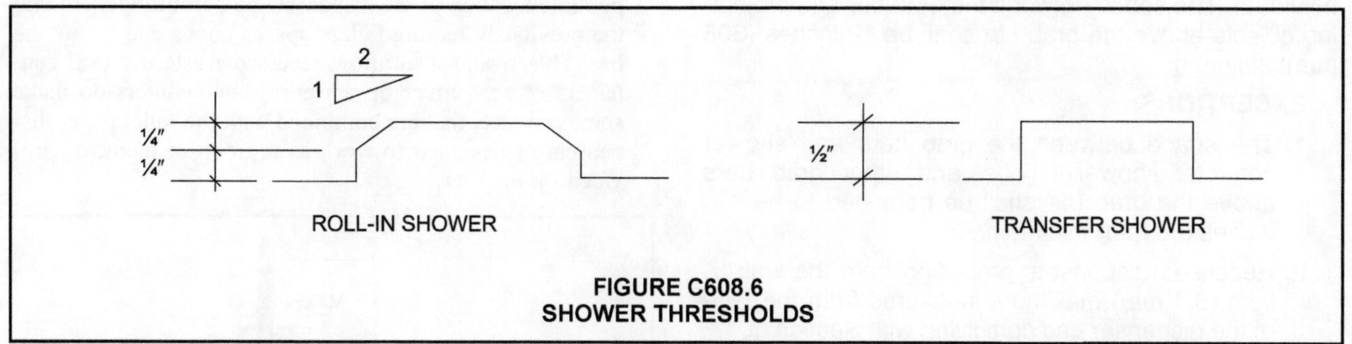

FIGURE C608.6
SHOWER THRESHOLDS

608.7 Shower Enclosures. Shower compartment enclosures for shower compartments shall not obstruct controls or obstruct transfer from wheelchairs onto shower seats.

❖ Enclosures must be mounted in a manner that allows the user full accessibility without defeating any of the design features required by the standard. Curtains on a standard rod would typically not block a transfer; however, shower doors would most likely be an obstruction. Tracks on the shower threshold may prevent access into the shower stall. Even in a transfer situation, the wheelchair user may need to move the small front wheels of the chair into the stall to make the transfer.

608.8 Water Temperature. Showers shall deliver water that is 120°F (49°C) maximum.

❖ The temperature limitation for the water is to prevent accidental scalding. Options for controlling the temperature of the water at the shower are a balanced-pressure, thermostatic, or a combination balanced-pressure/thermostatic valve.

609 Grab Bars

❖ These specific provisions for grab bars are referenced throughout the standard where it is necessary to install such features. When this section is referenced for blocking locations, the blocking should extend the full range of the permissible grab bar locations. The extent of the blocking must also include provisions for the mounting plates and adequate edge distance for the mounting screws.

609.1 General. Grab bars in accessible toilet or bathing facilities shall comply with Section 609.

❖ This section addresses grab bar requirements for shape, size, clearance, height and installation.

Many people with disabilities rely heavily on grab bars to maintain balance and prevent serious falls. Many brace their forearms between supports and walls to give them more leverage and stability in maintaining balance or for lifting. The clearance of $1^1/_2$ inches (38 mm) required between the bar and the wall surface is a safety clearance to prevent injuries from arms slipping through the opening. This clearance also provides a minimum space for gripping.

609.2 Cross Section. Grab bars shall have a cross section complying with Section 609.2.1 or 609.2.2.

❖ Grab bars can have a shape that is either round (Section 609.2.1) or a noncircular shape (Section 609.2.2) that is graspable (see Figure 609.2).

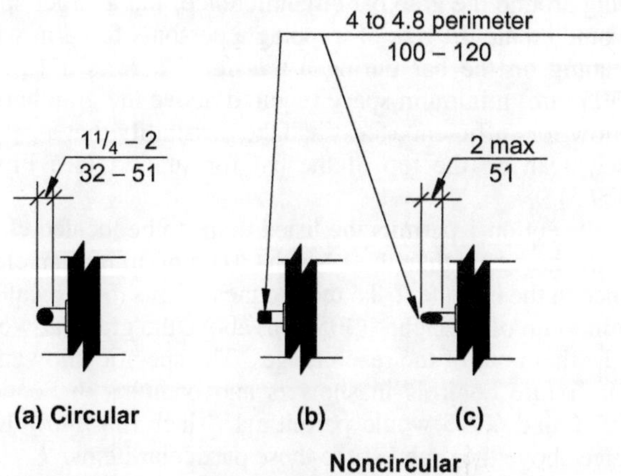

FIGURE 609.2
SIZE OF GRAB BARS

609.2.1 Circular Cross Section. Grab bars with a circular cross section shall have an outside diameter of $1^1/_4$ inch (32 mm) minimum and 2 inches (51 mm) maximum.

❖ The cross-sectional shape of a grab bar is limited in size to afford optimum graspability. The grab bar is typically a round section or shape such as a pipe. Equivalent gripping surface, though not specifically defined, pertains to the ability to wrap one's fingers completely around the bar to achieve a "power grip." A "pinch grip" does not provide the needed stability for which grab bars are used, even for people with ordinary hand dexterity.

609.2.2 Noncircular Cross Section. Grab bars with a noncircular cross section shall have a cross section dimension of 2 inches (51 mm) maximum, and a perimeter dimension of 4 inches (100 mm) minimum and 4.8 inches (120 mm) maximum.

❖ These provisions should allow an equivalent level of graspability for shapes other than the round bars in Section 609.2.1.

609.3 Spacing. The space between the wall and the grab bar shall be $1^1/_2$ inches (38 mm). The space between the grab bar and projecting objects below and at the ends of the grab bar shall be $1^1/_2$ inches (38 mm) minimum. The space between the grab bar and projecting objects above the grab bar shall be 12 inches (305 mm) minimum.

EXCEPTIONS:

1. The space between the grab bars and shower controls, shower fittings, and other grab bars above the grab bar shall be permitted to be $1^1/_2$ inches (38 mm) minimum.
2. Recessed dispensers projecting from the wall $^1/_4$ inch (6.4 mm) maximum measured from the face of the dispenser and complying with Section 604.7 shall be permitted within the 12-inch (305 mm) space above and the $1^1/_2$ inch (38 mm) spaces below and at the ends of the grab bar.

❖ The $1^1/_2$-inch (38 mm) spacing between the grab bar and the wall is absolute. Anything smaller would prevent gripping around the grab bar circumference, and a larger space would create the risk of trapping a person's forearm when leaning on the bar during a transfer. There is a 12-inch (305 mm) minimum space required above the grab bars to allow for sufficient access and the possibility that a person may lean on the top of the bar for support (see Figure 609.3).

Exception 1 permits the listed items to be located closer to the grab bars than the 12-inch (305 mm) minimum clearance in the main text. To require these items to be located a minimum of 12 inches (305 mm) above the grab bar would take them out of the reach ranges. The specific allowances for fixture controls in showers and bathtubs in Sections 607.6 and 608.5 would permit a $1^1/_2$-inch (38 mm) clearance above the grab bars to those particular items.

Exception 2 in Section 609.3 was developed in conjunction with the location of toilet paper dispensers in Section 604.7. When dispensers are located within the 12-inch (305 mm) space above or the $1^1/_2$-inch (38 mm) space below the grab bars, Exception 2 allows the use of recessed dispensers where they project a maximum of $^1/_4$ inch (19 mm) from the wall (see Commentary Figure C609.3). The use of recessed fixtures provides additional options for the possible location of the dispensers by permitting them into the previously required clear spaces above and below the bar. This would also allow recessed waste disposal containers or seat cover dispensers. Manufacturers do make some products that are combined with the toilet paper dispensers or designed to work as a group of elements provided for the user.

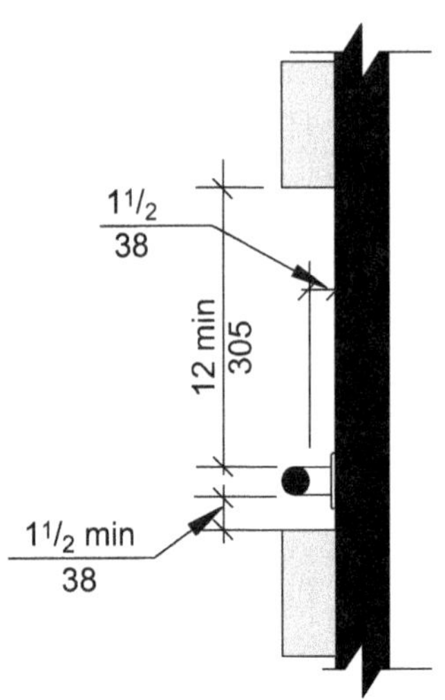

FIGURE 609.3
SPACING OF GRAB BARS

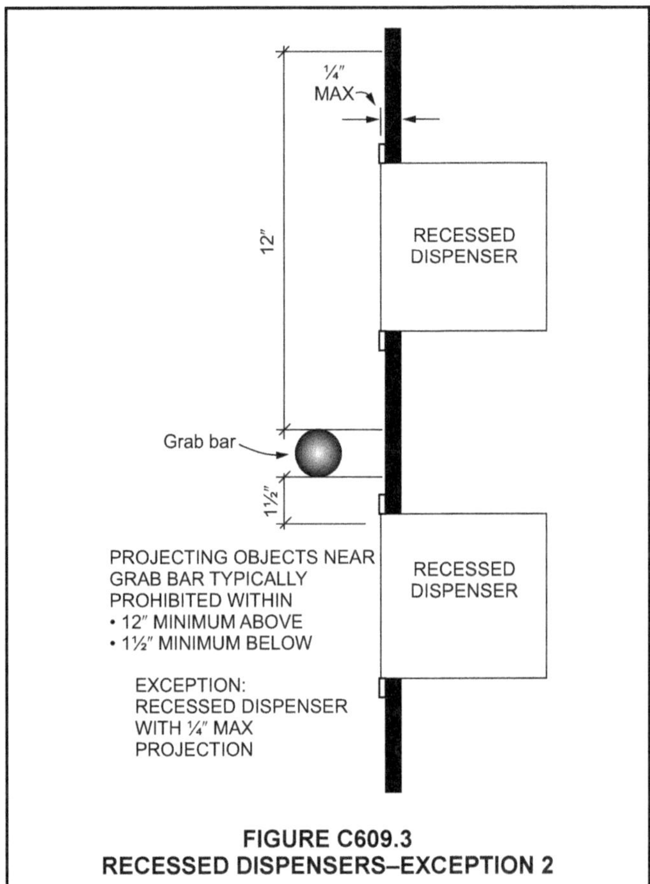

FIGURE C609.3
RECESSED DISPENSERS–EXCEPTION 2

609.4 Position of Grab Bars.

❖ The lengths and installation locations of grab bars are found/listed in the requirements specific to water closets, bathtubs and showers. This section address the height of the grab bars.

609.4.1 General. Grab bars shall be installed in a horizontal position, 33 inches (840 mm) minimum and 36 inches (915 mm) maximum above the floor measured to the top of the gripping surface or shall be installed as required by Items 1 through 3.

1. The lower grab bar on the back wall of a bathtub shall comply with Section 607.4.1.1 or 607.4.2.1.
2. Vertical grab bars shall comply with Sections 604.5.1, 607.4.1.2.2, 607.4.2.2, and 608.3.1.2.
3. Grab bars at water closets primarily for children's use shall comply with Section 609.4.2.

❖ The dimensions are from the floor to the top of the horizontal grab bar. Where multiple horizontal grab bars are provided on adjacent walls, the horizontal bars must be at the same elevation (see Sections 607.4 and 608.3).

Exception 1 is to allow for the double grab bar required on the rear wall at bathtubs.

Exception 2 reaffirms that vertical grab bar locations are fully addressed in listed sections.

Exception 3 allows for a different height allowance for grab bars adjacent to water closets specifically designed for use by children. The height of the grab bar is correlated to the height of the toilet seat in Section 604.11.

609.4.2 Position of Children's Grab Bars. At water closets primarily for children's use complying with Section 604.11, grab bars shall be installed in a horizontal position 18 inches (455 mm) minimum and 27 inches (685 mm) maximum above the floor measured to the top of the gripping surface. A vertical grab bar shall be mounted with the bottom of the bar located between 21 inches (535 mm) minimum and 30 inches (760 mm) maximum above the floor and with the centerline of the bar located between 34 inches (865 mm) minimum and 36 inches (915 mm) maximum from the rear wall.

❖ This section deals with the height of grab bars associated with water closets specifically designed for children. The height is adjusted to be coordinated with the height of the toilet seat. The vertical grab bar is located to assist children with mobility impairments to stand (see Figure 609.4.2).

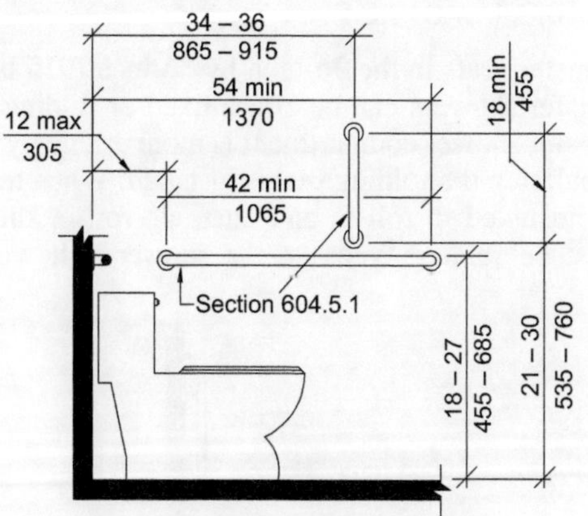

Note: For adult dimensions see Fig. 604.5.1

(a) Side Wall View

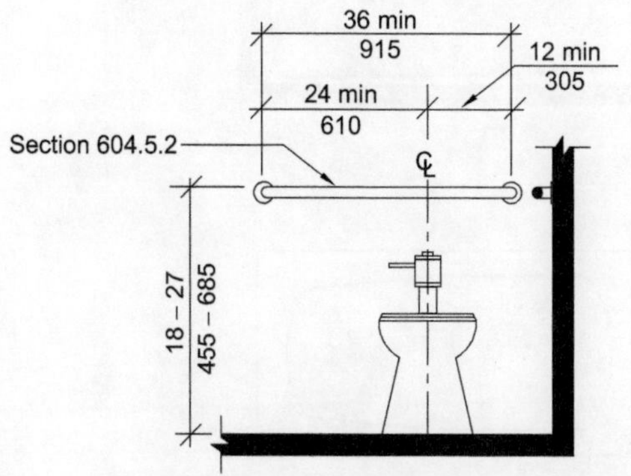

Note: For adult dimensions see Fig. 604.5.2

(b) Rear Wall View

FIGURE 609.4.2
POSITION OF CHILDREN'S GRAB BARS

609.5 Surface Hazards. Grab bars, and any wall or other surfaces adjacent to grab bars, shall be free of sharp or abrasive elements. Edges shall be rounded.

❖ Wall surfaces and other features adjacent to grab bars can be hazardous to users if they are abrasive or sharp. Cuts and abrasions may result, as well as the user's reluctance to use the bar when needed.

609.6 Fittings. Grab bars shall not rotate within their fittings.

❖ The bar must be firmly attached to the fittings that support the bar. If the bar rotates or spins within the fitting while the user is exerting a force on the bar, the person's grip may be lost, which could result in injury.

609.7 Installation and Configuration. Grab bars shall be installed in any manner that provides a gripping surface at the locations specified in this standard and does not obstruct the clear floor space. Horizontal and vertical grab bars shall be permitted to be separate bars, a single piece bar, or combination thereof.

❖ Grab bars that are wall mounted do not affect the measurement of required clear floor space where the space below the grab bar is clear and does not present a knee space encroachment as provided in Section 306. However, a floor-mounted grab bar system, depending on the specific configuration, may encroach on knee space and would affect how required clear floor space is measured. This requirement is included to ensure that the grab bar installation does not obstruct the required clear floor space. The horizontal bars on adjacent walls, or the horizontal/vertical bars on the same wall can be separate grab bars, or one continuous grab bar.

609.8 Structural Strength. Allowable stresses shall not be exceeded for materials used where a vertical or horizontal force of 250 pounds (1112 N) is applied at any point on the grab bar, fastener mounting device, or supporting structure.

❖ The structural strength of a grab bar is dependent on the material used as well as the design. This provision requires that all of the components of the grab bar be strong enough to resist a 250-pound (1112 N) concentrated force applied either horizontally or vertically. There is no way of knowing in which direction the forces will be applied to the grab bar in a real installation. For instance, a user may apply weight to the top, pull to the side to get up, push on the side to get up, pull up on the bar to avoid tipping over, and so on. This provision may be more difficult to meet for some installations than others. For example, floor-mounted grab bars may require elaborate anchoring devices and heavy-duty components to resist the horizontal forces. Further, the floor, wall or other structural element to which the bar is attached must be considered. Unless that element and the connection to it is able to transfer the loads, the strength of the grab bar itself will not compensate for the lack of stability in the connection.

Where the requirements for tubs and showers require a grab bar across a wall, the intent is to allow for there to be sufficient allowances for proper attachment at the ends of the bars. It is an important safety issue to reduce the chance of accidental pullout as much as possible.

610 Seats

❖ Seats are referenced from bathtubs and showers. Bathtubs may have removable seats in the tub or fixed seats at the head end of the tub (see Section 607.3). All three types of showers, transfer showers, roll-in showers and alternate roll-in showers must have seats. See Sections 608.2.1.3, 608.2.2.3 and 608.2.3.2 for where folding or fixed seat options are permitted.

610.1 General. Seats in accessible bathtubs and shower compartments shall comply with Section 610.

❖ This section addresses the size and shape for seats within bathtubs and showers that include a transfer seat. All seats must also meet the structural strength specified.

610.2 Bathtub Seats. The height of bathtub seats shall be 17 inches (430 mm) minimum and 19 inches (485 mm) maximum above the bathroom floor, measured to the top of the seat. Removable in-tub seats shall be 15 inches (380 mm) minimum and 16 inches (405 mm) maximum in depth. Removable in-tub seats shall be capable of secure placement. Permanent seats shall be 15 inches (380 mm) minimum in depth and shall extend from the back wall to or beyond the outer edge of the bathtub. Permanent seats shall be positioned at the head end of the bathtub.

❖ The 17-inch to 19-inch (430 to 485 mm) height for the tub seats is a typical seat height for wheelchairs (see Figure 610.2). This facilitates transfers and will effectively set a maximum rim height for the tub.

The depth of the seat is the measurement of the seat from front to back. In-tub seats work well for persons who want to bathe from the seat and not move down into the bottom of the tub. It is not required that an in-tub seat has back support. Some people would like the additional support, but others might consider it an obstruction to transfer.

Both this section and Section 607.3 require the permanent seat at the tub to be located at the head end, which is opposite the control wall. Some users prefer a seat at the head of the tub because they use the seat as a location to transfer down into the water. Most tubs are 30 inches (760 mm) wide, so the fixed bath seat will be at least that wide or slightly larger. There is not a maximum depth on the fixed tub seat, but if back support from the wall is desired, the depth should not be more than that proposed for benches in Section 903.

610.3 Shower Compartment Seats. The height of shower compartment seats shall be 17 inches (430 mm) minimum and 19 inches (485 mm) maximum above the bathroom floor, measured to the top of the seat. In transfer-type and alternate roll-in-type showers, the seat shall extend along the seat wall to a point within 3 inches (75 mm) of the compartment entry. In standard roll-in-type showers, the seat shall extend from the control wall to a point within 3 inches (75 mm) of the compartment entry. Seats shall comply with Section 610.3.1 or 610.3.2.

❖ Transfer seats in the 36-inch by 36-inch (915 by 915 mm) transfer showers can be either fixed or folding types. The transfer shower compartment is more usable by the general population if a folding seat is installed. When transfer seats are installed in roll-in and alternate roll-in showers, they must be folding types so the shower will work as both

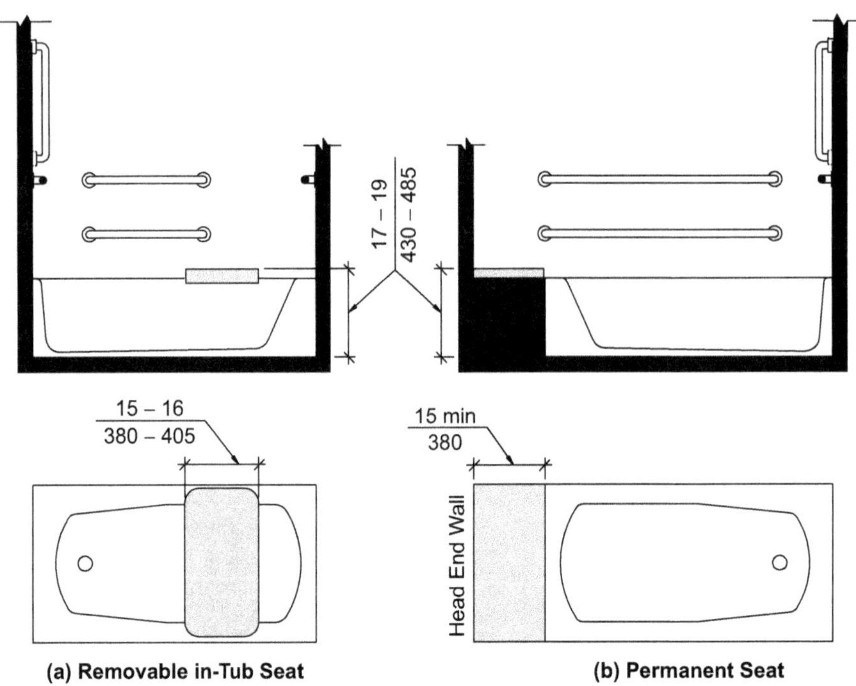

(a) Removable in-Tub Seat

(b) Permanent Seat

FIGURE 610.2
BATHTUB SEATS

transfer and roll-in. In a roll-in shower where the seat is located outside of the minimum floor space, a fixed seat can be an alternative (see Sections 608.2.1.3, 608.2.2.3 and 608.2.3.2).

The 17-inch to 19-inch (430 to 485 mm) height for the shower seats is a typical seat height for wheelchairs. This facilitates transfers.

The shape of the seat provides support when the user's back is placed in the corner for support while the shower is in use. The seat must be essentially the full depth of the stall; it must be within 3 inches (75 mm) of the front edge of the seat wall to minimize the distance between the seat and the wheelchair to facilitate a transfer. The seat wall must be free of grab bars to allow a person to slide onto the seat and a portion of the adjacent back wall must be without a grab bar so the person's back can be placed against the walls for support (see Sections 608.3.1, 608.3.2 and 608.3.3). An L-shaped seat allows the user to get additional stability from the adjacent walls.

610.3.1 Rectangular Seats. The rear edge of a rectangular seat shall be $2^1/_2$ inches (64 mm) maximum and the front edge 15 inches (380 mm) minimum and 16 inches (405 mm) maximum from the seat wall. The side edge of the seat shall be $1^1/_2$ inches (38 mm) maximum from the back wall of a transfer-type shower and $1^1/_2$ inches (38 mm) maximum from the control wall of a roll-in-type shower.

❖ Although the seat should extend the full width of the shower compartment, there are allowances for gaps at the sides—$1^1/_2$ inches maximum at the rear wall and 3 inches maximum at the opening. The total depth of the seat must be between 15 inches and 16 inches (380 and 405 mm). The maximum gap permissible across the back of the seat is $2^1/_2$ inches (64 mm) (see Figure 610.3.1)

610.3.2 L-Shaped Seats. The rear edge of an L-shaped seat shall be $2^1/_2$ inches (64 mm) maximum and the front edge 15 inches (380 mm) minimum and 16 inches (405 mm) maximum from the seat wall. The rear edge of the "L" portion of the seat shall be $1^1/_2$ inches (38 mm) maximum from the wall and the front edge shall be 14 inches (355 mm) minimum and 15 inches (380 mm) maximum from the wall. The end of the "L" shall be 22 inches (560 mm) minimum and 23 inches (585 mm) maximum from the main seat wall.

❖ The leg of the L-shaped seat is similar to that of the rectangular seat. The arm of the "L" shape of the seat is provided across the back wall. An L-shaped seat allows the user to get additional stability from the adjacent walls.

Although the seat should extend the full width of the shower compartment, there are allowances for gaps at the sides—$1^1/_2$ inches (38 mm) maximum at the rear wall and 3 inches (75 mm) maximum at the opening. The maximum gap permissible across the back of the seat is $2^1/_2$ inches (64 mm) (see Figure 610.3.2).

610.4 Structural Strength. Allowable stresses shall not be exceeded for materials used where a vertical or horizontal force of 250 pounds (1112 N) is applied at any point on the seat, fastener mounting device, or supporting structure.

❖ The seat and attachments must comply with the structural strength requirements to avoid failure and possible injury during use. Due to concerns with the failure of some folding seats, there is the option for fixed seats in transfer showers and roll-in showers (see Sections 608.2.1.3 and 608.2.2.3).

611 Washing Machines and Clothes Dryers

❖ For public use laundry facilities, the authority having jurisdiction will specify the number of washing machines and clothes dryers that must be accessible and comply with this section. Laundry equipment within an individual dwelling or sleeping unit in Accessible, Type A or Type B units is addressed in Chapter 10 with reference to this section as applicable.

611.1 General. Accessible washing machines and clothes dryers shall comply with Section 611.

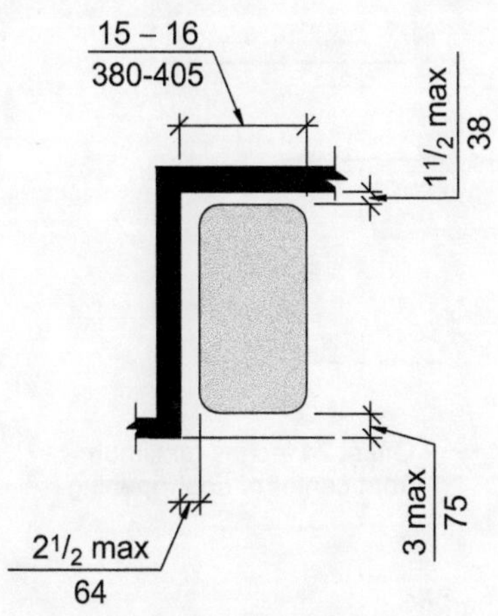

FIGURE 610.3.1
RECTANGULAR SHOWER COMPARTMENT SEAT

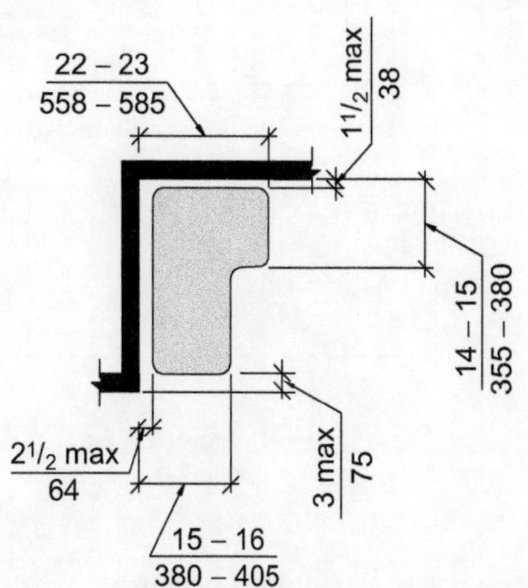

FIGURE 610.3.2
L-SHAPED SHOWER COMPARTMENT SEAT

❖ Laundry facilities present some complex problems of accessibility to the person in a wheelchair. The reach ranges provided in Section 308 do not include criteria for accessing things that require bending the elbow joint such as reaching over the top of and into the basket of a top loading clothes washing machine or down and into the front of a front-loading washer or dryer. Many devices are used to aid the user in reaching into these appliances to retrieve clothes at the bottom of the washer basket or rear of the dryer drum.

This standard provides specifics for top and front-loading laundry equipment and basically assumes separate pieces of equipment. Criteria included are clear floor space, height of the door and operational requirements for all operable parts (e.g., doors, lint traps) and controls (e.g., time or temperature settings, on/off control). It is not the intent of this standard to prohibit dual use equipment or stacked units if they meet the provisions in the subsection (see Section 103).

For examples of laundry rooms, see the commentary to Sections 1002.10 and 1003.10. Laundry equipment in Type B units has substantially different requirements (see Section 1004.10).

611.2 Clear Floor Space. A clear floor space complying with Section 305, positioned for parallel approach, shall be provided. For top loading machines, the clear floor space shall be centered on the appliance. For front loading machines, the centerline of the clear floor space shall be offset 24 inches (610 mm) maximum from the centerline of the door opening.

❖ The clearances differ between top loading and front-loading machines. For top loading machines, a 30-inch by 48 inch (760 by 1220 mm) clear floor space must be provided in front of and centered on top-loading washers and dryers to allow for access to the controls and access within the appliances themselves. With more and more front-loading machines being sold on the market, it is important to recognize the differences between front- and top-loading machines. Front-loading washers and dryers, especially those with drawers underneath, provide a higher level of access. Front-loading washers and dryers will permit the clear floor space to be offset up to a maximum of 24 inches (610 mm) from the center of the door opening. Allowing the clear floor space for front-loading machines to be offset is similar to what the standard permits in a kitchen for the refrigerator, and it recognizes that positioning the space directly in front of the door may prevent the door from opening and may be detrimental to access.

If access to the washer or dryer is located within an alcove, the clear floor space must also meet the alcove provisions in Section 305.7.

611.3 Operable Parts. Operable parts, including doors, lint screens, detergent and bleach compartments, shall comply with Section 309.

❖ The appliances must have controls that are provided with a clear floor space, within the reach ranges and can be operated with minimum hand dexterity. Operable parts include the on/off switch, any time/temperature water level settings, filters, doors, detergent and fabric softener ports, and anything unique to normal operation of the pieces of equipment. Please note that Section 309.3 references Section 308. Section 308.3.2 for obstructed side reach has an exception for laundry equipment. The exception allows for controls for the washer and dryer to be located on a panel over the back of the 36-inch (915 mm) high washer or dryer.

611.4 Height. Top loading machines shall have the door to the laundry compartment 36 inches (915 mm) maximum above the floor. Front loading machines shall have the bottom of the opening to the laundry compartment 15 inches (380 mm) minimum and 36 inches (915 mm) maximum above the floor.

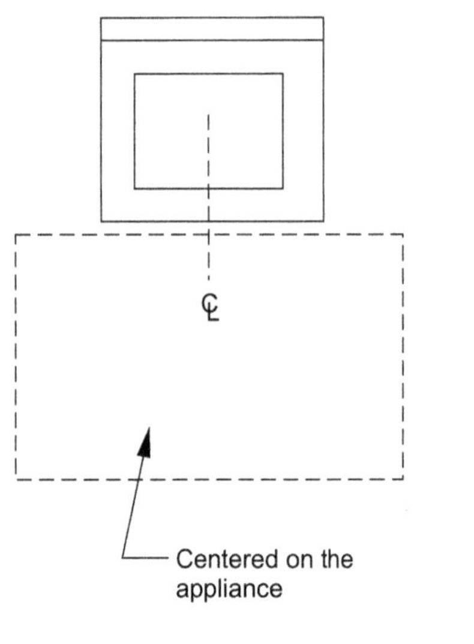

(a) Top Loading

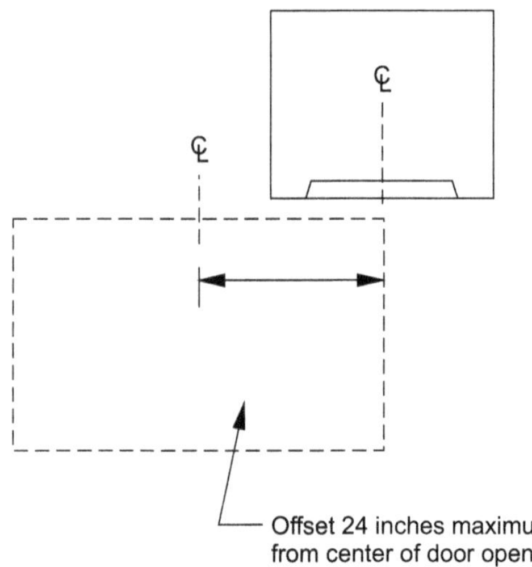

(b) Front Loading

FIGURE 611.2
CLEAR FLOOR SPACE

❖ The 36 inch (915 mm) height for top loading machines covers most commonly available top loading machines on the market. Operating a front-loading machine may be easier than operating a top loading machine. Some appliances have been developed with features to enhance accessibility. For example, some front-loader models are available with drawers under the units to raise the front-loading machines and provide easier access into the drum (see Figure 611.4).

612 Saunas and Steam Rooms

❖ This section is intended to be applicable to sauna and steam rooms. These provisions are not applicable to sauna and steam stalls or booths.

An item that was not addressed, which may be considered a safety issue or customer service issue, would be if the person using the sauna or a steam room would need to be able to move his or her chair out of the room him- or herself once he or she had transferred to the bench, or if it would be acceptable to have someone else remove and then bring the wheelchair back in. It would not be advisable to have a metal wheelchair remain in the hot or wet environment for an extended period of time.

612.1 General. Saunas and steam rooms shall comply with Section 612.

❖ This section provides reference to the bench requirements of Section 903, limits the potential for a door to swing into the required clear floor space serving the bench, and also requires that a turning space is provided within the room (see Commentary, Figure C612.1).

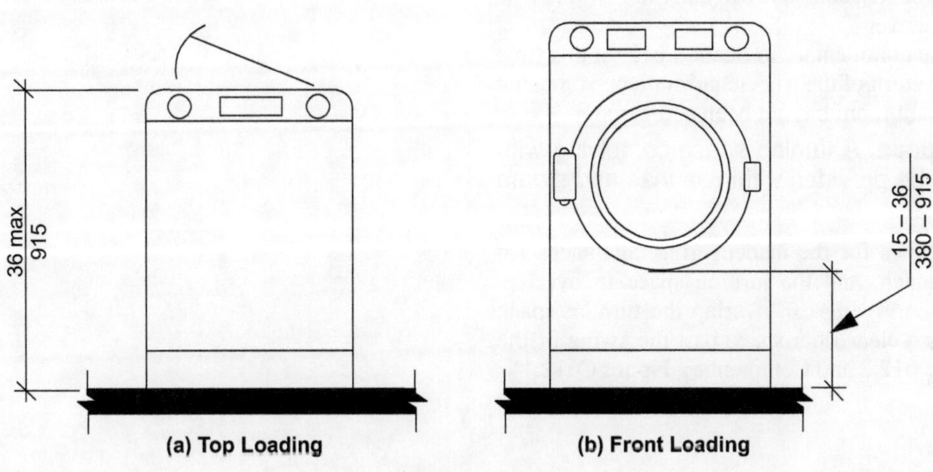

FIGURE 611.4
HEIGHT OF LAUNDRY EQUIPMENT

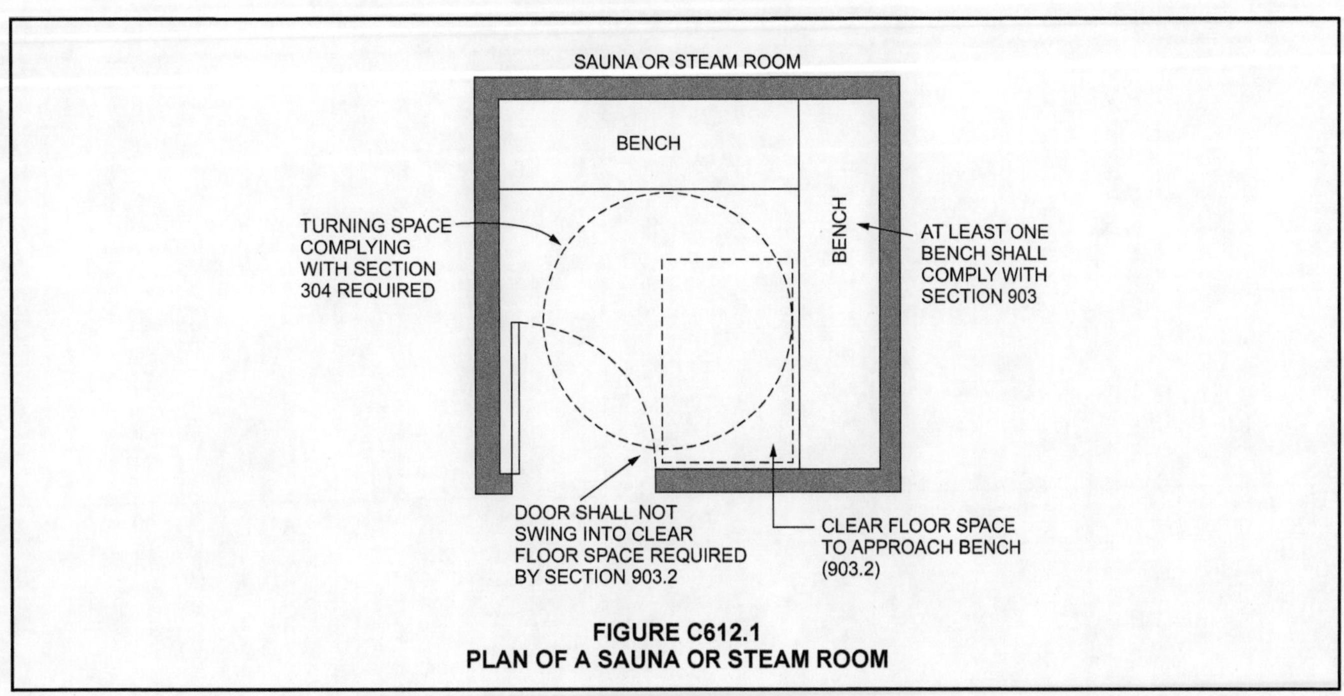

FIGURE C612.1
PLAN OF A SAUNA OR STEAM ROOM

612.2 Bench. Where seating is provided in saunas and steam rooms, at least one bench shall comply with Section 903. Doors shall not swing into the clear floor space required by Section 903.2.

❖ The bench requirements of Section 903 regulate the clear floor space and access to the bench; the size and height of the bench; require back support; regulate the structural strength; and state the need for slip-resistant surfaces on the seat. For additional information on the bench, see Section 903. While most facilities will include seating, it is important to note that this section does not require the bench but only regulates it where seating is provided.

Since someone could be transferring from their wheelchair to the bench, the door must not swing over the bench transfer location. Similar to the single occupant toilet room, this requirement would also ensure a wheelchair space available past the swing of the door into the room. The result would be that someone can enter the room, close the door and maneuver.

As noted in the commentary to Section 612, at this time the removal and return of the wheelchair for a person using the sauna and steam room has not been addressed.

612.3 Turning space. A turning space complying with Section 304 shall be provided within saunas and steam rooms.

❖ Section 301.2 allows for the maneuvering clearances for the doors and bench, and the turning space to overlap. Therefore, the door swing can overlap the turning space provided there is a clear floor space past the swing of the door (see Section 612.2 and Commentary Figure C612.1).

Chapter 7. Communication Elements and Features

❖ Chapter 7 includes elements that are used for communication of information. Information can be general (e.g., evacuation alarms, signage, detectable warnings) or private (e.g., phones, ATMs). Although the other chapters of this standard mainly dealt with mobility impairments, this chapter is more for persons with visual or hearing impairments.

- Communication features that are specific to dwelling units are covered in Section 1006.
- Section 701 is a general scoping provision that establishes that the requirements in this chapter are applicable when referenced by the authority having jurisdiction.
- Section 702 deals with visible and audible alarms. These devices are typically used to make occupants aware of an emergency evacuation necessary because of a fire in the building, but they can be used to inform occupants of other types of emergencies that may require evacuation or lock-down.
- Section 703 contains information on a variety of signage: tactile (i.e., raised and braille) and visual (i.e., text and pictograms). New technologies have also led to technical criteria for variable message signs (VMS) as well as remote infrared audible sign systems and pedestrian signals.
- Section 704 deals with telephone access for persons using wheelchairs and for persons with hearing impairments.
- Section 705 contains the technical criteria for detectable warnings on walking surfaces. The authority having jurisdiction dictates when the detectable warnings must be provided.
- Section 706 concerns assistive listening systems. These systems are commonly used in assembly spaces such as theaters, sports arenas and courtrooms.
- Section 707 provides tactile and audible requirements for ATMs and fare machines.
- Section 708 deals with two-way communication systems. These systems are commonly found at controlled entrances, within elevator cars (Section 407.4.10) or within areas of refuge.

701 General

❖ The national census has identified the population over 65 years of age as the fastest growing number in the United States. The percentage of people who have mobility, hearing and vision impairments increases as the general population of the United States ages. Following are brief descriptions of what constitutes a hearing or visual impairment.

"Blindness cuts you off from things; deafness cuts you off from people." — Helen Keller

Hearing Impairments

A hearing impairment is a full or partial decrease in the ability to detect or understand sounds. One American in 100 has a profound hearing loss; nearly one in 10 has a significant loss. Many hearing losses can be improved with hearing aids; however, a person with a moderate to profound hearing loss is dependent on visual cues for normal interaction, as well as to alert them to emergencies.

A hearing loss can be over the full range of frequencies or within a partial range, such as a high frequency range loss caused by exposure to loud noises. The U.S. Environmental Protection Agency (EPA) has set noise standards to protect people from these adverse health risks. The EPA has identified the level of 70 decibels for 24-hour exposure as the level necessary to protect the public from hearing loss. Normal speech sounds are within the 25 decibel to 35 decibel range. Living near an airport or a highway could expose someone to a 65 decibel to 75 decibel range and over time cause a hearing loss.

The severity of hearing loss is measured by how much louder, as measured in decibels, a sound must be made over the usual levels before being detected by an individual. The following list shows the rankings and their corresponding decibel ranges:

- Mild:
  - For adults: between 25 and 40 dB
  - For children: between 15 and 40 dB
- Moderate: between 41 and 55 dB
- Moderately severe: between 56 and 70 dB
- Severe: between 71 and 90 dB
- Profound: 90 dB or greater

Sound waves vary in amplitude and in frequency. Amplitude is the sound wave's highest point of oscillation. Frequency is the speed of sound divided by the wavelength of the sound wave, which is referred to as the pitch of the sound. The term "hearing impairment" is often reserved for people who have relative insensitivity to sound in the speech frequencies. Losing the ability to detect some frequencies creates some form of hearing impairment.

Many people with a hearing loss have better hearing in the lower frequency ranges (low tones), and cannot hear as well or at all in the higher frequencies. Noisy situations are especially difficult because hearing loss not only affects the ability to hear sounds, but also to localize and filter out background noise. People with unilateral hearing loss (single-sided deafness/SSD) lose their ability to localize sounds (i.e., unable to tell where a sound is coming from) and are unable to process out background noise in a noisy environment. A room with a high ceiling and hard surfaces for the walls and floors will have a lot of reverberation; therefore, acoustics can greatly affect a person's hearing ability. Difficulties can also arise for the listener trying to lip-read if the speaker is sitting with his back against the light source, obscuring his face.

Visual Impairments

The American Foundation for the Blind estimates that one in five people in the United States is visually impaired. "Visual impairment" is a term experts use to describe any kind of vision loss, whether it's someone who cannot see at all or someone who has partial vision loss. Some vision impairments can be improved with glasses or contacts, but not all. Persons with severe impairments may rely on a guide animal or a long cane for guidance.

Vision impairments in the young are more typically a result of an injury or congenital blindness. As part of the process of ageing, visual impairment may be caused by cataracts, diabetic retinopathy, glaucoma or macular degeneration.

Some people are completely blind, but many others have what's called legal blindness. They haven't lost their sight completely but have lost enough vision that they have to stand 20 feet (6.1 m) from an object to see it as well as someone with perfect vision could from 200 feet (61 m) away.

Color blindness is the inability to see parts of the color spectrum. This affects approximately 10 percent of males and 0.5 percent of females. People with color blindness usually have trouble discriminating reds and greens.

701.1 Scope. Communications elements and features required to be accessible by the scoping provisions adopted by the administrative authority shall comply with the applicable provisions of Chapter 7.

❖ The provisions in this chapter are intended to cover the requirements for communication features that are installed in a building. Even though signage is found in almost every building, other items are prescribed by the authority having jurisdiction (e.g., alarm systems) or are dependent on the type of activities within the building (e.g., assisted listening devices in a courthouse). Communication features specific to residential type facilities are specifically addressed in Section 1006. Note that these provisions apply to communication elements required in the scoping provisions (see Section 201). Understanding the scoping is important. As an example not every sign will be regulated. The provisions of Chapter 7 are only applicable to signs that are required to be provided or are required to be accessible when provided. For example, Sections 1007.9, 1110 and Appendix E107 of the 2012 *International Building Code*® (IBC®) or Sections 805.4 and 805.6.2 of A117.1 indicate certain signs that are required and expected to be accessible. Other signs such as advertisements may be in the same building, but they would not be required to comply with the provisions of this chapter.

702 Alarms

❖ Alarms serve to alert the occupants of a building of some event or condition. Fire, smoke, tornadoes, earthquakes and police emergencies are a few of the things for which people are notified by an audible or visual signal. These provisions address the technical requirements for the signaling devices used to notify occupants of fire emergencies (see Commentary Figure C702).

This standard does not mandate that fire alarm systems be installed in buildings. It provides only the technical requirements for such systems to be considered "accessible." The systems are typically mandated by the model codes, state laws or local ordinances. In alterations, where a new alarm system is installed or an existing system is replaced or upgraded, the degree of compliance is determined by the scope of the work and technical feasibility.

Audible alarms have been a standard feature of building construction since the early 1900s. However, visible signals did not appear, even in accessibility codes, until 1980. Early standards required relatively dim flashing lights at exit signs which were effective only along the exit route. As accessibility and building codes were revised, they began to incorporate alarm technology developed for use in schools for persons who are deaf and in factories where ambient noise levels made audible alarms ineffective.

The specifications in this section do not preclude the use of zoned or coded emergency alarm systems. In zoned systems, the visible alarm signals in an area flash whenever an audible signal sounds in the area. The standards regarding visible alarm signals provide comparable coverage and protection for persons who are deaf or hard of hearing, as well as for those depending on audible alarms. The provi-

FIGURE C702
AUDIBLE ALARM AND VISIBLE SIGNAL APPLIANCE

sions in this section for visible alarm signals were derived by studying facilities not designed for sleeping; e.g., business occupancies. In sleeping rooms, additional methods for waking sleeping persons who have hearing impairments may be necessary. For dwelling unit requirements see Section 1006.4.

Some facilities, for example, schools and courthouses, have started using the fire alarm system to make occupants aware of other types of emergencies, such as tornadoes or lock-downs. Typically, a different pattern is provided on the audible devices. Practice drills train the occupants to be aware of the differences. Facility alarm systems, other than the fire alarm systems, such as those used for tornado warnings and other emergencies, are not required to comply with the technical provisions in Section 702. However, every effort should be made to ensure that all occupants will be aware of any emergency. A full evaluation of the emergency evacuation system must be available in any building where fire safety and evacuation plans are required by the authority having jurisdiction.

702.1 General. Accessible audible and visible alarms and notification appliances shall be installed in accordance with NFPA 72 listed in Section 105.2.2, be powered by a commercial light and power source, be permanently connected to the wiring of the premises electric system, and be permanently installed.

❖ The model codes and NFPA 72 use the term "visible" alarms instead of "visual alarms." The terms are both intended to describe flashing light type alarms. A visible alarm provides persons with hearing loss the same warning delivered to hearing persons by an audible alarm. Unlike audible alarms, visible alarms must be located within the space they serve so that the signal is visible. NFPA 72, *National Fire Alarm Code*, is the nationally recognized technical standard for the installation of fire alarm systems. Because of the possible interpretation of language in NFPA 72 for allowance of radio-activated alarms, the A117.1 development committee wanted to emphasize that alarm systems must be permanently installed, not something that was handed to someone or moved around. Connection to the electrical system of the building will ensure that batteries do not run out, resulting in the units not operating.

Some hearing aids deactivate the amplification of a sound that could result in damage to residual hearing capabilities. Therefore, it is recommended that the maximum sound level of audible alarms be 110 decibels. This 110 decibel limit is the maximum allowed by NFPA 72, which is specified in this section to control alarm system installations. At locations where the alarm will not be heard above the ambient sound level, visible alarms must be provided.

Section 103 would allow for alternative alarm systems in situations where occupants may not be capable of self-preservation, such as a jail or hospital. For example, in hospitals, the activation of the alarm may cause undue concerns with bedridden patients, or startle doctors and nurses in an operatory. Alternative solutions that provide an equivalent level of safety in these situations are permitted. The first step is notification of trained personnel through a voice messaging system or audible code over an intercom system. Redundant protection, such as closure of doors to create separate smoke compartments/protected areas happens automatically. Trained personnel can then respond appropriately for possible evacuation or movement of patients to adjacent protected areas.

703 Signs

❖ The authority having jurisdiction establishes when accessible signage is required, typically by adoption of a building code; however, a designer or building owner may also choose to provide accessible signage at rooms that have permanent designations. The types of signage addressed in this section are visual signs (Section 703.2), tactile signs that include both raised letters and braille (Sections 703.3 and 703.4), pictograms (Section 703.5) and variable message signs (Section 703.7). The symbols for different accessible elements are indicated in Section 703.6.

Signage can include any combination of these types of signs (see Commentary Figure C703). Some of the requirements are repeated for each signage type. Rather than have the reader bounce around by referencing back, the commentary is repeated for each type of sign with most differences identified.

Examples of a signage type are those that provide audible information for persons with visual impairments. Technical requirements for remote infrared audible sign systems and pedestrian signals are provided in Sections 703.8 and 703.9.

FIGURE C703
TACTILE AND VISUAL SIGNAGE WITH PICTOGRAMS

703.1 General. Accessible signs shall comply with Section 703. Tactile signs shall contain both raised characters and braille. Where signs with both visual and raised characters are required, either one sign with both visual and raised characters, or two separate signs, one with visual, and one with raised characters, shall be provided.

❖ Much of the information contained in Section 703 was developed to assist the large number of people who are visually impaired but have some residual sight. In building complexes where finding locations independently on a routine basis is a necessity, such as in transportation terminals, tactile maps or prerecorded instructions are very helpful to visually impaired people. Several maps and auditory instructions have been developed and tested for specific applications. The types of maps or instructions are based on the information that must be communicated to the user, which in turn depends largely on the type of building as well as the user. Tactile signage is used where permanent signs are required to identify rooms and spaces such as, but not limited to, the following:

- Hotel guest rooms.
- Tenant space entrances.
- Entrances to apartment units.
- Patient rooms in medical facilities.
- Classrooms and offices in schools and colleges.
- Banquet and meeting rooms.
- Toilet and bathing rooms.
- Areas of refuge.

Landmarks easily distinguished by individuals with a visual impairment are useful as orientation cues. Such cues include changes in illumination level, bright colors, unique patterns, wall murals, location of special equipment or other architectural features. Many people with disabilities have head movement limitations and reduced peripheral vision. Thus, signage positioned perpendicular to the path of travel is easiest for them to notice. People generally distinguish signage within an angle of 30 degrees to either side of the centerline of their line of sight without being required to move their heads.

An important requirement in this section is the fact that "tactile" signs include both raised characters in accordance with Section 703.3 and braille complying with Section 703.4. This statement helps clarify the requirements by specifying the elements needed for each sign.

The last sentence of this section is also an important general provision to recognize. The option of using two separate signs will allow one sign to meet the visual character requirements and the other sign to comply with the raised character provisions. For example, a room might have a visual sign on or over the door to make it easier for people to see at a distance or over crowds and then provide a separate raised and braille sign at the jamb for persons with vision impairments.

The various subsections of Section 703.1 serve to provide scoping which directs the user to the various technical requirements for each type of sign. For example, the designation provisions of Section 703.1 would direct the user to the visual character requirements of Section 703.2 as well as the raised character provisions of Section 703.3. This type of information simply points to the proper type of sign characters needed. For example, the exception in Section 703.1.1 indicates that signs that are not located at a door to a space, such as a yard sign with a company's name on it, would not need to meet the raised character requirements of Section 703.3 because users would not be expected to walk up to the sign to feel it.

703.1.1 Designations. Interior and exterior signs identifying permanent rooms and spaces shall comply with Sections 703.1, 703.2, and 703.3.

EXCEPTION: Exterior signs that are not located at the door to the space they serve shall not be required to comply with Section 703.3.

❖ Where signs provide designations, labels or names for interior rooms or spaces, the signs must meet the general, visual and raised character provisions. Examples include room numbers in a school or hotel, room names in conference centers, restrooms, etc. Where signs are provided, they must meet both the visual character and raised character requirements. Compliance with the raised character requirements would also mean the information should be duplicated in braille as required by Section 703.3.1.

The exception eliminates the need for the sign to comply with the raised character provisions of Section 703.3. Where the sign is located in an exterior location where it is not effective or practical to provide signage that needs to be felt to be read, the sign would only need to meet the visual character requirements of Section 703.2. Examples would be the remote sign at the street indicating the name or occupant of the building, the building's address or the lane designation above a drive-up teller lane.

703.1.2 Directional and Informational Signs. Signs that provide direction to or information about interior spaces and facilities of the site shall comply with Section 703.2.

❖ Directional and information signs must meet the visual character requirements for font style, size, location, finish and contrast to be readable by persons with limited vision. See Section 703.2 for more information on the specific requirements. This requirement applies to signs providing direction to rooms or spaces and would include those that identify either the location of accessible elements or the egress route. Informational signs may include things such as occupant load, rules of conduct, employment laws, tenant advertising or signage that is changeable. These signs do not provide specific information about the facility or its interior spaces and are not required to be accessible in the visual sense. Building directories, elevator bank signage, toilet room locations, exit routes, etc., provide navigational information to building visitors and are therefore required to be accessible. Users should be certain to review the scoping provisions that direct signs to comply with the standard.

703.1.3 Pictograms. Where pictograms are provided as designations of permanent interior rooms and spaces, the pictograms shall comply with Section 703.5 and shall have text descriptors located directly below the pictogram field and complying with Sections 703.2 and 703.3.

EXCEPTION: Pictograms that provide information about a room or space, such as "No Smoking", occupant logos, and the International Symbol of Accessibility, are not required to have text descriptors.

❖ This section is similar in intent to the designation requirements of Section 703.1.1. Where pictograms are utilized to identify a space, such as the women's restroom, they must meet the size and contrast requirements for the pictorial portion, but must also include an equivalent text description beneath the graphic. The text within the description must comply with the visual and raised character requirements (see Commentary Figure C703.1.3). Additionally, the raised character text must be duplicated in braille as required by Section 703.3.1.

Where the pictogram is not serving as the designation for a room or space, the exception will eliminate the need for the text descriptor. Therefore, pictograms for information such as those for TTY devices, or others such as the occupant logos, "no smoking," and the International Symbol of Accessibility, are not required to have text descriptors and braille. This section and the exception reflect the A117.1 Committee's belief that text descriptors are not needed for many pictograms.

After looking at the exception, it is important to review the scoping document and the base paragraph of Section 703.1.3 so that the pictogram provisions are not misapplied. Looking at the exception might lead to the assumption that informational pictograms don't need the text descriptors but still need to meet the typical size and contrast requirements for pictograms. Notice however that the language of this section only applies where the pictogram is provided as a designation for a room or space. Therefore, the informational pictograms such as a "no smoking" sign or notifying occupants to not use the elevator during an emergency are not required to comply with Section 703.5 [see Commentary Figure 703.2(a)]. While pictograms used for purposes other than room designations do not have a specified size requirement, good guidance might be to use the A117.1 standard's height for visual characters when provided at the same viewing distance. For example, the wheelchair symbol at the accessible entrance should be at least 3 inches (76 mm) tall if viewed from about 15 feet (4.57 m) (see Table 703.2.4).

FIGURE C703.1.3
PICTOGRAM

703.2 Visual Characters.

❖ Examples of signs that provide visual information only would be exit signage, overhead signage and egress path information [see Commentary Figures C703.2(a) and (b)].

FIGURE C703.2(a)
VISUAL SIGNAGE

FIGURE C703.2(b)
VISUAL SIGNAGE

703.2.1 General. Visual characters shall comply with the following:

1. Visual characters that also serve as raised characters shall comply with Section 703.3, or
2. Visual characters on VMS signage shall comply with Section 703.7, or
3. Visual characters not covered in items 1 and 2 shall comply with Section 703.2.

EXCEPTION: The visual and raised requirements of item 1 shall be permitted to be provided by two separate signs that provide corresponding information provided one sign complies with Section 703.2 and the second sign complies with Section 703.3.

❖ This general section provides scoping and directs users to the various sections of the standard that apply to visual signs. For visual signage, the legibility of printed characters is a function of the viewing distance, character proportions, font, background contrast, the finish, lighting and whether the characters are static or variable.

There are essentially three separate types of visual characters addressed by the standard. In general, visual characters are regulated by the provisions of Section 703.2. Where VMS (variable message) signs are used, the characters are required to comply with the requirements for VMS that are found in Section 703.7. In those situations where a visual character is also expected to serve as a raised character, then Item 1 will direct the user to the provisions of Section 703.3.

The exception, which is applicable to Item 1, is essentially a repeat of the requirements found at the end of Section 703.1. This exception will direct the user to both the visual and the raised character requirements when a decision to provide two separate signs has been made.

703.2.2 Case. Characters shall be uppercase, lowercase, or a combination of both.

❖ Even though raised characters are required to be uppercase only (Section 703.3.3), visual signage can be uppercase and lowercase.

Where the visual characters also serve as raised characters, Section 703.2.1, Item 1, requires the sign to comply with the raised character requirements of Section 703.3 and therefore it must have uppercase letters (Section 703.3.3).

703.2.3 Style. Characters shall be conventional in form. Characters shall not be italic, oblique, script, highly decorative, or of other unusual forms.

❖ Visual signs are not required to be sans serif unlike tactiles signs (Section 703.3.4); however, typefaces without excessive flourishes or deviation in stroke width have been found to be the most legible. A severely nearsighted person has to be much closer to see a character of a given size accurately than a person with normal visual acuity.

Where the visual characters also serve as raised characters, Section 703.2.1, Item 1, requires the sign to comply with the raised character requirements of Section 703.3 and therefore they must be sans serif (Section 703.3.4).

Italic **Oblique** *script*
highly decorative
or other *unusual forms*

FIGURE C703.2.3
PROHIBITED CHARACTER STYLES

703.2.4 Character Height. The uppercase letter "I" shall be used to determine the allowable height of all characters of a font. The uppercase letter "I" of the font shall have a minimum height complying with Table 703.2.4. Viewing distance shall be measured as the horizontal distance between the character and an obstruction preventing further approach towards the sign.

EXCEPTION: In assembly seating where the maximum viewing distance is 100 feet (30.5 m) or greater, the height of the uppercase "I" of fonts shall be permitted to be 1 inch (25 mm) for every 30 feet (9145 mm) of viewing distance, provided the character height is 8 inches (205 mm) minimum. Viewing dis-

tance shall be measured as the horizontal distance between the character and where someone is expected to view the sign.

❖ Proportions of visual lettering are a function of character width (Section 703.2.5), height (Section 703.2.4), stroke width (Section 703.2.6) and character spacing (Section 703.2.7). The uppercase letter "I" in a font is the baseline to determine the "character height" for the entire font chosen for the sign. Therefore, some lowercase letters may actually be smaller than the minimum dimensions in Table 703.2.4 and the sign would still meet requirements. This same baseline is used to determine the relationship for character width, stroke width and spacing.

Character proportions in visual signage are very important to legibility. Very thick or thin characters are difficult to read. Characters placed close together can cause confusion with words like "MIN." The Society for Environmental Graphic Design (SEGD) recommends using the capital "O" and the capital "I" for calculating proportions for text. If numbers are used to identify spaces, use the numbers "0" and "1." Uniform stroke width also increases legibility.

The height for visual characters is based on viewing distance. If the sign is overhead, a person may need to stand back to read the sign. If moving forward to the signage is blocked by some type of barricade, the viewing distance is from that barricade.

Where the visual characters also serve as raised characters, Section 703.2.1, Item 1, requires the sign to comply with the raised character requirements of Section 703.3 and therefore the provisions of Section 703.3 will typically be the controlling factor. The general result of this for signage of both raised and visual characters is:

- Character width requirements in Sections 703.2.5 and 703.3.6 are the same.
- Character height requirements are specifically addressed in Section 703.3.5 and would control the character size.
- Specifics in Section 703.3.7.2 result in the minimum stroke width requirements being the same as those in Section 703.2.6. The maximum stroke width from Section 703.2.6 would also be applicable.
- Character spacing requirements in Section 703.3.8 are specific to a maximum character height of 2 inches (51 mm), however, the intent is to be consistent with the character spacing percentage in Section 703.2.7.

The exception addresses situations where the sign would be read from a great distance. This exception came about because of the development of the Variable Message Sign (VMS) provisions of Section 703.7 and the realization that when signs are viewed at greater distances, the standard does not adequately address how the characters should be dealt with and would literally require massive character heights if the general provisions of Section 703.2.4 were followed.

The general requirements for visual signage were originally developed for viewing within a room or space where someone could move forward for a better view, such as moving closer to the train schedule in Grand Central Station, rather than expecting the schedule to be read from every possible location within the room. When dealing with a sports venue or other types of assembly seating, it was realized that the signs had to be viewable from a person's seat without the person moving forward for better viewing.

In assembly seating, information is often presented in text form as well as audibly over the public address system. In large stadiums or venues, this text information is viewed at great distances, potentially as much as 600 feet (182.9 m) from some seats. While text information in these large assembly spaces is presented primarily in a VMS format, not all of it is always VMS. For example, a community sports facility may use a combination of fixed and VMS to minimize cost—characters that do not change very often, such as HOME and VISITOR on a scoreboard, may be fixed. Without an exception for visual character heights, these types of signs that comply with Table 703.2.4 and are viewed at great distances would result in signs that could be as large as the seating area.

The character height of 1 inch (25 mm) for every 30 feet (9145 mm) in the exception was based upon the most recent *Manual on Uniform Traffic Control Devices* (MUTCD) requirements. Though these signs are not dealing with traffic signs, MUTCD does address viewing distances for signs and is a standard that has been referenced by A117.1 for years. See A117.1 Sections 105.1 and 105.2.1 for additional information related to MUTCD.

TABLE 703.2.4. See page 7-8.

❖ The actual viewing distance for a person looking at a sign varies, depending on the height of the person, the height of sign and the number of lines of information. Character height requirements are calculated using the horizontal and vertical distances between the viewer and the sign as specified in the table. The "horizontal viewing distance" is the horizontal distance from the closest point a person can stand to view the sign, to the face of the sign. The vertical height is from the floor of the viewing position to the baseline of the highest line of the characters (see Commentary Figure C703.2.4). Section 703.2.9 requires that the base-

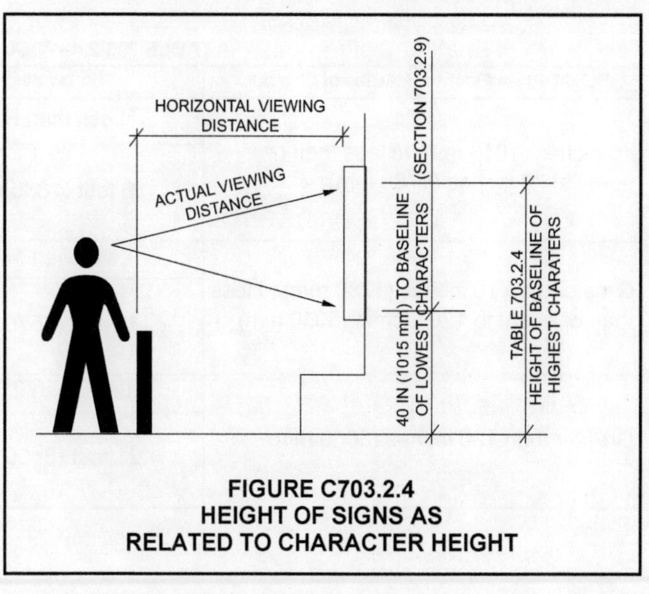

FIGURE C703.2.4 HEIGHT OF SIGNS AS RELATED TO CHARACTER HEIGHT

line of the lowest row of characters to be a minimum of 40 inches (1016 mm) above the floor. Specific requirements for visual signage in elevators are listed in Sections 407, 408 and 409, depending on the type of elevator.

703.2.5 Character Width. The uppercase letter "O" shall be used to determine the allowable width of all characters of a font. The width of the uppercase letter "O" of the font shall be 55 percent minimum and 110 percent maximum of the height of the uppercase "I" of the font.

❖ See the commentary to Section 703.2.4. For an example of proportion based on width, see Commentary Figure C703.3.6. Assuming characters within the font are proportional, some characters, such as "W," could actually be wider than the 110 percent required for the "O" and the font would still be compliant.

703.2.6 Stroke Width. The uppercase letter "I" shall be used to determine the allowable stroke width of all characters of a font. The stroke width shall be 10 percent minimum and 30 percent maximum of the height of the uppercase "I" of the font.

❖ Very thick or thin letters are difficult to read. See the commentary to Section 703.2.4 and Commentary Figure C703.2.6 for additional information. Stroke thickness within a font could vary, but should always stay within the 10 to 30 percent range.

703.2.7 Character Spacing. Spacing shall be measured between the two closest points of adjacent characters within a message, excluding word spaces. Spacing between individual characters shall be 10 percent minimum and 35 percent maximum of the character height.

❖ See the commentary to Section 703.2.4. The range in character spacing allows for locating sloped or curved letters closer to the adjacent letters so the font does not appear to have uneven spacing.

703.2.8 Line Spacing. Spacing between the baselines of separate lines of characters within a message shall be 135 percent minimum and 170 percent maximum of the character height.

EXCEPTION: In assembly seating where the maximum viewing distance is 100 feet (30.5 m) or greater, the spacing between the baselines of separate lines of characters within a message shall be permitted to be 120 percent minimum and 170 percent maximum of the character height.

❖ The character height is determined in Table 703.2.4 and is based on the uppercase letter "I;" therefore, line spacing is 135 percent to 170 percent of the uppercase letter "I" for the font used in the sign. This is measured from the highest letter in a row to the baseline of the row above. Tails of letters such as "g," "j" and "y" would not be considered. Equal spacing between lines increases legibility. If unrelated information is included on the same sign (e.g., signs in two languages), the line spacing may be larger between the two pieces of information.

Line spacing requirements for visual and raised character signs are the same (Section 703.3.9).

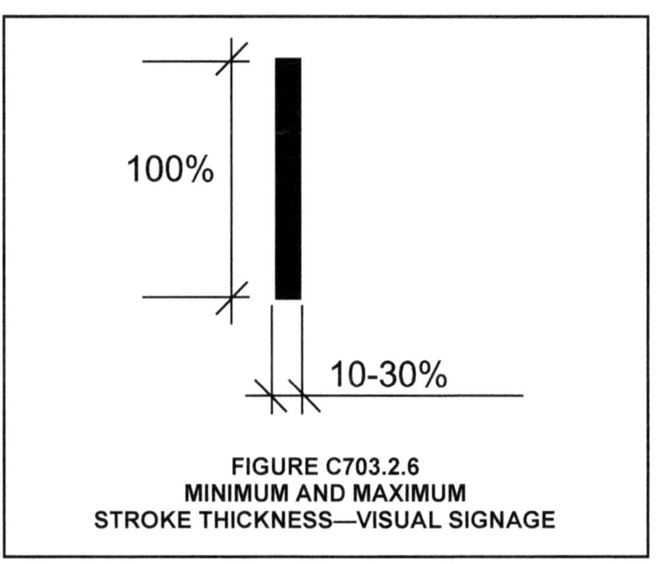

**FIGURE C703.2.6
MINIMUM AND MAXIMUM
STROKE THICKNESS—VISUAL SIGNAGE**

TABLE 703.2.4—VISUAL CHARACTER HEIGHT

Height above Floor to Baseline of Character	Horizontal Viewing Distance	Minimum Character Height
40 inches (1015 mm) to less than or equal to 70 inches (1780 mm)	Less than 6 feet (1830 mm)	$^5/_8$ inch (16 mm)
	6 feet (1830 mm) and greater	$^5/_8$ inch (16 mm), plus $^1/_8$ inch (3.2 mm) per foot (305 mm) of viewing distance above 6 feet (1830 mm)
Greater than 70 inches (1780 mm) to less than or equal to 120 inches (3050 mm)	Less than 15 feet (4570 mm)	2 inches (51 mm)
	15 feet (4570 mm) and greater	2 inches (51 mm), plus $^1/_8$ inch (3.2 mm) per foot (305 mm) of viewing distance above 15 feet (4570 mm)
Greater than 120 inches (3050 mm)	Less than 21 feet (6400 mm)	3 inches (75 mm)
	21 feet (6400 mm) and greater	3 inches (75 mm), plus $^1/_8$ inch (3.2 mm) per foot (305 mm) of viewing distance above 21 feet (6400 mm)

See the commentary to Section 703.2.4 for information addressing the exception. Where a sign is being viewed at these larger distances, the exception will permit a slightly reduced minimum line space. The 120-percent minimum character height spacing is similar to the criteria developed for Variable Message Sign (VMS) characters in Section 703.7 and was therefore included here for the visual signs.

703.2.9 Height Above Floor. Visual characters shall be 40 inches (1015 mm) minimum above the floor of the viewing position, measured to the baseline of the character. Heights shall comply with Table 703.2.4, based on the size of the characters on the sign.

EXCEPTION: Visual characters indicating elevator car controls shall not be required to comply with Section 703.2.9.

❖ This 40-inch (1015 mm) minimum measurement must be taken to the baseline of the lowest line of text. Because visual characters can be uppercase and lowercase, the baseline of the visual characters is the bottom edge of most of the letters, with the tail of some letters, like "g" and "j" going below the baseline. Note that Table 703.2.4 provides information based on the baseline to the highest line of information on the sign (see Commentary Figure C703.2.4).

Requirements for visual information on elevator car controls are contained in Sections 407, 408 and 409 depending on the type of elevator.

Where visual characters also serve as raised characters, Section 703.2.1 Item 1, requires the sign to comply with the raised character requirements of Section 703.3 and therefore they are required to comply with Sections 703.3.10 and 703.3.11. This would place the baseline of the lowest line of characters at a 48-inch (1219 mm) height versus the 40-inch (1015 mm) height specified in this section.

703.2.10 Finish and Contrast. Characters and their background shall have a non-glare finish. Characters shall contrast with their background, with either light characters on a dark background, or dark characters on a light background.

❖ A nonglare finish is typically matte or eggshell. Consideration must be given to light sources and the ambient lighting to prevent glare on sign surfaces. Light characters on a dark background are usually considered easier to read than dark characters on a light background; however, either is permitted. A contrast of at least 70 percent based on the light reflectance value (LRV) is recommended.

A nonglare finish (11- to 19-degree gloss on 60-degree glossimeter) is recommended. Research indicates that signs are more legible for persons with low vision when characters contrast with their background by 70 percent minimum. Contrast, in percent, is determined by:

$$\text{Contrast} = [(B1 - B2) / B1] \times 100$$

where $B1$ = light reflectance value (LRV) of the lighter area

and $B2$ = light reflectance value (LRV) of the darker area.

In any application neither white nor black is ever absolute; therefore, $B1$ will never equal 100, and $B2$ will always be greater than 0. The greatest readability is usually achieved with the use of light-colored characters or symbols on a dark background.

Examples of acceptable and unacceptable finishes, according to the Society for Environmental Graphic Design (SEGD), are included in Commentary Table C703.2.10.

If a sign contains both visual and tactile characters, it must comply with the finish and contrast requirements that are repeated in Sections 703.2.10 and 703.3.12. The raised characters and braille of tactile signage are addressed in the exception to Section 703.3.12 and would be exempt from the contrast requirement where separate visual characters are provided.

703.3 Raised Characters.

703.3.1 General. Raised characters shall comply with Section 703.3, and shall be duplicated in braille complying with Section 703.4.

❖ Persons who are blind read either tactile characters or braille; many of them do not read both. Therefore, tactile signs include both raised characters and braille. Both raised characters and braille are most legible when the raised profile in cross section (perpendicular to the face of the letter) is rounded or trapezoidal. Raised characters and braille having rectangular profiles are not as legible.

If a sign provides both raised and visual characters, the sign must comply with Section 703.3, as stated in Section 703.2.1, Item 1, if the visual characters also serve as raised characters. Where separate visual and raised characters are used, the sign must comply with Sections 703.2 and 703.3 as appropriate.

703.3.2 Depth. Raised characters shall be raised $^{1}/_{32}$ inch (0.8 mm) minimum above their background.

❖ Minimum projection of characters above the background is necessary to make the characters perceptible by touch. Height limitations keep the letters in a size range that can be distinguishable by a person reading them by touch (see Commentary Figure C703.3.2).

TABLE C703.2.10
FINISH AND CONTRAST RECOMMENDATIONS

MATERIALS	ACCEPTABLE	UNACCEPTABLE
Finish paints and inks	Eggshell	Gloss or semi-gloss
Acrylic sheet, mylar, frosted glass	Most nonglare types	Polished surface
Self-adhesive	Most nonglare types	Gloss
Metal	Certain satin or random brushed finishes	Polished or directional brushed finishes

703.3.3 Case. Characters shall be uppercase.

❖ The letters are raised so they can be read by touch; restricting the letters to uppercase allows for easier reading. Signage that is for visual only can be a combination of upper and lower case (Section 703.2.2).

703.3.4 Style. Characters shall be sans serif. Characters shall not be italic, oblique, script, highly decorative, or of other unusual forms.

❖ In typography, a sans serif typeface is one that does not have the small features called "serifs" at the end of strokes. Sans serif typefaces or a simple serif typeface without excessive flourishes or deviation in stroke width have been found to be the most legible. Where a person is reading the characters by touch, highly stylized fonts or characters with serifs add confusion when trying to determine what the character is. For an example of serif and sans serif typeface, see Commentary Figure C703.3.4. Commentary Figure C703.2.3 provides examples of character forms that are not permitted. Stroke thickness within a font can vary from top to bottom; however, uniform thickness is easier to read.

703.3.5 Character Height. The uppercase letter "I" shall be used to determine the allowable height of all characters of a font. The height of the uppercase letter "I" of the font, measured vertically from the baseline of the character, shall be $^{5}/_{8}$ inch (16 mm) minimum, and 2 inches (51 mm) maximum.

EXCEPTION: Where separate raised and visual characters with the same information are provided, the height of the raised uppercase letter "I" shall be permitted to be $^{1}/_{2}$ inch (13 mm) minimum.

❖ Proportions of raised character lettering are a function of character width (Section 703.3.6), character height (Section 703.3.5), stroke width (Section 703.3.7) and character spacing (Section 703.3.8). The uppercase letter "I" in a font is the baseline to determine the "character height" for the entire font chosen for the sign. Because raised character signs are all uppercase (Section 703.3.3) there probably will not be any smaller letters as in visual signs (Sections 703.2.2 and 703.2.4). This same baseline is used to determine the relationship for character width, stroke width and spacing.

Character proportions in tactile signage are very important to legibility. Very thick or thin characters are difficult to read. Characters placed close together can cause confusion with words like "MIN." The Society for Environmental Graphic Design (SEGD) recommends using the capital "O" and the capital "I" for calculating proportions for text. If numbers are used to identify spaces, use the numbers "0" and "1." Uniform stroke width also increases legibility.

Characters used for both visual and raised character signage can be $^{5}/_{8}$ inch to 2 inches (16 to 51 mm) in height (see Figure 703.3.5). If a sign is for tactile reading only (e.g., tactile exit signage), text can be as small as $^{1}/_{2}$ inch (13 mm).

FIGURE C703.3.4
SANS SERIF

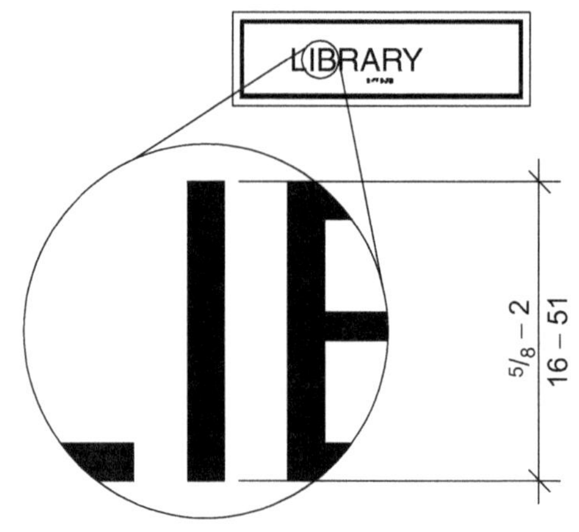

FIGURE 703.3.5
CHARACTER HEIGHT

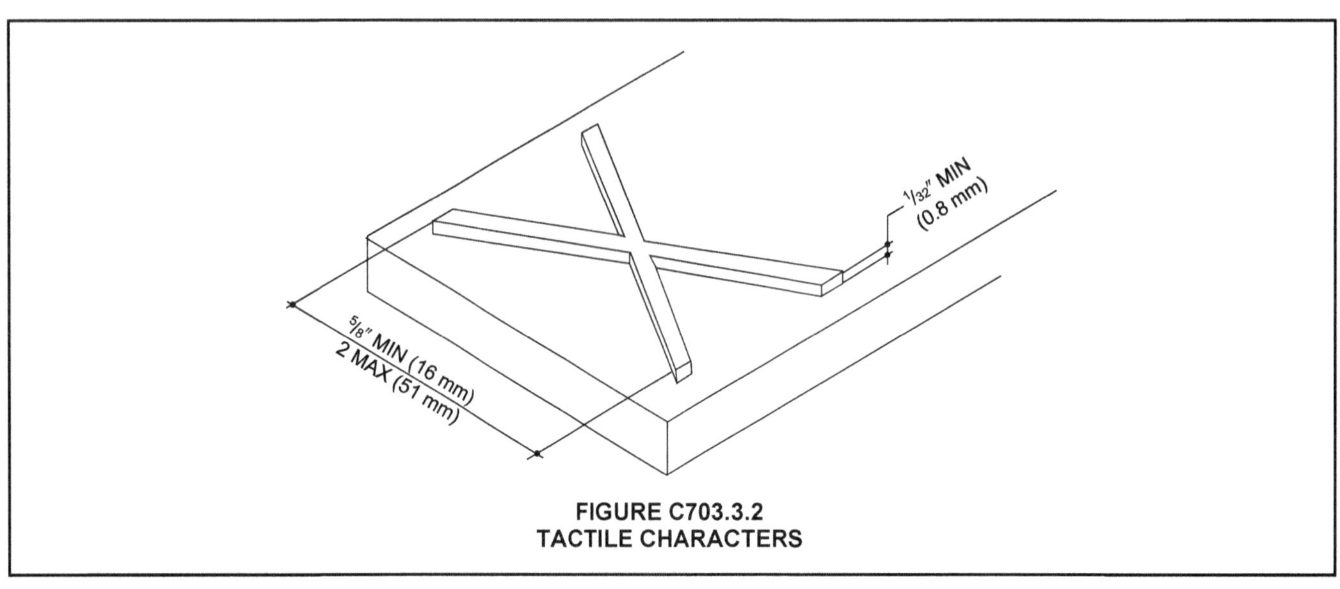

FIGURE C703.3.2
TACTILE CHARACTERS

703.3.6 Character Width. The uppercase letter "O" shall be used to determine the allowable width of all characters of a font. The width of the uppercase letter "O" of the font shall be 55 percent minimum and 110 percent maximum of the height of the uppercase "I" of the font.

❖ See the commentary to Section 703.3.5. For an example of proportion based on width, see Commentary Figure C703.3.6. Assuming characters within the font are proportional, some characters, such as "W," could actually be wider than the 110 percent required for the "O" and the font would still be compliant.

703.3.7 Stroke Width. Raised character stroke width shall comply with Section 703.3.7. The uppercase letter "I" of the font shall be used to determine the allowable stroke width of all characters of a font.

❖ Very thick or thin letters are difficult to read. See the commentary for Section 703.3.5 for additional information.

703.3.7.1 Maximum. The stroke width shall be 15 percent maximum of the height of the uppercase letter "I" measured at the top surface of the character, and 30 percent maximum of the height of the uppercase letter "I" measured at the base of the character.

❖ See the commentary for Section 703.3.7 and Commentary Figure C703.3.7. Stroke thickness within a font can vary from top to bottom; however, uniform thickness is easier to read.

703.3.7.2 Minimum. When characters are both visual and raised, the stroke width shall be 10 percent minimum of the height of the uppercase letter "I".

❖ There are additional minimum stroke width criteria when the sign includes both visual and raised characters The 10 percent minimum established by this section ensures that the characters can serve the visual function and comply with the requirements of Section 703.2.6 (see commentary, Sections 703.2.6 and 703.3.7 and Commentary, Figures C703.2.6 and C703.3.7.

703.3.8 Character Spacing. Character spacing shall be measured between the two closest points of adjacent raised characters within a message, excluding word spaces. Spacing between individual raised characters shall be 1/8 inch (3.2 mm) minimum measured at the top surface of the characters, 1/16 inch (1.6 mm) minimum measured at the base of the characters, and four times the raised character stroke width maximum. Characters shall be separated from raised borders and decorative elements 3/8 inch (9.5 mm) minimum.

❖ The range in character spacing allows for sloped or curved letters to be located closer to the adjacent letters so the font does not appear to have uneven spacing (see commentary, Section 703.3.5).

Raised borders that are located too close can be confusing and may be misread as a portion of a raised character or braille; therefore, they should be avoided or spaced away from the main text.

703.3.9 Line Spacing. Spacing between the baselines of separate lines of raised characters within a message shall be 135 percent minimum and 170 percent maximum of the raised character height.

❖ The character height is determined in Section 703.3.5 and is based on the uppercase letter "I;" therefore, line spacing is 135 percent to 170 percent of the uppercase letter "I" for the font used in the sign. Proportional spacing between lines increases legibility. If separate or nonrelated information appears on the same sign (e.g., signs in two languages), the line spacing may be larger between the two pieces of information. This line spacing requirement is intended to be applicable "within a message"; therefore, it is best to think of this similar to sentences or paragraphs. If it is a single thought or sentence, the line spacing requirements should apply. Where there is a different message or a different paragraph, the spacing between the two lines of text may exceed the 170-percent limit.

703.3.10 Height above Floor. Raised characters shall be 48 inches (1220 mm) minimum above the floor, measured to the baseline of the lowest raised character and 60 inches (1525 mm) maximum above the floor, measured to the baseline of the highest raised character.

EXCEPTION: Raised characters for elevator car controls shall not be required to comply with Section 703.3.10.

❖ To provide a consistent measuring point and to clarify the application of the requirements, the standard specifies that the height is measured to the baseline of both the highest

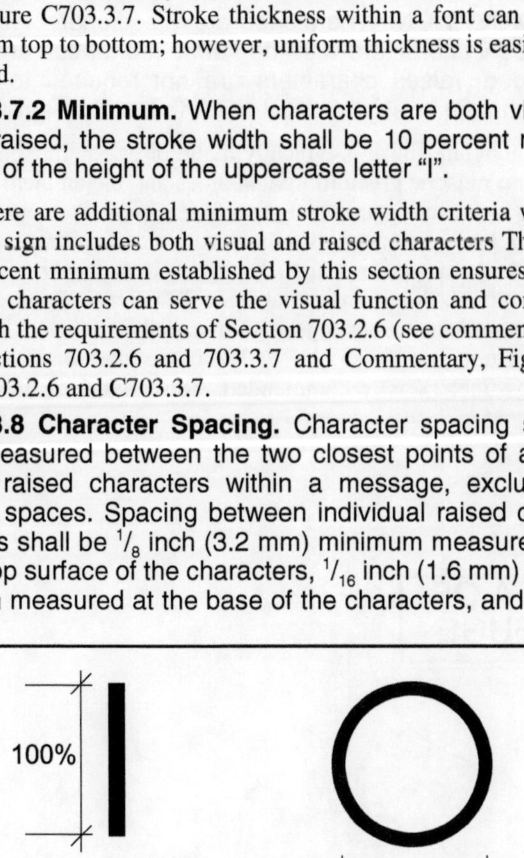

100%

55%-110%

FIGURE C703.3.6
CHARACTER WIDTH

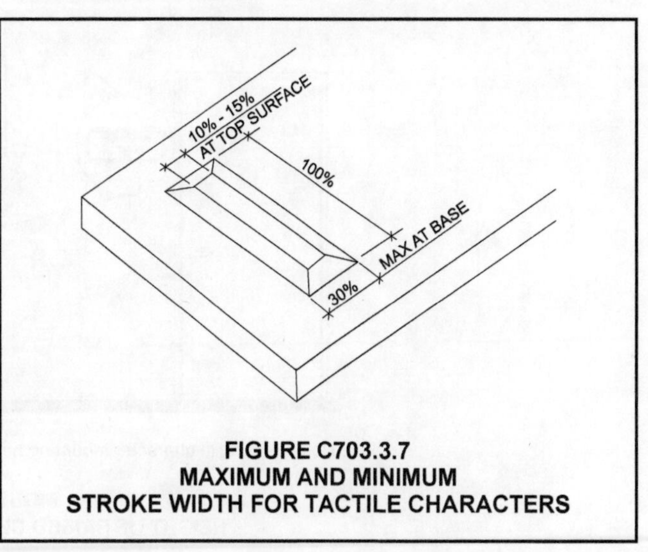

FIGURE C703.3.7
MAXIMUM AND MINIMUM
STROKE WIDTH FOR TACTILE CHARACTERS

and lowest lines of text (see Figure 703.3.10). The baseline of the raised characters is the bottom edge. Note that in addition to the baseline of the raised letters needing to be within 48 inches and 60 inches (1220 to 1525 mm), the braille must also be located within the same dimensions (Section 703.4.5). This is a convenient height in reading signs for a standing person. The raised character or braille signage need not be located within the reach ranges in Section 308 since it is used for people with visual impairments and the heights specified in Section 308 would place the sign too low for most users to read by touch.

Elevator car controls have requirements for raised characters or symbols and braille information. The height requirements for elevator car controls are addressed in Sections 407, 408 and 409, depending on the type of elevator.

703.3.11 Location. Where a sign containing raised characters and braille is provided at a door, the sign shall be alongside the door at the latch side. Where a sign containing raised characters and braille is provided at double doors with one active leaf, the sign shall be located on the inactive leaf. Where a sign containing raised characters and braille is provided at double doors with two active leaves, the sign shall be to the right of the right-hand door. Where there is no wall space on the latch side of a single door, or to the right side of double doors, signs shall be on the nearest adjacent wall. Signs containing raised characters and braille shall be located so that a clear floor area 18 inches (455 mm) minimum by 18 inches (455 mm) minimum, centered on the raised characters is provided beyond the arc of any door swing between the closed position and 45 degree open position.

> **EXCEPTION:** Signs containing raised characters and braille shall be permitted on the push side of doors with closers and without hold-open devices.

❖ To be usable by the visually impaired, signs with raised characters and braille are placed at consistent locations. In locations having double doors, tactile signs are mounted to the right of the right-hand door, as it is approached (see Figure 703.3.11). Thus, visually impaired travelers following customary pedestrian traffic patterns by traveling to the right side of corridors or spaces encounter signs before they encounter the associated doors.

Placement of raised character and braille signs adjacent to doors on the latch side will allow for a person to stand outside the swing of the door when reading the sign. In addition, signs located at the hinge side are obscured when doors are open. It is important that any fixed elements not obstruct access to the sign. The wheelchair maneuvering clearance required by Section 404.2.3 at the pull side of the doors should allow adequate space.

When adequate wall space is not available on the latch side, signs are to be placed on the adjacent wall (see Commentary Figure C703.3.11).

The exception allows for placing signs with raised characters and braille on the door in limited situations. With the closers operating, the door will never be held open, so the signage will always be readable.

703.3.12 Finish and Contrast. Characters and their background shall have a non-glare finish. Characters shall contrast with their background with either light characters on a dark background, or dark characters on a light background.

> **EXCEPTION:** Where separate raised characters and visual characters with the same information are provided, raised characters are not required to have nonglare finish or to contrast with their background.

❖ A nonglare finish is typically matte or eggshell. Consideration must be given to light sources and the ambient lighting to prevent glare on sign surfaces. Light characters on a dark background are usually considered easier to read than dark characters on a light background; however, either is permitted. A contrast of at least 70 percent based on the light reflectance value is recommended.

A nonglare finish (11- to 19-degree gloss on 60-degree glossimeter) is recommended. Research indicates that

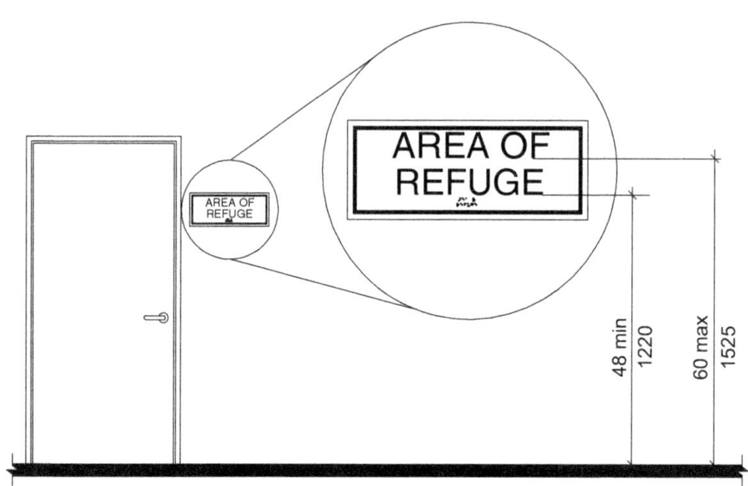

Note: For braille character mounting height see Section 703.4.5

FIGURE 703.3.10
HEIGHT OF RAISED CHARACTERS ABOVE FLOOR

signs are more legible for persons with low vision when characters contrast with their background by 70 percent minimum. Contrast, in percent, is determined by:

Contrast = $[(B1 - B2)/B1] \times 100$

where $B1$ = light reflectance value (LRV) of the lighter area

and $B2$ = light reflectance value (LRV) of the darker area.

In any application, neither white nor black is ever absolute; therefore, $B1$ will never equal 100, and $B2$ will always be greater than 0. The greatest readability is usually achieved with the use of light-colored characters or symbols on a dark background.

Examples of acceptable and unacceptable finishes, according to the Society for Environmental Graphic Design (SEGD) are included in Table C703.2.10.

If a sign uses characters that are both visual and raised, it must comply with the finish and contrast requirements that are repeated in Sections 703.2.10 and 703.3.12. The raised characters and braille of tactile signage are addressed in the exception to Section 703.3.12. When separate visual and raised character signage with the same information is provided, the raised character and braille sign can have little or no contrast, including being the same color as the background. Since contrast is important to users reading the sign through visual means and there is a separate sign meeting their needs, it is reasonable to not worry about contrast on the sign for users who will be reading the sign by touch as their fingers will not be able to detect a difference in contrast.

703.4 Braille

❖ Braille is read with a light sweeping touch using the pad of the finger, not the tip.

Braille can be Grade 1 or Grade 2. Section 703.4.1 specifies Grade 2 braille on signage. A character symbol is used to distinguish numbers from letters because the same characters are used for both. A character symbol is also used to indicate capitalization. Unlike raised characters (Section 703.3), which must be in all capitals, capitals for braille should be limited (Section 703.4.2). If a braille sign is all capitals, the capital symbol would be required before each letter.

703.4.1 General. Braille shall be contracted (Grade 2) braille and shall comply with Section 703.4.

❖ Grade 1 braille is a character-for-character translation of printed text. Grade 2 braille is standard literary braille in which numerous contractions shorten words (i.e., "contracted braille") (see Commentary Figure C703.4.1).

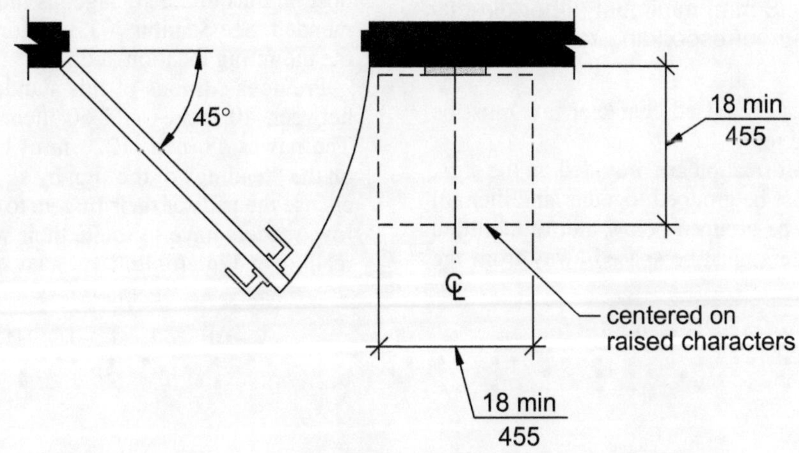

FIGURE 703.3.11
LOCATIONS OF SIGNS AT DOORS

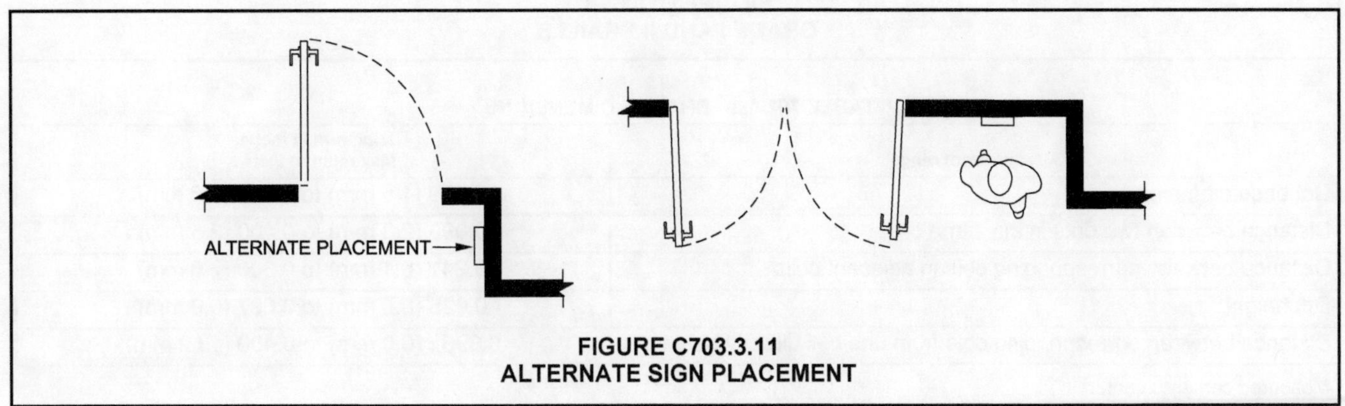

FIGURE C703.3.11
ALTERNATE SIGN PLACEMENT

703.4.2 Uppercase Letters. The indication of an uppercase letter or letters shall only be used before the first word of sentences, proper nouns and names, individual letters of the alphabet, initials, or acronyms.

❖ Standard 6-dot braille provides for 63 distinct characters, therefore, a number of distinct rule sets have been developed over the years to represent literary text, mathematics and science, computer software, music and other varieties of written material. Signage must follow the rules established for literary braille.

Section 703.4.1 specifies Grade 2 braille on signage. A character symbol is used to indicate capitalization. Unlike raised character signage, which must be in all capitals, capitals for braille should be limited to the items listed in this section. If a braille sign is all capitals, the capital symbol would be required before each letter.

703.4.3 Dimensions. Braille dots shall have a domed or rounded shape and shall comply with Table 703.4.3.

❖ It is important for readability that the vertical position of dots be rounded, not straight (i.e., mounds, not cylinders) (see Figure 703.4.3).

703.4.4 Position. Braille shall be below the corresponding text. If text is multilined, braille shall be placed below entire text. Braille shall be separated $^3/_8$ inch (9.5 mm) minimum from any other raised characters and $^3/_8$ inch (9.5 mm) minimum from raised borders and decorative elements. Braille provided on elevator car controls shall be separated $^3/_{16}$ inch (4.8 mm) minimum either directly below or adjacent to the corresponding raised characters or symbols.

❖ The braille equivalent of the raised character text must be located below the raised text.

If multiple lines of information are provided on the sign, all of the raised text must be grouped together and then all of the braille text must be grouped below that to facilitate reading. The braille letters must be spaced away from the raised character letters or borders so the fingers can be flush with the sign face (see Figure 703.4.4).

The elevator provisions in Sections 407 and 408 reference this section for the elevator car controls. Because of the control buttons and the configuration of the panel, the braille location is different from the signage requirements (i.e., location options and grouping).

703.4.5 Mounting Height. Braille shall be 48 inches (1220 mm) minimum and 60 inches (1525 mm) maximum above the floor, measured to the baseline of the braille cells.

EXCEPTION: Elevator car controls shall not be required to comply with Section 703.4.5.

❖ The lowest line of braille text must be located between 48 inches and 60 inches (1220 and 1525 mm) above the floor so that it can be located and reached by a person with visual impairments. The highest line of text must also be located with the baseline of the braille no more than 60 inches (1525 mm) above the floor. The raised character and braille signage need not be located within the reach ranges in Section 308 (see Figure 703.4.5).

All the signage information must work together. Note that Sections 703.3.1 and 703.4.4 require braille to be located under the raised character text information and Section 703.3.10 requires the raised characters to be located between 48 inches and 60 inches (1220 and 1525 mm) above the floor to the baseline of the text. Limiting obstructions under signage, as much as possible, is recommended. See Section 703.3.11 for additional discussion on the mounting location at doors.

Previous editions of this standard required braille to be between 40 inches and 60 inches (1015 and 1525 mm). The newer 48-inch (1220 mm) height limitation is based on the "reading" of the sign by standing users. Braille readers use the pads of their fingers to read. If the signage is too low, readers have to rotate their wrist, vastly complicating reading and intelligibility.

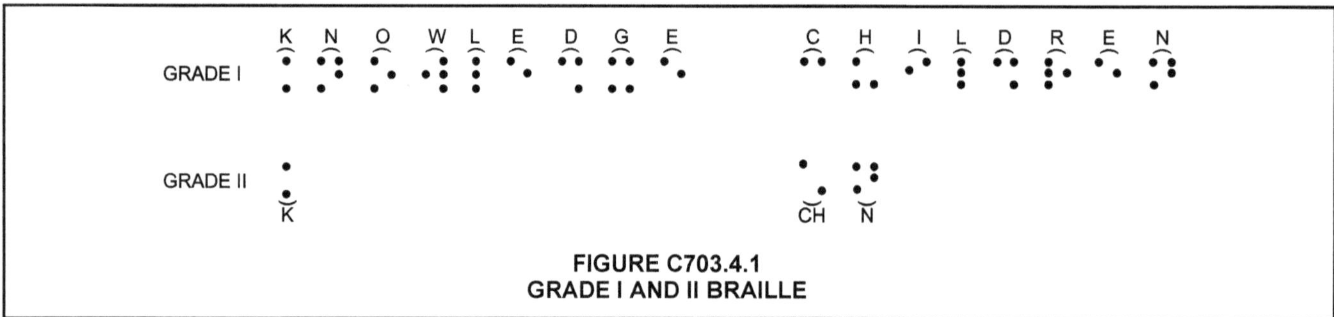

FIGURE C703.4.1
GRADE I AND II BRAILLE

TABLE 703.4.3—BRAILLE DIMENSIONS

Measurement range	Minimum in inches Maximum in inches
Dot base diameter	0.059 (1.5 mm) to 0.063 (1.6 mm)
Distance between two dots in the same cell	0.090 (2.3 mm) to 0.100 (2.5 mm)
Distance between corresponding dots in adjacent cells[1]	0.241 (6.1 mm) to 0.300 (7.6 mm)
Dot height	0.025 (0.6 mm) to 0.037 (0.9 mm)
Distance between corresponding dots from one cell directly below[1]	0.395 (10.0 mm) to 0.400 (10.2 mm)

[1]Measured center to center

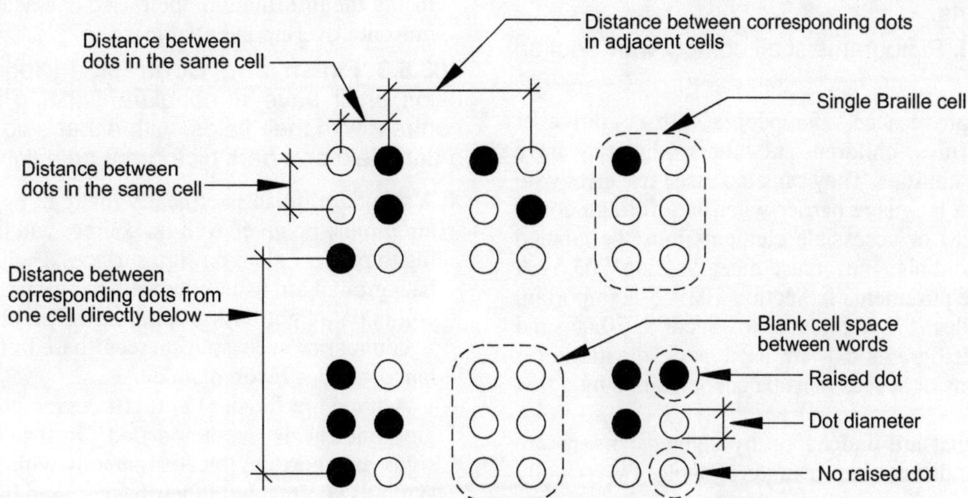

FIGURE 703.4.3
BRAILLE MEASUREMENT

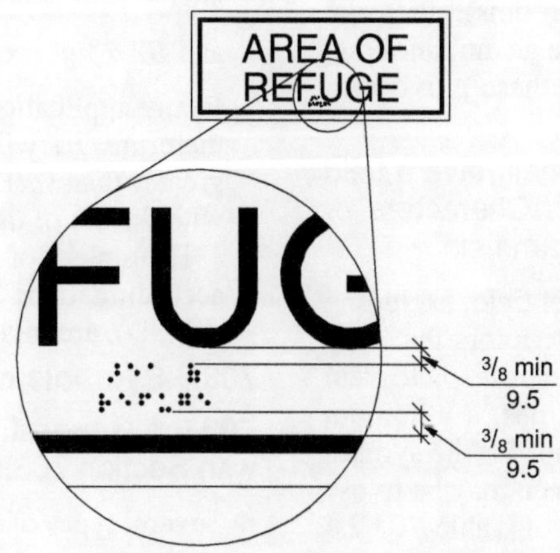

FIGURE 703.4.4
POSITION OF BRAILLE

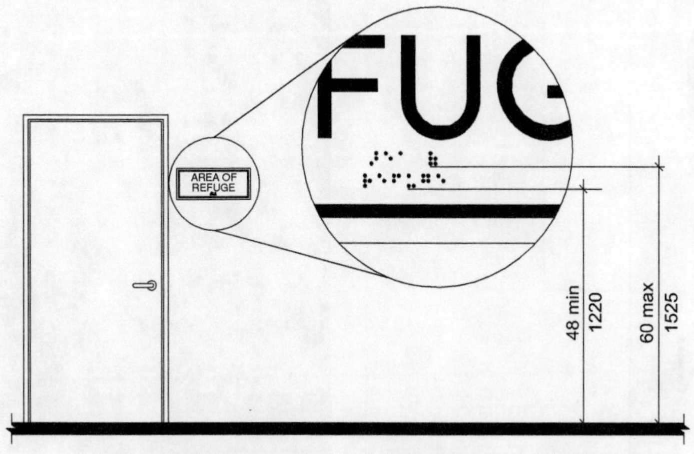

Note: For raised character mounting height see Section 703.3.10

FIGURE 703.4.5
HEIGHT OF BRAILLE CHARACTERS ABOVE FLOOR

703.5 Pictograms.

703.5.1 General. Pictograms shall comply with Section 703.5.

❖ Pictograms improve access for people with cognitive or learning disabilities, children and others who may have limited reading abilities. They can also assist travelers who may be facing a language barrier when in a foreign country. When spaces or accessible elements must be labeled with certain symbols, they must meet Section 703.5. A review of the requirements in Section 703.1.3 is important since it provides the reference to Section 703.5 and requires that pictograms that are used as designations for permanent rooms or spaces must be accompanied by a text descriptor.

Pictograms that are understood by sighted persons are frequently not discernible or interpretable by visually impaired persons; therefore, pictograms are often accompanied by the verbal equivalent in tactile (raised letters and braille) text descriptors complying with Section 703.3 (see Figure 703.5 and Commentary Figure C703.5.1). Requirements for text descriptors apply to pictograms used to label permanent rooms or spaces (e.g., restrooms). Pictorial symbols used for other types of signs (e.g., no smoking, occupant logos) are not required to meet these provisions, including access symbols.

703.5.2 Pictogram Field. Pictograms shall have a field 6 inches (150 mm) minimum in height. Characters or braille shall not be located in the pictogram field.

❖ The minimum height applies to the symbol field, excluding the raised characters and braille text descriptors that may be provided beneath the pictogram. Because pictogram symbols vary in their shape and proportions, a minimum size is specified for the background but not for the symbol itself. Although not required, good guidance may be to use the visual character height requirements of Table 703.2.4 as an indication of the size a symbol should be in order to be viewed at various heights and distances. To avoid confusing the information, the raised character text and braille must not overlap the pictogram.

703.5.3 Finish and Contrast. Pictograms and their fields shall have a nonglare finish. Pictograms shall contrast with their fields, with either a light pictogram on a dark field or a dark pictogram on a light field.

❖ A nonglare finish is typically matte or eggshell. Consideration must be given to light sources and the ambient lighting to prevent glare on sign surfaces. Light colors on a dark background are usually considered easier to read than dark colors on a light background; however, either is permitted. A contrast of at least 70 percent based on the light reflectance value is recommended.

A nonglare finish (11- to 19-degree gloss on 60-degree glossimeter) is recommended. Research indicates that signs are more legible for persons with low vision when symbols contrast with their background by 70 percent minimum. Contrast, in percent, is determined by:

Contrast = $[(B1 - B2)/B1] \times 100$

where $B1$ = light reflectance value (LRV) of the lighter area

and $B2$ = light reflectance value (LRV) of the darker area.

In any application neither white nor black is ever absolute; therefore, $B1$ will never equal 100, and B2 will always be greater than 0. The greatest readability is usually achieved with the use of light-colored symbols on a dark background.

Examples of acceptable and unacceptable finishes, according to the Society for Environmental Graphic Design (SEGD), are included in Commentary Table C703.2.10.

703.6 Symbols of Accessibility.

703.6.1 General. Symbols of accessibility shall comply with Section 703.6.

❖ Several types of access symbols are required by the authority having jurisdiction or other sections of this standard (e.g., accessible parking in Section 502.7) to identify

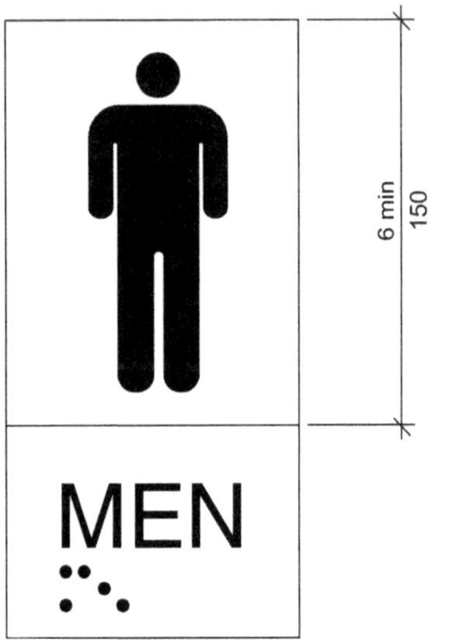

MEN

6 min
150

FIGURE 703.5
PICTOGRAM FIELD

FIGURE C703.5.1
PICTOGRAM

accessible elements. The standard includes four different symbols which help provide consistency so the accessible elements are easily identifiable in any building. Contrast is required, but size and color are not specified.

703.6.2 Finish and Contrast. Symbols of accessibility and their backgrounds shall have a non-glare finish. Symbols of accessibility shall contrast with their backgrounds, with either a light symbol on a dark background or a dark symbol on a light background.

❖ A nonglare finish is typically matte or eggshell. Consideration must be given to light sources and the ambient lighting to prevent glare on sign surfaces. Light characters on a dark background are usually considered easier to read than dark characters on a light background; however, either is permitted. A contrast of at least 70 percent based on the light reflectance value is recommended.

A nonglare finish (11 to 19 degree gloss on 60 degree glossimeter) is recommended. Research indicates that signs are more legible for persons with low vision when characters contrast with their background by 70 percent minimum. Contrast, in percent, is determined by:

Contrast = $[(B1 - B2)/B1] \times 100$

where $B1$ = light reflectance value (LRV) of the lighter area

and $B2$ = light reflectance value (LRV) of the darker area.

In any application neither white nor black is ever absolute; therefore, $B1$ will never equal 100, and $B2$ will always be greater than 0. The greatest readability is usually achieved with the use of light-colored characters or symbols on a dark background.

Examples of acceptable and unacceptable finishes, according to the Society for Environmental Graphic Design (SEGD), are included in Commentary Table C703.2.10.

703.6.3 Symbols.

703.6.3.1 International Symbol of Accessibility. The International Symbol of Accessibility shall comply with Figure 703.6.3.1.

❖ The model building codes require identification of certain accessible elements using the International Symbol of Accessibility (see Figure 703.6.3.1). The model codes do not require that all accessible elements be identified as accessible. Typically, elements such as inaccessible building entrances, inaccessible public toilets and bathing facilities, and elevators not serving an accessible route, must be marked with the International Symbol of Accessibility and directional signage indicating the accessible route to the nearest like accessible element. The International Symbol of Accessibility and appropriate directional signage are placed at inaccessible entrances indicating the direction to the nearest accessible entrance.

The International Symbol of Accessibility is used to label such items as accessible parking spaces, checkout aisles, dressing rooms, areas of refuge and exterior areas of rescue assistance. When not all similar elements are accessible, the International Symbol for Accessibility is used to identify such elements as the accessible passenger loading zone, entrances, exits, toilet and bathing rooms.

This emblem, depicting a person in a wheelchair, is standardized to be recognizable anywhere.

703.6.3.2 International Symbol of TTY. The International Symbol of TTY shall comply with Figure 703.6.3.2.

❖ This emblem depicts a telephone with a text type keypad indicating the telecommunication device can be used by typing messages on the keypad (see Figure 703.6.3.2).

In the 1960s, people who were deaf began using modified teletypewriters, which were in use at the time for printing stock quotes and typing messages to others who also had teletypewriters. They were referred to as TTYs. Technological advances in the 1970s produced smaller portable telecommunication devices for the deaf, or TDDs. During the 1980s, people with normal speech and hearing began using these telecommunication devices. The new term, "text telephone" (TT), was coined to indicate that the use of these devices was not limited to the deaf or hearing impaired. There were objections to the use of this designation by members of the deaf community who rely on American Sign Language to communicate. The objection was raised because the sign language for text telephone (TT) is also used for toilet. Telecommunications for the Deaf, Inc. conducted a national survey and found that deaf individuals preferred the term "teletypewriter" (TTY). TTYs are typically required by the jurisdiction's scoping requirements or the Americans with Disabilities Act and are based on the installation and location of public pay telephones. Unfortunately, due to the fact that fewer pay telephones are being provided in buildings, the availability of TTYs has been decreasing in recent years.

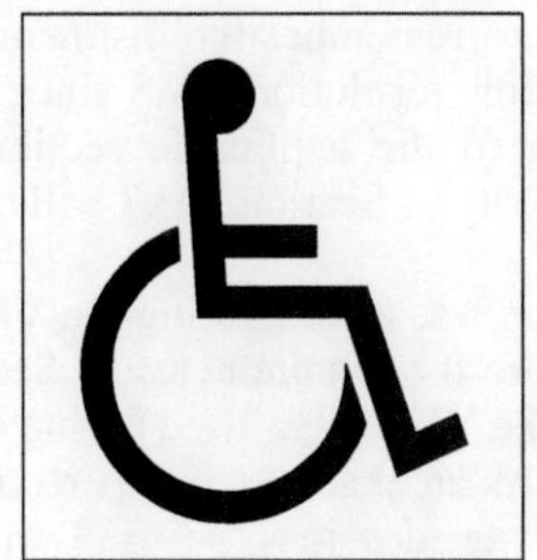

FIGURE 703.6.3.1
INTERNATIONAL SYMBOL OF ACCESSIBILITY

FIGURE 703.6.3.2
INTERNATIONAL TTY SYMBOL

703.6.3.3 Assistive Listening Systems. Assistive listening systems shall be identified by the International Symbol of Access for Hearing Loss complying with Figure 703.6.3.3.

❖ Assistive listening systems include such devices as amplifiers for the hearing impaired. The emblem depicts an ear with a diagonal stripe indicating hearing loss (see Figure 703.6.3.3).

This symbol can also be used to provide notice of auxiliary aids and services such as real time captioning or sign language/oral interpretation services.

703.6.3.4 Volume-Controlled Telephones. Telephones with volume controls shall be identified by a pictogram of a telephone handset with radiating sound waves on a square field complying with Figure 703.6.3.4.

❖ The volume control is a form of assistive listening device installed in a telephone. It controls the receiver part of the telephone only (see Figure 703.6.3.4).

703.7 Variable Message Signs.

❖ Variable message signs (VMS) are defined in Chapter 1 as electronic signs that have a message with the capacity to change by means of scrolling, streaming, or paging across a background. VMS signs are used in a number of locations and may sometimes be of a type that might not traditionally be considered as a "sign." As an example, it is fairly common for airports to use television monitors or other similar devices to display flight arrival/departure or gate information. Although not signs in the traditional sense, these VMS signs provide information that is important and of use to the occupants so they may easily and effectively use the space.

The variable message sign industry is rapidly evolving, and it is becoming increasingly common to see VMS, particularly LCD, plasma and fiber-optic displays, that have high resolution and may be as legible as signs having conventional visual characters. However, low resolution VMS, particularly signs that use either LED or electromechanical technology, will continue to be widely used in the foreseeable future and need also to be addressed within the standard.

The VMS provisions were developed by a task group of the A117.1 Committee who looked at research that had previously been done on VMS. This task group consisted of committee members representing regulatory, producer, professional and user perspectives, as well as outside individuals including manufacturers and people who had been conducting research on VMS. The task group looked at research that was sponsored by the U.S. Access Board and other identified research and then worked to develop the technical specifications for VMS that would make the signs easily visible to the users as well as easy for manufacturers to implement and for code officials to measure and enforce.

FIGURE 703.6.3.3
INTERNATIONAL SYMBOL OF ACCESS FOR HEARING LOSS

FIGURE 703.6.3.4
VOLUME-CONTROLLED TELEPHONE

703.7.1 General. High resolution variable message sign (VMS) characters shall comply with Sections 703.2 and 703.7.12 through 703.7.14. Low resolution variable message sign (VMS) characters shall comply with Section 703.7.

EXCEPTION: Theatrical performance related VMS signs, including but not limited to, text and translation delivery systems, surtitles and subtitles, shall not be required to comply with Section 703.7.1.

❖ VMS signs are classified as either high resolution or low resolution, based upon the definition and the vertical pixel count. Per the definition in Chapter 1, high resolution VMS characters are characters composed of pixels in an array with a vertical pixel count of 16 rows or greater. Low resolution characters have a vertical pixel count of 7 to 15 rows. The high resolution VMS signs are required to comply with the general visual character requirements of Section 703.2 as well as the VMS protective covering, brightness, and rate-of-change requirements in Section 703.7. The characters in low resolution VMS signs are required to follow all of the requirements of Section 703.7. It is important to remember the distinction between high resolution and low resolution VMS since this section provides direction to the applicable sections for each. As stated, the majority of Section 703.7 will only apply to low resolution VMS.

The exception was added during the VMS development process to ensure the requirements of Section 703.7 were not applied to the VMS signs used during or with theatrical performances. As an example, in a performing arts center, translations or surtitles may be used with vocal performances similar to the way subtitles are used with foreign languages in a film. While many of the technical provisions from Section 703.7 may help or improve the visible quality of these types of VMS signs, the standard did not consider these types of systems when the provisions were developed. One easy example to illustrate how the VMS provisions may not work for theatrical performances is the rate of change provisions of Section 703.7.14. If the translation or surtitles are to keep pace with the performance, it may be impossible to meet the rate of change provisions. Because these types of systems were not considered during the development stage of the VMS provisions, the committee decided to provide an exception and exclude these systems. A theater could use any or all of the provisions they believe were appropriate, but it would not be required.

703.7.2 Case. Low resolution VMS characters shall be uppercase.

❖ This section is similar to the provisions of Section 703.3. Signs having mixed case (e.g., capitalized words) are most legible for reading continuous text, and may be most legible for signs having conventional visual characters. However, the limitations of low resolution matrices are such that it is impossible to design fonts with lowercase characters that are highly legible. Low resolution matrices are often not capable of displaying lower case characters, like the "g" or "j," with descenders. The legibility difference to readers is because of the size contrast between the upper- and lowercase characters and because the lowercase characters may appear as a lower resolution and be harder to read (see Commentary Figure C703.7.2).

703.7.3 Style. Low resolution VMS characters shall be conventional in form, shall be san serif, and shall not be italic, oblique, script, highly decorative, or of other unusual forms.

❖ The restriction on character styles for low resolution VMS is similar to the general visual character requirements of Section 703.2.3. Because of the low resolution format, VMS characters with other than a fairly plain style would often not be legible or as easy to distinguish. While some research suggests that serifs appear to increase the legibility of continuous text, and may increase legibility of signs having conventional visual characters, the nature of low resolution matrices is such that styles having serifs are less legible than fonts without serifs. Therefore, the standard prohibits low resolution VMS fonts having serifs (see Commentary Figure C703.7.3).

Mixed Upper and Lower Case

Next Train
Boston 12:15
Platform 3

Upper Case Only

Lower Case without Descenders

abcdef9hijk
ABCDEFGHIJK

FIGURE C703.7.2
LOW RESOLUTION VMS EXAMPLES—CASE REQUIREMENT
(Graphic courtesy of Brian Iwerks, Daktronics)

7 Pixel Vertical Height - Sans Serif Font

NEXT TRAIN
BOSTON 12:15
PLATFORM 3

7 Pixel Vertical Height - Font with Serifs

NEXT TRAIN
BOSTON 12:15
PLATFORM 3

15 Pixel Vertical Height - Font with Serifs

NEXT TRAIN
BOSTON 12:15
PLATFORM 3

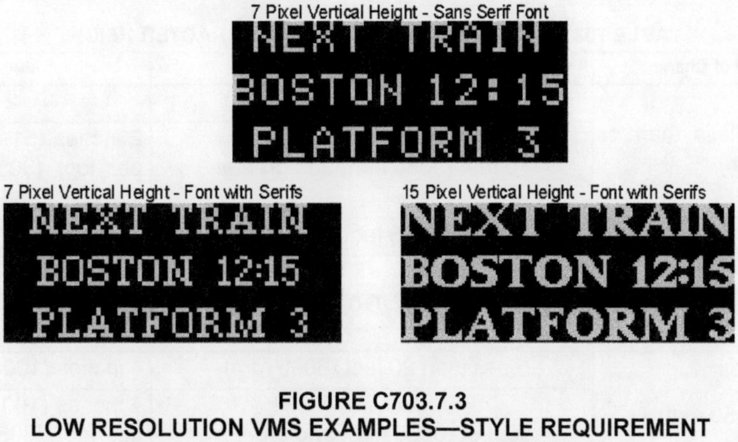

FIGURE C703.7.3
LOW RESOLUTION VMS EXAMPLES—STYLE REQUIREMENT
(Graphic courtesy of Brian Iwerks, Daktronics)

703.7.4 Character Height. The uppercase letter "I" shall be used to determine the allowable height of all low resolution VMS characters of a font. Viewing distance shall be measured as the horizontal distance between the character and an obstruction preventing further approach towards the sign. The uppercase letter "I" of the font shall have a minimum height complying with Table 703.7.4.

> **EXCEPTION:** In assembly seating where the maximum viewing distance is 100 feet (30.5 m) or greater, the height of the uppercase "I" of low resolution VMS fonts shall be permitted to be 1 inch (25 mm) for every 30 feet (9145 mm) of viewing distance, provided the character height is 8 inches (205 mm) minimum. Viewing distance shall be measured as the horizontal distance between the character and where someone is expected to view the sign.

❖ The character height, width and spacing requirements of Sections 703.7.4 through 703.7.9 recognize that VMS are not legible from as great a distance as conventional signs having the same character height, and that, in part because of the matrix nature of VMS, different font geometries and spacing enhance legibility. Since character height is more closely related to legibility than any other sign characteristic, it makes the requirements of Section 703.7.4, Table 703.7.4 and Section 703.7.5 some of the most important aspects of the VMS requirements.

There is no question that, for both readers with unimpaired and impaired vision, greater character height for low resolution VMS is necessary to make them legible from the same distances as signs having conventional visual characters. Character height is the factor that most influences legibility. The technical specifications for low resolution VMS character height (Table 703.7.4) (minimum of 2 inches (51 mm) in height, plus $^{1}/_{5}$ inch (5.1 mm) per foot of viewing distance above 10 feet) provides for 10 foot legibility for 2 inch characters, or a Legibility Index (LI) of 5 ft./in. (LI– legibility distance in feet per inch of character height). If we translate the specifications for visual character height in Table 703.2.4 to a legibility index, the resulting value is LI = 8 ft./in. While some of the research that was used in developing the VMS provisions recommends a LI of 3 ft./in. for VMS intended to be legible to persons having severe visual impairment, it also concluded that additional research was needed to determine optimal character height for persons with more moderate visual impairments. While the requirements in Table 703.7.4 are not as conservative as the research recommended value (LI = 3 ft./in.) it does provide for a lower LI than that for conventional signs. The A117.1 VMS task group and the research they studied did indicate that future research may determine that the LI should be even lower to achieve the same level of legibility as that provided in Table 703.2.4 for height of visual characters.

The exception recognizes that the general requirements for VMS were not ones that could readily be implemented in large assembly uses. There is, after all, a practical limitation to the overall size of these signs that can be used within the space. It is important to understand that the application of the exception is limited to assembly locations where viewing distances are 100 feet (30.5 mm) or greater and that the alternate height formula in the exception does not apply to other places in which large-format VMS may be used. Keep in mind that while a train station and a basketball arena might be the same size, the viewing distance is where the person can move to read the sign. In the train station, a person may walk forward for better viewing, thus possibly reducing the overall size of the sign. In the basketball arena, the viewpoint would be from every seat. See the commentary to Section 703.2.4 for information related to the selection of the 1-inch (25 mm) additional character height for every 30 feet (9045 mm) of viewing distance.

TABLE 703.7.4. See below.

❖ The actual viewing distance for a person looking at a sign varies, depending on the height of the person, the height of the sign and the number of lines of information. Character height requirements are calculated using the horizontal and vertical distances between the viewer and the sign as specified in the table. The "horizontal viewing distance" is the horizontal distance from the face of the sign to the closest point a person can stand to view the sign. Remember that in a large space such as an auditorium the sign would need to serve not only the people seated closest to the sign but also those seated farther back. Therefore in this situation, the viewing distance should consider that the person is not

TABLE 703.7.4—LOW RESOLUTION VMS CHARACTER HEIGHT

Height above Floor to Baseline of Character	Horizontal Viewing Distance	Minimum Character Height
40 inches (1015 mm) to less than or equal to 70 inches (1780 mm)	Less than 10 feet (3050 mm)	2 inches (51 mm)
	10 feet (3050 mm) and greater	2 inches (51 mm), plus $^{1}/_{5}$ inch (5.1 mm) per foot (305 mm) of viewing distance above 10 feet (3050 mm)
Greater than 70 inches (1780 mm) to less than or equal to 120 inches (3050 mm)	Less than 15 feet (4570 mm)	3 inches (75 mm)
	15 feet (4570 mm) and greater	3 inches (75 mm), plus $^{1}/_{5}$ inch (5.1 mm) per foot (305 mm) of viewing distance above 15 feet (4570 mm)
Greater than 120 inches (3050 mm)	Less than 20 feet (6095 mm)	4 inches (100 mm)
	20 feet (6095 mm) and greater	4 inches (100 mm), plus $^{1}/_{5}$ inch (5.1 mm) per foot (305 mm) of viewing distance above 20 feet (6095 mm)

allowed to approach the sign and therefore a greater viewing distance will exist and the character height will need to be increased. The vertical height is from the floor of the viewing position to the baseline of the highest line of the characters (see Commentary Figure C703.2.4). Section 703.7.9 requires that the baseline of the lowest row of characters to be a minimum of 40 inches (1015 mm) above the floor of the viewing position.

703.7.5 Character Width. The uppercase letter "O" shall be used to determine the allowable width of all low resolution VMS characters of a font. Low resolution VMS characters shall comply with the pixel count for character width in Table 703.7.5.

❖ Character proportion for low resolution VMS is more critical than for signs having conventional visual characters, and indicates that a layout of 5 by 7 pixels is the smallest matrix in which legible VMS can be produced. The examples shown in Commentary Figure C703.7.5 show the approximate end points of the range for character width specified in Section 703.2.5 (55 to 110 percent of the height of the uppercase letter "I") as well as the range for character width specified in Section 703.7.5 (70 to 90 percent). These examples are not at the precise minimum and maximum percentages specified because the matrix nature of low resolution VMS precludes this level of graphic precision. The character width range specified in the table was developed using a range for low resolution VMS of 70 percent minimum to 90 percent maximum of the uppercase "I," which is supported by research and is readily achievable in low resolution VMS technology. The table in the standard makes clear the extent of tolerance that is permissible in meeting the specification. In addition, it makes the provisions easier to design to and enforce.

TABLE 703.7.5. See below.

❖ This table incorporates the requirements of Sections 703.7.5, 703.7.6 and 703.7.7 for all of the various low resolution VMS character options. While the character height is included, it is based on the pixel count and would be dependent on and still need to meet the character height requirements of Section 703.7.4 and Table 703.7.4. Any of the listed pixel count character heights may be used for any size character. See the commentary to Section 703.7.4 related to the importance of this table to the VMS require-

Example 1

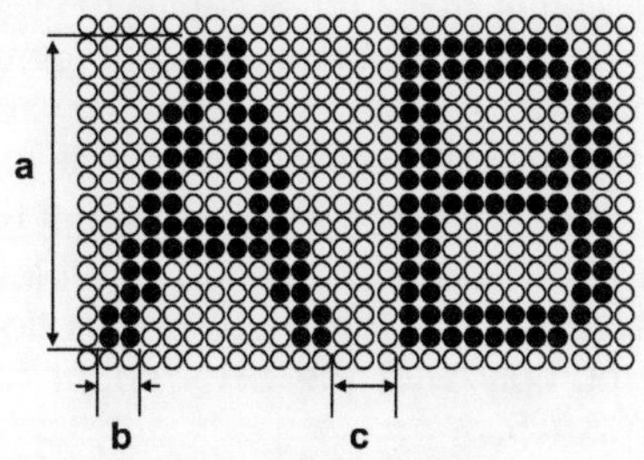

Example 2

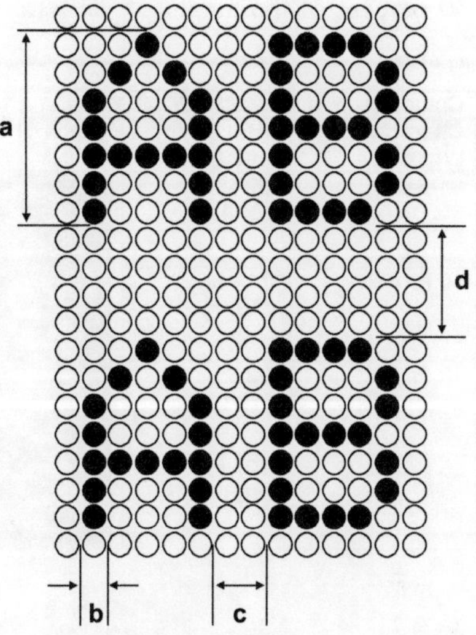

	Property	Example 1	Example 2
a	Character Height	14 Pixels	7 Pixels
b	Stroke Width	2 Pixels	1 Pixel
c	Character Spacing	3 Pixels	2 Pixels
d	Line Spacing		4 Pixels

FIGURE 703.7.5
LOW RESOLUTION VMS SIGNAGE CHARACTERS

TABLE 703.7.5—PIXEL COUNT FOR LOW RESOLUTION VMS SIGNAGE[1]

Character Height	Character Width Range	Stroke Width Range	Character Spacing Range
7	5-6	1	2
8	6-7	1-2	2-3
9	6-8	1-2	2-3
10	7-9	2	2-4
11	8-10	2	2-4
12	8-11	2	3-4
13	9-12	2-3	3-5
14	10-13	2-3	3-5
15	11-14	2-3	3-5

(1) Measured in pixels.

ments. Figure 703.7.5 of the standard shows two examples of how the provisions of this table apply to the various matrix arrays. See the commentary for Sections 703.7.5, 703.7.6 and 703.7.7 as well as Commentary Figures C703.7.5, C703.7.6 and C703.7.7 for examples of the various requirements and how they affect legibility.

703.7.6 Stroke Width. The uppercase letter "I" shall be used to determine the allowable stroke width of all low resolution VMS characters of a font. Low resolution VMS characters shall comply with the pixel count for stroke width in Table 703.7.5.

❖ Stroke width for low resolution VMS is more critical than for signs having conventional visual characters. While Section 703.2.6 will specify a stroke width for visual characters that is 10 to 30 percent of the height of the letter I, low resolution VMS signs will generally be closer to the 15- to 20-percent range. Although this range is not stated in the standard, it was the size used to establish the requirements of Section 703.7.6 and the corresponding stroke width pixel counts shown in Table 703.7.5. Because of the limitations of a pixel matrix array, some of the width values may fall outside of the 15- to 20-percent range but the legibility will generally be the best if it is within or very close to this range. The pixel counts specified for the stroke width will be readily achievable in low resolution VMS technology and provide a legible character.

The examples in Commentary Figure C703.7.6 show the end points of the range for stroke width specified in Section 703.2.6 for visual characters (10 to 30 percent of the height of the letter "I") as well as the range for stroke width specified in Section 703.7.6 and Table 703.7.5.

Comparison of Character Widths (Using a 14 Pixel High Font)

Character Width	Percentage of Height	Visual Characteristics	Comments
8 Pixels	57.1% (8/14)	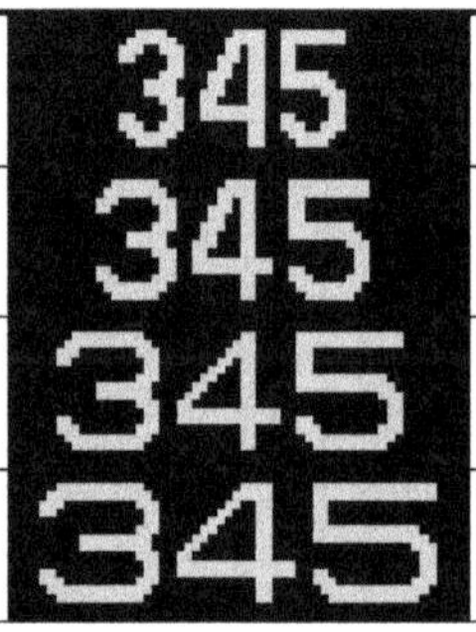 345	**Below Minimum** – (Not permitted) Can blur together, especially at lower resolutions
10 Pixels	71.4% (10/14)	345	**Minimum** – Easily legible
13 Pixels	92.9% (13/14)	345	**Maximum** – Easily legible
15 Pixels	107.1% (15/14)	345	**Above Maximum** – (Not permitted) Difficult to read

FIGURE C703.7.5
LOW RESOLUTION VMS EXAMPLES—CHARACTER WIDTH
(Graphic courtesy of Brian Iwerks, Daktronics)

Comparison of Stroke Widths Using a 7 Pixel High Font

Stroke Width	Percentage of Height	Visual Characteristics	Comments
1 Pixel	14.3% (1/7)	 345	**Permitted** - Very legible
2 Pixels	28.6% (2/7)	345	**Not permitted** - Runs together, difficult to read

Comparison of Stroke Widths Using a 14 Pixel High Font

Stroke Width	Percentage of Height	Visual Characteristics	Comments
1 Pixel	7.1% (1/14)	 345	**Not permitted** - Generally legible, but less than current standard allows
2 Pixels	14.3% (2/14)	345	**Minimum** - Very legible
3 Pixels	21.4% (3/14)	345	**Maximum** - Legible, but could blur together for those with low vision
4 Pixels	28.6% (4/14)	345	**Not permitted** - Very difficult to read

FIGURE C703.7.6
LOW RESOLUTION VMS EXAMPLES—STROKE WIDTH
(Graphic courtesy of Brian Iwerks, Daktronics)

703.7.7 Character Spacing. Spacing shall be measured between the two closest points of adjacent low resolution VMS characters within a message, excluding word spaces. Low resolution VMS character spacing shall comply with the pixel count for character spacing in Table 703.7.5.

❖ As mentioned with the other character features, the effect of character spacing has a greater influence on low resolution VMS signs than it does on the typical visual characters covered by Section 703.2. While visual characters are required by Section 703.2.7 to have a spacing of 10 to 35 percent of the character height, low resolution VMS will not work well in the lower portion of that range. The technical requirements for low resolution VMS were set up for the character spacing to be in the 22- to 35-percent range. Although this 22- to 35-percent range is not stated in the standard, it was the size used to establish the requirements of Section 703.7.7 and the corresponding character spacing pixel counts shown in Table 703.7.5. Because of the limitations of a pixel matrix array, some of the spacing values fall outside of the 22 to 35 percent range but the legibility will generally be the best if it is within or very close to this range.

The examples in Commentary Figure C703.7.7 show the end points of the range for visual character spacing specified in Section 703.2.7 (10 to 35-percent range) as well as the lower end point of the range specified in Section 703.7.7 and Table 703.7.5 for low resolution VMS. As the example shows, the lower end of the range for low resolution VMS (22 percent) provides a spacing that is readily achievable in VMS technology and results in legible characters.

703.7.8 Line Spacing. Low resolution VMS characters shall comply with Section 703.2.8.

❖ Since there was no research to indicate the requirements for line spacing for low resolution VMS needed to be different from the line spacing for signs having conventional visual characters, the standard will simply reference Section 703.2.8. This means that the line spacing between adjacent rows of text is 135 percent to 170 percent of the uppercase letter "I." Because Section 703.7.2 will require low resolution VMS signs to use uppercase characters, there will not be the same concern with descenders that was mentioned in the commentary for Section 703.2.8.

The reduction to the 120-percent spacing allowed by the exception in Section 703.2.8 came from work the A117.1 Committee's VMS task group had reviewed and developed. The 120-percent spacing would also be allowed here for low resolution VMS signs where they have the larger viewing distances mentioned.

703.7.9 Height Above Floor. Low resolution VMS characters shall be 40 inches (1015 mm) minimum above the floor of the viewing position, measured to the baseline of the character. Heights of low resolution variable message sign characters shall comply with Table 703.7.4, based on the size of the characters on the sign.

❖ The 40-inch (1015 mm) minimum height from the floor to the baseline of the text for low resolution VMS signs is the same as required for the general visual characters in Section 703.2.9. The important difference is the second sentence's reference to the character heights specified in Table 703.7.4. As discussed earlier in the commentary for Section 703.7.4, low resolution VMS characters must be larger than a typical visual character in order to be legible at the same distance.

703.7.10 Finish. The background of Low resolution VMS characters shall have a non-glare finish.

❖ The issues of finish and contrast are complex for VMS. VMS may be either directly visible, or may be covered by a protective layer. Therefore, the specifications regarding finish and contrast were divided into the four separate paragraphs of Sections 703.7.10 (finish), 703.7.11 (contrast), 703.7.12 (protective covering) and 703.7.13 (brightness).

Glare can be defined in a number of ways, however, when considering glare in relation to signs, the issue addressed by Section 703.2.10 for visual characters is that light reflecting off of the plane surfaces of characters or their background interferes with the ability to distinguish between characters and their background. Therefore, Section 703.2.10 requires that visual characters and their background have a nonglare finish.

Comparison of Character Spacing Using a 14 Pixel High Font

Stroke Width	Percentage of Height	Visual Characteristics	Comments
2 Pixels	14.3% (2/14)	 345	**Not permitted -** Narrow spacing tends to let characters run together
3 Pixels	21.4% (3/14)	345	**Minimum -** Legible, but could blur together for those with low vision
4 Pixels	28.6% (4/14)	345	**Permitted -** Easily read. While 5 pixel spacing is allowed, this mid-range value may be best.

FIGURE C703.7.7
LOW RESOLUTION VMS EXAMPLES—CHARACTER SPACING
(Graphic courtesy of Brian Iwerks, Daktronics)

Low resolution VMS signs are typically comprised of LED pixels that are turned off or on, or pixel elements that are flipped electromechanically to display a light or a dark side. LEDs are not plane surfaces; therefore, this type of glare does not occur with them. The bright sides of flip-element VMS must have highly reflective plane surfaces because their brightness comes from reflected light. It is the nonpixel background of VMS signs that needs to be nonglare.

703.7.11 Contrast. Low resolution VMS characters shall be light characters on a dark background.

❖ Research on low resolution VMS shows unquestionably that light-on-dark contrast orientation for VMS signs provide better legibility than dark on light. Therefore, low resolution VMS signs are limited to light-on-dark contrast. It is important that this difference between the low resolution VMS and the general visual or raised character requirements of Sections 703.2.10 and 703.3.12 are noticed and understood.

The light-on-dark contrast orientation is the current industry practice for VMS and therefore compliance with this requirement should not be a problem.

During the time period that the VMS provisions were being developed, the light-on-dark orientation was also expected to be recommended for highway signs in the next edition of the MUTCD, (*Manual on Uniform Traffic Control*) which is referenced in Section 105.2.1 of A117.1. While highway signs and VMS are different, it does show that in specific situations the light-on-dark contrast is preferred to provide better visibility. The MUTCD Committee has been working on VMS and sign legibility requirements during the same period as the A117.1 Committee and has reached similar conclusions.

703.7.12 Protective Covering. Where a protective layer is placed over VMS characters through which the VMS characters must be viewed, the protective covering shall have a non-glare finish.

❖ VMS signs are frequently covered by a protective layer. Even if the VMS character and background elements have a nonglare finish, if the covering is not nonglare, the sign will be hard to read at various times or positions.

703.7.13 Brightness. The brightness of variable message signs in exterior locations shall automatically adjust in response to changes in ambient light levels.

❖ As legibility of signs having conventional visual characters is strongly influenced by illumination, legibility of VMS is strongly influenced by the brightness of the sign itself. Research does not yet support tight specifications for brightness. However, VMS can be both too dim to be easily read, and too bright, causing blooming (in which bright characters appear larger, and the defining spaces within and between them smaller, leading to illegibility). It is common in the industry to use VMS that respond to ambient light in situations where there is wide variability in ambient light, particularly outdoors. Requiring that VMS in exterior locations respond to ambient light will at least result in application of widely used, and relatively inexpensive, systems that measure ambient light and adjust emitted light where they are most needed. To say just what the relationship should be between ambient light and brightness of the VMS would require a table, and there is no research to date to support this kind of specificity for other than highway use. The next MUTCD, which is adopted by reference in Section 105.2.1, is expected to require adjustment to ambient light for VMS intended to be read by drivers.

703.7.14 Rate of Change. Where a VMS message can be displayed in its entirety on a single screen, it shall be displayed on a single screen and shall remain motionless on the screen for a minimum 3 seconds or one second minimum for every 7 characters of the message including spaces whichever is longer.

❖ The intent of the rate of change provisions was simply to say that if it is possible to display an entire VMS message at one time, the message should be displayed in its entirety. Where the length of the message exceeds the capacity of the screen, the standard specifies a minimum length of time the message must be displayed before transitioning to the remaining portion of the message. The A117 Committee did recognize that the reference to a "single screen" may create some confusion because some large VMS signs may be comprised of multiple smaller screens. Regardless of whether the VMS is a single screen or comprised of multiple screens, the intent remains the same: that if the message can be displayed on the sign "in its entirety" at a single time, that is the preferred option. Where it cannot be done at the same time, then the rate-of-change requirements apply.

Research has shown VMS messages that move across the sign area are more difficult to read, especially for readers with visual impairments, than those that are displayed without moving. There has not yet been conclusive research on the effects on legibility, especially for readers with impaired vision, of type of change (streaming vs. paging), or rate of change. Therefore, the VMS task group and A117.1 Committee were not able to write or include a specification that deals with these VMS characteristics. However, VMS messages that are short may fit in their entirety on the sign on which they are displayed, therefore they do not need to change by streaming from right to left, or scrolling from bottom to top. Therefore, the requirement is that "Where a VMS message can be displayed entirely on a single screen, it shall remain motionless....

Even if VMS messages fit on a sign, the nature of VMS is that the message will change from time to time. If messages change too fast, there is not enough time for them to be read. The length of time the message shall remain motionless is based on the literature on reading rate for people with low vision. Given that reading signs requires scanning to find the sign, as well as sometimes maintaining fixation on a sign while the reader is in motion (e.g. reading the name of the transit station from the vehicle, as the vehicle pulls in), the proposed reading rate provided (seven characters per second) is, if not optimal for people with impaired vision, a very conservative estimate. Based on some of the reviewed research, the optimal duration for motionless VMS for people with visual impairments may actually be longer than the seven characters per second specified.

The current VMS industry default for the minimum amount of time a message is motionless, independent of length of message, seems to be 2 seconds. However, a 3-second minimum was likely to be required (as recommended in the MUTCD) for highway signs based on driver comprehension. The minimum 3-second motionless time included in Section 703.7.14 is a conservative estimate of the amount of time that might be optimal for readers with impaired vision, but it is readily achievable in the industry, even though it is longer than current industry practice.

703.8 Remote Infrared Audible Sign (RIAS) Systems.

❖ Remote infrared audible sign systems are a form of wireless communication that provides a means of way-finding for persons with visual impairments. The system is typically made up of portable personal receivers and multiple fixed transmitters at key doors or elements you want people to be able to locate and that a person will carry.

The system consists of audio signals transmitted by invisible infrared light beams. The receivers decode the signal and deliver voice messages through a speaker or headset. The signals are directional, and the beam width and distance can be adjusted. The system can work both indoors and outside.

As an example of how the system would work, assume a corridor serving a hotel conference center/ballroom area is equipped with an RIAS. When a person wearing a portable receiver walks out of a ballroom and into a corridor he/she may hear "exterior door" when turning to the right or "hotel lobby" when turning to the left. Assuming a left turn toward the lobby they may then hear announcements for other doors such as "men's restroom on left" or "Ballroom A" as they approach or pass those particular doors. As mentioned previously the signals can be directionally focused and varied so a user may hear general information at any point in the corridor (such as the "hotel lobby" announcement) while others such as the "Ballroom A" comment may be limited to only the area adjacent to the ballroom entry doors. This would allow persons to find these rooms as they passed them but not be overwhelmed with multiple or conflicting audible signals throughout the entire corridor length.

703.8.1 General. Remote Infrared Audible Sign Systems shall comply with Section 703.8.

❖ To work effectively, the transmitters (Section 703.8.2) installed in the buildings must be compatible with the receivers (Section 703.8.3) that are provided to or purchased by the persons using the system.

703.8.2 Transmitters. Where provided, Remote Infrared Audible Sign Transmitters shall be designed to communicate with receivers complying with Section 703.8.3.

❖ The transmitters are intended to be compatible with a variety of receivers. Typically the transmitters are installed in a building and the individuals will bring in their own receivers (see commentary, Section 703.8).

703.8.3 Infrared Audible Sign Receivers.

❖ Receivers are hand held or may be worn around the neck similar to a name tag and must meet frequency, optical power density, audio output, reception range and power ration specified in the following subsections.

703.8.3.1 Frequency. Basic speech messages shall be frequency modulated at 25 kHz, with a +/- 2.5 kHz deviation, and shall have an infrared wavelength from 850 to 950 nanometer (nm).

❖ See the commentary to Sections 703.8 and 703.8.3.

703.8.3.2 Optical Power Density. Receiver shall produce a 12 decibel (dB) signal-plus-noise-to-noise ratio with a 1 kHz modulation tone at +/- 2.5 kHz deviation of the 25 kHz subcarrier at an optical power density of 26 picowatts per square millimeter measured at the receiver photosensor aperture.

❖ See the commentary to Sections 703.8 and 703.8.3.

703.8.3.3 Audio Output. The audio output from an internal speaker shall be at 75 dBA minimum at 18 inches (455 mm) with a maximum distortion of 10 percent.

❖ See the commentary to Sections 703.8 and 703.8.3.

703.8.3.4 Reception Range. The receiver shall be designed for a high dynamic range and capable of operating in full-sun background illumination.

❖ The "full-sun" background illumination requirement will help in situations such as the example in Section 703.8. If the person were to turn toward the "exterior door" and it was a glass storefront-type door, the intent is the RIAS announcement would still be audible and the sunlight streaming through the glass door would not interfere with or eliminate the announcement (see commentary, Sections 703.8 and 703.8.3).

703.8.3.5 Multiple Signals. A receiver provided for the capture of the stronger of two signals in the receiver field of view shall provide a received power ratio on the order of 20 dB for negligible interference.

❖ See the commentary to Sections 703.8 and 703.8.3.

703.9 Pedestrian Signals. Accessible pedestrian signals shall comply with Section 4E.06-Accessible Pedestrian Signals, and Section 4E.09-Accessible Pedestrian Signal Detectors, of the Manual on Uniform Traffic Control Devices listed in Section 105.2.1.

EXCEPTION: Pedestrian signals are not required to comply with the requirement for choosing audible tones.

❖ Audible signals, provided at locations where traffic is controlled by traffic lights, allow for persons with vision impairments to know when they can cross the street. The sound also provides some directional information so people can stay in the crosswalk.

704 Telephones

❖ Public telephones are mounted in a variety of ways: in telephone booths, on wall surfaces, recessed in walls, enclosed in an alcove, on pylons and others. Providing access to make the telephones usable for persons with disabilities is the purpose of these provisions (see Commentary Figure C704).

FIGURE C704
TELEPHONES

Many individuals with hearing impairments use certain assistive devices in their daily lives. Individuals can communicate by telephone using telecommunication devices for the deaf (TDD). This device looks like a typewriter or computer keyboard and transmits typed text over the telephone. Other names in common use are textphone and minicom. A videophone can be used for distance communication using sign language. In 2004, mobile textphone devices came onto the market for the first time allowing simultaneous two-way text communication. There are telephone relay services so that a hearing impaired person can communicate with a hearing person via a human translator. Wireless, internet and mobile phone/SMS text messaging have taken over the role of the TDD in areas where mobile service is available. Video conferencing is also a new technology that permits signed conversations as well as permitting an American Sign Language-English (ASL) interpreter to voice and sign conversations between a hearing impaired and hearing person, negating the need to use a TTY or computer keyboard.

704.1 General. Accessible public telephones shall comply with Section 704.

❖ Phones that may be addressed by the authority having jurisdiction are public phones, closed circuit phones for controlled access and phones at security glazing. The provisions are for persons using wheelchairs and persons with hearing and speech impairments. One phone can meet the requirements for both.

704.2 Wheelchair Accessible Telephones. Wheelchair accessible public telephones shall comply with Section 704.2.

EXCEPTION: Drive up only public telephones are not required to comply with Section 704.2.

❖ Telephones that are usable by persons in wheelchairs must comply with provisions for access and operable parts.

Since this section is intended to address wheelchair accessible telephones, the exception exempts any telephone that is only available in a drive up situation. This will exempt the drive up telephone from all of the requirements of Section 704.2 and not just the space requirements of Section 704.2.1. This exception was added into A117.1 to coordinate with a similar exception that is found in the ADA standard.

704.2.1 Clear Floor Space. A clear floor space complying with Section 305 shall be provided. The clear floor space shall not be obstructed by bases, enclosures, or seats.

❖ The clear floor space requirements are determined by a forward or parallel approach, and whether the phone is located in an alcove. Many elements found in typical mounting arrangements will restrict the clear floor space. Care must be taken to ensure that such elements do not interfere with the clear floor space required to make the telephone usable. Telephones, enclosures, support col-

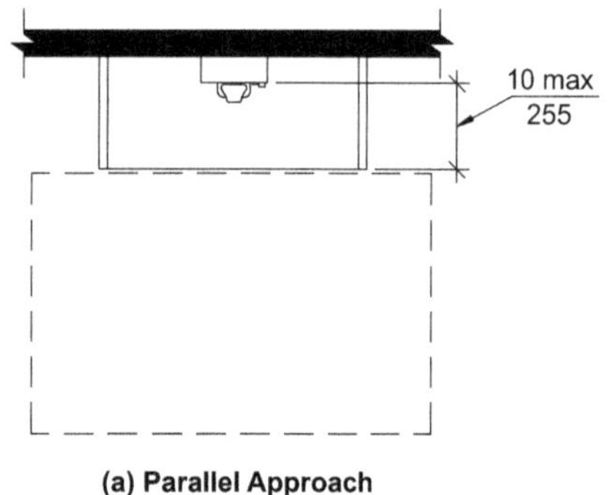

(a) Parallel Approach

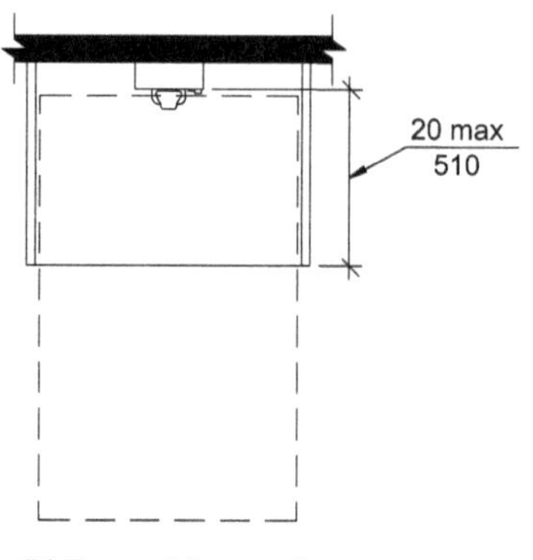

(b) Forward Approach

FIGURE 704.2.1
CLEAR FLOOR SPACE FOR TELEPHONES

umns, shelves and related telephone book storage are examples of the types of elements that could possibly obstruct or interfere with the clear floor space. An accessible route must be provided to the clear floor space based on Section 305.6. A turning space is not required; however, if provided, it can use the knee and toe clearances available under any built-in seats or counters.

704.2.1.1 Parallel Approach. Where a parallel approach is provided, the distance from the edge of the telephone enclosure to the face of the telephone shall be 10 inches (255 mm) maximum.

❖ The parallel approach allows a side reach for a person using a wheelchair. Only 10 inches (255 mm) is allowed from the edge of the telephone enclosure to the face of the telephone unit to ensure the receiver and controls are within the reach range. This is consistent with the maneuvering clearance provided for a side reach in accordance with Section 308.3.1. A parallel approach may provide better access for person using scooters.

704.2.1.2 Forward Approach. Where a forward approach is provided, the distance from the front edge of a counter within the enclosure to the face of the telephone shall be 20 inches (510 mm) maximum.

❖ An option for an accessible phone is to provide a front approach with knee and toe clearances under the phone. If a counter is provided, the face of the phone can be a maximum of 20 inches (510 mm) back from the front edge of the counter. This allows for the controls and receiver to be within reach ranges. If the surrounding booth or walls create an alcove, the requirements of Section 305.7 are also applicable.

704.2.2 Operable Parts. Operable parts shall comply with Section 309. Telephones shall have push button controls where service for such equipment is available.

❖ For users with limited hand dexterity, push button controls are beneficial. Operable parts would include items such as the key pad, coin slots, coin return, credit card swipes, volume controls, handsets or other types of receivers. The reference to Section 309 will also impose the reach range limits of Section 308 based upon the reference in Section 309.3.

704.2.3 Telephone Directories. Where provided, telephone directories shall comply with Section 309.

❖ The reference to Section 309 addresses the general provisions for making an object accessible for those who are mobility impaired. It includes provisions for maneuvering spaces for wheelchairs and reach ranges. Care should be taken so that the telephone directories or their storage space do not interfere or obstruct the clear floor space, knee and toe clearance where a forward approach is used, or access to the phone itself.

704.2.4 Cord Length. The telephone handset cord shall be 29 inches (735 mm) minimum in length.

❖ This minimum cord length will accommodate a standing person, a person using a wheelchair or scooter and a portable TTY.

704.2.5 Hearing-Aid Compatibility. Telephones shall be hearing aid compatible.

❖ Many persons who are hard of hearing use hearing aids to enhance their ability to hear. To be accessible, telephones must be compatible with hearing aids. This is not the same as a volume control (Section 704.3). A federal law, the Hearing Aid Compatibility Act of 1998, requires all public telephones installed in the U.S. to be hearing-aid compatible. A compatible phone generates a magnetic field that can be "translated" by hearing aids with a "T" switch, which activates a telecoil. This normally results in a clearer signal than having the hearing aid reamplify the audible output of the handset. It is important that the compatible phones be shielded or located away from other electromagnetic sources that can interfere with the T-switch transmission.

704.3 Volume-control Telephones. Public telephones required to have volume controls shall be equipped with a receiver volume control that provides a gain adjustable up to 20 dB minimum. Incremental volume controls shall provide at least one intermediate step of gain of 12 dB minimum. An automatic reset shall be provided.

❖ Volume control ranges reflect a 20 dB minimum in order to make them usable. The volume control is equipped with automatic reset, which protects the next user from a potentially damaging loud volume.

Volume controls are located either on the base or on the handset. Volume controls located in handsets are most commonly used in retrofitting existing phones. Telephones that have a volume control are identified by the volume control telephone symbol in Section 703.6.3.4.

704.4 TTY. TTYs required at a public pay telephone shall be permanently affixed within, or adjacent to, the telephone enclosure. Where an acoustic coupler is used, the telephone cord shall be of sufficient length to allow connection of the TTY and the telephone receiver.

❖ Requiring permanently affixed equipment precludes an arrangement that requires the user to ask an employee of an establishment to hook up a TTY. It ensures that, where required, the equipment will be available. An acoustic coupler is a device that allows the telephone receiver to be fitted into it, or with digital phones a digital/analog converter is needed. The signals will then be transmitted through the coupler to the TTY (see Commentary Figure C704.4).

The TTY is a device that allows persons with hearing or speech impairments to communicate over the telephone. Like computers with modems, TTYs provide a keyboard for input and some type of visual output. Typed messages are converted in audible tones, which are transmitted through the phone lines to a receiver unit (see Section 106.5, definition for TTY).

Signage is required at phones indicating the location of the TTY. The symbol is the International Symbol of TTY shown in Section 703.6.3.2.

Although not stated within the standard, it is important to ensure an outlet or other electrical service is provided for the TTY. If the TTY is a separate element from the telephone, the TTY may not function without a source of power.

FIGURE C704.4
TTY

704.5 Height. When in use, the touch surface of TTY keypads shall be 34 inches (865 mm) minimum above the floor.

EXCEPTION: Where seats are provided, TTYs shall not be required to comply with Section 704.5.

❖ The 34-inch (865 mm) height for the TTY keypad will be accessible for a person using a wheelchair or a standing person. If a seat is provided, the TTY keypad can be at a lower height. Compliance with Section 704.2.2 and the operable parts reach ranges should be evaluated. If the TTY and reach range requirements cannot be met on a single phone, it may dictate that the TTY is installed beneath a phone other than the wheelchair accessible telephone.

704.6 TTY Shelf. Where public pay telephones designed to accommodate a portable TTY are provided, they shall be equipped with a shelf and an electrical outlet within or adjacent to the telephone enclosure. The telephone handset shall be capable of being placed flush on the surface of the shelf. The shelf shall be capable of accommodating a TTY and shall have a vertical clearance 6 inches (150 mm) minimum in height above the area where the TTY is placed.

❖ Some people travel with their own portable TTY units. These requirements ensure that electrical power and a surface with enough vertical clearance to place the equipment are provided to make a portable TTY usable at public pay telephones. To accommodate the full range of models, it is suggested that the shelf should provide a minimum clearance of 10 inches (255 mm) and have the electrical outlet less than 3 feet (915 mm) from the shelf.

704.7 Protruding Objects. Telephones, enclosures, and related equipment shall comply with Section 307.

❖ Telephone equipment and enclosures are often installed projecting from walls, pylons and posts. Such projections may be detrimental to the visually impaired person. Persons who are blind and depend on canes to detect obstructions are particularly affected by such projections. Projections under which canes can sweep without being detected present a potential danger to the cane user. Telephones must be located so that they are not along a walking path, are recessed, have side panels with the bottom edge below 27 inches (685 mm) or are otherwise configured so that they do not violate the protruding-object provisions in Section 307.

705 Detectable Warnings

❖ Detectable warnings are required by this standard at raised marked crossings (Section 406.12 and also Commentary Figure C705) and where a circulation path crosses train tracks (Section 805.10). They are also generally required by the jurisdiction's scoping requirements at the drop-off edge of transportation platforms such as train loading platforms (see Section 805.5.2). Depending upon the jurisdiction's scoping provisions, they may also be required at other locations as a means of warning for the visually impaired. Detectable warnings are not required by this standard at curb ramps (Section 406.13), islands or cut-through medians (Section 406.14), but if provided, should comply with the provisions in this section.

FIGURE C705
RAISED MARKED CROSSING

705.1 General. Detectable warning surfaces shall comply with Section 705.

❖ Detectable warnings provide a tactile clue for persons with visual impairments when they approach some type of edge. Detectable warnings are commonly used at platform edges, at the bottom of curb ramps, at traffic islands, at the front of stores along the edge of the parking lot or at the top of stairways.

Detectable warnings are intended to alert pedestrians of a hazard. Research indicates the most effective detectable warnings:

- Have a unique texture distinction from other common surfaces in the environment.
- Adjoin the hazard to signal the change.
- Extend beyond the average stride length so a person can detect and still have time to react before encountering the hazard.

At the time of the writing of this commentary, the U.S. Access Board has a committee that is reviewing the requirements for public rights of way, including detectable warnings. Users should remember to review the appropriate scoping document. Requirements for detectable warnings will generally differ depending on whether the work is on private property, public property or located within a public right-of-way.

705.2 Standardization. Detectable warning surfaces shall be standard within a building, facility, site, or complex of buildings.

EXCEPTION: In facilities that have both interior and exterior locations, detectable warnings in exterior locations shall not be required to comply with Section 705.4.

❖ Recognition of, and quick response to, detectable warnings is maximized by standardization of material as well as surface texture and color. Provision of too many different types of detectable and tactile warnings or failure to standardize such warnings weakens their usefulness. Detectable and tactile warnings are also visual signals to guide dogs because dogs are trained to respond to a large variety of visual cues.

The exception is in recognition that requirements for resiliency and sound-on-cane contact are applicable only in interior environments.

705.3 Contrast. Detectable warning surfaces shall contrast visually with adjacent surfaces, either light-on-dark or dark-on-light.

❖ Different colors for the main floor surface and for the domes and their immediate surrounding surfaces assists persons with vision impairments to identify the location of detectable warnings. When choosing a color, keep in mind persons with color blindness as well as the issue of contrast. The recommended minimum light reflectance contrast is 70 percent.

705.4 Interior Locations. Detectable warning surfaces in interior locations shall differ from adjoining walking surfaces in resiliency or sound-on-cane contact.

❖ Interior applications require that the warning feature contrast in resilience or sound when sensed with a cane. This requirement is not applicable for exterior locations (Section 705.2 Exception).

705.5 Truncated Domes. Detectable warning surfaces shall have truncated domes complying with Section 705.5.

❖ Truncated domes are typically placed in a strip 24 inches (610 mm) wide. The technical specifications for the detectable warning truncated domes are found within the four subsections that follow (see Figure 705.5).

705.5.1 Size. Truncated domes shall have a base diameter of 0.9 inch (23 mm) minimum and 1.4 inch (36 mm) maximum, and a top diameter of 50 percent minimum and 65 percent maximum of the base diameter.

❖ See Figure 705.5 for a graphic indication of dome size.

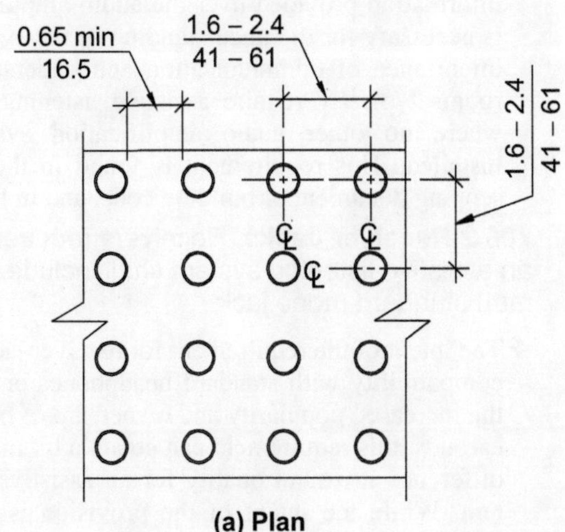

(a) Plan

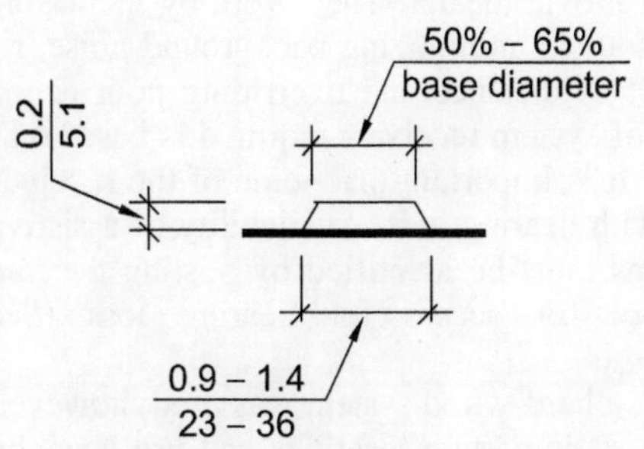

(b) Elevation (Enlarged)

FIGURE 705.5
TRUNCATED DOME SIZE AND SPACING

705.5.2 Height. Truncated domes shall have a height of 0.2 inch (5.1 mm).

❖ See Figure 705.5 for a graphic indication of dome size.

705.5.3 Spacing. Truncated domes shall have a center-to-center spacing of 1.6 inches (41 mm) minimum and 2.4 inches (61 mm) maximum, and a base-to-base spacing of 0.65 inch (16.5 mm) minimum, measured between the most adjacent domes on the grid.

❖ See Figure 705.5 for a graphic indication of dome size.

705.5.4 Alignment. Truncated domes shall be aligned in a square grid pattern.

❖ See Figure 705.5 for a graphic indication of dome alignment. The square grid pattern was chosen over the diagonal grid pattern so persons using a wheelchair can locate their wheels between rows of domes to cross the detectable warning. The diagonal grid used in the past was difficult to maneuver over and could cause some discomfort for persons using wheelchairs as they crossed them.

705.6 Transportation Platform Edges. Detectable warning surfaces at transportation platform boarding edges shall extend the full length of the public use areas of the platform. The detectable warning surface shall extend 24 inches (610 mm) from the boarding edge of the platform.

❖ Section 805.5.2 requires that detectable warnings are installed at the edge of a transportation boarding platform unless the people are kept away from the edge by a screen or guard. Section 705.6 provides the specifications for the location of where the detectable warning is to be installed. The public portions of the platform are to be equipped with the detectable warnings to alert the users of the drop-off. Although the platform or a walking surface may continue past the public portion, the detectable warning may be stopped at the point where the public is not to continue beyond. The warning should be installed at the edge of the platform and then extend back from the edge 24 inches. This 24-inch (610 mm) distance provides adequate visual and tactile notification to the users to warn of the drop-off location.

706 Assistive Listening Systems

❖ Assistive listening systems are required by the model codes in assembly areas, such as a live theater, lecture hall, courtroom or movie theater. They work by increasing the loudness of sounds, minimizing background noise, reducing the effect of distance and overriding poor acoustics. The number of system receivers required is based on seating capacity. It is important that some of the receivers be compatible with hearing aids. Availability of assistive listening systems must be identified by posting the international symbol for access for hearing loss (Section 703.6.3.3).

In the past, a hard-wired system was used; however, listeners had to sit in certain locations and use headphones. With the new technologies, almost all assisted listening systems are wireless. Portable systems are feasible for special accommodations; however, the required systems must be permanently installed.

The three types of wireless devices are the FM system, the audio induction loop and the infrared system. Each system has advantages and benefits for particular uses.

All three types of systems require that the person who is speaking use a microphone. Sound is converted and transferred by radio waves (FM), invisible light waves (infrared) or electromagnetic field (audio induction loop) to the listener. The listener uses a receiver with headphones to hear the speaker. If the listener wears hearing aids or a cochlear implant processor which has a telecoil (T-coil), a neckloop can be used in place of the headphones with the FM or infrared systems. Neckloops transmit the sound directly from the receiver into the aid or processor. Sound provided by an audio induction loop can be heard by a wearer of hearing aids or a cochlear implant processor with T-coils, without an additional receiver or neckloop. All systems can be integrated with existing PA systems.

There is no difference in the amount of understanding provided by the three systems (refer to Commentary Table C706) which are used as public accommodations, as long as they are of good quality. The choice of which system should be provided will depend on other factors, such as the need for confidentiality.

No matter what system is used, selection of the microphone is critical. For best sound quality microphones should:

- Limit background noise,
- Provide the highest gain signal,
- Accommodate speech over all frequencies and
- Be used with an automatic mixer where multiple microphones are used.

706.1 General. Accessible assistive listening systems in assembly areas shall comply with Section 706.

❖ An assistive listening system is used in conjunction with an audio amplification system to assist those individuals who are hard of hearing to have the same audio information as is being transmitted to the general public at the event. The scoping provisions from the jurisdiction having authority typically require these systems when the audio information provided over the audio amplification system is necessary for the understanding of the event. Due to the importance of communication and understanding, courtrooms typically require assistive listening systems even where no other audio amplification system is being installed. This requirement is found in the jurisdiction's scoping document or building code, and in federal law.

706.2 Receiver Jacks. Receivers required for use with an assistive listening system shall include a $^1/_8$ inch (3.2 mm) standard mono jack.

❖ The intent of the requirement for receiver jacks is to ensure compatibility with standard headphones or earbuds. With the increased popularity and ownership of headphones and earbuds, this requirement can create a bit of confusion and difference in sound quality for an assistive listening system. While the intent of the provision is to ensure that users can plug in their own headphones to the system, the fact that the standard specifies a "mono" jack will result in the users hearing the sound differently than what is being heard through the remainder of the audio system. Monaural or monophonic sound (mono) is created by an amplifier transmitting a single signal whereas a stereophonic (stereo) sound is produced by transmitting two independent signals through two separate channels. Stereo systems are the most common today and are best used to replicate the sensation of hearing an orchestra or band performance since the independent signals allow for different sounds or instruments in the right and left channels reproducing the sound of individual instruments or performers being located in different areas of the auditorium. The mono system tends to work best for speeches or panel discussions and will produce the exact same sound level in each speaker of the headphone since it is receiving a single signal channel. While a mono system may not produce the depth or location sensation that stereo can provide, it remains the standard for various communication systems including assistive listening devices.

706.3 Receiver Hearing-aid Compatibility. Receivers required to be hearing aid compatible shall interface with telecoils in hearing aids through the provision of neck loops.

❖ The intent of the requirement for receivers is to ensure compatibility with hearing aids. The neck loops are essentially a personal audio induction loop that the user can place around their neck similar to a lanyard instead of placing a headphone or earbud over or into their ears.

706.4 Sound Pressure Level. Assistive listening systems shall be capable of providing a sound pressure level of 110 dB minimum and 118 dB maximum, with a dynamic range on the volume control of 50 dB.

❖ The increase in sound levels should allow the user to hear above the ambient noise of the room.

706.5 Signal-to-noise Ratio. The signal-to-noise ratio for internally generated noise in assistive listening systems shall be 18 dB minimum.

❖ The electronic noise in the system can be a problem for the listener. The tolerance of noise to the amount of noise in the system is the signal to noise ratio.

706.6 Peak Clipping Level. Peak clipping shall not exceed 18 dB of clipping relative to the peaks of speech.

❖ The distortion caused when the gain of an amplifier is increased to a point where the high points, or peaks, of the signal or waveform are cut off at a level where the amplifying circuits are driven beyond their overload point. This is also called over-modulation. Peak clipping can be avoided by gain reduction, compression of the signal or the use of a limiter.

Table C706
SUMMARY OF ASSISTIVE LISTENING DEVICES

SYSTEM	ADVANTAGES	DISADVANTAGES	TYPICAL APPLICATIONS
INDUCTION LOOP Transmitter: Transducer wired to induction loop around listening area. Receiver: Self-contained induction receiver or personal hearing aid with telecoil	Accommodate a large group of people or an individual based on size of loop Cost-effective Low maintenance Easy to use Unobtrusive May be possible to integrate into existing public address system. Some hearing aids can function as receivers	With large loops, signal spills over to adjacent rooms Susceptible to electrical interference Limited portability Inconsistent signal strength Head position affects signal strength Lack of standards for induction coil performance Receivers with a telecoil are required for people who do not have a telecoil in their hearing aid	Meeting areas Theaters Churches and Temples Conference rooms Classrooms TV viewing
FM Transmitter: Flashlight sized worn by speaker Receiver: With personal hearing aid via DAI or induction neck loop and telecoil; or self-contained with earphone(s)	Highly portable Can be used indoors or outdoors Covers large areas Different channels allow use by different groups within the same facility High user mobility Variable for large range of hearing losses	Signal spills over to adjacent rooms Subject to interference High cost of receivers Equipment obtrusive Custom fitting to individual user may be required	Classrooms Tour Groups Meeting areas Outdoor events One-on-one
INFRARED Transmitter: Emitter in line-of-sight with receiver Receiver: Self-contained or with personal hearing aid via DAI or induction neck loop and telecoil	Easy to use Ensures privacy or confidentiality Moderate cost Can often be integrated into existing public address system	Line-of-sight required between emitter and receiver Ineffective outdoors Limited portability Requires installation	Theaters Churches and Temples Auditoriums Meetings requiring confidentiality Courtrooms

Source: Rehab Brief, National Institute on Disability and Rehabilitation Research, Washington, DC, Vol. XII, No. 10, (1990).

707 Automatic Teller Machines (ATMs) and Fare Machines

❖ Although this section is specifically geared toward ATMs and fare machines, similar machines must comply as much as applicable. For example, there are now machines that dispense lottery tickets, or many movie theaters allow people to buy tickets through an automated machine (see Commentary Figure C707). The jurisdiction's scoping requirements should also be reviewed since general vending machines, change machines and others may need to follow the requirements of Section 707.

FIGURE C707
ATM
(Photo courtesy of United Spinal Association)

707.1 General. Accessible automatic teller machines and fare machines shall comply with Section 707.

❖ Requirements are applicable to automatic teller machines wherever walk-up access is provided, and to fare machines such as those in transportation facilities. Basic accessibility is provided by requiring a way to the machine, clear floor space, height, reach range and display requirements.

707.2 Clear Floor Space. A clear floor space complying with Section 305 shall be provided in front of the machine.

> **EXCEPTION:** Clearfloor space is not required at drive up only automatic teller machines and fare machines.

❖ The ATM can be accessed by either a front approach or a parallel approach. A clear floor space is not required at drive-up facilities. With a front approach, clearance must be provided to the front of the unit because effective reach is not much past the toes of the person in the wheelchair. Providing knee and/or toe clearance would make access easier because it would allow for a closer approach. Where a parallel approach is provided, the clear floor space should be centered on the controls.

707.3 Operable Parts. Operable parts shall comply with Section 309. Unless a clear or correct key is provided, each operable part shall be able to be differentiated by sound or touch, without activation.

> **EXCEPTION:** Drive up only automatic teller machines and fare machines shall not be required to comply with Section 309.2 or 309.3.

❖ All operable parts, including items such as keypad, deposit slots, money or ticket dispensing and coin slots, must be within the 15-inch to 48-inch (380 to 1220 mm) reach range. To assist persons with visual impairments, each operable part must be distinguishable by either touch or sound without activation. For example, the keypad can meet the provisions of Section 707.5 and raised symbols as shown in Table 707.6.1 can be provided on the function keys. This allows the user to be certain of the key or discern its function before pressing it. Where a clear or correct key is provided, the standard will allow the keys or parts to be activated upon touching since the user would be able to correct their entry by using the clear or correct key. Drive-up machines are not required to provide the clear floor space or reach ranges in Section 309, but the operable parts must still meet the operational requirements in Section 309.4. Controls for user activation must:

- Be automatic or operable with one hand;
- Operate without tight grasping, pinching or twist of the wrist;
- Require no more than 5 pounds (22 N) force to activate.

707.4 Privacy. Automatic teller machines shall provide the opportunity for the same degree of privacy of input and output available to all individuals.

❖ In addition to people with visual impairment, people who are short of stature cannot effectively block the video screen with their bodies, so they may prefer to use speech output. Screen output users can benefit from an option to render the screen blank, thereby affording them greater privacy and personal security.

An audio output or large print display that can be seen or heard by persons other than the person using the machine may create a privacy concern. Options could be a telephone handset or audio plugs so that a person could use a headset to hear audio output during the transaction.

707.5 Numeric Keys. Numeric keys shall be arranged in a 12-key ascending or descending telephone keypad layout. The number Five key shall have a single raised dot.

❖ Telephone keypads have numbers in an ascending order [Figure 707.5(a)] while computer keypads have numbers in a descending order [Figure 707.5(b)]. Both types of keypads are acceptable. The number 5 key must be designated tactilely with a raised dot.

707.6 Function Keys. Function keys shall comply with Section 707.6.

❖ Function keys are the buttons on an ATM or fare machine other than numeric keypads. Examples on an ATM are the

"Enter" or "Clear" button. Examples on a fare machine might be the key for the desired station or zone or add/subtract value keys used to change the amount of money you want on the transportation card. Cues for the visually impaired are arrangement, marking and color coding.

707.6.1 Raised Symbols. Function key surfaces shall have raised symbols as shown in Table 707.6.1.

❖ It is not the intent to require these particular function keys, but if provided, the use of consistent standardized raised cues on the typical function keys will provide additional assistance for persons with visual impairments.

TABLE 707.6.1—RAISED SYMBOLS

Key Function	Description of Raised Symbol	Raised Symbol
Enter or Proceed:	CIRCLE	○
Clear or Correct:	LEFT ARROW	←
Cancel:	"X"	X
Add Value:	PLUS SIGN	+
Decreased Value:	MINUS SIGN	-

707.6.2 Contrast. Function keys shall contrast visually from background surfaces. Characters and symbols on key surfaces shall contrast visually from key surfaces. Visual contrast shall be either light-on-dark or dark-on-light.

EXCEPTION: Raised symbols required by Section 707.6.1 shall not be required to comply with Section 707.6.2.

❖ The function buttons/keys must contrast with the surrounding surfaces. The first sentence of the requirement is for the keys themselves, while the second sentence addresses a separate issue and is applicable to any visual numbers or characters on the keys or buttons. The exception is really related to the second sentence. As stated in the exception, where the symbol on the key surface is for a tactile purpose and not for a visual identification, the raised symbol is not required to contrast with the key surface itself but the key itself should still contrast with the background surface. not the tactile symbols in Section 707.6.1. A contrast of at least 70 percent based on the light reflectance value is recommended (see commentary, Section 703.2.10).

707.7 Display Screen. The display screen shall comply with Section 707.7.

❖ Video display screens are found on almost all ATMs and some fare machines. Even though tactile cues used for keys would not be technically feasible, the screens can improve access with good design for viewing height, contrast and fonts.

707.7.1 Visibility. The display screen shall be visible from a point located 40 inches (1015 mm) above the center of the clear floor space in front of the machine.

EXCEPTION: Drive up only automatic teller machines and fare machines shall not be required to comply with Section 707.7.1.

❖ The average eye height for an adult male using a wheelchair is from 43 inches to 51 inches (1090 to 1295 mm). The visibility of the screen is also an issue for persons who are short of stature.

The screen need not be located at 40 inches (1015 mm) above the floor, but rather it must be seen from a point 40 inches (1015 mm) above the floor. This requirement is not applicable for drive-up machines.

707.7.2 Characters. Characters displayed on the screen shall be in a sans serif font. The uppercase letter "I" shall be used to determine the allowable height of all characters of the font. The uppercase letter "I" of the font shall be $^3/_{16}$ inch (4.8 mm) minimum in height. Characters shall contrast with their background with either light characters on a dark background, or dark characters on a light background.

❖ In typography, a sans serif typeface is one that does not have the small features called "serifs" at the end of strokes. Sans serif typefaces or a simple serif typeface without excessive flourishes or deviation in stroke width have been

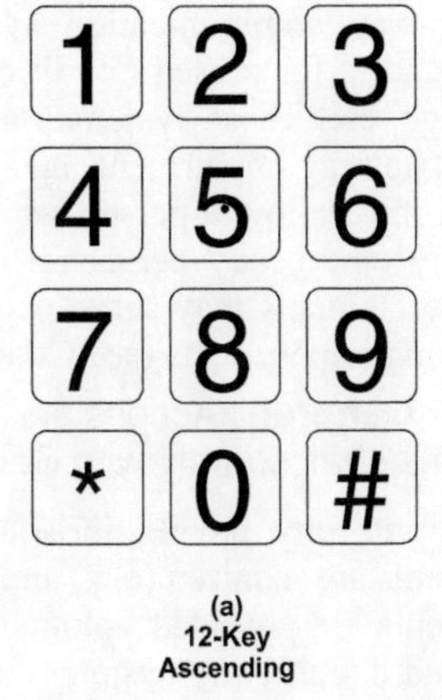

(a)
12-Key
Ascending

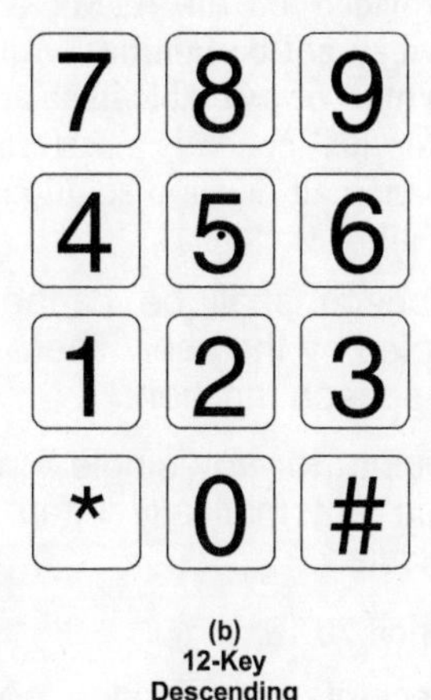

(b)
12-Key
Descending

FIGURE 707.5
NUMERIC KEY LAYOUT

found to be the most legible. A severely nearsighted person has to be much closer to see a character of a given size accurately than a person with normal visual acuity. For an example of serif and sans serif typeface, see Commentary Figure C703.3.4.

The Society for Environmental Graphic Design (SEGD) recommends using the capital "O" and the capital "I" for calculating proportions for text. If numbers are used to identify spaces, use the numbers "0" and "1." Uniform stroke width also increases legibility. See Section 703.2 for additional guidance on visual characters.

Light characters on a dark background are usually considered easier to read than dark characters on a light background; however, either is permitted. A contrast of at least 70 percent based on the light reflectance value is recommended. Possible glare on the screen should also be considered.

707.8 Speech Output. Machines shall be speech enabled. Operating instructions and orientation, visible transaction prompts, user input verification, error messages, and all displayed information for full use shall be accessible to and independently usable by individuals with vision impairments. Speech shall be delivered through a mechanism that is readily available to all users including, but not limited to, an industry standard connector or a telephone handset. Speech shall be recorded or digitized human, or synthesized.

EXCEPTIONS:

1. Audible tones shall be permitted in lieu of speech for visible output that is not displayed for security purposes, including but not limited to, asterisks representing personal identification numbers.
2. Advertisements and other similar information shall not be required to be audible unless they convey information that can be used in the transaction being conducted.
3. Where speech synthesis cannot be supported, dynamic alphabetic output shall not be required to be audible.

❖ Visual instructions are provided on all ATMs or fare machines for persons who may not be familiar with their operation. This information must be available in an audible format as well. The intent for this section is a performance standard so that manufacturers can develop solutions that take advantage of new technologies.

707.8.1 User Control. Speech shall be capable of being repeated and interrupted by the user. There shall be a volume control for the speech function.

EXCEPTION: Speech output for any single function shall be permitted to be automatically interrupted when a transaction is selected.

❖ See the commentary to Section 707.8.

707.8.2 Receipts. Where receipts are provided, speech output devices shall provide audible balance inquiry information, error messages, and all other information on the printed receipt necessary to complete or verify the transaction.

EXCEPTIONS:

1. Machine location, date and time of transaction, customer account number, and the machine identifier shall not be required to be audible.
2. Information on printed receipts that duplicates audible information available on-screen shall not be required to be presented in the form of an audible receipt.
3. Printed copies of bank statements and checks shall not be required to be audible.

❖ Information available on the printed receipt must be available audibly, the same as the requirements for audio output for performing the transaction (Section 707.8).

The exceptions are recognition of irrelevant information, duplicated information or information that may be lengthy.

707.9 Input Controls. At least one tactually discernible input control shall be provided for each function. Where provided, key surfaces not on active areas of display screens shall be raised above surrounding surfaces. Where membrane keys are the only method of input, each shall be tactually discernable from surrounding surfaces and adjacent keys.

❖ Not all machines use standard key pads or buttons. The intent for this section is a performance standard so that manufacturers could develop solutions that can take advantage of new technologies.

707.10 Braille Instructions. Braille instructions for initiating the speech mode shall be provided. Braille shall comply with Section 703.4.

❖ Braille instructions must be provided to initiate the speech output required in Section 707.8. Braille must be the Grade 2 literary braille specified in Section 703.4. This information should also be available on a sign for persons who may have difficulty reading the display screen.

708 Two-way Communication Systems

❖ Two-way communication systems are used at security entrances, for closed circuit entry systems, from areas of refuge, etc. These systems must be available for a person with hearing impairments and, in the case of an area of refuge, must allow a person who cannot exit the building to notify emergency personnel of their location. Therefore, these elements may serve people with mobility, visual or hearing impairments (see Commentary Figure C708).

708.1 General. Accessible two-way communication systems shall comply with Section 708.

❖ The authority having jurisdiction specifies where these systems are required (e.g., areas of refuge), however, when systems are provided voluntarily (e.g., security entrances, closed circuit entry systems) the systems should still comply. In addition, the system must also meet the general requirement for operable parts in Section 309.

FIGURE C708
EXAMPLE OF TWO-WAY COMMUNICATION SYSTEM

708.2 Audible and Visual Indicators. The system shall provide both visual and audible signals.

❖ Different systems and purposes will result in different application needs. Visual indicators, such as a flashing light or text output, as appropriate, will make this system available to persons with hearing impairments. Audible information, provided by a speaker or a recording, as appropriate, will make this system available to persons with vision impairments. The importance of providing both visual and audible signals can be highlighted by the example of a two-way communication system within an area of refuge. If a person needing assistance activates the system, it is important for them to know their call has been answered and that assistance is on the way. If the communication device does not provide both visual and audible signals, a person with either visual or hearing impairments might be unaware that their call had been answered or that help was being sent to assist them.

708.3 Handsets. Handset cords, if provided, shall be 29 inches (735 mm) minimum in length.

❖ If a telephone handset is used, the cord must be a minimum of 29 inches (740 mm) long to allow use by either a standing person or a person using a wheelchair or scooter. The handset should also be configured to address the needs of persons who have hearing impairments. See the provisions for telephones in Section 704 for additional information.

708.4 Telephone entry systems. Telephone entry systems shall comply with ANSI/DASMA 303 listed in Section 105.2.7.

❖ These types of systems are most commonly found at the front entrance to an apartment complex, but are increasingly used as part of the security for limited-access areas in facilities such as courthouses or high-tech facilities. The DASMA standard provides appropriate references for all general requirements to make the system accessible, while giving performance criteria on location, placement, visual user directions, audible user directions, volume level, call status, controls and input devices.

ANSI/DASMA 303 is titled *Performance Criteria for Accessible Communications Entry Systems.* It was developed with the input of various users, producers, and others with a general interest in these types of entry systems. It provides a uniform means of evaluating the performance of accessible communication entry systems.

DASMA 303 is available for viewing and for downloading free of charge at the DASMA web site, http://www.dasma.com.

Chapter 8. Special Rooms and Spaces

❖ Chapter 8 contains the technical requirements for spaces with unique types of usage. This includes assembly seating; dressing, fitting and locker rooms; kitchens and kitchenettes; transportation facilities; holding and housing cells and courthouses.

- Section 801 is a general statement about the Chapter 8 criteria being applicable for the special types of spaces addressed in this chapter when required by the authority having jurisdiction.
- Section 802 contains criteria for fixed assembly seating arrangements.
- Section 803 provides technical criteria for spaces where a person may need to change clothes, such as a dressing room, fitting room or locker room.
- Section 804 addresses requirements for kitchens that are found outside of a Type A or Type B dwelling unit. "Kitchens" in Accessible Units (Section 1002.12) references Section 804 for requirements. There are also provisions for kitchenettes and wet bars that may be found in such areas as office break rooms.
- Section 805 deals with all types of transportation facilities such as bus stops and train stations.
- Section 806 contains requirements for holding cells and housing cells, such as those found in police stations, jails and courthouses.
- Section 807 addresses criteria unique to courtrooms.

801 General

801.1 Scope. Special rooms and spaces required to be accessible by the scoping provisions adopted by the administrative authority shall comply with the applicable provisions of Chapter 8.

❖ The provisions in this chapter are intended to state requirements for the specialized use areas that may not be addressed elsewhere in the standard but are required for accessibility and usability by people with physical impairments. It is not the intent for the provisions in this chapter to exclude the application of any provision required elsewhere. All applicable accessibility requirements contained elsewhere in this standard, or required in the scoping documents adopted by the administrative authority, are to be applied in addition to the requirements in this chapter. Note that these provisions apply to these special rooms and spaces when required by the scoping provisions (see Section 201).

802 Assembly Areas

802.1 General. Wheelchair spaces and wheel chair space locations in assembly areas with spectator seating shall comply with Section 802. Team and player seating shall comply with Sections 802.2 through 802.6.

❖ Although there are many types of assembly areas, the criteria in this section deal specifically with fixed seating arrangements. These requirements can be applicable to a variety of venues, including spaces such as theaters, sports arenas, churches, courtroom gallery seating, lecture halls, grandstands at high school football fields and bleachers at Little League baseball parks. Planned wheelchair positions for viewing speakers, performances, sporting events or other productions in a place of assembly enhance the viewing for those persons using wheelchairs and the general safety of the entire audience (see Commentary Figure C802.1).

In the past, many places of assembly placed persons using wheelchairs in aisles and cross aisles, drawing unnecessary attention to the person with a disability and possibly obstructing required aisles for everyone. Having persons in wheelchairs sit in ramped aisles also made for unstable seating. Creating a special section where persons using wheelchairs were segregated was not a successful solution. Often, these areas did not provide a view similar to the options available to the general audience.

The criteria in this section have been extensively expanded in this edition to address concerns about dispersion and line of sight for seating locations for persons using wheelchairs or scooters and their companions. Wheelchair spaces are locations for individuals using a wheelchair or scooter. The number of wheelchair spaces required is based on the number of seats in the venue and is specified by the authority having jurisdiction. When benches, bleachers or pews are provided, per most building codes, the number of seats is typically based on one occupant for each 18 inches (455 mm) of seating length.

Each "wheelchair space" must have an associated companion seat (Section 802.7). The requirements for size (Sections 802.3 and 802.4), approach (Section 802.5), overlap (Section 802.5.1), integration (Section 802.6) and companion seat adjacency and alignment (Section 802.7) must work together for proper placement of the wheelchair space within the seating rows.

Groups of wheelchair spaces and their associated companion spaces are called "wheelchair space locations." Concerns about the quality and variety of choices of the wheelchair seating are addressed in sections on integration (Section 802.6), line of sight (Section 802.9), and dispersion of locations from side-to-side (Section 802.10.1), front-to-back (Section 802.10.2) and by type (Section 802.10.3). There are also unique requirements for movie theaters (Section 802.10.4).

Designated aisle seats are those that can be used by persons with mobility impairments who have difficulty moving into the aisle accessway between rows (Section 802.8).

Where team and play seating is required to be accessible, the wheelchair space in that area must meet size, slope, approach and integration. An accessible route must be available both from any locker rooms to the team seating, and from the team seating to the edge of the area of sports activity [see Section 106.5 and Chapter 11 and Commentary Figure C802.1(g)].

(a) STADIUMS

(b) THEATERS

(C) OUTSIDE BLEACHERS

(d) INSIDE BLEACHERS

(e) COURTROOMS

(f) LECTURE HALL

FIGURE C802.1
ASSEMBLY SEATING

FIGURE C802.1(g)
TEAM SEATING

802.2 Floor Surfaces. The floor surface of wheelchair space locations shall have a slope not steeper than 1:48 and shall comply with Section 302.

❖ The wheelchair space location must be substantially level for safety and comfort. See Section 302 for surface requirements.

The wheelchair space will typically have more depth than one row of general seats. When the wheelchair space is in seating having a tiered or sloped floor, a curb or barrier may be necessary at the edge of a raised wheelchair space location to provide a higher level of safety for persons who may be sitting near the edge of that raised area. If the drop-off is high enough, a guard may be required by the building code for issues of safety with the minimum height determined by whether or not it constrains the line of sight for a person seated on that wheelchair space location (see Commentary Figure C802.2).

802.3 Width. A single wheelchair space shall be 36 inches (915 mm) minimum in width. Where two adjacent wheelchair spaces are provided, each wheelchair space shall be 33 inches (840 mm) minimum in width.

❖ The width of a single wheelchair space is 6 inches (150 mm) greater than the clear floor or ground space required by Section 305 for maneuvering clearances within seating. When two wheelchair spaces are provided adjacent to each other, a slightly narrower wheelchair space is permitted because they share maneuvering space (see Figure 802.3 and Commentary Figure C802.3).

Note that Section 802.7 requires a companion seat on at least one side of each wheelchair space; therefore, the maximum number of wheelchair spaces immediately adjacent to each other would be two.

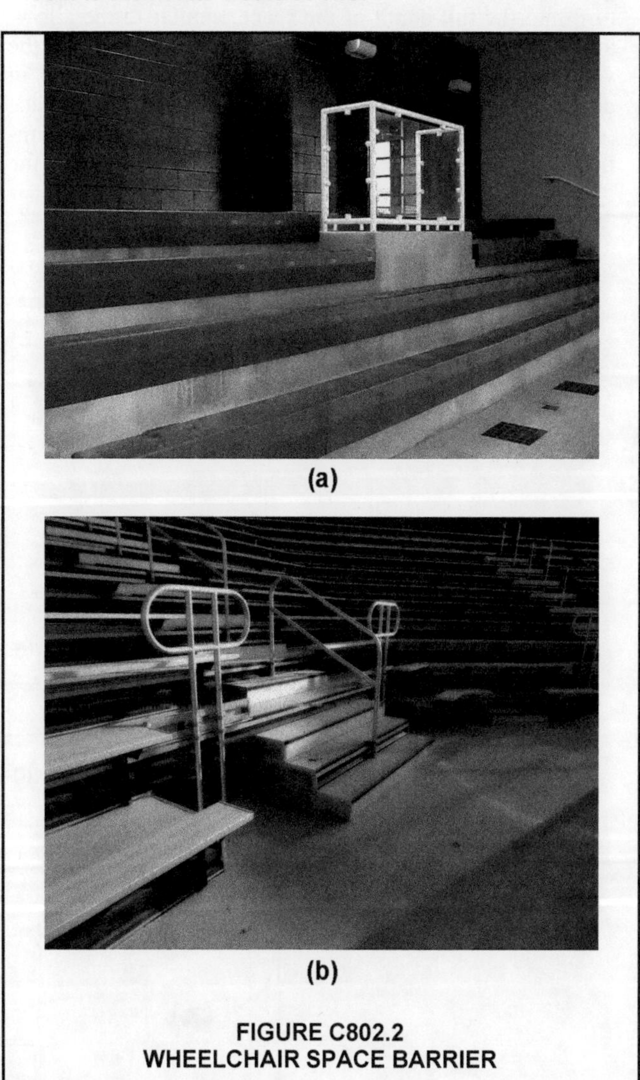

(a)

(b)

FIGURE C802.2
WHEELCHAIR SPACE BARRIER

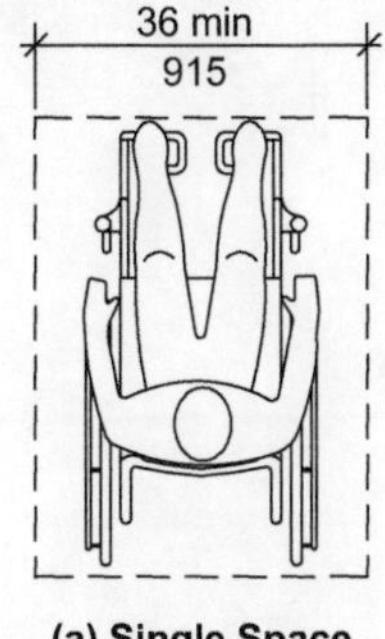

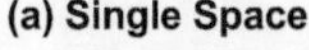

(a) Single Space

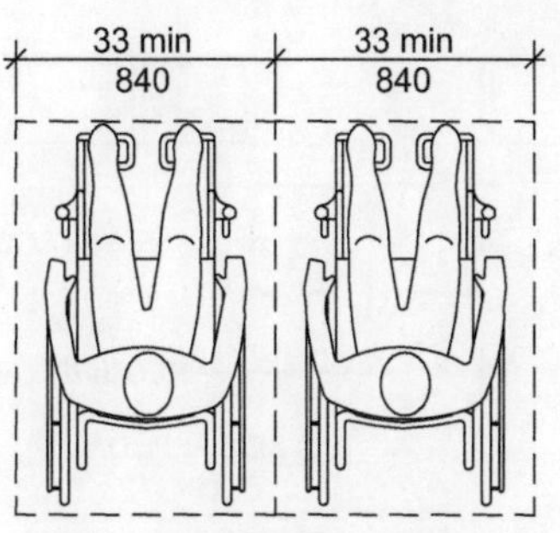

(b) Multiple Adjacent Spaces

FIGURE 802.3
WIDTH OF A WHEELCHAIR SPACE IN ASSEMBLY AREAS

802.4 Depth. Where a wheelchair space can be entered from the front or rear, the wheelchair space shall be 48 inches (1220 mm) minimum in depth. Where a wheelchair space can only be entered from the side, the wheelchair space shall be 60 inches (1525 mm) minimum in depth.

❖ When a person can pull into a wheelchair space forward or backward, the required depth is the same as a clear floor or ground space (Section 305.3). If a person can make a full turn into the full depth of the space, similar to the allowances for turns along accessible routes in Chapter 4, the wheelchair space is required to be 48 inches (1220 mm) in depth minimum. Side approach to the wheelchair space requires maneuvering into a position with movements similar to parallel parking. This requires more space than the forward or rear approach. The parallel approach depth is similar to that required for the alcove provisions (Section 305.7) (see Figure 802.4 and Commentary Figure C802.3). Note that Section 802.5 requires that the approach to a wheelchair space be from an accessible route; therefore, a side approach wheelchair space will be a single wheelchair space requiring both greater width and depth than clear floor or ground space.

802.5 Approach. The wheelchair space shall adjoin an accessible route. The accessible route shall not overlap the wheelchair space.

❖ An accessible route must connect the wheelchair viewing space with the accessible entrances and any services, such as beverage and food stands, souvenir stands, toilet rooms, etc. The wheelchair space cannot overlap the accessible

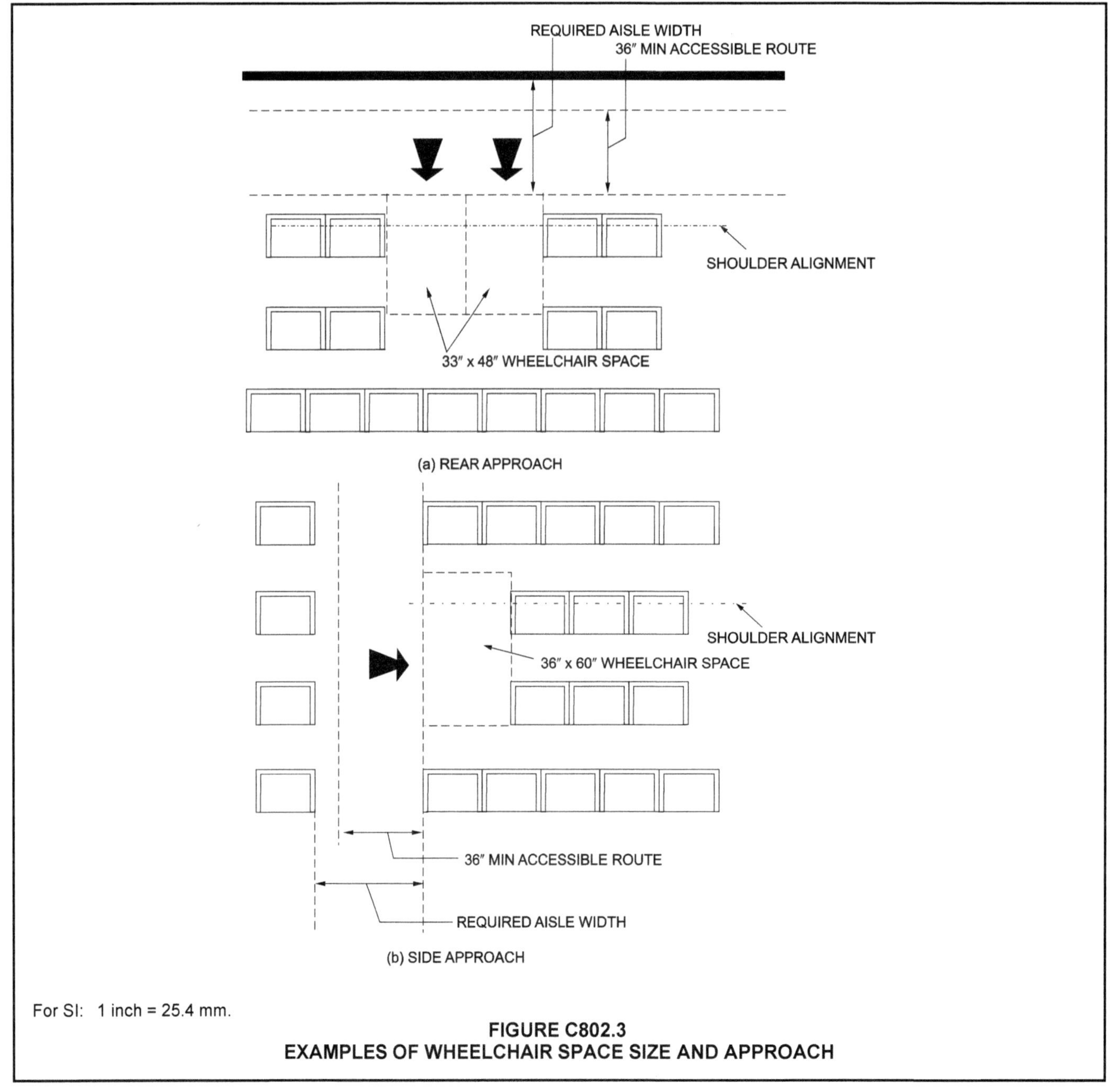

FIGURE C802.3
EXAMPLES OF WHEELCHAIR SPACE SIZE AND APPROACH

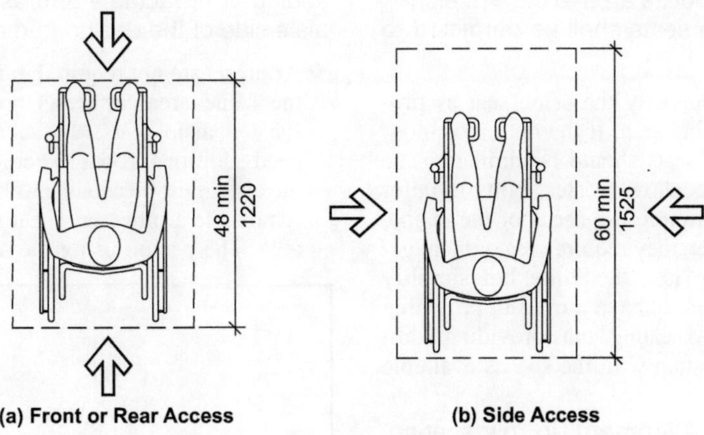

(a) Front or Rear Access (b) Side Access

FIGURE 802.4
DEPTH OF A WHEELCHAIR SPACE IN ASSEMBLY AREAS

route, so the wheelchair space must either be the end point of an accessible route, or the route must be along one side of the wheelchair space. The route cannot pass through one wheelchair space to get to another wheelchair space (see Commentary Figure C802.3).

The location of the accessible route and aisle (Section 802.5.1) should be measured from the wheelchair space when the wheelchair is positioned for shoulder alignment with the companion seat (Section 802.7.2). The wheelchair user should not have to move forward to get out of the aisle or accessible route, even when additional space is provided in front of the space.

802.5.1 Overlap. A wheelchair space shall not overlap the required width of an aisle.

❖ The intent of this requirement is that a person occupying the wheelchair space would not obstruct the main exit paths from seating areas, i.e., the aisle, similar to other seats (see Commentary Figure C802.3 and Section 802.5).

Seating arrangements include aisles and aisle accessways. An aisle accessway is the narrow path between the rows of seats that connect to an aisle. An aisle is the path that connects aisle accessways to other components of the exit system. The minimum clear width of both aisles and aisle accessways is defined in the building codes. Where aisles are wider than required, the wheelchair space is permitted to overlap the portion of the aisle that is in excess of the width required. Note that Section 802.7.2 requires shoulder alignment between a wheelchair space and the associated companion seat. Therefore, a wheelchair space often overlaps an aisle accessway but never a minimum width aisle. A person using a wheelchair can move forward or backward slightly to allow someone to get to their seat from the aisle and down the aisle accessway, similar to a seated person standing up to let someone by. The number of seats along an aisle accessway is very limited compared to an aisle. Even though the wheelchair space must overlap an aisle accessway, the wheelchair space is not permitted to overlap the required width of an aisle.

802.6 Integration of Wheelchair Space Locations. Wheelchair space locations shall be an integral part of any seating area.

❖ Each wheelchair space location must be within its associated seating area as much as possible. Note that Section 802.10.3 requires wheelchair spaces to be dispersed into each type where there are multiple distinct seating areas. However, complete integration of wheelchair spaces is limited. For example, guards may be required around wheelchair space locations where they must be elevated for line of sight over standing spectators to prevent someone from accidentally rolling off the edge of the elevated area. Guard requirements can be found in the building codes.

802.7 Companion Seat. A companion seat, complying with Section 802.7, shall be provided beside each wheelchair space.

❖ Locating a wheelchair space next to a seat for a companion allows wheelchair users and at least one person accompanying them to be seated together. The companion seat should be similar to the adjacent seating and placed so that someone in a wheelchair could align their shoulders with their companion to ensure a viewing experience similar to that of others attending the event (Sections 802.7.1 and 802.7.2).

A "wheelchair space location" that follows the repeating pattern of companion seat, two wheelchair spaces, companion seat along a row would allow for the companion to be someone in a seat or someone using a wheelchair.

The Department of Justice (DOJ) has a ticketing policy that allows for persons using one of the wheelchair spaces to purchase up to three seats for companions. This policy would allow for this purchase to include another wheelchair space and a chair can be placed in that space. This ticketing policy will not affect the layout of wheelchair spaces and companion seats as required by this standard.

802.7.1 Companion Seat Type. The companion seat shall be equivalent in size, quality, comfort and amenities to the seats in the immediate area to the wheelchair space location. Companion seats shall be permitted to be moveable.

❖ The companion seat is essentially the same seat as provided elsewhere in the seating area. If the option of movable seats is chosen, those seats should be similar to the fixed seating. Movable seats allow greater ability to tailor the wheelchair seating location to the needs of the people wanting to sit there; however, they require greater management. Fixed seats promote less flexibility but simplify operation policies. Some venues have moved to providing a mixture of fixed and loose seating, thus providing additional flexibility and integration with the spaces available for wheelchair seating.

802.7.2 Companion Seat Alignment. In row seating, the companion seat shall be located to provide shoulder alignment with the wheelchair space occupant. The shoulder of the wheelchair space occupant shall be measured either 36 inches (915 mm) from the front or 12 inches (305 mm) from the rear of the wheelchair space. The floor surface for the companion seat shall be at the same elevation as the wheelchair space floor surface.

❖ This provision provides the same interaction potential between the person using the wheelchair and the person sitting next to them as for any other seated pair. The seating should be at the same floor elevation, and the shoulders of both people should align. In a front or rear approach space with a 48-inch (1220 mm) depth, the shoulder alignment is both 12 inches (305 mm) from the back and 36 inches (915 mm) from the front. This allows space for the back wheels of a wheelchair.

In a side approach space, with a 60-inch depth (1525 mm), the shoulder alignment would be 36 inches (915 mm) from the front. However, because the person in a wheelchair aligns with the companion chair, both would have similar lines of sight regardless of whether it is 36 inches (915 mm) from the front or 12 inches (305 mm) from the back of a side approach space. The overriding criterion is the person in a wheelchair and the companion be able to sit side by side with lines of sight similar to those of other spectators (see Commentary Figure C802.7.2).

802.8 Designated Aisle Seats. Designated aisle seats shall comply with Section 802.8.

❖ Designated aisle seats are seats located along the aisles in a fixed seating arrangement. These seats need not be located directly on an accessible route. The authority having jurisdiction determines the percentage of aisle seats required to serve as designated aisle seats. The designated aisle seats are used by persons with mobility impairments that make it difficult for them to move laterally in the aisle accessways between the seating rows. For a description of aisles and aisle accessways, see the commentary for Section 802.5.1 (see Commentary Figure C802.8).

802.8.1 Armrests. Where armrests are provided on seating in the immediate area of designated aisle seats, folding or retractable armrests shall be provided on the aisle side of the designated aisle seat.

❖ Armrests are not required, but if provided for the seating in the same area, armrests are also required for the designated aisle seats. To accommodate persons who may need additional room to get into the seat, the armrest along the aisle must be capable of being moved out of the way. A removable armrest or a seat with no armrest is not acceptable. The person using the seat may need the armrest for

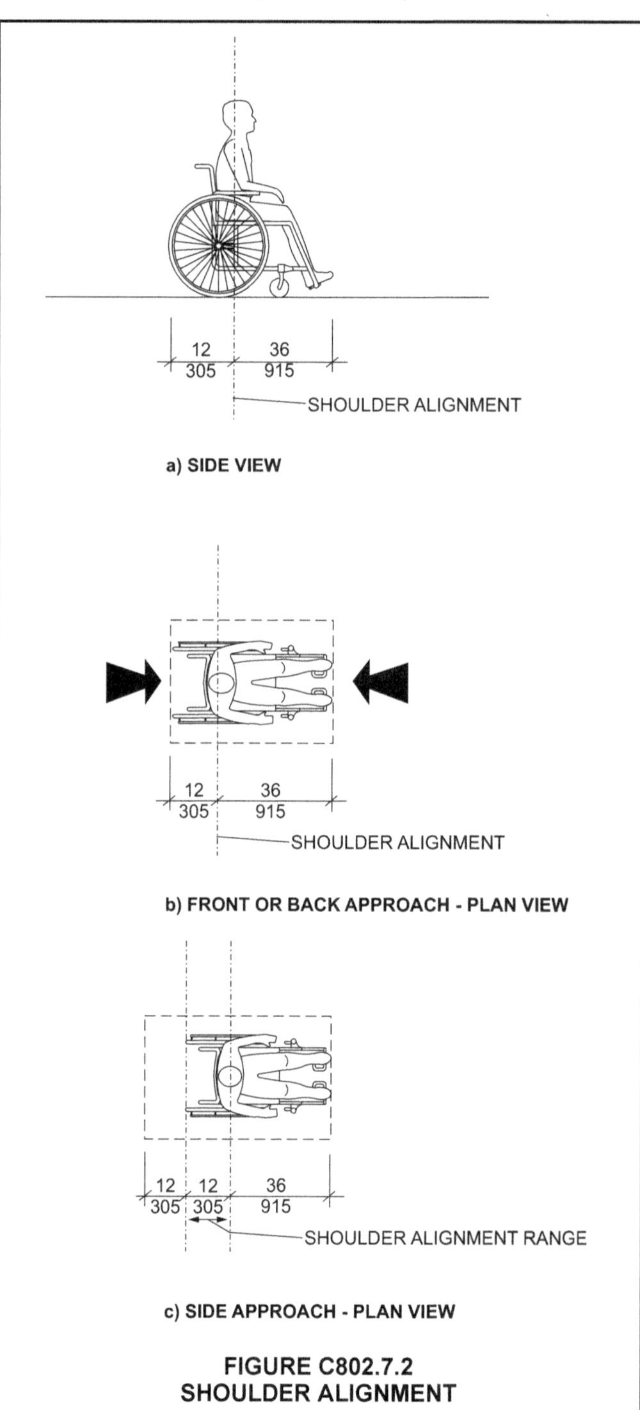

FIGURE C802.7.2
SHOULDER ALIGNMENT

support or assistance to raise or lower themselves in the seat.

End caps on pew-type seating (e.g., typically found in religious facilities or courtroom galleries) (see Commentary Figure C802.8.1) are not considered armrests.

FIGURE C802.8
DESIGNATED AISLE SEATS

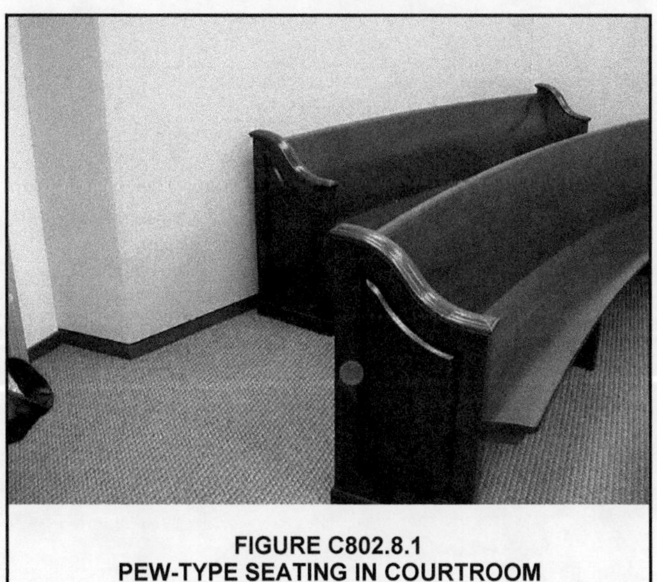

FIGURE C802.8.1
PEW-TYPE SEATING IN COURTROOM

802.8.2 Identification. Each designated aisle seat shall be identified by the International Symbol of Accessibility.

❖ The designated aisle seats must be designated with the symbol associated with wheelchair access; however, this does not mean the designated aisle seats are intended for transfer. The intent is to have a consistent symbol for this type of seating.

802.9 Lines of Sight. Where spectators are expected to remain seated for purposes of viewing events, spectators in wheelchair space locations shall be provided with a line of sight in accordance with Section 802.9.1. Where spectators in front of the wheelchair space locations will be expected to stand at their seats for purposes of viewing events, spectators in wheelchair space locations shall be provided with a line of sight in accordance with Section 802.9.2.

❖ A variety of locations and views must be available to the spectator using a wheelchair. This requirement precludes the grouping of all wheelchair spaces into one area because that would limit the sight line options available for the persons using wheelchairs and their companions. Although the average adult male seated in a wheelchair has an eye height of 43 to 51 inches (1090 to 1295 mm), the eye height of the companion will depend on the seat provided and average adult anthropometrics. The line of sight must be considered for both types of viewing.

The line of sight is dependent on the events that will occur in the venue. For example, in a courtroom or opera house, the seating is designed for spectators that remain seated. Even though the audience in a courtroom may rise for the entrance of the judge, or stand in a theater for an ovation at the end of a performance, the audience does not typically stand during the event. In religious facilities, participants may stand for part of the services, but this is for group participation, not to view an event; therefore, seating in religious facilities is designed assuming seated spectators.

In most sports facilities, the audience is expected to stand during exciting and critical times of the event; therefore, wheelchair seating must be designed for persons in wheelchairs to see over spectators standing in front of them. The intent is to provide a line of sight for the spectator in a wheelchair the same as, or better than, that of an adjacent standing spectator. A tennis stadium is an example of a sports facility where spectators are not expected to stand at exciting and critical times, so seating could be designed for seated spectators.

Within a luxury box or suite, because it is reasonable to assume the people in this area know each other and would be accommodating, line of sight over standing spectators would not be required in the suite.

The options covered in Section 802.9 deal with typical venues. In a unique situation, such as a planetarium or Omnimax theater, the seating arrangement should provide alternatives that meet the intent (see Section 103).

802.9.1 Line of Sight over Seated Spectators. Where spectators are expected to remain seated during events, spectators seated in a wheelchair space shall be provided with lines of sight to the performance area or playing field comparable to that provided to seated spectators in closest proximity to the wheelchair space location. Where seating provides lines of sight over heads, spectators in wheelchair space locations shall be afforded lines of sight complying with Section 802.9.1.1. Where wheelchair space locations provide lines of sight over the shoulder and between heads, spectators in wheelchair space locations shall be afforded lines of sight complying with Section 802.9.1.2.

❖ The line of sight from the spectator to the event depends upon several factors, which may include items such as the vertical rise between rows of seats, the location of the focal point and/or points and the extent of events to be viewed. The line of sight may be provided between the heads of the audience members sitting in the rows in front or provided over the heads of audience members. A spectator in a wheelchair must be provided the same or better line of sight than that provided for the general seating, whether it is between heads or over heads.

Note that this does not require that seating be designed for spectators to see over or between heads of the spectators in front of them, but if the facility is designed in this manner, the wheelchair spaces must have a view that is the same or better than the average spectator.

802.9.1.1 Lines of Sight over Heads. Spectators seated in a wheelchair space shall be afforded lines of sight over the heads of seated individuals in the first row in front of the wheelchair space location.

❖ In facilities where the lines of sight for spectators are designed to be unobstructed by the head of an average height spectator, spectators in wheelchairs shall be provided lines of sight unobstructed by the head of an average height spectator (see Figure 802.9.1.1).

The average eye height of someone in a wheelchair is at least as high as the average eye height of a general spectator; therefore, this is typically not a problem when there is no significant difference in the vertical rise between rows of seats and those rows having wheelchair spaces.

802.9.1.2 Lines of Sight between Heads. Spectators seated in a wheelchair space shall be afforded lines of sight over the shoulders and between the heads of seated individuals in the first row in front of the wheelchair space location.

❖ The basic requirement is to provide for a line of sight similar to that provided to the surrounding seating arrangements (see commentary, Section 802.9.1.1 and Figure 802.9.1.2).

802.9.2 Line of Sight over Standing Spectators. Wheelchair spaces required to provide a line of sight over standing spectators shall comply with Section 802.9.2.

❖ In venues where the typical crowd behavior is to stand during exciting and critical times of an event, spectators in wheelchairs shall be provided the same line of sight as adjacent standing spectators. If the spectators are expected to stand, and wheelchair locations are provided where the line of sight would be over that area to the event, the line of sight for the wheelchair space and the associated companion seat must be provided over the standing spectators. The designer should use the eye level of an average adult male to determine the line of sight for standing spectators.

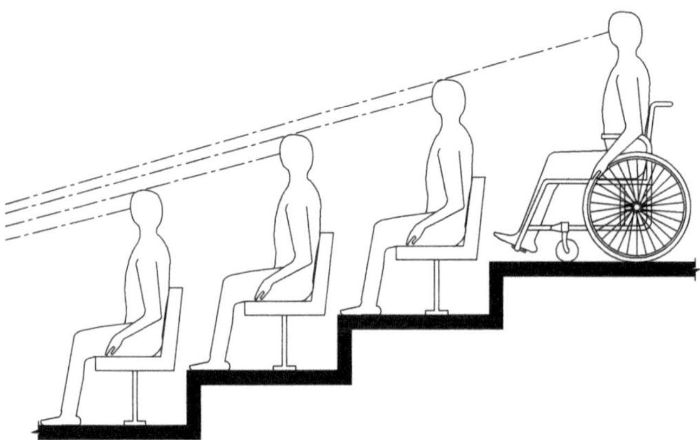

FIGURE 802.9.1.1
LINES OF SIGHT OVER THE HEADS OF SEATED SPECTATORS

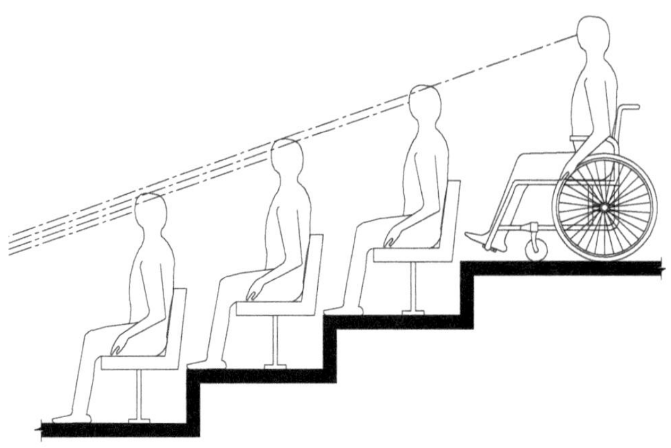

FIGURE 802.9.1.2
LINES OF SIGHT BETWEEN THE HEADS OF SEATED SPECTATORS

802.9.2.1 Distance from Adjacent Seating. The front of the wheelchair space in a wheelchair space location shall be 12 inches (305 mm) maximum from the back of the chair or bench in front.

❖ The distance between the wheelchair space and the chair in the row immediately in front is an essential criterion to provide spectators in wheelchairs with the same line of sight as standing spectators because lines of sight are based on geometry. When the wheelchair platform is at an elevation above the seating tread in front in accordance with Table 802.9.2.2 and the wheelchair space is located 12 inches (305 mm) from the chair in front, the spectator in a wheelchair is provided essentially the same lines of sight as standing spectators. Wheelchair spaces that are located closer than 12 inches (305 mm) to the row immediately in front would have better lines of sight and wheelchair spaces that are located more than 12 inches (305 mm) would see less than standing spectators. However, the designer could provide a sight line analysis to demonstrate essentially the same lines of sight as an alternative approach to Table 802.9.2.2 in support of more than 12 inches (305 mm) (see Section 103). As seen in Figure 802.9.2, the wheelchair space location may overlap two or more rows of seats with the total depth.

802.9.2.2 Height. The height of the floor surface at the wheelchair space location shall comply with Table 802.9.2.2. Interpolations shall be permitted for riser heights that are not listed in the table.

❖ Table 802.9.2.2 provides the minimum height of the wheelchair space location above the tread of the row of seats in front to achieve a line of sight for persons in wheelchairs over spectators standing in front of them. Notes in Table 809.2.2 and Figure 802.9.2 provide the technical criteria based on basic geometry, assuming looking down towards an event. This type of configuration is typical for sports arenas looking down on a playing field or court. If a specific configuration is not indicated, interpolation between numbers is permitted to allow this table to cover a full range of seating options.

For example, the "tread" of a wheelchair space location associated with seating having 33-inch (835 mm) row spacing and 15-inch (380 mm) high rise between rows requires 43 inches (1090 mm) minimum height above the tread of the row in front of the wheelchair space, interpolated between 12- and 16-inch (305 and 405 mm) riser height. Likewise, the "tread" of a wheelchair space location associated with seating having 36- or 40-inch (915 or 1015 mm) row spacing and 15-inch (380 mm) high rise between rows also requires 43 inches (1090 mm) minimum height above the tread of the row in front of the wheelchair space; interpolation relates only to the height of the riser. Although this will typically result in a raised area, the wheelchair space location must be integrated into the seating as much as possible (see Section 802.6). Complete integration of wheelchair spaces is in conflict with this requirement for lines of sight over standing spectators. Building codes may require guards around wheelchair space locations because of the tread elevation of the wheel-

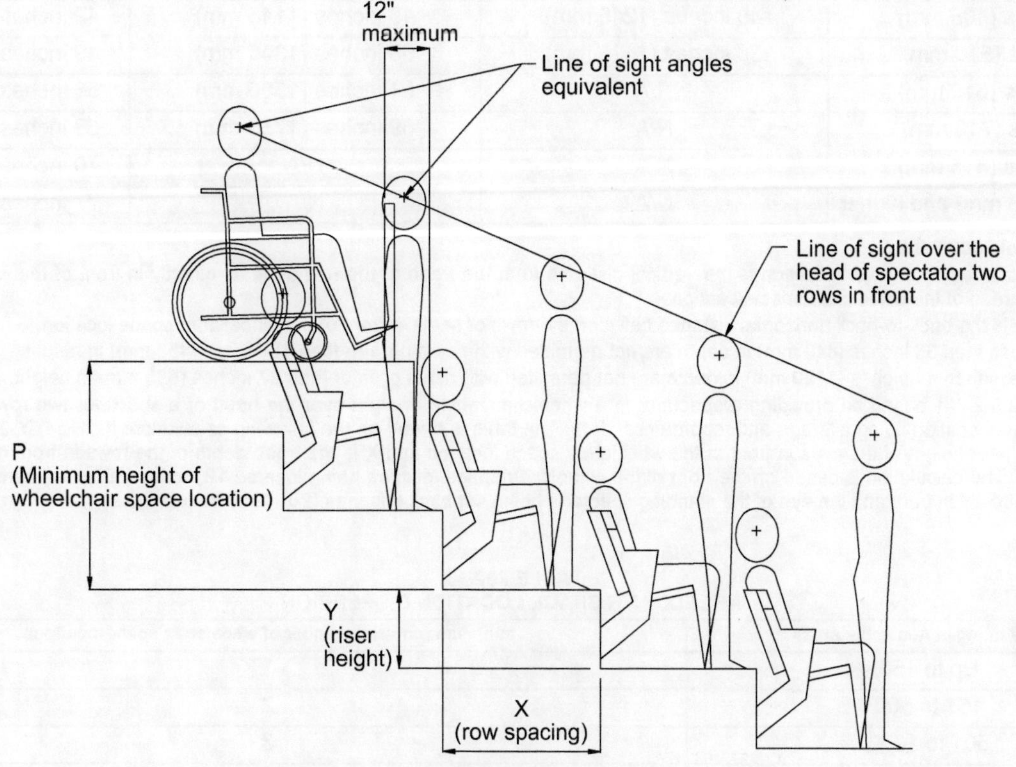

FIGURE 802.9.2
LINES OF SIGHT OVER STANDING SPECTATORS

chair space location, or some other type of edge protection for safety reasons may be provided where guards are not required. If guards or barriers interfere with the line of sight, the building codes include unique provisions for sight line-constrained rails.

802.10 Wheelchair Space Dispersion. The minimum number of wheelchair space locations shall be in accordance with Table 802.10. Wheelchair space locations shall be dispersed in accordance with Sections 802.10.1, 802.10.2 and 802.10.3. In addition, wheelchair space locations shall be dispersed in accordance with Section 802.10.4 in spaces utilized primarily for viewing motion picture projection. Once the required number of wheelchair space locations has been met, further dispersion is not required.

❖ A wheelchair space location may include one wheelchair space and one companion seat or multiple wheelchair spaces and companion seats. Note that Section 802.7 requires a companion seat on at least one side of each wheelchair space; therefore, the maximum number of wheelchair spaces immediately adjacent to each other would be two. The number of wheelchair spaces required is greater than the number of wheelchair space "locations" required. Although similar in name, there are unique requirements for each of these defined terms (see Section 106.5). To provide a variety of choices for seating options, the wheelchair space locations must be dispersed to at least the minimum number of options indicated in Table 802.10. It is, of course, permitted to further disperse wheelchair space locations to more locations than the number required.

A common term in the assembly seating industry is to call the entire seating arrangement the "seating bowl." The seating bowl may be on one large sloped floor, a series of tiers or even a series of totally different floor levels (e.g., balconies). The seating bowl may totally surround the event, such as a theater in the round or a basketball arena; be in a U-shape, such as in smaller baseball parks; be on two straight sides, commonly found at a high school football stadium; or only on one side, such as in a movie projection theater, playhouse or performing arts center. The possible configurations are endless.

TABLE 802.9.2.2
REQUIRED WHEELCHAIR SPACE LOCATION ELEVATION OVER STANDING SPECTATORS

Riser height	Minimum height of the wheelchair space location based on row spacing[1]		
	Rows less than 33 inches (840 mm)[2]	Rows 33 inches (840 mm) to 44 inches (1120 mm)[2]	Rows over 44 inches (1120 mm)[2]
0 inch (0 mm)	16 inches (405 mm)	16 inches (405 mm)	16 inches (405 mm)
4 inches (100 mm)	22 inches (560 mm)	21 inches (535 mm)	21 inches (535 mm)
8 inches (205 mm)	31 inches (785 mm)	30 inches (760 mm)	28 inches (710 mm)
12 inches (305 mm)	40 inches (1015 mm)	37 inches (940 mm)	35 inches (890 mm)
16 inches (405 mm)	49 inches (1245 mm)	45 inches (1145 mm)	42 inches (1065 mm)
20 inches (510 mm)[3]	58 inches (1475 mm)	53 inches (1345 mm)	49 inches (1245 mm)
24 inches (610 mm)	N/A	61 inches (1550 mm)	56 inches (1420 mm)
28 inches (710 mm)[4]	N/A	69 inches (1750 mm)	63 inches (1600 mm)
32 inches (815 mm)	N/A	N/A	70 inches (1780 mm)
36 inches (915 mm) and higher	N/A	N/A	77 inches (1955 mm)

Footnotes to Table 802.9.2.2

[1]The height of the wheelchair space location is the vertical distance from the tread of the row of seats directly in front of the wheelchair space location to the tread of the wheelchair space location.

[2]The row spacing is the back-to-back horizontal distance between the rows of seats in front of the wheelchair space location.

[3]Seating treads less than 33 inches (840 mm) in depth are not permitted with risers greater than 18 inches (455 mm) in height.

[4]Seating treads less than 44 inches (1120 mm) in depth are not permitted with risers greater than 27 inches (685 mm) in height.

NOTE: Table 802.9.2.2 is based on providing a spectator in a wheelchair a line of sight over the head of a spectator two rows in front of the wheelchair space location using average anthropometrical data. The table is based on the following calculation: [(2X+34)(Y-2.25)/X]+(20.2-Y) where Y is the riser height of the rows in front of the wheelchair space location and X is the tread depth of the rows in front of the wheelchair space location. The calculation is based on the front of the wheelchair space location being located 12 inches (305 mm) from the back of the seating tread directly in front and the eye of the standing spectator being set back 8 inches (205 mm) from the riser.

TABLE 802.10
WHEELCHAIR SPACE LOCATION DISPERSION

Total seating in Assembly Areas	Minimum required number of wheelchair space locations
Up to 150	1
151 to 500	2
501 to 1000	3
1001 to 5,000	3, plus 1 additional space for each 1,000 seats or portions thereof above 1,000
5,001 and over	7, plus 1 additional space for each 2,000 seats or portions thereof above 5,000

When looking at the total seating arrangement or seating bowl, the intent is to disperse side to side, across or around the event (horizontal dispersion), front to back from the event (vertical dispersion) and by type of seating (e.g., box seats, seats with or without backs, reserved seating/open seating areas).

Because of the unique viewing angles inherent in the stadium style seating, now commonly offered in theaters used for viewing motion pictures, there are additional requirements for these types of venues in Section 802.10.4.

Note that dispersion is integrally related with the accessible means of egress provisions of the building code. Typically, building codes require at least two accessible means of egress where more than one exit is required. Therefore, there are practical limitations to dispersion because of accessible means of egress. In addition, dispersion is also integrally related to lines of sight over standing spectators because vertical heights necessary for such lines of sight affect options for accessible routes and accessible means of egress (see Section 802.9.2).

802.10.1 Horizontal Dispersion. Wheelchair space locations shall be dispersed horizontally to provide viewing options. Two wheelchair spaces shall be permitted to be located side-by-side.

EXCEPTION: Horizontal dispersion shall not be required in assembly areas with 300 or fewer seats if the wheelchair space locations are located within the 2nd and 3rd quartile of the row length. Intermediate aisles shall be included in determining the total row length. If the row length in the 2nd and 3rd quartile of the row is insufficient to accommodate the required number of companion seats and wheelchair spaces, the additional companion seats and wheelchair spaces shall be permitted to extend into in the 1st and 4th quartile of the row.

❖ Horizontal dispersion is required in order to provide viewing options around the event in a circular or U-shaped seating bowl, or from left to right in a straight line seating bowl. Horizontal dispersion does not require every wheelchair space to be separated from every other wheelchair space. To allow for a companion to also use a wheelchair, two wheelchair spaces may be located between two companion seats.

While no specific criteria for dispersion are required, it is recommended that to be considered a different location, the wheelchair spaces should be a minimum of 10 intervening seats apart. This is just a suggestion, because there are such a large number of configuration options.

The exception is to allow for the wheelchair space locations to provide for a better line of sight than the average line of sight provided for the seating bowl. For example, in a high school football stadium with seats down one or both sides of the field from goal line to goal line, if the wheelchair space locations are between the 25 yard lines, further horizontal dispersion is not required. These seats are considered in the location that is better than 50 percent of the general seating.

802.10.2 Dispersion for Variety of Distances from the Event. Wheelchair space locations shall be dispersed at a variety of distances from the event to provide viewing options.

EXCEPTIONS:

1. In bleachers, wheelchair space locations provided only in rows at points of entry to bleacher seating shall be permitted.
2. Assembly areas utilized for viewing motion picture projections with 300 seats or less shall not be required to comply with Section 802.10.2.
3. Assembly areas with 300 seats or less other than those utilized for viewing motion picture projections shall not be required to comply with Section 802.10.2 where all wheelchair space locations are within the front 50 percent of the total rows.

❖ Wheelchair space locations also need to provide a choice of seating from the front to the back of the seating bowl, to provide for additional viewing angles. Typically the building codes provide for vertical dispersion to different floor levels (e.g., balcony or box seating levels). This provision is for distance from the event within any seating bowl. Keep in mind that the seating bowl may be on one large sloped floor, a series of tiers or even a series of totally different floor levels (e.g., balconies).

Again, while no specific criteria for separation is provided, it is recommended that to be considered a separate wheelchair space location, the wheelchair spaces should be separated by a minimum of five intervening rows. This is just a suggestion, because there are such a large number of configuration options.

Bleacher seating is typically provided on its own structural frame. Benches mounted on a sloped or tiered floor integral with the building's floor or roof framing are not bleachers. Folding bleachers are common in schools and portions of some sporting venues. Because of safety concerns with providing accessible routes into the portable or collapsible types of bleacher seating, the exception allows for all bleacher wheelchair space locations to be incorporated into the first row of bleacher seating [see Commentary Figures C802.10.2(a) and (b)].

Even though Exception 2 would allow small motion picture theaters to not have dispersion front to back, the motion picture theater would still have to comply with the dispersion requirements in Sections 802.10.1 and 802.10.4.

Exception 3 is in recognition of what is considered the better half of the seating when moving from front to back. The exception provides wheelchair space locations with a better line of sight than the average provided for the seating bowl. For example, in a typical auditorium with a front stage, if the wheelchair spaces are within the front half of the rows, further dispersion is not required. These seats are considered to be in a location that is better than 50 percent of the general seating. Due to the greater variety of viewing angles in stadium style movie projection theaters, this exception is not permitted for that particular type of seating arrangement.

(a)

(b)

FIGURE C802.10.2
BLEACHER SEATING EXAMPLES

802.10.3 Dispersion by Type. Where assembly seating has multiple distinct seating areas with amenities that differ from other distinct seating areas, wheelchair space locations shall be provided within each distinct seating area.

❖ Some venues offer a variety of types of seating; others venues have only one type of seats. Some examples would include a portion of the seating having back support and a portion that has no back support, or areas with reserved seating and areas with open seating, areas that have food or drink services available and areas that do not have such services. This provision is not meant to imply anything other than either the physical characteristics of the seats or the level of service provided.

802.10.4 Spaces Utilized Primarily for Viewing Motion Picture Projections. In spaces utilized primarily for viewing motion picture projections, wheelchair space locations shall comply with Section 802.10.4.

❖ Most theaters designed in recent decades for viewing motion pictures have been designed using a tiered seating arrangement called "stadium style." A limited number still include the older style sloped floor seating, sometimes in rows in front of the stadium style seating. The intent of this stadium style is to allow for a more unobstructed view of the movie screen. Although viewing angles differ greatly in this type of venue, the main idea is that for stadium style seating, the best seats are in about the middle of the seating. The best seats in an older style low-sloped floor seating would include the rear of the seating because of the better viewing angle relationship to the screen.

The average movie theater being constructed today is typically between 150 and 300 seats. Multiplex style theaters may have one or more larger auditoriums with between 300 and 500 seats.

802.10.4.1 Spaces with Seating on Risers. Where tiered seating is provided, wheelchair space locations shall be integrated into the tiered seating area.

❖ When stadium style seating is provided, at least some of the wheelchair spaces must be integrated into the tiers. If sloped seating is also provided, some of the wheelchair spaces may be located in the sloped seating if they also comply with the minimum distance from the screen indicated in Section 802.10.4.2.

802.10.4.2 Distance from the Screen. Wheelchair space locations shall be located within the rear 60 percent of the seats provided.

❖ Because viewing angles are different for a screen on a wall versus a three-dimensional event on a stage or playing field, there are specific criteria for wheelchair space locations to be further back from the screen. The intent is for a person using a wheelchair to view the screen in a location that has desirable viewing angles that minimize head movement in order to see the full screen. Wheelchair spaces located in the front of the movie seating rows would have steeper vertical viewing angles compared to seats in the rear of the movie seating rows. This provision requires that the wheelchair spaces be located in the more desirable seating of the theater. It would prohibit locating wheelchair spaces where viewing angles are too acute, which is especially important for those having limited range of head movement.

The requirement for variety of distances from the event is forgiven by Exception 2 of Section 802.10.2 for movie theaters with no more than 300 seats; however, all of the wheelchair space locations must be located in the rear 60 percent of the seats. Movie theaters having more than 300 seats are required to vertically disperse wheelchair space locations, all of which must still be located in the rear 60 percent of the seats.

When designing these types of facilities, it is important to consider the accessible route requirements for both ingress and egress from the wheelchair spaces. Access to the tiered seating, along with the exit dispersion requirements for safe evacuation found in the building codes, must be considered together.

803 Dressing, Fitting, and Locker Rooms

❖ The intent of this section is to provide requirements that allow a person using a mobility aid to have the ability to change clothes. Examples of these types of facilities include, but are not limited to, dressing or fitting rooms in clothing retailers; dressing rooms or locker rooms in sports recreational facilities including swimming pools; and locker rooms where staff persons change from street clothes to uniforms. Spaces that provide self-storage lockers, such as at a bus depot or museum, must meet the provisions for lockers in Section 905, but not the locker room provisions of this section [see Commentary Figures C803(a) and C803(b)].

FIGURE C803(a)
LOCKER AREA

FIGURE C803(b)
LOCKER ROOM

Dressing rooms in theaters may also need to comply with work station or work surface requirements found in the scoping documents and Section 902.

Small dressing areas are often provided immediately in front of individual shower stalls in facilities such as community pools or health clubs. Although not true dressing rooms, these are changing areas [see Commentary Figure C803(c) and C803.1].

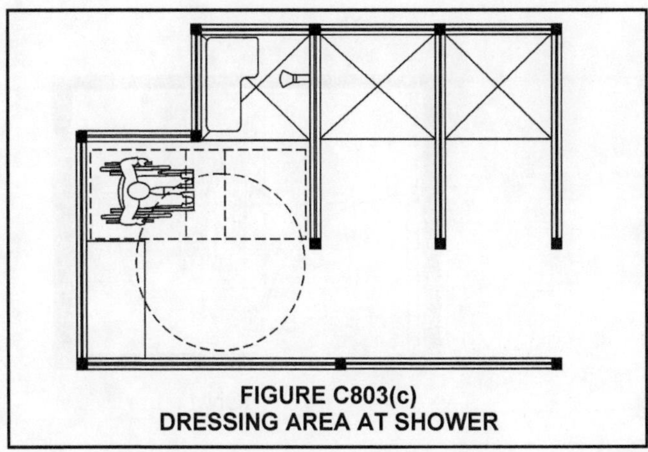

FIGURE C803(c)
DRESSING AREA AT SHOWER

803.1 General. Accessible dressing, fitting, and locker rooms shall comply with Section 803.

❖ When required to be accessible, all of these facilities must be located on an accessible route and have doors, clear floor space and operable parts that meet the requirements established and discussed in the following sections. Benches are also required within the rooms (see Commentary Figure C803.1).

803.2 Turning Space. A turning space complying with Section 304 shall be provided within the room.

❖ A 60-inch-diameter (1525 mm) turning circle or a 60-inch T-turn space is required somewhere within the dressing, fitting or locker room. This section does not require individual dressing or fitting rooms to be provided; however, when they are provided, the turning space must be available within the accessible changing room. When an open multiple occupant room is provided, such as a locker room, the turning space can be anywhere in the general room space. One side of the turning space can use the toe clearances under the bench required in Section 803.4 (see Commentary Figure C803.1).

803.3 Door Swing. Doors shall not swing into the room unless a clear floor space complying with Section 305.3 is provided within the room, beyond the arc of the door swing.

❖ When a door opens into a single-user room or space, sufficient maneuvering space must be provided within the room for a person using a wheelchair to enter the room and close the door, use the facilities, and then be able to reopen the door and exit without undue difficulty.

The door swing may encroach into a clear floor space within a room or space because it is assumed that no one will be using the facility while the door is being opened. If a 30-inch by 48-inch (760 by 1220 mm) clear floor space is provided beyond the arc of the door swing, this will allow a person using a wheelchair to enter the room and close the door. Once the door is closed, the turning space required in Section 803.2 provides sufficient maneuvering space within the room for a person using a wheelchair to use the fixtures, reopen the door and exit without undue difficulty. This is consistent with the single occupant bathroom provisions in Section 603.2.2, Exception 2 (see Commentary Figure C803.1).

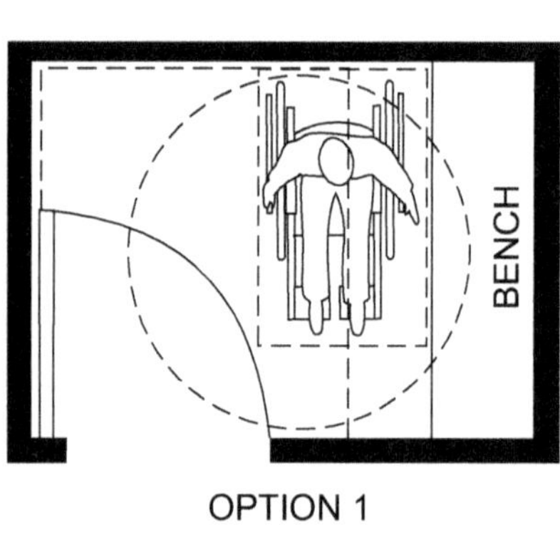

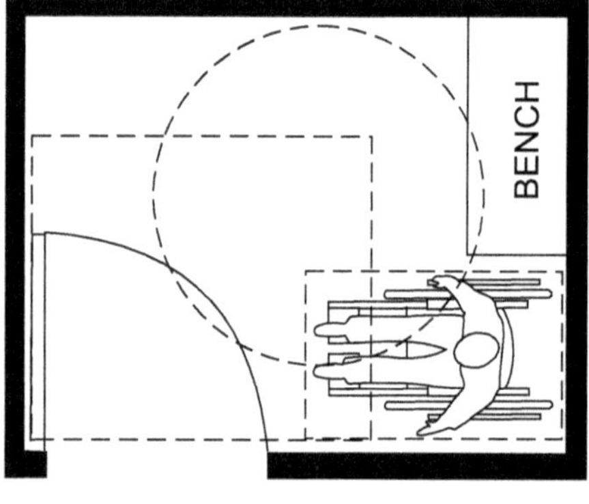

- TURNING SPACE CAN USE TOE CLEARANCE UNDER BENCH
- DOOR CAN SWING OVER TURNING SPACE IF A 30 IN. x 48 IN. WHEELCHAIR SPACE IS AVAILABLE PAST THE DOOR SWING
- BENCH REQUIREMENTS IN SECTION 903

**FIGURE C803.1
DRESSING ROOM**

803.4 Benches. A bench complying with Section 903 shall be provided within the room.

❖ In areas such as dressing rooms and locker rooms, where people may need to get out of their wheelchair to dress or undress, an accessible bench is required.

When common access lockers are provided along a wall for temporary storage, a bench is not required because this situation is not considered a locker room. An example is storage lockers for bags or purses available to the public in a museum or bus station.

Accessible benches must be mounted against a wall to provide a stable surface to lean against or to provide back support (see Section 903). When considering the relationship of clear floor space to the bench, a primary consideration is transfer between a wheelchair and the bench. This can be accomplished by one of two ways. One, by placing the wheelchair at the end of the bench, allowing side transfer between two seats that face the same direction. For an ideal side transfer, the clear floor space would extend beyond the wall at the back of the bench so that the wheelchair seat and the bench seat align. Alternatively, a bench with a back support could be provided where a transfer space with seat alignment would be available. It is important to recognize that an armrest at the ends of bench is a barrier for side transfer from an end. Secondly, placing the wheelchair in front and parallel to a bench allows a person to slide sdeways onto the front of the bench. If the bench is located across the width of the dressing room, the bench needs to be at least 60 inches (1525 mm) long due to the alcove provisions in Section 305.7. This extra length allows for someone to position their chair so they could slide onto the bench from the side that works best for them (see Commentary Figure C803.1 for both options).

In a locker room, the accessible bench should be located so that transfer to the bench is not necessary for access to an accessible locker. An accessible locker need not be within the reach range for the bench, but it is more user friendly if they are close.

Providing a grab bar on a side wall would exceed code requirements and possibly aid transfer to the bench; however, a grab bar should not be provided over the back of the bench [see Commentary Figure 903.2(b)]. A grab bar on the rear wall would cause a problem with using the wall for back support.

803.5 Coat Hooks and Shelves. Accessible coat hooks provided within the room shall accommodate a forward reach or side reach complying with Section 308. Where provided, a shelf shall be 40 inches (1015 mm) minimum and 48 inches (1220 mm) maximum above the floor.

❖ Where coat hooks are provided in accessible locker rooms, dressing rooms and fitting rooms, the hooks may be accessed using either a forward approach or a parallel approach with the appropriate clear floor or ground space. Coat hooks located near or above obstructions must comply with the reach range requirements described in Section 308. The type of obstruction that must be overcome will determine the maximum allowable mounting height of coat hooks.

The location of the bench in the space (Section 803.4) should be taken into account in the design of the room. When items are hung on the coat hook, they should not obstruct the bench. Although not required, it would be more user friendly to locate at least one hook within reach of the bench so that it could be used while changing.

Fold down shelves are permitted in fitting and dressing rooms. This is typically the type of shelf used to hold a purse or bag, similar to those found in toilet stalls. The provisions in this section are intended to establish the mounting height only. A fold down shelf in the down position may overlap, but should not obstruct any of the required accessible provisions, such as clear floor space, wheelchair turning space, or the area over the bench. Fold down shelves must be designed and constructed to support the live loads for the anticipated use of the shelf. Fixed shelves or fold down shelves may be provided at other heights if they do not overlap or obstruct the required clearances for the accessible elements. If a fold down shelf is intended to serve as a working surface (e.g., baby changing table), Section 902 is applicable.

804 Kitchens and Kitchenettes

❖ The intent of this section is to provide technical requirements for full kitchens and kitchenettes that are in shared spaces. Examples of shared kitchens are those within community buildings or some congregate residences where residents may prepare their own food, such as in dormitories or group homes. Requirements for kitchens associated with Accessible dwelling or sleeping units reference this section from Section 1002.12.

Kitchenettes, even though they do have elements similar to kitchens, do not include a stove, cooktop or range. Kitchenettes may also be referred to as wet bars or coffee counters. These types of facilities are common in offices or employee lounge areas. The food preparation and cleanup chores in these types of facilities are minimal; therefore, specific requirements for kitchenettes are addressed throughout this section by exceptions (see Commentary Figure C804).

FIGURE C804
EXAMPLE OF KITCHENETTE

Commercial kitchens are addressed as employee work areas and specifically addressed as such in scoping requirements. Kitchens that are part of Type A and Type B dwelling units are specifically addressed in Chapter 10.

Note that there are no requirements for kitchens to comply with Section 905 for accessible storage elements. If upper cabinets were required to be within reach range, the counter would not have enough vertical clearance for many of the small appliances, such as coffee makers. The bottom shelf of base cabinets is outside of the reach range. Basically, the requirements for access to appliances (Section 804.5) and clearances in the kitchen allow a person to at least get adjacent to most of the cabinets in the kitchen, as well as leaving storage options open for standing persons that are sharing the same kitchen. To improve access to kitchen storage areas, a designer could include additional drawers, slide out shelving or lazy susans in lower cabinets or pantry cabinets.

804.1 General. Accessible kitchens and kitchenettes shall comply with Section 804.

❖ The design of kitchens usable by a person with a disability demands careful consideration and thoughtful planning. Careful location of appliances, plumbing fixtures and cabinetry is essential to achieve the required maneuvering clearances and clear floor spaces that are required in the necessary functions in an accessible and functional kitchen. Careful design will produce a kitchen that provides an accessible and functionally efficient kitchen that is easily usable by a person with a disability or mobility impairment, as well as an able-bodied person.

Although not as complicated as a full kitchen design, accessible kitchenettes should be designed so that they are useable by persons with or without mobility impairments.

804.2 Clearance. Where a pass-through kitchen is provided, clearances shall comply with Section 804.2.1. Where a U-shaped kitchen is provided, clearances shall comply with Section 804.2.2.

EXCEPTION: Spaces that do not provide a cooktop or conventional range shall not be required to comply with Section 804.2 provided there is a 40-inch (1015 mm) minimum clearance between all opposing base cabinets, counter tops, appliances, or walls within work areas.

❖ Kitchens include requirements for clearances between cabinets or appliances; the clearance requirements in referenced Sections 804.2.1 and 804.2.2 are different because the two floor plan types are unique and require different types of spaces for maneuvering. The difference in the arrangement of fixtures and appliances also creates a different set of requirements for access into and egress from each kitchen type.

The exception is meant to exempt kitchenettes and wet bars from the pass through and clearance requirements for kitchens. Since the assumption is that kitchenettes are not used for heavy duty food preparation or the associated clean-up, the user clearance is 40 inches (1015 mm) minimum, even if the area is confined with walls.

It is not the intent of these provisions to prohibit other types of kitchen layouts, such as L-shaped or kitchens with islands. If other layouts are used, the key considerations would be maneuvering for access to appliances, the sink and the work surface.

804.2.1 Pass-through Kitchens. In pass-through kitchens where counters, appliances or cabinets are on two opposing sides, or where counters, appliances or cabinets are opposite a parallel wall, clearance between all opposing base cabinets, counter tops, appliances, or walls within kitchen work areas shall be 40 inches (1015 mm) minimum. Pass-through kitchens shall have two entries.

❖ Pass-through kitchens are typically laid out with all the appliances, counters and sink in straight lines. The appliances and fixtures can be located along one side of the kitchen, or they can be located along both sides of the kitchen. A pass-through kitchen must be open on both ends. If the pass-through kitchen is enclosed at one end by a wall or counter, the kitchen is then considered to be a U-shaped kitchen and must comply with the provisions in Section 804.2.2. The clearances in this section are the clear open space between the faces of opposing cabinets and/or appliances or a wall opposite the cabinet/appliances (see Figure 804.2.1).

The need for a turning space in a pass-through kitchen is not intended to increase the 40-inch (1015 mm) width between opposing cabinets. The knee and toe clearances under the work surface (Section 804.3) or the sink (Section 804.4) may be used to provide the turning space within the kitchen. In most pass-through designs, a turning space is also available beyond each end of the kitchen.

804.2.2 U-Shaped Kitchens. In kitchens enclosed on three contiguous sides, clearance between all opposing base cabinets, countertops, appliances, or walls within kitchen work areas shall be 60 inches (1525 mm) minimum.

❖ U-shaped kitchens are kitchens with cabinets and appliances on three contiguous sides. In such an arrangement, 60-inch (1525 mm) clearance is required between the faces of opposing cabinets and appliances to make all sides usable (see Figure 804.2.2).

Galley-style kitchens with cabinets/counters on two opposing sides of a walking path and a wall at one end are considered U-shaped kitchens and require a 60-inch (1525 mm) minimum clear space.

804.3 Work Surface. At least one work surface shall be provided in accordance with Section 902.

EXCEPTION: Spaces that do not provide a cooktop or conventional range shall not be required to provide an accessible work surface.

❖ An accessible work surface is a critical component of a kitchen for wheelchair users. Without an accessible work surface, many of the tasks necessary for preparing a meal, such as mixing, chopping, cutting and cleaning become very difficult, and for some wheelchair users, routine tasks may even become impossible. Sections 804.5.5.2 and 804.5.5.3 require an accessible work surface immediately adjacent to the oven. It is not the intent of this provision to require all work surfaces in the kitchen to meet Section 902. See the commentary in Section 902 for technical requirements.

If the space under the work surface is to be used for a wheelchair turning space, the minimum width of the clearance will be 36 inches (915 mm) instead of 30 inches (760 mm) (see Section 304.3.2 and Commentary Figure C804.3).

The intent of the exception is to allow kitchenettes and wet bars to not include accessible work surfaces because major food preparation or clean-up is not expected in these areas.

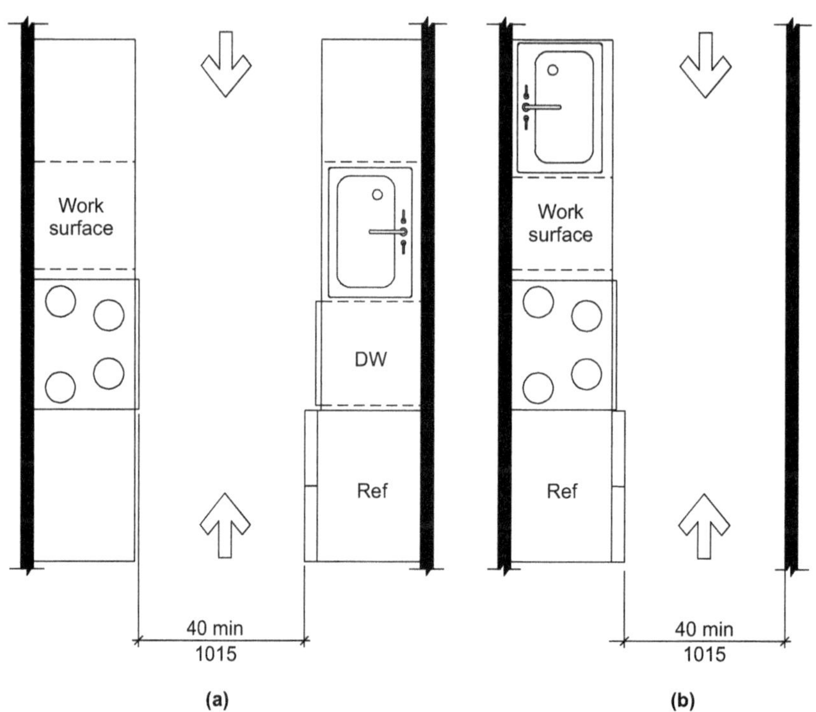

FIGURE 804.2.1
PASS-THROUGH KITCHEN CLEARANCE

804.4 Sinks. The sink shall comply with Section 606.

❖ Sinks in kitchens shall have knee and toe clearances that allow for a front approach (including protection from the pipes), a maximum rim height of 34 inches (865 mm), and faucets that meet operable parts requirements. If a double bowl sink is installed, these requirements can be applied to only one bowl. This allows for the second bowl to be deeper or to include a garbage disposal (see Commentary Figure C804.4).

If the space under the sink is to be used for a wheelchair turning space, the minimum width of the clearance will be 36 inches (915 mm) instead of 30 inches (760 mm) (see Section 304.3.2).

Per Section 606.2, Exception 1, a side approach is a permitted alternative for sinks in kitchenettes. The sink must still meet the 34-inch (760 mm) maximum rim height provisions and have faucets that meet operable parts provisions (see Commentary Figure C804).

804.5 Appliances. Where provided, kitchen appliances shall comply with Section 804.5.

❖ Any kitchen appliance installed should meet the general requirements for clear floor space (Section 804.5.1), and any controls must be within reach range and meet operable parts provisions (Section 804.5.2). If the appliance has a door that opens for operation, the door may overlap, but not obstruct, the clear floor space. Additional provisions are included for dishwashers, ranges, cooktops, ovens and refrigerator/freezers (Sections 804.5.3 through 804.5.6).

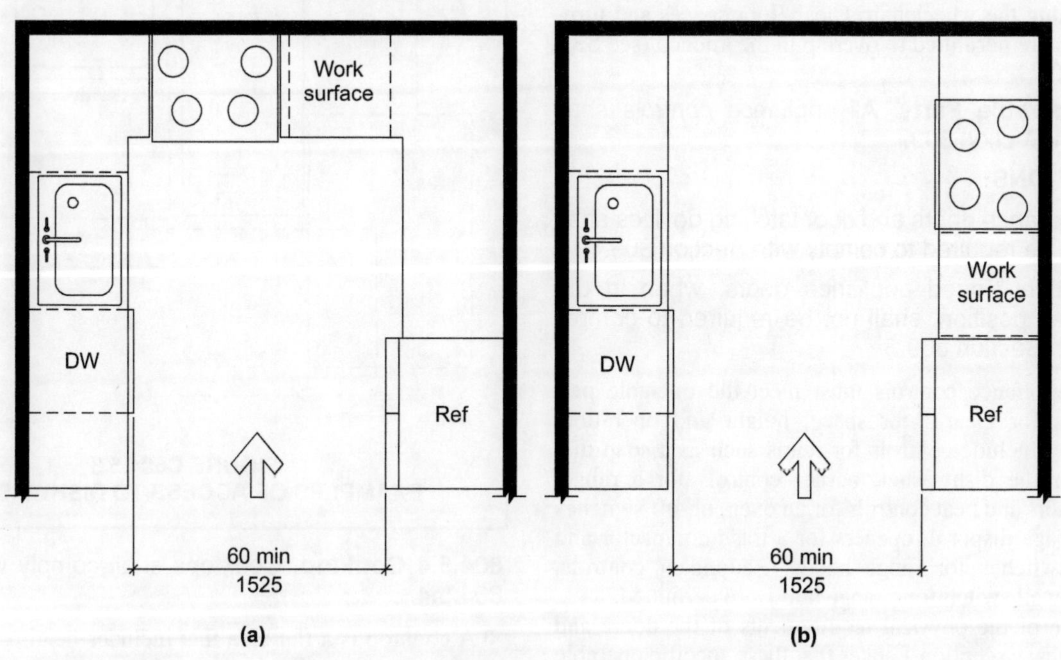

FIGURE C804.2.2
U-SHAPED KITCHEN CLEARANCE

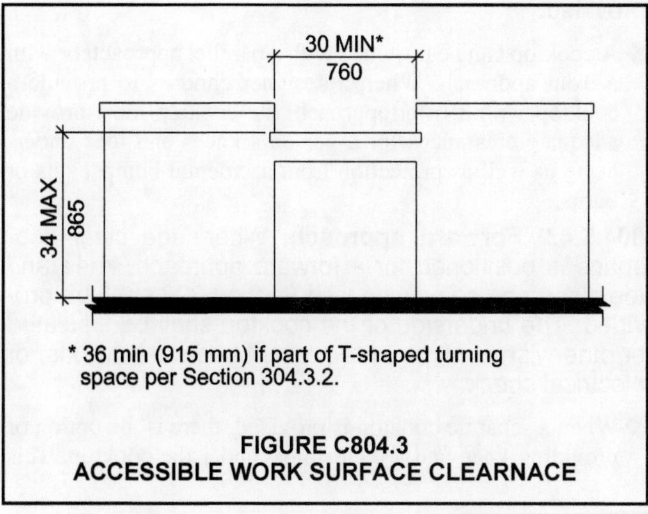

FIGURE C804.3
ACCESSIBLE WORK SURFACE CLEARNACE

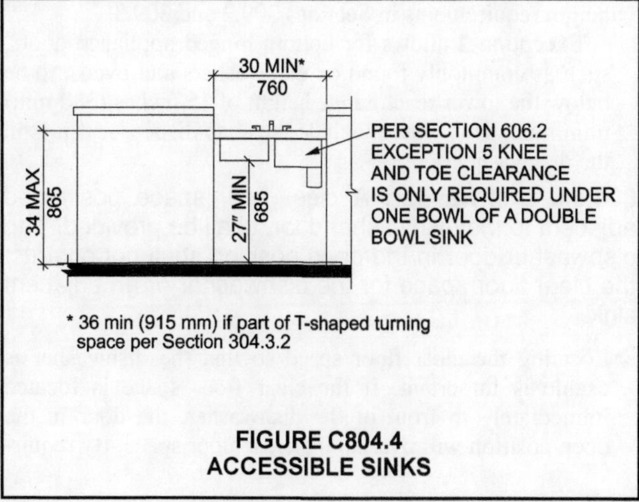

FIGURE C804.4
ACCESSIBLE SINKS

804.5.1 Clear Floor Space. A clear floor space complying with Section 305 shall be provided at each kitchen appliance.

❖ Unless provisions specific to a fixture or appliance are given in the following sections, a 30-inch by 48-inch (760 by 1220 mm) clear floor space must be provided that allows a forward or parallel approach to the appliance. It is important to plan the kitchen and clear floor spaces in consideration for the way a person in a wheelchair uses the fixture or appliance. For instance, the easiest way to use the burners on the top of a range from a wheelchair is by a parallel approach, although access to the oven portion of the range may be best from a different angle. It is also important to consider how these fixtures and appliances are used in conjunction with one another. To move items from an oven to a preparation area and then to a serving dish may require an adjacent counter surface to place the item while repositioning the wheelchair. Clear floor spaces and turning spaces are permitted to overlap in the kitchen (see Section 301.2).

804.5.2 Operable Parts. All appliance controls shall comply with Section 309.

EXCEPTIONS:

1. Appliance doors and door latching devices shall not be required to comply with Section 309.4.
2. Bottom-hinged appliance doors, when in the open position, shall not be required to comply with Section 309.3.

❖ Kitchen appliance controls must meet the operable part provisions for clear floor space, height and operation. These may include controls for items such as a soap dispenser for the dishwasher, burner controls for a range, lights, timers and heat controls for an oven, on-off switches for a garbage disposal, openers for a trash compactor and exhaust switches for range hoods. Redundant controls, such as a wall switch for a range hood, are permitted.

Because of the physical requirements of the doors and door latches, Exception 1 states that these specific operable parts are not required to meet the one-hand, no-tight-pinching/grasping and the 5-pound (22 N) maximum force requirements in Section 309.4 for operable parts. Doors and door latches do have to meet the clear floor space and height requirements in Sections 309.2 and 309.3.

Exception 2 allows for bottom hinged appliance doors, such as commonly found on dishwashers and ovens, to be below the lower reach range height of 15 inches (380 mm) minimum. This would include the soap dispenser if it is in the dishwasher door.

804.5.3 Dishwasher. A clear floor space positioned adjacent to the dishwasher door, shall be provided. The dishwasher door in the open position shall not obstruct the clear floor space for the dishwasher or an adjacent sink.

❖ Locating the clear floor space so that the dishwasher is usable is important. If the clear floor space is located immediately in front of the dishwasher, the door in the open position will overlap the clear floor space. By requiring that the clear floor space not be obstructed by the dishwasher door, either the clear floor space must be located past the door, or the door could overlap the toe clearance when a minimum of 9 inches (225 mm) clearance under the open door is provided. It is important to locate the clear floor space so the dishwasher can be easily loaded and unloaded. Often, it is desirable to load the dishwasher from the sink area; therefore, it may be helpful to locate the sink and dishwasher adjacent to each other. Where a dishwasher is located adjacent to the clear floor space for a sink, the single clear floor space can be used to serve both the sink and the dishwasher (see Commentary Figure C804.5.3).

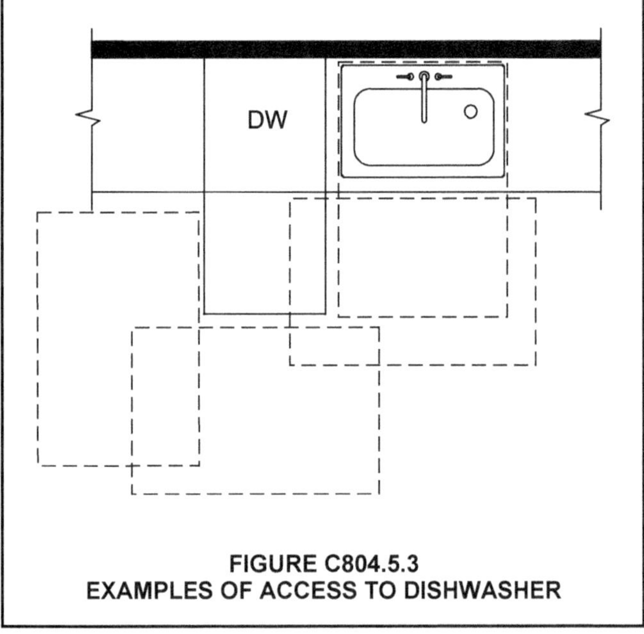

FIGURE C804.5.3
EXAMPLES OF ACCESS TO DISHWASHER

804.5.4 Cooktop. Cooktops shall comply with Section 804.5.4.

❖ A cooktop is a flat area that includes heating elements for preparing food. Cooktops can be electric, gas or induction. A cooktop can be separate, or the top part of a range.

804.5.4.1 Approach. A clear floor space, positioned for a parallel or forward approach to the cooktop, shall be provided.

❖ A cooktop can be provided with a parallel approach or with a front approach. When a designer chooses to provide a cooktop with a front approach, the cooktop must provide adequate clearances for a person's knees and toes underneath as well as protection from accidental bumps, cuts or burns.

804.5.4.2 Forward approach. Where the clear floor space is positioned for a forward approach, knee and toe clearance complying with Section 306 shall be provided. The underside of the cooktop shall be insulated or otherwise configured to prevent burns, abrasions, or electrical shock.

❖ When a separate cooktop is provided, there is the option of providing knee and toe clearance under the cooktop. This makes it easier for someone using a wheelchair to access the pots and pans on burners and keep an eye on what they are cooking. Since the cooktop can get very hot, there is a requirement for some type of heat shielding from the underside of the appliance.

If the forward approach option is chosen, this space cannot count as the required accessible work surface in the kitchen (see Sections 804.3 and 804.6.5).

804.5.4.3 Parallel approach. Where the clear floor space is positioned for a parallel approach, the clear floor space shall be centered on the appliance.

❖ A parallel approach is typically used when a cooktop has a cabinet or oven below, or it is part of a range (see Commentary Figure C804.5.4.3). The centering allows for someone to reach all the burners, regardless of the direction of approach.

804.5.4.4 Controls. The location of controls shall not require reaching across burners.

❖ To reduce the chance of accidental scalding or burns, access to controls for the burners on either a cooktop or range must not require reaching across burners. Controls can be provided on the front, center or side of the burners. Access to controls for the oven that is part of the range must also be located so that a person using the range does not have to reach across burners to access the oven controls (Section 804.5.5.4).

804.5.5 Oven. Ovens shall comply with Section 804.5.5.

❖ Ovens may be part of a range, or they may be the built-in wall type. Usability of the oven must be considered when choosing placement and options. Wall mounted ovens may provide better access in an accessible kitchen because the height makes access easier for persons using wheelchairs. A person would not have to reach both down and over the door to reach the rack or item in the oven. Although most standard wall ovens come with a bottom hinged door, some manufacturers are starting to offer microwave/oven combinations with a side swing door or oven racks that pull out all the way without tilting.

804.5.5.1 Clear floor space. A clear floor space shall be provided. The oven door in the open position shall not obstruct the clear floor space for the oven.

❖ Locating the clear floor space so that the oven is usable is important. If the clear floor space is located immediately in front of the oven, the door in the open position will overlap the clear floor space. By requiring that the clear floor space not be obstructed by the oven door, either the clear floor space must be located past the door, or the door could overlap the toe clearance if there was a minimum of 9-inch (225 mm) clearance under the door when open. It is important to locate the clear floor space so the oven can be easily accessed for moving food in and out. Ranges must be able to meet the clearances for cooktops with the oven door shut, and the clearances for ovens with the oven door open (see Commentary Figure C804.5.4.3).

804.5.5.2 Side-Hinged Door Ovens. Side-hinged door ovens shall have a work surface complying with Section 804.3 positioned adjacent to the latch side of the oven door.

❖ If a side opening wall oven is chosen, to facilitate transfer of dishes into and out of the oven, the latch side should be adjacent to a counter space that also serves as an accessible work surface (Sections 804.3 and 902).

804.5.5.3 Bottom-Hinged Door Ovens. Bottom-hinged door ovens shall have a work surface complying with Section 804.3 positioned adjacent to one side of the door.

❖ If a bottom-hinged oven is chosen, to facilitate transfer of dishes into and out of the oven, an adjacent counter space that is also configured as an accessible work surface must be provided (Sections 804.3 and 902) (see Commentary Figure C804.5.4.3).

804.5.5.4 Controls. The location of controls shall not require reaching across burners.

❖ Access to oven controls that are part of a range must not require reaching across burners. Controls for wall ovens must be within reach ranges, 15 to 48 inches (380 to 1220 mm) in height.

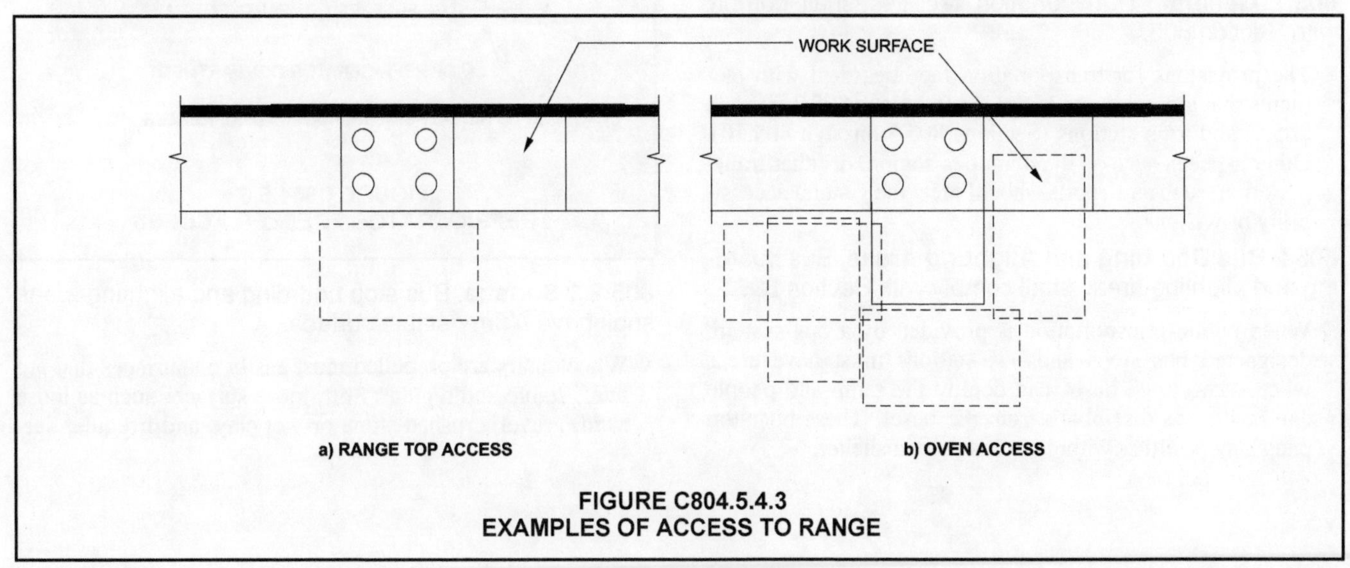

FIGURE C804.5.4.3
EXAMPLES OF ACCESS TO RANGE

804.5.6 Refrigerator/Freezer. Combination refrigerators and freezers shall have at least 50 percent of the freezer compartment shelves, including the bottom of the freezer, 54 inches (1370 mm) maximum above the floor when the shelves are installed at the maximum heights possible in the compartment. A clear floor space, positioned for a parallel approach to the refrigerator/freezer, shall be provided. The centerline of the clear floor space shall be offset 24 inches (610 mm) maximum from the centerline of the appliance.

❖ The position for the parallel approach to the refrigerator and freezer must consider how the person using a wheelchair will access the interior with the door open (see Commentary Figure C804.5.6).

Refrigerator/freezer choices can have the freezer on the top, on the bottom or side by side. If a top freezer option is chosen, a freezer with the bottom of the compartment at a maximum of 54 inches (1370 mm) above the ground (assuming one shelf in the freezer) will meet the freezer compartment requirements. If a bottom freezer option is chosen, at least one shelf in the freezer compartment should be 15 inches (380 mm) minimum above the floor. Side-by-side refrigerator/freezers provide the most usable freezer compartment; however, clear floor spaces for both sides must be provided for the unit. Locating refrigerators so the doors swing back 180 degrees (3.1 rad) can provide greater accessibility for a person using a wheelchair. Although not specifically mentioned, if a refrigerator has ice or water provided through the door, or inside the appliance, that feature is considered part of the refrigerator/freezer. Therefore, those elements must also have a clear floor space for access and meet reach range and operable parts requirements.

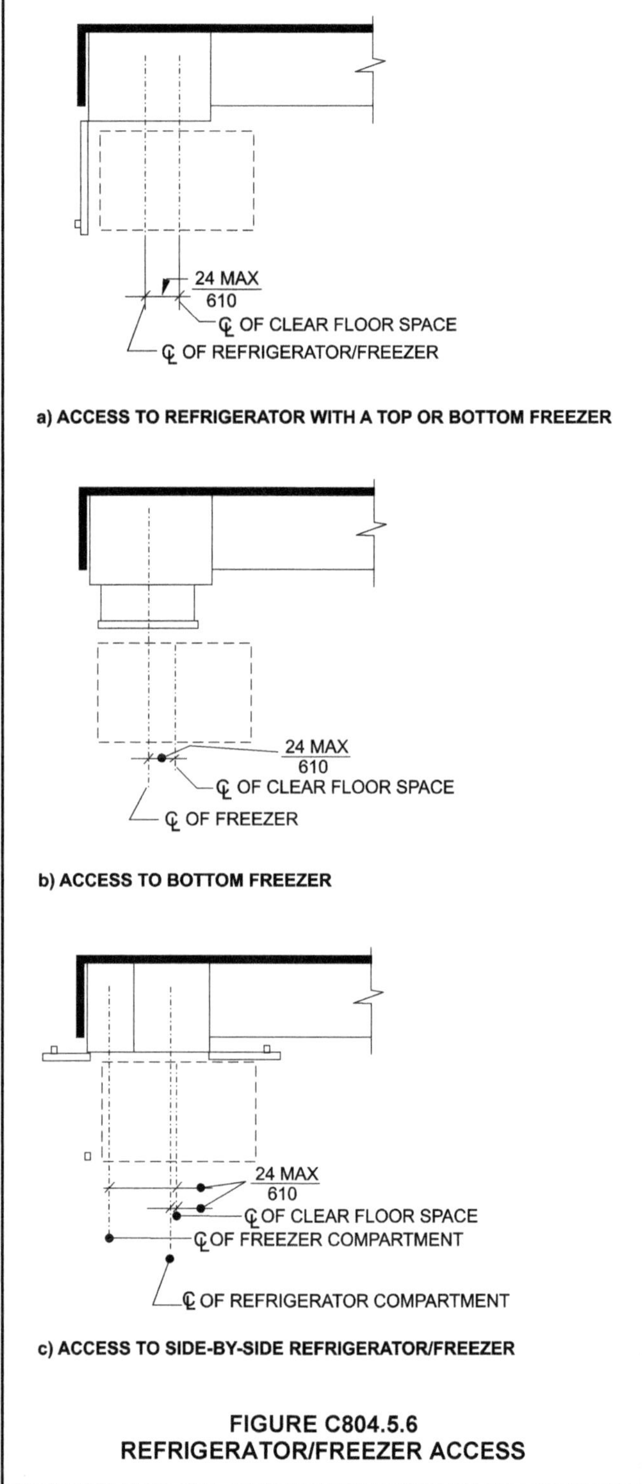

FIGURE C804.5.6
REFRIGERATOR/FREEZER ACCESS

805 Transportation Facilities

❖ Access to transportation facilities is essential for persons with disabilities, not only for reasons of equivalent access, but also because many people with disabilities cannot drive or cannot afford special converted vehicles. They rely on public transportation to get everywhere.

805.1 General. Transportation facilities shall comply with Section 805.

❖ The provisions for transportation facilities deal with elements that are unique to bus stops (Sections 805.2 through 805.4) and train stations (Sections 805.5 through 805.10). Other aspects, such as the main bus station, or other transportation, such as airports, should meet the general accessibility provisions.

805.2 Bus Boarding and Alighting Areas. Bus boarding and alighting areas shall comply with Section 805.2.

❖ When public transportation is provided by a bus system, designated bus stops and bus stations must have areas where "kneeling" buses can deploy the ramp and people can board and disembark from the buses. These bus stop pads may be either within or outside of a shelter.

805.2.1 Surface. Bus stop boarding and alighting areas shall have a firm, stable surface.

❖ Wheelchairs are propelled most easily on surfaces that are hard, stable and regular. Soft, loose surfaces such as loose sand, gravel, crushed stone or wet clay, and irregular surfaces such as cobblestone, significantly impede movement of a wheelchair.

A stable surface is one that remains unchanged by contaminants or applied force, so that when the contaminant or force is removed, the surface returns to its original condition. A firm surface resists deformation by either indentation or particles moving on its surface. It is not the intent of the standard to require only paved surfaces; however, any other type (e.g., wood chips, gravel) would need to be evaluated.

805.2.2 Dimensions. Bus stop boarding and alighting areas shall have a 96-inch (2440 mm) minimum clear length, measured perpendicular to the curb or vehicle roadway edge, and a 60-inch (1525 mm) minimum clear width, measured parallel to the vehicle roadway.

❖ The size of the area for the bus stop pad would allow adequate space for the kneeling bus ramp to deploy and the person using the wheelchair or scooter to board or disembark from the bus (see Figure 805.2.2 and Commentary Figure C805.2.2).

805.2.3 Slope. The slope of the bus stop boarding and alighting area parallel to the vehicle roadway shall be the same as the roadway, to the maximum extent practicable. The slope of the bus stop boarding and alighting area perpendicular to the vehicle roadway shall be 1:48 maximum.

❖ The bus stop pad should slope with the road in the direction of travel and level back from the road edge.

805.2.4 Connection. Bus stop boarding and alighting areas shall be connected to streets, sidewalks, or pedestrian paths by an accessible route complying with Section 402.

❖ An accessible route must be available to and from the bus stop pad.

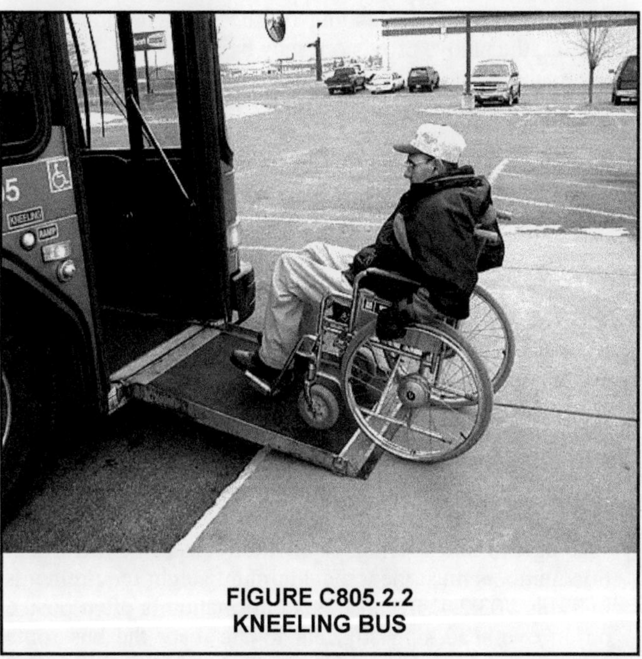

FIGURE C805.2.2
KNEELING BUS

805.3 Bus Shelters. Bus shelters shall provide a minimum clear floor space complying with Section 305 entirely within the shelter. Bus shelters shall be connected by an accessible route complying with Section

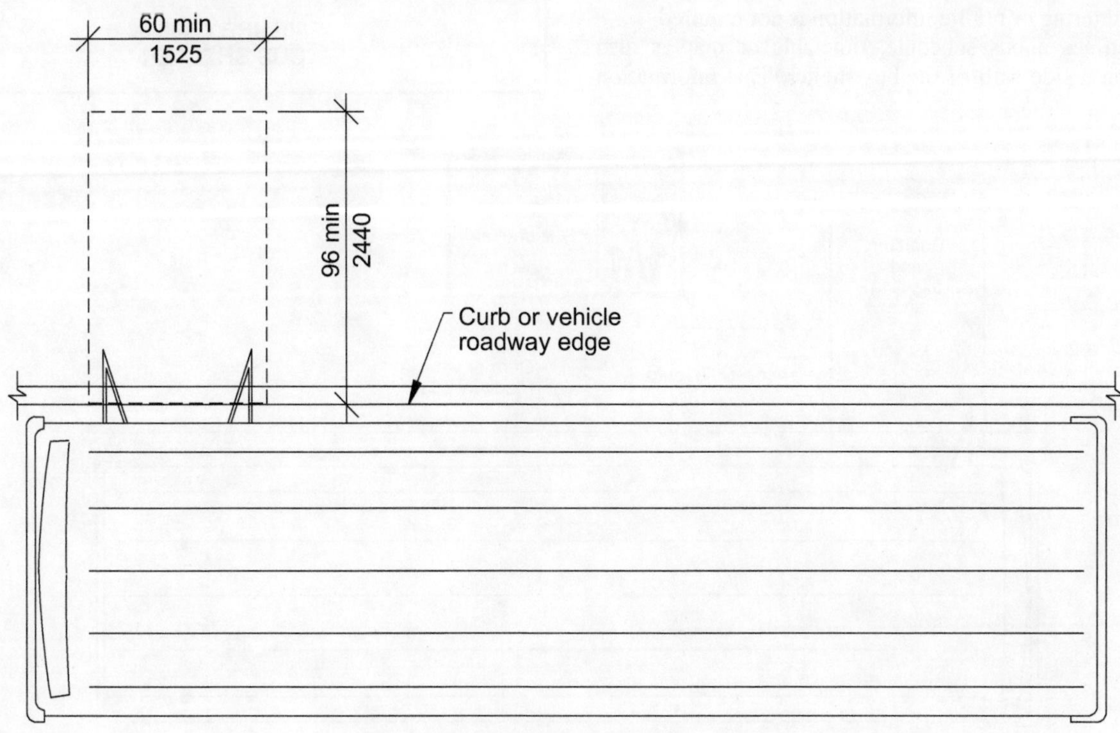

FIGURE 805.2.2
SIZE OF BUS BOARDING AND ALIGHTING AREA

402 to a boarding and alighting area complying with Section 805.2.

❖ Where bus shelters are provided, there must be within the bus shelter at least one 30-inch by 48-inch (762 by 1220 mm) clear floor space for people using wheelchairs or scooters to wait. Depending on the configuration of the shelter, the alcove provisions may be applicable. The waiting space in the bus shelter and the bus stop pad must be connected by an accessible route (see Figure 805.3 and Commentary Figure C805.3).

805.4 Bus Signs. Bus route identification signs shall have visual characters complying with Sections 703.2.2, 703.2.3, and 703.2.5 through 703.2.8. In addition, bus route identification numbers shall be visual characters complying with Section 703.2.4.

EXCEPTION: Bus schedules, timetables and maps that are posted at the bus stop or bus bay shall not be required to comply with Section 805.4.

❖ The intent is that bus route information should be made accessible to persons with vision impairments as much as possible. Route identification signs must meet the requirements for visual characters for case, style, character width, spacing and line spacing. In addition, bus route identification numbers must meet the minimum height requirements in Table 703.2.4. Because bus information is often posted on an overhead sign adjacent to the road, the bus route identification number will typically be over 2 inches (50 mm) in height. Although not listed as a requirement, high contrast and low glare requirements in Section 703.2.10 may be beneficial to make bus information readable. Another option would be a sign that complies with the variable message signage requirements in Section 703.7. Raised lettering or braille information is not required.

Sometimes a bus schedule, timetable or map is also posted on a side wall of the bus shelter. This information need not meet the visual signage requirements in this section.

805.5 Rail Platforms. Rail platforms shall comply with Section 805.5.

❖ Rail platforms may be elevated so that the edge of the platform lines up with the floor of the rail car. To provide open access to the cars, there are no guards provided along this edge. The requirements for slope and detectable warnings

FIGURE C805.3
BUS SHELTER

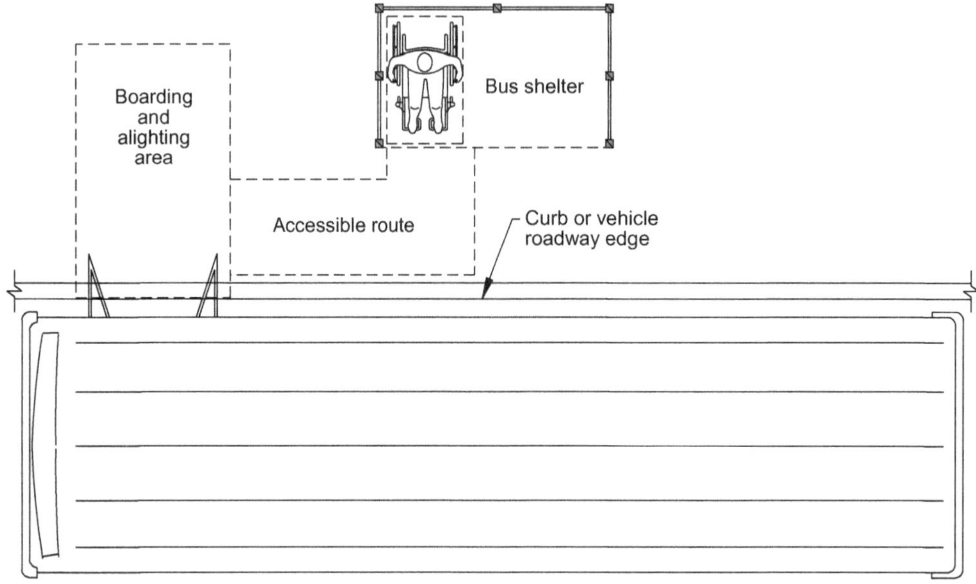

FIGURE 805.3
BUS SHELTERS

in the subsections address safety concerns for this condition.

805.5.1 Slope. Rail platforms shall not exceed a slope of 1:48 in all directions.

EXCEPTION: Where platforms serve vehicles operating on existing track or track laid in existing roadway, the slope of the platform parallel to the track shall be permitted to be equal to the slope (grade) of the roadway or existing track.

❖ So that a person using a mobility device does not have to deal with a slope while on a train platform or while entering or exiting the cars, the platform must be basically level.

The exception allows for existing train systems to remain in operation even if they cannot meet the current provisions for level platforms as long as the platform matches the slope of the rails.

805.5.2 Detectable Warnings. Platform boarding edges not protected by platform screens or guards shall have a detectable warning complying with Section 705.

❖ Detectable warnings along the edge of the platform will alert persons with visual impairments of the edge of the platform. This is also a good safety feature that helps keep passengers from standing too close to the edge (see Commentary Figure C805.5.2).

FIGURE C805.5.2
PLATFORM EDGE

805.6 Rail Station Signs. Rail station signs shall comply with Section 805.6.

EXCEPTION: Signs shall not be required to comply with Sections 805.6.1 and 805.6.2 where audible signs are remotely transmitted to hand-held receivers, or are user- or proximity-actuated.

❖ It is important that information designating stations and routes be available for persons with visual impairments. Another option would be a sign that complies with the variable message signage requirements in Section 703.7. This section does not require signage, but requires equivalent access to the information when signage is provided.

The exception allows for new technology available for persons with visual impairments.

Emerging technologies such as an audible sign system using infrared transmitters and receivers may provide greater accessibility in the transit environment than traditional braille and raised letter signs. The transmitters are placed on or next to the print signs and transmit their information to an infrared receiver that is held by a person. By scanning an area, the person will hear the sign. This means that signs can be placed well out of reach of braille readers, even on parapet walls and on walls beyond barriers. Additionally, such signs can be used to provide a way of finding information that cannot be efficiently conveyed on braille signs.

805.6.1 Entrances. Where signs identify a station or a station entrance, at least one sign with raised characters and braille complying with Sections 703.3 and 703.4 shall be provided at each entrance.

❖ At each signed entrance to a station, a sign adjacent to that entrance with both raised letters and braille shall also be provided.

805.6.2 Routes and Destinations. Lists of stations, routes and destinations served by the station that are located on boarding areas, platforms, or mezzanines shall have visual characters complying with Section 703.2. A minimum of one sign with raised characters and braille complying with Sections 703.3 and 703.4 shall be provided on each platform or boarding area to identify the specific station.

EXCEPTION: Where sign space is limited, characters shall not be required to exceed 3 inches (75 mm) in height.

❖ Route lists must meet the visual contrast, style and size requirements in Section 703.2. At least one sign with raised and braille characters must be provided on each platform to identify the station. Route maps need not comply with these signage requirements.

The exception is in recognition of limitations for location when a large amount of information must be provided at a high location. Table 703.2.4 requires that characters exceed 3 inches (75 mm) when the viewing distance is greater than 21 feet (6400 mm).

805.6.3 Station Names. Stations covered by this section shall have identification signs with visual characters complying with Section 703.2. The signs shall be clearly visible and within the sight lines of a standing or sitting passenger from within the vehicle on both sides when not obstructed by another vehicle.

❖ Train disembark location is important information for passengers. Signage on the platform indicating the name of the station must be visible to all passengers in the train cars. This may require several signs along the length of the platform.

805.7 Public Address Systems. Where public address systems convey audible information to the public, the same or equivalent information shall be provided in a visual format.

❖ When announcements are made regarding bus or train arrivals and departures, the same information must be available for persons with hearing impairments.

805.8 Clocks. Where clocks are provided for use by the public, the clock face shall be uncluttered so that its elements are clearly visible. Hands, numerals and digits shall contrast with the background either light-on-dark or dark-on-light. Where clocks are installed overhead, numerals and digits shall be visual characters complying with Section 703.2.

❖ Departures and arrivals from transportation facilities are controlled by timed schedules. To assist persons in getting to the right place at the right time, the time is often prominently displayed in the stations. The time display can be a standard clock face or digital. Whatever option is chosen, the display must meet the visual contrast, style and height for the characters. A clock face should also meet the visual contrast requirements and be free of any types of additional information or advertising.

805.9 Escalators. Where provided, escalators shall have a 32-inch (815mm) minimum clear width, and shall comply with Requirements 6.1.3.5.6-Step Demarcations, and 6.1.3.6.5-Flat Steps of ASME A17.1/CSA B44 listed in Section 105.2.5.

EXCEPTION: Existing escalators shall not be required to comply with Section 805.9.

❖ Even though escalators are not part of an accessible route for persons using wheelchairs or scooters, they may be usable by people with mobility impairments.

ASME A17.1 for safety for elevators also includes escalator provisions. ASME A17.1, Section 6.1.3.5.6, deals with the stripe along the front edge and side of each step. ASME A17.1, Section 6.1.3.6.5, deals with the required flat area at the top and bottom of the escalator. These requirements will help persons with vision and mobility impairments negotiate the escalators. New escalators in transportation facilities must provide a minimum clear width of 32 inches (815 mm).

805.10 Track Crossings. Where a circulation path crosses tracks, it shall comply with Section 402 and shall have a detectable warning 24 inches (610 mm) in depth complying with Section 705 extending the full width of the circulation path. The detectable warning surface shall be located so that the edge nearest the rail crossing is 6 foot (1830 mm) minimum and 15 foot (4570 mm) maximum from the centerline of the nearest rail.

EXCEPTION: Openings for wheel flanges shall be permitted to be $2^1/_2$ inches (64 mm) maximum.

❖ When a person with mobility impairments must cross over a track system, the rails may cause a problem. With the reference to the accessible route provisions in Section 402, the opening limitations (Section 302.3) and change in elevation (Section 303) are applicable. Therefore, the path must provide a surface level with the top of the rails, and the gap between the path and the sides of the rails must be limited to $^1/_2$ inch (13 mm) maximum.

In order for track crossings to be detectable by persons with vision impairments while they are still a safe distance away from the tracks, a detectable warnings shall be provided between 6 feet and 15 feet (1830 mm to 4570 mm) back from the tracks. This will allow enough room for a gate to move down for both pedestrians and cars when a train is approaching (see Commentary Figure C805.10).

The exception allows for the necessary additional clearance for wheel flanges at rails. In most rail systems, this $2^1/_2$-inch (63 mm) gap would be limited to the gap on the inside of the rails as indicated in Figure 805.10.

806 Holding Cells and Housing Cells

❖ The administrative authority will specify which holding cells and housing cells are required to be accessible.

Generally, for holding cells, the requirements are for one of each type at each location. For example, in a courthouse, there may be men's, women's and juvenile holding cells at a main entry level (e.g., different types) and lower capacity holding cells adjacent to the courtrooms where criminal cases are heard (e.g., different locations). At least one accessible cell must be provided to serve each courtroom

FIGURE 805.10
TRACK CROSSINGS

to avoid having to move the entire proceeding to accommodate a person who uses a wheelchair. If a pair of cells equally serve more than one courtroom, only one cell must be accessible.

Housing cells in jails may vary based on the security level within the facility or the need (e.g., daily housing, hospital cells, isolation cells). Because of security and safety concerns, Accessible cells must be available in each type, but can be grouped in the facility.

806.1 General. Holding cells and housing cells shall comply with Section 806.

❖ Persons may be incarcerated before, during and after a trial. Holding cells are used for short term incarcerations, and are those commonly found within police stations and in courthouses. Housing cells are used for more long term incarceration and are typically found in jails. Holding cells often have bench seating, and may include a water closet and lavatory within the cell. Housing cells often include a water closet, a lavatory and a bed within the cell, and may also include a shower, bench and working surface. The nature of the facility causes almost everything to be built-in when in high security situations (see Commentary Figure C806.1). Shared spaces available to Accessible jail housing cells must also be accessible. For example, if bathing facilities are provided in a common area, the bathing facility must be accessible.

Of concern are persons with mobility impairments (Section 806.2) as well as those with hearing impairments (Section 806.3).

FIGURE C806.1
ACCESSIBLE HOUSING CELL

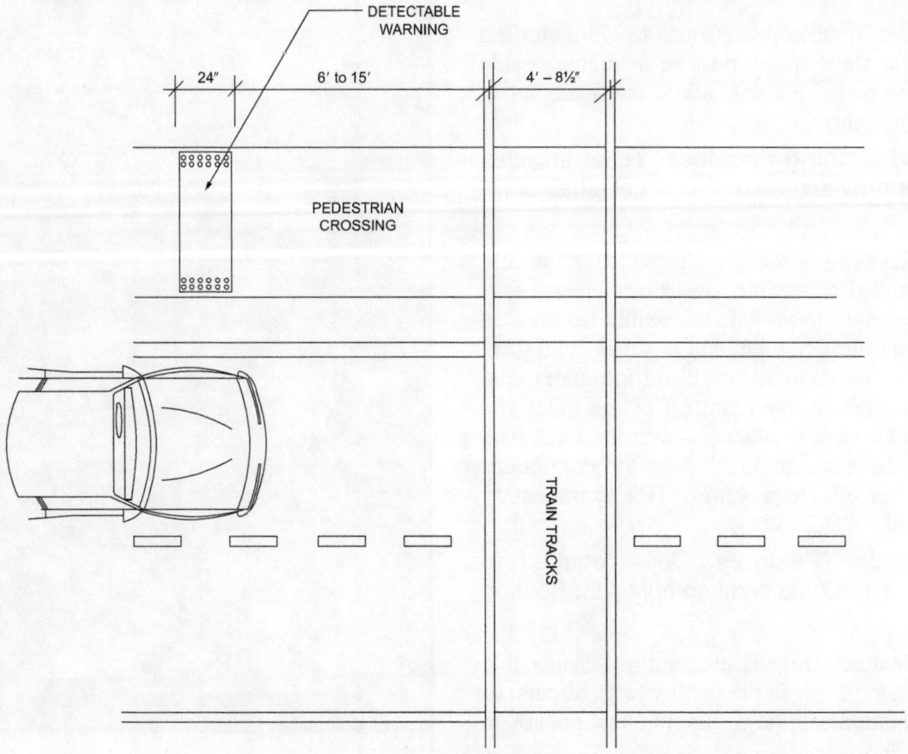

FIGURE C805.10
TRACK CROSSINGS AND TACTILE WARNINGS

806.2 Features for People Using Wheelchairs or Other Mobility Aids. Cells required to have features for people using wheelchairs or other mobility aids shall comply with Section 806.2.

❖ A person with mobility impairments may be using a wheelchair, scooter, walker or other type of mobility device. The cell must be designed so that a person can access and use all elements provided in the cell.

806.2.1 Turning Space. Turning space complying with Section 304 shall be provided within the cell.

❖ Either a 60-inch-diameter (525 mm) circle or a T-shaped turning space must be available within the cell. The turning space can use any knee and toe clearances available under the bed, bench, lavatory or work surfaces in the room. The door to the cell can be sliding or swing into or out of the cell. If the door swings into the cell, a 30-inch by 48-inch (760 by 1220 mm) clear floor space should be provided past the swing of the door, similar to the single occupant toilet room or dressing room.

806.2.2 Benches. Where benches are provided, at least one bench shall comply with Section 903.

❖ If a bench is provided within the cell, the bench must be either against a wall or provide back support. Technical criteria, including bench size and space for a transfer, are defined in Section 903.

806.2.3 Beds. Where beds are provided, clear floor space complying with Section 305 shall be provided on at least one side of the bed. The clear floor space shall be positioned for parallel approach to the side of the bed.

❖ If beds are provided in the cell, a 30-inch by 48-inch (760 by 1220 mm) clear floor space must be available beside and parallel to the bed. This will allow for someone to transfer into bed at night.

806.2.4 Toilet and Bathing Facilities. Toilet facilities or bathing facilities provided as part of a cell shall comply with Section 603.

❖ If a water closet, lavatory or shower is provided in the cell, it must be constructed accessible. Security concerns will dictate some alternatives to provide accessible features. In every instance, regardless of toilet and lavatory configuration, adequate space needs to be provided for inmates who use wheelchairs to transfer onto and off of the toilet and have knee and toe clearances under the lavatory. Grab bars may be constructed with an infill plate or continuous mounting bracket for suicide prevention (see Commentary Figures C604.5 and C806.2.4).

806.3 Communication Features. Cells required to have communication features shall comply with Section 806.3.

❖ Communication features in cells are those elements that impart information to people in the facility (e.g., alarms) or for persons to communicate (e.g., pay phones, phones at security glazing).

806.3.1 Alarms. Where audible emergency alarm systems are provided to serve the occupants of cells, visible alarms complying with Section 702 shall be provided.

EXCEPTION: In cells where inmates or detainees are not allowed independent means of egress, visible alarms shall not be required.

❖ The authority having jurisdiction determines when a general emergency alarm system is required throughout a building that contains housing or holding cells. If it is the intent for persons in cells to react or self-evacuate during an emergency situation, both audible and visible alarms must be provided so that they alert persons in the cells. The alarm system must be installed in accordance with NFPA 72. If security personnel dictate how and when persons in the cells will evacuate, the alarm system is not required to notify the cell residents.

806.3.2 Telephones. Where provided, telephones within cells shall have volume controls complying with Section 704.3.

❖ Pay phones may be available in some holding and housing cell areas. At a minimum, these phones must have the volume control requirements in Section 704.3. These phones may also need to meet the pay phone provisions in Section 704.

When phones are part of visitor areas with security glazing, all the phones must have a volume control in accordance with Section 704.3 (see Commentary Figure 806.3.2).

FIGURE C806.2.4
ACCESSIBLE HOUSING CELL TOILET AND LAVATORY

FIGURE C806.3.2
VISITOR AREA WITH PHONES

807 Courtrooms

❖ The sixth and seventh amendments in the Bill of Rights guarantee all Americans the right to a public trial and trial by a jury. To guarantee the rights of persons with disabilities, it is important that courthouses be accessible. Minimal requirements for the courtrooms are addressed in this section.

Courtrooms are unique spaces. Historically, the judge's bench is raised for reasons of decorum. Today there is also the issue of safety for the judge in situations where the parties in the courtroom may become agitated to the point of violence. Once the judge is elevated, other portions of the courtroom are also raised to facilitate interaction between the judge and the courthouse staff, as well as to provide important lines of sight among participants. As a result, providing adequate access to all areas of a courtroom can be a challenge.

Scoping provisions in the building code typically require approach, entry and exit for employee work areas. In the situation of employee work areas in courtrooms, the vertical portion of the accessible route can be planned for future installation, rather than initial installation. An accessible route is always required to the jury box and witness box.

For additional information on this topic, the U.S. Access Board Courthouse Access Advisory Committee has developed a report that clarifies minimum federal requirements, as well as recommendations for best design practices.

The Access Board organized the Courthouse Access Advisory Committee in 2004 to promote accessibility in the design of court facilities. The committee's November 15, 2006, "Final Report" provides design guidance and best-practice recommendations to achieve access in courthouses, including courtrooms. Available free of charge at www.access-board.gov/caac/report.htm, the report also includes sample plans and educational strategies for disseminating the information to a variety of audiences. Although focused on the design of new facilities, it can also be used as a resource in the retrofit of existing facilities.

807.1 General. Courtrooms shall comply with Section 807.

❖ All parts of a courtroom must be accessible, and the space must meet the general requirements for these areas. For example, the gallery area seating must meet the assembly seating provisions in Section 802 (see Commentary Figure C807.5), or the gate in the bar must meet the provisions in Section 404. Elements particular to courtrooms include witness stands, jury boxes, judges' benches, clerks' stations, other work stations, and assistive listening systems (Section 706), among others. Design is complicated because it must achieve access effectively while preserving traditional and necessary features of courtroom design.

There are also very different styles of courtrooms. See Commentary Figures C807.1(a) through (c) for examples

FIGURE C807.1(a)
COURTROOM FOR PANEL OF JUDGES

FIGURE C807.1(b)
CRIMINAL COURTROOM WITH JUDGE AND JURY

of a courtroom for a panel of judges, a criminal courtroom with a judge and jury, and a traffic/small claims court with a judge and no jury. Access to courtrooms would also include support spaces such as the jury deliberation room [see Commentary Figure C807.1(d)].

FIGURE C807.1(c)
TRAFFIC/SMALL CLAIMS COURT

FIGURE C807.1(d)
JURY DELIBERATION ROOM

807.2 Turning Space. Where provided, each area that is raised or depressed shall provide a turning space complying with Section 304.

> **EXCEPTION:** Levels of jury boxes not required to be accessible are not required to comply with Section 807.2.

❖ When a judge's bench area, clerk's station, witness box, jury box or other defined area is raised or depressed, that area must include a turning space. The intent is that a person could turn around to be able to go back up or down the ramp or onto the platform lift. If the platform includes an accessible work surface, the knee and toe clearances under that work area can be used to provide the turning space.

Where a jury box has two tiers, only one wheelchair space is required (see Section 807.3); therefore, the exception is for the level that does not include the wheelchair space [see Commentary Figure C807.3(c)].

807.3 Clear Floor Space. Within the defined area of each jury box and witness stand, a clear floor space complying with Section 305 shall be provided.

> **EXCEPTION:** In alterations, wheelchair spaces are not required to be located within the defined area of raised jury boxes or witness stands and shall be permitted to be located outside these spaces where ramps or platform lifts restrict or project into the means of egress required by the administrative authority.

❖ A person who uses a mobility device such as a scooter or wheelchair must be able to testify from within the witness stand or serve as a member of the jury. Typically, half-height walls define these areas.

For example, sometimes witness boxes are raised, and sometimes not. If the area is raised, both a turning space (Sections 304 and 807.2) and a clear floor space are required (Section 305). The clear floor space should be positioned so that the person testifying can face in the same direction as anyone else testifying from the witness box. If the space is confined, the alcove provisions are applicable [see Commentary Figure C807.3(a)].

FIGURE C807.3(a)
WITNESS BOX

Jury boxes are often two levels. Sometimes both levels are raised, and sometimes only the second level is raised. A space for a juror using a wheelchair or scooter must be available within the jury box [see Commentary Figure C807.3(b)]. The juror must be able to face in the same direction as the rest of the jurors. If the wheelchair space is confined by the half-height wall or the other raised areas, the alcove provisions are applicable. This is different from the wheelchair space provided in the gallery seating because there are no requirements for companion seats, or shoulder alignment with other jurors [see Commentary Figure C807.3(c)].

807.4 Courtroom Stations. Judges' benches, clerks' stations, bailiffs' stations, deputy clerks' stations, court reporters' stations and litigants' and counsel stations shall comply with Section 902.

❖ Work station counter or desk surfaces provided within the courtroom must be constructed accessible. What stations are provided depend on the type of courtroom. This includes the counselors' tables and the speaking lectern (see Commentary Figure C807.4).

The lectern must be usable by both standing persons and persons using wheelchairs; therefore, the lectern work sur-

**FIGURE C807.3(b)
JURY BOX**

**FIGURE C807.4
COUNSELOR'S TABLE AND LECTERN**

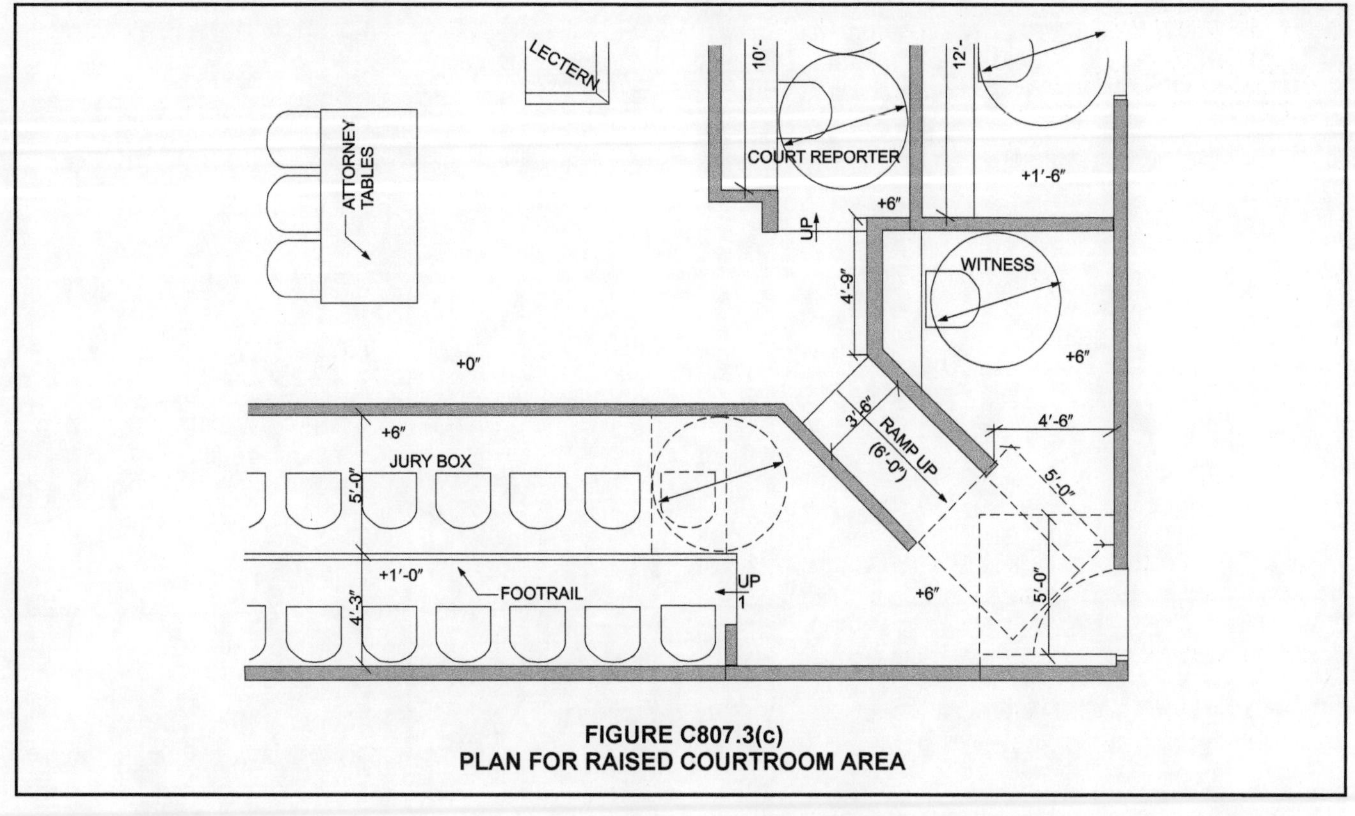

**FIGURE C807.3(c)
PLAN FOR RAISED COURTROOM AREA**

face should be adjustable mechanically. In addition to the work surface and knee and toe clearance requirements in Section 902, it is important to keep a line of sight between the judge and lawyer. The surrounding edges should lower with the work surface to maintain sightlines.

807.5 Gallery seating. Gallery seating shall comply with Section 802.

❖ Gallery seating is handled the same as any type of fixed seating used to view an event. A wheelchair clear floor space integrated into the gallery seating with a companion seat (including shoulder alignment) is required (see Commentary Figure C807.5). The number of wheelchair spaces depends on the number of gallery seats provided. The scoping provisions are found in the building codes.

Courtrooms are also required to provide designated aisle seating. Where courtrooms provide bench style seating with endcaps, the endcaps are not considered armrests (see commentary, Section 802.8.1).

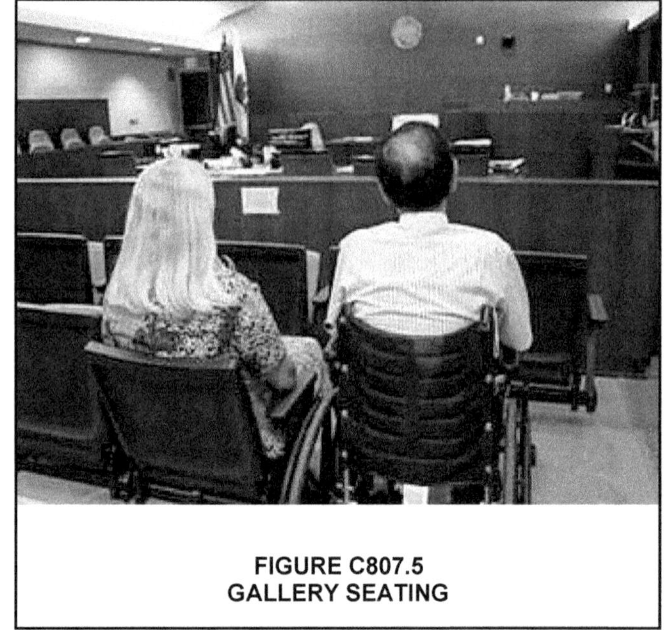

FIGURE C807.5
GALLERY SEATING

Chapter 9. Built-in Furnishings and Equipment

❖ Chapter 9 contains the technical requirements for built-in furnishings and equipment that were not addressed in other chapters. Parts of this chapter are referenced from other chapters, similar to the building blocks in Chapter 3. For example, the work surface section is referenced for the work surfaces in kitchens.

- Section 901 is a general statement about the Chapter 9 criteria being applicable for the special types of elements addressed in this chapter where required by the authority having jurisdiction.
- Section 902 states criteria for fixed dining surfaces, such as bars, booths or banquette tables, or work surfaces, such as study carrels in libraries or check writing stations in banks.
- Section 903 contains technical criteria for benches required in spaces where persons may need to change their clothes, such as dressing rooms, fitting rooms or locker rooms.
- Section 904 addresses requirements for sales and service counters that are commonly found in grocery stores, banks or mercantile establishments.
- Section 905 provides technical criteria for storage facilities, such as pantries, supply closets or coat closets.

901 General

901.1 Scope. Built-in furnishings and equipment required to be accessible by the scoping provisions adopted by the administrative authority shall comply with the applicable provisions of Chapter 9.

❖ Sections 902 through 905 contain the provisions necessary for accessibility to furnishings and equipment that are built into a building or structure as permanent elements. The elements included in this section are not intended to be a comprehensive list of everything that can be built into a building, but rather a listing of elements typically found in most building types. Elements that are not specifically described in this section, but are similar in nature and similar in use to the elements that are described in this section, must be made accessible to the extent possible for similar elements where specific detailed provisions are stated. Note that these provisions apply to these built-in furnishings and equipment when required by the scoping provisions (see Section 201).

902 Dining Surfaces and Work Surfaces

❖ The requirements in this section establish the necessary dimensions and clearances that must be maintained to provide access to built-in tables or counters that are used for dining surfaces and work surfaces.

Dining surfaces are tables or counters where people consume food or drink, such as fixed tables in restaurants, picnic tables in park shelters, or bars in nightclubs or ice cream parlors. Dining surfaces are typically provided with loose seats, booth seating or fixed stools, but they can also have adjacent standing space.

Work surfaces include tables and counters intended to be accessible surfaces where work can be performed, such as writing, filling out forms, operating a computer, preparing food, reading, personal grooming, etc. Examples include writing counters in banks, admission counters in hospitals, reading and writing surfaces in libraries and classrooms, student laboratory stations and baby changing stations. Counters at visitor areas in courthouses and correctional and detention facilities would be considered a work surface [see Commentary Figure C902(a) through (f)].

Seating, counters and work surfaces that must be accessible must be located on an accessible route.

902.1 General. Accessible dining surfaces and work surfaces shall comply with Section 902.

EXCEPTION: Dining surfaces and work surfaces primarily for children's use shall be permitted to comply with Section 902.5.

❖ Built-in work counters and surfaces are designed for a vast number of reasons, built to a wide variety of sizes and shapes, and use many of the available building materials. It is not always necessary for an entire counter or work surface to be accessible, but people with physical disabilities must have access to a portion of these building elements. This is also true for fixed tables with seating. Not only must a percentage of the tables be accessible, but if fixed seating is provided, a loose seat or open space for a wheelchair location must be available at those accessible tables.

The heights for adults are different than for children; therefore, an option that allows for accessible location when tables or work surfaces are designed for children is given in Section 902.4. Examples would be a reading counter in the children's section of a library or work counters or tables in a preschool or elementary classroom.

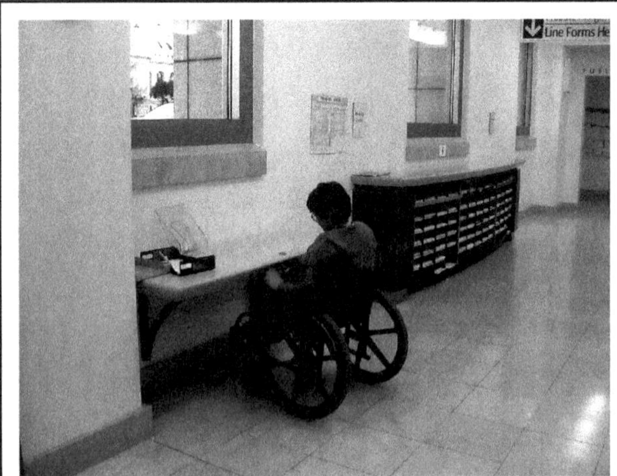

(a) FORM COUNTER

(b) LIBRARY CARRELS

(c) BOOTH SEATING

(d) PICNIC TABLE

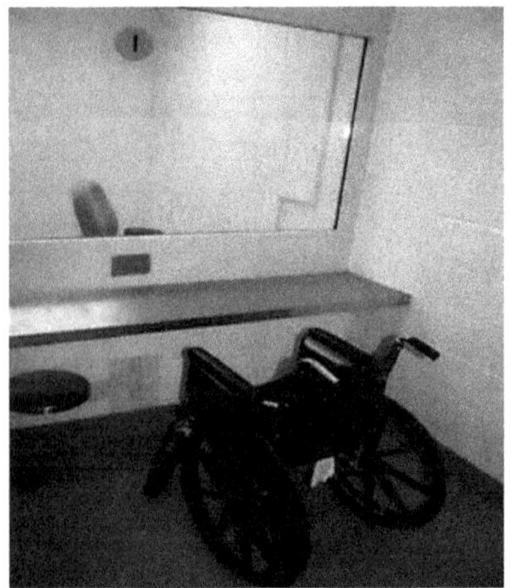

(e) VISITOR WINDOW

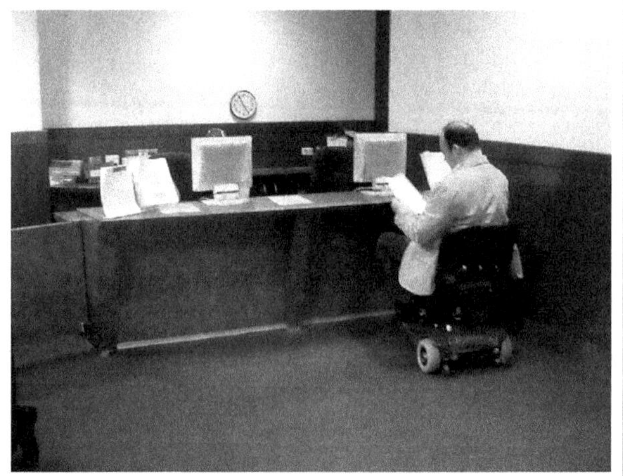

(f) RESOURCE CENTER

FIGURE C902
EXAMPLES OF DINING AND WORK SURFACES

902.2 Clear Floor Space. A clear floor space complying with Section 305, positioned for a forward approach, shall be provided. Knee and toe clearance complying with Section 306 shall be provided.

EXCEPTIONS:

1. At drink surfaces 12 inches (305 mm) or less in depth, knee and toe space shall not be required to extend beneath the surface beyond the depth of the drink surface provided.
2. Dining surfaces that are 15 inches (380 mm) minimum and 24 inches (610 mm) maximum in height are permitted to have a clear floor space complying with Section 305 positioned for a parallel approach.

❖ In addition to providing counters or work surfaces at an accessible height (Section 902.3), a work surface or dining surface must be on an accessible route and have adequate clearances under that surface. Although some items in this standard have an option of a front approach or a parallel approach, a front approach is required at dining and work surfaces.

The 30-inch by 48-inch (760 by 1220 mm) clear floor or ground space (Section 305) is required at all accessible built-in furnishings to provide maneuvering space that will allow access to the seating spaces at counters and work surfaces. If the area under the work surface is confined in some way by items such as walls, a privacy shield, table legs, etc., the provisions for alcoves are applicable. This could result in a minimum required width of 36 inches (915 mm).

The space for a person using a wheelchair is permitted to project under tables, counters and work surfaces to the extent described in Section 306. Clearances for a person's knees and toes are required. The arms on a wheelchair or the chest of the person using the wheelchair will limit the amount someone can move forward under a counter or table. If objects are located under the surface adjacent to the knee and toe space (e.g., cable tray, support), it is advisable to protect the person using the surface from injury by padding or rounding any sharp edges or locate these items as far past the knee and toe clearances as practical.

Although not required, design is improved if the clear floor space at accessible furnishings does not interfere with the path of travel for other people using aisles adjacent to accessible features so persons sitting in the wheelchair locations will not be continually jostled. For example, locate the wheelchair seating in a restaurant so that when a person is using that space, people moving to and from other tables or waiters and waitresses serving the tables can have a clear path past the person without bumping them, squeezing past or having to ask them to move.

The exceptions address types of dining and drinking surfaces where people use the surface just to set drinks or food down for convenience, not necessarily to eat at the surface as at a dining table. Examples of drink rails and side tables are illustrated in Commentary Figures C902.2(a) and (b).

902.3 Exposed Surfaces. There shall be no sharp or abrasive surfaces under the exposed portions of dining surfaces and work surfaces.

❖ Limitations to exposed surfaces are an issue of safety. When a person using a wheelchair moves under a surface, there should be no sharp objects that could cause bruises or cuts. This is especially important for persons using wheel-

FIGURE C902.2(a)
DRINK SURFACE
(Photo courtesy of Populous)

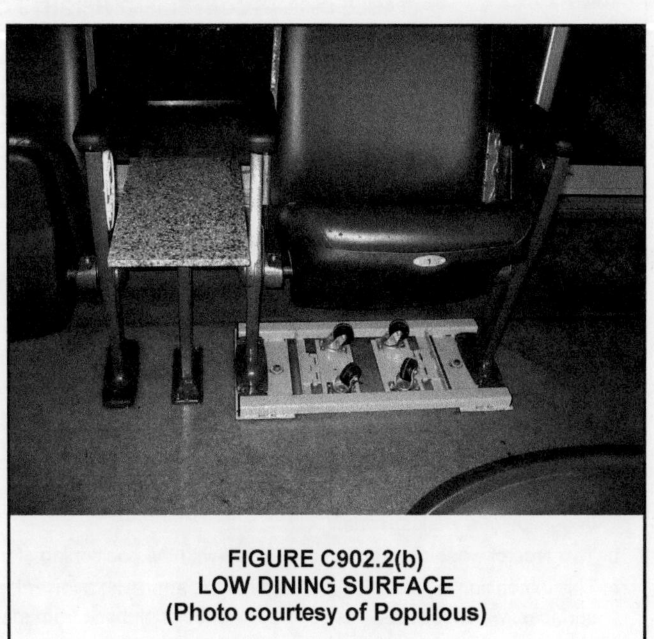

FIGURE C902.2(b)
LOW DINING SURFACE
(Photo courtesy of Populous)

chairs who have no pain sensation in their legs and do not realize when an injury has occurred.

902.4 Height. The tops of dining surfaces and work surfaces shall be 28 inches (710 mm) minimum and 34 inches (865 mm) maximum in height above the floor.

❖ The height of any type of table top, counter, work surface or similar furnishing is determined by the intended use, as well as by the needs of the person using the wheelchair. These provisions apply to the specific furnishing and do not change because of the particular occupancy of the building.

Dining surfaces can be of a variety of configurations. When booths are installed for accessible seating, the accessible space can be either at the side or end of the table. Tables with booth seating on one side and loose chairs on the other side are called banquettes. If accessible seating is provided at a bar, the length of the accessible section should be a minimum of 60 inches (1525 mm) to better accommodate a companion at the same level.

Different types of work require different work surface heights for comfort and ease of use. Light detailed work, such as writing, requires a work surface close to elbow height for a standing person. Heavy manual work such as rolling dough requires a work surface height about 10 inches (255 mm) below elbow height for a standing person. The principle of a high work surface for light detailed work and a low work surface for heavy manual work also applies for seated persons; however, the limiting condition for seated manual work is knee clearance under the work surface.

Commentary Table C902.4 lists convenient work surface heights for seated persons. The great variety of heights for comfort and optimal performance indicates a need for alternatives or a compromise in height if both people who stand and people who sit are using the same counter area. Service counters serve as duty stations for employees who require knee clearances and may double as temporary work surfaces for persons using wheelchairs having a need to complete forms or work directly with personnel.

902.5 Dining Surfaces and Work Surfaces for Children's Use. Accessible dining surfaces and work surfaces primarily for children's use shall comply with Section 902.5.

EXCEPTION: Dining surfaces and work surfaces used primarily by children ages 5 and younger shall not be required to comply with Section 902.5 where a clear floor space complying with Section 305 is provided and is positioned for a parallel approach.

❖ When designing spaces where a high percentage of the users are children, such as schools, libraries, museums or community centers, a designer/owner may want to provide areas specifically sized for the comfort of children. If a designer/owner wants to provide an accessible dining or work surface specifically designed for the use of children from age 6 to 12 years, they must follow the provisions in the following sections. If the children using the surface are 5 years or younger, a counter of any height may be provided as long as a 30-inch by 48-inch (760 by 1220 mm) clear floor space is provided that allows for a side approach. Typically, with children of that age, the table height is lower than 26 inches (660 mm), which would not allow for normal knee and toe clearances.

902.5.1 Clear Floor Space. A clear floor space complying with Section 305, positioned for forward approach, shall be provided. Knee and toe clearance complying with Section 306 shall be provided.

EXCEPTION: A knee clearance of 24 inches (610 mm) minimum above the floor shall be permitted.

❖ This child provision allows for consideration of child appropriate sizes. The basic requirement is that a typical adult-sized clear floor space along with knee and toe clearances is provided at the accessible dining or work surface

TABLE C902.4—CONVENIENT HEIGHTS OF WORK SURFACES FOR SEATED PEOPLE[a]

CONDITIONS OF USE	SHORT WOMEN		TALL MEN	
	inches	mm	inches	mm
Seated in a wheelchair				
Manual work				
Desk or removable armrests	26	660	30	760
Fixed, full-size armrests[b]	32[c]	815	32[c]	815
Light, detailed work				
Desk or removable armrests	29	735	34	865
Fixed, full-size armrests[b]	32[c]	815	34	865
Seated in a 16-inch (405 mm) high chair				
Manual work	26	660	27	685
Light, detailed work	28	710	31	785

a. All dimensions are based on a work-surface thickness of $1^1/_2$ inches (38 mm) and a clearance of $1^1/_2$ inches (38 mm) between legs and the underside of a work surface.

b. This type of wheelchair does not interfere with the positioning of a wheelchair under a work surface.

c. This dimension is limited by the height of the armrests; a lower height would be prefereable. Some people in this group perfer lower work surfaces, which required positioning the wheelchair back from the edge of the counter.

(see Sections 902.2 and 902.4). The exception allows for the height required for the knee space to be reduced to 24 inches (610 mm) instead of the standard 27 inches (685 mm) minimum. This will in turn allow for the lower table/counter service height permitted in Section 902.5.2.

902.5.2 Height. The tops of tables and counters shall be 26 inches (660 mm) minimum and 30 inches (760 mm) maximum above the floor.

❖ This child provision allows for consideration of child appropriate sizes. The lower knee clearances permitted with the exception in Section 902.5.1 will allow for the lower table/counter surface height. The allowances for adult table/counter surface heights are addressed in Section 902.4.

903 Benches

❖ The section on benches is referenced in the requirements for saunas (Section 612.2), dressing, fitting and locker rooms (Section 803.4) and holding and housing cells (Section 806.2.2).

The scoping provisions in the applicable building code may require accessible benches at other locations.

903.1 General. Accessible benches shall comply with Section 903.

❖ For dressing, fitting and locker rooms, the intent is that if a person using a wheelchair needs to transfer, or a person with mobility impairments or balance problems needs to sit down to change any item of clothing, that a seat is available. In a locker room, the bench must be located so that it does not require transfer to the bench to access the accessible lockers. At the same time, the bench is not required to have reach range to the lockers, but it is more user friendly if they are in proximity. Storage lockers for bags or purses provided for the public in a museum are not intended to allow for changing; therefore a bench is not required.

For security reasons in housing and holding cells sometimes the only seat provided is a bench seat. In an Accessible housing cell, a person may need to transfer to a bench for grooming activities.

903.2 Clear Floor Space. A clear floor space complying with Section 305, positioned for parallel approach to the bench seat, shall be provided.

❖ When considering the relationship of clear floor space to the bench, a primary consideration is transfer between a wheelchair and the bench. This can be accomplished by placing the wheelchair at the end of the bench, allowing

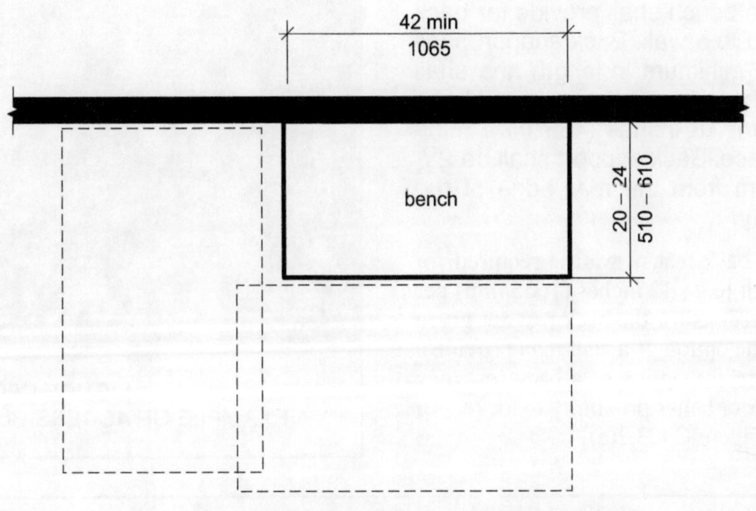

(a) Bench Size and Options for Clear Floor Space

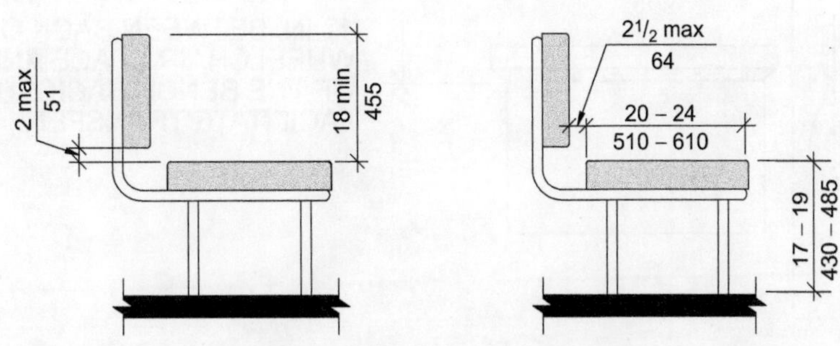

(b) Bench Back Support and Seat Height

FIGURE 903
BENCHES

transfer between two seats that face the same direction. To accomplish this, however, the clear floor space must be located at the open end of the bench so the side of the wheelchair is parallel to the end of the bench [see Figure 903(a)]. Transfer is easier if the seat on the wheelchair and the bench line up. If possible, the clear floor space provided for transfer should be 12 inches (305 mm) back from the back of the seat [see Commentary, Figure C903.2(a)]. It is also important to recognize the barrier introduced by arm-rests at the ends of benches.

Installing a grab bar on a side wall would exceed code requirements and possibly aid transfer to the bench; however, a grab bar should never be installed over the back of the bench. A grab bar on the rear wall would cause a problem with using the wall for back support [see Commentary, Figure C903.2(b)].

903.3 Size. Benches shall have seats 42 inches (1065 mm) minimum in length, and 20 inches (510 mm) minimum and 24 inches (610 mm) maximum in depth.

❖ The 42-inch (1065 mm) dimension is the overall length of the bench and the 20- to 24-inch (510 to 610 mm) dimension is the seat depth. The length will allow for a person to put their leg up on the bench lengthwise for assistance in changing clothes. A user may need to brace themselves into the corner for added support, so a much longer bench is not recommended.

903.4 Back Support. The bench shall provide for back support or shall be affixed to a wall. Back support shall be 42 inches (1065 mm) minimum in length and shall extend from a point 2 inches (51 mm) maximum above the seat surface to a point 18 inches (455 mm) minimum above the seat surface. Back support shall be $2^1/_2$ inches (64 mm) maximum from the rear edge of the seat measured horizontally.

❖ Back support by either a back rest or wall is required for the full length of the bench [e.g., 42 inches (1665 mm) per Section 903.3]. The dimensions for the back rest are given in Figure 903. Although the option of a wall may provide a corner location for support, the option of a back rest may allow for an easier transfer or better proximity to lockers or hooks (see Commentary Figure C903.2(a)].

903.5 Height. The top of the bench seat shall be 17 inches (430 mm) minimum and 19 inches (485 mm) maximum above the floor, measured to the top of the seat.

EXCEPTION: Benches primarily for children's use shall be permitted to be 11 inches (280 mm) minimum and 17 inches (430 mm) maximum above the floor, measured to the top of the seat.

❖ The height of the bench seating area above the floor is critical for the wheelchair user to make a safe and comfortable transfer from the wheelchair to the bench. For a comfortable transfer, the height of the bench seat should be as close as possible to the seat height of the wheelchair. The seat height of most standard wheelchairs is about 17 inches (430 mm).

The exception allows a lower bench height when designing for children.

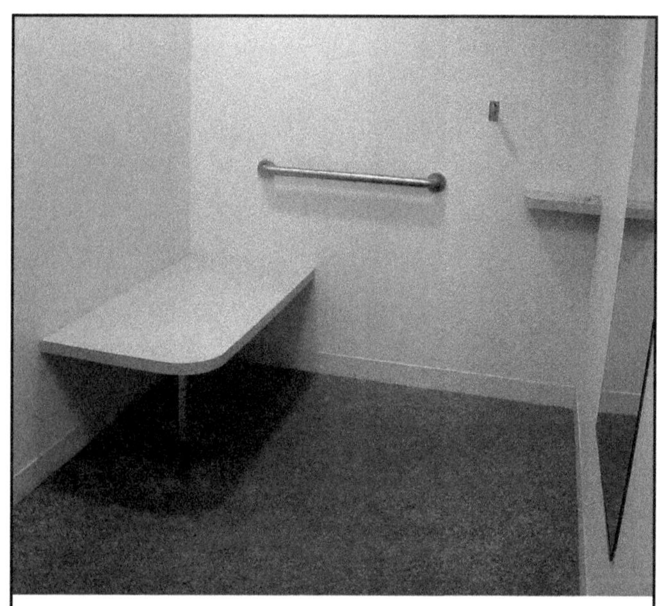

FIGURE C903.2(b)
EXAMPLE OF ACCESSIBLE DRESSING ROOM

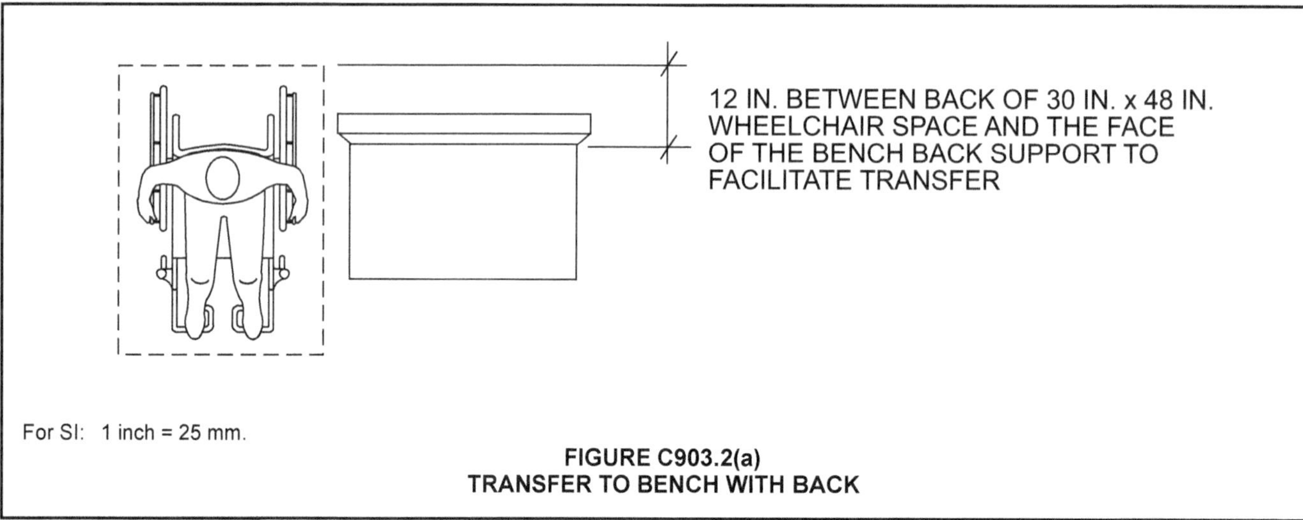

FIGURE C903.2(a)
TRANSFER TO BENCH WITH BACK

903.6 Structural Strength. Allowable stresses shall not be exceeded for materials used where a vertical or horizontal force of 250 pounds (1112 N) is applied at any point on the seat, fastener mounting device, or supporting structure.

❖ The structural loads required in this section are to be applied to the bench seat material, as well as to the structural components that support the bench seat. One of the options is for the bench to be fixed to the wall along the long side of the bench. It is not the intent to require all or any of the structural loads to be supported from the wall at the long side of the bench. The only requirement is for the bench to be adjacent to the wall for back support. It is the responsibility of the bench designer to provide the prescribed structural support of the bench. Consideration must also be given to the structural support system to ensure that the system itself does not create an obstacle that will make the bench inaccessible.

903.7 Wet Locations. Where provided in wet locations the surface of the seat shall be slip resistant and shall not accumulate water.

❖ Wet locations such as showers, saunas, steam rooms and pool bathhouses are generally more hazardous because of the presence of moisture and standing water. Wheelchair users quite often use the surface on the bench for support while making a wheelchair transfer. Benches in these types of locations must be made of nonslip materials. The materials must be certified as being nonslip while wet. A material that is considered nonslip only when dry does not comply with the intent of this requirement. Bench seats must also be installed with a minimum degree of slope to allow water to drain off the seat surface. The surface can have a minimum of perforations to prevent water from ponding on the seat. If perforated seat material is used, care must be taken to ensure that the perforations do not become a hazard.

904 Sales and Service Counters

❖ This section addresses all types of sales and service counters where transactions take place at or over the counter. The key is how the customer is expected to interact with the employee at that counter, or if they are expected to access items themselves. Examples are checkout counters in grocery stores, counters for pick-up such as a dry-cleaner, reception counters at the front of an office, car rental and airline counters in airports, counters used for viewing merchandise, fast food ordering counters, cafeteria lines, etc.

Simply providing a cash register at a counter is not intended to automatically trigger the checkout aisle requirements. The provisions in Section 904.4 were written for the standard conveyor belt to bagger type of checkout aisle commonly found in grocery stores. The provisions for service counters or windows in Section 904.3 are intended to cover locations where transactions take place, such as a bank teller window or a hotel check-in counter. The designer should follow the provisions based on the use of the counter and what type of interaction occurs at that location. For example, many drugstores have one or two counters with cash registers at the front of the store. Customers typically bring up several items to purchase that they have gathered from throughout the store. The counter at this location may follow the provisions for check-out aisles, even if they do not have a conveyor belt. However, there are also cash registers at several other locations, such as the photo order window, the cosmetic counter and at the pharmacy. At these locations the customer is typically coming in for an item that is handed to them by the employee. Although someone could take additional items to any of those locations, the number is usually limited to a few items. These locations would most likely be considered sales or service counters.

Food service line requirements in Section 904.5 were developed for cafeteria style dining or portions of fast food restaurants where customers help themselves, such as condiment or drink service areas. The portion of the counter where customers order food in a fast food restaurant is most likely a sales or service counter.

904.1 General. Accessible sales and service counters and windows shall comply with Section 904 as applicable.

EXCEPTION: Drive up only sales or service counters and windows are not required to comply with Section 904.

❖ Where sales and service counters and windows are required by the administrative authority to be accessible for use by the public, the provisions of this section apply. Typical scoping provisions are for one at each location or each type when these counters are dispersed. When they are grouped, as in the front of a large store, a minimum percentage is typically required. When not all aisles are accessible, the accessible aisles will be signed.

Drive up windows are common at fast food restaurants, banks and pharmacies. Drive up windows are not required to provide clear floor space or height limitations.

904.2 Approach. All portions of counters required to be accessible shall be located adjacent to a walking surface complying with Section 403.

❖ Adjacent to the accessible portion of the counter should be a level floor surface that is part of an accessible route. At a hotel checkout counter, this may be only a small portion. At a cafeteria line or checkout aisle, this may be along the entire line.

If a queue or waiting line defined by permanent walls or rails is part of the access to the sales or service counter, checkout aisles or food service line, the clearances must be maintained in this portion as well.

904.3 Sales and Service Counters. Sales and service counters shall comply with Section 904.3.1 or 904.3.2. The accessible portion of the countertop shall extend the same depth as the sales and service countertop.

❖ A sales or service counter may be accessed by either a parallel or a forward approach. The use of the counter should dictate when a forward approach with knee and toe clearances should be used. An example would be when the customer/employee interaction requires some type of filling out of forms.

This section is applicable at sales or service windows too. Not providing a counter surface is not intended to be an exemption from this requirement.

904.3.1 Parallel Approach. A portion of the counter surface 36 inches (915 mm) minimum in length and 36 inches (915 mm) maximum in height above the floor shall be provided. Where the counter surface is less than 36 inches (915 mm) in length, the entire counter surface shall be 36 inches (915 mm) maximum in height above the floor. A clear floor space complying with Section 305, positioned for a parallel approach adjacent to the accessible counter, shall be provided.

❖ Typically, service counters are designed and used from both sides at the same time. An employee will address the counter from one side while the other side is used for customers. Sales and service counters are designed using a vast assortment of materials, and the sizes and shapes are limited only by the imagination of architects and designers. Because sales and service counters can take on many shapes and be constructed to a wide variety of sizes it is important to establish guidelines that will ensure a portion of the counter will contain an area that is accessible for someone using a wheelchair. The 36-inch (915 mm) height will allow for a standard counter height. The width of the accessible counter must be at least 36 inches (915 mm) minimum. For interaction between the customer/employee, the 36-inch (915 mm) height must be the full depth of the counter. A shelf under a higher window is not adequate (see Commentary Figure C904.3.1).

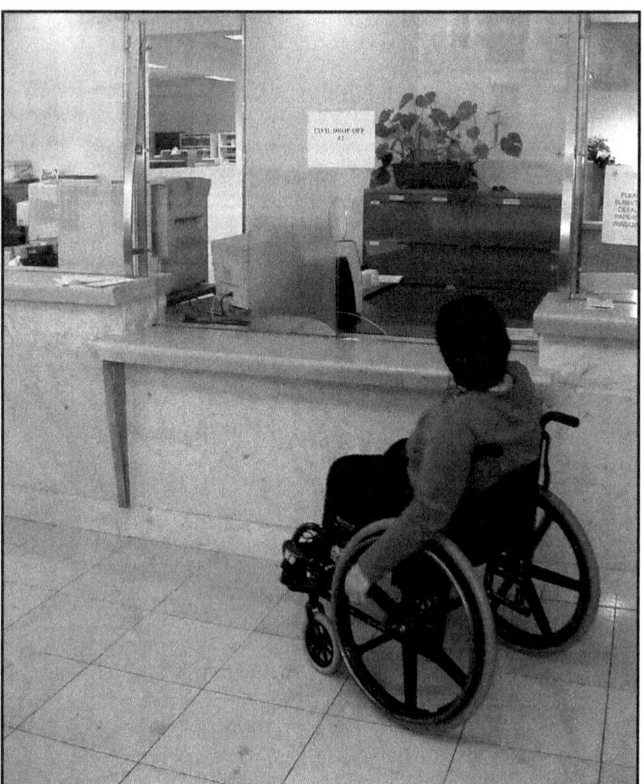

FIGURE C904.3.1
SERVICE COUNTER PARALLEL APPROACH

904.3.2 Forward Approach. A portion of the counter surface 30 inches (760 mm) minimum in length and 36 inches (915 mm) maximum in height above the floor shall be provided. A clear floor space complying with Section 305, positioned for a forward approach to the accessible counter, shall be provided. Knee and toe clearance complying with Section 306 shall be provided under the accessible counter.

❖ Sometimes a service counter can be the location where someone may need to fill out forms or access information. In these cases, the service window should have a forward approach with knee and toe clearances similar to a work surface (see Section 902 and Commentary Figure C904.3.2).

FIGURE C904.3.2
SERVICE COUNTER FORWARD APPROACH

904.4 Checkout Aisles. Checkout aisles shall comply with Section 904.4.

❖ Accessible checkout aisles, such as those found in grocery stores, must meet the provisions for the aisle, counter and any check writing surface. See the commentary to Section 904 for an explanation of the difference between a checkout aisle and a sales and service counter (see Commentary, Figure C904.4).

904.4.1 Aisle. Aisles shall comply with Section 403.

❖ The aisle between the checkout counter and any other obstruction, such as a wall or another checkout counter, must have a clear width of 36 inches (915 mm) minimum. If getting into or out of the aisle would require making a tight turn around an obstruction, the requirements of Section 403.5.1 may result in a 42-inch (1065 mm) minimum aisle width.

904.4.2 Counters. The checkout counter surface shall be 38 inches (965 mm) maximum in height above the floor. The top of the counter edge protection shall be 2 inches (51 mm) maximum above the top of the counter surface on the aisle side of the checkout counter.

❖ A 2-inch-high (50 mm) ledge is permitted along the edge of accessible checkout counters so that food will not tip off the conveyor belt as it moves forward. The 38-inch-high (965 mm) checkout aisle will still allow a person using a wheelchair to be able to see the merchandise (see Figure 904.4.2).

904.4.3 Check Writing Surfaces. Where provided, check writing surfaces shall comply with Section 902.4.

❖ If a surface is provided for customers to write checks or sign a credit card slip, the height of that surface must be between 28 inches and 34 inches (710 and 865 mm) high. The reference to Section 902.3 does not require any knee or toe clearances under that surface. A side approach would be permitted.

The intent is not to prohibit an additional check writing surface at a higher level. With the checkout counter at 38 inches (965 mm) in height (Section 904.4.2), it is not possible to meet both requirements at the same location. A small pull-out shelf or fixed shelf at the lower height may be provided for this condition. If a pull-out shelf is provided, it must meet the operable parts provisions in Section 309 and be operable with only one hand without tight grasping.

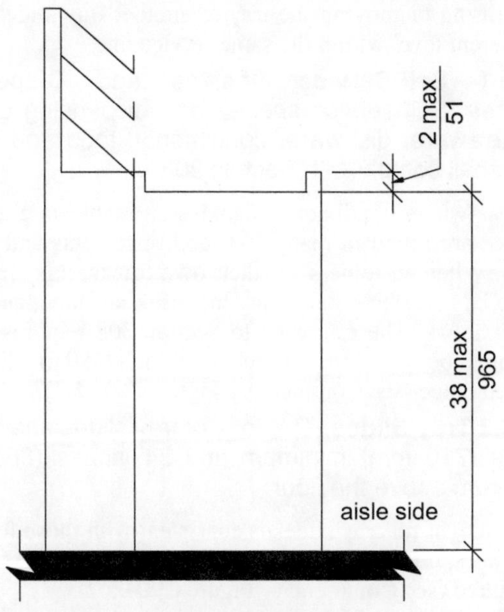

FIGURE 904.4.2
HEIGHT OF CHECKOUT COUNTERS

FIGURE C904.4
CHECKOUT AISLE

904.5 Food Service Lines. Counters in food service lines shall comply with Section 904.5.

❖ Unlike the requirements for service windows or work surfaces that require portions of counters to be accessible, the provisions in this section apply to the entire length of the tray slide. The height must be maintained throughout the tray slide without requiring the user to interrupt progress by lifting or moving the tray to another tray slide or to a different level within the same service line.

904.5.1 Self-Service Shelves and Dispensing Devices. Self-service shelves and dispensing devices for tableware, dishware, condiments, food and beverages shall comply with Section 308.

❖ Areas where condiments, napkins and tableware are provided are found in many fast food restaurants and cafeterias. When customers get their own drinks, this area must also be accessible, including the drink machine, cups, lids and straws. The reference to Section 308 requires everything to be within the 15-inch to 48-inch (380 to 1220 mm) reach range (see Commentary Figure C904.5.1).

904.5.2 Tray Slides. The tops of tray slides shall be 28 inches (710 mm) minimum and 34 inches (865 mm) maximum above the floor.

❖ The height for tray slides is consistent with those for work surfaces; however, knee and toe clearances are not required (see Commentary Figure C904.5.2).

The standard 24-inch (610 mm) maximum reach range should be considered when designing for access to the food. Not all portions must be within the reach range (e.g., food layout and suitable utensils can be a factor).

904.6 Security Glazing. Where counters or teller windows have security glazing to separate personnel from the public, a method to facilitate voice communication shall be provided. Telephone handset devices, if provided, shall comply with Section 704.3.

❖ For security reasons, some service windows may have glazing at the window. Examples would be bank teller windows, currency exchanges or sign-in windows at controlled facilities. Security glazing may include voice communication methods such as openings, grilles, slats, talk-through baffles, intercoms, assistive listening systems (Section 706) or telephone handsets. If the system of choice includes telephone handsets, volume controls (Section 704.3) are required.

Visiting areas in judicial facilities and detention and correctional facilities are considered as two work surfaces separated by security glazing. Therefore, in addition to providing accessible stations (e.g., typically 5 percent) in accordance with the authority having jurisdiction, all stations must meet the security glazing provisions for persons on both sides [see Commentary Figures C904.6(a) and C904.6(b)].

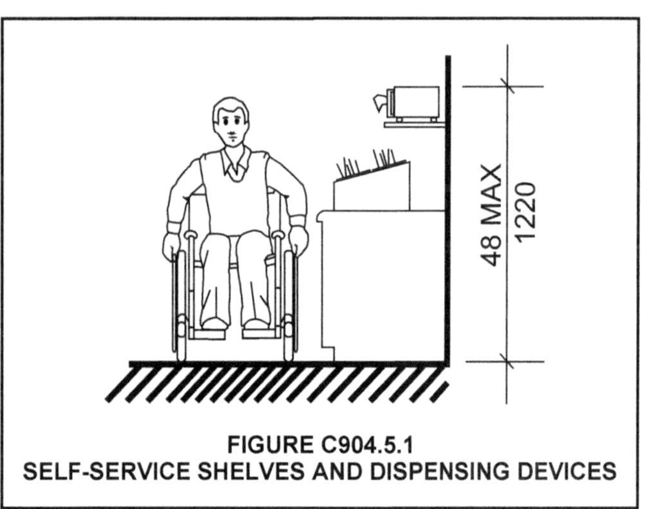

FIGURE C904.5.1
SELF-SERVICE SHELVES AND DISPENSING DEVICES

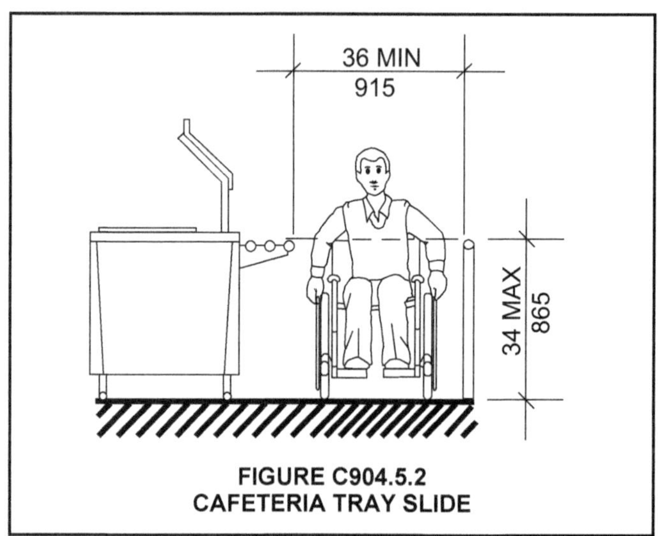

FIGURE C904.5.2
CAFETERIA TRAY SLIDE

FIGURE C904.6(a)
SECURITY GLAZING AT TICKET WINDOWS

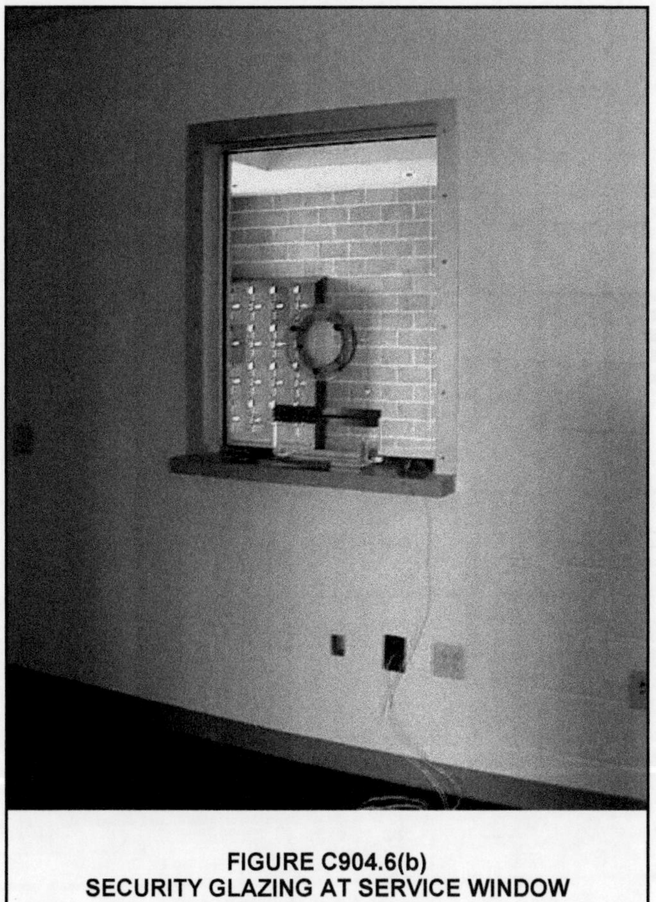

FIGURE C904.6(b)
SECURITY GLAZING AT SERVICE WINDOW

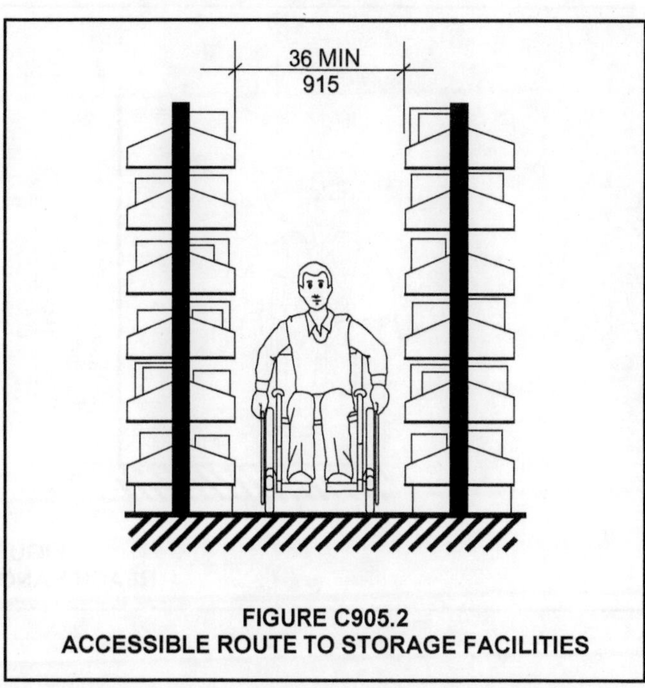

FIGURE C905.2
ACCESSIBLE ROUTE TO STORAGE FACILITIES

905 Storage Facilities

❖ An accessible storage facility is defined as one that complies with the provisions of this section. The components required to make a storage facility accessible are addressed in this section, including the approach, reach ranges and hardware that allows operation by a person with a physical disability.

Examples of storage facilities include shelves, cabinets, clothes rods, drawers, mail boxes, storage lockers, etc.

905.1 General. Accessible storage facilities shall comply with Section 905.

❖ The provisions in this section are not intended to determine whether or when a storage facility must be accessible. The provisions in this section are the minimum standards necessary to ensure that a storage facility is accessible when required by the administrative authority.

905.2 Clear Floor Space. A clear floor space complying with Section 305 shall be provided.

❖ To be usable by a person with a disability, storage facilities must have a 30-inch by 48-inch (760 by 1220 mm) clear floor or ground space to position a wheelchair so that the user can reach the stored items. This clear floor space must be on an accessible route (see Commentary Figure C905.2).

905.3 Height. Accessible storage elements shall comply with at least one of the reach ranges specified in Section 308.

❖ Once a wheelchair is positioned for forward or parallel approach at a storage facility, the facility is still not usable unless the stored items are kept within reach ranges that allow the wheelchair user to reach and retrieve them. Typically, this would include shelving or clothes rods between 15 inches and 48 inches (380 and 1220 mm) above the floor (see Commentary Figure C905.3). Reaching over an obstruction may reduce the high reach to 44 inches (1115 mm) (see Section 308 for full requirements).

Providing additional shelves or clothes rods above or below reach ranges is acceptable.

905.4 Operable Parts. Operable parts of storage facilities shall comply with Section 309.

❖ This reference reflects the more general need to consider those persons with limited physical dexterity. Hardware requiring tight grasping, pinching or twisting of the wrist is undesirable. Touch latches, levers and U-shaped pulls are acceptable because they do not require great dexterity. These issues are addressed in Section 309.4. The general reference to Section 309 results in the operable parts needing to meet clear floor space (Section 309.2) and height restrictions (Section 309.3), as well as the requirements for the storage element itself as addressed in Sections 905.2 and 905.3.

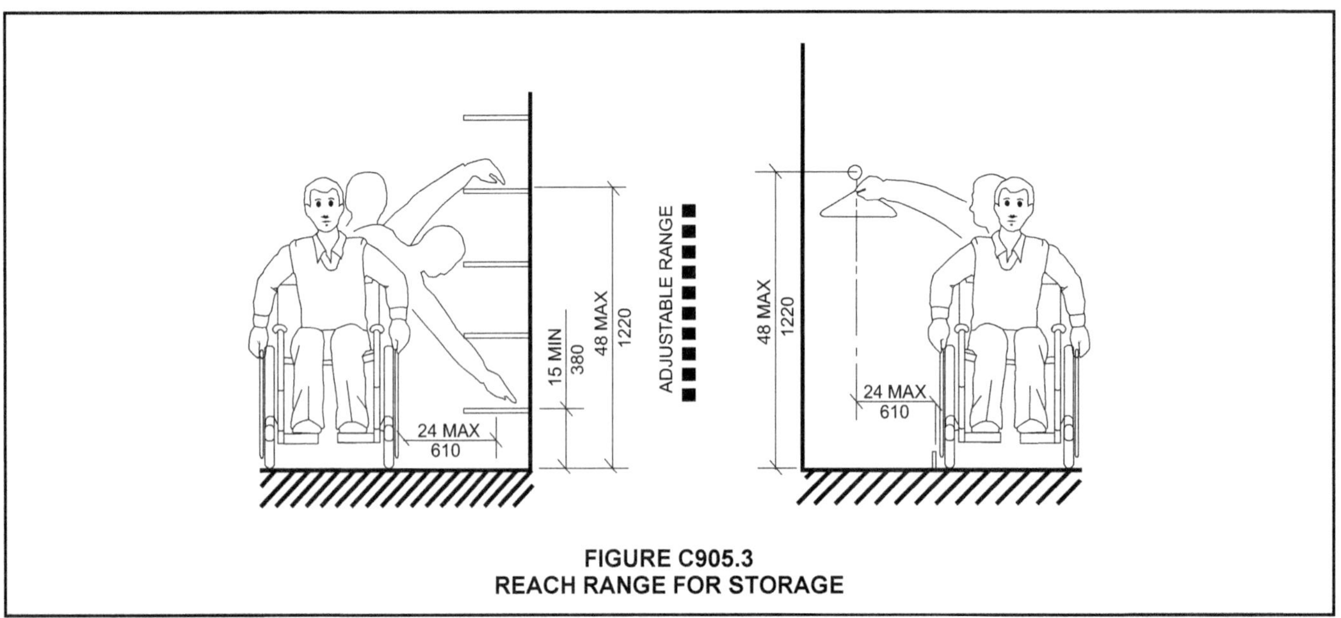

FIGURE C905.3
REACH RANGE FOR STORAGE

Chapter 10. Dwelling Units and Sleeping Units

❖ Chapter 10 contains the technical requirements for Accessible, Type A, Type B and Type C dwelling and sleeping units. See the commentary at the beginning of Sections 1002, 1003, 1004 and 1005 for a description of the different types of units and history.

- Section 1001 is a general statement about the Chapter 10 criteria being applicable for the Accessible, Type A, Type B and Type C dwelling and sleeping units addressed in this chapter where any or all such units are required by the authority having jurisdiction. This scoping criterion provides information on "what, where and how many." Technical criteria in this chapter are the "how."
- Section 1002 details technical criteria for Accessible dwelling and sleeping units.
- Section 1003 states technical criteria for Type A dwelling and sleeping units.
- Section 1004 provides technical criteria for Type B dwelling and sleeping units.
- Section 1005 covers technical criteria for Type C dwelling units.
- Section 1006 contains criteria for accessible communication features such as those used for emergency evacuations (e.g., fire alarms, smoke detectors) and announcing visitors (e.g., doorbells, voice or visual communication between the apartment and the building entrance).

Chapter 10 provides users with all of the technical requirements for each level of accessibility of dwelling and sleeping units. The technical criteria are stated in the section for the specific type of unit or a reference is provided to the location of the technical requirement either in another section of Chapter 10 or one of the other chapters of the standard. A section in Chapters 1 through 9 or in Chapter 11 is not used for dwelling or sleeping unit design unless it is specifically referenced in Chapter 10. For example, Section 1003.12.3 provides the requirements for a kitchen work surface in a Type A unit; however, neither Section 804.3 nor 902, which address work surfaces in kitchens in other occupancies, is referenced. On the other hand, for an Accessible unit, Section 1002.12 refers the user to Section 804 for the design of a kitchen or kitchenette and Section 902 for the work surface. For the Type A unit work surface, the standards of Sections 804.3 and 902 do not apply; for the Accessible unit work surface they do.

- Each of the subsections in Sections 1002, 1003 and 1004 for Accessible, Type A or Type B dwelling or sleeping units is set up in the same order. This allows for easy comparison between the three unit types. The layout of Section 1005 for the Type C units does not follow this format since its accessibility requirements are more limited.
- 100*.1 is a general reference to the section requirements.
- 100*.2 has criteria for the primary entrance to the unit.
- 100*.3 provides accessible route requirements throughout the inside of the unit.
- 100*.4 deals with the walking surfaces that are part of the accessible route in Section 100*.3.
- 100*.5 is for the doors and doorways within the unit. In Type B units there are separate criteria for the primary entrance door and the other doors and doorways in the unit.
- 100*.6 is a reference to the general ramp provisions in Section 405.
- 100*.7 indicates that a private residence elevator (Section 409) is an option to provide an accessible route within the unit. Passenger elevators and LULAs in accordance with Sections 407 and 408 are also acceptable as alternatives because they result in a higher level of accessibility.
- 100*.8 indicates that a platform lift (i.e., not a chair lift) in accordance with Section 410 can also serve as part of an accessible route within a unit.
- 100*.9 provides technical criteria for the referenced list of operable parts. It is important to note that the items that must meet operable parts provisions are not the same in Accessible, Type A and Type B units. For example, appliance controls, plumbing controls and door hardware are not required to meet the operable parts requirements in Type B units.
- 100*.10 states the applicable provisions for laundry facilities installed within the unit. Laundry facilities in a shared or common location for residents must match the level or accessibility for the units they serve.
- 100*.11 contains options for bathrooms. Note that the two alternatives in Type B units are called Option A and Option B. Although some people confuse this nomenclature with Type A units, the Option A and Option B bathrooms are limited to Type B units.
- 100*.12 deals with kitchen requirements within units. Kitchenettes or wet bars must comply as applicable.
- 100*.13 deals with provisions for accessible windows. Type B units do not require accessible windows.
- 100*.14 deals with storage facilities such as closets, cabinets and shelving other than those in the kitchen area. Type B units do not include requirements for storage facilities.
- 100*.15 deals with requirements related to beds in an Accessible unit. The standard does not contain requirements for beds in Type A or Type B units.

1001 General

❖ Dwelling units and sleeping units are defined in Section 106.5.

A dwelling unit contains independent facilities for living, sleeping, eating, cooking and sanitation (i.e., living room, bedroom, a full kitchen and a bathroom). This group covers all types of units that individuals or families think of as their house and a minimal number of transient lodging facilities. Examples are: apartments, condominiums, townhouses, single-family homes and residential type hotel guestrooms.

A sleeping unit is something that is not a full dwelling unit. It can be just a sleeping area, such as a dorm room with access to gang bathrooms and no cooking facilities. A sleeping unit can include either sanitation or cooking, but not both (i.e., the unit is a space to live and sleep, but shares a bathroom outside the unit and/or does not include a full kitchen). This group covers all types of congregate living arrangements and most transient lodging. Examples are: guestrooms in hotels and motels; bedrooms in dormitories, boarding houses, sorority houses, fraternity houses, halfway houses, group homes, monasteries, convents, assisted living facilities and nursing homes; and sleeping cells in jails.

1001.1 Scoping. Dwelling units and sleeping units required to be Accessible units, Type A units, Type B units, Type C (Visitable) units or units with accessible communication features by the scoping provisions adopted by the administrative authority shall comply with the applicable provisions of Chapter 10.

❖ The requirements of this chapter are intended to provide the technical criteria for accessibility within dwelling and sleeping units for Accessible, Type A, Type B or Type C units when scoped by the authority having jurisdiction (see Section 201). Scoping may also include dwelling or sleeping units that require accessible communication features, regardless of whether the unit is accessible in other ways. For example, an apartment building may have requirements for visible alarm notification appliances (e.g., visible fire alarms and smoke detectors) or entry systems (e.g., closed circuit communication systems) to all floors in a building, including upper floors without elevator access.

The model codes contain scoping criteria for the three levels of accessibility in dwelling and sleeping units (Accessible, Type A and Type B). The level of accessibility increases based on the anticipated needs. At this point, the model codes do not contain scoping criteria for Type C (Visitable) units, and those units would only be required if the jurisdiction provided specific scoping provisions for those units (see Section 201).

While the terminology of having an "Accessible"-type-dwelling unit may initially be confusing, it is important to always notice the distinction between an "Accessible" unit (with a capital "A") and elements that are accessible (with a lower case "a"). The capital "A" is used when referencing the Accessible dwelling units that are described in detail in Section 1002. These units are constructed to be fully accessible (all features are built and installed at the time of initial construction); whereas, the Type A and Type B units allow certain items to be adapted or installed when the occupant needs or desires them. It is confusing, but all three unit types (Accessible, Type A and Type B) are considered as being accessible (lower case "a"). It is important to recognize and remember the distinction between the capital "A" Accessible and the lower case "a" accessible.

The model codes provide scoping criteria for accessibility in all types of places where people live, eat and sleep. Types of dwelling units are addressed, including apartments, condominiums and townhouses. Typically single-family detached homes are exempted, but a homeowner may choose to follow these criteria to build an accessible home. The model codes also contain scoping criteria for congregate living facilities, such as assisted-living facilities, group homes, shelters, nursing homes, boarding houses, dormitories, convents, monasteries, fraternities and sororities. Even though each person's accommodations may not contain all the elements listed in Chapter 10, they must comply with the applicable provisions. For example, a boarding house may have a private or semiprivate sleeping room with a private bath, but additional living space and possibly a kitchen area common to a group of rooms. If the boarding house sleeping rooms are scoped for Type B units, the sleeping rooms, bathrooms and all shared/common spaces for residents must have a minimum level of accessibility consistent with Type B unit criteria.

The International Code Council, including ICC A117.1, is working toward coordinating with federal requirements such as the Americans with Disabilities Act (ADA) and the Fair Housing Act (FHA). For example, ADA deals with transient facilities such as a typical hotel. A percentage of the hotel rooms must be constructed as Accessible units. FHA deals mostly with permanent housing, such as apartments. Apartment buildings are required to contain Type B units. In some situations ADA and FHA overlap, such as in dormitories and nursing homes. In these situations, the model codes require a percentage of units to be Accessible units and a percentage of units to be Type B units. These examples are illustrations only. For full criteria, see the scoping in the model codes.

ICC A117.1 has typically been certified as a "safe harbor" document for compliance with the Fair Housing Act Accessibility Guidelines (FHAG). At publication time of this commentary, A117.1-2009 has not received formal safe harbor status from the U.S. Department of Housing and Urban Development. However, since each edition of the standard including and since 1986 (1986, 1992, 1998 and 2003) has been approved as a safe harbor document, ICC does anticipate that the 2009 edition will ultimately be accepted as a safe harbor document. The provisions for Type B units within the standard are intended to be consistent with FHAG. The Type A and Accessible units exceed FHAG so they would be permitted to replace any unit that is required to be a Type B unit.

1002 Accessible Units

❖ Accessible units are considered to provide a higher level of accessibility than both Type A and Type B units. Therefore, compliance with the provisions in Section 1002 would exceed Type A and Type B requirements. The Accessible unit has all accessible features installed at the time of construction; whereas Type A and Type B units may have some elements, such as grab bars, installed later when the occupant needs them.

For the design of an Accessible unit, the requirements in Sections 1002.1 through 1002.15 must be met. The technical criteria are either specifically stated in these sections or a reference is given to another section of the standard that contains the applicable technical standard. If a technical standard in another chapter is not referenced, it is not applicable to the design of an Accessible unit.

1002.1 General. Accessible units shall comply with Section 1002.

❖ An Accessible dwelling or sleeping unit must comply with all the provisions in this section. Accessible units are constructed wheelchair accessible. See the scoping documents for when Accessible dwelling and sleeping units are required. Accessible units are typically required in transient facilities such as hotels or facilities where there is a high anticipation of people who may need these facilities, such as nursing homes.

1002.2 Primary Entrance. The accessible primary entrance shall be on an accessible route from public and common areas. The primary entrance shall not be to a bedroom unless it is the only entrance.

❖ In an apartment-type unit, the main entrance is typically into a central living area, so this should also be the accessible entrance for the unit. The accessible entrance cannot be a "back door" entrance, such as a patio door or through a bedroom.

In an efficiency unit or sleeping unit where the main living area is also the bedroom, this entrance may serve as the accessible entrance, and is acceptable by the last sentence of this section. It is not the intent of this section to require an entry vestibule or second room. Having the limiter of "unless it is the only entrance" helps to resolve the uncertainty that occurs where the unit is either an efficiency unit or a sleeping unit in a hotel, dormitory, assisted living facility and so forth and entry is through the "bedroom." Without that added limitation, the standard would not be as clear as to the proper application of this requirement for this common entry arrangement.

This accessible unit entrance must be connected by an accessible route to an accessible building entrance and all public or shared areas intended for the use of the residents of that unit. This includes areas such as the building lobby, mailboxes, garbage chutes or dumpsters, shared laundry facilities and recreational facilities, such as exercise rooms or pools. See also Section 1002.5 for requirements for the accessible entrance door to the unit.

In facilities such as hotels or nursing homes, the changing of linens or removal of garbage may be the responsibility of employees rather than residents. In these situations, the areas such as laundry rooms and garbage disposal areas should be regulated under the employee work area provisions and are not required to be accessible to the residents of the dwelling units.

1002.3 Accessible Route. Accessible routes within Accessible units shall comply with Section 1002.3.

❖ The accessible route within the unit must meet the provisions for location, turning space and components. In the 2003 edition of the standard, this section contained an added sentence dealing with limited size exterior spaces such as faux balconies. This requirement has been revised and relocated to Section 1002.5, Exception 6, in the 2009 edition of the standard. See the commentary for Section 1002.5 for information regarding these limited size exterior spaces.

1002.3.1 Location. At least one accessible route shall connect all spaces and elements that are a part of the unit. Accessible routes shall coincide with or be located in the same area as a general circulation path.

EXCEPTION: An accessible route is not required to unfinished attics and unfinished basements that are part of the unit.

❖ A route must be available to all living spaces within the unit, to all stories in the unit as well as any raised or sunken floor areas.

In a congregate living arrangement, this also includes access to shared spaces such as the bathroom and living or eating areas.

The accessible route should be equivalent and consistent with the general circulation path. The intent of this sentence is similar to what was described in Section 1002.1 from the aspect that the accessible route should not be a back door or secondary route where the person using the accessible route would have a less desirable path of travel. In earlier editions of the standard, this section listed specific rooms or areas that the accessible route was not to pass through. The current wording in the second sentence of this section ensures equal treatment and makes it easier to determine what locations are acceptable for the route. As long as the accessible route within the unit is the same as the route used by everyone else, it should not make any difference which rooms or spaces the accessible route goes through.

Based on the exception, unfinished attics and basements are not required to be on an accessible route because these spaces do not include living space for the unit. Where the basement or attic is finished, an accessible route is required to those levels and those portions of the unit.

1002.3.2 Turning Space. All rooms served by an accessible route shall provide a turning space complying with Section 304.

EXCEPTIONS:

1. A turning space shall not be required in toilet rooms and bathrooms that are not required to comply with Section 1002.11.2.
2. A turning space is not required within closets or pantries that are 48 inches (1220 mm) maximum in depth.

❖ Turning spaces are required in each room. This turning space can be circular or T-shaped. The turning spaces can include knee and toe clearances under fixtures, counters, shelves, etc. Using the option of a T-shaped space may help minimize the size impact of this requirement. For example, in a kitchen or bathroom a T-shaped turning space with the base or one arm extending beneath the required accessible sink, work surface, lavatory or vanity may reduce the room size from that needed by a circular turning space.

The first exception coordinates with Section 1002.11, which only requires one toilet and bathing room within the unit to be accessible. Any additional toilet and bathing facilities would, therefore, be exempt from both the accessibility requirements (Section 1002.11.2) and the need for a turning space within the room.

Exception 2 removes the requirement for the turning space when the room under consideration is a closet or a pantry of limited depth. The 48-inch (1220 mm) depth was selected to coordinate with the clear floor space size and to limit the likelihood that a person would move far enough into the space where they could potentially become trapped if the door were to be closed behind them. With such a shallow depth, it is reasonable to permit a person to either back into or out of the space and not require a turning space to maneuver within the closet or pantry. Based on the discussions at the All7.1 committee meeting, the 48-inch (1220 mm) depth should be measured to the location where someone would move into the closet, for example, the edge of the hanging clothes that may be on the wall opposite the door. When dealing with a pantry, it would be reasonable to measure to the edge of the permanent shelves (see Commentary Figure C1002.3.2).

Although Exception 2 eliminates the turning space within the closet or pantry, the door should be evaluated and in compliance with Section 1002.5 if it is for user passage. Although the door will not need the maneuvering clearances on the inside of the closet or pantry, the door should be wide enough to comply with Section 404 if the user will be entering the closet or pantry area. If the user will just be reaching into the space from a clear floor space located outside of the closet or pantry, the door would not be considered as being "intended for user passage."

See the storage requirements from Section 1002.14. While the exception in Section 1002.14 will typically exempt a pantry, a closet may be regulated and need to provide a clear floor space and storage elements within the specified reach range.

1002.3.3 Components. Accessible routes shall consist of one or more of the following elements: walking surfaces with a slope not steeper than 1:20, doors and doorways, ramps, elevators, and platform lifts.

❖ In many ways, this section serves as a setup to transition from the accessible route requirements of Section 1002.3 to the actual technical requirements found within Sections 1002.4 through 1002.8. The accessible route throughout the unit should be on level surfaces. When a transition is needed between levels or stories, either a ramp, elevator or platform lift can be used (see commentary, Sections 1002.6, 1002.7 and 1002.8).

1002.4 Walking Surfaces. Walking surfaces that are part of an accessible route shall comply with Section 403.

❖ The reference to Section 403 requires walking surfaces that are generally level to be stable and firm with a clear width of 36 inches (915 mm). For example, carpet must have a firm cushion or no cushion at all. Heavy pile or thick padding under carpeting makes it difficult for a person using a wheelchair to turn or move forward.

1002.5 Doors and Doorways. The primary entrance door to the unit, and all other doorways intended for user passage, shall comply with Section 404.

EXCEPTIONS:

1. Existing doors to hospital patient sleeping rooms shall be exempt from the requirement for space at the latch side provided the door is 44 inches (1120 mm) minimum in width.
2. In toilet rooms and bathrooms not required to comply with Section 1002.11.2, maneuvering clearances required by Section 404.2.3 are not required on the toilet room or bathroom side of the door.
3. A turning space between doors in a series as required by Section 404.2.5 is not required.
4. Storm and screen doors are not required to comply with Section 404.2.5.
5. Communicating doors between individual sleeping units are not required to comply with Section 404.2.5.
6. At other than the primary entrance door, where exterior space dimensions of balconies are less than the required maneuvering clearance, door maneuvering clearance is not required on the exterior side of the door.

❖ The primary entrance door should be the main door used to access the unit. Any doors that a person walks through in the unit must also be accessible. This includes doors to all

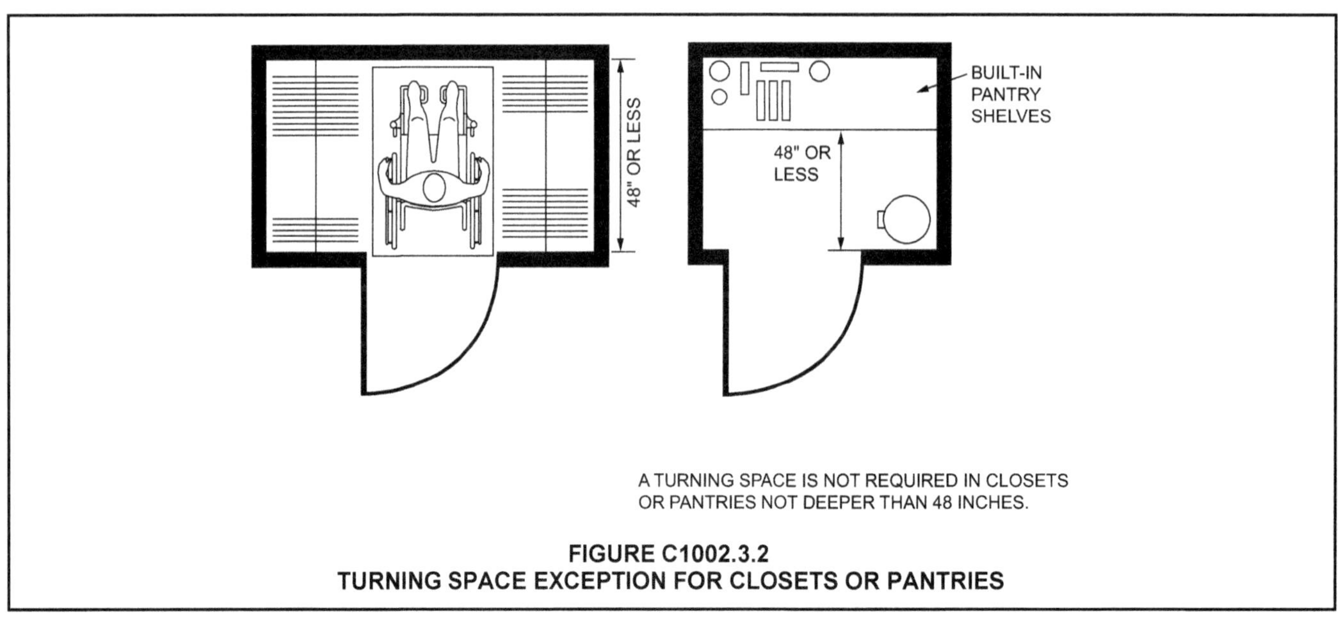

FIGURE C1002.3.2
TURNING SPACE EXCEPTION FOR CLOSETS OR PANTRIES

rooms, walk-in closets, bathrooms, balconies, etc. Doors to spaces such as reach-in closets are not required to meet the provisions for Section 404 since they are not "intended for user passage."

The requirements include 32-inch (815 mm) clear width, maneuvering clearances, thresholds, lever hardware, door opening force, door surface on the push side and vision lite locations.

The exceptions address a number of situations to either coordinate with other provisions of this standard or to clarify when certain aspects of the door provisions may be modified (see Commentary Figure C1002.5).

The first exception helps to limit the impact of the door-maneuvering requirements on an existing door in a hospital. The scoping document specifies that a percentage of the hospital patient sleeping rooms are required to meet Accessible unit requirements. In new construction, doors to Accessible units must meet the provisions in Section 404, including maneuvering clearances. In existing hospital patient sleeping rooms, the additional maneuvering clearance on the latch side of 44-inch-wide (1120 mm) doors is not required.

Exception 2 removes the door-maneuvering clearance requirement from the toilet room or bathroom side of the door when that space is not required to be accessible. This coordinates with Section 1002.11, which only requires one toilet or bathing facility in the unit to be accessible. This exception also matches a similar exception that applied to Type A dwelling units (Section 1003.5, Exception 2) and was in the 2003 edition of the standard.

The exceptions that reference Section 404.2.5 eliminate the need to comply with the doors-in-series requirements. These exceptions address two issues related to the provisions of Section 404.2.5. First of all, if there is a small entrance hall or vestibule within a dwelling unit, the turning space should not be required. This recognizes that within a dwelling unit there is less danger of entrapment within this area as there would be within an exterior vestibule in a public area or commercial building. Second, storm or screen doors, as well as the communicating doors between guestrooms, are not intended to be considered as doors in a series. Although the exceptions dealing with storm/screen doors and the communicating doors between dwelling units only refer to Section 404.2.5, it would be illogical to apply the maneuvering clearances of Section 404.2.3 separately to each door and the space between them. When the doors are placed closely together as these types of doors are, it is appropriate to consider both of the doors as being a single doorway. If they are viewed as separate doors, then this standard would generally require a 48-inch (1220 mm) front approach between the two doors and a 12-inch (305 mm) latch side clearance would be required.

Exception 6 addresses an issue that was initially placed into Section 1002.3 of the 2003 edition of the standard. The original intent was to address items such as faux balconies (balconies of very limited size that were not intended to be occupied) from the turning space and door approach requirements. Rather than addressing an arbitrary deck size of 30 inches (760 mm) as was previously done (see the 2003 edition of A117.1, Section 1002.3), the exception applies to any space having a dimension less than the required maneuvering clearance that Section 404.2.3 would require on the exterior side of the door. The phrase "at other than the primary entrance door" was included to clarify that the exception was trying to address faux balconies and did not apply to an exterior location that could serve as the entry to the unit. This viewpoint is also supported by the inclusion of the word "balconies." By using the word "balconies," this section is intended to exempt small exterior balconies but would not apply to a deck that is associated with a ground-floor dwelling unit. Where a ground-floor unit is provided with an exterior deck, it does not face the same limitations that may restrict above-grade balconies from becoming larger.

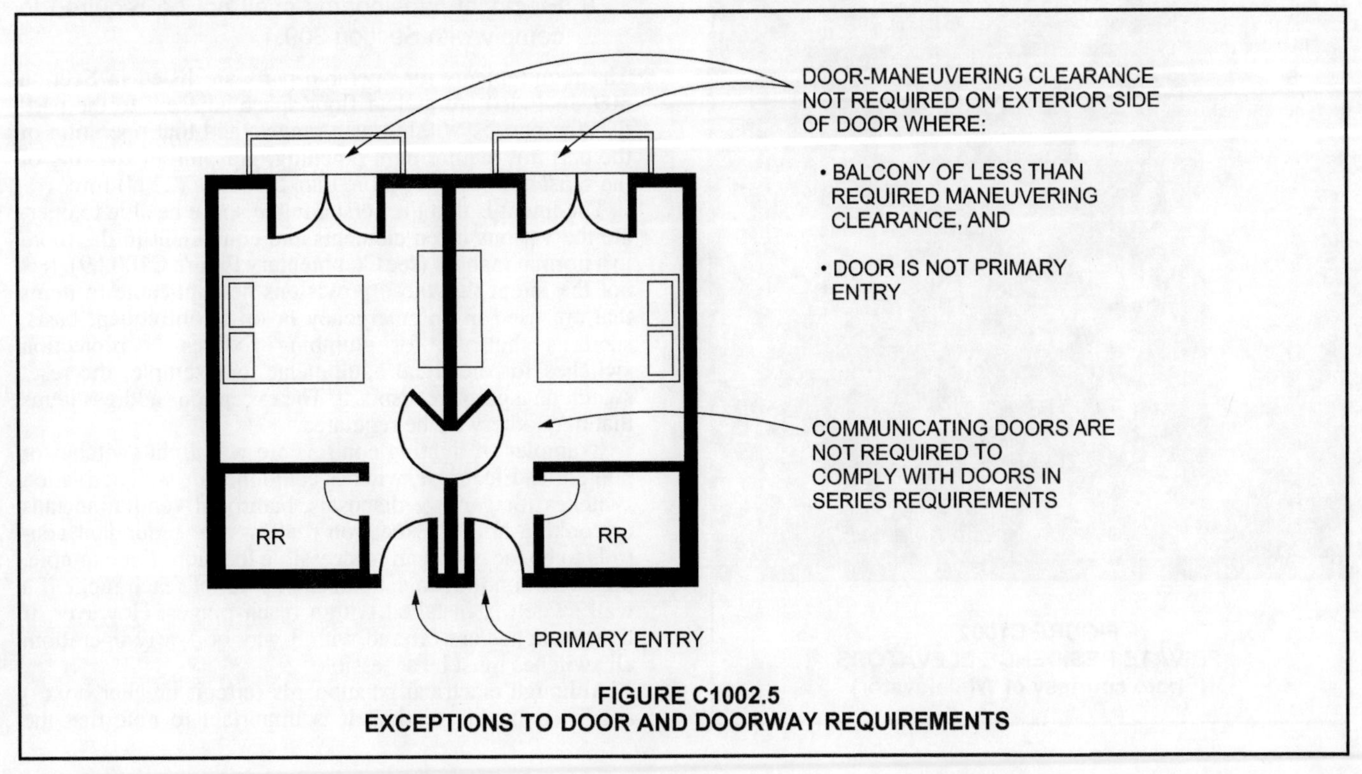

FIGURE C1002.5
EXCEPTIONS TO DOOR AND DOORWAY REQUIREMENTS

1002.6 Ramps. Ramps shall comply with Section 405.

❖ Ramps that serve as part of the accessible route into or through an Accessible dwelling or sleeping unit must meet the general ramp provisions in Section 405.

Ramps providing a change in elevation greater than 6 inches (150 mm) require handrails on both sides. The local building code should be consulted when guards are required along ramps. Ramps must have a landing at both the top and the bottom of every ramp segment, so a ramp cannot extend up to the face of a door. The ramp landing and door-maneuvering space (Section 1002.5) are permitted to overlap (Section 301.2).

1002.7 Elevators. Elevators within the unit shall comply with Section 407, 408, or 409.

❖ Elevators installed within a single dwelling unit or providing private access to a single dwelling unit are permitted to be passenger elevators, LULAs or private residence elevators. Refer to ASME A17.1 for limitations of use. For an example of a private residence elevator see Commentary Figure C1002.7.

Section 1002.3.1 requires an accessible route throughout an Accessible unit. If an Accessible unit is multistory, elevators or platform lifts (Section 1002.8) can serve as part of the accessible route within an individual unit. Although a common-use elevator is often used for residents to access common areas in a building (e.g., mail room, lobby, laundry room), it is not the intent to allow the use of a common-use elevator to provide access to multiple levels of the same unit. The accessible route should be contained within the unit.

FIGURE C1002.7
PRIVATE RESIDENCE ELEVATORS
(Photo courtesy of Wheelovator)

1002.8 Platform Lifts. Platform lifts within the unit shall comply with Section 410.

❖ Platform lifts can be used within individual dwelling units to serve as part of an accessible route between levels or to provide access into an individual unit. The lift must be a platform (wheelchair) lift in accordance with ASME A18.1, not a chair lift (e.g., flip-down seat). Platform lifts may be incline or vertical lifts. The current ASME A18.1 standard limits the maximum rise to 12 feet (3660 mm) (see ASME A18.1 for limitations of use).

1002.9 Operable Parts. Lighting controls, electrical panelboards, electrical switches and receptacle outlets, environmental controls, appliance controls, operating hardware for operable windows, plumbing fixture controls, and user controls for security or intercom systems shall comply with Section 309.

EXCEPTIONS:

1. Receptacle outlets serving a dedicated use.
2. Where two or more receptacle outlets are provided in a kitchen above a length of counter top that is uninterrupted by a sink or appliance, one receptacle outlet shall not be required to comply with 309.
3. Floor receptacle outlets.
4. HVAC diffusers.
5. Controls mounted on ceiling fans.
6. Where redundant controls other than light switches are provided for a single element, one control in each space shall not be required to be accessible.
7. Reset buttons and shut-offs serving appliances, piping and plumbing fixtures.
8. Electrical panelboards shall not be required to comply with Section 309.4.

❖ The requirements for operable parts are listed in Section 309. Included are a clear floor space adjacent to the part; that the part be within reach ranges; and that operation of the part not require tight pinching, grasping or twisting of the wrist to operate or more than 5 pounds (22 N) force.

The intent is that the person in the space be able to operate the various listed elements and equipment in the room in a normal manner (see Commentary Figure C1002.9). It is not the intent that these provisions be applicable to items that are used in an emergency or on an infrequent basis, such as shut-offs for plumbing fixtures or protection switches for electrical equipment, for example, the reset switch on a garbage disposal. The exceptions address items that may otherwise be regulated.

Examples of lighting controls are wall light switches or pull cords. Electrical switches could include wall activation switches for garbage disposals, bathroom ventilation fans or cooking hoods. Exception 6 allows for redundant controls to be located in an inaccessible location. For example, the switch on the range hood can be out of reach range if a wall switch is installed within reach ranges. However, if light switches are offered with 3-way or 4-way operation, all switches must be accessible.

Although electrical panelboards (circuit breaker boxes) are listed in this section, it is important to note that the inclusion of panelboards does not mean that they are required to be placed within the unit but simply that they are accessible where they are installed within the units and are available for operation or use by the occupants. The location and additional access requirements for panelboards are found in the National Fire Protection Association's *National Electrical Code*® (NFPA 70). If the panelboards are located within the unit, they should allow for the occupants to have access to and reach them. Exception 8 exempts circuit breakers, fuses and panelboard latches as well as the circuit breakers or fuses within them from the operation requirements of Section 309.4. A panelboard must have a clear floor space in front and be within reach range and height requirements in accordance with Sections 309.2 and 309.3.

Receptacle outlets are typically the standard duplex wall outlets located around a room or over a counter. Note that there are several exceptions for receptacle outlets. Outlets that serve a dedicated purpose (Exception 1), such as the outlet for a washer/dryer, refrigerator or stove, need not be accessible. These items are typically plugged in all the time. The model electrical code requires outlets spaced at a maximum of 12 feet (3660 mm) apart in most rooms. In spaces with very tall windows or along balcony guards, there may not be wall space for the required electrical outlets. Large rooms may need outlets located toward the center of the room. When floor outlets are used, these outlets do not need to be accessible (Exception 3). Exception 2 is used when dealing with outlets over kitchen counters. In kitchens, per the model electrical code, one outlet is required over each section of counter top with a maximum spacing of 4 feet (1220 mm). If an appliance or sink is located along a counter top, the counter on each side is considered a separate section, and an outlet must be installed on each side. In a kitchen in an Accessible unit, the sink and the work surface must be at a maximum height of 34 inches (865 mm), although the remainder of the counters can be located at any height, typically 36 inches (915 mm). Accessible outlets could be provided over the sink and work surface. However, with the obstructed side reach range requirements in Section 308.3.2, outlets cannot be located over the standard 36-inch-high (915 mm) counter and be considered accessible. Exception 2 allows for one outlet per counter section to not be accessible if the remainder of the outlets are accessible. An alternative that would provide an accessible outlet is to locate an outlet on the side or front surface of the lower cabinet. This is commonly done on kitchen island counters; however, this will reduce drawer space. This same problem is not typically found in bathrooms because bathroom counter heights are typically between 29 and 34 inches (735 and 865 mm) high.

Environmental controls can include ceiling fans or heating and air-conditioning thermostats. A common error for locating the thermostat is to specify the electrical box at 48 inches (1220 mm) high, not noting that the actual control is on the top of the thermostat box, thus placing the control out of the reach range. Exception 4 does exempt the heating and air-conditioning diffusers from being accessible. They need to be on or near the floor and near the ceiling to circulate the air in the room effectively. Exception 5 exempts controls mounted on ceiling fans. Typically the on-off and speed for ceiling fans are controlled from a wall switch, but there may be a switch on the fan itself for reversing the direction of the blades.

Appliance controls vary greatly and may include the key pad for temperature and type of cooking (e.g., bake/broil)

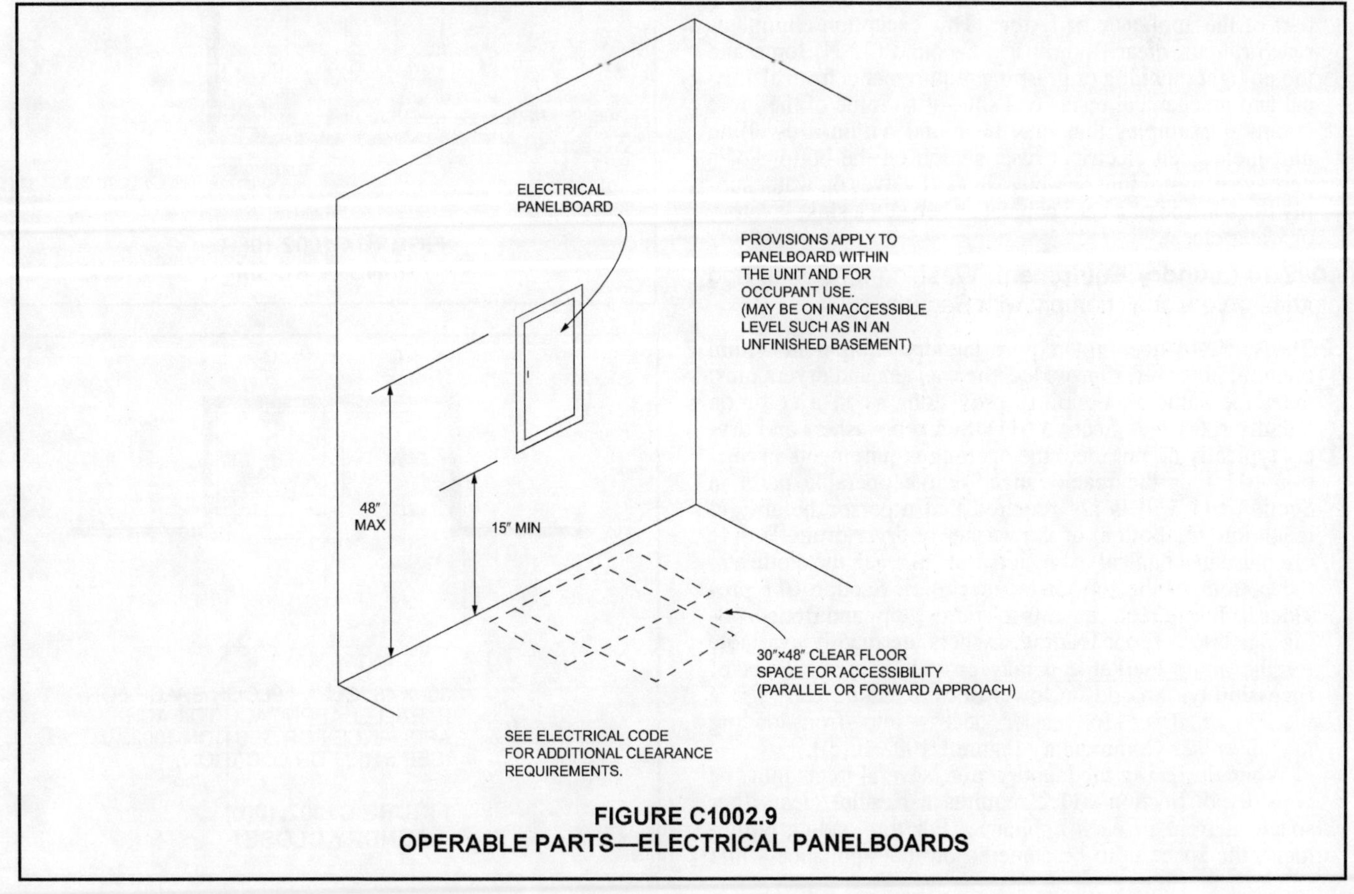

FIGURE C1002.9
OPERABLE PARTS—ELECTRICAL PANELBOARDS

on ovens, knobs for burner settings on stove tops, door handles to access the interior of the appliance, water/ice dispensers on refrigerators, latches for self-cleaning ovens, soap containers on dishwashers and clothes washers, lint trays on dryers, etc. The specifics for appliance controls in Section 804.5.2 allow some exceptions for appliance doors in kitchens. Laundry equipment is specifically addressed in Section 611.3.

Operating hardware for operable windows includes locks and opening devices for windows that must be ac-cessible in accordance with Section 1002.13. Although Section 309.4 is not referenced for window operation at this time, in order to meet the operating force requirements if desired, most windows need add-on devices for opening.

Plumbing fixture controls include faucets in showers, tubs and sinks, and flush valves on toilets. Lever-type handles are much easier to operate than knobs for those with limited hand motion or strength. See the specifics in Sections 604.6, 606.4, 607.5, 607.6, 608.4 and 608.5 for plumbing controls.

Security or intercom systems may include activation keypads or access to a phone or speaker. Refer to Sections 708, 1006.5, 1006.6 and 1006.7 for additional specifics for communication features.

Operable parts on doors are regulated under Section 1002.5 by a reference to Sections 404.2.6 and 404.3.5.

Exception 7 for reset buttons and shut-offs is intended to cover any of the elements in the base paragraph and allow electrical switches and various shut-offs to be exempt from all of the requirements of Section 309. Inclusion of this exception clarifies that these controls are not typically considered as being regulated by the standard. These types of switches or controls are not intended for everyday usage but are for protecting appliances or allowing them to be disconnected to be serviced. They may even be built in as a part of the appliance or fixture. This exception eliminates reach ranges, clear floor space, 5-pound (22 N) force and the no tight pinching or grasping requirements from electrical and mechanical resets and shut-offs. Some of the more common examples that may be found within a dwelling unit include an electrical reset switch on the bottom of a garbage disposal unit or water shut-off valves on water supply lines inside of a base cabinet or beneath a sink, lavatory or water closet.

1002.10 Laundry Equipment. Washing machines and clothes dryers shall comply with Section 611.

❖ The standard does not require laundry equipment within the unit; however, if provided, the washers and dryers must meet the same accessibility provisions as in a common laundry room (see Section 611). Stacked washers and dryers typically do not meet the opening requirements in Section 611.4 or the reach range for the operable parts in Section 611.3. It is not required that a person be able to reach into the bottom of the washer or dryer drum. People often use mechanical extension arms to reach the clothes in the bottom of the top loader machines. Section 611 provides differing requirements to address top- and front-loading machines. Front-loading washers are readily available for the home market and may provide a higher level of accessibility. An add-on lower drawer feature can raise a washer or dryer for easier access into front-loading machines [see Commentary Figure C1002.10(c)].

When designing the laundry area, several items must be considered. Section 611.2 requires a parallel clear floor space in front of each appliance. For top-loading equipment, the space is to be centered on that appliance while front-loading machines will permit the space to be offset up to 24 inches (610 mm) from the centerline (see Figure 611.2). Designers must understand the clear floor space centering requirement since it necessitates additional space on each side of each laundry appliance.

When laundry equipment is installed in a room, Section 1002.3.2 requires a turning space within the room, and Section 1002.5 requires maneuvering clearance at the door. To provide a more user friendly space, even though an accessible work surface is not required, if a counter for folding is provided within the room, knee and toe clearances should be available for that work surface. If a laundry sink is provided, scoping documents typically exempt service sinks from knee and toe clearances because of the needed depth of the sink, but it would be better design to provide a parallel approach to that sink to allow for use [see Commentary Figure C1002.10(a)].

When laundry equipment is installed in a closet, the clear floor space can be located 10 inches (255 mm) back from the face of the units (Section 308.3.1) which would allow for the wall thickness, but may necessitate either sliding closet doors or no doors, so the doors will not block the clear floor space [see Commentary Figure C1002.10(b)].

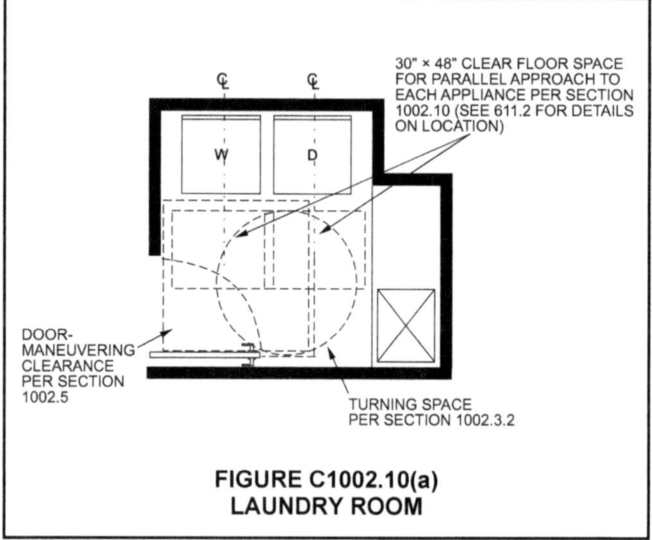

FIGURE C1002.10(a)
LAUNDRY ROOM

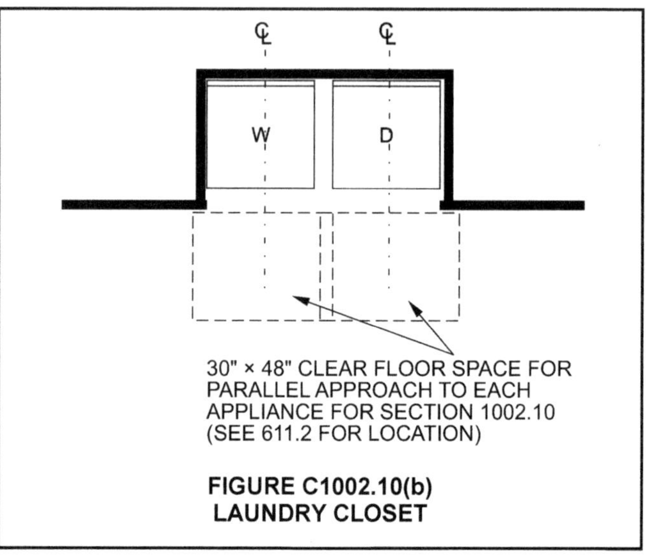

FIGURE C1002.10(b)
LAUNDRY CLOSET

FIGURE C1002.10(c)
EXAMPLE OF LAUNDRY ROOM

1002.11 Toilet and Bathing Facilities. At least one toilet and bathing facility shall comply with Section 1002.11.2. All other toilet and bathing facilities shall comply with Section 1002.11.1

❖ Every Accessible unit must have at least one bathroom constructed as fully accessible in accordance with the requirements in Sections 603 through 610. This includes grab bars installed at the water closet and tub or shower, a water closet that allows for a side transfer, a front approach lavatory and an accessible bathing fixture (i.e., either tub or shower). Unlike Type A and Type B unit bathrooms, the lavatory or any other fixture in the required accessible toilet/bathing room may not overlap the clear floor space required for the water closet. Where the unit has more than one toilet or bathing area, the additional bathrooms are not required to include maneuvering clearances for an accessible bathroom, but must include the blocking or reinforcement in the walls to allow for the future installation of grab bars and shower seat. This will allow the occupant to install the grab bars or shower seat when and if they desire them without making it a major project that would require the wall surface to be removed and replaced. This requirement for reinforcement helps to ensure that the Accessible units comply with this important provision from the federal Fair Housing Act and the Type B unit requirements.

1002.11.1 Grab Bars and Shower Seat Reinforcement. At fixtures in toilet and bathing facilities not required to comply with Section 1002.11.2, reinforcement in accordance with Section 1004.11.1 shall be provided.

EXCEPTION: Reinforcement is not required where Type B units are not provided in the structure.

❖ Because toilet and bathing areas complying with Section 1002.11.2 require the installation of grab bars and a shower seat at the time of initial construction, this section will only address the other toilet and bathing areas within the unit that are not required to be accessible. Section 1004.11.1 typically requires all toilets and bathing areas within the unit be equipped with reinforcement to allow for the future installation of grab bars and shower seats. This is an important feature that allows for this portion of the dwelling unit to be adaptable and permits the higher level Accessible unit to substitute for and still meet all of the requirements for the Type B and federal Fair Housing required units. Therefore when the Type B units are not required to be provided, the exception will allow these additional toilet and bathing areas to be built without the required reinforcement.

The exception is dealing with facilities, such as hotels and hospitals, that are not scoped to include Type B units. In these situations, since the facility is not required to comply with the Fair Housing Act, Type B criteria are not applicable.

1002.11.2 Accessible Toilet and Bathing Facility. At least one toilet and bathing facility shall comply with Section 603. At least one lavatory, one water closet and either a bathtub or shower within the unit shall comply with Sections 604 through 610. The accessible toilet and bathing fixtures shall be in a single toilet/bathing area, such that travel between fixtures does not require travel through other parts of the unit.

❖ Every Accessible unit must have at least one bathroom constructed as fully accessible in accordance with the requirements in Sections 603 through 610. Therefore all of the fixtures and elements in that toilet or bathing area are accessible just as they would be for any public facility. This includes grab bars installed at the water closet and tub or shower, a water closet that allows for a side transfer, a front approach lavatory and an accessible bathing fixture (i.e., either a tub or shower). Instead of duplicating the requirements here in the Accessible unit provisions, the standard simply provides references to the appropriate sections of Chapter 6.

The intent of the last sentence of this section is to ensure that the accessible bathing and toilet facilities are located in a single area of the unit and not dispersed throughout various portions of the unit. This provision should not be construed as prohibiting the accessible elements from being located in different rooms or compartments within the same area. In many residential uses it is common for a master suite to have the lavatory located in a central open space with perhaps the toilet or toilet and bathing fixture located in an adjacent separate room that can be closed off for privacy. This type of arrangement is allowed by the standard. The standard prevents placing the accessible bathing element in the master bathroom while the accessible toilet and lavatory are located in another bathroom serving a separate bedroom or perhaps in the general living area of the home.

1002.11.2.1 Vanity Counter Top Space. If vanity counter top space is provided in dwelling or sleeping units not required to be Accessible units within the same facility, equivalent vanity counter top space, in terms of size and proximity to the lavatory, shall also be provided in Accessible units.

❖ Accessible dwelling units are commonly scoped for hotels, dormitories, assisted living facilities or nursing homes. In these residential and institutional types of facilities, a counter space is typically provided for a person to place grooming items while using the lavatory. Counters are provided either within a bathroom or immediately adjacent (e.g., lavatory located adjacent to a room with a water closet and tub). The same type of counter space should be available for the use of the person within the Accessible unit as that which is provided in other similar units.

1002.11.2.2 Mirrors. Mirrors above accessible lavatories shall have the bottom edge of the reflecting surface 40 inches (1015 mm) maximum above the floor.

❖ This section does not require mirrors over lavatories or the installation of any mirror at all. It simply regulates the mirror's height if it is installed above the accessible lavatory.

The standard lavatory or counter height within bathrooms varies from 29 inches to 34 inches (735 to 865 mm), which coordinates with the 34-inch (865 mm) maximum height that is required for the accessible lavatory by Section 606.3. Counters or wall-mounted lavatories typically have a 4-inch-high (100 mm) backsplash. The normal eye level of a person using a wheelchair, 43 inches to 51 inches (1090 to 1295 mm), provides an angle of incidence sufficient for a reflection from a mirror with a maximum bottom edge 40 inches (1015 mm) above the floor. This allows for an adequate field of view for the desired bathing or grooming activities while allowing for clearance over the backsplash on the lavatory or counter [see Commentary Figure C102(a)].

If mirrors are to be used by both ambulatory people and wheelchair users, design standards recommend 74-inch (1880 mm) height, minimum, at the topmost edge. In rooms with multiple lavatories, the 40-inch (1015 mm) minimum height requirement only applies to the mirror over the designated accessible sink.

1002.12 Kitchens and kitchenettes. Kitchens and kitchenettes shall comply with Section 804. At least one work surface, 30 inches (760 mm) minimum in length, shall comply with Section 902.

EXCEPTION: Spaces that do not provide a cooktop or conventional range shall not be required to provide an accessible work surface.

❖ Kitchens and kitchenettes within an Accessible unit must be constructed accessible in accordance with Section 804. This would include minimum clearances, a front approach sink and an accessible work surface, along with access to each appliance. The requirement for an accessible work surface in this section is redundant with Section 804.3. Notice that the oven requirements of Section 804.5.5 will require the work surface to be adjacent to the oven.

The work surface is not required if the area is not equipped with a cooktop, range or conventional oven. Therefore, items such as a wet bar or small kitchenette with only a microwave oven would not need to provide the accessible work surface. The exception will generally be used for Accessible sleeping units (e.g., a hotel room or assisted living facility room) or for wet bars and kitchenettes within dwelling units. The fact that only a small 30-inch (760 mm) length is required for the work surface is important because it helps to clarify it is acceptable for standard cabinetry which is 36 inches (915 mm) in height to be used for most of the kitchen while only the work surface and sink would need to be at the lower 34-inch (915 mm) maximum height. Section 1002.3.2 requires a turning space within the room. If the space under the sink or the work surface is used as part of a T-turn, the width must be a minimum of 36 inches (915 mm).

1002.13 Windows. Windows shall comply with Section 1002.13.

❖ For those windows that must be operated by the occupants, it is logical to ensure that they meet a certain minimum level of requirements. Currently, double-hung windows typically need a minimum of 25 pounds (110 N) to operate, and casement windows need a minimum of $8^1/_2$ pounds (37.4 N) to operate. In order for window operation to meet a 5 lbs. (22 N) force, an add-on arm must be added. Windows that are required for natural ventilation or emergency escape and egress have requirements in the section below. A designer could choose to provide access to other operable windows in the unit; however, this is not a requirement so that design options for Accessible units would not be limited, such as high or low hopper-style windows, windows over the sink in kitchens, window raised for privacy in bathroom, etc.

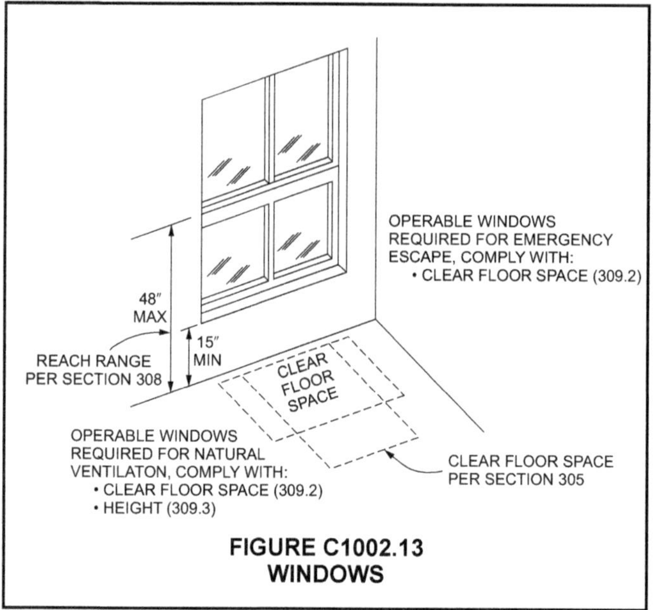

FIGURE C1002.13 WINDOWS

1002.13.1 Natural ventilation. Operable windows required to provide natural ventilation shall comply with Sections 309.2 and 309.3.

❖ The jurisdiction's scoping document will provide information regarding where operable windows are required for natural ventilation. The model building codes generally impose the requirement for natural ventilation if a mechanical ventilation system is not provided or possibly for certain specific occupancies. Where the windows are required for natural ventilation purposes, all of the required windows must meet the clear floor space and have the operable parts within reach ranges (see Commentary Figure C1002.13).

1002.13.2 Emergency escape. Operable windows required to provide an emergency escape and rescue opening shall comply with Section 309.2.

❖ Emergency escape and rescue openings allow the occupants to escape from a unit if their primary means of egress is blocked or unavailable. They also allow for emergency personnel to gain access to the unit from the exterior in order to facilitate a rescue. The jurisdiction's scoping document (i.e., building code) will provide information regarding where openings are required for emergency escape and rescue. The model building codes generally impose the requirement for these openings in sleeping areas or basements. This section of the standard will only impose the requirement for a clear floor space in front of the window (see Commentary Figure C1002.13). Building codes will typically address items such as sill height, height of hardware and minimum sizes for the opening.

1002.14 Storage Facilities. Where storage facilities are provided, at least one of each type shall comply with Section 905.

EXCEPTION: Kitchen cabinets shall not be required to comply with Section 1002.14.

❖ Storage facilities, other than those in kitchen cabinets, are scoped so that "at least one of each type" is made accessible. As an example, the types of storage facilities that may be affected by this requirement are tenant storage lockers/closets that may be located in a common area of an apartment building, an outdoor storage closet on the balcony of the dwelling unit, bathroom cabinets, linen cabinets, or a private storage closet within a garage. Storage facilities must have a clear floor space in front of the storage element. At least a portion of each storage facility provided, such as shelves or rods, must be within the 15-inch to 48-inch (350 to 1220 mm) reach range. A standard closet organizer with a high-low rod for a portion of the closet meets this provision. If there are doors or drawers, the latches and knobs must be easily operable by a person with limited hand movement and strength. If this is a reach-in closet, the door does not have to meet the clear width, threshold or maneuvering clearance requirements in Section 1002.5.

Kitchen cabinets are not regulated by this section based upon the exception. The special work environment and concentrated amount of storage allows for unique consideration. Kitchen cabinets are extremely difficult to make fully accessible, particularly in a small kitchen with limited options. The lower shelf in typical base cabinets is below the reach range while all shelves in upper cabinets are typically beyond reach ranges. Stationary appliances in lower cabinets (i.e., range, dishwasher, garbage disposal) eliminate most of the lower cabinet storage options. Note that the 2009 standard does not address kitchen cabinet storage as it had in earlier editions where a percentage of shelf space was required to be accessible. This requirement sometimes forced the removal of the upper cabinets or where the bottom shelf is within the reach range, the counter top will not fit many of the standard household appliances such as microwaves, blenders, toasters or coffee pots. Being able to move within the kitchen (via the appliance clearance requirements and width between counters) would provide access to most base cabinets, drawers and counter storage. Therefore, the clear space aspect of accessibility is generally taken care of and there is no need to be more specific. The addition of user-friendly items such as pull-out shelves in lower cabinets or a Lazy Susan in corner cabinets is fairly easy to accomplish. Pantry-type cabinets with or without pull-out elements provide readily accessible storage (see Commentary Figure C1002.14). Using extended reaching tools will allow limited access to upper cabinets. While a person with limited reach range might be unable to reach into all the cabinets, his or her family can still utilize the additional cabinets or the space may be used for storage of infrequently used items.

FIGURE C1002.14
EXAMPLES OF KITCHEN PANTRY STORAGE

1002.15 Beds. In at least one sleeping area, a minimum of five percent, but not less than one bed shall comply with Section 1002.15.

❖ The intent of all three of these sections is to make at least one of the beds within every Accessible unit usable by a person using a wheelchair. The phrase "in at least one sleeping area" is important to allowing the requirement to apply to a number of different situations where an Accessible unit may be provided. The primary intent of that phrase is similar to the requirement for toilet and bathing facilities (Section 1002.11.2), where "at least one" facility within the Accessible unit is regulated. In a unit where there are multiple bedrooms or sleeping areas, only one of them would require the complying bed. On the other hand, the language does not allow the provision to be applied across the entire building but is instead applied to each unit. For example, in a typical college dormitory or hotel, the bed requirements would not apply to only a single sleeping area or unit in the structure but would be applied individually within each Accessible unit in the building. The jurisdiction's scoping document or the model building code provides the scoping for the number of Accessible units, while Section 1002.15 addresses the number of sleeping areas within the unit that are regulated. In a large dormitory or barracks-type setting where all of the beds are in the same room or area, the requirement for "a minimum of 5 percent" means that if there were more than 20 beds within the space, more than one of them would be regulated.

1002.15.1 Clear Floor Space. A clear floor space complying with Section 305 shall be provided on both sides of the bed. The clear floor space shall be positioned for parallel approach to the side of the bed.

EXCEPTION: Where a single clear floor space complying with Section 305 positioned for parallel approach is provided between two beds, a clear floor space shall not be required on both sides of the bed.

❖ To be considered accessible, the bed must be approachable from either side in order to accommodate wheelchair users who may need to transfer from a particular side due to their mobility impairment. The alternative that is allowed by the exception applies when a bed is provided on both sides of a single-approach location. Common examples of where the exception may be applied are in the sleeping rooms of nursing homes or hotels where two beds are placed in the room.

1002.15.2 Bed Frames. At least one bed shall be provided with an open bed frame.

❖ The open bed frame is intended to allow the use of a bed lift such as a Hoyer lift to be used to transfer either to or from the bed. If the bed is installed on a solid platform, as is common at many hotels, the platform does not allow for the supports of the lifts to move under the bed. Having the open bed frame allows the legs of the lift to extend under the bed and provides a greater base of support for the lift so that it is stable and secure during the transfer. Although the language of Section 1002.15.2 could be viewed as meaning that any one bed within the unit could have the open frame, the language of Section 1002.15 should be used so that the bed with the open frame is also the bed served by the clear floor space. This is a reasonable interpretation since it will allow the person to maneuver adjacent to the bed before using the lift or allow an assistant to maneuver the lift into the clear floor space before transferring the person back to the bed (see Commentary Figure C1002.15.2).

1003 Type A Units

❖ Type A units are considered to provide a higher level of accessibility than Type B units, but less accessibility than Accessible units. Therefore, compliance with the provisions in Section 1003 would exceed Type B requirements and compliance with Section 1002 would exceed Type A requirements.

For the design of a Type A unit, the requirements in Sections 1003.1 through 1003.14 must be met. The technical criteria are either specifically stated in these sections or the section contains a reference to another section of the standard that contains the applicable technical standard. If a technical standard in another chapter is not referenced, it is not applicable to the design of a Type A unit.

1003.1 General. Type A units shall comply with Section 1003.

❖ A Type A dwelling or sleeping unit must comply with all the provisions in this section. Type A units have some elements constructed wheelchair accessible [e.g., 32-inch (815 mm)] clear doors with maneuvering clearances, controls within reach ranges) and some elements that allow for planning for those elements to be made accessible (e.g., sink and work space in the kitchen, lavatory in the bathroom). When fully adapted, the Type A units come close to meeting the level of access found in Accessible units. The bathrooms, depending on the configuration, may have a lesser level of accessibility. See the scoping documents for when Type A dwelling and sleeping units are required. Type A units are typically found in large apartment buildings.

Historically the Type A unit had been called the Adaptable dwelling unit in the A117.1 editions prior to 1998. The idea of Adaptable dwelling units was added into the model building codes in the mid-1970s. When Type B units were added, the name of this type of unit was changed to Type A.

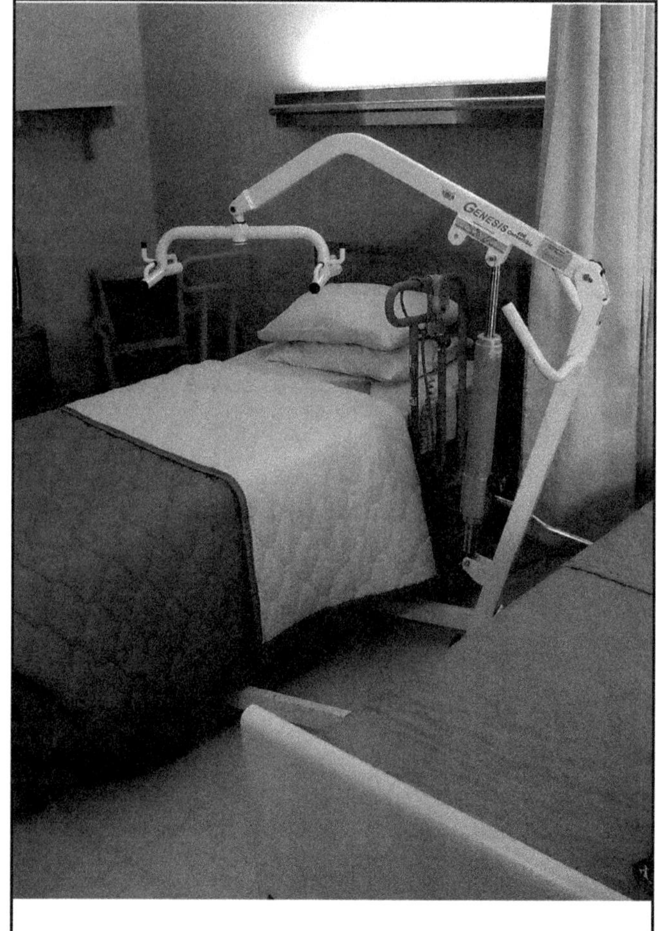

FIGURE C1002.15.2
OPEN BED FRAME FOR BED LIFT

1003.2 Primary Entrance. The accessible primary entrance shall be on an accessible route from public and common areas. The primary entrance shall not be to a bedroom unless it is the only entrance.

❖ In an apartment type unit, the main entrance is typically into a central living area, so this should also be the accessible entrance for the unit. The accessible entrance cannot be a "back door" entrance, such as a patio door or through a bedroom.

In an efficiency unit or sleeping unit where the main living area is also the bedroom, this entrance may serve as the accessible entrance, and is acceptable by the last sentence of this section. It is not the intent of this section to require an entry vestibule or second room. Having the limiter of "unless it is the only entrance" helps to resolve the uncertainty that occurs where the unit is either an efficiency unit or a sleeping unit in a hotel, dormitory, assisted living facility and so forth and entry is through the "bedroom." Without that added limitation, the standard would not be as clear as to the proper application of this requirement for this common entry arrangement.

This accessible unit entrance must be connected by an accessible route to an accessible building entrance and all public or shared areas intended for the use of the residents of that unit. This includes areas such as the building lobby, mailboxes, garbage chutes or dumpsters, shared laundry facilities and recreational facilities, such as exercise rooms or pools. Also see Section 1002.5 for requirements for the accessible entrance door to the unit.

In facilities such as hotels or nursing homes, the changing of linens or removal of garbage may be the responsibility of employees rather than residents. In these situations, the areas such as laundry rooms and garbage disposal areas should be regulated under the employee work area provisions and are not required to be accessible to the residents of the dwelling units.

1003.3 Accessible Route. Accessible routes within Type A units shall comply with Section 1003.3.

❖ The accessible route within the unit must meet the provisions for location, turning space and components. In the 2003 edition of the standard, this section contained an added sentence dealing with limited size exterior spaces such as faux balconies. This requirement has been revised and relocated to Section 1003.5, Exception 6, in the 2009 edition of the standard. See the commentary to Section 1003.5 for information regarding these limited size exterior spaces.

1003.3.1 Location. At least one accessible route shall connect all spaces and elements that are a part of the unit. Accessible routes shall coincide with or be located in the same area as a general circulation path.

EXCEPTION: An accessible route is not required to unfinished attics and unfinished basements that are part of the unit.

❖ A route must be available to all living spaces within the unit. A route must be available to all stories in the unit, as well as any raised or sunken floor areas. In a congregate living arrangement, this also includes access to shared spaces such as the bathroom and living or eating areas.

The accessible route should be equivalent and consistent with the general circulation path. The intent of this sentence in the standard is similar to what was described in Section 1003.2 from the aspect that the accessible route should not be a backdoor or secondary route where the person using the accessible route would have a less desirable path of travel. When only one accessible route is available to certain spaces, the route should not be through areas that are subject to locking such as bathrooms or closets. This is not intended to prohibit access through spaces controlled by the individual. For example, a master suite with the closet accessed through the bathroom would not be blocking access for the occupant of that bedroom. On the other hand, the access to the pool area in the apartment complex should not be through a changing room that may be subject to being locked and therefore limiting access. In earlier editions of the standard, this section listed specific rooms or areas that the accessible route was not to pass through. The current wording in the second sentence of this section ensures equal treatment and makes it easier to determine what locations are acceptable for the route. As long as the accessible route within the unit is the same as the route used by everyone else, it should not make any difference which rooms or spaces the accessible route goes through.

Based on the exception, unfinished attics and basements are not required to be on an accessible route because these spaces do not include living space for the unit. Where the basement or attic is finished, an accessible route is required to those levels and portions of the unit.

1003.3.2 Turning Space. All rooms served by an accessible route shall provide a turning space complying with Section 304.

EXCEPTIONS:

1. A turning space is not required in toilet rooms and bathrooms that are not required to comply with Section 1003.11.2.
2. A turning space is not required within closets or pantries that are 48 inches (1220 mm) maximum in depth.

❖ Turning spaces are required in each room. This turning space can be circular or T-shaped. The turning spaces can include knee and toe clearances under fixtures, counters, shelves, etc. Remembering the option of using a T-shaped space may help minimize the size impact of this requirement. For example, in a kitchen or bathroom, a T-shaped turning space with the T-base or one T-arm extending beneath the required sink, work surface, lavatory or a vanity may reduce the room size to less than that needed by a circular turning space.

The first exception coordinates with Sections 1003.11 and 1003.11.2. In Type A units with multiple bathrooms, only one bathroom must meet the clearances in Section 1003.11.2. The bathroom that is not accessible does not require a turning space within the room. The bathroom that serves as the accessible bathroom is allowed to have the turning space utilize the knee and toe clearances under the lavatory (e.g., after cabinetry is removed), rather than at the time of initial construction.

Exception 2 removes the requirement for the turning space when the room under consideration is a closet or a pantry of limited depth. The 48-inch (1220 mm) depth was selected to coordinate with the clear floor space size and to limit the likelihood that a person would move far enough into the space where they could potentially become trapped if the door were to be closed behind them. With such a shallow depth, it is reasonable to permit a person to either back into or out of the space and not require a turning space to maneuver within the closet or pantry. Based on the discussions at the A117.1 committee meeting, the 48-inch (1220 mm) depth should be measured to the location where someone would move into the closet, for example, edge of the hanging clothes that may be on the wall opposite the door. When dealing with a pantry, it would be reasonable to measure to the edge of the permanent shelves (see Commentary Figure C1002.3.2.)

Although Exception 2 eliminates the turning space within the closet or pantry, the door should be evaluated and in compliance with Section 1003.5 if it is for user passage. Although the door will not need the maneuvering clearances on the inside of the closet or pantry, the door should be wide enough to comply with Section 404 if the user will be entering the closet or pantry area. If the user will just be reaching into the space from a clear floor space located outside of the closet or pantry, the door would not be considered as being "intended for user passage."

See the storage requirements from Section 1002.14. While the exception in Section 1002.14 will typically exempt a pantry, a closet may be regulated and need to provide a clear floor space and storage elements within the specified reach range.

1003.3.3 Components. Accessible routes shall consist of one or more of the following elements: walking surfaces with a slope not steeper than 1:20, doors and doorways, ramps, elevators, and platform lifts.

❖ In many ways, this section serves as a setup to transition from the accessible route requirements of Section 1003.3 to the actual technical requirements found within Sections 1003.4 through 1003.8. The accessible route throughout the unit should be on level surfaces. When a transition is needed between levels or stories, either a ramp, elevator or platform lift can be used (see commentary, Sections 1003.6, 1003.7 and 1003.8).

1003.4 Walking Surfaces. Walking surfaces that are part of an accessible route shall comply with Section 403.

❖ Section 403 requires walking surfaces to be stable and firm and generally level with a clear width of 36 inches (915 mm). For example, carpet must have a firm cushion or no pad. Heavy pile or thick padding under carpets makes it difficult for a person using a wheelchair to turn or move forward. Thick padding underfoot is also a tripping hazard for persons who shuffle or do not or cannot lift their feet as they walk.

1003.5 Doors and Doorways. The primary entrance door to the unit, and all other doorways intended for user passage, shall comply with Section 404.

EXCEPTIONS:

1. Thresholds at exterior sliding doors shall be permitted to be $^{3}/_{4}$ inch (19 mm) maximum in height, provided they are beveled with a slope not greater than 1:2.
2. In toilet rooms and bathrooms not required to comply with Section 1003.11.2, maneuvering clearances required by Section 404.2.3 are not required on the toilet room or bathroom side of the door.
3. A turning space between doors in a series as required by Section 404.2.5 is not required.
4. Storm and screen doors are not required to comply with Section 404.2.5.
5. Communicating doors between individual sleeping units are not required to comply with Section 404.2.5.
6. At other than the primary entrance door, where exterior space dimensions of balconies are less than the required maneuvering clearance, door maneuvering clearance is not required on the exterior side of the door.

❖ The primary entrance door should be the main door used to access the unit—typically the front door. Any doors that a person walks through in the unit must also be accessible. This includes doors to all rooms, walk-in closets, bathrooms, balconies, etc. Doors to spaces such as reach-in closets are not required to meet the provisions for Section 404 since they are not "intended for user passage."

Requirements include 32-inch (815 mm) clear width, maneuvering clearances, thresholds, lever hardware, door opening force, bottom door surface on the push side and vision lite locations.

Section 404.2.4 requires a $^{1}/_{2}$-inch (13 mm) maximum threshold. Exception 1 allows a $^{3}/_{4}$-inch (19 mm) threshold at exterior sliding doors. This typically occurs most often at an exterior balcony or deck.

Section 1003.11 states that only one bathroom in a multibathroom unit must be accessible in accordance with Section 1003.11.2. Per Exception 2, maneuvering clearance is not required on the inside of the door to the inaccessible bathroom, but is required on the outside of the door.

The exceptions that reference Section 404.2.5 eliminate the need to comply with the doors in series requirements. These exceptions address two issues related to the provisions of Section 404.2.5. First, if there is a small entrance hall or vestibule within a dwelling unit, the turning space should not be required. This recognizes that within a dwelling unit there is less danger of entrapment within this area as there would be within an exterior vestibule in a public area or commercial building. Second, storm or screen doors, as well as the communicating doors between units, are not intended to be considered as doors in a series. Although the exceptions dealing with storm/screen doors and the communicating doors between dwelling units only refer to Section 404.2.5, it would be illogical to apply the maneuvering clearances of Section 404.2.3 separately to each door and the space between them. When the doors are placed closely together, as these types of doors are, it is appropriate to consider both of the doors as being a single doorway. If they are viewed as separate doors, then this standard would generally require a 48-inch (1220 mm) front approach between the two doors and a 12-inch (305 mm) latch side clearance could be required.

Exception 6 addresses an issue that was initially placed into Section 1003.3 of the 2003 edition of the standard. The original intent was to address items such as faux balconies (balconies of very limited size that were not intended to be occupied) from the turning space and door approach requirements. Rather than addressing an arbitrary deck size of 30 inches (760 mm), as was previously done (see the 2003 edition of A117.1, Section 1003.3), the exception applies to any space having a dimension less than the required maneuvering clearance that Section 404.2.3 would require on the exterior side of the door. The phrase "at other than the primary entrance door" was included to clarify that the exception was trying to address faux balconies and did not apply to an exterior location that could serve as the entry to the unit. This viewpoint is also supported by the inclusion of the word "balconies." By using the word "balconies," this section is intended to exempt small exterior balconies but would not apply to a deck that is associated with a ground-floor dwelling unit. Where a ground-floor unit is provided with an exterior deck, it does not face the same limitations that may restrict above-grade balconies from becoming larger (see Commentary Figure C1002.5).

1003.6 Ramps. Ramps shall comply with Section 405.

❖ Ramps that serve as part of the accessible route into or through a Type A dwelling or sleeping unit must meet the general ramp provisions in Section 405.

Ramps provided for a change in elevation greater than 6 inches (150 mm) require handrails on both sides. The local building code should be consulted when guards are required along ramps. Ramps must have a landing at both the top and the bottom, so a ramp cannot extend up to the face of a door. The ramp landing and door-maneuvering space (Section 1003.5) are permitted to overlap (Section 301.2).

1003.7 Elevators. Elevators within the unit shall comply with Section 407, 408, or 409.

❖ Elevators installed within a single dwelling unit or providing private access to a single dwelling unit are permitted to be passenger elevators, LULAs or private residence elevators. Refer to ASME A17.1 for limitations of use.

Section 1003.3.1 requires an accessible route throughout a Type A unit. If a Type A unit is multistory, elevators or platform lifts (Section 1003.8) can serve as part of the accessible route within an individual unit. Even though a common-use elevator is often used for residents to access common areas in a building (e.g., mail room, lobby, laundry room), it is not the intent to allow the use of a common-use elevator for access to multiple levels of the same unit. The accessible route should be contained within the unit.

1003.8 Platform Lifts. Platform lifts within the unit shall comply with Section 410.

❖ Platform lifts can be used within individual dwelling units to serve as part of an accessible route (Section 1003.3.1) between levels or to provide access into an individual unit. The lift must be a platform (wheelchair) lift in accordance with ASME A18.1, not a chair lift (e.g., flip-down seat). Platform lifts may be inclined lifts or vertical lifts. The current ASME A18.1 standard limits the maximum rise to 12 feet (3660 mm) (see ASME A18.1 for limitations of use).

1003.9 Operable Parts. Lighting controls, electrical panelboards, electrical switches and receptacle outlets, environmental controls, appliance controls, operating hardware for operable windows, plumbing fixture controls, and user controls for security or intercom systems shall comply with Section 309.

EXCEPTIONS:

1. Receptacle outlets serving a dedicated use.
2. Where two or more receptacle outlets are provided in a kitchen above a length of counter top that is uninterrupted by a sink or appliance, one receptacle outlet shall not be required to comply with Section 309.
3. Floor receptacle outlets.
4. HVAC diffusers.
5. Controls mounted on ceiling fans.
6. Where redundant controls other than light switches are provided for a single element, one control in each space shall not be required to be accessible.
7. Reset buttons and shut-offs serving appliances, piping and plumbing fixtures.
8. Electrical panelboards shall not be required to comply with Section 309.4.

❖ The requirements for operable parts are listed in Section 309. Included is a clear floor space adjacent to the part; that the part be within reach ranges; and that operation of the part not require tight pinching, grasping or twisting of the wrist to operate or more than 5 pounds (22 N) force.

The intent is that the person in the space be able to operate the various listed elements and equipment in the room in a normal manner (see Commentary Figure C1003.9). It is not the intent that these provisions be applicable to items that are used in an emergency or on an infrequent basis, such as shut-offs for plumbing fixtures or protection switches for electrical equipment, such as the reset switch on a garbage disposal. The exceptions address items that may otherwise be regulated.

Examples of lighting controls are wall light switches or pull cords. Electrical switches could include wall activation switches for garbage disposals, bathroom ventilation fans or cooking hoods. Exception 6 allows for redundant controls located in an inaccessible location. For example, the switch on the range hood can be out of reach range if a wall switch is installed within reach ranges. However, if light switches are offered with 3-way or 4-way operation, all switches must be accessible.

Although electrical panelboards (circuit breaker boxes) are listed in this section, is important to note that the inclusion of panelboards does not mean that they are required to be placed within the unit but simply that they are accessible where they are installed within the units and are available for operation or use by the occupants. The location and additional access requirements for panelboards are found in the National Fire Protection Association's *National Electrical Code* (NFPA 70). If the panelboards are located within the unit, they should allow for the occupants to have access to and reach them. Exception 8 exempts circuit breakers, fuses and panelboard latches as well as the circuit breakers or fuses within them from the operation requirements of Section 309.4. A panelboard must have a clear floor space in front and be within reach range and height requirements per Sections 309.2 and 309.3 (see Commentary Figure C1002.9).

Receptacle outlets are typically the standard duplex wall outlets located around a room or over a counter. Note that there are several exceptions for receptacle outlets. Outlets that serve a dedicated purpose (Exception 1), such as the outlet for a washer/dryer, refrigerator or stove, need not be accessible. These items are typically plugged in all the time. The model electrical code requires outlets spaced at a maximum of 12 feet (3660 mm) apart in most rooms. In spaces with very tall windows or along balcony guards there may not be wall space for the required electrical outlets. Large rooms may need outlets located toward the center of the room. When floor outlets are used, these outlets do not need to be accessible (Exception 3). Exception 2 is used when dealing with outlets over kitchen counters. In kitchens, per the model electrical code, one outlet is required over each section of counter top with a maximum spacing of 4 feet (1220 mm). If an appliance or sink is located along a counter top, the counter on each side is considered a separate section and an outlet must be installed on each side. In a kitchen in a Type A unit, the sink and the work surface must be adjustable to a maximum height of 34 inches (865 mm), while the remainder of the counters can be located at any height, typically 36 inches (915 mm). Outlets could be installed over the sink and work surface so they would be accessible when those areas were modified. However, with the obstructed side reach range requirements in Section 308.3.2, outlets cannot be located over the standard 36-inch-high (915 mm) counter and be accessible. Exception 2 allows for one outlet per counter section to not be accessible if the remainder of the outlets are accessible. An alternative is to locate an outlet on the side or front surface of the lower cabinet. This is commonly done on kitchen island counters; however, this will reduce drawer space. This same problem is not typically found in bathrooms because bathroom counter heights are typically installed between 29 and 34 inches (735 and 865 mm) high.

FIGURE C1003.9
EXAMPLES OF OPERABLE PARTS

Environmental controls can include ceiling fans or heating and air-conditioning thermostats. A common error when locating the thermostat is to center the electrical box at 48 inches (1220 mm) high, not noting that the actual control is at the top of the thermostat box, thus placing the control out of reach range. Exception 4 does exempt the heating and air-conditioning diffusers from being accessible. They need to be on or near the floor and ceiling to circulate the air in the room effectively. Exception 5 exempts controls mounted on ceiling fans. Typically the on-off and speed for ceiling fans are controlled from a wall switch, but there may be a switch on the fan itself for reversing the direction of the blades.

Appliance controls vary greatly and may include the key pad for temperature and type of cooking (e.g., bake/broil) on ovens, knobs for burner settings on stove tops, door handles to access the interior of the appliance, water/ice dispensers on refrigerators, latches for self-cleaning ovens, soap containers in dishwashers and clothes washers, lint trays in dryers, etc. The specifics for appliance controls in Section 1003.12.5.1 allow for some exceptions for appliance doors in kitchens. Laundry equipment is specifically addressed in Section 1003.10 with a reference that includes Section 611.3 for operable parts.

Operating hardware for operable windows includes locks and opening devices for windows that must be accessible in accordance with Section 1003.13. Although Section 309.4 is not referenced for window operation at this time, in order to meet the operating force requirements if desired, most windows need add-on devices for opening.

Plumbing fixture controls would include faucets in showers, tubs and sinks, and flush valves on toilets. Lever-type handles are much easier to operate than knobs for those with limited hand mobility or strength. See Sections 1003.11.2.4.6, 606.4, 607.5, 607.6, 608.4 and 608.5 for more information on plumbing controls.

Security or intercom systems may include activation keypads or access to a phone or speaker. Refer to Sections 708, 1006.5, 1006.6 and 1006.7 for additional specifics for communication features that are part of security or intercom systems.

Operable parts on doors are regulated under Section 1003.5 through a reference to Sections 404.2.6 and 404.3.5.

Exception 7 for reset buttons and shut-offs is intended to cover any of the elements in the base paragraph and allow electrical switches and various shut-offs to be exempt from all of the requirements of Section 309. Inclusion of this exception clarifies that these controls are not typically considered as being regulated by the standard. These types of switches or controls are not intended for everyday usage but are for protecting appliances or allowing them to be disconnected for service. They may even be built in as a part of the appliance or fixture. This exception will eliminate the reach ranges, clear floor space, 5-pound (22 N) force, and the no tight-pinching or grasping requirements. Some of the more common examples that may be found within a dwelling unit would include an electrical reset switch on the bottom of a garbage disposal unit or the water shut-off valves that may be found on water supply lines in a base cabinet or beneath a sink, lavatory or water closet.

1003.10 Laundry Equipment. Washing machines and clothes dryers shall comply with Section 611.

❖ The standard does not require laundry equipment within the unit; however, if provided, the washers and dryers must meet the same accessibility provisions as in a common-use laundry room (see Section 611).

Laundry facilities present some complex problems of accessibility to the person in a wheelchair. The reach ranges in Section 308 do not include criteria for accessing things that require bending the elbow joint such as reaching over the top of and into the basket of a top-loading clothes washing machine or down and into the front of a front-loading washer or dryer. Many devices are available to aid the user in reaching into these appliances to retrieve clothes at the bottom of the washer basket or rear of the dryer drum.

This standard includes specifics for top- and front-loading laundry equipment and basically assumes separate pieces of laundry equipment (see Commentary Figure C1003.10). Criteria included are clear floor space, height of the door handles and operational requirements for all operable parts (e.g., doors, lint traps) and controls (e.g., time or temperature settings, on/off control). It is not the intent of this standard to prohibit dual use equipment or stacked units if they show equivalent or greater levels of accessibility (see Section 103). However, stacked washers and dryers typically do not meet the door height limitations in Section 611.4 or the reach range for the operable parts in Section 611.3. Front-loading washers are now readily available for the home market and may provide a higher level of accessibility. An add-on base/drawer feature can raise the washer and dryer for easier access into the drum [see Commentary Figure C1002.10(c)].

When designing the laundry area, several items must be considered. Section 611.2 requires a parallel clear floor space in front of each appliance. For top-loading equipment the space is to be centered on that appliance while front-loading machines will permit the space to be offset up to 24 inches (610 mm) from the centerline (see Figure 611.2). Designers must understand the clear floor space

FIGURE C1003.10
EXAMPLES OF LAUNDRY ROOM

centering requirement since it will typically require that the laundry area be large enough to provide approximately 10 to 12 inches (255 to 305 mm) between the appliances and the nearest side wall or obstruction.

When laundry equipment is placed in a room, Section 1003.3.2 requires a turning space within the room, and Section 1003.5 requires maneuvering clearance at the door. If a counter for folding is provided within the room, to provide a more user-friendly space, even though an accessible work surface is not required, knee and toe clearances should be available for that work surface. If a laundry sink is installed, scoping documents typically exempt it from knee and toe clearances because of the needed depth of the sink. A better design provides adequate space for a parallel approach to laundry sinks. [see Commentary Figure C1002.10(a)].

When laundry equipment is installed in a closet, the clear floor space can be located 10 inches (255 mm) back from the face of the units (Section 308.3.1), which would allow for the jamb thickness, but may necessitate either sliding closet doors or no doors so the doors will not block the clear floor space [see Commentary Figure C1002.10(b)]. This standard does not address whether removal of the doors by an occupant can be considered an adaptable feature.

1003.11 Toilet and Bathing Facilities. At least one toilet and bathing facility shall comply with Section 1003.11.2. All toilet and bathing facilities shall comply with Section 1003.11.1.

❖ Every Type A unit must have at least one bathroom constructed to be accessible in accordance with the requirements in Section 1003.11.2. A bathroom includes at least one lavatory, one water closet and either a bathtub or a shower. Unlike the Accessible unit requirements of Section 1002.11, removable cabinetry can be installed beneath the lavatory and the lavatory may be located to overlap the required clearance around the water closet. Where the unit has more than one toilet room or bathing room, the additional bathing/toilet rooms are not required to be accessible, but must include blocking or reinforcement in the walls to allow for the future installation of grab bars and shower seat. This will allow the occupant to install the grab bars or shower seat when and if they desire them without making it a major project that would require the wall covering to be removed and replaced. This requirement for blocking/reinforcement helps to ensure that the Type A units comply with this important provision from the federal Fair Housing Act and the Type B unit requirements.

The inaccessible bathroom(s) must have blocking in the walls for the future installation of grab bars (see Sections 1003.11 and 1003.11.1); however, the fixture clearances and other items under the other subsections of Section 1003.11.2 are not required. Exception 1 for Section 1003.3.2 exempts the inaccessible bathroom from having a turning space within the room. Section 1003.5, Exception 2, exempts the door to the inaccessible bathroom from maneuvering clearances on the inside of the bathroom. This ensures that Type A unit bathroom requirements are not less than what is required for Type B unit bathrooms.

1003.11.1 Grab Bar and Shower Seat Reinforcement. Reinforcement shall be provided for the future installation of grab bars complying with Section 604.5 at water closets; grab bars complying with Section 607.4 at bathtubs; and for grab bars and shower seats complying with Sections 608.3, 608.2.1.3, 608.2.2.3 and 608.2.3.2 at shower compartments.

EXCEPTIONS:

1. At fixtures not required to comply with Section 1003.11.2, reinforcement in accordance with Section 1004.11.1 shall be permitted.
2. Reinforcement is not required in a room containing only a lavatory and a water closet, provided the room does not contain the only lavatory or water closet on the accessible level of the dwelling unit.
3. Reinforcement for the water closet side wall vertical grab bar component required by Section 604.5 is not required.
4. Where the lavatory overlaps the water closet clearance in accordance with the exception to Section 1003.11.2.4.4 reinforcement at the water closet rear wall for a 24-inch (610 mm) minimum length grab bar, centered on the water closet, shall be provided.

❖ In Type A unit bathrooms, blocking must be provided for the future installation of grab bars at the water closet and bathtub or shower. This requirement is applicable to all toilet and bathing facilities and elements within the unit (see Section 1003.11). Therefore, the general requirements of the base paragraph apply to any shower, tub or water closet that is installed within the unit. This section assumes the grab bars or shower seat are not installed during the initial construction but will be added when the occupant desires them. Users should be certain to remember this section so that they do not require the grab bars to actually be installed when dealing with the bathing fixture requirements that simply direct them to Section 607 or 608. The reference to water closets (Section 604.5), bathtubs (Section 607.4) and showers (Section 608) provides the information for the length and location of the grab bars and the location of shower seats. Shower seat requirements are found in the various subsections of Section 608 and the details for the seat are in Section 610. The blocking must be sized to cover the range for the height of the grab bars and the minimum lengths. Allowance must also be made for the attachment of the grab bars. The escutcheon plates at the ends of the bars are larger than the bars, and a minimum edge distance must be allowed for secure embedment of the screws used to attach the bar to the wall (see Commentary Figure C1003.11.1).

Exception 1 helps ensure the Type A units meet or exceed the requirements for a Type B unit. To fully understand the application of the exception, it is important to remember that the base paragraph requires every water closet, bathtub and shower to provide reinforcement, which would allow for the future installation of grab bars or shower seat in compliance with the specified sections of Chapter 6. This exception allows the reinforcement for fixtures that are not required to be accessible fixtures from Section 1003.11.2 to have either blocking to support the normally required grab bars from Chapter 6 or blocking that meets the Type B requirements from Section 1004.11.1. The "fixtures not required to comply with Section 1003.11.2" would include any of the three mentioned fixtures (water closets, bathtubs or showers) that are located in a bathroom that is not required to be accessible, but it would also pick up any extra fixtures that may be provided within the accessible bathroom. As an example, in a secondary bathroom (one not required to comply with Section 1003.11.2), the side wall next to the water closet could have blocking installed to allow a 24-inch-long (610 mm) grab bar instead of the normally required 42-inch-long (1067 mm) grab bar (see 1004.11.1, Exception 4). Another example is that because Section 1003.11.2 regulates "either a bathtub or a shower, " if complying blocking was installed in the walls adjacent to the tub (see Section 607.4) then the shower seat blocking could be eliminated based on Exception 7 to Section 1004.11.1. This second

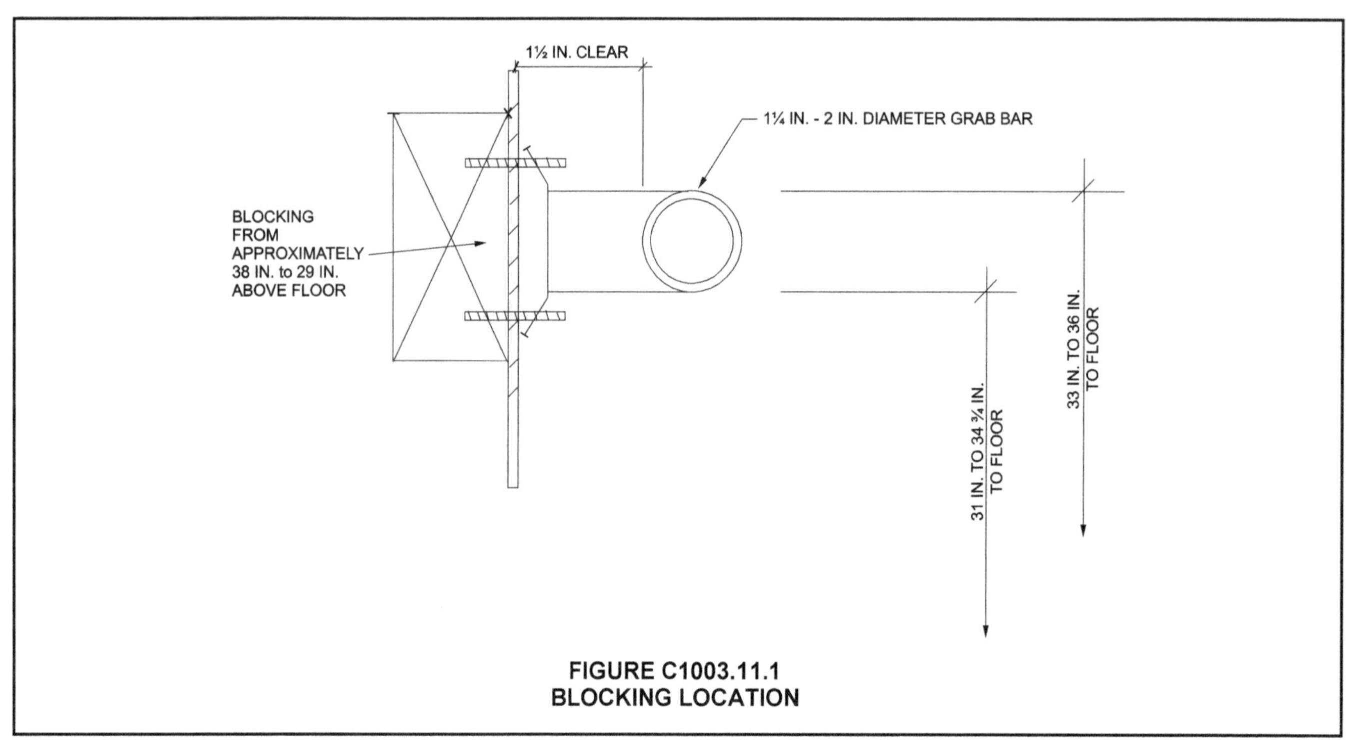

FIGURE C1003.11.1
BLOCKING LOCATION

example points out an important aspect of Section 1003.11.1, which is the fact that blocking is required for all bathtubs, showers and water closets within the unit, including those extra bathing fixtures within the Section 1003.11.2 compliant bathroom.

Exception 2 will exempt a toilet room with only a water closet and a lavatory, often referred to as a powder room or a half-bath. If this toilet room is the only restroom on the accessible level, it must contain blocking in the walls at the water closet. If other toilet facilities are provided on that floor level, blocking is not required in the powder room.

The water closet side wall vertical grab bar that is specified in Section 604.5.1 is not required in Type A units based on Exception 3. While the vertical grab bar would be helpful to aid people to rise from or sit on the water closet, the exception recognizes that windows are often located on the wall adjacent to the water closet within dwelling units.

Exception 4 has the same intent as Section 604.5.2, Exception 1, by allowing a reduced grab bar length where a lavatory is installed in the clear floor space at the side of the water closet (Section 1003.11.2.4.4, Exception). This fourth exception allows the rear wall grab bar reinforcement to be shorter when the lavatory is so close to the water closet that it will conflict with the typical 36-inch-long (915 mm) grab bar installation (Section 604.5.2).

1003.11.2 General. At least one toilet and bathing facility shall comply with Section 1003.11.2. At least one lavatory, one water closet and either a bathtub or shower within the unit shall comply with Section 1003.11.2. The accessible toilet and bathing fixtures shall be in a single toilet/bathing area, such that travel between fixtures does not require travel through other parts of the unit.

❖ When a Type A unit has multiple bathrooms, only one bathroom in the unit must be accessible. Unlike an Accessible unit, there are provisions that allow for planning for the future installation of grab bars, and installing cabinetry under the lavatory. There are also allowances for lavatories to overlap the clearance for the water closet in Type A units that are not permitted in Accessible units.

Bathroom requirements in Type A units result in a higher level of accessibility than required for Type B dwelling units. Users should be certain to not confuse the Option A bathroom requirements (Section 1004.11.3.1) of a Type B dwelling unit with those requirements for bathrooms in a Type A unit (Section 1003.11).

In Type A units the bathroom has certain elements that are constructed accessible, and certain elements that are permitted to be adaptable. Because these types of units are typically required where the residents are nontransient, the unit bathroom can be adapted post occupancy based on the needs of the resident.

Although only one bathroom needs to comply with Section 1003.11.2, each bathroom needs to be located on an accessible route (Section 1003.3.1) and have accessible doors (Section 1003.5). The bathroom chosen to be accessible must include a turning space (Section 1003.3.2). Because the exception to Section 1003.11.2.2 allows for cabinetry to be installed under the lavatory, the turning space can rely on the knee and toe clearance that would be available under the lavatory when and if the bathroom is adapted for accessibility in the future.

Items specifically addressed for the designated accessible toilet or bathing room are door swing, a lavatory, a mirror, a water closet and a bathing facility. Notice also that the reinforcement for grab bars and shower seats (Section 1003.11.1) is required in *all* toilet and bathing facilities of the unit (Section 1003.11). Based on the scoping within Section 1003.11.2, where two lavatories are provided in the same room, only one is required to meet the provisions in this section. Where a bathtub and a separate shower are provided in the same room, only one bathing facility is required to meet the access provisions in this section, although reinforcement (Section 1003.11.1) is required for both bathing fixtures.

The intent of the last sentence of this section is to ensure that the accessible bathing and toilet area is located in a single area of the unit and not dispersed throughout various portions of the unit. This provision should not be construed as prohibiting the accessible elements from being located in different rooms within the same area. In many residential uses, it is common for a master suite to have the lavatory located in a central open space with perhaps the toilet or toilet and bathing fixture located in a separate room that can be closed off to allow privacy. This type of arrangement is allowed by the standard. The text is trying to prevent something like placing the accessible bathing fixture in the master bathroom while the accessible toilet and lavatory are located in a bathroom serving a separate bedroom or perhaps in the general living area of the home.

1003.11.2.1 Doors. Doors shall not swing into the clear floor space or clearance for any fixture.

EXCEPTION: Where a clear floor space complying with Section 305.3 is provided within the room beyond the arc of the door swing.

❖ The door to the accessible bathroom must not swing into the bathroom and over the clear floor space for the lavatory, water closet, tub or shower. However, the exception allows that where a 30-inch by 48-inch (760 by 1220 mm) wheelchair space is provided past the swing of the door, the door can swing over the fixture clearances. With this configuration, someone could enter the room, maneuver away from the door to close it, and then maneuver to access the fixtures. Based on Section 305.4, the 30-inch by 48-inch (760 by 1220 mm) wheelchair space required by the exception can include knee and toe clearances under the lavatory. However, the maneuvering clearances for the door itself are to be unobstructed and are not allowed to include knee and toe clearances beneath any fixture (Section 404.2.3).

1003.11.2.2 Lavatory. Lavatories shall comply with Section 606.

EXCEPTION: Cabinetry shall be permitted under the lavatory, provided the following criteria are met:

(a) The cabinetry can be removed without removal or replacement of the lavatory;

(b) The floor finish extends under the cabinetry; and

(c) The walls behind and surrounding the cabinetry are finished.

❖ The lavatory is one of the elements that is permitted to be adaptable in a Type A unit. The base requirements are for a lavatory with a maximum height of 34 inches (865 mm), a clear floor space for a front approach with associated knee and toe clearances underneath the lavatory and faucets that meet operable parts requirements. Pipes underneath must be padded or configured to prevent accidental contact that may result in injury. This is the same as required in an Accessible unit.

The exception allows for installation of cabinetry under the lavatory or counter top. The intent of other requirements is to ensure that the modification be accomplished with the minimum amount of additional work in the space. Preplanning allows for an easy modification rather than becoming a major remodeling project to make the bathroom look "finished." A design with a lavatory supported on a vanity cabinet that must be removed, requiring reinstallation of a lavatory and installation of new floor coverings, new trim, new wall painting, etc., does not comply with this exception.

An alternative could be a pedestal lavatory, if the pedestal does not interfere with knee and toe clearances.

Lavatories in Type B units require a lesser level of access (e.g., parallel approach), but they may use either of the options permitted for lavatories in a Type A unit because this is considered to result in a higher level of access.

The reference to Section 606 in the base paragraph includes all subsections (Section 606.1 through 606.6). The provisions in Section 606.5 for a lavatory with enhanced reach range probably will never apply within a Type A unit because the model building code only requires this feature where there are six or more lavatories installed within the toilet or bathing room. However, nothing would prevent the use of these provisions and they would improve access for many.

1003.11.2.3 Mirrors. Mirrors above accessible lavatories shall have the bottom edge of the reflecting surface 40 inches (1015 mm) maximum above the floor.

❖ This section does not require mirrors over lavatories or the installation of any mirror at all. It simply regulates the mirror's height if it is installed above the accessible lavatory.

The standard lavatory or counter height within bathrooms varies from 29 inches to 34 inches (735 to 865 mm), which coordinates with the 34-inch (865 mm) maximum height that is required for the accessible lavatory by Section 606.3. Counters or wall-mounted lavatories typically have a 4-inch-high (100 mm) backsplash. The normal eye level of a person using a wheelchair, 43 inches to 51 inches (1090 to 1295 mm), provides an angle of incidence sufficient for a reflection from a mirror with a maximum bottom edge 40 inches (1015 mm) above the floor. This allows for an adequate field of view for the desired bathing or grooming activities while allowing for clearance over the backsplash on the lavatory or counter [see Commentary Figure C102(a)].

If mirrors are to be used by both ambulatory people and wheelchair users, design standards recommend 74-inch (1880 mm) height, minimum, at the topmost edge. In rooms with multiple lavatories, the 40-inch (1015 mm) minimum height requirement only applies to the mirror over the designated accessible sink.

1003.11.2.4 Water Closet. Water closets shall comply with Section 1003.11.2.4.

❖ This section primarily provides the scoping for the various subsections that affect the water closets within a Type A unit. The specific requirements dictate the location of the water closet (a wall behind and to one side), the clear floor space around the water closet, as well as the seat height and location of flush controls. When all these features are provided, the water closet will be accessible. It is important to remember the scoping from Sections 1003.11 and 1003.11.2, these provisions only apply to one water closet within one toilet facility in the unit.

Although not directly addressed in this section, the reinforcement requirements from Section 1003.11.1 should be reviewed to ensure that grab bars may be easily installed by the occupants when and if they are desired.

Reinforcement for the future installation of grab bars is required for all of the water closets (Section 1004.11.1) except for powder rooms covered by Exception 2 in Section 1003.11.1.

1003.11.2.4.1 Location. The water closet shall be positioned with a wall to the rear and to one side. The centerline of the water closet shall be 16 inches (405 mm) minimum and 18 inches (455 mm) maximum from the sidewall.

❖ In Type A units the water closet must be positioned adjacent to a wall so the wall-mounted grab bars can be installed in the future. The relationship between the wall and the water closet is the same as in an Accessible unit.

Sixteen inches to 18 inches (405 to 455 mm) has been established as the optimal dimension from a side wall or partition to the center line of the water closet to allow optimum bearing and reach for the grab bar. Once everything is installed, this 2-inch (50 mm) tolerance addresses differences that occur between the plumbing rough-in and the finished wall to water closet measurement.

1003.11.2.4.2 Clearance Width. Clearance around the water closet shall be 60 inches (1525 mm) minimum in width, measured perpendicular from the side wall.

❖ The 2009 edition of the standard revised the format of the clearance provisions and separated the clearance width, depth and overlap provisions into small sections so that the requirements can be easily stated and determined. However, all three of these provisions work in conjunction with each other and are not truly independent requirements. It is how they coordinate that determines if the water closet is accessible and what the final clearance requirements are.

Basically, the water closet must be set in a clear floor space that is at least 60 inches (1525 mm) in depth when measured from the side wall. This requirement is the same as for a water closet in an Accessible unit (Section 1002.11.2) or an accessible public restroom (Section 604.3.1). This 60-inch (1525 mm) width is intended to allow a user to do a side transfer from a wheelchair onto the water closet. The 60-inch (1525 mm) clear width, with no other fixtures in the space, provides approximately 30 inches (760 mm) between the water closet and the nearest wall or fixture on the open side of the water closet. This space allows the wheelchair user to back into the space and accomplish a side transfer as shown in Commentary Figure C604.3.1(a).

The overlap requirements of Section 1003.11.2.4.4 are important to this width clearance since it indicates that only specific elements such as grab bars, coat hooks and the wheelchair turning space or clear floor space for other fixtures may overlap or encroach into the 60-inch (1525 mm) space. The overlap provisions continue to state that "no other fixtures or obstructions shall be located within the required water closet clearance." Therefore, under the general provisions of Sections 1003.11.2.4.2 and 1003.11.2.4.4, the standard will not allow any type of obstruction within the 60-inch (1525 mm) width. See Figure 1003.11.2.4(b) and Sections 1003.11.2.4.3 and 1003.11.2.4.4 for additional related information.

1003.11.2.4.3 Clearance Depth. Clearance around the water closet shall be 56 inches (1420 mm) minimum in depth, measured perpendicular from the rear wall.

❖ As mentioned in the commentary to Section 1003.11.2.4.2, the requirements of this section must be viewed together with the clearance width requirements of Section 1003.11.2.4.2 and the overlap provisions of Section 1003.11.2.4.4.

This general 56-inch (1420 mm) depth requirement for the water closet's clear space is again identical to that required in an Accessible unit (Section 1002.11.2) or an accessible public restroom (Section 604.3.2). In addition, this clearance may only have very limited items within it and as stated in Section 1003.11.2.4.4, "no other fixtures or obstructions shall be located within the required...clearance."

A review of the exception in Section 1003.11.2.4.4 shows that a second option is available if the depth of the clear floor space is increased to 66 inches (1675 mm) minimum measured from the back wall. This second option allows for a lavatory to be placed on the rear wall near the water closet if the depth of the clear floor space is increased to 66 inches (1675 mm). With the lavatory overlapping the general minimum clear floor space for the water closet, there is not adequate space for a side transfer. The 10 inches (255 mm) of extra depth will allow for the wheelchair to be positioned to allow for a diagonal or front transfer to the water closet [see Commentary Figure C604.3.1(b)].

See commentary Sections 1003.11.2.4.2 and 1003.11.2.4.4 for related information.

1003.11.2.4.4 Clearance Overlap. The required clearance around the water closet shall be permitted to overlap the water closet, associated grab bars, paper dispensers, coat hooks, shelves, accessible routes, clear floor space required at other fixtures, and the wheelchair turning space. No other fixtures or obstructions shall be located within the required water closet clearance.

EXCEPTION: A lavatory measuring 24 inches (610 mm) maximum in depth and complying with Section 1003.11.2.2 shall be permitted on the rear wall 18 inches (455 mm) minimum from the centerline of the water closet to the side edge of the lavatory where the clearance at the water closet is 66 inches (1675 mm) minimum measured perpendicular from the rear wall.

❖ Requirements for clearances (Sections 1003.11.2.4.2 and 1003.11.2.4.3) and overlap (Section 1003.11.2.4.4) must be viewed in conjunction (see commentary, Sections 1003.11.2.4.2 and 1003.11.2.4.4 for related information). The provisions basically allow either a side or diagonal transfer to the water closet for a person using a wheelchair.

The overlaps that are permitted are intended to allow for access to the water closet, and for everything a person needs to reach from the water closet (e.g., grab bars, toilet

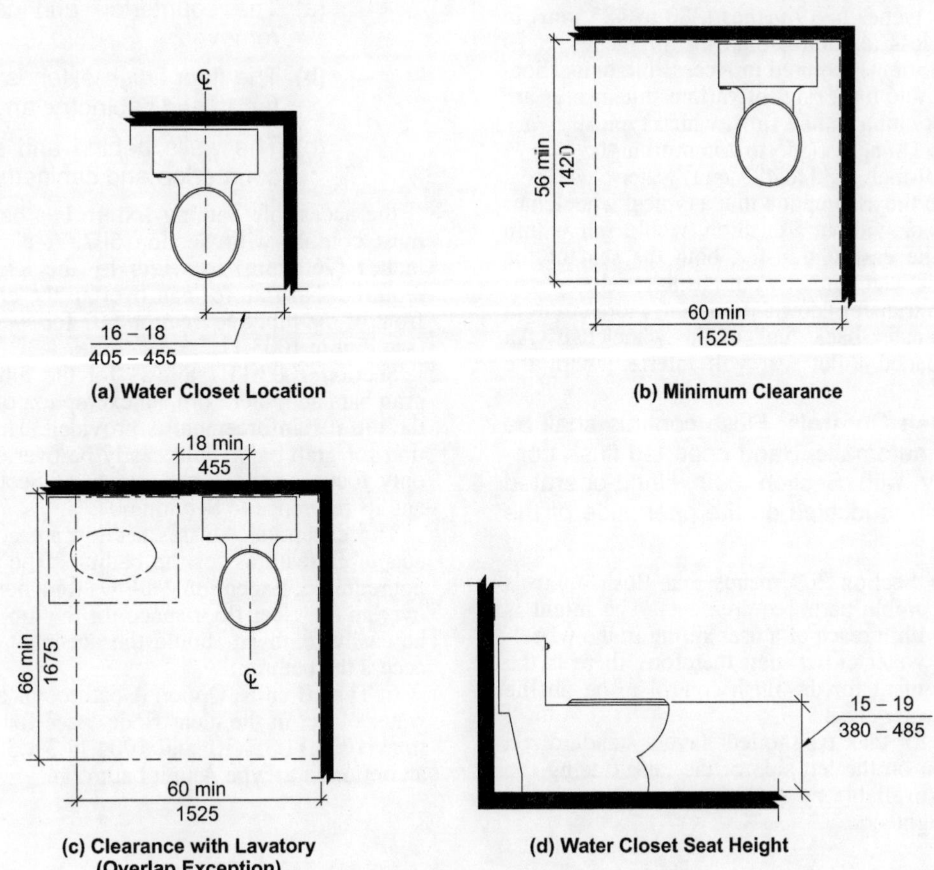

(a) Water Closet Location

(b) Minimum Clearance

(c) Clearance with Lavatory (Overlap Exception)

(d) Water Closet Seat Height

FIGURE 1003.11.2.4
WATER CLOSETS IN TYPE A UNITS

paper dispensers, etc.). Although shelves can overlap the clear floor space, the intent is that shelves must not obstruct access to the water closet or the future installation of grab bars.

The exception allows a lavatory to be placed within the clear floor space serving the water closet [see Figure 1003.11.2.4(c)] when the depth of the clearance is increased (see commentary Section 1003.11.2.4.3 for discussion related to the exception). It should be noted that this exception for the lavatory is not allowed within an Accessible unit or a public restroom. The reduced level of access that the lavatory obstruction creates is only acceptable within a Type A or Type B dwelling or sleeping unit (Section 1004.11.3.1.2.2, Exception).

The lavatory's 24-inch (610 mm) maximum depth specified in the exception was selected to ensure the Type A units are consistent with the Type B provisions of Section 1004.11.3.1.2.2.4 and may therefore serve as a compliant alternate to the Type B units. While the exception specifically says a "lavatory," there is no reason that a lavatory with cabinetry should not be allowed provided it complies with the exception in Section 1003.11.2.2.

1003.11.2.4.5 Height. The top of the water closet seat shall be 15 inches (380 mm) minimum and 19 inches (485 mm) maximum above the floor, measured to the top of the seat.

❖ Preferences for the heights of toilet seats vary considerably among persons with disabilities. Higher seats are an advantage to some ambulatory persons with disabilities, but a disadvantage for some wheelchair users and others. The allowance for 15 inches to 19 inches (380 to 485 mm) in Type A units is less restrictive than the 17 inches to 19 inches (430 to 485 mm) required in Accessible units (Section 604.4). Seats and filler rings of various thicknesses are available to adapt china fixture rims, which typically vary from 14 inches to 18 inches (355 to 455 mm) high.

A 17-inch to 19-inch (430 to 485 mm) water closet seat height is based on the assumption that a typical wheelchair seat height, with or without a cushion, would fall within that range. For the easiest transfer, both the seat of the wheelchair and the water closet would be as level as possible. It is easier to transfer "down" to a seat, more strength is required to transfer back "up" to the wheelchair. An upward spring-loaded toilet seat will interfere with the user's transfer.

1003.11.2.4.6 Flush Controls. Flush controls shall be hand-operated or automatic. Hand operated flush controls shall comply with Section 309. Hand-operated flush controls shall be located on the open side of the water closet.

❖ The reference to Section 309 means that flush controls must meet all operable parts requirements. The intent is that controls be within reach of a user sitting in the wheelchair, not on the water closet seat; therefore, there is the additional requirement for the flush control to be on the open side of the water closet.

Flush controls for tank-type toilets have a standardized mounting location on the left side of the tank (facing the tank). Tanks are available by special order with controls mounted on the right side.

The requirement for the control to be located on the open side is not intended to prohibit a top-of-tank flush control as long as the control is within reach ranges. In theory, any control located from the centerline of the water closet towards the open side can meet the open side requirement. The flush control can also be located on the wall or some other location provided it complies with the operable parts requirements.

1003.11.2.5 Bathing Fixtures. The accessible bathing fixture shall be a bathtub complying with Section 1003.11.2.5.1 or a shower compartment complying with Section 1003.11.2.5.2.

❖ This section coordinates with the provisions of Section 1003.11.2 to indicate either a bathtub or a shower must comply with the applicable sections and be the accessible bathing fixture. Remember that although only one of the fixtures is required to be accessible, all bathing facilities throughout the unit must comply with the reinforcement provisions in Section 1003.11.1 (see Section 1003.11).

1003.11.2.5.1 Bathtub. Bathtubs shall comply with Section 607.

EXCEPTIONS:

1. The removable in-tub seat required by Section 607.3 is not required.
2. Counter tops and cabinetry shall be permitted at one end of the clearance, provided the following criteria are met:
   (a) The countertop and cabinetry can be removed;
   (b) The floor finish extends under the countertop and cabinetry; and
   (c) The walls behind and sur-rounding the countertop and cabinetry are finished.

❖ If the accessible bathing fixture is a bathtub, the bathtub must comply with Section 607. A clear floor space 30 inches (760 mm) in width by the length of the tub is required. No fixtures can overlap the clear floor space in front of the tub. See Section 607 for specific requirements (see Figure 1003.11.2.5.1).

Section 1003.11.1 allows for the future installation of grab bars and, therefore, an exemption of grab bars around the tub if reinforcement is provided. This general exemption for grab bars could easily be overlooked if designers only focus on the requirements of Section 1003.11.2.5.1 and its reference to Section 607.

The exceptions in this section are concerned with the adaptable features for the bathtub. The removable seat is not required. Exception 2 allows for a portion of a vanity to overlap the clear floor space for the tub if this portion can be easily removed should the occupant need the space to access the bathtub.

In Type B units, Option A bathrooms allow a lavatory or water closet in the clear floor space for the bathtub (Sections 1004.11.3.1.3.1 and 1004.11.3.1.3.2), but this is not an option in a Type A unit bathroom.

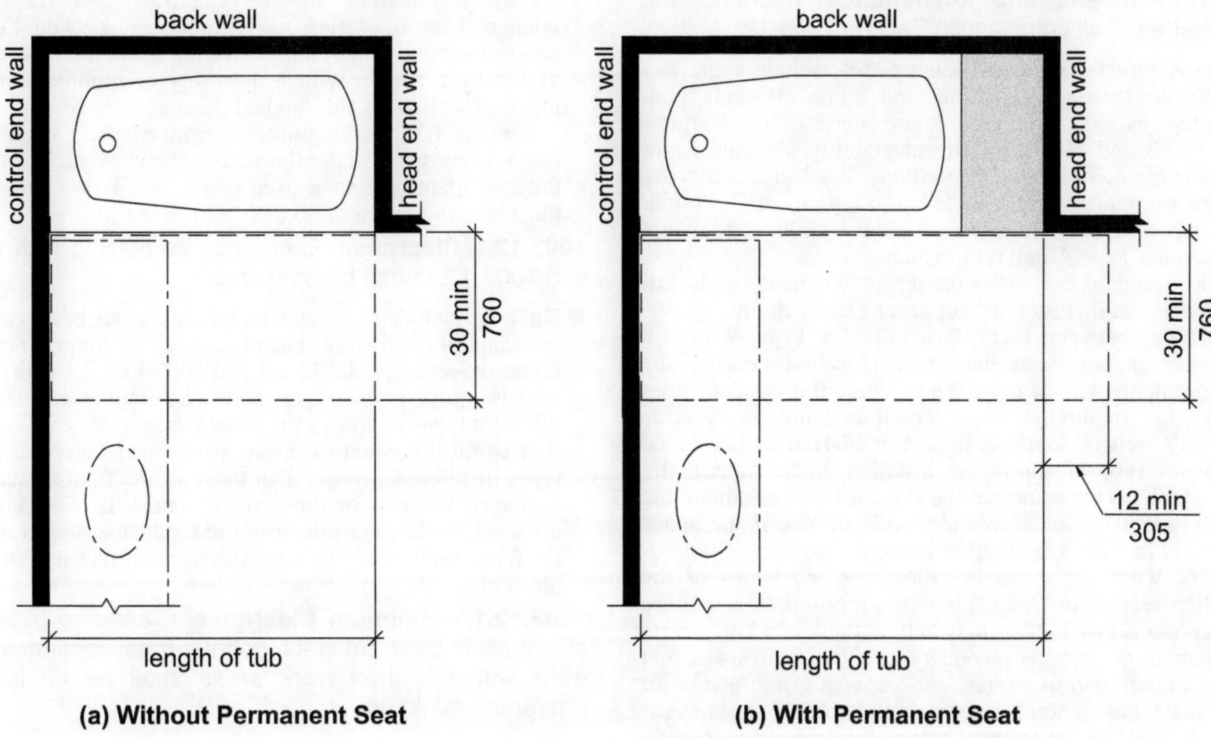

(a) Without Permanent Seat **(b) With Permanent Seat**

**FIGURE 1003.11.2.5.1
CLEARANCE FOR BATHTUBS IN TYPE A UNITS**

1003.11.2.5.2 Shower. Showers shall comply with Section 608.

> **EXCEPTION:** At standard roll-in shower compartments complying with Section 608.2.2, lavatories, counter tops and cabinetry shall be permitted at one end of the clearance, provided the following criteria are met:
>
> (a) The countertop and cabinetry can be removed;
>
> (b) The floor finish extends under the countertop and cabinetry; and
>
> (c) The walls behind and surrounding the countertop and cabinetry are finished.

❖ If the accessible bathing fixture is to be a shower, it can be a transfer shower, roll-in shower or alternate roll-in shower as specified in Section 608. A lavatory can overlap the clear floor space in front of the roll-in shower (Section 608.2.2.2). A lavatory with removable cabinetry can be installed in the clear floor space for the roll-in shower, based on the exception and the options for lavatories in Section 1003.11.2.2. The wording of the exception will allow an extended counter top or cabinet to be installed, provided it is removable and meets the three criteria in the exception. Compliance with this exception will allow the occupant to remove the cabinetry should they need the space to access the shower. This is consistent with the exception permitted for bathtubs (Section 1003.11.2.5.1). The result is that at roll-in showers, either a lavatory or counter can overlap the clear floor space for the roll-in shower if it has removable cabinetry (see Figure 1003.11.2.5.2).

Section 1003.11.1 is concerned with the adaptable features for the showers. Seats and grab bars are not required to be installed at the time of construction if reinforcement is provided for future installation when the occupant desires them.

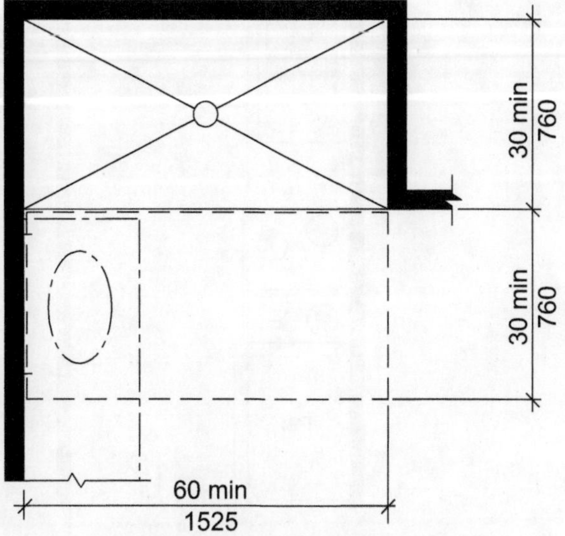

Note: Lavatory permitted per Section 608.2.2

**FIGURE 1003.11.2.5.2
STANDARD ROLL-IN TYPE
SHOWER COMPARTMENT IN TYPE A UNITS**

1003.12 Kitchens and kitchenettes. Kitchens and kitchenettes shall comply with Section 1003.12.

❖ Type A unit kitchens and kitchenettes include some elements constructed accessible and some elements constructed as adaptable for future needs. See Sections 1003.12.3 and 1003.12.4 for adaptability allowances for work surfaces and sinks, respectively. If a designer chooses to use some of the Accessible unit requirements for kitchens, this results in a higher level of accessibility and would exceed the Type A unit requirements.

The standard combines the terms "kitchens" and "kitchenettes" in this section, but never clearly defines or differentiates between them. Generally for Type A units it will not matter what the space is called because the requirements will be consistent. Where the standard does vary the requirements (Accessible units in Section 1002.12, general kitchens in Section 804), it will be based upon the type of appliances installed. In Sections 804.3 and 1002.12, for example, the standard will eliminate the requirement for an accessible work surface if the space does not include a cooktop or conventional range. Regardless of what the space is called, the provisions of the kitchen section in Chapter 8 will apply unless a specific exception is provided. It may help to think of a kitchenette as a small or perhaps secondary kitchen in the space that may contain a refrigerator, and perhaps a microwave or hot plate but generally not a built-in cooktop, conventional oven or conventional range. A kitchenette typically includes a sink; therefore, a wet bar within a unit should comply with kitchenette provisions.

The design of kitchens usable by a person with a disability demands careful consideration and thoughtful planning. Careful location of appliances, plumbing fixtures and cabinetry is essential to achieve the required maneuvering clearances and clear floor spaces required to perform the necessary functions in an accessible and functional kitchen. Careful design will produce a kitchen that is accessible and functionally efficient, and that is easily usable by a person with a disability or mobility impairment, as well as an able-bodied person.

Section 1003.3.2 requires a turning space within the room. If the space under the sink or the work surface (once they are adapted) is to be used as part of a T-turn, the width must be a minimum of 36 inches (915 mm).

1003.12.1 Clearance. Clearance complying with Section 1003.12.1 shall be provided.

❖ Kitchens include requirements for clearances between cabinets and/or appliances. The clearance requirements in referenced Sections 1003.12.1.1 and 1003.12.1.2 are different because floor plan arrangements are unique and require different types of spaces for maneuvering.

It is not the intent of these provisions to prohibit other types of kitchen layouts than those in the figures, such as L-shaped kitchens or those with islands. If other layouts are used, the key considerations are maneuvering to access the fixed appliances, the sink, the work surface and storage elements.

1003.12.1.1 Minimum Clearance. Clearance between all opposing base cabinets, counter tops, appliances, or walls within kitchen work areas shall be 40 inches (1015mm) minimum.

❖ The minimum clear width between opposing cabinets/appliances, or a cabinet/appliance and wall or other type of obstruction, is 40 inches (1015 mm). This measurement is face-to-face and does not include cabinet/appliance handles (see Figure 1003.12.1.1).

Galley-style kitchens are typically laid out with all the appliances, counters and sink in straight or parallel lines.

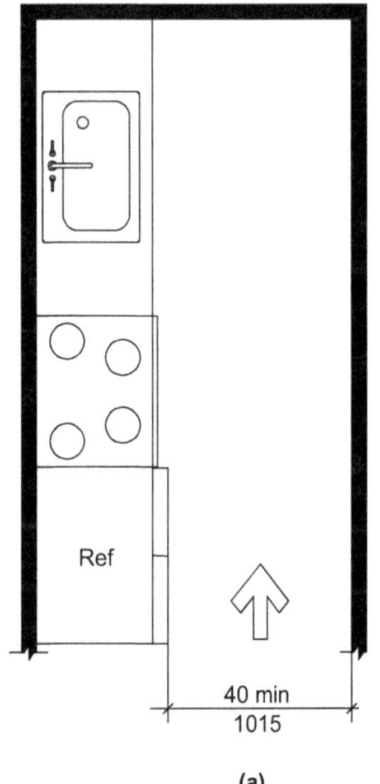

(a)

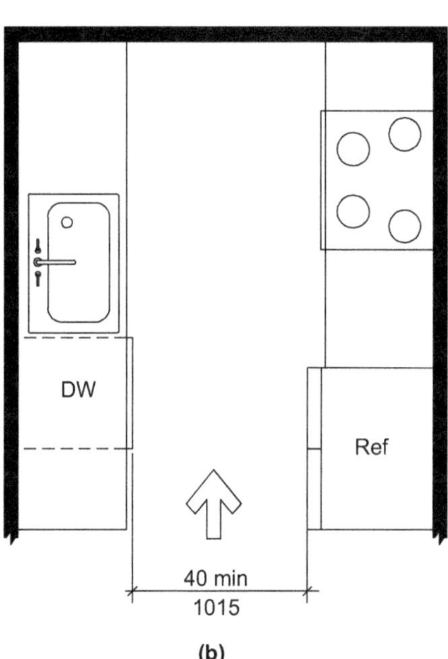

(b)

FIGURE 1003.12.1.1
MINIMUM KITCHEN CLEARANCE IN TYPE A UNITS

The appliances and fixtures can be located along one side of the kitchen, or they can be located along both sides of the kitchen. Unlike a pass-through kitchen (Section 804.2.1) that is required to have two entries, a Type A unit galley-style kitchen may be open on one end or both ends.

The need for a turning space in a kitchen is not intended to increase the 40-inch (1015 mm) width between opposing cabinets. The knee and toe clearances under the work surface (Section 1003.12.3) and/or under the sink (Section 1003.12.4), once adapted, are available for use as part of the required turning space within the kitchen. Unlike Accessible unit kitchens (Sections 1002.12 and 804.2.2), a galley-style kitchen in a Type A unit with an opening on only one end is not considered a U-shaped kitchen and is not required to comply with the U-shaped kitchen provisions of Section 1003.12.1.2 (see commentary, Section 1003.12.1.2 for additional related discussion).

1003.12.1.2 U-Shaped Kitchens. In kitchens with counters, appliances, or cabinets on three contiguous sides, clearance between all opposing base cabinets, countertops, appliances, or walls within kitchen work areas shall be 60 inches (1525 mm) minimum.

❖ U-shaped kitchens are kitchens with cabinets and appliances on three contiguous sides. In such an arrangement, 60 inches (1525 mm) of face-to-face clearance is required between opposing cabinets and/or appliances to make all three sides usable (see Figure 1003.12.1.2).

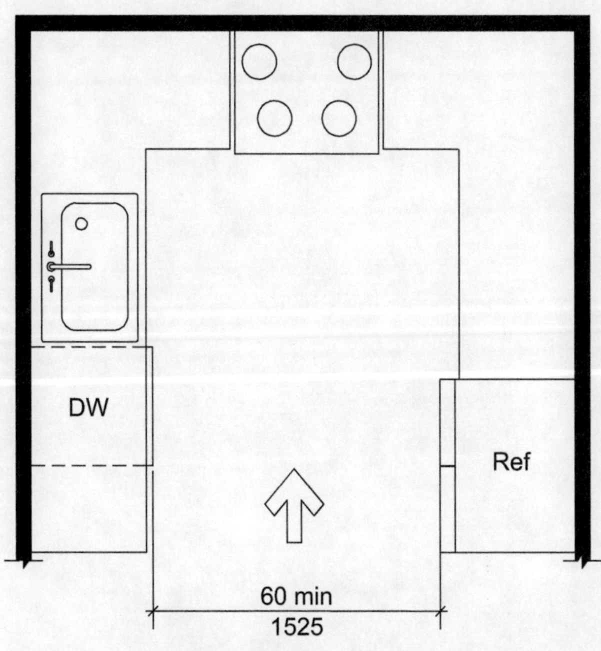

FIGURE 1003.12.1.2
U-SHAPED KITCHEN CLEARANCE IN TYPE A UNITS

Unlike Accessible unit kitchens (Sections 1002.12 and 804.2.2), a two-sided galley-style kitchen in a Type A unit with an opening on only one end is not considered a U-shaped kitchen and does not require a 60-inch (1525 mm) clear floor space between cabinets. The key for a U-shaped kitchen in a Type A unit is the need to be able to turn 90 degrees (1.6 rad) to reach an appliance or use a counter or cabinet on the third wall. Virtually every nonpass-through kitchen could be considered a U-shaped kitchen when using the general kitchen requirements and the Accessible unit requirements of Chapter 8 and Section 1002.12.

1003.12.2 Clear Floor Space. Clear floor spaces required by Sections 1003.12.3 through 1003.12.5 shall comply with Section 305.

❖ The clear floor space for the work surface, sink and appliances is 30 inches by 48 inches (760 by 1220 mm) (Section 305.3). Where knee and/or toe clearances are provided, the clear floor space can extend underneath (e.g., under a sink or work surface, or under the door of an oven or dishwasher in the down position). If a knee space is confined on three sides, the alcove provisions in Section 305.7 are applicable.

1003.12.3 Work Surface. At least one section of counter shall provide a work surface 30 inches (760 mm) minimum in length complying with Section 1003.12.3.

❖ An accessible work surface is a critical component of a kitchen for persons who use wheelchairs. Without an accessible work surface, many of the tasks necessary for preparing a meal, such as mixing, chopping, cutting and cleaning, become very difficult, and for some people routine tasks may even become impossible. Although Accessible units require the accessible work surface adjacent to the oven (Section 1002.12 references Sections 804.5.5.2 and 804.5.5.3), Type A units are required only to have a counter surface (not work surface) adjacent to ovens (Sections 1003.12.5.5.2 and 1003.12.5.5.3). Therefore, the work surface can be located anywhere within the kitchen. It is not the intent of this provision to require all work surfaces in the kitchen to meet this section, only a 30-inch (760 mm) minimum length segment. The provisions in this section are consistent with the general requirements for accessible work surfaces in Section 902.

If the space under the work surface is to be used as part of a T-turning space, the minimum width of the clearance will be 36 inches (915 mm) instead of 30 inches (760 mm) (see Section 304.3.2) (see Figure 1003.12.3).

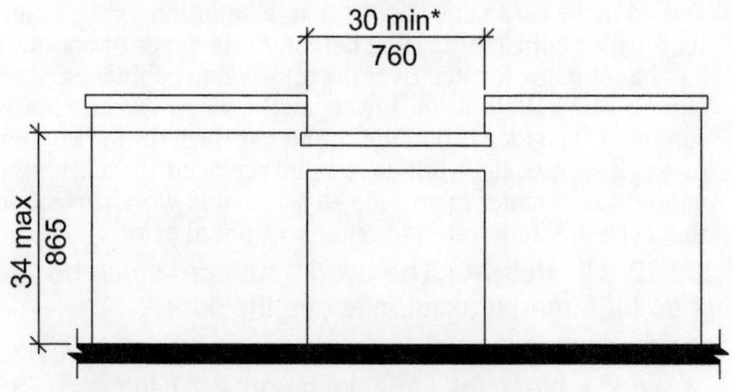

FIGURE 1003.12.3
WORK SURFACE IN KITCHEN FOR TYPE A UNITS

1003.12.3.1 Clear Floor Space. A clear floor space, positioned for a forward approach to the work surface, shall be provided. Knee and toe clearance complying with Section 306 shall be provided. The clear floor space shall be centered on the work surface.

EXCEPTION: Cabinetry shall be permitted under the work surface, provided the following criteria are met:

(a) The cabinetry can be removed without removal or replacement of the work surface,

(b) The floor finish extends under the cabinetry, and

(c) The walls behind and surrounding the cabinetry are finished.

❖ In addition to installing counters or work surfaces at an accessible height (Section 1003.12.3.2), a work surface must be on an accessible route and have adequate clearances under that surface. Although some items in a kitchen have an option of a front approach or a parallel approach, a front approach is always required at work surfaces.

The 30-inch by 48-inch (760 by 1220 mm) clear floor space (Section 305) is required by Sections 1003.12.2 and 1003.12.3.1. If this space is also used for a T-turn, a 36-inch (915 mm) minimum width is required (Sections 304.3 and 1003.3.2).

The space for a person using a wheelchair is permitted to project under the work surfaces to the extent described in Section 306. Clearances for a person's knees and toes are required. The arms on a wheelchair or the chest of the person using the wheelchair will limit the amount someone can move forward under a counter.

Some kitchen designs include a desk-type work area so that the accessible work surface is available at the time of initial construction (see Commentary Figure C1003.12.3.1). However, the intent of the exception is for the work surface to be one of the adaptable elements in a Type A unit. Planning for the work surface to be made accessible in the future requires a removable cabinet under that portion of the counter and the floor treatment to be installed under that cabinet. The back wall should be finished and the cabinets on each side should be ordered with finished side panels. This way, when the cabinet is removed, the space looks like it was always there. The counter must either be located at the height between 29 inches and 34 inches (735 and 865 mm) at installation, or the counter must be adjustable to that height. Some types of counters can have seams located over the removable cabinet, so they can be reinstalled at the lower height when the cabinet is removed. The idea is that the counter surface for the kitchen or work surface does not have to be replaced. Adapting the cabinets or counter to provide an accessible work surface in the Type A kitchen should require minimal effort.

1003.12.3.2 Height. The work surface shall be 34 inches (865 mm) maximum above the floor.

EXCEPTION: A counter that is adjustable to provide a work surface at variable heights 29 inches (735 mm) minimum and 36 inches (915 mm) maximum above the floor, or that can be relocated within that range without cutting the counter or damaging adjacent cabinets, walls, doors, and structural elements, shall be permitted.

❖ Different types of work require different work surface heights for comfort and ease of use. Light detailed work such as writing requires a work surface close to elbow height for a standing person. Heavy manual work such as rolling dough requires a work surface height about 10 inches (255 mm) below elbow height for a standing person. The principle of a high work surface for light detailed work and a low work surface for heavy manual work also applies for seated persons; however, the limiting condition for seated manual work is the vertical clearance under the work surface.

Table C902.4 lists convenient work surface heights for seated persons. The great variety of heights for comfort and optimal performance indicates a need for alternatives or a compromise in height if both sitting and standing persons use the same counter area.

The intent of the exception is to allow adjustment of the counter height from the standard 36 inches (915 mm) to the desired height between 29 inches and 34 inches (735 and 865 mm). [Section 902.4 allows for 28 inches (710 mm).] The intent is not that the counter surface be mechanically adjustable, but rather that it be planned for adjustment of the counter without replacement of the counter or surrounding cabinets. Some types of counters allow for locating seams along the sides of the removable cabinet so that the piece can be reinstalled at a lower height when this area is adapted to be accessible.

FIGURE C1003.12.3.1 EXAMPLE OF BUILT-IN WORK SURFACE

1003.12.3.3 Exposed Surfaces. There shall be no sharp or abrasive surfaces under the exposed portions of work surface counters.

❖ Hot, cold and abrasive surfaces may cause harm to people using wheelchairs because their ability to feel and react to such hazards may be diminished significantly by paralysis or loss of sensation. Protection can be provided by padding, apron walls, recessing the pipes, etc.

If objects are located under the surface above or adjacent to the knee and toe space (including counter supports), it is advisable to protect the person using the surface from injury by padding or rounding any sharp edges, or locating these items as far past the knee and toe clearances as practical.

1003.12.4 Sink. The sink shall comply with Section 1003.12.4.

❖ The kitchen sink must have knee and toe clearances that allow for a front approach (including protection from the pipes), a maximum rim height of 34 inches (865 mm), and faucets that meet operable parts requirements (see Figure 1003.12.4). If a double bowl sink is installed, these requirements can apply to only one bowl. This allows for the second bowl to be deeper or include a garbage disposal.

The intent of the wording "the sink" is to limit the accessibility requirements to the main kitchen sink and therefore not apply the requirements to a separate bar or prep sink that may also be in the same room. The use of the plural "sinks" in earlier editions of the standard would have seemingly required all of the sinks to comply.

If the space under the sink is to be used for a T-turn space, the minimum width of the clearance will be 36 inches (915 mm) instead of 30 inches (760 mm) (see Section 304.3).

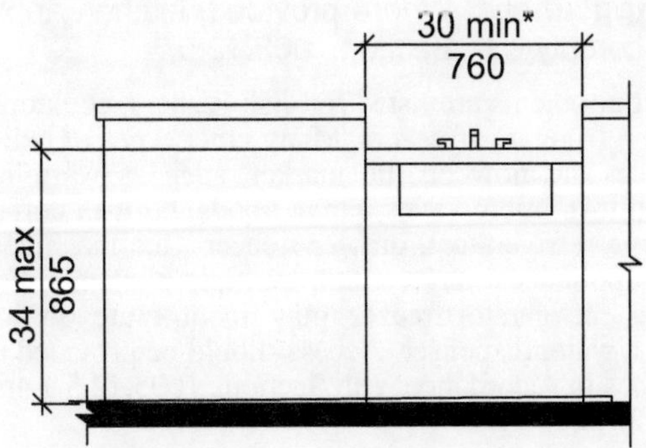

* 36 in. (915 mm) min. if part of T-shaped turning space per Sections 304.3.2 and 1003.3.2

FIGURE 1003.12.4
KITCHEN SINK FOR TYPE A UNITS

1003.12.4.1 Clear Floor Space. A clear floor space, positioned for a forward approach to the sink, shall be provided. Knee and toe clearance complying with Section 306 shall be provided.

EXCEPTIONS:

1. The requirement for knee and toe clearance shall not apply to more than one bowl of a multi-bowl sink.
2. Cabinetry shall be permitted to be added under the sink, provided the following criteria are met:
   (a) The cabinetry can be removed without removal or replacement of the sink,
   (b) The floor finish extends under the cabinetry, and
   (c) The walls behind and surrounding the cabinetry are finished.

❖ In addition to being at an accessible height (Section 1003.12.4.2), a kitchen sink must be on an accessible route and have adequate clearances under that surface. Although some items in a kitchen have an option of a front approach or a parallel approach, a front approach is required at sinks in a Type A unit.

The 30-inch by 48-inch (760 mm by 1220 mm) clear floor space (Sections 305 and 1003.12.2) is required. If this space is also used for a T-turn, a 36-inch (915 mm) width is required (Sections 304.3 and 1003.3.2).

The space for a person using a wheelchair is permitted to project under the sink to the extent described in Section 306. Clearances for a person's knees and toes are required. The arms on a wheelchair or the chest of the person using the wheelchair will limit the amount someone can move forward under a counter.

Users who are familiar with earlier editions of the standard may notice that the requirement for the clear floor space to be centered on the bowl of the sink has been deleted in the 2009 edition. Centering of the space is important for a parallel approach but not for a forward approach. While it generally may be the best practice to center the clear floor space, it may also create difficulties for certain types of sinks or unnecessarily limit the design options. The previous requirement for the clear floor space to be centered on the kitchen sink in a Type A unit would appear to have been unjustified or unnecessary given that the centering requirement did not apply to lavatories in the bathroom or to the kitchen sink in an Accessible unit or in other kitchens (Section 606.2).

Given that many kitchen sinks may include a garbage disposal unit beneath the sink, drains and faucets at varying locations, or that some sinks come with multiple bowls and even different sizes of bowls, it would appear that the requirement for centering may not always be possible with a forward approach or that it may not provide the best access. Eliminating the centering requirement made the Type A units consistent with the Accessible units and the general kitchen requirements of Section 804 that have apparently provided adequate access in the past without having this requirement [see Commentary Figure C1003.12.4.1(b)].

Based on Exception 1, the knee and toe clearances are required on only one bowl of a multibowl sink. Typical sink widths would result in the clear floor space extending under the side of the second bowl [see Commentary Figure C1003.12.4.1(a)]. If the garbage disposal has sharp edges, protection should be provided as noted in Section 1003.12.4.4.

The intent of Exception 2 is for the sink to be one of the adaptable elements in a Type A unit. Planning for the sink to be made accessible in the future requires a removable cabinet under that portion of the counter, and the floor treatment to be installed under that cabinet. The back wall should be finished and the cabinets on each side should be ordered with finished side panels. This way, when the cabinet is removed, the space looks like it was always there. The sink must either be located at the height between 29 inches and 34 inches (735 and 865 mm) at installation, or the counter must be adjustable to that height. Some types of counters can have seams located over the removable cabinet, so they can be reinstalled at the lower height when the cabinet is removed. The plumber should install the supply and drain lines at a location that would allow for the future lowering of the sink. The idea is that neither the sink nor the counter surface for the kitchen or around the sink would have to be replaced. Providing an accessible sink in the Type A kitchen should require minimal effort.

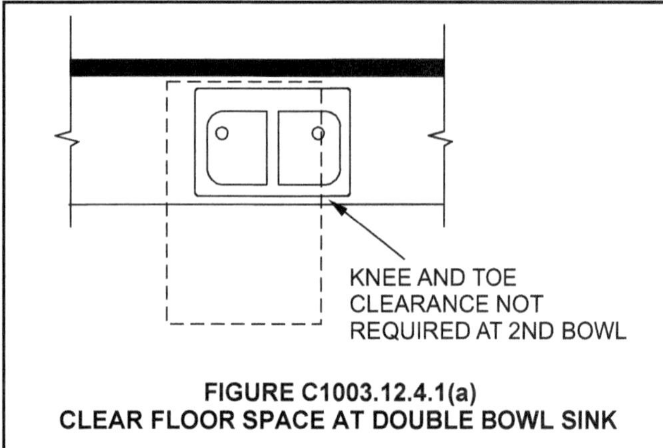

FIGURE C1003.12.4.1(a)
CLEAR FLOOR SPACE AT DOUBLE BOWL SINK

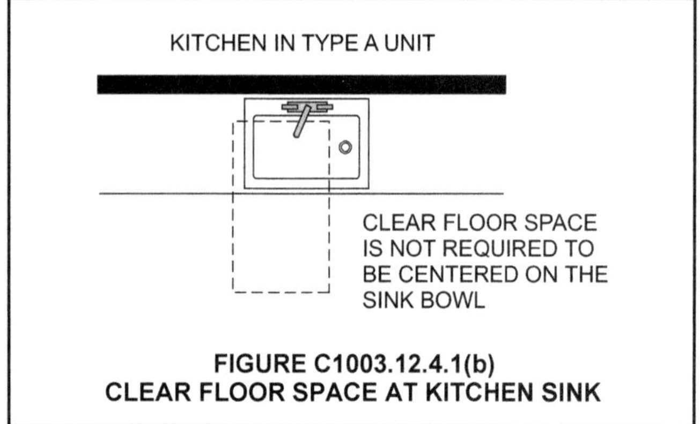

FIGURE C1003.12.4.1(b)
CLEAR FLOOR SPACE AT KITCHEN SINK

1003.12.4.2 Height. The front of the sink shall be 34 inches (865 mm) maximum above the floor, measured to the higher of the rim or counter surface.

EXCEPTION: A sink and counter that is adjustable to variable heights 29 inches (735 mm) minimum and 36 inches (915 mm) maximum above the floor, or that can be relocated within that range without cutting the counter or damaging adjacent cabinets, walls, doors and structural elements, provided rough-in plumbing permits connections of supply and drain pipes for sinks mounted at the height of 29 inches (735 mm), shall be permitted.

❖ The top rim of the sink for over-mount sinks or the counter height for under-mount sinks must be at a maximum height of 34 inches (865 mm). This will allow for about a $6^1/_2$-inch-deep (165 mm) sink and still have a 27-inch-high (685 mm) knee clearance.

The intent of the exception is to allow adjustment of the counter surrounding the sink from the standard 36-inch (915 mm) height to the desired height between 29 inches and 34 inches (735 and 865 mm). [Section 902.3 allows for 28 inches (710 mm).] The intent is not that the sink be mechanically adjustable, but rather that the counter be adjustable without replacement of the counter or surrounding cabinets. Some types of counters allow location of seams along the sides of the removable cabinet, so the counter and sink can be reinstalled at a lower height when this area is adapted to be accessible. Note that the supply and drain lines must be installed to permit the sink to be adjusted to the 29-inch (735 mm) height.

1003.12.4.3 Faucets. Faucets shall comply with Section 309.

❖ Any faucet controls that are provided, including the temperature and water flow, hand spray, spigot swivel, etc., must meet the operable parts provisions of Section 309. Single-lever controls for the faucet typically are the easiest for persons with limited hand mobility to use.

1003.12.4.4 Exposed Pipes and Surfaces. Water supply and drain pipes under sinks shall be insulated or otherwise configured to protect against contact. There shall be no sharp or abrasive surfaces under sinks.

❖ Hot, cold and abrasive surfaces may cause harm to a person using a wheelchair because their ability to feel and react to such hazards may be significantly diminished by paralysis or loss of sensation.

This protection can be provided by padding, apron panels, recessing the pipes, etc. The performance level of the insulation is not specified, but should be adequate to protect against the expected hazard. This protection is not intended to be the type of insulation required for steam pipes, hot water heating pipes or other types of system piping.

1003.12.5 Appliances. Where provided, kitchen appliances shall comply with Section 1003.12.5.

❖ Specific requirements are listed for dishwashers, cooktops, ovens, and refrigerator/freezers. Many other types of built-in appliances are now on the market, such as warming drawers, built-in microwaves, range hoods, built-in coffee centers, wine refrigerators, drawer freezers, ice machines, etc. Some appliances may contain multiple elements. For example, a refrigerator/freezer may incorporate an ice maker and a water dispenser. Access should be provided to all appliances in accordance with Sections 1003.12.5.1 and 1003.12.5.2.

1003.12.5.1 Operable Parts. All appliance controls shall comply with Section 1003.9.

EXCEPTIONS:

1. Appliance doors and door latching devices shall not be required to comply with Section 309.4.
2. Bottom-hinged appliance doors, when in the open position, shall not be required to comply with Section 309.3.

❖ Appliance controls must meet the clear floor space, reach range and operable parts requirements in Section 309. Section 1003.9, Exception 6, does exempt the redundant controls. For example, controls on range hoods do not have to be within reach ranges if redundant accessible controls are provided. Remember also that Exception 7 in Section

1003.9 will exempt controls that are not for general use but serve as resets or shut-offs for the appliances.

Per Exception 1, appliance doors and door latches do not have to meet the operable parts requirements for operation with one hand, no tight pinching, grasping or twisting of the wrist or the 5 pounds (22 N) force found in Section 309.4. Because a door seal is necessary for some appliances (ovens, refrigerators, freezers) the 5 pound (22 N) force limit is waived. Other door latch examples would be the lever for sealing a dishwasher door or the mechanical latch on self-cleaning oven doors. Generally, the grasping portion of hardware used to open an appliance door does have to meet the clear floor space and height requirements in Sections 309.2 and 309.3.

Exception 2 allows a downward opening appliance door to be out of the 15-inch to 48-inch (380 to 1220 mm) reach range required in Section 309.3. A dishwasher or range door in the down position can be as low as 9 or 10 inches (230 or 255 mm) from the floor.

1003.12.5.2 Clear Floor Space. A clear floor space, positioned for a parallel or forward approach, shall be provided at each kitchen appliance.

❖ Although the 30-inch by 48-inch (760 by 1220 mm) clear floor space at appliances can be a side approach or front approach, typical use of an appliance must be considered. For example, a side approach to a cooktop allows access to all the burners, but a front approach, because of the difficulty reaching forward beyond wheelchair kick plates, would probably allow access to only the front burners. Most stationary appliances must have the door near fully open for access (e.g., dishwasher, oven, refrigerator, trash compactor). Clear floor space can overlap the knee and/or toe clearances available when the door is open.

The provisions of Section 301.2 are important to remember when locating an appliance and its associated clear floor space. Based on the general provision in Section 301.2, while each appliance is required to have a clear floor space providing access to it, there is nothing that prevents the clear floor spaces for the various appliances from overlapping. A review of each of the sections should be undertaken since there are some specific requirements that help ensure the kitchen and appliances are usable. For example, Section 1003.12.5.3 indicates the dishwasher door in the open position shall not obstruct the clear floor space for the dishwasher or adjacent sink. A similar requirement in Section 1003.12.5.5.1 for the oven will ensure that the oven door, when in the open position, will not obstruct the clear floor space serving the oven.

1003.12.5.3 Dishwasher. A clear floor space, positioned adjacent to the dishwasher door, shall be provided. The dishwasher door in the open position shall not obstruct the clear floor space for the dishwasher or an adjacent sink.

❖ It is important to locate the clear floor space so the dishwasher can be easily loaded and unloaded. No portion of an open dishwasher door (bottom hinged) can overlap the designated clear floor space unless the door in the full open/down position has knee or toe clearance below. Dishwashers with bottom-hinged doors can be installed to provide 9-inch (230 mm) vertical toe clearance below the door. Note that toe clearance can only utilize a maximum of 6 inches (150 mm) horizontally below an overhang. Drawer-style dishwashers will provide toe space [9-inch (230 mm) vertical] when installed at normal height and possibly knee space (27-inch vertical) if installed higher. Often, it is desirable to load the dishwasher from the sink area; therefore, it may be helpful to locate the sink and dishwasher adjacent to each other. Where a dishwasher is located adjacent to the forward approach clear floor space for a sink, the sink clear floor space can be used to serve both the sink and the dishwasher [see Commentary Figures C1003.12.5.3(a) and (b)]. The exception for sink knee and toe clearances in Section 1003.12.4 is still applicable.

FIGURE C1003.12.5.3(a)
EXAMPLE OF ACCESS TO DISHWASHER

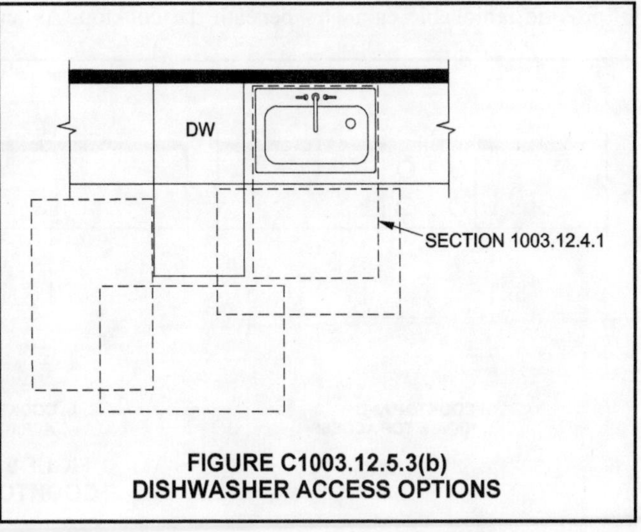

FIGURE C1003.12.5.3(b)
DISHWASHER ACCESS OPTIONS

1003.12.5.4 Cooktop. Cooktops shall comply with Section 1003.12.5.4.

❖ The provisions of this section apply to either a separate cooktop or to the cooktop that is a part of a range. The provisions of the 2009 edition of the standard eliminated the requirements for a "range" and now simply address the various elements separately with the cooktop being regulated by this section and the oven being regulated by Section 1003.12.5.5. Both sets of requirements will apply to a range since it does include both a cooktop and an oven.

1003.12.5.4.1 Approach. A clear floor space, positioned for a parallel or forward approach to the cooktop, shall be provided.

❖ The type of approach used for a cooktop is entirely the designer's decision. It will depend on whether the cooktop is a separate element, a part of a range or located where it does not have cabinetry installed beneath it. Depending on the type of approach selected, either Section 1003.12.5.4.2 or 1003.12.5.4.3 will be used (see Commentary Figure C1003.12.5.4).

1003.12.5.4.2 Forward approach. Where the clear floor space is positioned for a forward approach, knee and toe clearance complying with Section 306 shall be provided. The underside of the cooktop shall be insulated or otherwise configured to protect from burns, abrasions, or electrical shock.

❖ Where a forward approach is used, the space for a person using a wheelchair is required to project under the cooktop to the extent described in Section 306. Clearances for a person's knees and toes are required. The arms on a wheelchair or the chest of the person using the wheelchair will limit the amount someone can move forward under a cooktop or counter.

Hot, sharp or abrasive surfaces may cause harm to a person using a wheelchair because their ability to feel and react to such hazards may be diminished significantly by paralysis or loss of sensation. Cooktops are generally enclosed by the cabinetry they are built into, but the protection can be provided by any means that adequately separates or protects the user.

If the space under the cooktop is to be used for a T-turning space, the minimum width of the clearance will be 36 inches (915 mm) (see Section 304.3.2).

Because cooktops are allowed to use either a forward or a parallel approach, this section does not contain the option to provide removable cabinetry beneath the cooktop. As an alternate design that would provide future users more options, it would be acceptable to design the cooktop for a parallel approach at the time of initial construction but to also design for a future option of a forward approach by using removable cabinetry as allowed by the exception in other sections of the standard.

1003.12.5.4.3 Parallel approach. Where the clear floor space is positioned for a parallel approach, the clear floor space shall be centered on the appliance.

❖ A parallel or side approach to a cooktop tends to allow access to all the burners but can also be a bit difficult since it also requires the lifting of pans to the side. Where a parallel approach is used, the clear floor space must be centered on the appliance. Centering of the space is important for a parallel approach but not as important for a forward approach.

1003.12.5.4.4 Controls. The location of controls shall not require reaching across burners.

❖ To reduce the chance of accidental scalding or burns, access to controls for the burners on a cooktop or a cooktop that is part of a range must not require reaching across burners. Controls can be provided on the front, center or side of the burners. If the cooktop is part of a range, access to controls for the oven must also be located so a person using the oven does not have to reach across burners to access the oven controls (Section 1003.12.5.5.4). Unlike ovens, there is no requirement for a counter top or work surface adjacent to a cooktop. However, best design practice would have a portion of the counter at the same level as the burners [i.e., typical 36-inch (915 mm) height] so that someone with limited strength could slide pots over without a drop down [i.e., work surface is 29 inches to 34 inches (735 to 865 mm) in height].

1003.12.5.5 Oven. Ovens shall comply with Section 1003.12.5.5. Ovens shall have controls on front panels, on either side of the door.

❖ The provisions of this section apply to either a separate oven or to an oven that is a part of a range. The provisions of the 2009 edition of the standard eliminated the requirements for a "range" and now address the various elements separately with the oven being regulated by this section and the cooktop being regulated by Section 1003.12.5.4. Both sets of requirements apply to a range since they include both a cooktop and an oven.

Access to oven controls that are part of a range must not require reaching across burners (Section 1003.12.5.5.4).

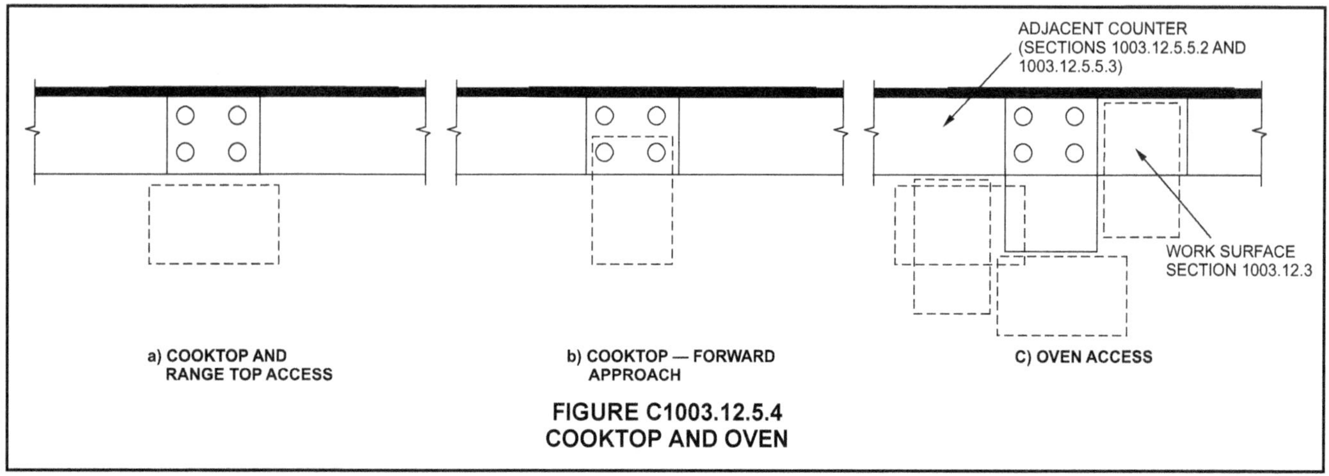

FIGURE C1003.12.5.4
COOKTOP AND OVEN

Due to a bit of a quirk in the standard's development process, the Type A unit's oven provisions actually have two sections that regulate the location of the controls. This section requires the controls to be located on the front panel of the oven and to either side of the door while Section 1003.12.5.5.4 simply limits reaching over the burners of a cooktop. The fact that requirements exist in both sections will not create a conflict but could create confusion, especially because they differ from the requirements for kitchens in Chapter 8 and in Accessible units. While it seems that the A117.1 Committee's intent was to have eliminated the control requirements from Section 1003.12.5.5 and only keep those in Section 1003.12.5.5.4, similar to how Sections 804.5.5 and 804.5.5.4 work, that was not the result and so users are left with what the standard actually says. With this text remaining here in Section 1003.12.5.5, an oven with controls located above or below the oven door is not permitted in a Type A unit. This will affect many commonly selected ranges or wall ovens. Controls for ovens must be within reach ranges based on the provisions of Sections 1003.9 and 1003.12.5.1.

1003.12.5.5.1 Clear floor space. A clear floor space shall be provided. The oven door in the open position shall not obstruct the clear floor space for the oven.

❖ A person must be able to fully open the oven door and reach the oven racks. Therefore, how the oven is used must be considered when determining the clear floor space location. Wall-mounted ovens may have better access because the height makes access easier for persons using wheelchairs (see Commentary Figure C1003.12.5.5). A person would not have to reach both down and over the door to reach the rack or item in the oven. Another option to increase access would be racks that pull out all the way without tilting. See Commentary Figure C1003.12.5.4(b) for various options to access an oven.

FIGURE C1003.12.5.5
EXAMPLE OF A WALL OVEN

1003.12.5.5.2 Side-Hinged Door Ovens. Side-hinged door ovens shall have a countertop positioned adjacent to the latch side of the oven door.

❖ Though most standard ovens come with a bottom-hinged door, some manufacturers are starting to offer microwave/oven combinations with a side swing door. If a side opening oven is chosen, to facilitate transfer of heavy or hot dishes into and out of the oven, the latch side must be adjacent to a counter space. Notice that this section does not specify a minimum length for the countertop next to the oven, but a countertop is available on the latch side. An accessible work surface located adjacent to the oven could serve as this counter space and a minimum 30-inch (760 mm) length could result in improved access for the oven. Note that the work surface in a Type A unit kitchen can be located anywhere in the kitchen [see Commentary Figure C1003.12.5.4(b) and Section 1003.12.3].

1003.12.5.5.3 Bottom-Hinged Door Ovens. Bottom-hinged door ovens shall have a countertop positioned adjacent to one side of the door.

❖ If a bottom-hinged oven is chosen to facilitate transfer of heavy or hot dishes into and out of the oven, counter space must be located adjacent to the oven on either side. The fold-down-type doors are often used as the shelf for dishes, but this is not recommended by the manufacturer. Notice that this section does not specify a minimum length for the countertop adjacent to the oven. An accessible work surface located adjacent to the oven could serve as this counter space and since Section 1003.12.3 requires a minimum 30-inch (760 mm) length could result in improved access for the oven; however, in a Type A unit kitchen, the work surface can be located anywhere in the kitchen [see Commentary Figure C1003.12.5.4(b) and commentary, Section 1003.12.3].

1003.12.5.5.4 Controls. The location of controls shall not require reaching across burners.

❖ To reduce the chance of accidental scalding or burns, access to controls for the oven must not require reaching across the burners of a cooktop. See the commentary to Section 1003.12.5.5, which also regulates the control location and would require the oven controls to be on a front panel and not above the oven door. The requirements of Section 1003.12.5.5.4 would seem to be adequate in protecting the users since they match those of Section 804.5.5.4 for general kitchens and those of Accessible units, but since Section 1003.12.5.5 does have a specific statement regarding the control location, users should be aware of it.

1003.12.5.6 Refrigerator/Freezer. Combination refrigerators and freezers shall have at least 50 percent of the freezer compartment shelves, including the bottom of the freezer 54 inches (1370 mm) maximum above the floor when the shelves are installed at the maximum heights possible in the compartment. A clear floor space, positioned for a parallel approach to the refrigerator/freezer, shall be provided. The centerline of the clear floor space shall be offset 24 inches (610 mm) maximum from the centerline of the appliance.

❖ The position for the parallel approach to the refrigerator and freezer must consider how the person using a wheelchair will access the interior with the door open [see Commentary Figure C1003.12.5.6(a)].

Refrigerator/freezer choices can have the freezer on the top, on the bottom or side by side. If a top freezer option is chosen, a freezer with the bottom of the compartment at a maximum of 54 inches (1370 mm) above the ground (assuming one shelf in the freezer) will meet the freezer compartment requirements. Bottom freezer access is not specifically addressed; however, the intent is if a bottom freezer option is chosen, at least one shelf in the freezer compartment must be 15 inches (380 mm) minimum above the floor. Bottom freezers may be a side-hinged door with interior pull-out drawers or a pull-out door/drawer. A clear floor space must be available with the freezer door fully open. Side-by-side refrigerator/freezers provide the easiest access to the freezer compartment; however, a clear floor space for each door is necessary [see Commentary Figure C1003.12.5.6(b)]. Locating refrigerators so the doors are able to swing back a full 180 degrees (3 rad) can provide greater accessibility for a person using a wheelchair.

In recognition that there are a variety of appliance options and the clear floor space must allow access to the appliance, the standard will allow the clear floor space to be offset as much as 24 inches (610 mm) from the center of the appliance. Requiring the space to be centered on the appliance, while perhaps the best option once the doors are open, could in fact prevent the user from being able to open the doors. The actual offset should be kept to the smallest distance that allows the user to open the refrigerator or freezer and still access the various areas of the appliance. Therefore, it is generally better if the accessible route to the refrigerator/freezer is large enough to allow maneuvering to approach, open and then move to a proper position for using the appliance. Fortunately, refrigerators are available in a tremendous range of sizes and configurations. An individual should be able to find one that best suits his or her situation.

Although not specifically mentioned, if a refrigerator has ice or water available through the door or inside the appliance, that feature is considered part of the refrigerator/freezer. Therefore, those elements must also have a clear floor space for access and meet reach range and operable parts requirements.

1003.13 Windows. Windows shall comply with Section 1003.13.

❖ For those windows that must be operated by the occupants, it is logical to ensure that they meet a certain minimum level of requirements. Currently, double-hung windows typically need a minimum of 25 pounds (110 N) to operate, and casement windows need a minimum of $8^1/_2$ pounds (37.4 N) to operate. In order for window operation to meet a 5-pound (22 N) force, an add-on arm must be added. Windows that are required for natural ventilation or emergency escape and egress have requirements in the next two sections. A designer could choose to provide access to other operable windows in the unit; however, this is not a

FIGURE C1003.12.5.6(a)
EXAMPLE OF ACCESS TO REFRIGERATOR/FREEZER

requirement so that design options for Accessible units would not be limited, such as high or low hopper-style windows, windows over the sink in kitchens, window raised for privacy in bathroom, etc.

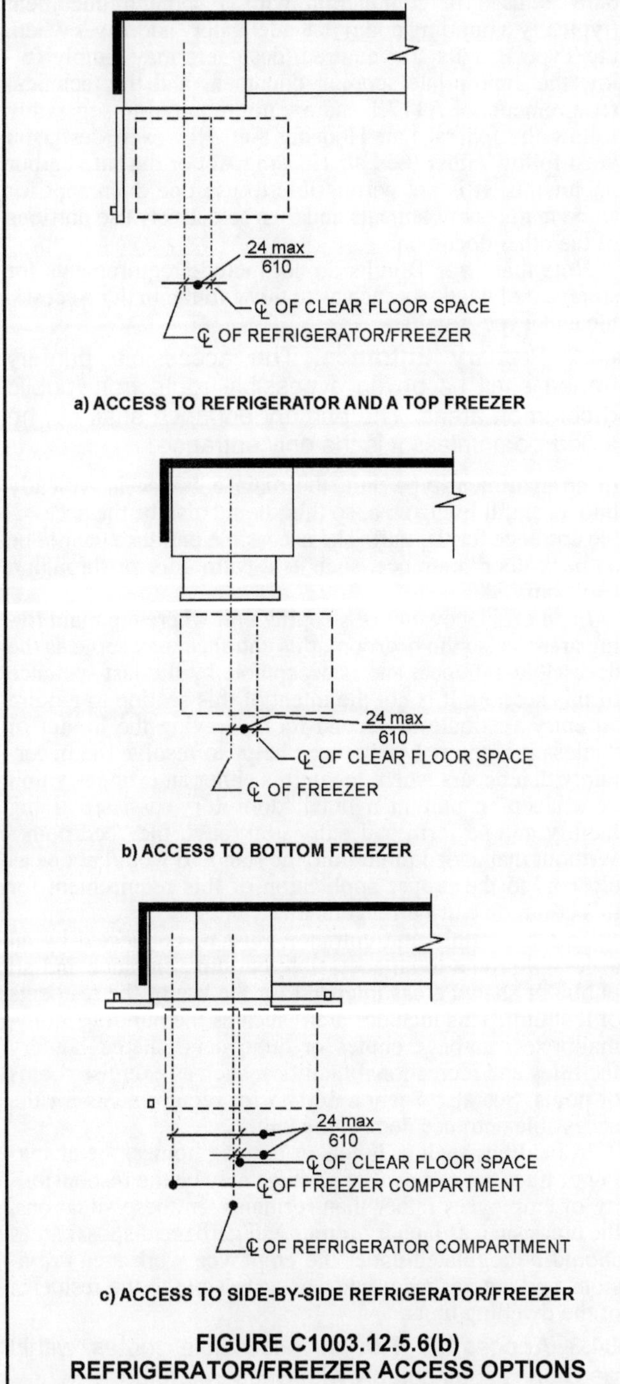

**FIGURE C1003.12.5.6(b)
REFRIGERATOR/FREEZER ACCESS OPTIONS**

1003.13.1 Natural ventilation. Operable windows required to provide natural ventilation shall comply with Sections 309.2 and 309.3.

❖ The jurisdiction's scoping document will provide information regarding where operable windows are required for natural ventilation. The model building codes generally impose the requirement for natural ventilation if a mechanical ventilation system is not provided or possibly for certain specific occupancies. Where the windows are required for natural ventilation purposes, all of the required windows must meet the clear floor space and have the operable parts within reach ranges (see Commentary Figure C1002.13).

1003.13.2 Emergency escape. Operable windows required to provide an emergency escape and rescue opening shall comply with Section 309.2.

❖ Emergency escape and rescue openings allow the occupants to escape from a unit if their primary means of egress is blocked or unavailable. They also allow for emergency personnel to gain access to the unit from the exterior in order to facilitate a rescue. The jurisdiction's scoping document (i.e., building code) will provide information regarding where openings are required for emergency escape and rescue. The model building codes generally impose the requirement for these openings in sleeping areas or basements. This section of the standard will only impose the requirement for a clear floor space in front of the window (see Commentary Figure C1002.13), but building codes will typically address items such as sill height, height of hardware and minimum sizes for the opening.

1003.14 Storage Facilities. Where storage facilities are provided, at least one of each type shall comply with Section 905.

> **EXCEPTION:** Kitchen cabinets shall not be required to comply with Section 1003.14.

❖ Storage facilities, other than those in kitchen cabinets, are scoped so that "at least one of each type" is made accessible. As an example, the types of storage facilities that may be affected by this requirement are tenant storage lockers/closets that may be located in a common area of an apartment building, an outdoor storage closet on the balcony of the dwelling unit, bathroom cabinets, linen cabinets or a private storage closet within a garage. The reference to Section 905 results in requirements for a clear floor space, the height of the storage and operable parts to enter or use the elements (see commentary, Section 905). Storage facilities must have a clear floor space in front of the storage element. At least a portion of each storage facility provided, such as shelves or rods, must be within the 15-inch to 48-inch (350 to 1220 mm) reach range. A standard closet organizer with a high-low rod for a portion of the closet meets this provision. If there are doors or drawers, the latches and knobs must be easily operable by a person with limited hand movement and strength. If this is a reach-in closet, the door does not have to meet the clear width, threshold or maneuvering clearance requirements in Section 1003.5 because the door is not "intended for user passage."

Kitchen cabinets are not regulated by this section based upon the exception. The special work environment and concentrated amount of storage allows for unique consideration. Kitchen cabinets are extremely difficult to make fully accessible, particularly in a small kitchen with limited options. The lower shelf in typical base cabinets is below the reach range while all shelves in upper cabinets are typically beyond reach ranges. Stationary appliances in lower cabinets (i.e., range, dishwasher, garbage disposal) eliminate most of the lower cabinet storage options. Note that the 2009 standard does not address kitchen cabinet storage as it had in earlier editions where a percentage of shelf space was required to be accessible. This requirement sometimes forced the removal of the upper cabinets or where the bottom shelf is within the reach range, the counter top will not fit many of the standard household appliances such as microwaves, blenders, toasters or coffee pots. Being able to move within the kitchen (via the appliance clearance requirements and width between counters) would provide access to most base cabinets, drawers and counter storage. Therefore, the clear space aspect of accessibility is generally taken care of and there is no need to be more specific. The addition of user-friendly items such as pull-out shelves in lower cabinets or a Lazy Susan in corner cabinets is fairly easy to accomplish. Pantry-type cabinets with or without pull-out elements provide readily accessible storage (see Commentary Figure C1002.14). Using extended reaching tools will allow limited access to upper cabinets. While a person with limited reach range might be unable to reach into all the cabinets, his or her family can still utilize the additional cabinets or the space may be used for storage of infrequently used items.

1004 Type B Units

❖ Accessible units and Type A units are considered to provide a higher level of accessibility than Type B units. Therefore, compliance with the provisions in Section 1002 or 1003 will meet or exceed Type B requirements.

For the design of a Type B unit, the requirements in Sections 1004.1 through 1004.12 must be met. The technical criteria are either specifically stated in these sections or the section contains a reference to another section of the standard that contains the applicable technical standard. If a technical standard in another chapter is not referenced, it is not applicable to the design of a Type B unit.

1004.1 General. Type B units shall comply with Section 1004.

❖ A Type B dwelling or sleeping unit must comply with all the provisions in this section. Type B units are intended to be consistent with the Fair Housing Accessibility Guidelines (FHAG) (see Section 101). The scoping documents (typically, state or local building codes) identify when Type B dwelling units and/or Type B sleeping units are required. Type B units are typically found where four or more attached units are constructed at the same time and the units are intended to be occupied as a residence. This can include both institutional and residential-type facilities—mostly long-term living arrangements, but not always.

The Type B unit was first added to the 1998 edition of ICC/ANSI A117.1. Both the 1998 and 2003 editions of ICC A117.1 have been designated as "safe harbor" documents for compliance with FHAG by Housing and Urban Development (HUD). At the time this commentary is being published, HUD has begun its review of the 2009 edition of the standard, but has not completed it to determine whether safe harbor status will be granted. ICC believes that the 2009 edition of the standard will receive HUD approval just as did previous editions. Although the 1986 and 1992 editions of A117.1 are also considered "safe harbor" documents, they did not contain requirements specifically to match FHAG, but did contain criteria for units that provided a higher level of access, commonly referred to as Accessible units and Adaptable units. Adaptable units are now called Type A.

Users should be certain to understand the importance of the safe harbor status that HUD has granted to the various A117.1 standards. What this means is that the A117.1 standard provides technical requirements that are consistent and typically either meet or exceed the technical provisions from the FHAG. Therefore, when the A117.1 standard is used in conjunction with a scoping document (typically a building code) that adequately addresses where the Type B units are required, designers may simply follow the appropriate scoping document and the technical requirements of A117.1 and are not required to separately follow the federal Fair Housing Act. However, designers must follow either the Fair Housing Act or the safe harbor documents. It is not permissible to use one document for some features or elements and then selectively use portions of the other document.

Note that Type B units do not include requirements for storage and windows such as to those found in the Accessible and Type A units.

1004.2 Primary Entrance. The accessible primary entrance shall be on an accessible route from public and common areas. The primary entrance shall not be to a bedroom unless it is the only entrance.

❖ In an apartment-type unit, the main entrance is typically into a central living area, so this should also be the accessible entrance for the unit. The accessible entrance cannot be a "back door" entrance, such as a patio door or through a bedroom.

In an efficiency unit or sleeping unit where the main living area is also the bedroom, this entrance may serve as the accessible entrance, and is acceptable by the last sentence of this section. It is not the intent of this section to require an entry vestibule or second room. Having the limiter of "unless it is the only entrance" helps to resolve the uncertainty that occurs where the unit is either an efficiency unit or a sleeping unit in a hotel, dormitory, assisted living facility and so forth and entry is through the "bedroom." Without that added limitation, the standard would not be as clear as to the proper application of this requirement for this common entry arrangement.

This accessible unit entrance must be connected by an accessible route to an accessible building entrance and all public or shared areas intended for the use of the residents of that unit. This includes areas such as the building lobby, mailboxes, garbage chutes or dumpsters, shared laundry facilities and recreational facilities, such as exercise rooms or pools. See also Section 1004.5 for requirements for the accessible entrance door to the unit.

In facilities such as hotels or nursing homes, the changing of linens or removal of garbage may be the responsibility of employees rather than residents. In these situations, the areas such as laundry rooms and garbage disposal areas should be regulated under the employee work area provisions and are not required to be accessible to the residents of the dwelling units.

1004.3 Accessible Route. Accessible routes within Type B units shall comply with Section 1004.3.

❖ Type B units differ from Accessible and Type A units in that the accessible route does not require a turning space anywhere within the unit. The accessible route in the Type B units must meet the provisions for location and components only.

1004.3.1 Location. At least one accessible route shall connect all spaces and elements that are a part of the unit. Accessible routes shall coincide with or be located in the same area as a general circulation path.

EXCEPTIONS:

1. An accessible route is not required to unfinished attics and unfinished basements that are part of the unit.
2. One of the following is not required to be on an accessible route:
   - 2.1 A raised floor area in a portion of a living, dining, or sleeping room; or
   - 2.2 A sunken floor area in a portion of a living, dining, or sleeping room; or
   - 2.3 A mezzanine that does not have plumbing fixtures or an enclosed habitable space.

❖ A route must be available to all living spaces within the unit. The provisions were written assuming a single-story unit; however, this could include multiple stories within an individual unit. In a congregate living arrangement, this accessible route would also include access to shared spaces such as the bathroom and living or eating areas (Section 1004.2).

The accessible route should be equivalent and consistent with the general circulation path. The intent of this sentence in the standard is similar to what was described in Section 1004.2 from the aspect that the accessible route should not be a backdoor or secondary route where the person using the accessible route would have a less desirable path of travel. In earlier editions of the standard this section listed specific rooms or areas that the accessible route was not to pass through. The current wording in the second sentence of this section ensures equal treatment and makes it easier to determine what locations are acceptable for the route. As long as the accessible route within the unit is the same as the route used by everyone else, it should not make any difference which rooms or spaces the accessible route goes through.

In a Type B unit, certain portions of a multilevel unit do not need to be on an accessible route. The first exception addresses unfinished attics and basements. Unfinished attics and basements do not need to be on an accessible route because these spaces do not include living space for the unit. This exception was applicable for Accessible and Type A units in earlier editions of the standard and was included here for the Type B units in the 2009 edition of the standard because the Type B units provide a lower level of accessibility. This exception is also consistent with the multistory unit exception that is found in the FHA and the building code. When discussing the inclusion of this exception, the A117.1 Committee did state that it believed the doors to these spaces were still a "user passage doorway" (see Section 1004.5.2) and that the door width and size requirements were still regulated. Therefore, the committee's intent was that this exception does not exempt doors to these unfinished spaces from complying with Section 1004.5.

The second exception addresses three specific items within a multilevel unit that may not need to be on an accessible route. This includes either a raised area, a sunken area or a mezzanine within the unit [see Commentary Figures C1004.3.1(a) and (b)]. See the scoping documents for exemptions for multistory units.

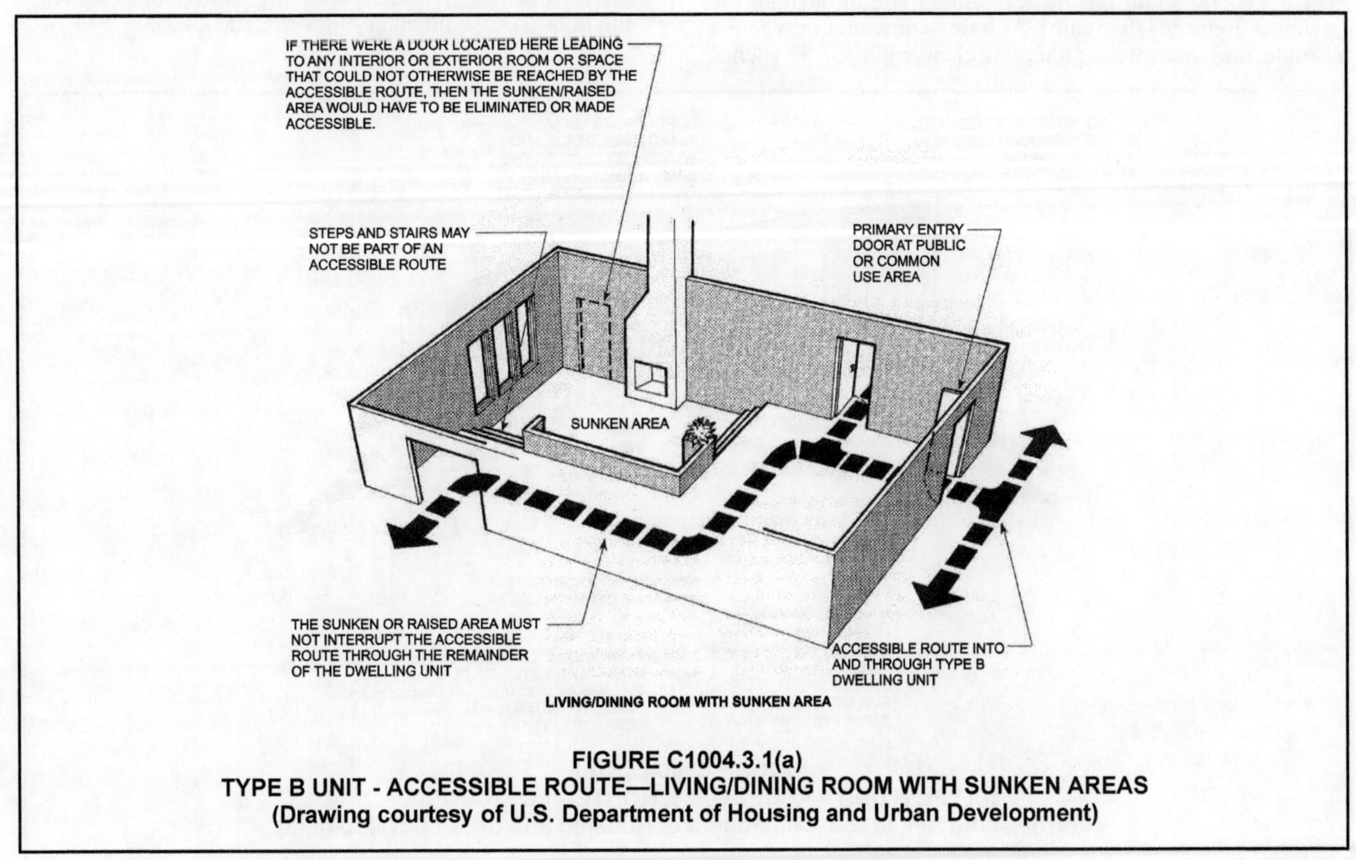

FIGURE C1004.3.1(a)
TYPE B UNIT - ACCESSIBLE ROUTE—LIVING/DINING ROOM WITH SUNKEN AREAS
(Drawing courtesy of U.S. Department of Housing and Urban Development)

In the scoping provisions found in the model codes and the Fair Housing Act, there are exceptions for multistory units without elevator service, as well as to a second level in multistory dwelling units with elevator access to only the first level. See the scoping documents for specific provisions. See Section 201 and the preface for an explanation of scoping provisions and technical requirements.

1004.3.2 Components. Accessible routes shall consist of one or more of the following elements: walking surfaces with a slope not steeper than 1:20, doors and doorways, ramps, elevators, and platform lifts.

❖ In many ways, this section serves as a setup to transition from the accessible route requirements of Section 1004.3 to the actual technical requirements found in Sections 1004.4 through 1004.8. The accessible route throughout the unit should be on level surfaces. When a transition is needed between levels or stories, either a ramp, elevator or platform lift can be used (see commentary, Sections 1004.6, 1004.7 and 1004.8).

1004.4 Walking Surfaces. Walking surfaces that are part of an accessible route shall comply with Section 1004.4.

❖ An accessible route in public areas must comply with Section 403, including floor surfaces (Section 302), slope, change in level (Section 303) and clear width. Within the Type B unit, walking surfaces need to comply with only the requirements for width and change in level. What this most often represents is that Type B units can have carpets with higher pile and thicker padding than what is permitted in the building corridors.

1004.4.1 Clear Width. Clear width of an accessible route shall comply with Section 403.5.

❖ The general width for the accessible route throughout the unit is 36 inches (915 mm). At framed openings or where a route may narrow, a minimum clear width of 32 inches (815 mm) provides adequate clearance. However, if an opening or another type of restriction along a route is more than 24 inches (610 mm) deep, it must be a minimum of 36 inches (915 mm) wide (see Commentary Figure C403.5). This allows for framed openings, pilasters or other minimal protrusions along the accessible route.

For the width requirements at doors, see Section 1004.5. It is not the intent of this section to require the clear widths at turns (Section 403.5.1) or passing spaces (Section 403.5.2) within the Type B unit.

1004.4.2 Changes in Level. Changes in level shall comply with Section 303.

EXCEPTION: Where exterior deck, patio or balcony surface materials are impervious, the finished exterior impervious surface shall be 4 inches (100 mm) maximum below the floor level of the adjacent interior spaces of the unit.

❖ A change in level means a change in elevation between horizontal walking surfaces in the direction of travel along an accessible route. The general limits are $^1/_4$-inch (6 mm) maximum vertical change or $^1/_2$-inch (13 mm) maximum with a beveled edge. These provisions are covered in Section 303, which is generally applicable to all floor surfaces on an accessible route. In addition, more than $^1/_2$ inch (13 mm) is considered a tripping hazard for ambulatory persons (see commentary, Section 303).

The exception allows for a maximum 4-inch (100 mm) change between the interior finished floor and an exterior deck surface. This dimension does not include the threshold permitted in Section 1004.5.2.2. This change in elevation is permitted only at doors other than the primary entrance. The change in elevation allows for concerns about water infiltration and/or wind resistance for that secondary opening—typically a sliding patio door or a swinging door (see Commentary Figure C1004.4.2).

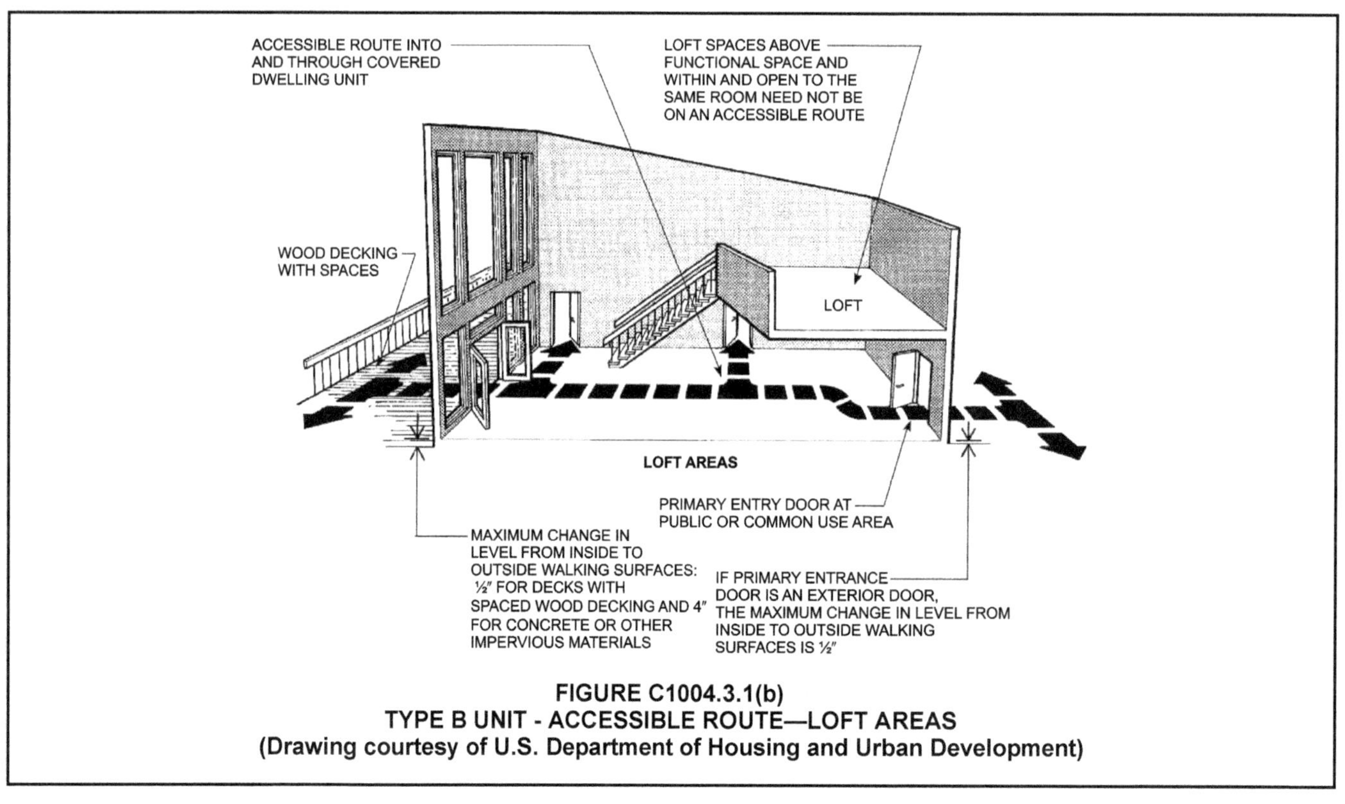

FIGURE C1004.3.1(b)
TYPE B UNIT - ACCESSIBLE ROUTE—LOFT AREAS
(Drawing courtesy of U.S. Department of Housing and Urban Development)

1004.5 Doors and Doorways. Doors and doorways shall comply with Section 1004.5.

❖ Two types of doors are addressed in this section: the door that serves as the primary entrance door to the unit and other doors within the unit intended for people to pass through. This includes doors leading to private areas that are part of the unit, such as attached private garages or balconies.

1004.5.1 Primary Entrance Door. The primary entrance door to the unit shall comply with Section 404.

EXCEPTION: Storm and screen doors serving individual dwelling or sleeping units are not required to comply with Section 404.2.5.

❖ The primary entrance door should be the main door used to access the unit. Although this may be somewhat interpre-

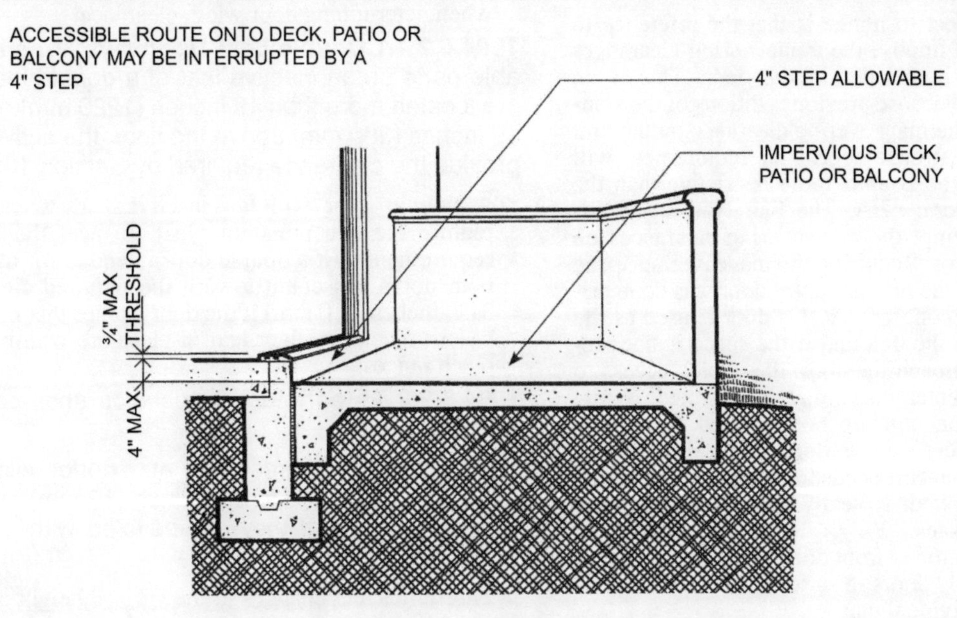

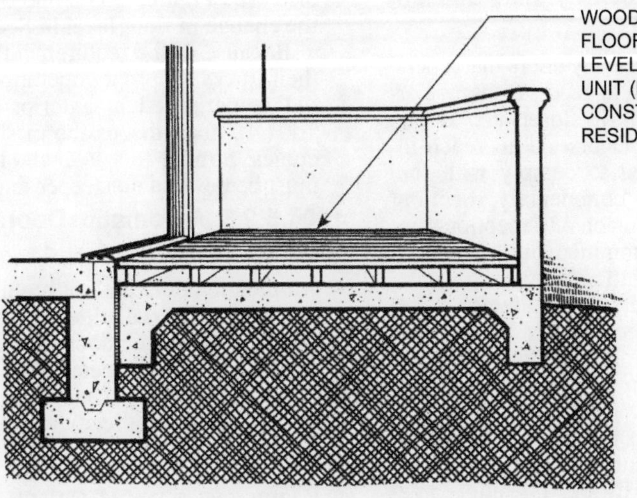

FIGURE C1004.4.2
EXTERIOR DECK CHANGE IN ELEVATION
(Drawing courtesy of U.S. Department of Housing and Urban Development)

tive in some units, it is typically the "front" door to the unit. See Section 1004.2 for additional information.

The primary entrance door to the Type B unit must meet all the provisions for doors that are located along an accessible route (see Section 404). This includes the requirements for 32-inch (815 mm) clear width, thresholds, lever hardware, door opening force, bottom door surface on the push side and vision lite location, which typically result in a 36-inch (915 mm) door leaf. Door hardware must be installed between 34 inches and 48 inches (865 and 1220 mm) above the floor.

One important aspect to notice is that the reference to Section 404 will also impose the maneuvering clearances (Section 404.2.3) to both sides of the door. This is an important distinction because previous editions of the standard did not require the maneuvering clearance on the unit side of the primary entrance door. This requirement will also make A117.1 Type B units more restrictive than the provisions of the federal FHA. The Fair Housing provisions continue to exempt the maneuvering clearances on the unit side of the door. Requiring the maneuvering space on the interior side of the primary entry door was done primarily to address the concern that this door is used as the means of egress from the unit and if the space is not provided to properly approach the door, then quick access to the door during an emergency may be affected. While other doors within the unit are not required to provide maneuvering clearances, those doors typically can be removed by the occupants if needed. The option of removing the primary entry door typically does not exist due to security or weather issues.

Based on the exception, a front door with a screen/storm door is not considered "doors in series" provided the door is only serving an individual unit.

If an automatic door is installed, the provisions of Section 404.3 are applicable. While this requirement is not stated directly as it is in Section 1004.5.2.3 for user passage doorways, because the base paragraph refers to all of Section 404, this requirement is also applicable to the primary entrance door.

1004.5.2 User Passage Doorways. Doorways intended for user passage shall comply with Section 1004.5.2.

❖ Doors "intended for user passage" are any doors that a person is expected to pass fully through to access a space. For example, doorways to rooms or walk-in closets are "doorways intended for user passage." Doorways to reach-in pantries or closets are not required to comply with the requirements in this section (see commentary, Section 1004.3.1). When discussing the inclusion of Exception 1 in Section 1004.3.1, the A117.1 Committee did state that doors to unfinished basements and attics are "user passage doorways" and that door width and size requirements are regulated. Therefore, the committee's intent is that the exception in Section 1004.3.1 does not exempt doors to those unfinished spaces from complying with Section 1004.5.2.

Doors within Type B units must meet the clear width and threshold requirements in the subsections that follow. Maneuvering clearances, lever hardware, opening force limits, etc., are not required.

1004.5.2.1 Clear Width. Doorways shall have a clear opening of $31^3/_4$ inches (805 mm) minimum. Clear opening of swinging doors shall be measured between the face of the door and stop, with the door open 90 degrees.

❖ The opening is measured with the door open 90 degrees (1.6 rad), even if the door can open wider. The intent of the $31^3/_4$-inch (810 mm) dimension is to allow for a 2-foot, 10-inch (865 mm) door. The 32-inch (815 mm) clearance at the primary entrance door (Section 1004.5.1) typically requires a 36-inch (915 mm) door.

Although the standard does not specifically reference door hardware, it is not the intent to include hardware when determining door width clearance.

1004.5.2.1.1 Double Leaf Doorways. Where the operable parts on an inactive leaf of a double leaf doorway are located more than 48 inches (1220 mm) or less than 15 inches (380 mm) above the floor, the active leaf shall provide the clearance required by Section 1004.5.2.1.

❖ A double door with an inactive leaf would generally require the one remaining leaf to meet the clear width requirements. At a double door intended for user passage, both doors can count toward the required clear width of $31^3/_4$ inches (810 mm) if the door latches that hold the inactive or secondary door leaf in place are within the normal reach ranges.

1004.5.2.2 Thresholds. Thresholds shall comply with Section 303.

> **EXCEPTION:** Thresholds at exterior sliding doors shall be permitted to be $^3/_4$ inch (19 mm) maximum in height, provided they are beveled with a slope not steeper than 1:2.

❖ Thresholds and changes in the surface height at doorways are difficult for persons using a wheelchair who also may have low stamina or restrictions in arm movement because complex maneuvering is required to get over the level change when operating the door.

The reference to Section 303 effectively establishes $^1/_2$ inch (13 mm) as the maximum change in elevation for a threshold at a doorway. Where a threshold exceeds $^1/_4$ inch (6 mm) in height, the edge of the threshold must be beveled (see Figures 303.2 and 303.3). This is in addition to the change in floor level in Section 1004.4.2.

Because of the requirements for sliding doors to stay in their tracks for proper operation, a $^3/_4$-inch (19 mm) threshold is permitted at exterior sliding doors. See Section 1004.4.2 for a discussion of sliding doors at patios or balconies. Similar to a $^1/_2$-inch (13 mm) threshold, the edges must be beveled no steeper than 1:2.

1004.5.2.3 Automatic Doors. Automatic doors shall comply with Section 404.3.

❖ Automatic doors are not required within Type B dwelling units, but if installed, they must meet the general provisions for automatic doors in Section 404.3.

This item is not specifically listed in Accessible or Type A dwelling units because the general reference to Section 404 for all doors already requires this.

1004.6 Ramps. Ramps shall comply with Section 405.

❖ Ramps that serve as part of the accessible route into or through a Type B dwelling or sleeping unit must meet the general ramp provisions in Section 405. See Sections 1004.3.1 and 1004.4.2 for levels within a Type B unit that do not have to be on an accessible route.

Ramps for a change in elevation greater than 6 inches (150 mm) will require handrails on both sides. The local building code should be consulted regarding guard requirements along ramps. Ramps must have a landing at both the top and the bottom, so a ramp cannot extend up to the face of a door.

1004.7 Elevators. Elevators within the unit shall comply with Section 407, 408, or 409.

❖ Elevators installed within a single dwelling unit or providing private access to a single dwelling unit are permitted to be passenger elevators, LULAs or private residence elevators. Refer to ASME A17.1 for limitations of use.

Refer to the scoping documents for requirements when elevators are installed for general access in the building and within individual units. In the model code and Fair Housing Act Accessibility Guidelines, when there are no elevators in the building, multistory units are exempted from Type B requirements. When a common elevator is available in the building, the units on levels served by the elevator must meet Type B unit requirements. The elevator must serve the primary entry into the unit and that level must include at least a toilet room (i.e., powder room with water closet and lavatory) and a living space. When an elevator is provided for access within an individual dwelling unit (e.g., a multistory townhouse), the Type B unit requirements are applicable to all levels served by the elevator. In all cases, an accessible route must be provided from the site arrival point, through the accessible entrance, to the elevator.

Another example of elevators being used in relation to Type B dwelling units is when dwelling units are located above other uses, such as parking, business or mercantile. Be certain to review the jurisdiction's scoping requirements since the determination regarding where Type B units are required is heavily dependent on whether the building or unit contains an elevator.

1004.8 Platform Lifts. Platform lifts within the unit shall comply with Section 410.

❖ Platform lifts can be used to provide access to a dwelling unit or within an individual dwelling unit to serve as part of an accessible route between levels. The lift must be a platform (wheelchair) lift in accordance with ASME A18.1, not a chair lift (e.g., flip-down seat). Platform lifts may be incline lifts or vertical lifts. The current edition of ASME A18.1 limits the maximum rise to 12 feet (3660 mm) (see ASME A18.1 for limitations of use).

1004.9 Operable Parts. Lighting controls, electrical switches and receptacle outlets, environmental controls, electrical panelboards, and user controls for security or intercom systems shall comply with Sections 309.2 and 309.3.

EXCEPTIONS:

1. Receptacle outlets serving a dedicated use.
2. Where two or more receptacle outlets are provided in a kitchen above a length of counter top that is uninterrupted by a sink or appliance, one receptacle outlet shall not be required to comply with Section 309.
3. Floor receptacle outlets.
4. HVAC diffusers.
5. Controls mounted on ceiling fans.
6. Controls or switches mounted on appliances.
7. Plumbing fixture controls.
8. Reset buttons and shut-offs serving appliances, piping and plumbing fixtures.
9. Where redundant controls other than light switches are provided for a single element, one control in each space shall not be required to be accessible.
10. Within kitchens and bathrooms, lighting controls, electrical switches and receptacle outlets are permitted to be located over cabinets with counter tops 36 inches (915 mm) maximum in height and $25^1/_2$ inches (650 mm) maximum in depth.

❖ The general requirements for operable parts are listed in Section 309. By a more specific reference to Sections 309.2 and 309.3 (and not Section 309.4), operable parts in Type B units require a clear floor space adjacent to the part and that part is to be within reach ranges. Section 309.4, which is not included by reference, is the section that would normally require that operation of the part does not require any tight pinching, grasping or twisting of the wrist to operate or more than 5 pounds (22 N) force. While it would be a good design practice to still consider the provisions of Section 309.4, it is not a requirement for the items listed in Section 1004.9.

The intent is for the person in the space to be able to operate the equipment in the room in a normal manner. It is not the intent that these provisions be applicable to items such as shut-offs for plumbing fixtures or protection switches for electrical equipment, such as the reset switch on a garbage disposal. These reset buttons or shut-off controls are addressed by Exception 8. Exception 8 is intended to cover any of the elements in the base paragraph and allow electrical switches and various shut-offs to be exempt from the requirements of Section 309. Inclusion of this exception clarifies that these controls are not typically considered as being regulated by the standard. These types of switches or controls are not intended for everyday usage but are for protecting appliances or allowing them to be disconnected to be serviced. Two examples that may be found within a dwelling unit are the electrical reset switch on the bottom of a garbage disposal unit and the water shut-off valves on water supply lines beneath a sink, lavatory or water closet.

Examples of lighting controls are wall light switches or pull cords. If light switches are offered with 3-way or 4-way operation, all switches must be accessible (note that Exception 9 excludes "light switches" from the redundant control exception). Other types of switches could include wall activation switches for garbage disposals, bathroom ventilation fans or cooking hoods. Exception 9 allows for redundant controls to be located in an inaccessible location. For example, where multiple controls can operate a single element, one of those controls does not need to be accessible. Exception 6 exempts any electrical switches mounted on appliances, such as the cooking hoods. Bathroom ventilation fans shall be accessible as part of the environmental controls.

Receptacles are typically the standard duplex wall outlets located around a room or over a counter. Note that there are several exceptions for electrical receptacles. Receptacles that serve a dedicated purpose (Exception 1), such as the receptacle for a washer/dryer, refrigerator or stove, need not be accessible. These items are typically plugged in all the time and located behind the stationary appliance. The model electrical code requires electrical receptacles spaced at a maximum of 12 feet (3660 mm) apart in most rooms. In spaces with very tall windows or along balcony guards there may not be wall space for the required electrical receptacles. Large rooms may need receptacles located toward the center of the room. When floor receptacles are used, they do not need to be accessible (Exception 3). Exception 2 is used when dealing with receptacles over kitchen counters. In kitchens, per the model electrical code, one receptacle is required over each section of counter top with a maximum spacing of 4 feet (1220 mm). If an appliance or sink is located along a counter top, the counter on each side is considered a separate section, and a receptacle must be installed on each side. Exception 2 allows for one receptacle per counter section to not be accessible if the remainder of the outlets are accessible. An alternative is to locate a receptacle on the side or front surface of the lower cabinet. This is commonly done on kitchen island counters; however, this will reduce drawer space.

In a kitchen in a Type B unit, the counters can be located at any height, typically 36 inches (915 mm). However, with the obstructed side reach range requirements in Section 308.3.2 (which is referenced from Section 309.3), receptacles generally cannot be located over the standard 36-inch-high (915 mm) counter and be accessible, since the height of the obstruction is to be limited to 34 inches (865 mm) or less. In addition, the standard generally limits the depth of the obstruction to a maximum of 24 inches (610 mm). Because Type B units were intended to meet the requirements of the Fair Housing Act and the FHA design requirements intended to allow conventional cabinets, Exception 10 was added to specifically allow the reach to be over a 36-inch-high (915 mm) counter. Exception 10 also will allow the reach depth to be over a 24-inch-deep (610 mm) base cabinet that has the typical $1^1/_2$-inch 38 mm) counter top extending over the base cabinet. Without Exception 10, it would not be possible to use conventional cabinets and still provide access to the outlets, controls and switches that are located over the cabinets. This same problem is typically not as big of an issue in bathrooms because bathroom counter heights are typically between 29 and 34 inches (735 and 865 mm) high and the controls or switches may be located on a side wall near the front of the cabinet.

Environmental controls can include ceiling fans or heating and air-conditioning thermostats. A common error for locating the thermostat is to specify the electrical box at 48 inches (1220 mm) high, not noting that the actual control is on the top of the thermostat box, thus placing the control out of the reach range. Exception 4 does exempt the heating and air-conditioning diffusers from being accessible. They need to be on or near the floor and near the ceiling to circulate the air in the room effectively. Exception 5 exempts controls mounted on ceiling fans. Typically the on-off and speed for ceiling fans are controlled from a wall switch, but there may be a switch on the fan itself for reversing the direction of the blades.

For Type B units (unlike Accessible and Type A units), Exception 6 exempts all appliance-mounted controls. Appliance controls vary greatly and may include the key pad for temperature and type of cooking (e.g., bake/broil) on ovens, knobs for burner settings on stove tops, door handles to access the interior of the appliance, water/ice dispensers on refrigerators, latches for self-cleaning ovens, soap containers in dishwashers and clothes washers, lint trays in dryers, etc.

In Type B units, plumbing fixture controls are exempted per Exception 7. Plumbing fixture controls would include faucets in showers, tubs and sinks, and flush valves on toilets, which do have accessibility requirements in Accessible and Type A units.

Accessible windows and window hardware are covered in Accessible and Type A units; however, they are not required in Type B units.

Although electrical panelboards (circuit breaker boxes) are listed in this section, it is important to note that their inclusion does not mean that they are required to be placed within the unit but that they are accessible wherever they are installed within the units and are available for operation or use by the occupants. The location and additional access requirements for panelboards are found in the NFPA's *National Electrical Code®* (NFPA 70). If the panelboards are located within the unit, they should allow for the occupants to have access to and reach them (see Commentary Figure C1002.9). It is also important that users understand that including panelboards in this section makes the Type B units more restrictive than the FHA. Fair Housing excludes panelboards and circuit breakers completely from the occupant control requirements while the A117.1 standard will regulate the clear floor space and height to access the panelboard.

Security or intercom systems may include activation keypads or access to a phone or speaker. Refer to Sections 1006.5, 1006.6 and 1006.7 for additional specifics for communication features that are part of security or intercom systems.

Operable parts on the primary entrance door to the units are regulated under Section 1004.5.1 through a reference to Sections 404.2.6 and 404.3.5. Door hardware on other doors within the unit is not regulated (see Section 1004.5.2).

1004.10 Laundry Equipment. Washing machines and clothes dryers shall comply with Section 1004.10.

❖ The standard does not require laundry equipment in the unit; however, where they are provided in units, washers and dryers must meet the minimal level of accessibility in Section 1004.10.1. These provisions are less than those in a common laundry room (see Section 611).

When designing the laundry area, several items must be considered. Section 1004.10.1 requires a parallel clear floor space in front of each top-loading appliance, and forward or parallel approach in front of each front-loading machine.

Though not specifically referenced, the requirements of Section 611.2 regarding the location of the clear floor space should be followed for guidance. This would center the clear floor space on a top-loading appliance and allow up to a 24-inch (610 mm) offset for either a forward or parallel approach to a front-loading machine [see Commentary Figure C1004.10(c)]. The ICC A117.1 did not state this requirement because clearances at laundry equipment are not required by the Fair Housing Act (FHA). This means that the ICC A117.1 requirements in Section 1004.10.1 exceed the requirements of the FHA simply by requiring the clear floor space. It is for that same reason that the standard no longer requires the clear floor space be centered on the laundry equipment in a Type B unit.

The orientation of the clear floor space at a front-loading appliance is another important distinction for the Type B unit. While the general laundry provisions of Section 611 and, therefore, those of the Accessible and Type A units (Sections 1002.10 and 1003.10) will only accept a parallel approach, the Type B units will accept either a parallel or forward approach. The option for a forward approach to top-loading washers and dryers was not added to the standard in order that the requirements in Section 611 and those of the Accessible and Type A units could match the requirements of Section 611.2 in the federal *2010 ADA Standards for Accessible Design*.

When laundry equipment is located in a room, turning spaces and maneuvering clearances are not required as they are for an Accessible unit and Type A unit. A service/laundry sink does not need be accessible; however, it would be a better design to provide a parallel or side approach to that sink for potential use [see Commentary Figure C1004.10(a)].

When laundry equipment is located in a closet, the clear floor space can be located 10 inches (255 mm) back from the face of the units (Section 308.3.1), which allows for the wall thickness, but may necessitate either sliding closet doors or no doors so the doors will not block the clear floor space [see Commentary Figure C1004.10(b)]. This standard does not address whether removal of the doors could be considered an adaptable feature.

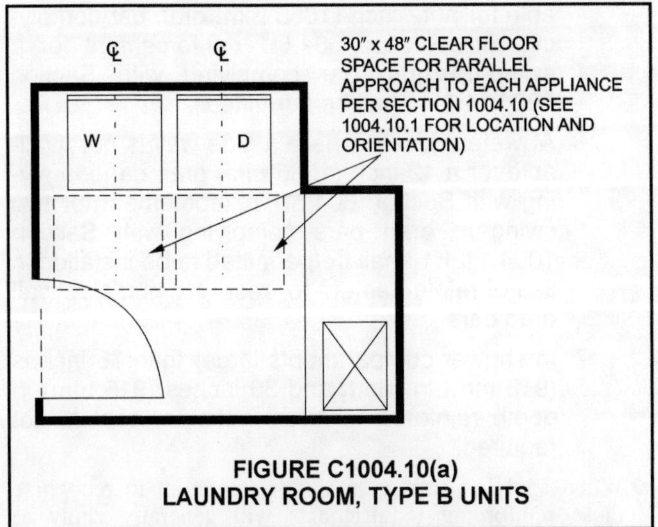

FIGURE C1004.10(a)
LAUNDRY ROOM, TYPE B UNITS

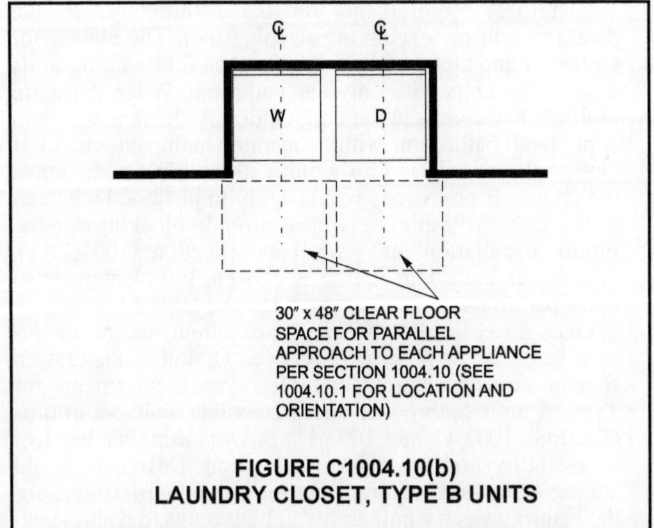

FIGURE C1004.10(b)
LAUNDRY CLOSET, TYPE B UNITS

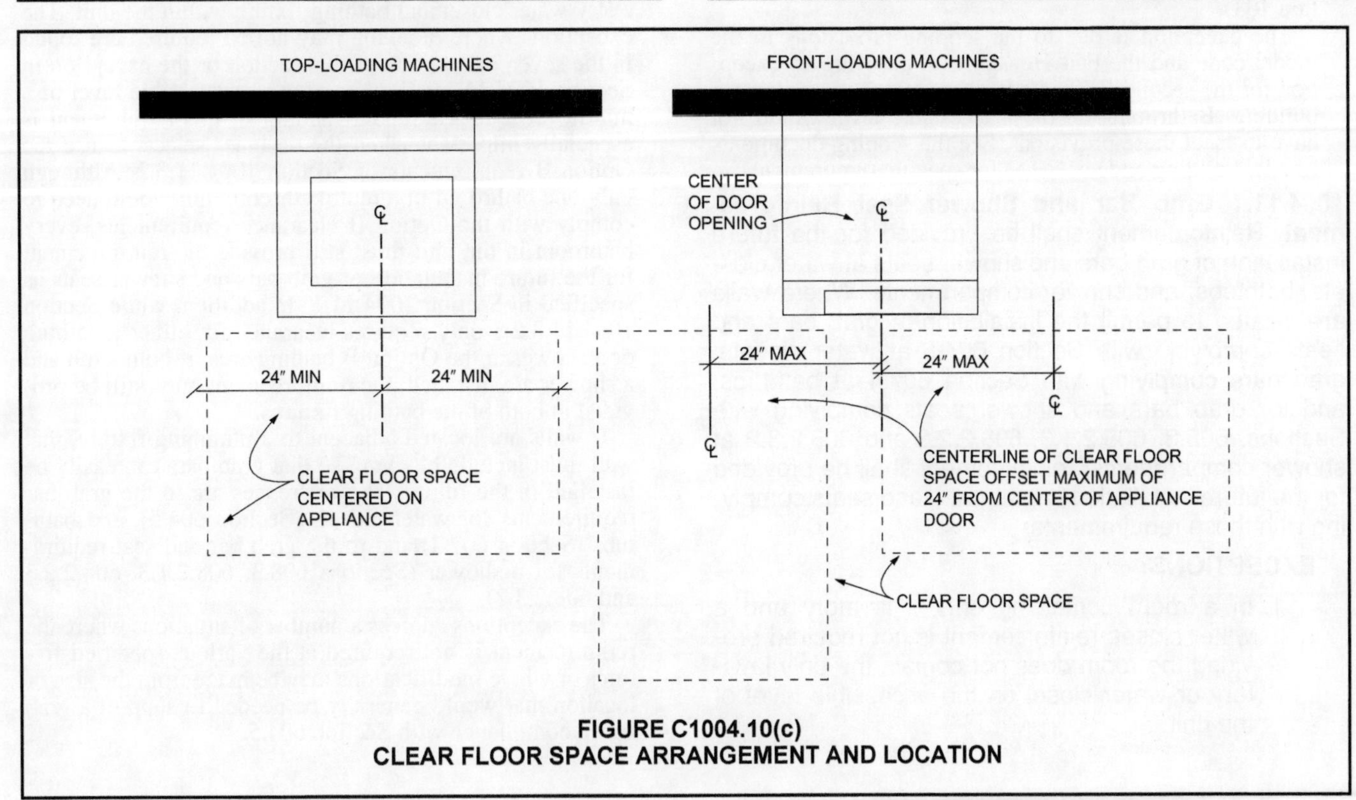

FIGURE C1004.10(c)
CLEAR FLOOR SPACE ARRANGEMENT AND LOCATION

1004.10.1 Clear Floor Space. A clear floor space complying with Section 305.3, shall be provided. A parallel approach shall be provided for a top loading machine. A forward or parallel approach shall be provided for a front loading machine.

❖ See Section 1004.10.

1004.11 Toilet and Bathing Facilities. Toilet and bathing fixtures shall comply with Section 1004.11.

EXCEPTION: Fixtures on levels not required to be accessible.

❖ Type B units allow for minimal access into a bathroom. Bathroom requirements for Accessible units and Type A units provide for a higher level of accessibility.

In Type B units, designers can choose to meet either Option A (Section 1004.11.3.1) or Option B (Section 1004.11.3.2) requirements for the bathroom(s) in the dwelling unit or serving the sleeping unit. The choice for Option A and Option B is available even for dwelling units or sleeping units with only one bathroom. When there are multiple bathrooms in the unit, Option A clearances would apply to all bathrooms within the unit. On the other hand, if Option B was selected for a unit with multiple bathrooms, the Option B provisions would apply to just one bathroom in the unit. All bathrooms must provide blocking for the future installation of grab bars (Section 1004.11.1). Whichever bathroom option is chosen, the clearances in those bathrooms must also meet Section 1004.11.2.

Once an option is chosen, the requirements are exclusive, there can be no mixing between Option A and Option B requirements within a unit. However, requirements for Type A unit bathrooms and Accessible unit bathrooms (Sections 1002.11 and 1003.11) provide a higher level of accessibility and are always an option. Designers could choose to exceed requirements for individual fixtures, for the bathroom as a whole or for all bathrooms in a unit (Section 103).

The exception is due to the scoping provisions in the model code and the Fair Housing Act allowing an exception for the second floor in a multistory unit in an elevator building. Bathrooms on the inaccessible level would not have to meet these provisions. See the scoping documents (model building code or FHA) for specific requirements.

1004.11.1 Grab Bar and Shower Seat Reinforcement. Reinforcement shall be provided for the future installation of grab bars and shower seats at water closets, bathtubs, and shower compartments. Where walls are located to permit the installation of grab bars and seats complying with Section 604.5 at water closets; grab bars complying with Section 607.4 at bathtubs; and for grab bars and shower seats complying with Sections, 608.3, 608.2.1.3, 608.2.2.3 and 608.2.3.2 at shower compartments; reinforcement shall be provided for the future installation of grab bars and seats complying with those requirements.

EXCEPTIONS:

1. In a room containing only a lavatory and a water closet, reinforcement is not required provided the room does not contain the only lavatory or water closet on the accessible level of the unit.
2. At water closets reinforcement for the side wall vertical grab bar component required by Section 604.5 is not required.
3. At water closets where wall space will not permit a grab bar complying with Section 604.5.2, reinforcement for a rear wall grab bar 24 inches (610 mm) minimum in length centered on the water closet shall be provided.
4. At water closets where a side wall is not available for a 42-inch (1065 mm) grab bar complying with Section 604.5.1, reinforcement for a sidewall grab bar, 24 inches (610 mm) minimum in length, located 12 inches (305 mm) maximum from the rear wall, shall be provided.
5. At water closets where a side wall is not available for a 42-inch (1065 mm) grab bar complying with Section 604.5.1 reinforcement for a swing-up grab bar complying with Section 1004.11.1.1 shall be permitted.
6. At water closets where a side wall is not available for a 42-inch (1065 mm) grab bar complying with Section 604.5.1 reinforcement for two swing-up grab bars complying with Section 1004.11.1.1 shall be permitted to be installed in lieu of reinforcement for rear wall and side wall grab bars.
7. In shower compartments larger than 36 inches (915 mm) in width and 36 inches (915 mm) in depth reinforcement for a shower seat is not required.

❖ When applying this section it is important to recognize these reinforcing requirements will generally apply to every water closet and bathing fixture within the unit. The exceptions where blocking may not be required are found in the seven exceptions of this section or the exception in Section 1004.11 for fixtures on a nonaccessible level of a multilevel unit. The understanding of this requirement is especially important when the designer selects to use the Option B requirements of Section 1004.11.3.2. Although only one bathroom in a multibathroom unit would need to comply with the Option B clearance requirements, every bathroom in the unit must still provide the reinforcement for the future installation of grab bars and shower seats as specified in Section 1004.11.1. In addition, while Section 1004.11.3.2.3 only requires clearance for either a bathtub or a shower in the Option B bathing area, if both a tub and a shower are installed, the reinforcement must still be provided in both of the bathing fixtures.

If walls are located adjacent to a plumbing fixture, that wall must include blocking so that grab bars can easily be installed in the future. The references are to the grab bar requirements for water closets (Section 604.5), and bathtubs (Section 607.4) and to the grab bar and seat requirements for a shower (Sections 608.3, 608.2.1.3, 608.2.2.3 and 608.2.3.2).

The exceptions address a number of situations where the reinforcement is not required at the various specified fixtures or where modifications may be made from the size or location that would generally be needed to support a grab bar in compliance with Section 604.5.

If there is a toilet room with only a water closet and a lavatory installed in it, Exception 1 may sometimes be used to eliminate the reinforcement requirement for that toilet room. These types of rooms are often referred to as a powder room or a half-bath. If this toilet room is the only toilet facility on the accessible level, it must contain blocking in the walls at the water closet. If other facilities are provided on that level, blocking is not required in the powder room. The language in the exception related to being "on the accessible level of the unit" coordinates with the scoping provisions in the model code and the Fair Housing Act, which allow an exception for the second floor in a multistory unit in an elevator building (see these documents for specific requirements).

To fully understand the exceptions it is important to remember that, unlike Accessible or Type A units, Type B units do not require the water closet be located with walls behind and to one side. In a Type B unit, it is permissible to have the water closet located in an area without a side wall or in an area where a bathing fixture or lavatory may be located to the sides. This difference in the location requirements of Section 1004.11.3.1.2, as compared to Sections 604.2, 1002.11.2 and 1003.11.2.4.1, also results in the need for using Exceptions 2 through 6 in some toilet rooms.

The water closet side wall vertical grab bar that is specified in Section 604.5.1 is not required in Type B units, based on Exception 2. This exception will, therefore, eliminate the reinforcement that may be needed within the wall to support the bar. While the vertical grab bar would be helpful to aid people to rise from or sit on the water closet, the exception recognizes that windows are often located on the wall adjacent to the water closet within dwelling units or that a side wall may not be provided.

Section 604.5.2 addresses requirements for the rear wall grab bar at water closets and generally requires the grab bar to be a minimum of 36 inches (915 mm) in length. Because a vanity, lavatory or other obstruction may be located in the clear floor space for the water closet in a Type B unit (Section 1004.11.3.1.2.2.4) or the rear wall may be of a very limited length, Exception 3 allows the grab bar to be shortened to 24 inches (610 mm) in length and therefore allows the reinforcement to be reduced accordingly.

Exception 4 is conceptually similar to Exception 3 but deals with the side wall versus the rear wall. Where the side wall is not long enough to accommodate the generally required 42-inch-long (1065 mm) grab bar (Section 604.5.1), Exception 4 will allow the grab bar length to be 24 inches (610 mm) minimum in length, which will change the reinforcement requirement. This may occur when the water closet is adjacent to a shower or tub enclosure or the door into the room is on the side wall. Blocking for a shorter bar is acceptable [see Commentary Figure C1004.11.1(a)].

Generally grab bars are required on the side and rear wall at water closets. Exceptions 5 and 6 allow reinforcement for swing-up grab bars complying with Section 1004.11.1.1 to be used. The difference between Exceptions 5 and 6 is that Exception 5 addresses a single swing-up grab bar replacing a side wall grab bar, while Exception 6 addresses two swing-up grab bars as replacement for both the side wall and rear wall grab bars at a water closet.

Type B units are the only unit type where blocking for swing-up grab bars or the installation of swing-up grab bars is permitted instead of the blocking or installation of fixed rear and side grab bars. See Section 1004.11.1.1 for swing-up grab bar requirements. Per Exception 6, two swing-up grab bars are permitted in place of the rear and side grab bars. Using swing-up grab bars may be helpful where there are no walls adjacent to the water closet, where additional space adjacent to the water closet is needed to allow for someone to assist a user, or where the occupant may be using mobility aids such as a walker or cane and the purpose of the grab bar is more for assistance in rising or sitting (an up or down movement) instead of a transfer (pulling to the side). Exception 5 may be used anywhere a side wall is not available for the generally required 42-inch (1065 mm) minimum length grab bar. This arrangement could occur in Option A bathrooms in Type B units where the water closet is located between a tub and a lavatory; therefore, a wall is located only behind the water

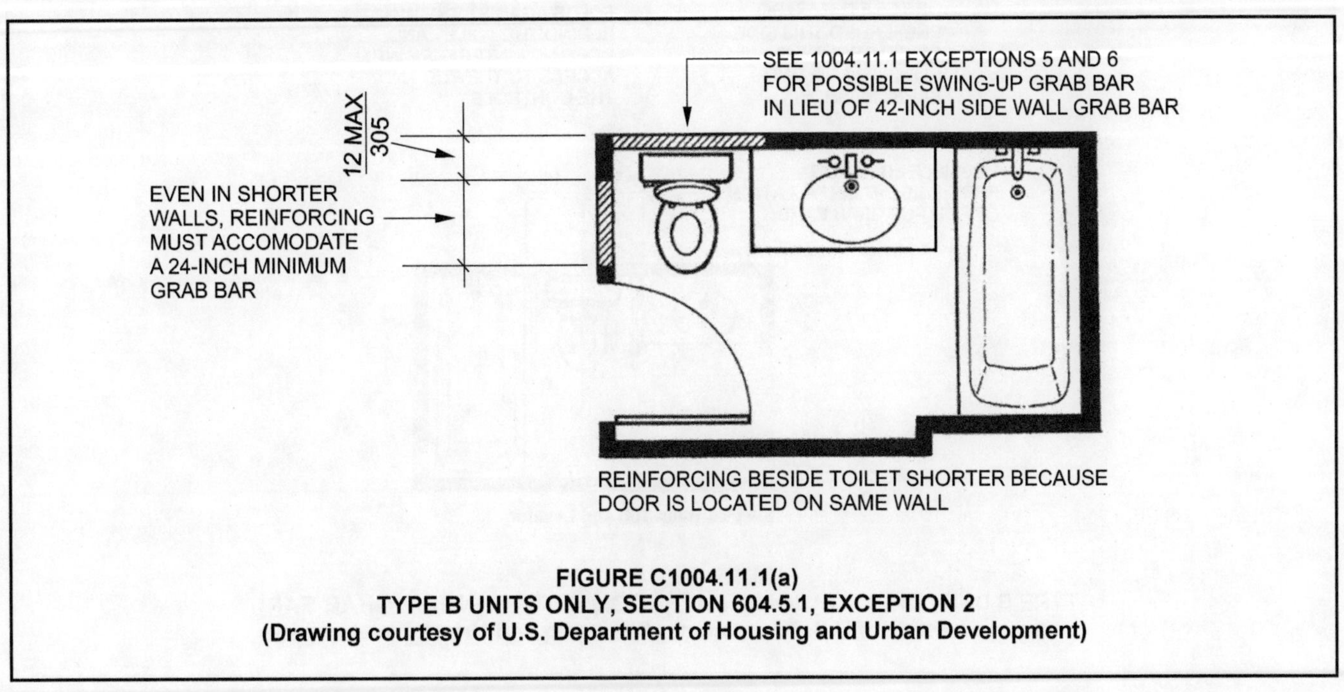

FIGURE C1004.11.1(a)
TYPE B UNITS ONLY, SECTION 604.5.1, EXCEPTION 2
(Drawing courtesy of U.S. Department of Housing and Urban Development)

closet. For persons with mobility impairments, Option A configurations allow a person to sit down at (or transfer to) the water closet, swing up the bar and then transfer to the tub. Although a swing-up grab bar is not ideal for transfer to a water closet, providing a fixed grab bar between water closet and tub would block access to the tub. Therefore the swing-up grab bar is a viable alternative for the side grab bar and can reduce the chance of a fall getting in and out of the tub [see Commentary Figure C1004.11.1(b)].

Exception 7 allows the reinforcement for the seat to be eliminated in a shower larger than 36 inches by 36 inches (915 by 915 mm). This size limitation is intended to coordinate with the transfer shower requirements of Section 608.2.1. If the shower is 36 inches by 36 inches, it can easily be adapted by the installation of grab bars and a seat to become a transfer shower when needed. The seat reinforcement would not be required in a shower stall of a larger size because the stall may be so long that the user is not able to reach the controls from a fixed seat at the opposite end of the stall. Although the exception would eliminate the requirement for seat reinforcement in larger showers, it would be better accessibility wise if the designer gave additional thought to the control and seat locations for the proposed configuration. With a little thought, the designer may be able to locate the controls so they could be reached from the future seat location and from outside of the shower. This would provide the user with a more usable shower that is easier to adapt when the need arises.

1004.11.1.1 Swing-up Grab Bars. A clearance of 18 inches (455 mm) minimum from the centerline of the water closet to any side wall or obstruction shall be provided where reinforcement for swing-up grab bars is provided. When the approach to the water closet is from the side, the 18 inches (455 mm) minimum shall be on the side opposite the direction of approach. Reinforcement shall accommodate a swing-up grab bar centered $15^3/_4$ inches (400 mm) from the centerline of the water closet and 28 inches (710 mm) minimum in length, measured from the wall to the end of the horizontal portion of the grab bar. Reinforcement shall accommodate a swing-up grab bar with a height in the down position of 33 inches (840 mm) minimum and 36 inches (915 mm) maximum. Reinforcement shall be adequate to resist forces in accordance with Section 609.8.

EXCEPTION: Where a water closet is positioned with a wall to the rear and to one side, the centerline of the water closet shall be 16 inches (405 mm) minimum and 18 inches (455 mm) maximum from the sidewall.

❖ Swing-up grab bars are permitted as an option in Type B units only. The intent of the 18-inch (455 mm) minimum centerline dimension for the swing-up grab bars is to ensure adequate space to the nearest obstruction to install and locate the swing-up bar in the same general position relative to the water closet as if there was a wall-mounted grab bar (see Figure 1004.11.1.1 and Commentary Figure C1004.11.1.1). The exception addresses situations where a wall is installed and could be used for supporting a typical side wall grab bar. Where a wall is provided on the side of the water closet, the exception will allow a clearance of 16 to 18 inches (405 by 455 mm) similar to what is allowed by Sections 604.2 and 1004.11.3.1.2.1. Side wall mounted grab bars tend to be more stable and secure and, therefore, the exception allows the wall for a side wall grab bar versus the swing-up grab bar.

Because swing-up grab bars are supported only at the one end and cantilevered from that point, the amount of stress that is placed on the reinforcement and connections is greater than a typical side wall grab bar that is supported at multiple points. The standard reminds the user the general grab bar strength requirements of Section 609.8 need to be considered and addressed for both the vertical and horizon-

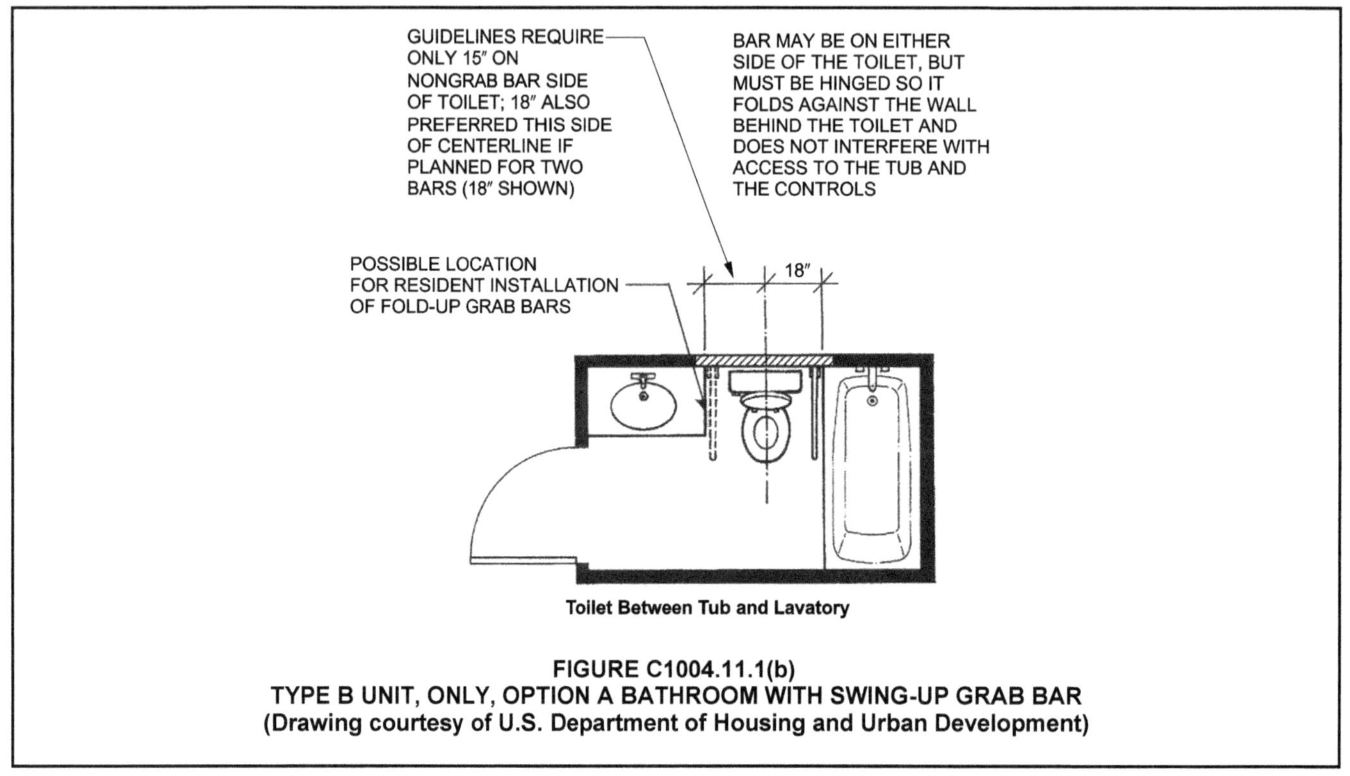

FIGURE C1004.11.1(b)
TYPE B UNIT, ONLY, OPTION A BATHROOM WITH SWING-UP GRAB BAR
(Drawing courtesy of U.S. Department of Housing and Urban Development)

tal forces placed on the swing-up grab bar and reinforcement. Designers need to consider these forces and directions to ensure that the reinforcement, structure and connections supporting it are adequate to withstand the forces and provide for a secure and stable swing-up grab bar.

The 28-inch (710 mm) minimum length is based on three considerations: 1) the length is comparable with the shorter length permitted in Section 1004.11.1, Exception 4; 2) the support for this length/cantilever is achievable with a standard wall system; 3) this length is commonly available so that future modification is readily achievable (see Commentary Figure C1004.11.1.1).

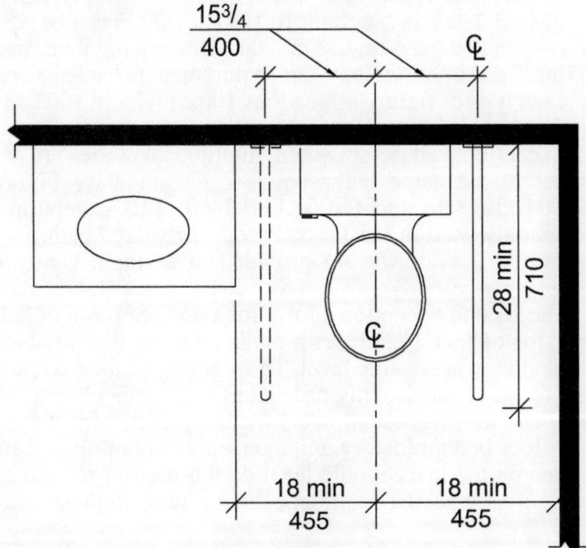

FIGURE 1004.11.1.1
SWING-UP GRAB BAR FOR WATER CLOSET

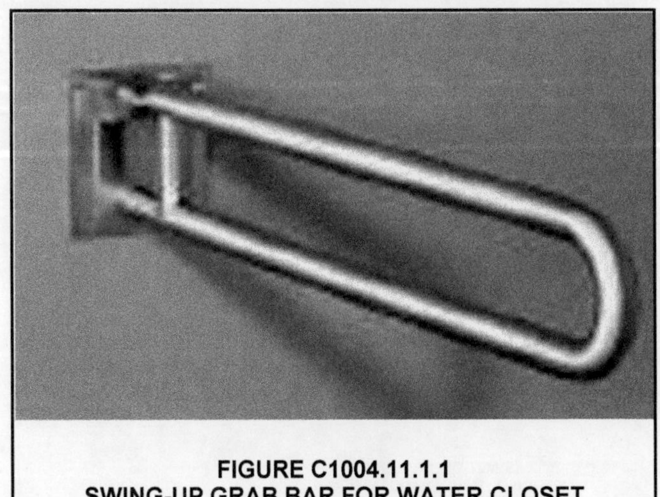

FIGURE C1004.11.1.1
SWING-UP GRAB BAR FOR WATER CLOSET

1004.11.2 Clear Floor Space. Clear floor spaces required by Section 1004.11.3.1 (Option A) or 1004.11.3.2 (Option B) shall comply with Sections 1004.11.2 and 305.3.

❖ In Type B units, the designer chooses to comply with either Option A (Section 1004.11.3.1) or Option B (Section 1004.11.3.2) bathroom requirements. Regardless of which clearance design option is selected, the door swing and knee and toe clearance requirements of Sections 1004.11.2.1 and 1004.11.2.2 must be applied.

The reference to Section 305.3 and the 30-inch by 48-inch (760 by 1220 mm) clear floor space may appear to be redundant given the specific clearance provisions in Option A and Option B. Having this extra reference does help when looking at the requirement in Section 1004.11.2.1. The wording in that section helps serve as a reminder that the clearances at fixtures (Section 1004.11.3.1 or 1004.11.3.2) are often of a different size and configuration than the floor space (Section 305.3). The intent is to make sure that a properly sized space for a person using a wheelchair is available at each fixture and that the maneuvering clearances for accessing the fixture are not obstructed.

1004.11.2.1 Doors. Doors shall not swing into the clear floor space or clearance for any fixture.

EXCEPTION: Where a clear floor space complying with Section 305.3, excluding knee and toe clearances under elements, is provided within the room beyond the arc of the door swing.

❖ The door to the bathroom must not swing into the bathroom and over the clearances and floor space needed for access to the lavatory, water closet, tub or shower. However, the exception allows that where a 30-inch by 48-inch (760 by 1220 mm) clear floor space for a wheelchair is located past the swing of the door, the door can swing over the fixture clearances. With this configuration, someone can enter the room, close the door and then maneuver to access the fixtures. The portion of the exception, "excluding knee and toe clearances," indicates that even though knee and toe clearances are not required in Type B unit bathrooms, this particular wheelchair space cannot use any knee and toe clearances. Therefore the 30-inch by 48-inch (760 by 1220 mm) space truly must be open and unobstructed and would not be allowed to use knee and toe space beneath a fixture as Section 1004.11.2.2 would typically allow.

1004.11.2.2 Knee and Toe Clearance. Clear floor space at fixtures shall be permitted to include knee and toe clearances complying with Section 306.

❖ Provisions in Type B dwelling unit bathrooms are for a parallel approach to fixtures and do not require knee and toe clearances; however, if a designer chooses to provide knee and toe clearances, for example under a lavatory, this would be acceptable.

This provision is not applicable to the exception in Section 1004.11.2.1.

1004.11.3 Toilet and Bathing Areas. Either all toilet and bathing areas provided shall comply with Section 1004.11.3.1 (Option A), or one toilet and bathing area shall comply with Section 1004.11.3.2 (Option B).

❖ When dealing with Type B units, the designer has the choice between two bathroom design options. These two options are available regardless of the number of bathrooms within the unit. Where multiple bathrooms are located within the same unit, a designer can choose to have either all the bathrooms meet Option A bathroom clearances, or have one bathroom meet the Option B bathroom clearances. When a unit has only one bathroom, a designer still has the choice of Option A or Option B since building that one bathroom to the Option A provisions would meet the requirement for "all toilet and bathing areas" in the unit to be Option A; or making that one bathroom an Option B design would ensure that "one toilet and bathing area" within the unit was an Option B bathroom.

The primary difference between the two bathroom design options is that an Option B bathroom provides greater clear access to the tub than does an Option A bathroom. Option B bathrooms, with a clear floor space in front of the bathtub, are considered to provide a higher level of access for persons using wheelchairs than Option A bathrooms. On the other hand, physical therapists will advise persons with mobility impairments to sit on a toilet to disrobe and then move to the bathtub. Therefore, the Option A bathroom could be considered more user friendly for a person with mobility impairments.

The selection of the Option A or Option B bathroom is truly the designer's choice. Neither the model building code nor the FHA require or specify which design is needed in a particular unit or that a certain mixture of the various options be provided within a building or project.

1004.11.3.1 Option A. Each fixture provided shall comply with Section 1004.11.3.1.

EXCEPTIONS:

1. Where multiple lavatories are provided in a single toilet and bathing area such that travel between fixtures does not require travel through other parts of the unit, not more than one lavatory is required to comply with Section 1004.11.3.1.
2. A lavatory and a water closet in a room containing only a lavatory and water closet, provided the room does not contain the only lavatory or water closet on the accessible level of the unit.

❖ The general configuration for an Option A bathroom is with the lavatory, water closet and tub along one common plumbing wall [see Commentary Figure C1004.11.3.1(a)]. The general configuration for an Option B bathroom is with the tub on one side and the water closet and lavatory on the other side [see Commentary Figure C1004.11.3.1(a)].

If Option A bathrooms are chosen, each fixture in the bathroom must meet the clearance requirements in this section. This requirement for "each fixture" to comply will be discussed later in Section 1004.11.3.1.3. For now it is important that users realize the standard does regulate "each fixture" and does not limit this requirement to "at least one" of each type of fixture as Sections 1002.11.2 and 1003.11.2 do for Accessible and Type A units.

Exception 1 addresses where multiple lavatories are provided in the same bathroom [see Commentary Figures C1004.11.3.1(b) and C1004.11.3.1(c)]. This exception is commonly used in master bathrooms or shared bathrooms where two lavatories are provided in a single vanity or counter space.

The second exception allows for a powder room or half-bath to not have clearances provided it is not the only bathroom on the accessible level. The wording of the exception is a result of the scoping provisions in the model code and the Fair Housing Act allowing for an exception for the second floor in a multistory unit in an elevator building. Bathrooms on the inaccessible level do not need to meet these provisions. Specific requirements are stated in these docu-

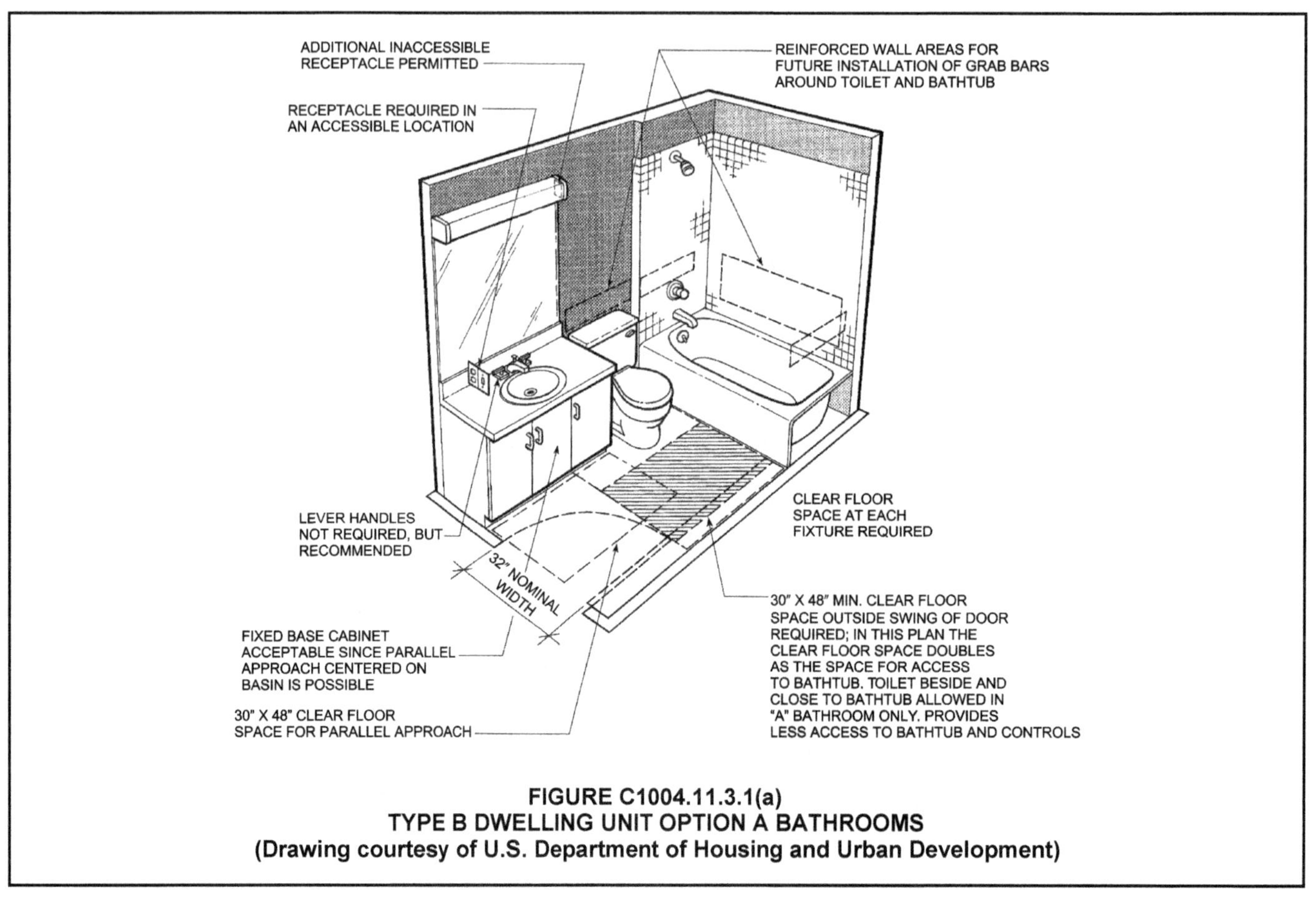

FIGURE C1004.11.3.1(a)
TYPE B DWELLING UNIT OPTION A BATHROOMS
(Drawing courtesy of U.S. Department of Housing and Urban Development)

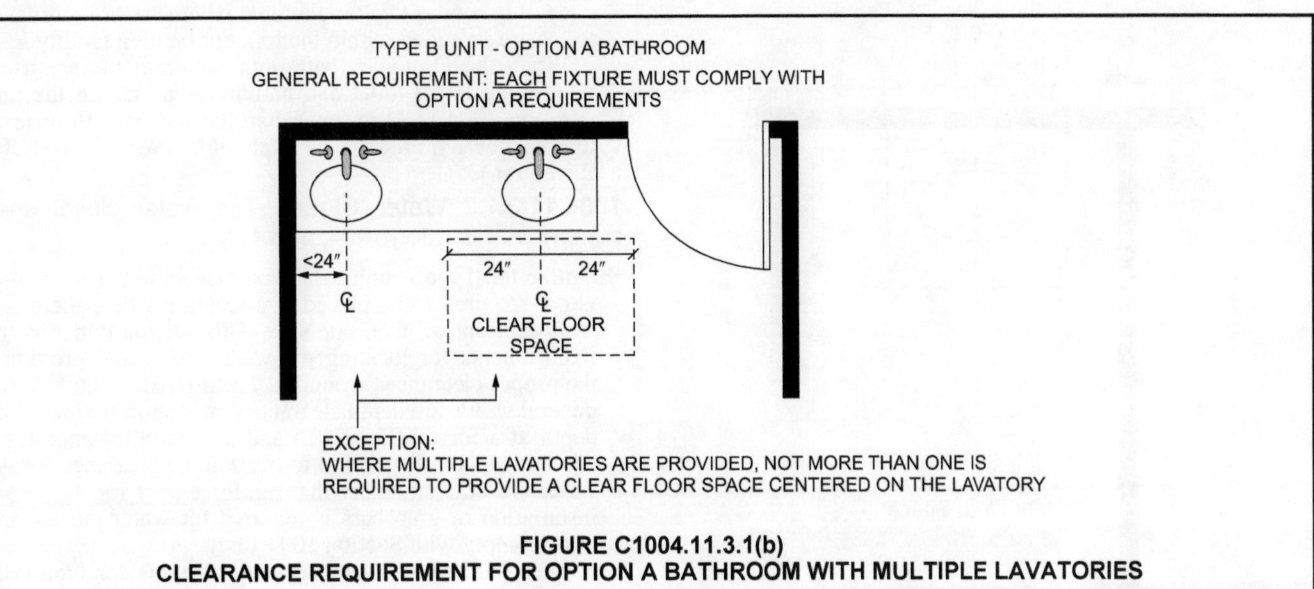

FIGURE C1004.11.3.1(b)
CLEARANCE REQUIREMENT FOR OPTION A BATHROOM WITH MULTIPLE LAVATORIES

ments. Where applying Exception 2, be certain to see Exception 1 in Section 1004.11.1 as it will also eliminate the requirement for grab bar reinforcement in these limited bathrooms.

Users should remember that the clearances contained in Section 1004.11.3.1 must also be designed to comply with the clear floor space provisions of Section 1004.11.2.

When comparing the Option A bathroom requirements with those in the Accessible and Type A units and also with those of the Type B unit with Option B bathrooms, users will note that the standard does not contain a sentence similar to those other units stating that the accessible toilet and bathing fixtures "shall be in a single toilet/bathing area, such that travel between fixtures does not require travel through other parts of the unit" (Sections 1002.11.2, 1003.11.2, and 1004.11.3.2). This sentence is not needed with the Option A bathrooms because the Option A provisions apply to every toilet and bathing area within the unit (Section 1004.11.3) whereas Accessible units and Type A units only regulate one toilet and bathing area within the unit (Sections 1002.11.2, 1003.11.2 and 1004.11.3).

FIGURE C1004.11.3.1(c)
MULTIPLE LAVATORIES

1004.11.3.1.1 Lavatory. A clear floor space complying with Section 305.3, positioned for a parallel approach, shall be provided at a lavatory. The clear floor space shall be centered on the lavatory.

EXCEPTION: A lavatory complying with Section 606 shall be permitted. Cabinetry shall be permitted under the lavatory provided the following criteria are met:

(a) The cabinetry can be removed without removal or replacement of the lavatory; and

(b) The floor finish extends under the cabinetry; and

(c) The walls behind and surrounding the cabinetry are finished.

❖ The clear floor space requirement for Option A and Option B lavatories is the same; however, Option B has an additional height requirement (see Section 1004.11.3.2.1.1).

A 30-inch by 48-inch (760 by 1220 mm) parallel space centered on the lavatory will allow a person using a wheelchair to approach the lavatory and use it for bathing. Because the wheels of a wheelchair typically extend at least 12 inches (305 mm) behind the back of the wheelchair seat, the center of the lavatory must be at least 24 inches (610 mm) from an adjacent wall or other obstruction [see Figure 1004.11.3.1.1 and Commentary Figure C1004.11.3.1(b)].

The intent of the exception is to allow the more accessible lavatory options permitted in Accessible units or Type A units (see Section 1003.11.2.2). Although the reference to Section 606 would result in faucets having to meet operable parts requirements (Section 606.4), the specific exception for plumbing fixtures in Type B units in Section 1004.9, Exception 7, negates that requirement. In addition, the exception allows removable cabinetry that is not permitted by Section 606 but is reasonable in Type A (Section 1003.11.2.2) and Type B units where the occupants can adapt certain elements or fixtures as they need or desire.

The reference to Section 606 in the exception includes all subsections (Section 606.1 through 606.6). However, the enhanced reach range requirements of Section 606.5 are generally not applicable because the model building

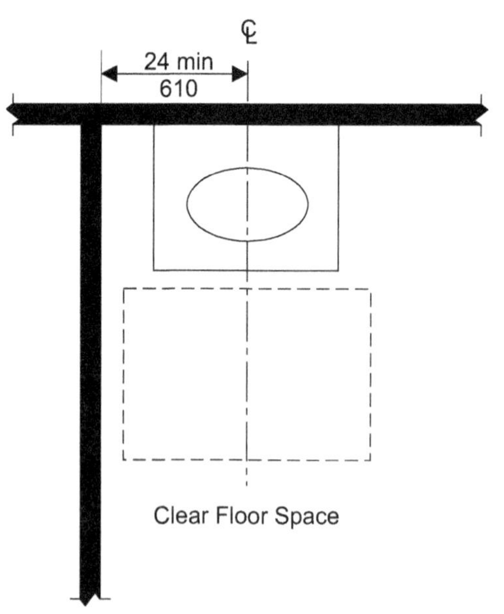

FIGURE 1004.11.3.1.1
LAVATORY IN TYPE B UNITS—OPTION A BATHROOMS

code only scopes this requirement where six or more lavatories are provided within the toilet or bathing facility.

When the Option A bathroom requirements are used, they apply to all toilet and bathing areas within the unit (Section 1004.11.3) except when located on a floor level that is not required to be accessible (Section 1004.11, Exception).

1004.11.3.1.2 Water Closet. The water closet shall comply with Section 1004.11.3.1.2.

❖ Unlike the Type A units, the water closet in a Type B unit is not required to be placed at a location where there is a wall adjacent to it on one side. This section contains the requirements for locating the water closet and providing the proper clearances around it. The provisions include the general width and depth clearances, an option for increased depth at a forward approach and also an allowance for a vanity or other obstruction to overlap the clearance for the water closet. Remember that reinforcement for the future installation of grab bars is required for water closets and must comply with Section 1004.11.1.

The water closet clearance requirements for Option A and Option B bathrooms are the same. Although the requirements for the water closet clearances are the same, Option A bathrooms allow a configuration with the water closet located between the tub and lavatory (Section

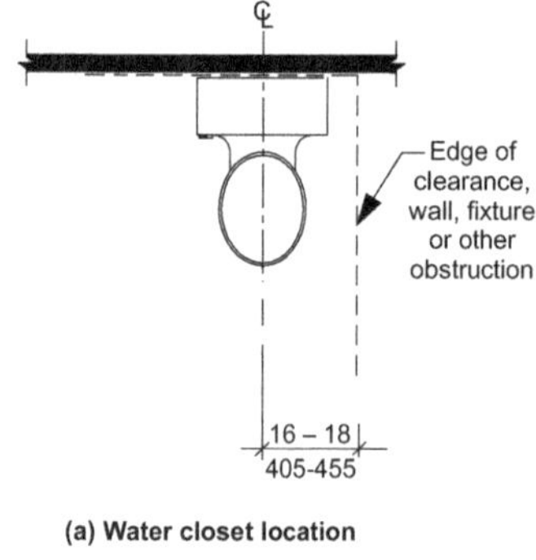

(a) Water closet location

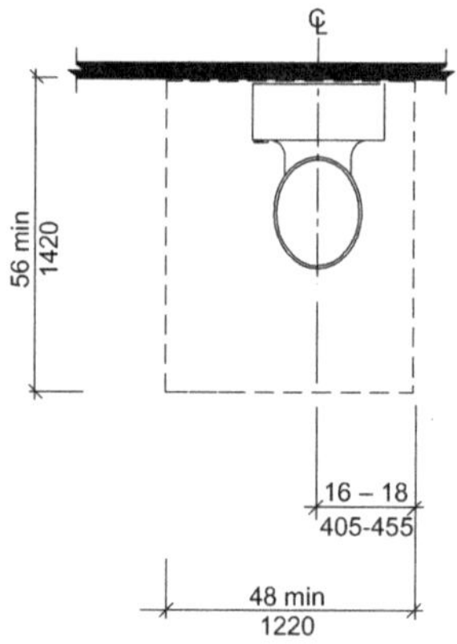

(b) Clearance width and depth

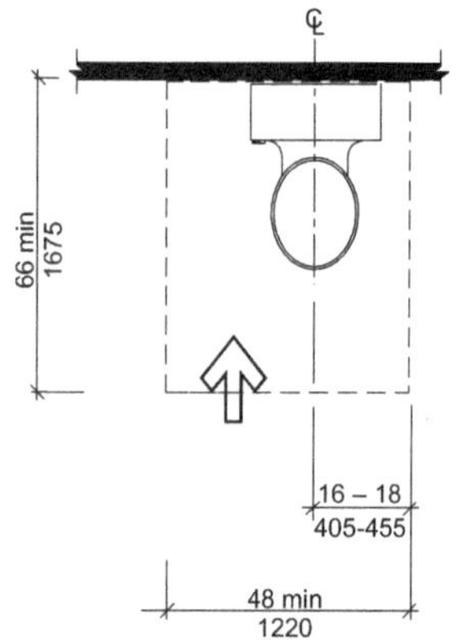

(c) Increased clearance depth – forward approach

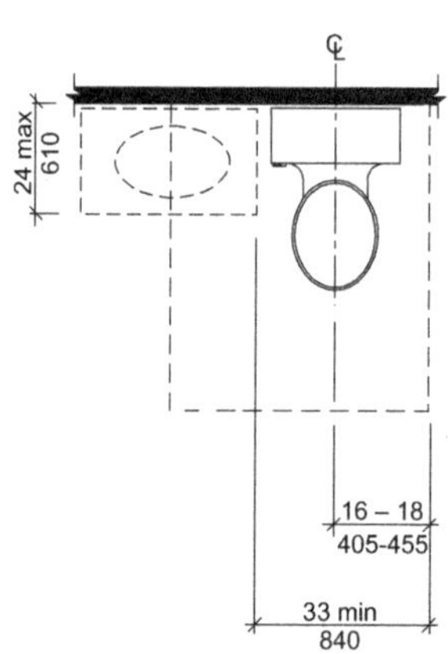

(d) Clearance with lavatory overlap

FIGURE 1004.11.3.1.2
CLEARANCE AT WATER CLOSETS IN TYPE B UNITS

1004.11.3.1.3.2), while the Option B bathrooms do not allow the water closet to encroach into the tub's clear floor space.

When Option A toilet room requirements are used, these water closet requirements apply to all toilet areas within the unit (Section 1004.11.3) unless they are located on a floor level that is not required to be accessible (Section 1004.11, Exception). In addition, reinforcement for the future installation of grab bars is also required for all of the water closets (Section 1004.11.1) unless it is in a powder room covered by Exception 1 in Section 1004.11.1 or on an inaccessible level using the exception in Section 1004.11.

1004.11.3.1.2.1 Location. The centerline of the water closet shall be 16 inches (405 mm) minimum and 18 inches (455 mm) maximum from one side of the required clearance.

❖ This provision is really tied to the 48-inch (1220 mm) clearance width requirement of Section 1004.11.3.1.2.2.1. The requirement places the water closet off center and to one side of the 48-inch (1220 mm) minimum width space. This location is best depicted in Figure 1004.11.3.1.2(b) and (c). Placing the water closet to one side will ensure that an open space of at least 30 to 32 inches (760 to 815 mm) in width would remain between the centerline of the water closet and the open side of the original 48-inch (1220 mm) clearance. The 16- to 18-inch (405 to 455 mm) dimension may be located to either side of the water closet; it is not required to be located to the right side of the fixture (when looking at the water closet) as is shown in Figure 1004.11.3.1.2(b) and (c).

The 16- to 18-inch (405 to 455 mm) clearance from the centerline of the water closet coordinates with the future grab bar installation provisions and puts the grab bar in a usable location on the far side of the water closet. For situations where the plans are for a swing-up grab bar, the 18-inch (455 mm) minimum is needed for clearances (Section 1004.11.1.1). However, when plans are for mounting the grab bar on the wall, exceeding 18 inches (455 mm) could place the wall-mounted bar past the reach of a person attempting a transfer. The 16- to 18-inch (405 to 455 mm) range also provides a tolerance to help address the difficulties of placing the water closet at a specific location when the drainage piping may be installed prior to walls or fixtures being constructed, finished or installed.

1004.11.3.1.2.2 Clearance. Clearance around the water closet shall comply with Sections 1004.11.3.1.2.2.1 through 1004.11.3.1.2.2.3.

> **EXCEPTION:** Clearance complying with Sections 1003.11.2.4.2 through 1003.11.2.4.4.

❖ There are three choices for the clearances around the water closet. The decision regarding which of the three to use is left entirely up to the designer. The options are:

(a) Minimum of 48-inch (1220 mm) width and 56-inch (1420 mm) depth (Sections 1004.11.3.1.2.2.1 and 1004.11.3.1.2.2.2),

(b) Minimum of 48-inch width and 66-inch (1675 mm) depth (Sections 1004.11.3.1.2.2.1 and 1004.11.3.1.2.2.3), or.

(c) Minimum of 60-inch (1525 mm) width and either a 56- or 66-inch (1420 mm or 1675 mm) depth (Sections 1003.11.2.4.2 through 1003.11.3.1.2.2.3).

The third option is from the Type A unit provisions and is allowed based on the exception in Section 1004.11.3.1.2.2. This last option allows for either a parallel or forward approach, and is intended to allow the Type B dwelling unit to meet the same clearances as required for water closets in the more accessible Type A units. Because of the resultant dimensions, this third option can be used to allow either the side or forward approach to the water closet.

1004.11.3.1.2.2.1 Clearance Width. Clearance around the water closet shall be 48 inches (1220 mm) minimum in width, measured perpendicular from the side of the clearance that is 16 inches (405 mm) minimum and 18 inches (455 mm) maximum from the water closet centerline.

❖ In a Type B unit, the width required for a clear floor space for water closets is smaller than the width required for Type A units (Section 1003.11.2.4.2) or for Accessible units (Sections 1002.11.2 and 604.3.1). It is this reduced water closet clearance that is the main feature that makes the water closets in a Type B unit less accessible than those of a Type A unit. The water closet must be located off center within this 48-inch (1220 mm) width as required in Section 1004.11.3.1.2.1 (see commentary, Section 1004.11.3.1.2.1). The 16-inch to 18-inch (405 to 455 mm) clearance is to allow for the water closet to be adjacent to a wall and allow for the proper placement of a grab bar on the adjacent wall.

1004.11.3.1.2.2.2 Clearance Depth. Clearance around the water closet shall be 56 inches (1420 mm) minimum in depth, measured perpendicular from the rear wall.

❖ The general depth requirement for the water closet clearance is based on a parallel approach where the water closet will be accessed from the side. The 56-inch (1420 mm) requirement coordinates with the identical dimension that is required in a Type A unit (Section 1003.11.2.4.3) or an Accessible unit (Sections 1002.11.2 and 604.3.2). It is important to note that this dimension is measured forward from the wall surface behind the water closet as shown in Figure 1004.11.3.1.2(b).

1004.11.3.1.2.2.3 Increased Clearance Depth at Forward Approach. Where a forward approach is provided, the clearance shall be 66 inches (1675 mm) minimum in depth, measured perpendicular from the rear wall.

❖ Where the water closet is approached from a forward direction, this section requires the depth of the clearance around the water closet to be increased from the 56 inches (1420 mm) that are generally required by Section 1004.11.3.1.2.2.2. The 66-inch (1675 mm) depth that this section requires is measured from the wall surface behind the water closet as shown in Figure 1004.11.3.1.2(c). This 66-inch (1675 mm) depth requirement coordinates with the identical dimension required in a Type A unit where a lavatory is allowed to obstruct the clearance width (Section 1003.11.2.4.4, Exception) and helps to compensate for the reduced width that is allowed by Section 1004.11.3.1.2.2.1 and the potential obstruction allowed by Section 1004.11.3.1.2.2.4.

1004.11.3.1.2.2.4 Clearance Overlap. A vanity or other obstruction 24 inches (610 mm) maximum in depth, measured perpendicular from the rear wall, shall be permitted to overlap the required clearance, provided the width of the remaining clearance at the water closet is 33 inches (840 mm) minimum.

❖ A vanity or other obstruction is allowed within either the 48-inch by 56-inch (1220 by 1420 mm) minimum clearance required by Sections 1004.11.3.1.2.2.1 and 1004.11.3.1.2.2.2 or the 48-inch by 66-inch (1220 by 1675 mm) minimum clearance required by Sections 1004.11.3.1.2.2.1 and 1004.11.3.1.2.2.3. This vanity or other obstruction must not project into the clearance depth more than 24 inches (610 mm) from the back wall. It must also be located so that the space in which the water closet is located remains at least 33 inches (840 mm) in width (see Figure 1004.11.3.1.2).

The absolute closest the vanity can be located to the centerline of the water closet is 15 inches (380 mm) on the side of the approach [assuming 18 inches (455 mm) on the side away from the direction of approach]. However, the actual distance between the centerline of the water closet and the edge of the vanity or obstruction will depend on the location of the water closet within the space (Section 1004.11.3.1.2.1). It is better to measure the 33-inch (840 mm) dimension from the edge of the designed clearance width versus measuring from the centerline of the water closet. If the designer prefers to dimension the vanity's location off of the centerline of the water closet, it would be best to use a minimum 17-inch (430 mm) distance. That 17-inch (430 mm) dimension would provide the required 33-inch (840 mm) clearance regardless of the whether the water closet was located using the minimum or maximum dimensions specified in Sections 1004.11.3.1.2.1 and 1004.11.3.1.2.2.1.

1004.11.3.1.3 Bathing Fixtures. Where provided, a bathtub shall comply with Section 1004.11.3.1.3.1 or 1004.11.3.1.3.2 and a shower compartment shall comply with Section 1004.11.3.1.3.3.

❖ Bathing facilities can either be a bathtub or shower. Provisions address a parallel or forward approach to a bathtub and access to a standard shower stall. A bathtub constructed in accordance with Section 607 or a roll-in shower, alternate roll-in shower or transfer shower constructed in accordance with Section 608 would result in a higher level of accessibility and would be acceptable.

There are three choices for the clearances in front of the bathtub. The arrows in Figures 1004.11.3.1.3.1 and 1004.11.3.1.3.2 indicate the anticipated approach direction to a bathtub. The designer can use any of the three choices. Section 1004.11.3.1.3.3 is intended to address a transfer-type shower.

See Section 1004.11.1 for reinforcement requirements for the future installation of grab bars and shower seats. The provisions of Section 1004.11.1 apply to all bathing fixtures within the unit.

Remember that when Option A bathroom criteria are used, these bathing fixture requirements will apply to all bathing areas within the unit (Section 1004.11.3) unless they are located on a floor level that is not required to be accessible (Section 1004.11, Exception).

The language of this section should be reviewed carefully based on HUD's interpretation of the Fair Housing requirements. While this section will allow for either a bathtub or a shower to be installed as the required bathing facility, according to HUD, if a tub and a shower are both installed in the same bathroom, then both must be made accessible. This interpretation from HUD is based on the fact that this section states "where provided" a bathtub must comply with the listed sections while a shower must comply with its appropriate section. Therefore, if both types of bathing fixtures are provided in a single bathroom, then both of them must be accessible.

1004.11.3.1.3.1 Parallel Approach Bathtubs. A clearance 60 inches (1525 mm) minimum in length and 30 inches (760 mm) minimum in width shall be provided in front of bathtubs with a parallel approach. Lavatories complying with Section 606 shall be permitted in the clearance. A lavatory complying with Section 1004.11.3.1.1 shall be permitted at one end of the bathtub if a clearance 48 inches (1220 mm) minimum in length and 30 inches (760 mm) minimum in width is provided in front of the bathtub.

❖ Two options exist for bathtubs with a parallel approach. The figures show a standard 60-inch-long (1525 mm) tub. This could also be a 30-inch by 60-inch (760 by 1525 mm) shower stall.

If a 30-inch by 48-inch (760 by 1220 mm) wheelchair space is available in front of the tub, a lavatory with a parallel approach can be located at the end of the tub [see Figure 1004.11.3.1.3.1(b)].

Alternatively, a 30-inch-wide (760 mm) space for the length of the tub [60-inch (1525 mm) minimum] must be provided. A lavatory constructed for a front approach with knee and toe clearances can overlap the tub space clearance [see Figure 1004.11.3.1.3.1(a)]. Although not mentioned, installing removable cabinetry under the lavatory consistent with Type A units is also viable (Section 1003.11.2.5.1, Exception 2).

1004.11.3.1.3.2 Forward Approach Bathtubs. A clearance 60 inches (1525 mm) minimum in length and 48 inches (1220 mm) minimum in width shall be provided in front of bathtubs with a forward approach. A water closet and a lavatory shall be permitted in the clearance at one end of the bathtub.

❖ Figure 1004.11.3.1.3.2 shows a standard 60-inch (1525 mm) tub. This could also be a 30-inch by 60-inch (760 by 1525 mm) shower stall. With a perpendicular approach to the tub, the depth of the clearance must be 48-inches (1220 mm). A water closet, a lavatory or both can be located within this clear floor space. To see an illustration of how both fixtures are allowed to overlap the 48-inch (1220 mm) clearance width, see Figure 1004.11.3.1.2(d) and Commentary Figure C1004.11.3.1.3.2. This arrangement would be similar to the water closet requirements of Sections 1004.11.3.1.2.2.1 and 1004.11.3.1.2.2.4 (see commentary, Sections 1004.11.3.1.2.2.1 and 1004.11.3.1.2.2.4).

This configuration is often viewed as a good alternative for persons with mobility impairments or the elderly. Physical therapists teach people to sit on the toilet to disrobe, adjust the tub water, and then move into the tub to reduce the chance of falls while getting into and out of the bathtub.

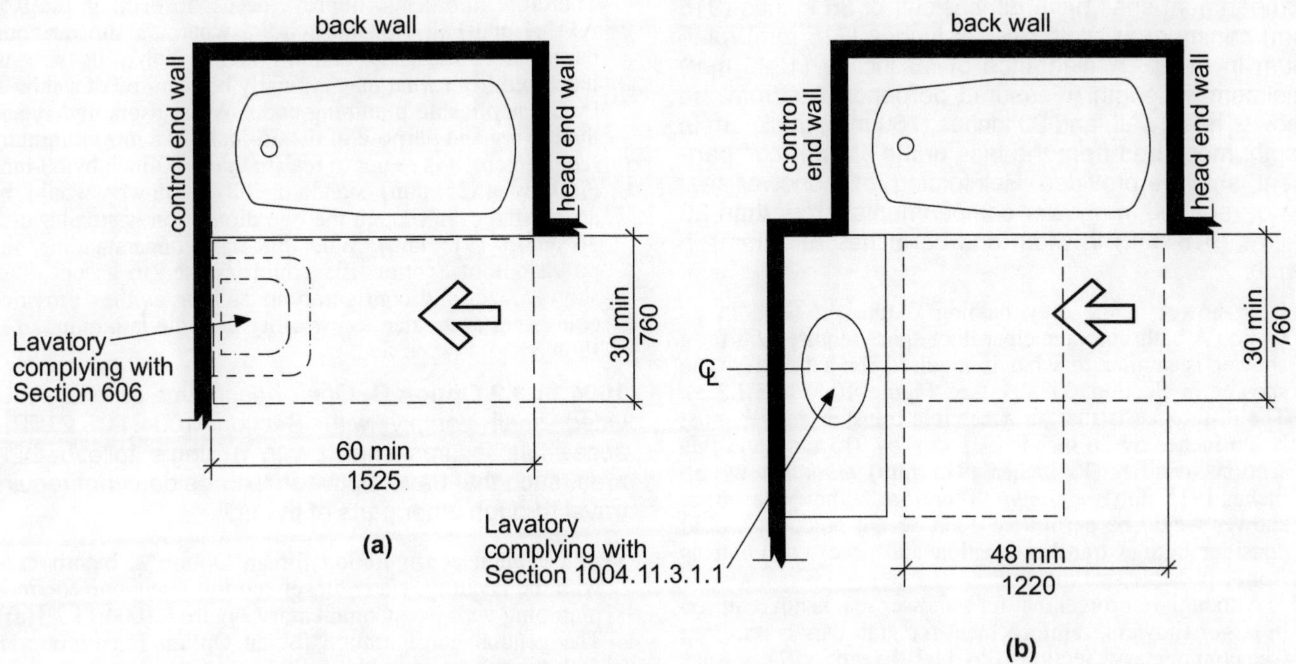

FIGURE 1004.11.3.1.3.1
PARALLEL APPROACH BATHTUB IN TYPE B UNITS—OPTION A BATHROOMS

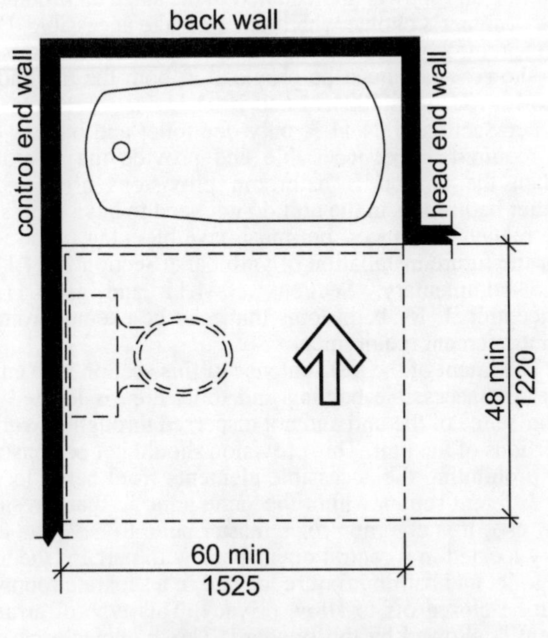

FIGURE 1004.11.3.1.3.2
FORWARD APPROACH BATHTUB IN TYPE B UNITS—OPTION A BATHROOMS

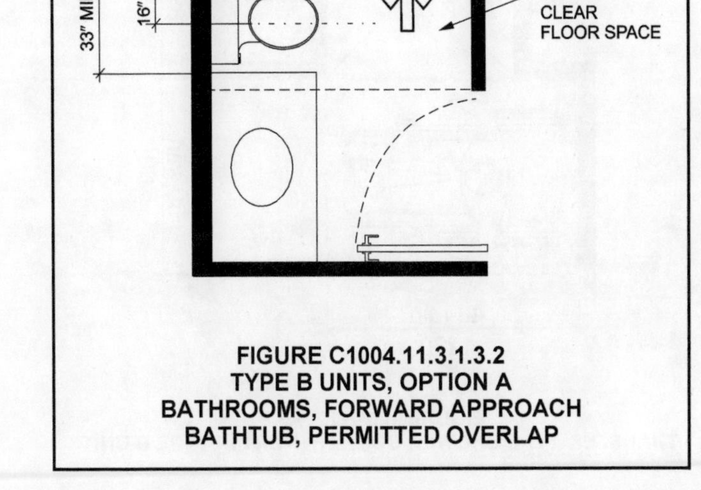

FIGURE C1004.11.3.1.3.2
TYPE B UNITS, OPTION A BATHROOMS, FORWARD APPROACH BATHTUB, PERMITTED OVERLAP

1004.11.3.1.3.3 Shower Compartment. If a shower compartment is the only bathing facility, the shower compartment shall have dimensions of 36 inches (915 mm) minimum in width and 36 inches (915 mm) minimum in depth. A clearance of 48 inches (1220 mm) minimum in length, measured perpendicular from the shower head wall, and 30 inches (760 mm) minimum in depth, measured from the face of the shower compartment, shall be provided. Reinforcing for a shower seat is not required in shower compartments larger than 36 inches (915 mm) in width and 36 inches (915 mm) in depth.

❖ If a shower is the only bathing fixture provided in an Option A bathroom, the clear floor space requirement for a shower is similar to what is required for a transfer-type shower in Section 608.2.1 (see Figure 1004.11.3.1.3.3). The difference is that an accessible transfer shower must be 36 inches by 36 inches (915 mm by 915 mm) and this section specifies 36 inches (915 mm) *minimum* by 36 inches (915 mm) *minimum*. Therefore, although a larger shower would be permitted, good design practices would consider both a transfer location and access to controls from a possible seat location.

Although reinforcement for a shower seat is not required in larger showers, reinforcement for grab bars is required (see commentary, Section 1004.11.1, Exception 7).

Although this section and the Fair Housing requirements specify a minimum 36-inch by 36-inch (915 by 915 mm) requirement for a shower when it is the only bathing facility, larger configurations can be accepted. A roll-in shower (Section 608.2.2) or alternative roll-in shower (Section 608.2.3) would be permitted as alternatives that result in a higher level of accessibility. The 36-inch by 36-inch (915 by 915 mm) requirement is specified not only because that size allows for the shower to be adapted to become a transfer shower but also because the model plumbing codes would typically allow a shower to be of a smaller size. Model plumbing codes typically allow a shower compartment to be a minimum of 900 square inches (580 644 mm^2) in area with a minimum dimension of 30 inches (760 mm). Therefore in order to improve access to bathing, the ICC A117.1 and Fair Housing require where "a shower compartment is the only bathing facility" that its size be increased from what may typically be required of a shower by the applicable plumbing code. When users understand the history and purpose of the 36-inch (915 mm) minimum requirement, it is easier to realize that a 30-inch by 60-inch (760 by 1525 mm) standard roll-in shower would be acceptable even though the one dimension is smaller than 36 inches (915 mm). With this same understanding, the provisions of Section 103 could be used to accept other shower sizes and configurations as long as they provided equivalent or greater accessibility than the minimum sized shower that is specified.

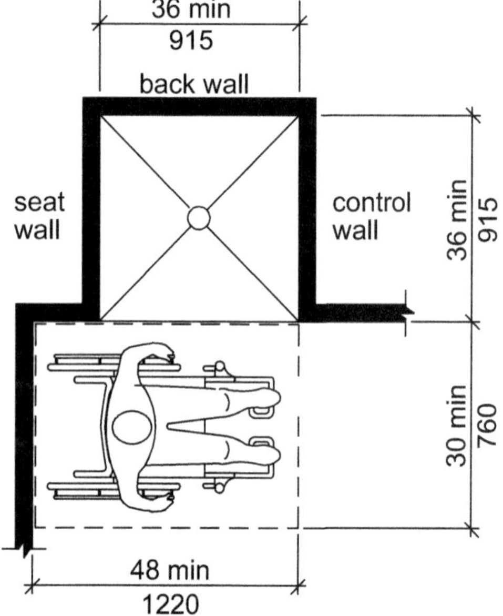

FIGURE 1004.11.3.1.3.3
TRANSFER-TYPE SHOWER COMPARTMENT IN TYPE B UNITS

1004.11.3.2 Option B. One of each type of fixture provided shall comply with Section 1004.11.3.2. The accessible fixtures shall be in a single toilet/bathing area, such that travel between fixtures does not require travel through other parts of the unit.

❖ The general configuration for an Option A bathroom is with the lavatory, water closet and tub along one common plumbing wall [see Commentary Figure C1004.11.3.1(a)]. The general configuration for an Option B bathroom is with the tub on one side and the water closet and lavatory on the other side (see Commentary Figure C1004.11.3.2). The primary difference between the two bathroom design options is that an Option B bathroom provides greater clear access to the tub than does an Option A bathroom. Option B bathrooms, with a clear floor space in front of the bathtub, are considered to provide a higher level of access for persons using wheelchairs than Option A bathrooms.

The base requirement is that if Option B bathrooms are chosen, each type of fixture in one bathroom must meet the clearance requirements in this section. Therefore, when two lavatories are installed in the same bathroom, only one is required to meet clearance requirements. If a separate bathtub and shower are installed in the same bathroom, it is the designer's choice which one to make accessible. However, reinforcement for the future installation of grab bars or shower seats must be provided at both the tub and the shower (Sections 1004.11 and 1004.11.1).

Per Section 1004.11.3, only one toilet and bathing area is required to be accessible and provide the clearances when the Option B bathroom provisions are selected. Other bathrooms in the unit do not need to have accessibility related clearances, but must have blocking in the walls for the future installation of grab bars (Section 1004.11.1). See commentary, Sections 1004.11 and 1004.11.1.1, Exception 1, for bathrooms that may be exempt from the reinforcement requirement.

The intent of the last sentence of this section is to ensure that the accessible bathing and toilet area is located in a single area of the unit and not dispersed throughout various portions of the unit. This provision should not be construed as prohibiting the accessible elements from being located in different rooms within the same area. In many residential uses it is common for a master suite to have the lavatory located in a central open space with perhaps the toilet or toilet and bathing fixture located in a separate room that can be closed off to allow privacy. This type of arrangement is allowed by the standard. This prevents accessible bathing elements in the master bathroom while the accessible toilet and lavatory are located in a bathroom serving a separate bedroom or perhaps in the general living area of the home. This requirement is needed in the Option B section since only one bathroom is required to be accessible. It is not needed in Section 1004.11.3.1 because every toilet and bathing area within the unit must be accessible if the Option A bathroom requirements are selected (Section 1004.11.3).

Users should remember that the clearances contained in Section 1004.11.3.2 must also be designed to comply with the clear floor space provisions of Section 1004.11.2.

1004.11.3.2.1 Lavatory. Lavatories shall comply with Sections 1004.11.3.1.1 and 1004.11.3.2.1.1.

❖ The clear floor space requirement for Option A and Option B lavatories is the same; however, Option B has an additional height requirement. In an Option B bathroom the lavatory is limited to a 34 inch (865 mm) maximum height (Section 1004.11.3.2.1.1). See Figure 1004.11.3.2.1 and Section 1004.11.3.2.1.1 and the commentary for information related to the clearance at the accessible lavatory.

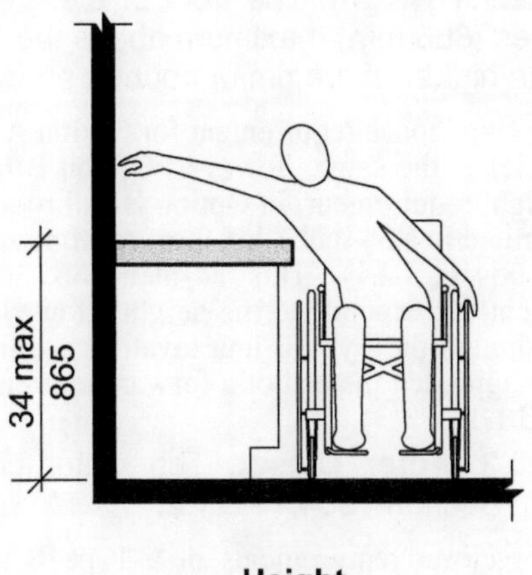

FIGURE 1004.11.3.2.1
LAVATORY IN TYPE B UNITS—OPTION B BATHROOMS

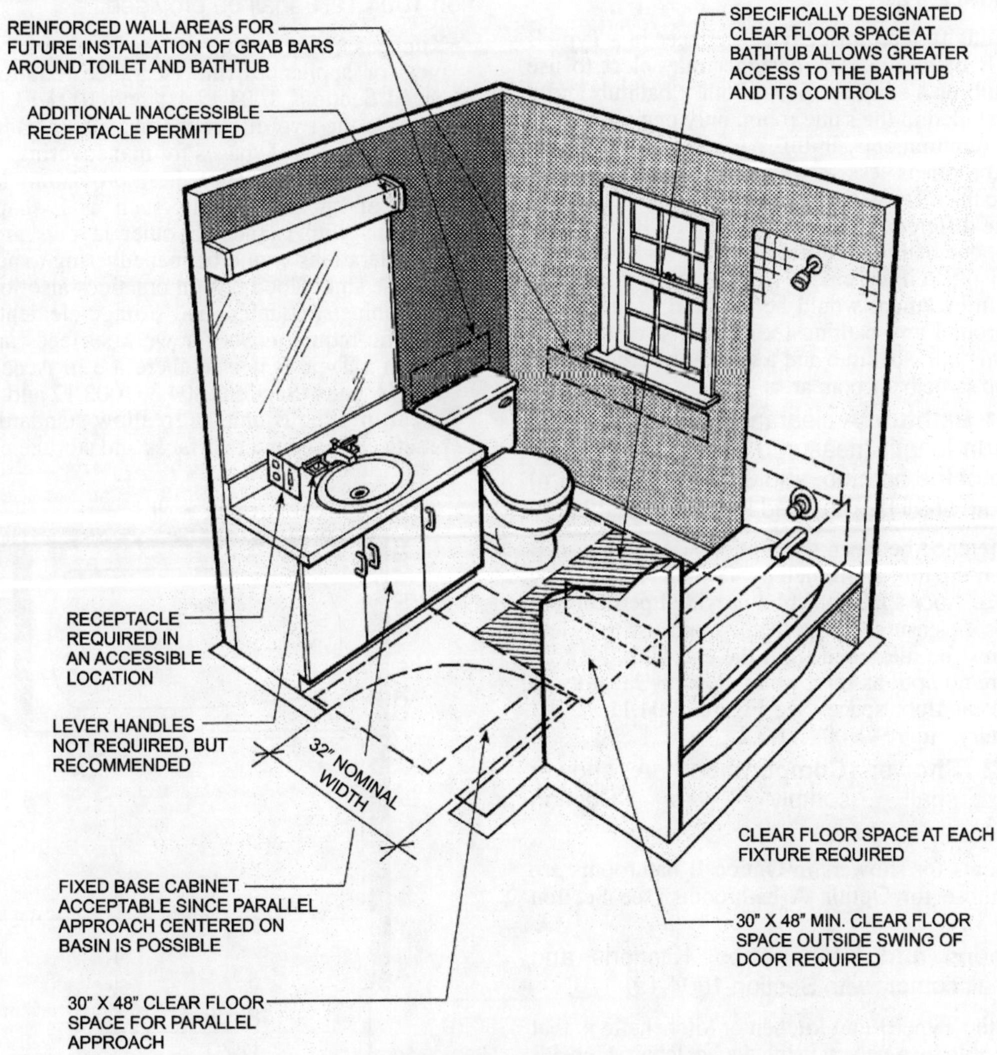

REINFORCED WALL AREAS FOR FUTURE INSTALLATION OF GRAB BARS AROUND TOILET AND BATHTUB

ADDITIONAL INACCESSIBLE RECEPTACLE PERMITTED

SPECIFICALLY DESIGNATED CLEAR FLOOR SPACE AT BATHTUB ALLOWS GREATER ACCESS TO THE BATHTUB AND ITS CONTROLS

RECEPTACLE REQUIRED IN AN ACCESSIBLE LOCATION

LEVER HANDLES NOT REQUIRED, BUT RECOMMENDED

32" NOMINAL WIDTH

CLEAR FLOOR SPACE AT EACH FIXTURE REQUIRED

FIXED BASE CABINET ACCEPTABLE SINCE PARALLEL APPROACH CENTERED ON BASIN IS POSSIBLE

30" X 48" MIN. CLEAR FLOOR SPACE OUTSIDE SWING OF DOOR REQUIRED

30" X 48" CLEAR FLOOR SPACE FOR PARALLEL APPROACH

FIGURE C1004.11.3.2
TYPE B DWELLING UNIT OPTION B BATHROOM
(Drawing courtesy of U.S. Department of Housing and Urban Development)

1004.11.3.2.1.1 Height. The front of the lavatory shall be 34 inches (865 mm) maximum above the floor, measured to the higher of the rim or counter surface.

❖ The clear floor space requirement for Option A and Option B lavatories is the same; however, Option B has an additional height requirement. In Option B bathrooms the lavatory is limited to a 34 inch (865 mm) maximum height (see Figure 1004.11.3.2.1). This 34-inch (865 mm) height requirement corresponds to the height allowed by Section 606.3, although the Type B unit lavatory is allowed to use a parallel approach instead of a forward approach (Section 1004.11.3.1.1).

1004.11.3.2.2 Water Closet. The water closet shall comply with Section 1004.11.3.1.2.

❖ The water closet requirements in a Type B unit are the same for Option A and Option B bathrooms (see Section 1003.11.3.1.2).

1004.11.3.2.3 Bathing Fixtures. The accessible bathing fixture shall be a bathtub complying with Section 1004.11.3.2.3.1 or a shower compartment complying with Section 1004.11.3.2.3.2.

❖ Only one bathing fixture must have clearances in a Type B unit, Option B bathroom. The designer may elect to use either a bathtub or a shower. When both a bathtub and a shower are installed in the same room, only one must meet the clearance requirements. In this particular instance, the Option B bathroom is less restrictive than the Option A bathroom. See the discussion with Section 1004.11.3.1.3 to understand the difference and why the Option B bathroom only regulates one bathing fixture.

Because of the reinforcement requirements in Section 1004.11.1, reinforcement would be required in any walls constructed around any bathing fixture. This requirement would apply to both a bathtub and a shower where they are installed in the same bathroom area.

1004.11.3.2.3.1 Bathtub. A clearance 48 inches (1220 mm) minimum in length measured perpendicular from the control end of the bathtub, and 30 inches (760 mm) minimum in width shall be provided in front of bathtubs.

❖ The main difference between the Option A and Option B bathrooms is at the tub. A 30-inch by 48-inch (760 mm by 1220 mm) clear floor space must be provided perpendicular to the tub. To ensure access to the controls, the clear floor space must be measured from the end with the controls. There are no options for a water closet or lavatory to overlap this clear floor space. See Figure 1004.11.3.2.3.1 and Commentary Figure C1004.11.3.2.

1004.11.3.2.3.2 Shower Compartment. A shower compartment shall comply with Section 1004.11.3.1.3.3.

❖ The requirements for showers in Option B bathrooms are the same as those for Option A bathrooms (see Section 1004.11.3.1.3.3).

1004.12 Kitchens and kitchenettes. Kitchens and kitchenettes shall comply with Section 1004.12.

❖ The intent of the Type B unit kitchen or kitchenette is that the space is usable by a person using a wheelchair. Consideration must be given for wheelchair access to the general kitchen area, sink and appliances. The Type B unit kitchen does not include some of the access requirements found in Type A units, such as adaptability for front approach at the sink or a work surface, or a turning space within the room. A side approach to the kitchen sink is permitted. Type B and Type A units are similar in their requirements for clearances in the kitchen and approach to the appliances. If a designer chooses to use some of the Type A unit requirements for kitchens, the higher level of accessibility that results would exceed the Type B unit requirements.

Careful design will produce a kitchen with a minimal-level accessible and functionally efficient kitchen that is easily usable by most persons with a disability or mobility impairment, as well as by able-bodied persons.

This section applies the same criteria to kitchenettes as it does to kitchens. Therefore, regardless of what the space is called or whether there is another full kitchen elsewhere within the unit, any type of wet bar, kitchenette or similar space would be regulated by the provisions of Section 1004.12. Although kitchenettes are not defined within the standard, a review of Sections 804 and 1002.12 would indicate the standard typically considers a kitchenette as being a space that does not have a cooktop or conventional range.

1004.12.1 Clearance. Clearance complying with Section 1004.12.1 shall be provided.

❖ Kitchens include requirements for clearances between cabinets or appliances; the clearance requirements in referenced Sections 1004.12.1.1 and 1004.12.1.2 are different because the two different floor plan arrangements require different types of spaces for maneuvering.

It is not the intent of these provisions to prohibit other types of kitchen layouts, such as L-shaped kitchens or kitchens with islands. If other layouts are used, the key considerations would be maneuvering to access appliances and the sink. Good design practices also look for access to the cabinets, counters and storage elements. There are no specific requirements for work surfaces and kitchen storage in a Type B unit as there are in Accessible units and Type A units (Sections 804.3, 1002.12 and 1003.12.3). The intent in Type B units is to allow standard kitchen design practices for counter surfaces and storage elements.

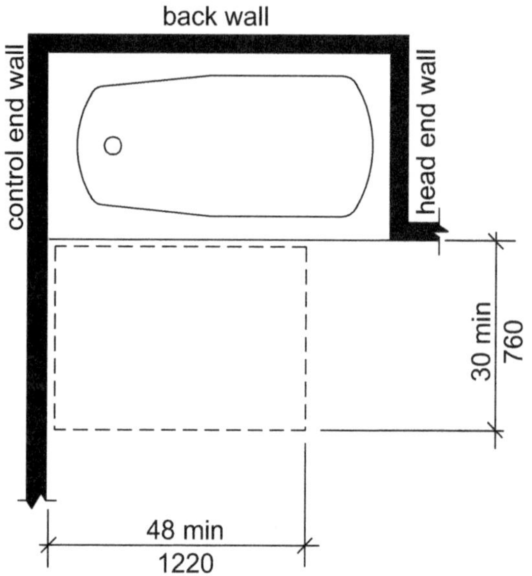

FIGURE 1004.11.3.2.3.1 BATHROOM CLEARANCE IN TYPE B UNITS—OPTION B BATHROOMS

1004.12.1.1 Minimum Clearance. Clearance between all opposing base cabinets, counter tops, appliances, or walls within kitchen work areas shall be 40 inches (1015 mm) minimum.

❖ The minimum clear width between opposing cabinets/appliances, or a cabinet/appliance and wall or other type of obstruction, is 40 inches (1015 mm). This measurement does not include cabinet/appliance handles (see Figure 1004.12.1.1).

Galley-style kitchens are typically laid out with all the appliances, counters and sink in straight lines. The appliances and fixtures can be located along one side of the kitchen, or they can be located along parallel sides of the kitchen. Unlike a pass-through kitchen required for an Accessible unit (Sections 1002.12. and 804.2.1), a Type B unit and Type A unit (Section 1003.12.1.1) galley kitchen may be open on one or both ends.

Although this section only mentions kitchens, based upon the scoping in Section 1004.12, this 40-inch (1015 mm) clearance requirement also applies to kitchenettes.

1004.12.1.2 U-Shaped Kitchens. In kitchens with counters, appliances, or cabinets on three contiguous sides, clearance between all opposing base cabinets, countertops, appliances, or walls within kitchen work areas shall be 60 inches (1525 mm) minimum.

❖ U-shaped kitchens are kitchens with counters, cabinets or appliances on three contiguous sides. In such an arrangement, a 60-inch (1525 mm) clearance is required between the faces of opposing cabinets and appliances to make all sides usable (see Figure 1004.12.1.2).

Unlike Accessible unit kitchens (Section 1002.12 and 804.2.2), in Type B units and Type A units (Section 1003.12.1.2), a galley-style kitchen with an opening on only one end is not considered a U-shaped kitchen and would not need to have a 60-inch (1525 mm) clear floor space between cabinets. The key for when a U-shaped kitchen is required in a Type B unit is the need to be able to turn 90 degrees (1.6 rad) to reach an appliance or use a counter or cabinet located on the third side.

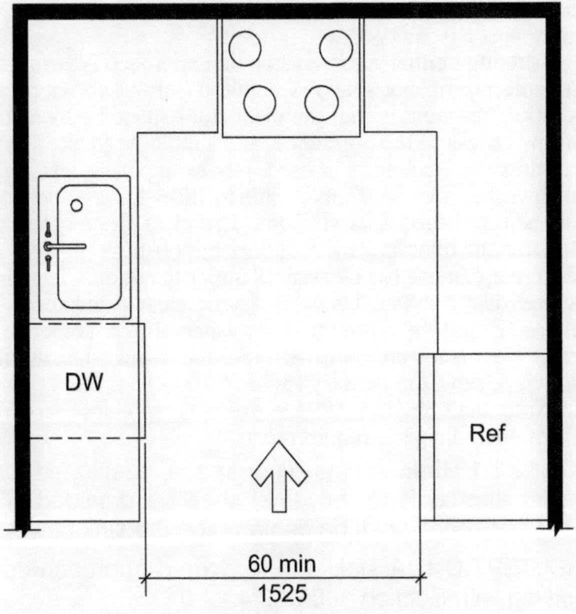

FIGURE 1004.12.1.2
U-SHAPED KITCHEN CLEARANCE IN TYPE B UNITS

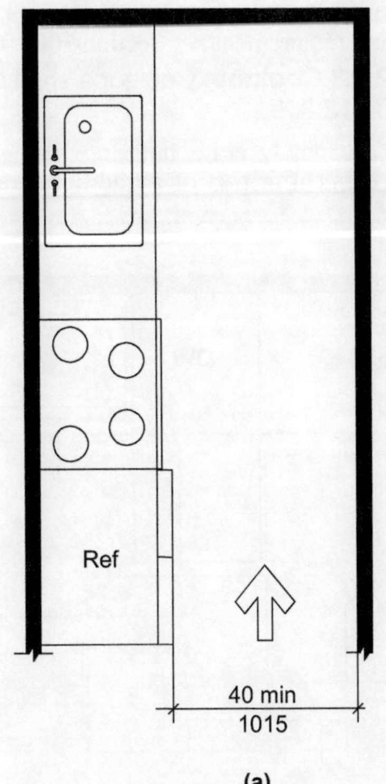

(a)

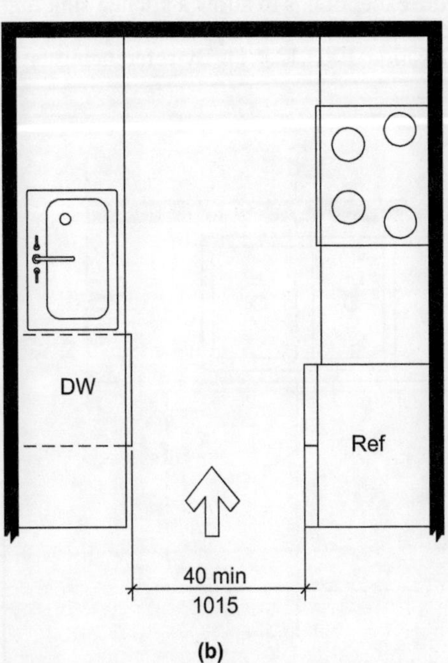

(b)

FIGURE 1004.12.1.1
MINIMUM KITCHEN CLEARANCE IN TYPE B UNITS

1004.12.2 Clear Floor Space. Clear floor space at appliances shall comply with Sections 1004.12.2 and 305.3.

❖ The clear floor space for the sink, dishwasher, cooktop, oven, refrigerator/freezer and trash compactor must be 30 inches by 48 inches (760 by 1220 mm) (Section 305.3). The intent is that all built-in appliances, not just the ones specifically listed, have a clear floor space. For example, if a built-in microwave is provided in the kitchen, a clear floor space is needed.

Although either a forward or side approach is permitted, a centering of that space is required only at cooktops and sinks. The intent is that the clear floor space be located to allow access to the appliance, and should be located based on how the appliance is used. For example, access to the dishwasher may be from the side to allow for the door to be opened and the racks slid out. The clear floor space can overlap the door as long as it does not obstruct the door—a designer can use toe clearances under the door. Clear floor spaces can overlap. Using the same clear floor space for the sink and an adjacent dishwasher allows someone to rinse the dishes and put them into the dishwasher without moving (see Commentary Figure C1004.12.2.2).

Note that Section 1004.9 exempts appliance controls from operable parts requirements.

1004.12.2.1 Sink. A clear floor space, positioned for a parallel approach to the sink, shall be provided. The clear floor space shall be centered on the sink bowl.

EXCEPTION: A sink with a forward approach complying with Section 1003.12.4.1.

❖ Although some items in a kitchen have an option of a front approach or a parallel approach, a parallel approach is generally required at sinks. Whether the sink is a single bowl or double bowl, the clear floor space must be centered on the unit (see Commentary Figure C1004.12.2.1). As a plumbing fixture, Section 1004.9, Exception 7, exempts the faucets from operable parts requirements.

The intent of the exception is to allow a kitchen sink that could be adapted to allow a forward approach as allowed in a Type A unit (Section 1003.12.4.1). By referencing only the one section in Section 1003.12.4, the sink would not be required to comply with the height, faucet or exposed surface requirements of that section. This permits the sink to be designed for a forward approach with the proper knee and toe clearances. The use of the exceptions in Section 1003.12.4.1 would be permissible and therefore removable base cabinetry could be installed, closing off the forward approach knee and toe clearance when not needed. A sink complying with Section 1003.12.4.1 and Exception 2 of that section would still be capable of meeting the base requirements of Section 1004.12.2.1 but would also provide additional options for improving access in the future.

1004.12.2.2 Dishwasher. A clear floor space, positioned for a parallel or forward approach to the dishwasher, shall be provided. The dishwasher door in the open position shall not obstruct the clear floor space for the dishwasher.

❖ Locating the clear floor space so that the dishwasher is usable is important. If the clear floor space is located immediately in front of the dishwasher, a bottom-hinged door in the open position will overlap the clear floor space and prevent fully opening the dishwasher. By requiring that the clear floor space be positioned beyond the swing of the dishwasher door, either the clear floor space must be located past the door, or the door could overlap the toe clearance if there was a minimum 9-inch (230 mm) clearance under the door when open. It is important to locate the clear floor space so that the dishwasher can be easily loaded and unloaded. Often, it is desirable to load the dishwasher from the sink area; therefore, it may be helpful to locate the sink and dishwasher adjacent to each other. Where a dishwasher is located adjacent to the clear floor space for a sink, the single clear floor space can be used to serve both the sink and the dishwasher (see Commentary Figure C1004.12.2.2).

Controls for a dishwasher are exempted from the operable parts requirement per Section 1004.9, Exception 6.

1004.12.2.3 Cooktop. Cooktops shall comply with Section 1004.12.2.3.

❖ Cooktops may be either built into the cabinetry as a standalone element or part of a traditional range with an oven

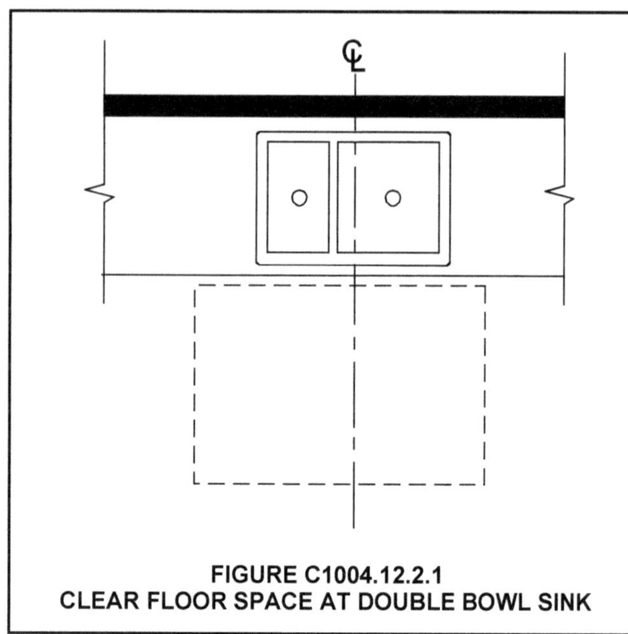

FIGURE C1004.12.2.1
CLEAR FLOOR SPACE AT DOUBLE BOWL SINK

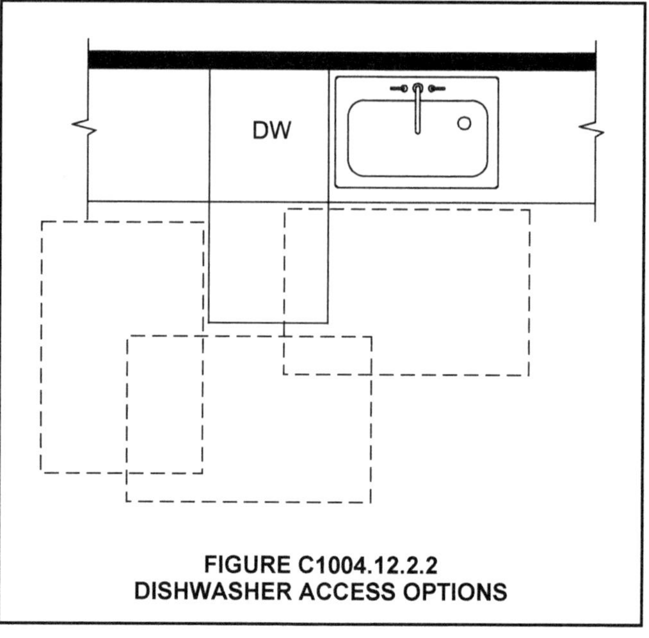

FIGURE C1004.12.2.2
DISHWASHER ACCESS OPTIONS

located below. Where a cooktop is a part of a range, the requirements of this section apply to the cooktop portion of the appliance.

Controls for a cooktop, as well as any associated kitchen exhaust hood, are exempted from the operable parts requirement per Section 1004.9, Exception 6.

1004.12.2.3.1 Approach. A clear floor space, positioned for a parallel or forward approach to the cooktop, shall be provided.

❖ The designer can elect to provide a cooktop with either a parallel approach or a front approach dependent upon the type of appliance selected and the desired kitchen layout. Depending on the type of approach selected, the requirements of the following two subsections must be met.

1004.12.2.3.2 Forward approach. Where the clear floor space is positioned for a forward approach, knee and toe clearance complying with Section 306 shall be provided. The underside of the cooktop shall be insulated or otherwise configured to prevent burns, abrasions, or electrical shock.

❖ When a designer chooses a front approach, the cooktop must have adequate clearances for a person's knees and toes underneath, as well as protection from accidental bumps, cuts or burns.

1004.12.2.3.3 Parallel approach. Where the clear floor space is positioned for a parallel approach, the clear floor space shall be centered on the appliance.

❖ A traditional range includes both a cooktop and an oven. A range must be located for a parallel approach, not a front approach (see Commentary Figure C1004.12.2.3.3) because wheelchair footplates can stop people from reaching forward past their toes. A parallel or side approach to a cooktop tends to allow access to all the burners but can also be a bit difficult since it also requires the lifting of pans to a person's side. Where a parallel approach is used, the clear floor space must be centered on the appliance. Centering of the space is important for a parallel approach but not as important for a forward approach.

1004.12.2.4 Oven. A clear floor space, positioned for a parallel or forward approach adjacent to the oven shall be provided. The oven door in the open position shall not obstruct the clear floor space for the oven.

❖ Ovens may be either built into the cabinetry as a stand-alone element or they may be a part of a traditional range with a cooktop located above it. Where an oven is a part of a range the requirements of this section apply only to the oven portion of the appliance.

Access to the ovens can be either via a parallel approach or a front approach (see Commentary Figure C1004.12.2.3.3). While a typical oven will not allow full knee and toe clearances beneath it, the oven door may be located high enough to allow a forward approach to include toe space beneath the door when the oven is opened. A wall oven that is elevated may provide adequate space beneath the open oven door to allow both knee and toe clearance and therefore allow the forward approach clear floor space to get closer to the oven.

Usability of the oven must be considered when choosing placement and options. A person must be able to open the oven door fully and reach the oven racks. Wall-mounted ovens may provide better access for persons using wheelchairs or persons who have difficulty bending down. Although most ovens have a bottom hinge door, some manufacturers are starting to offer microwave/oven combinations with a side swinging door. Other options that increase access include racks that pull all the way out without tipping, or doors that can support the weight of a full pan.

Placement of the oven next to a counter surface or accessible work surface assists in transfer of hot dishes out of the oven, but is not required in a Type B unit, as it is in an Accessible unit (Sections 1002.12., 804.5.5.2 and 804.5.5.3) or a Type A unit (Sections 1003.12.5.5.2 and 1003.12.5.5.3).

Controls for a range or wall oven are exempted from the operable parts requirement per Section 1004.9, Exception 6.

1004.12.2.5 Refrigerator/Freezer. A clear floor space, positioned for a parallel approach to the refrigerator/freezer, shall be provided. The centerline of the clear floor space shall be offset 24 inches (610 mm) maximum from the centerline of the appliance.

❖ The position for the parallel or forward approach to the refrigerator and freezer must consider how the person using a wheelchair will access the interior with the door open.

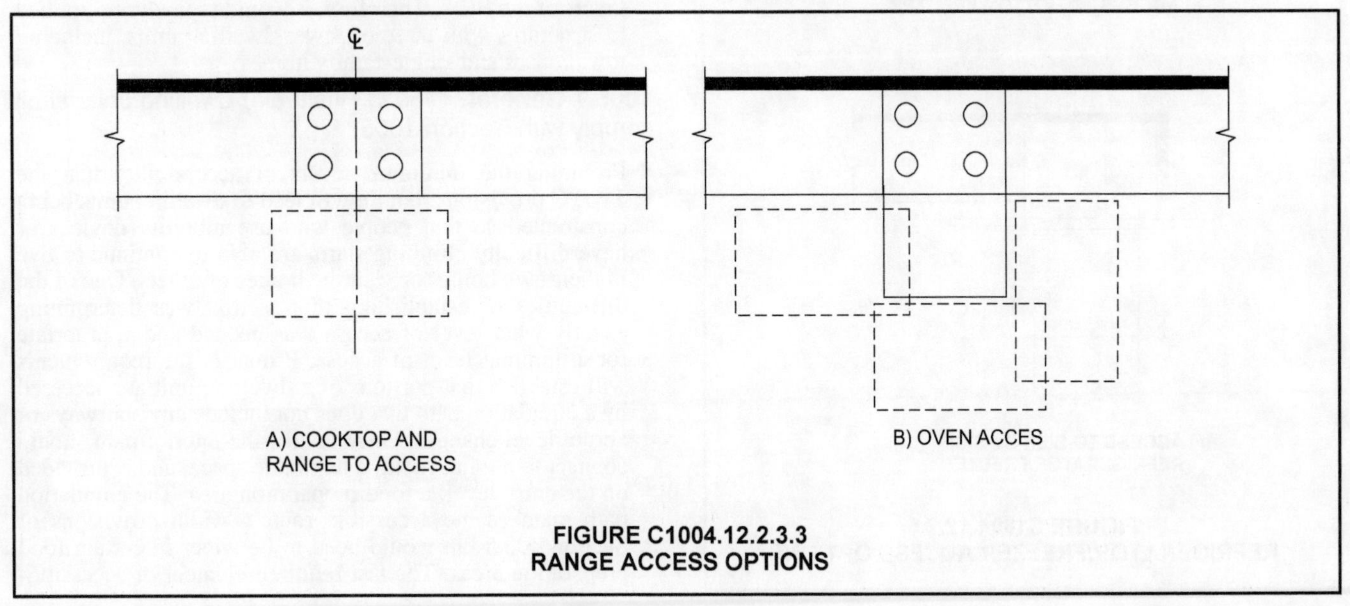

FIGURE C1004.12.2.3.3
RANGE ACCESS OPTIONS

Refrigerator/freezer choices can have the freezer on the top, on the bottom or side by side. Side-by-side refrigerator/freezers have the most accessible freezer compartment; however, clear floor spaces for both sides must be considered for the unit (see Commentary Figure C1004.12.2.5). Bottom freezers are typically pull-out drawers, so a clear floor space must be available with the freezer door/drawer fully open. While this section does require a parallel approach, it will allow a maximum offset of 24 inches (610 mm) between the centerline of the appliance and the centerline of the clear floor space. This offset requirement is helpful when facing a variety of appliance types and door configurations and may improve access to certain appliances or portions of them. Locating refrigerators so the doors swing back 180 degrees (3 rad) can result in greater accessibility for a person using a wheelchair.

Although not specifically mentioned, if a refrigerator dispenses ice or water through the door, or inside the appliance, that feature is considered part of the refrigerator/freezer. Therefore, those elements must also have a clear floor space for access.

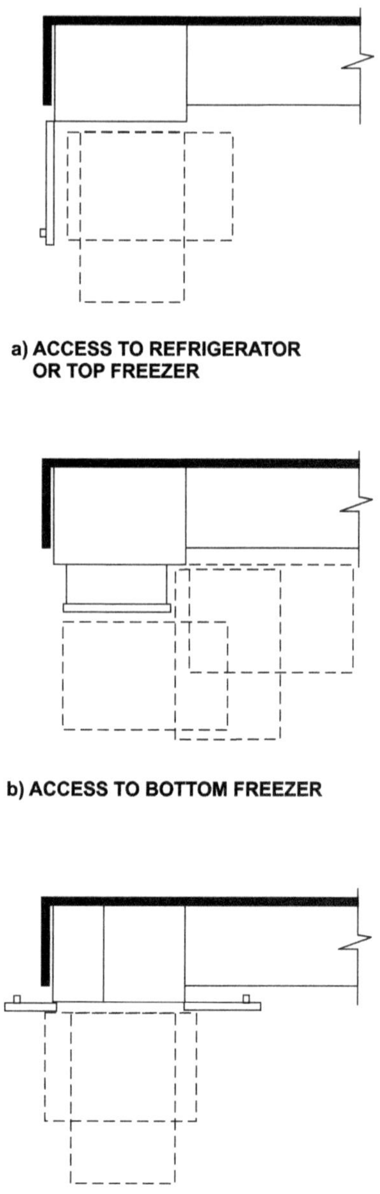

a) ACCESS TO REFRIGERATOR OR TOP FREEZER

b) ACCESS TO BOTTOM FREEZER

c) ACCESS TO SIDE-BY-SIDE REFRIGERATOR/FREEZER

FIGURE C1004.12.2.5
REFRIGERATOR/FREEZER ACCESS OPTIONS

1004.12.2.6 Trash Compactor. A clear floor space, positioned for a parallel or forward approach to the trash compactor, shall be provided.

❖ The trash compactor is similar to the dishwasher and oven in that it must be open for use. Therefore, the clear floor space should be located so that it does not obstruct the door of the trash compactor in the open position.

1005 Type C (Visitable) Units

❖ The Type C (Visitable) unit requirements are a new feature that was added into the 2009 edition of the standard. The purpose of this section is to include the technical criteria the A117.1 Committee determined would be necessary to provide a level of accessibility for dwelling units that are visitable or will allow for "aging-in-place" features. A number of communities across the country have begun to develop or require homes to provide some basic level of accessibility. As these types of developments or rules have been adopted, each community had to create its own technical requirements. These local ordinances have typically required zero-step entrances, wider interior doors and a few additional access features, but the requirements varied. By providing the Type C provisions in the standard, the A117.1 Committee has taken a step to provide consistency throughout the country and a model of what is believed to be a minimum level of accessibility to accomplish the purpose of visitable or inclusive design.

Currently neither model building codes nor the standard address the scoping requirements for when and in what quantity the Type C (visitable) units would be required. This type of scoping would be developed by the jurisdiction as specified in Sections 201 and 202. During the A117.1 standard development process it was the committee's assumption that these units would generally be applied to dwellings that were not regulated by the requirements of the FHA. Therefore, it would typically be applied to structures with three or fewer dwelling units, including townhouses and single-family homes.

1005.1 General. Type C (Visitable) dwelling units shall comply with Section 1005.

❖ Providing the minimum levels of accessibility that the Type C provisions require will lead to dwelling units being constructed so that people who use mobility devices or have difficulty climbing stairs are able to continue to live in their own homes or visit the homes of others. One of the difficulties of establishing this section was determining exactly what level of access was needed and appropriate for a minimal level of access. Primarily the requirements will establish that portions of a dwelling unit are accessed by a circulation path that does not include any stairways or abrupt level changes. Once inside, the interior path should connect to a toilet room, a habitable space, and if provided on the entry level, a food preparation area. The circulation path matches the accessible route's width provisions of Section 403.5 but would need to be wider in certain food preparation areas. The last required element of accessibility is that most lighting controls and receptacle outlets must be located within the specified reach range.

When these few access features are provided, people with mobility impairments can visit the homes of friends or family. Furthermore, these features may permit residents who are injured, who develop a disability or who are recovering from an operation to remain living in their homes for a short time, even if lacking a full bathroom and a separate designated sleeping space, while they plan and make any additional renovations they may need or while seeking a different place to reside.

1005.2 Unit Entrance. At least one unit entrance shall be on a circulation path complying with Section 1005.5 from a public street or sidewalk, a dwelling unit driveway, or a garage.

❖ The provision requires at least one entrance to be accessible, but unlike the Accessible, Type A or Type B units, this section does not mandate that the primary entry be selected or limit the path within the unit. In lieu of the primary entry, other viable options would be the door into the home from the garage or a door off a back patio.

1005.3 Connected Spaces. A circulation path complying with Section 1005.5 shall connect the unit entrance complying with Section 1005.2 and with the spaces specified in Section 1005.4.

❖ The route provided into and through the dwelling should meet most provisions of accessible routes but, since it does not meet all requirements, it should not be called an "accessible route." To avoid confusion with other requirements of the standard, the term "circulation path" is used within the requirements.

Unlike the accessible route requirements within an Accessible, Type A or even a Type B unit, the circulation path within a Type C unit is only required to serve a limited number of locations and is not required to access all rooms or spaces within the unit. In this situation, the circulation path is only required to connect from the accessible unit entry to the toilet/bathing room, a minimally sized habitable space and any food preparation area on the entry level of the unit.

1005.4 Interior Spaces. The entrance level shall include a toilet room or bathroom complying with Section 1005.6 and one habitable space with an area 70 square feet (6.5 m^2) minimum. Where a food preparation area is provided on the entrance level, it shall comply with Section 1005.7.

Exception: A toilet room or bathroom shall not be required on an entrance level with less than 120 square feet (11.1 m^2) of habitable space.

❖ The only space that will be guaranteed to be on the accessible level is a habitable space. The standard defines habitable in Section 106.5 as "A space in a building for living, sleeping, eating or cooking." and then continues to say "Bathrooms, toilet rooms, closets, halls, storage or utility spaces and similar areas are not considered habitable spaces."

In many situations a toilet or bathing room would also be required on the accessible entry level. However, based on the exception, this space may not be required if the entry level is of a very limited size. See Section 1005.6 for details of what this space is required to include.

A food prep area on the entry level is regulated if provided, but the standard does not mandate that a food prep area be included on the accessible level. The food prep area could be something as simple as a kitchenette or wet bar area with some type of cooking appliance or it could be a complete kitchen. Since food preparation and consumption is such an important part of living, having a useable food prep area on the accessible level will greatly improve the dwelling's usefulness in meeting the intent of a Type C unit.

1005.5 Circulation Path. Circulation paths shall comply with Section 1005.5.

❖ The route provided into and through the dwelling should meet most provisions of an accessible route but, since it does not meet all the requirements, it should not be called an "accessible route" (see commentary, Section 1005.3). To avoid confusion with other requirements of the standard, the term "circulation path" is used within the Type C unit requirements.

1005.5.1 Components. The circulation path shall consist of one or more of the following elements: walking surfaces with a slope not steeper that 1:20, doors and doorways, ramps, elevators complying with Sections 407 through 409, and wheelchair (platform) lifts complying with Section 410.

❖ This section identifies the various types of architectural elements that contribute to an accessible circulation path. In effect, any surface that a person can travel using a wheelchair to reach an accessible element or required area of the dwelling unit can be a part of the accessible circulation path if it complies with the provisions of Section 1005.5 or the various referenced sections. If a circulation path is constructed to meet the requirements for an accessible route in Chapter 4, that would provide a higher level of access and would be acceptable as a replacement for a circulation path.

By the definition for ramps in Section 106.5, any walking surface that slopes at 1:20 (1 inch rise to 20 inches of run) or less is considered a sloped walkway. Walking surfaces that slope from 1:20 up to 1:12 (1-inch rise to 12 inches of run) are considered to be accessible ramps (Section 405). Where greater changes in level are made, the standard will allow for an elevator or platform lift to be used. While a stairway may be the most common means of moving from various levels within a dwelling unit, it is not considered as providing an accessible circulation path and therefore is not listed in this section.

1005.5.2 Walking Surfaces. Walking surfaces with slopes not steeper than 1:20 shall comply with Section 303.

❖ In order to ensure that the circulation path is usable to the greatest number of people, this section references the change in level requirements of Section 303. Abrupt changes in elevation can create a significant barrier for a person using a wheelchair because of the small caster wheels on most wheelchairs. Compliance with Section 303 will limit the level changes along the circulation path so they can be negotiated by a person using a wheelchair with minimal difficulty and not present an unreasonable tripping hazard for other users.

1005.5.2.1 Clear Width. The clear width of the circulation path shall comply with Section 403.5.

❖ The circulation path matches the accessible route's width provisions of Section 403.5 but would need to be wider in certain food preparation areas. This section requires the general circulation path to be 36 inches (915 mm) in clear width and allows a reduction at limited spaces to a 32-inch (815 mm) clearance (Section 403.5, Exception). Where the circulation is through the food preparation area, a minimum width of 40 inches (1015 mm) will typically be required between opposing base cabinets, counter tops, walls and appliances.

1005.5.3 Doors and Doorways. Doors and doorways shall comply with Section 1005.5.3.

❖ Because both doors and doorways may create obstructions that would interfere with movement along an accessible route, the standard requires that they comply with the provisions found within this section. This section is not as limiting as the general door requirements of Section 404 or even those found within the Type B units. The doors and doorways along the circulation path of a Type C unit are only regulated for their clear width and the level change at thresholds. Other provisions such as maneuvering clearances, hardware and opening force are not regulated within the Type C units.

1005.5.3.1 Clear Width. Doorways shall have a clear opening of $31^3/_4$ inches (805 mm) minimum. Clear opening of swinging doors shall be measured between the face of the door and stop, with the door open 90 degrees.

❖ The provisions of this section match what is required for user passage doors and doorways within a Type B dwelling unit. The opening is measured with the door open 90 degrees (1.6 rad), even if the door can open wider. The intent of the $31^3/_4$-inch (810 mm) dimension is to allow for a 2-foot, 10-inch (865 mm) door leaf to be used.

Although the standard does not specifically mention door hardware, it is not the intent to include hardware when determining door width clearance. The clear width is typically measured from the face of the door to the nearest stop or frame element on the opposite side of the opening.

1005.5.3.2 Thresholds. Thresholds shall comply with Section 303.

Exception: Thresholds at exterior sliding doors shall be permitted to be $^3/_4$ inch (19 mm) maximum in height, provided they are beveled with a slope not steeper than 1:2.

❖ Thresholds and changes in the surface height at doorways are difficult for persons using a wheelchair who also may have low stamina or restrictions in arm movement because complex maneuvering is required to get over the level change when operating the door.

The reference to Section 303 effectively establishes $^1/_2$ inch (13 mm) as the maximum change in elevation for a threshold at a doorway. Where a threshold exceeds $^1/_4$ inch (6 mm) in height, the edge of the threshold must be beveled (see Figures 303.2 and 303.3).

Because of the requirements for sliding doors to stay in their tracks for proper operation, a $^3/_4$-inch (19 mm) threshold is permitted at exterior sliding doors. Similar to a $^1/_2$-inch (13 mm) threshold, the edges must be beveled.

1005.5.4 Ramps. Ramps shall comply with Section 405.

Exception: Handrails, intermediate landings and edge protection are not required where the sides of ramp runs have a vertical drop off of $^1/_2$ inch (13 mm) maximum within 10 inches (255 mm) horizontally of the ramp run.

❖ The standard provides an exception to eliminate handrails or edge protection on ramps that move up with the surrounding grade. Residents of single-family homes often prefer not to have obstructions such as handrails and edge protection along their walkways where they can prevent circulation to portions of the yard or appear different from neighboring homes. This exception reflects the A117.1 Committee's belief that handrails and edge protection can be added by an owner when and if needed. When developing these provisions, the committee did not believe that every home subject to the modest requirements for Type C units should incur the added cost associated with providing handrails at the time of initial construction where the drop-off is so limited.

1005.5.4.1 Clear Width. The clear width of the circulation path shall comply with Section 403.5.

❖ This section is somewhat redundant and is used to make the format consistent within the various circulation path elements. Notice that a width section is provided for walking surfaces (Section 1005.5.2.1), doors and doorways (Section 1005.5.3.1), and herein for ramps.

One aspect that this format does change is that by referencing Section 403.5, the ramp circulation path may be 36 inches (915 mm) in width and that measurement could allow for handrails to project into the ramp width for a limited distance and amount. While the general ramp provisions in Section 405.5 would generally prohibit handrails and handrail supports from projecting into the required width of a ramp, by this section referencing Section 403.5 it will allow the handrails to reduce the ramp to a 32-inch (815 mm) width provided the width is not reduced for a distance of more than 24 inches (610 mm) in the direction of travel. While it may be better design practice to make ramps 36 inches (915 mm) in width between any handrails for their entire length, the standard will allow the ramps in Type C units to be reduced for the limited distances.

1005.6 Toilet Room or Bathroom. At a minimum, the toilet room or bathroom required by Section 1005.4 shall include a lavatory and a water closet. Reinforcement shall be provided for the future installation of grab bars at water closets. Clearances at the water closet shall comply with Section 1004.11.3.1.2.

❖ A toilet room or bathroom must be provided that allows for clearances and blocking at the water closet. Clearances and the type of approach are not indicated for the lavatory or any bathing facilities that are provided. Providing clearances at these elements would be best design practice, but clearances are not specifically required.

1005.7 Food Preparation Area. At a minimum, the food preparation area shall include a sink, a cooking appliance, and a refrigerator. Clearances between all opposing base cabinets, counter tops, appliances or walls within the food preparation area shall be 40 inches (1015 mm) minimum in width.

Exception: Spaces that do not provide a cooktop or conventional range shall be permitted to provide a clearance of 36 inches (915 mm) minimum in width.

❖ Although visitability requirements or policies do not always specify access to kitchens and eating areas, they have been included in the standard to address the goals of the Type C unit. The food preparation area may, however, simply be an auxiliary kitchen such as a bar area with a small refrigerator and microwave. It is important to note that this requirement is scoped by Section 1005.4 and would only be applicable where a food preparation area is provided on the entrance level.

1005.8 Lighting Controls and Receptacle Outlets. Receptacle outlets and operable parts of lighting controls shall be located 15 inches (380 mm) minimum and 48 inches (1220 mm) maximum above the floor.

Exception: The following shall not be required to comply with Section 1005.8.

1. Receptacle outlets serving a dedicated use.
2. Controls mounted on ceiling fans and ceiling lights.
3. Floor receptacle outlets.
4. Lighting controls and receptacle outlets over countertops.

❖ The requirement for electrical outlets and light switches to be within reach range heights is a limited application of operable parts requirements found in Accessible, Type A, and Type B units. There are no requirements for other operable parts, such as appliances, plumbing fixtures, door hardware, electrical panels and so on. The exceptions are intended to exempt lighting controls and receptacles that are typically located out of the accessible reach ranges. Exception 4 is intended to allow for electrical outlets or switches to be located over a standard 36-inch-high (915 mm) kitchen counter.

1006 Units with Accessible Communication Features

❖ Section 1006 contains criteria for accessible communication features such as those used for emergency evacuations (e.g., fire alarms, smoke detectors) and announcing visitors (e.g., doorbells, voice or visual communication between an apartment and the building entrance).

Sections 1006.2 through 1006.4 work together for the emergency alarm system. Sections 1006.5 through 1006.7 deal with communication between entrances and occupants.

1006.1 General. Units required to have accessible communication features shall comply with Section 1006.

❖ The provisions of this section are the technical criteria for accessible communication features within dwelling units when scoped by the authority having jurisdiction (see Section 201). Scoping may include dwelling units that are not accessible in other ways (i.e., other than Accessible units, Type A units, Type B units or Type C units). For example, an apartment building may have requirements for visible alarm notification appliances (e.g., visible fire alarms and smoke detectors) or entry systems (e.g., closed circuit communication systems) to all floors in a building, including upper floors without elevator access.

The model codes have scoping criteria for accessibility in all types of places where people live, eat and sleep. Types of dwelling units are addressed, including apartments, condominiums and townhouses. Typical single-family detached homes are exempted, but a homeowner may choose to follow these criteria to build an accessible home. Scoping criteria for accessible communication features typically include apartments, condominiums and townhouses—all of which are typical dwelling units. Scoping criteria may include other types of places where people live—congregate living arrangements such as assisted living facilities, group homes, shelters, nursing homes, boarding houses, dormitories, convents, monasteries, fraternities and sororities. Scoping for transient-type lodging, such as hotels and motels, is often addressed separately, but may also include provisions for accessible communication features.

1006.2 Unit Smoke Detection. Where provided, unit smoke detection shall include audible notification complying with NFPA 72 listed in Section 105.2.2.

❖ In occupancies with sleeping areas, occupants must be notified in a fire so they can promptly evacuate the premises. Dwelling unit or sleeping unit smoke detection is typically provided by a single-station or multiple-station smoke alarm.

A single-station smoke alarm is a self-contained alarm device that detects visible or invisible particles of combustion. Its function is to detect a fire in the immediate area of the detector location. Where single-station smoke alarms are interconnected with other single-station devices, they are considered a multiple-station smoke alarm system. Single-station smoke alarms are not capable of notifying or controlling any other fire protection equipment or system. They may be battery powered, directly connected to the building power supply or both.

Multiple-station smoke alarms are self-contained smoke-activated alarm devices that can be interconnected with other devices, so all integral or separate alarms will operate when any one device is activated.

Model codes typically specify where dwelling or sleeping unit smoke detection will be required within a dwelling or sleeping unit. In dwelling units, this is typically outside each sleeping area, in each sleeping room and on each story in a multistory unit. In congregate living arrangements requirements are similar. In hotels, dormitories or other types of sleeping units, the smoke alarms must be in sleeping rooms and in any room between the sleeping room and the entrance to the unit (e.g., living area of a suite). Smoke alarms must be interconnected within the unit (i.e., activation of one smoke alarm will set off all smoke alarms within the unit).

For successful smoke alarm operation and performance, single- and multiple-station smoke alarms must be listed in accordance with UL 217 and installed to comply with the model code and NFPA 72, which contains the minimum requirements for the selection, installation, operation and maintenance of fire warning equipment for use in family living units. Model codes and NFPA 72 use the term "smoke alarms" rather than "smoke detectors" because they are independent of a fire alarm system and include an integral alarm notification device.

This section requires that the unit smoke detectors have an audible notification in accordance with NFPA 72. NFPA 72 requires a minimum average ambient sound level for smoke alarms in the private mode to be greater than 10 dBa above average ambient sound level or 5 dBa above the maximum sound level (NFPA 72, Section 7.4.3). Within a sleeping area, the audible alarm requirement is to be at least 15 dB above the average ambient sound level, 5 dB above the maximum sound level or at least 75 dBA, whichever is greater (NFPA 72, Section 7.4.4).

1006.3 Building Fire Alarm System. Where a building fire alarm system is provided, the system wiring shall be extended to a point within the unit in the vicinity of the unit smoke detection system.

❖ In residential facilities, a building fire alarm system, dwelling unit smoke alarms and a sprinkler system are parts of an overall fire protection system for a building. These elements are considered part of the active fire safety provisions. They are directed at containing and abating the fire once it has erupted, as well as providing notification to occupants and emergency responders to emergency situations. The requirements are generally based on what the building is used for, and the height and area of the building. These are factors that most affect fire-fighting capabilities and the relative hazard of a specific space.

Building fire alarms include both audible and visible alarm requirements (see Section 702) and are intended to serve as a general evacuation alarm system. Model codes typically require a building fire alarm system in apartment buildings that have basement dwelling units, apartment buildings four stories or higher and apartment buildings with 16 or more apartments. Check with the authority having jurisdiction for specifics. Activation of the smoke alarms within a unit and the building fire alarm system are typically independent.

This section requires that when there is a building fire alarm system, the wiring be extended into each unit in the area of one of the smoke alarms. The intent is that the resident of that unit can request standard smoke alarms be switched out to smoke alarms that have both audible and visible notification appliances, rather than just audible. With the wiring in place, the smoke alarms in the unit can be hooked up so the activation of the building alarm system will also activate the smoke alarms in that unit. Because multiple-station smoke alarms are already interconnected, the wiring from the building alarm system need be extended to only one smoke alarm. It is not the intent for the activation of the smoke alarm to activate the building alarm system.

It is not the intent of this section to require wiring for full visible alarm coverage within the dwelling unit in permanent residential facilities. See the scoping provisions of the model codes for coverage of the building alarm audible and visible alarms. Model codes do scope a certain number of sleeping units in transient lodging and assisted living facilities to have full visible and audible alarm coverage.

1006.4 Visible Notification Appliances. Visible notification appliances, where provided within the unit as part of the unit smoke detection system or the building fire alarm system, shall comply with Section 1006.4.

❖ Requirements for visible alarms within the unit and the public spaces and common spaces in the building are intended to alert individuals with hearing impairments of a possible emergency situation. The model codes scope where visible alarm coverage is required; therefore, this section does not require visible alarms, but indicates that when they are installed they should meet the provisions in the following subsections.

1006.4.1 Appliances. Visible notification appliances shall comply with Section 702.

❖ Both the required visible alarm coverage in the public and common areas of the building and the smoke alarms with a visible component should meet the applicable provisions in NFPA 72. NFPA does not require the same area coverage, flash rate or intensity for the visible notification in the smoke detectors as it requires for the visible appliances in the building alarm system.

1006.4.2 Activation. All visible notification appliances provided within the unit for smoke detection notification shall be activated upon smoke detection. All visible notification appliances provided within the unit for building fire alarm notification shall be activated upon activation of the building fire alarm in the portion of the building containing the unit.

❖ Once the dwelling unit smoke alarms are connected to the building alarm system, the dwelling unit smoke alarms should activate when there is either smoke detected within the unit or when the building alarm system is activated.

The intent is that a resident can request installation of smoke alarms with both visible and audible notification (e.g., flashing lights and horns) within their unit as a reasonable modification. The wiring that allows for the preplanning for this is required by Section 1006.3. Because the smoke alarms have their own power, this should not increase the power requirements for the building alarm system.

1006.4.3 Interconnection. The same visible notification appliances shall be permitted to provide notification of unit smoke detection and building fire alarm activation.

❖ This section clarifies that the flashing lights in the smoke alarms can serve to notify the dwelling occupants of both smoke within the unit and the general building evacuation alarm.

1006.4.4 Prohibited Use. Visible notification appliances used to indicate unit smoke detection or building fire alarm activation shall not be used for any other purpose within the unit.

❖ The lights in the smoke alarms for alarm notification should not be used for other purposes, such as means of egress emergency lighting, or other types of emergency notification, such as tornado warnings or for nonemergency items such as notification of doorbell activation or telephone ringing.

1006.5 Unit Primary Entrance. Communication features shall be provided at the unit primary entrance complying with Section 1006.5.

❖ When the authority having jurisdiction requires communication features at individual dwelling unit entrances, those systems shall comply with the notification and identification requirements listed in the subsections that follow.

1006.5.1 Notification. A hard-wired electric doorbell shall be provided. A button or switch shall be provided on the public side of the unit primary entrance. Activation of the button or switch shall initiate an audible tone within the unit.

❖ The doorbell, as an operable part, should have a clear floor space and be located within reach ranges. Best design practice allows for an adjustment of the tone and/or volume of the bell within the unit for persons with hearing losses. The adjustment in tone rather than just volume would be beneficial for persons with hearing loss in a specific range.

1006.5.2 Identification. A means for visually identifying a visitor without opening the unit entry door shall be provided. Peepholes, where used, shall provide a minimum 180-degree range of view.

❖ Visual identification could be by the use of a peephole, a door with inset lites or side lites, or a video monitoring system. It could be anything that allows for a person inside the unit to see who is outside without opening the door. If a peephole is used, the eye height of an average person in a wheelchair is 43 inches to 51 inches (1090 mm to 1295 mm), so that range would be considered an accessible height. A door can have both a high and a low peephole to accommodate standing and sitting persons. The bottom edge of door lite glazing must be below 43 inches (1090 mm) (see Section 404.2.11).

1006.6 Site, Building, or Floor Entrance. Where a system permitting voice communication between a visitor and the occupant of the unit is provided at a location other than the unit entry door, the system shall comply with Section 1006.6.

❖ When the authority having jurisdiction requires communication features at a building entrance or similar location, those systems must comply with the interface requirements listed in the subsections. Systems at these locations typically involve a phone, intercom, video relay or some combination of these.

1006.6.1 Public or Common-Use Interface. The public or common-use system interface shall include the capability of supporting voice and TTY communication with the unit interface.

❖ For a person visiting in the building, the option of some type of TTY system, either built in or a portable that could be plugged in, must be considered because either the visitor or the person living in the unit could be hearing impaired. TTY specifications for phone systems are found in Sections 704.4, 704.5 and 704.6.

1006.6.2 Unit Interface. The unit system interface shall include a telephone jack capable of supporting voice and TTY communication with the public or common-use system interface.

❖ For persons living in the building, the option of some type of TTY system, either built in or a portable that could be plugged in, must be considered because either the visitor or the person living in the unit could be hearing impaired. TTY specifications for phone systems are found in Sections 704.4, 704.5 and 704.6.

1006.7 Closed-Circuit Communication Systems. Where a closed-circuit communication system is provided, the public or common-use system interface shall comply with Section 1006.6.1, and the unit system interface in units required to have accessible communication features shall comply with Section 1006.6.2.

❖ Two-way communication systems are used at security entrances, for closed-circuit entry systems, from areas of refuge, etc. These systems must be available for persons with hearing impairments. Persons with hearing impairments will need TTY capability the same as required for the public or common-use interface. For additional information on two-way communication systems, see Section 708.

Chapter 11. Recreational Facilities

❖ Chapter 11 contains the technical requirements for a variety of recreational facilities. However, it is not the intent of these provisions to change the nature of the games played. Therefore, basically a route is required to recreational facilities. Only for the specific facilities listed in this chapter are additional criteria required for ways to access or participate in the activity.

- Section 1101 is a set of specific exceptions for recreational facilities.
- Section 1102 deals with permanent amusement rides.
- Section 1103 provides criteria for recreational boating facilities including boat slips, boat launch ramps and boarding piers.
- Section 1104 requires an accessible route within spaces with exercise equipment.
- Section 1105 includes specific criteria for accessible locations on fishing piers.
- Section 1106 requires an accessible route to different points within a golf course. However, some areas allow for golf carts to be used to provide the accessible route.
- Section 1107 requires half of the holes in a miniature golf course to allow for access.
- Section 1108 provides a variety of options for children to access equipment on playgrounds. This section also addresses the soft-contained play areas commonly located within malls or fast food establishments.
- Section 1109 provides options for allowing persons with mobility problems access into swimming pools, wading pools and hot tubs/spas. Criteria vary depending on the type of pool (i.e., lazy river, lap, wave) and the size of the pool.
- Section 1110 includes criteria for accessible firing positions within shooting ranges.

1101 General

1101.1 Scope. Recreational facilities required to be accessible by the scoping provisions adopted by the administrative authority shall comply with the applicable provisions of Chapter 11.

❖ The intent for this chapter is to provide specifications for elements within different sports facilities that will create a general level of accessibility for individuals. Persons with mobility impairments will be able to access the sports facility so that they can participate to the best of their individual ability. Although the provisions of this chapter may improve the design and usability of all buildings, it is important to note that the section is qualified by the phrase "required by the administrative authority." This is intended to be consistent with the fact that scoping provisions are not included in this standard (see commentary, Chapter 2).

Where the administrative authority requires recreational facilities to be on an accessible route, supporting areas are also expected to be accessible. This would include provisions addressed elsewhere in this standard such as: parking, locker rooms, team or player seating, toilet rooms, shower rooms and concession stands.

1101.2 Special Provisions.

❖ Special provisions are basically a series of exceptions for recreational facilities.

1101.2.1 General Exceptions. The following shall not be required to be accessible or to be on an accessible route:

1. Raised structures used solely for refereeing, judging, or scoring a sport.
2. Water Slides.
3. Animal containment areas that are not for public use.
4. Raised boxing or wrestling rings.
5. Raised diving boards and diving platforms.
6. Bowling lanes that are not required to provide wheelchair spaces.
7. Mobile or portable amusement rides.
8. Amusement rides that are controlled or operated by the rider.
9. Amusement rides designed primarily for children, where children are assisted on and off the ride by an adult.
10. Amusement rides that do not provide amusement ride seats.

❖ These specific portions or areas of sports activities are exempted both from accessibility for that particular element as well as an accessible route to that element. These exceptions often coordinate with the provisions found later in this chapter. Some are coordinated with the scoping requirements anticipated to come from the administrative authority.

Exception 1 exempts areas that are raised so that referees, judges or scorers can see the field of play. An example would be the net judge at a professional tennis match.

Exceptions 2 and 5 are for water slides and diving boards associated with swimming pools [see Commentary Figure C1101.2.1(a)]. Section 1109.1.1, Exception 3, also exempts the catch pools associated with water slides from accessible means of entry.

Exception 4 is for animal containment areas, such as fields, barns or kennels used to exercise or house animals, that are not open to the public. An example might be the wildlife areas in a zoo. An accessible route would be required to the viewing areas [see Commentary Figure C1101.2.1(b)].

Exception 6 exempts bowling lanes that are not required to be accessible. Scoping documents typically specify 5 percent of bowling lanes and the associated team and player seating area to be accessible [see Commentary Figure C1101.2.1(c)].

Exceptions 7 through 10 are for the amusement ride provisions in Section 1102. This would exempt amusement rides that are relocated with the traveling carnival (Exception 7); rides operated by the rider, such as bumper cars or go-carts [Exception 8, see Commentary Figure C1101.2.1(d)]; rides primarily for children, such as merry-go-rounds (Exception 9); and rides that do not provide seats, such as water flume rides where people go through the ride on inner tubes (Exception 10). Note that "amusement ride seats" are defined in Section 106.5 as a seat that is built-in or mechanically fastened to an amusement ride.

1101.2.2 Area of Sport Activity. Areas of sport activity shall be served by an accessible route and shall not be required to be accessible except as provided in Chapter 11.

❖ "Area of sports activity" is defined in Section 106.5 as a space where play or practice of a sport occurs. This encompasses an extremely large variety of spaces, both indoors and outdoors. However, the intent is not to change the nature of the game; therefore, the requirement is for an accessible route to the field or play area. The area of sports activity itself is not required to meet accessible features for surfaces, accessible routes or protruding objects (see Commentary Figure C1101.2.2 for examples of areas of sports activity). It is not the intent that persons who use wheelchairs be excluded, but rather that they can participate to the best of their unique abilities.

FIGURE C1101.2.1(a)
WATER SLIDES

FIGURE C1101.2.1(c)
BOWLING LANES

FIGURE C1101.2.1(b)
ZOO

FIGURE C1101.2.1(d)
BUMPER CARS

Areas of sports activities include all the areas specifically described in this chapter. For these areas, certain specific criteria are expected. Areas of sports activity also include areas such as skating rinks, baseball fields, running tracks, ski slopes, tennis courts and football fields. The extent of the play area varies. For example, football fields are defined by boundary lines. In addition, a safety border is provided along both sides of the field and "end zones" on both ends. The purpose of those areas is that players may run or be pushed out of the play area and into these zones. Therefore, in football, the field and the side and end zones are included in the area of sports activity.

1101.2.3 Recreational Boating Facilities. Operable parts of cleats and other boat securement devices shall not be required to comply with Section 308.

❖ This limited exception for boat securement devices is intended to be coordinated with the recreational boating requirements in Section 1103. Boat cleats are typically bolted directly to the dock; therefore, boat cleats are not required to be located within reach ranges (see Commentary Figure C1101.2.3). Keep in mind that a clear floor space and a route to the cleats are still required. The reach range exceptions do not apply to other controls and operating mechanisms such as water and electrical hookups.

(a) SKATEBOARD PARK

(b) BASKETBALL COURT

(c) SKI SLOPES

(d) ICE RINKS

(e) RUNNING TRACK

(f) SOCCER FIELD

FIGURE C1101.2.2
AREA OF SPORTS ACTIVITY EXAMPLES

FIGURE C1101.2.3
EXAMPLE OF BOAT CLEAT

1101.2.4 Exercise Machines and Equipment. Exercise machines and exercise equipment shall not be required to comply with Section 309.

❖ Section 1104 provides criteria for accessible routes within rooms and spaces that include exercise machines and equipment. The equipment itself is not required to be altered or revised to meet any of the operable parts requirements in Section 309.

1101.3 Protruding Objects. Protruding objects on circulation paths shall comply with Section 307.

EXCEPTIONS:

1. Within areas of sport activity, protruding objects on circulation paths shall not be required to comply with Section 307.
2. Within play areas, protruding objects on circulation paths shall not be required to comply with Section 307 provided that ground level accessible routes provide vertical clearance complying with Section 1108.2.

❖ Section 1101.3 simply repeats the basic requirement that circulation paths must meet the protruding object requirements in Section 307. The real intent of this requirement being repeated here is to set up the exceptions. Exception 1 allows for objects on a playing field to literally be protruding objects. For example, this would allow for a volleyball net to be located so that the net would not be detectable. Exception 2 allows for objects within a playground setup to be protruding objects provided the vertical clearance at the accessible routes to ground-level play components is at least 80 inches (2030 mm) (see Sections 1108.2 and 1108.4).

1102 Amusement Rides

❖ This section is applicable for amusement rides that are not exempted under Section 1101.2.1, Exceptions 7 through 10. Section 106.5 defines "amusement rides" as a system that moves people through a fixed course within a defined area for purposes of amusement (see Commentary Figure C1102). Therefore, this section is primarily intended to address permanent rides with seats that move people through a fixed course. This section is not applicable to trams or gondolas that are designed primarily to transport people. An example of a ride to transport people would be the monorail that transports visitors between parks in Disneyland in Florida.

Other definitions that are important to application of this section are amusement attraction, amusement ride, amusement ride seat, and transfer device.

FIGURE C1102
EXAMPLE OF AMUSEMENT RIDE

1102.1 General. Accessible amusement rides shall comply with Section 1102.

❖ Criteria in this section address routes to the load and unload areas in amusement rides, and transfer onto and off the ride.

1102.2 Accessible Routes. Accessible routes serving amusement rides shall comply with Chapter 4.

EXCEPTIONS:

1. In load or unload areas and on amusement rides, where complying with Section 405.2 is not structurally or operationally feasible, ramp slope shall be permitted to be 1:8 maximum.
2. In load or unload areas and on amusement rides, handrails provided along walking surfaces complying with Section 403 and required on ramps complying with Section 405 shall not be required to comply with Section 505 where complying is not structurally or operationally feasible.

❖ Accessible routes connect accessible elements. For amusement rides, an accessible route is required to connect arrival points to the load and unload areas of a ride. Vertical access can be provided by passenger elevators, limited use/limited application (LULA) elevators, platform lifts or ramps. The exceptions are allowances for breaks from the ramp requirements due to structural or operational issues. Exception 1 allows for a steeper ramp (1:8 maximum) where it is structurally or operationally infeasible to meet the typical ramp slopes (1:12 maximum). This would be where the accessible route leads directly to the ride due to space limitations on the ride. This exception would not typically be used along the queue lines. Exception 2 is for handrails along ramps where it is structurally or operationally infeasible to provide them.

If the accessible route is different from the typical queue line, signage should be provided at the start of the queue. Signage should also indicate the type of access provided (i.e., wheelchair spaces or transfer seats).

1102.3 Load and Unload Areas. A turning space complying with Sections 304.2 and 304.3 shall be provided in load and unload areas.

❖ A level turning circle or T-turn must be provided in load and unload areas. A good location would depend on the location of the route and access to the transfer device or wheelchair space provided on the ride.

1102.4 Wheelchair Spaces in Amusement Rides. Wheelchair spaces in amusement rides shall comply with Section 1102.4.

❖ There are three options for providing an accessible amusement ride: a wheelchair space on the ride (Section 1102.4), a seat on the ride that someone transfers to (Section 1102.5) or a seat on the ride that is accessed from a transfer device (Section 1102.6). This section addresses requirements for wheelchair seats on the ride (see Commentary Figure C1102.4.4.1).

1102.4.1 Floor Surface. The floor surface of wheelchair spaces shall be stable and firm.

❖ The size of the wheelchair space is indicated in Section 1102.4.4.1 as 30 inches by 48 inches (760 by 1220 mm). Section 1102.4.4.2 requires maneuvering space. The entire floor area should provide a stable surface.

1102.4.2 Slope. The floor surface of wheelchair spaces shall have a slope not steeper than 1:48 when in the load and unload position.

❖ The floor of the ride may slope during the course of the ride. Where this occurs, safety concerns may require someone to lock their brakes, or possibly utilize tie-down devices. However, when the ride is in the load and unload position, the surface should be level.

1102.4.3 Gaps. Floors of amusement rides with wheelchair spaces and floors of load and unload areas shall be coordinated so that, when amusement rides are at rest in the load and unload position, the vertical difference between the floors shall be within plus or minus $^5/_8$ inch (16 mm) and the horizontal gap shall be 3 inches (75 mm) maximum under normal passenger load conditions.

EXCEPTION: Where complying is not operationally or structurally feasible, ramps, bridge plates, or similar devices complying with the applicable requirements of 36 CFR 1192.83(c), listed in Section 105.2.11, shall be provided.

❖ It is important to coordinate the floor of the wheelchair space on the ride and the floor of the load and unload areas. The vertical difference must be less than $^5/_8$ inch (16 mm) and any horizontal gap must be less than 3 inches (76 mm) [see Commentary Figure C1102.4.3(a)]. Where these limitations cannot be met on the ride, the exception allows for bridge plates or ramps to provide a way for someone to move from the boarding areas to the ride [see Commentary Figures C1102.4.3(b, c and d)].

1102.4.4 Clearances. Clearances for wheelchair spaces shall comply with Section 1102.4.4.

EXCEPTIONS:

1. Where provided, securement devices shall be permitted to overlap required clearances.
2. Wheelchair spaces shall be permitted to be mechanically or manually repositioned.
3. Wheelchair spaces shall not be required to comply with Section 307.4.

❖ Wheelchair spaces must comply with requirements for size of space, size of access opening, clearances and protrusions listed in the subsections. The exceptions address areas where securement devices are required; instances when the wheelchair space may be repositioned (i.e., use of a turntable); and instances where the 80-inch (2030 mm) vertical clearance is not required over the wheelchair space. This allows for the wheelchair to be restrained for safety reasons, the rider to be repositioned so they can face the direction of the ride movement, and that the ride may move through confined spaces. The 80-inch (2030 mm) clearance is required along the accessible route from the entry point to the load and unload areas.

1102.4.4.1 Width and Length. Wheelchair spaces shall provide a clear width of 30 inches (760 mm) minimum and a clear length of 48 inches (1220 mm) minimum measured to 9 inches (230 mm) minimum above the floor.

❖ The relationship between the size and location of the opening in the cab wall and the orientation of the wheelchair space should be considered in design. This can be front entry, side entry or front entry with a turntable. Within the cab, the wheelchair space must be a minimum of 30 inches by 48 inches (760 by 1220 mm). The 9-inch (230 mm) height allows for toe clearance height with no protrusions (see Commentary Figure C1102.4.4.1).

1102.4.4.2 Side Entry. Where wheelchair spaces are entered only from the side, amusement rides shall be designed to permit sufficient maneuvering clearance for individuals using a wheelchair or mobility aid to enter and exit the ride.

❖ If the wheelchair space is accessed by a side entry, sufficient maneuvering space must be allowed. The provisions for alcoves in Section 305.7 and possible turning space must be considered. For example, a side entry with a 42-inch (1065 mm) door would need a clear floor space of 60 inches by 36 inches (914 mm).

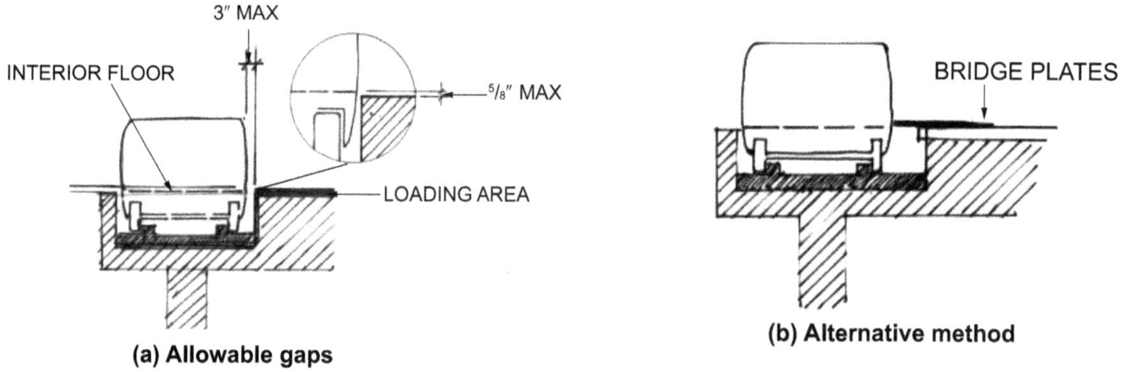

3″ MAX
INTERIOR FLOOR
$^5/_8$″ MAX
LOADING AREA

(a) Allowable gaps

BRIDGE PLATES

(b) Alternative method

RAMP UP

(c) Alternative method

RAMP DOWN

(d) Alternative method

FIGURE C1102.4.3
ALLOWABLE GAP AND ALTERNATIVE METHODS
(Drawing courtesy of U.S. Access Board)

48″ MIN
30″ MIN
25″ MAX
OBJECTS MAY PROTRUDE A MAXIMUM OF 25″ IF ABOVE 27″ FROM FLOOR
BETWEEN 9″ AND 27″ ABOVE THE FLOOR, OBJECTS MAY PROTRUDE TO A MAXIMUM OF 6″
6″
27″ KNEE CLEARANCE
9″
9″ VERTICAL TOE CLEARANCE (NO PROTRUSIONS ALLOWED)

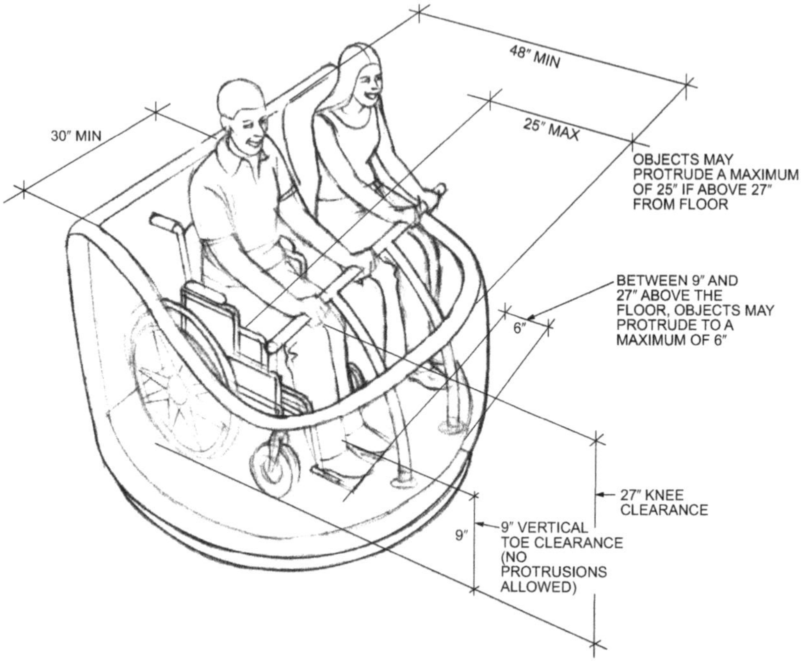

FIGURE C1102.4.4.1
ALLOWABLE PROTRUSIONS INTO WHEELCHAIR SPACES
(Drawing courtesy of U.S. Access Board)

1102.4.4.3 Permitted Protrusions in Wheelchair Spaces. Objects are permitted to protrude a distance of 6 inches (150 mm) maximum along the front of the wheelchair space, where located 9 inches (230 mm) minimum and 27 inches (685 mm) maximum above the floor of the wheelchair space. Objects are permitted to protrude a distance of 25 inches (635 mm) maximum along the front of the wheelchair space, where located more than 27 inches (685 mm) above the floor of the wheelchair space.

❖ The permitted protrusions into the wheelchair space are consistent with the knee and toe clearances and depth under a counter as indicated in Chapter 3 (see Figure 1102.4.4.3 and Commentary Figure C1102.4.4.1).

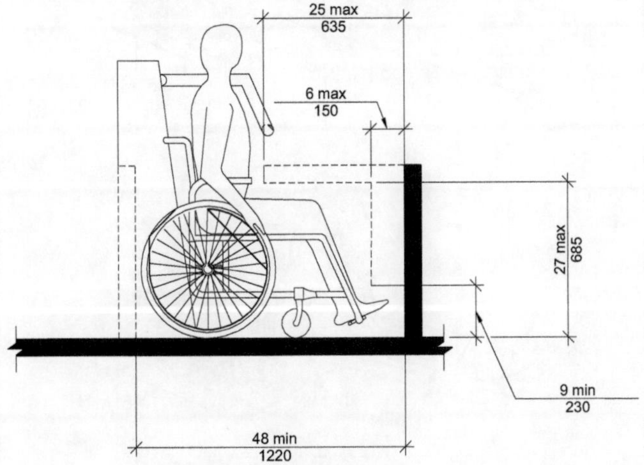

**FIGURE 1102.4.4.3
PROTRUSIONS IN WHEELCHAIR
SPACES IN AMUSEMENT RIDES**

1102.4.5 Ride Entry. Openings providing entry to wheelchair spaces on amusement rides shall provide a clear width of 32 inches (815 mm) minimum.

❖ The provisions for ride openings to access the wheelchair space are consistent with doors in Chapter 4; however, in confined spaces with a side approach, 32 inch (815 mm) clear width would not be sufficient to access the space. For a side approach, a 42-inch (1065 mm) door associated with a clear floor space of 36 inches (915 mm) wide and 60 inches (1525 mm) deep would be required for access.

1102.4.6 Approach. One side of the wheelchair space shall adjoin an accessible route when in the load and unload position.

❖ This reiterates the basic requirement that the wheelchair space be located directly on an accessible route.

1102.4.7 Companion Seats. Where the interior width of the amusement ride is greater than 53 inches (1345 mm), seating is provided for more than one rider, and the wheelchair is not required to be centered within the amusement ride, a companion seat shall be provided for each wheelchair space.

❖ Part of the amusement ride experience is enjoying the ride with a companion. If there are seats for more than one rider in the car and the ride car is more than 53 inches (1345 mm) wide, a companion seat should be provided. If the weight of the wheelchair raises an issue regarding the center of gravity, this would be considered a technical reason to not provide a companion seat.

1102.4.7.1 Shoulder-to-Shoulder Seating. Where an amusement ride provides shoulder-to-shoulder seating, companion seats shall be shoulder-to-shoulder with the adjacent wheelchair space.

EXCEPTION: Where shoulder-to-shoulder companion seating is not operationally or structurally feasible, complying with this requirement shall be required to the maximum extent practicable.

❖ Where seating is provided for a companion, there should be shoulder alignment, similar to assembly seating when viewing an event. The exception addresses structural or operation issues.

1102.5 Amusement Ride Seats Designed for Transfer. Amusement ride seats designed for transfer shall comply with Section 1102.5 when positioned for loading and unloading.

❖ There are three options for providing an accessible amusement ride: a wheelchair space on the ride (Section 1102.4), a seat on the ride that someone transfers to (Section 1102.5) or a seat on the ride that is accessed from a transfer device (Section 1102.6). This section addresses requirements for seats designed for transfer (see Commentary Figure C1102.5). To go on the ride, a person will transfer from their wheelchair or mobility device to a ride seat. Transfer should be independently manageable. While there are different options for transfer; however, clear floor space and the height of the seat are critical for safe transfer. Considerations of gripping surfaces, seat padding, possible obstruction and support after transfer are important.

1102.5.1 Clear Floor Space. A clear floor space complying with Section 305 shall be provided in the load and unload area adjacent to the amusement ride seats designed for transfer.

❖ The size of the wheelchair space is typically 30 inches by 48 inches (760 by 1220 mm). However, if the transfer space for the wheelchair is at all restricted, the alcove provisions may also be applicable.

1102.5.2 Transfer Height. The height of amusement ride seats designed for transfer shall be 14 inches (355 mm) minimum and 24 inches (610 mm) maximum measured from the surface of the load and unload area.

❖ While good design would try for a seat height of 17 inches to 19 inches (430 to 485 mm), to allow for ride options, the limits are extended to a height of 14 inches to 24 inches (355 by 610 mm).

1102.5.3 Transfer Entry. Where openings are provided for transfer to amusement ride seats, the openings shall provide clearance for transfer from a wheelchair or mobility aid to the amusement ride seat.

❖ Sufficient space for transfer is required. However, since there is such a variety of amusement rides and transfer systems, what constitutes adequate space differs (see Commentary Figure C1102.5.3).

1102.5.4 Wheelchair Storage Space. Wheelchair storage spaces complying with Section 305 shall be provided in or adjacent to unload areas for each required amusement ride seat designed for transfer and shall not overlap any required means of egress or accessible route.

❖ It is not always convenient for a wheelchair or mobility device to remain where the person transferred from it during the time they are on the ride. A wheelchair storage space must be provided in or near the unloading area. For safety reasons, the wheelchair storage space cannot block accessible routes or general means of egress.

1102.6 Transfer Devices for Use with Amusement Rides. Transfer devices for use with amusement rides shall comply with Section 1102.6 when positioned for loading and unloading.

❖ There are three options for providing an accessible amusement ride: a wheelchair space on the ride (Section 1102.4), a seat on the ride that someone transfers to (Section 1102.5) or a seat on the ride that is accessed from a transfer device (Section 1102.6). Transfer to a ride can be direct from the wheelchair to the ride seat, or with a transfer device. Transfer devices can be permanent or moveable. A variety of designs are viable provided they are reliable and sturdy (see Commentary Figure 1102.5.3).

1102.6.1 Clear Floor Space. A clear floor space complying with Section 305 shall be provided in the load and unload area adjacent to the transfer device.

❖ The size of the wheelchair space is typically 30 inches by 48 inches (760 by 1220 mm). However, if the transfer space for the wheelchair is at all restricted, the alcove provisions may also be applicable.

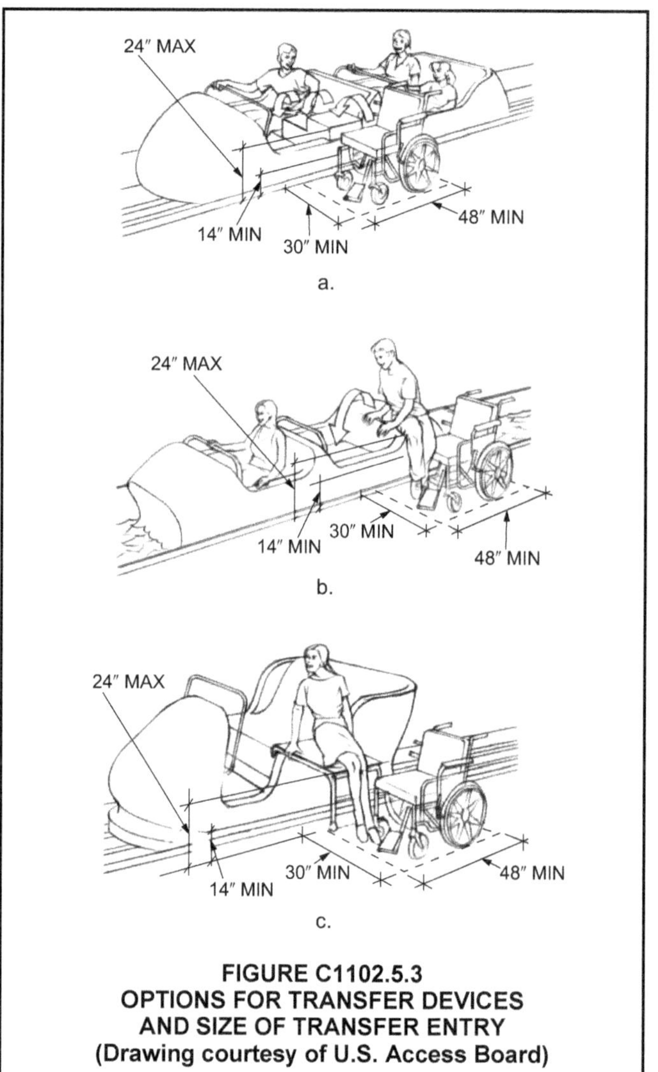

FIGURE C1102.5.3
OPTIONS FOR TRANSFER DEVICES AND SIZE OF TRANSFER ENTRY
(Drawing courtesy of U.S. Access Board)

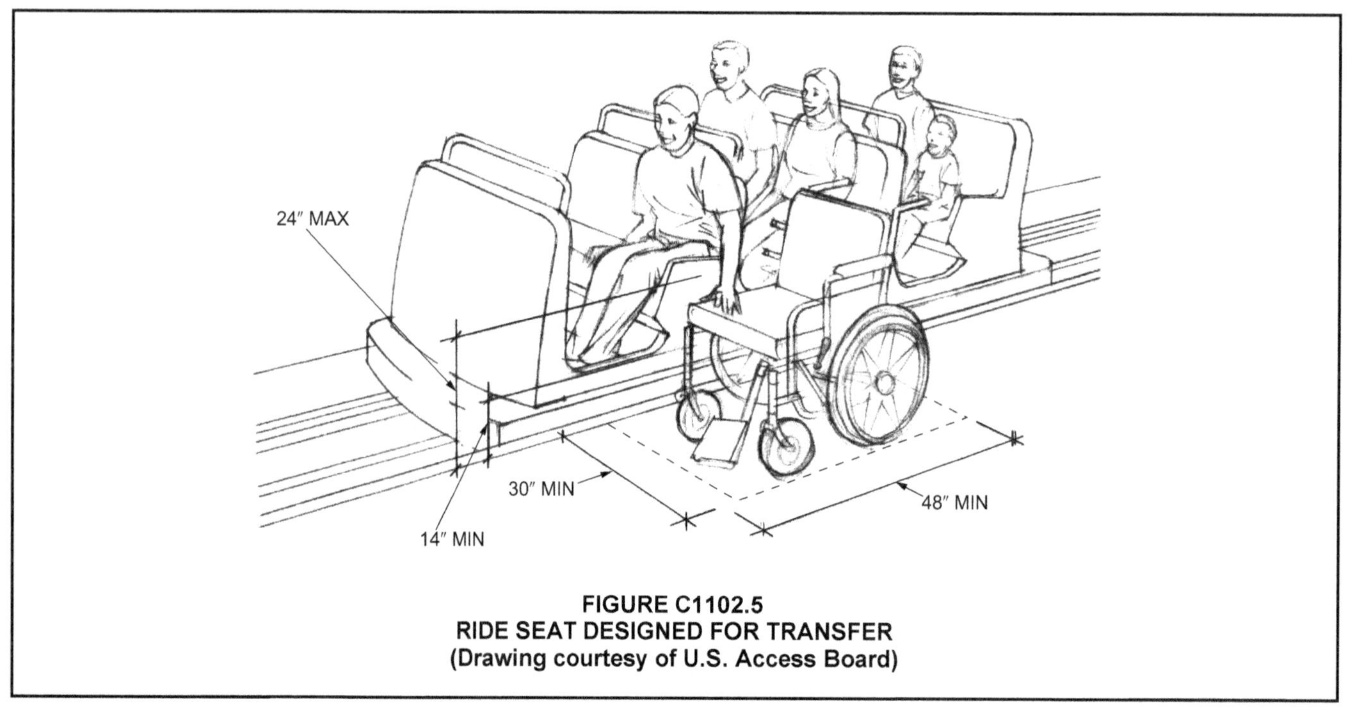

FIGURE C1102.5
RIDE SEAT DESIGNED FOR TRANSFER
(Drawing courtesy of U.S. Access Board)

1102.6.2 Transfer Height. The height of transfer device seats shall be 14 inches (355 mm) minimum and 24 inches (610 mm) maximum measured from the load and unload surface.

❖ While good design would try for a seat height of 17 inches to 19 inches (430 to 485 mm), to allow for ride options, the limits are extended to a height of 14 inches to 24 inches (355 to 610 mm).

1102.6.3 Wheelchair Storage Space. Wheelchair storage spaces complying with Section 305 shall be provided in or adjacent to unload areas for each required transfer device and shall not overlap any required means of egress or accessible route.

❖ It is not always convenient for a wheelchair or mobility device to remain where the person transferred from it during the time they are on the ride. A wheelchair storage space must be provided in or near the unloading area. For safety reasons, the wheelchair storage space cannot block accessible routes or general means of egress.

1103 Recreational Boating Facilities

❖ This section addresses recreational boating facilities (see Commentary Figure C1103). The emphasis is placed on access for persons with disabilities to the boating facilities and use of the various elements.

Definitions that are relevant to this section are boarding pier, boat launch ramp, boat slip and gangway.

It is not the intent of this section to apply to docks for passenger vessels or ferry docks. Nor is it the intent for these provisions to apply to boats that are permanently docked and used for other purposes, for example, restaurants, casinos or museums.

1103.1 General. Accessible recreational boating facilities shall comply with Section 1103.

❖ Recreational boating facilities can include fixed or floating piers and docks. Access is required to marinas, launching facilities, and piers and docks designed for recreational boats. The facility can have any number of boat slips. The size of boats intended to be addressed varies from canoes and rowboats to large sailboats and powerboats. How many and what types of boat slips are required to be accessible, or how many embarking locations on a boarding pier are required to be accessible, is scoped by the authority having jurisdiction.

1103.2 Accessible Routes. Accessible routes serving recreational boating facilities, including gangways and floating piers, shall comply with Chapter 4 except as modified by the exceptions in Section 1103.2.

❖ Accessible routes connect accessible elements. For boating facilities, an accessible route is required to connect arrival points to the piers that contain boat slips and any boarding piers at boat launch ramps. The exceptions found in Sections 1103.2.1 and 1103.2.2 are specific to the route for access to different types of piers: those used for boat slips and those used for boarding and associated with boat launch ramps.

An option to providing accessible gangways, would be providing vertical access via elevators, LULA elevators or platform lifts.

1103.2.1 Boat Slips. An accessible route shall serve boat slips.

EXCEPTIONS:

1. Where an existing gangway or series of gangways is replaced or altered, an increase in the

FIGURE C1103
EXAMPLE OF BOAT SLIPS

length of the gangway shall not be required to comply with Section 1103.2.

2. Gangways shall not be required to comply with the maximum rise specified in Section 405.6.
3. Where the total length of a gangway or series of gangways serving as part of a required accessible route is 80 feet (24 m) minimum, gangways shall not be required to comply with Section 405.2.
4. Where facilities contain fewer than 25 boat slips and the total length of the gangway or series of gangways serving as part of a required accessible route is 30 feet (9145 mm) minimum, gangways shall not be required to comply with Section 405.2.
5. Where gangways connect to transition plates, landings specified by Section 405.7 shall not be required.
6. Where gangways and transition plates connect and are required to have handrails, handrail extensions shall not be required. Where handrail extensions are provided on gangways or transition plates, the handrail extensions shall not be required to be parallel with the floor.
7. The cross slope specified in Sections 403.3 and 405.3 for gangways, transition plates, and floating piers that are part of accessible routes shall be measured in the static position.
8. Changes in level complying with Sections 303.3 and 303.4 shall be permitted on the surfaces of gangways and boat launch ramps.
9. Cleats and other boat securement devices shall not be required to comply with Section 309.3.

❖ A boat slip is a location along a pier where a boat is berthed or moored and used for embarking and disembarking (see Section 106). For purposes of these requirements, boat slips are boarding piers not associated with boat launch ramps (see Section 1103.2.2).

FIGURE C1103.2.1(a)
EXAMPLE OF GANGWAY

A gangway is a sloped walkway that links structures or land with a floating pier [see Section 106 and Commentary Figure C1103.2.1(a)]. The exceptions allow for the varying water levels caused by water influx or tides. There are no exceptions for the accessible route between fixed piers and structures or land.

Exception 1: Where an existing gangway is replaced or altered, the gangway is not required to be increased in length in order to meet the new accessible route requirements. This exception applies to boat slips and boarding piers associated with boat launch ramps.

Exception 2: Typical ramps are limited to a 30-inch (760 mm) rise between landings. Gangways do not have a limit for rise between landings. This exception applies to boat slips and boarding piers associated with boat launch ramps.

Exceptions 3 and 4: For piers with more than 25 slips, when a gangway has to have a length of greater than 80 feet (24 400 m) to connect the land to the floating pier, the gangway can have a slope steeper than the standard ramp slope of 1:12. For smaller piers, 25 slips or fewer, where a gangway has a length of greater than 30 feet, the gangway can have a slope steeper than 1:12.

Exception 5: Transition plates are sloped surfaces located at the end of a gangway that allow for the rise and fall of the water levels at this connection point. Gangways are not required to have landings where a transition plate is provided. If the slope of the transition place is greater than 1:20, there must be a landing at the end of the transition plate on the end opposite the gangway [see Commentary Figure C1103.2.1(b)].

Exception 6: Ramps with a rise of greater than 6 inches (150 mm) are required to have handrails (see Section 405.8). If both the gangway and transition plates are required to have handrails, handrail extensions are not required at the break between the gangway and transition plate. This location needs to be flexible and handrail extensions would conflict with one another. Where handrail extensions are provided at either gangways or transition plates, the handrail extensions should be designed so that they are as close to parallel to the pier as possible (see Section 505.10.1). This is not always possible due to the changes in water level. This exception applies to boat slips and boarding piers associated with boat launch ramps.

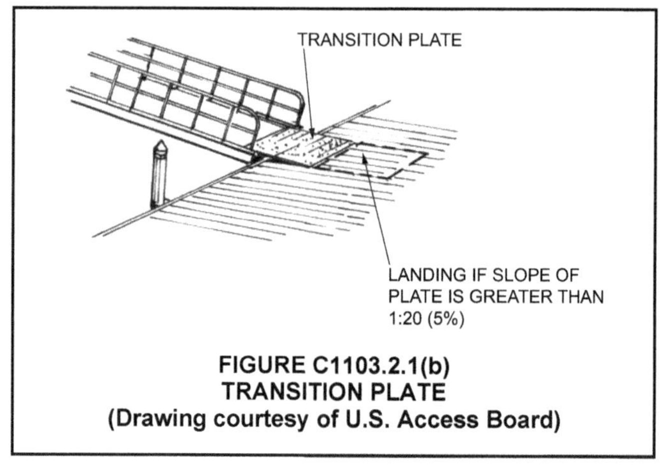

FIGURE C1103.2.1(b)
TRANSITION PLATE
(Drawing courtesy of U.S. Access Board)

Exception 7: The cross slope of gangways, transition plates and floating piers must not exceed 1:48 (see Sections 403.3 and 405.3). Once in place, these elements may lift or twist due to wind and waves. The cross slope is measured when the elements are not moving. When floating piers are grounded out due to low water conditions, the cross slope requirements are not applicable. This exception applies to boat slips and boarding piers associated with boat launch ramps.

Exception 8: Along the gangway, vertical changes in level are limited to $^1/_4$ inch (6 mm) maximum, and beveled changes in level are limited to $^1/_2$ inch (13 mm) maximum (see Sections 303.3 and 303.4). This exception applies to boat slips and boarding piers associated with boat launch ramps.

Exception 9: Cleats and other boat securement devices are not required to meet the reach ranges. These elements are typically placed on the pier surface so they are reachable from both the pier and the boat (see Section 1101.2.3). Keep in mind that a clear floor space and a route to the cleats are still required. The reach range exceptions do not apply to other controls and operating mechanisms such as water and electrical hookups.

1103.2.2 Boarding Piers at Boat Launch Ramps. An accessible route shall serve boarding piers.

EXCEPTIONS:

1. Accessible routes serving floating boarding piers shall be permitted to use Exceptions 1, 2, 5, 6, 7 and 8 in Section1103.2.1.
2. Where the total length of the gangway or series of gangways serving as part of a required accessible route is 30 feet (9145 mm) minimum, gangways shall not be required to comply with Section 405.2.
3. Where the accessible route serving a floating boarding pier or skid pier is located within a boat launch ramp, the portion of the accessible route located within the boat launch ramp shall not be required to comply with Section 405.

❖ A boarding pier is a pier where a boat is temporarily moored for purposes of embarking and disembarking (see Section 106). A boat launch ramp is a sloped surface designed for launching and retrieving trailered boats to and from a body of water (see Section 106). The accessible route is only required to and along the boarding pier, not to the boat launch ramp. Boarding piers that are not associated with boat launch ramps are addressed in Section 1103.2.1. There are no accessibility requirements for boat launch ramps, with or without an associated boarding pier.

A gangway is a sloped walkway that links structures or land with a floating pier. The exceptions allow for the varying water levels caused by water influx or tides. There are no exceptions for the accessible route between fixed piers and structures or land.

See the commentary to Section 1103.2.1 for the gangway exceptions addressed in Exception 1.

Per Exception 2, where the length of the gangway leading to the boarding pier exceeds 30 feet (9145 mm), the gangway may slope at greater than the normal ramp slope (1:12).

Where the accessible route serving a floating boarding pier is located within the boat launch ramp, the ramp requirements do not apply. For example, a chain of float on a boat launch ramp is used as the accessible boarding pier. At high tide, the entire chain floats and the board pier is accessible. At low tide, the floats rest on the boat launch ramp, matching the slope of the ramp. The boarding pier, while resting on the boat launch, is not required to comply with the ramp provisions.

1103.3 Clearances. Clearances at boat slips and on boarding piers at boat launch ramps shall comply with Section 1103.3.

❖ A boat slip is a location along a pier where a boat is berthed or moored and used for embarking and disembarking. Boarding piers are similar locations, but associated with boat launch ramps. Allowance for access to the boats from the piers is addressed in Sections 1103.3.1 and 1103.3.2. Piers that are not intended for embarking and disembarking, such as fuel piers, are not required to meet the clearance requirements.

Accessible boat slips are not required to be marked or reserved as are accessible parking spaces for cars. Ensuring that accessible slips are available for persons who may need them is an operational issue.

1103.3.1 Boat Slip Clearance. Boat slips shall provide clear pier space 60 inches (1525 mm) minimum in width that extend the full length of the boat slips. Each 10 feet (3050 mm) of linear pier edge serving boat slips shall contain at least one continuous clear opening 60 inches (1525 mm) minimum in width.

EXCEPTIONS:

1. Clear pier space shall be permitted to be 36 inches (915 mm) minimum in width and 24 inches (610 mm) maximum in length, provided that multiple 36-inch (915 mm) wide segments are separated by segments that are 60 inches (1525 mm) minimum in width and 60 inches (1525 mm) minimum in length.
2. Edge protection shall be permitted at the continuous clear openings, provided the edge protection is 4 inches (100 mm) maximum in height and 2 inches (51 mm) maximum in width.
3. In existing piers, clear pier space shall be permitted to be located perpendicular to the boat slip and shall extend the width of the boat slip, where the facility has at least one boat slip complying with Section 1103.3, and further compliance with Section 1103.3 would result in a reduction in the number of boat slips available or result in a reduction of the widths of existing slips.

❖ The number of boat slips and dispersion requirements come from the authority having jurisdiction. If boat slips are not identified or demarcated by length, typically each 40 feet (12.2 m) of boat slip edge along the perimeter of the pier will be counted as one boat slip. The pier serving the accessible boat slip must extend the full length of the slip and be at least 60 inches (1525 mm) wide. The 60-inch (1525 mm) width is the minimum necessary for persons with disabilities to have space next to their boat to use a chair lift or other transfer device for getting on and off their boat. Every 10 feet (3050 mm) of linear pier edge must have at least 5 feet (1.52 m) of opening to the boat that is not obstructed by items such as piles, fixed equipment or storage, or electrical hook ups [see Figure 1103.3.1(a) and Commentary Figure C1103.3.1(a)].

Exception 1: The 60-inch (1525 mm) width of the pier can be reduced to 36 inches (515 mm) wide for sections 24 inches (610 mm) long as long as the narrowed sections are separated by at least 60 inches (1525 mm) in length. This is similar to the idea of corridors narrowing down for short sections (see Section 403.5). This allows the pier to be 60 inches (1525 mm) wide, but still have piles or equipment on the pier within that width [see Figure 1103.3.1(b) and Commentary Figure C1103.3.1(b)].

Exception 2: Edge protection is not required along the accessible pier. However, if it is provided, it should not be more than 2 inches (51 mm) wide and 4 inches (100 mm) high [see Figure 1103.3.1(c) and Commentary Figure C1103.3.1(c)].

Exception 3: This exception is for alterations within existing piers. The facility must provide at least one accessible boat slip. However, if adding additional accessible boat slips would result in a reduction in the number of slips within the facility, there is an allowance for providing an accessible area for the boats at either the end of the piers, or perpendicular to the boat slips rather than parallel.

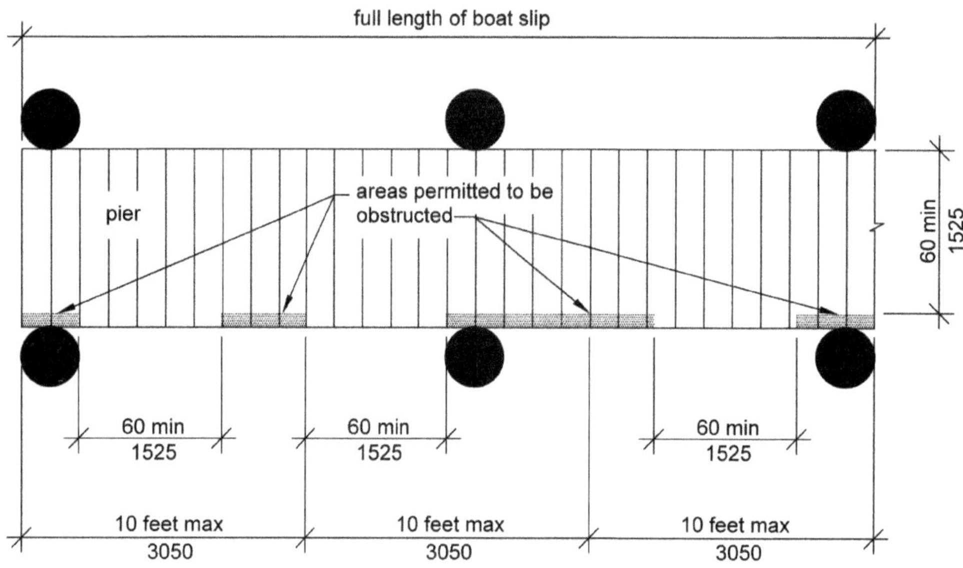

FIGURE 1103.3.1(a)
BOAT SLIP CLEARANCE

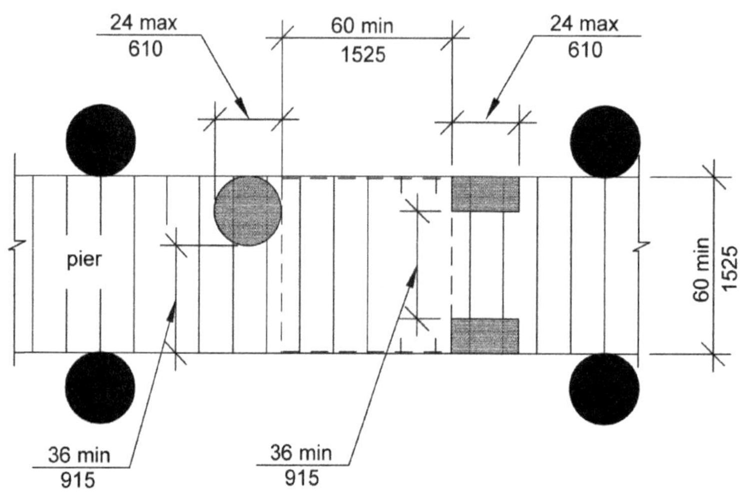

FIGURE 1103.3.1(b)
(EXCEPTION 1) CLEAR PIER SPACE REDUCTION AT BOAT SLIPS

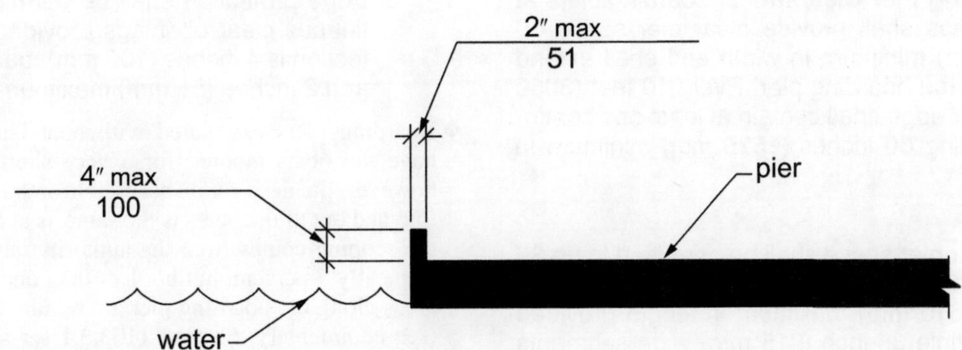

FIGURE 1103.3.1(c)
(EXCEPTION 2) EDGE PROTECTION AT BOAT SLIPS

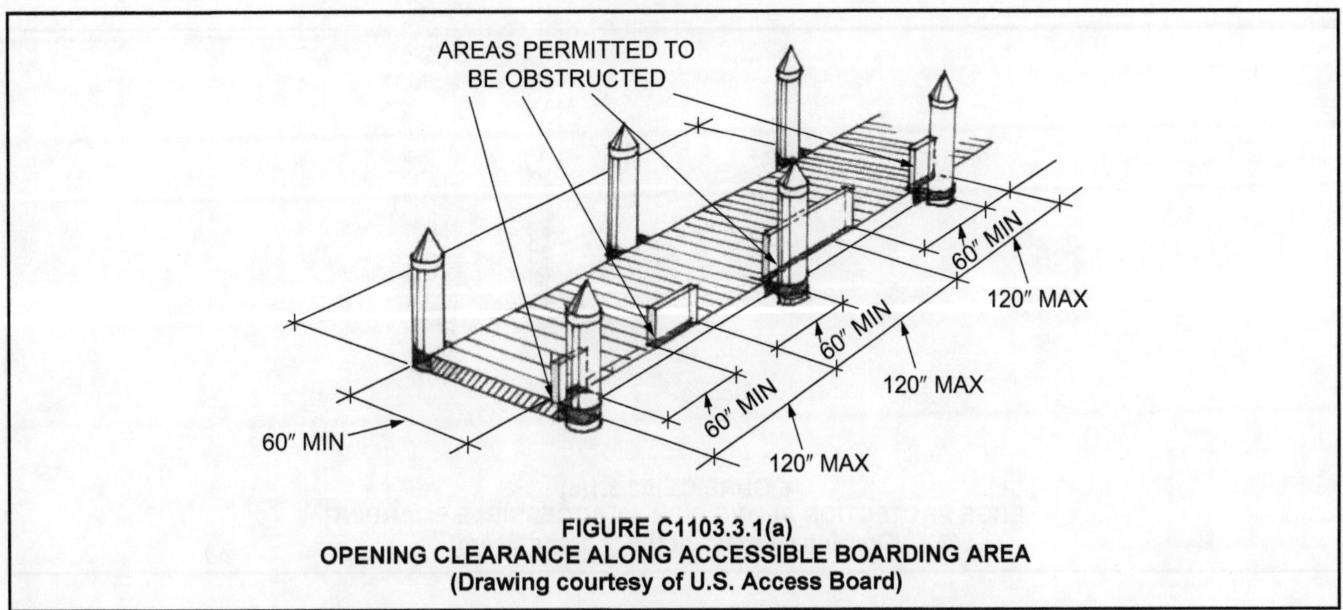

FIGURE C1103.3.1(a)
OPENING CLEARANCE ALONG ACCESSIBLE BOARDING AREA
(Drawing courtesy of U.S. Access Board)

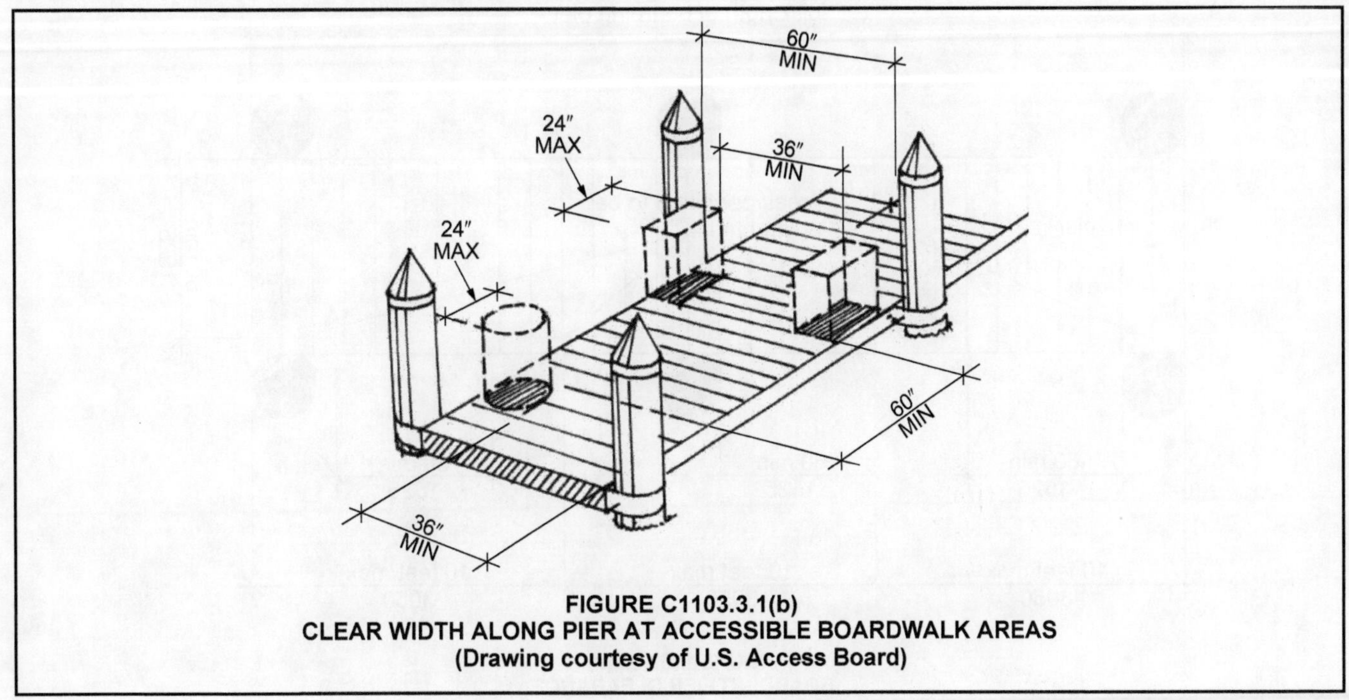

FIGURE C1103.3.1(b)
CLEAR WIDTH ALONG PIER AT ACCESSIBLE BOARDWALK AREAS
(Drawing courtesy of U.S. Access Board)

1103.3.2 Boarding Pier Clearances. Boarding piers at boat launch ramps shall provide clear pier space 60 inches (1525 mm) minimum in width and shall extend the full length of the boarding pier. Every 10 feet (3050 mm) of linear pier edge shall contain at least one continuous clear opening 60 inches (1525 mm) minimum in width.

EXCEPTIONS:

1. The clear pier space shall be permitted to be 36 inches (915 mm) minimum in width and 24 inches (610 mm) maximum in length provided that multiple 36-inch (915 mm) wide segments are separated by segments that are 60 inches (1525 mm) minimum in width and 60 inches (1525 mm) minimum in length.
2. Edge protection shall be permitted at the continuous clear openings provided the edge protection is 4 inches (100 mm) maximum in height and 2 inches (51 mm) maximum in width.

❖ Boarding piers associated with boat launch ramps only have the boats moored for a very short period of time, however, the need for an accessible area to provide a route into and out of the boats is the same as at boat slips. Again, the scoping comes from the authority having jurisdiction. Typically 5 percent, but not less than one, off all boarding areas along the boarding pier are required to be accessible (see commentary, Section 1103.3.1 for an explanation of the requirements at the embarking and disembarking areas along these piers [see Figures 1103.3.2(a), (b) and (c) and Commentary Figures C1103.3.1(a), (b) and (c)].

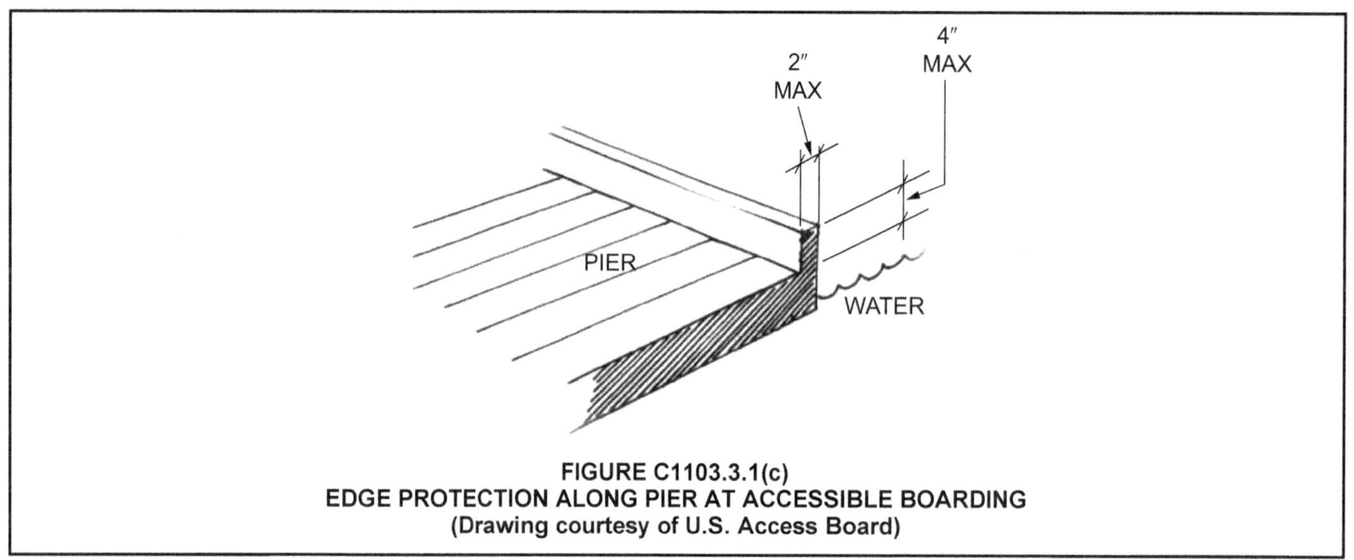

FIGURE C1103.3.1(c)
EDGE PROTECTION ALONG PIER AT ACCESSIBLE BOARDING
(Drawing courtesy of U.S. Access Board)

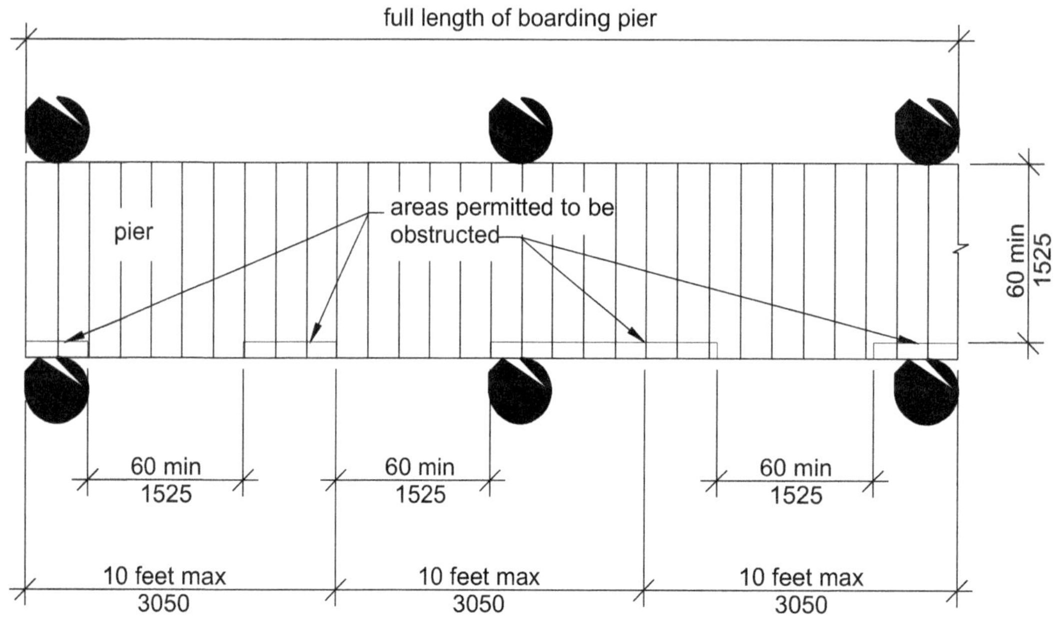

FIGURE 1103.3.2(a)
BOARDING PIER CLEARANCE

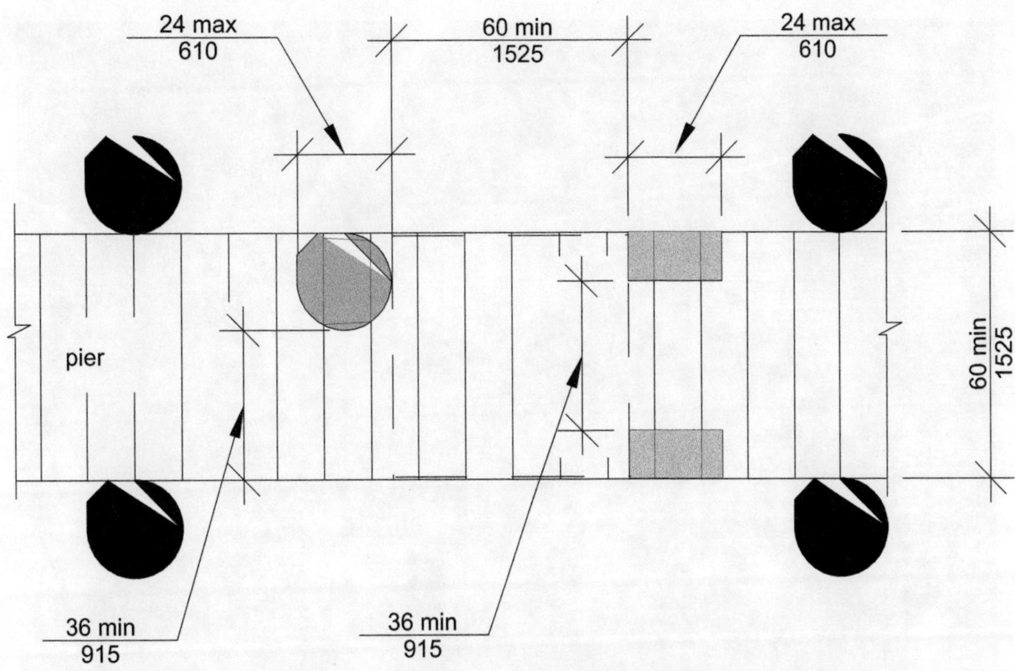

FIGURE 1103.3.2(b)
(EXCEPTION 1) CLEAR PIER SPACE REDUCTION AT BOARDING PIERS

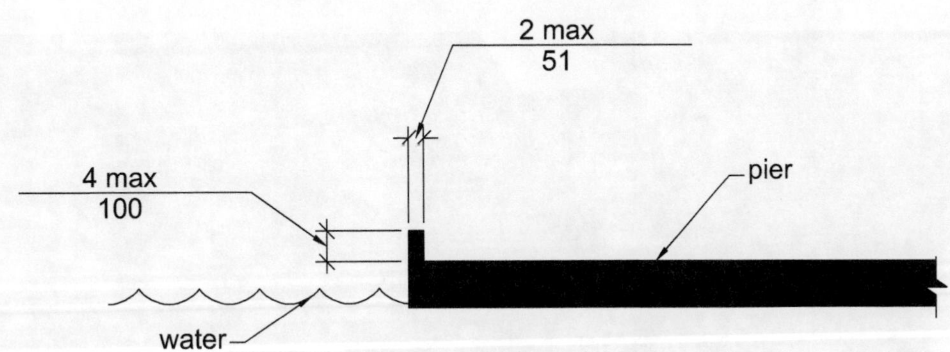

FIGURE 1103.3.2(c)
(EXCEPTION 2) EDGE PROTECTION AT BOARDING PIERS

1104 Exercise Machines and Equipment

❖ Exercise equipment is often provided in health clubs, in schools as part of the sports programs and in hotels and apartments as an amenity for guests and residents (see Commentary Figure C1104).

1104.1 Clear Floor Space. Accessible exercise machines and equipment shall have a clear floor space complying with Section 305 positioned for transfer or for use by an individual seated in a wheelchair. Clear floor spaces required at exercise machines and equipment shall be permitted to overlap.

❖ Section 1101.2.2 requires an accessible route throughout the space, with the intent of connecting the accessible exercise equipment required by the authority having jurisdiction. Typically this is one or each type of equipment provided. A clear floor space is required so that a person can transfer onto the equipment or use the equipment while still in their wheelchair; therefore, the appropriate location is dependent on the machine being considered. This clear floor space is at least 30 inches by 48 inches (760 by 1220 mm), however, where the clear floor space is obstructed on three sides by walls or the equipment itself, the clear floor space must meet the alcove provisions.

The purpose of Section 1102.4 is to reinforce that it is not the intent to require the actual equipment to be altered to be considered accessible. The exercise equipment is not required to meet operable parts requirements.

(a)

(b)

FIGURE C1104
EXAMPLE OF EXERCISE EQUIPMENT

1105 Fishing Piers and Platforms

❖ The intent of this section is to address piers or platforms that are designed specifically for the activity of fishing. Structures that were not built for fishing, even if used by people to fish, are not covered. Piers used for access to boats are addressed in Section 1103. The scoping for which fishing piers are required to be accessible is through the authority having jurisdiction. Access is required to every fishing pier or platform [see Commentary Figures C1105(a), (b) and (c)].

1105.1 Accessible Routes. Accessible routes serving fishing piers and platforms, including gangways and floating piers, shall comply with Chapter 4.

EXCEPTIONS:

1. Accessible routes serving floating fishing piers and platforms shall be permitted to use Exceptions 1, 2, 5, 6, 7 and 8 in Section 1103.2.1.
2. Where the total length of the gangway or series of gangways serving as part of a required accessible route is 30 feet (9145 mm) minimum, gangways shall not be required to comply with Section 405.2.

❖ Access to floating fishing piers and platforms typically includes some form of gangway, similar to floating piers for docks. Therefore, Exception 1 references the allowances for gangways in Section 1103.2.1. A gangway is a sloped walkway that links structures or land with a floating pier. The exceptions allow for the varying water levels caused by water influx or tides. This includes specific exceptions for some items related to maximum rise, transition plates, handrails and cross slope. There are no exceptions for the accessible route between fixed piers and structures or land ([see Commentary Figures C1105.1(a) and (b)].

Gangways that are 30 feet (9145 mm) or less in length must be designed to provide a maximum slope of 1:12, similar to a standard ramp. In accordance with Exception 2, gangways that are longer than 30 feet (9145 mm) do not have to meet any slope limitations. For example, if the change in elevation between a floating pier and the land is greater than 30 inches (760 mm), the gangway would have to be longer than 30 feet (9145 mm) to provide the accessible route. As water levels raise and lower, the slope of the gangway would also rise and fall. Designers are encouraged to have the gangway slope 1:12 or less when possible to allow for independent access. Remember that the reference to Section 1103.2, Exception 2, allows for ramps to not have required landings at a 30-inch (760 mm) rise; therefore, gangways can be any length.

1105.2 Railings. Where provided, railings, guards, or handrails shall comply with Section 1105.2.

❖ It is important to note that railings, guards and handrails are unique elements as defined by the building codes adopted by the jurisdiction. Handrails are located between 34 inches (865 mm) and 38 inches (965 mm) in height and are required along ramps and stairways. Handrails are for support while traveling along those sloped surfaces, but

(a)

(b)

(c)

FIGURE C1105(a), (b) and (c)
EXAMPLE OF FISHING PIERS

also are required as a safety measure for someone to grab in case of a fall. Guards are a minimum of 42 inches (1065 mm) in height and are the entire vertical barrier that is intended to prevent people from falling off the edge of a walking surface due to safety issues. Openings in guards are limited to 4 inches (100 mm) maximum to prevent children from falling through them. The authority having jurisdiction may require guards due to the height of the pier and/or the depth and speed of the water below the pier. Any other barrier provided along a pier or platform would be considered a railing.

It is not the intent of this section to require a guard or rail (see Commentary Figure C1105.2).

1105.2.1 Height. A minimum of 25 percent of the railings, guards, or handrails shall be 34 inches (865 mm) maximum above the ground or deck surface.

EXCEPTION: Where a guard complying with the applicable building code is provided, the guard shall not be required to comply with Section 1105.2.1.

❖ Along the portion of the pier intended for fishing, at least 25 percent of the railing must be at or below 34 inches (865 mm) high. This will allow a person sitting in a wheelchair or scooter to be able to reach over the railing to fish. If the authority having jurisdiction requires guards to be provided, the exception would allow the entire guard to be at a higher height to address safety concerns for everyone.

FIGURE C1105.1(a) and (b)
EXAMPLE OF ACCESSIBLE ROUTES TO FISHING PIERS

1105.2.1.1 Dispersion. Railings, guards, or handrails required to comply with Section 1105.2.1 shall be dispersed throughout the fishing pier or platform.

❖ The accessible fishing locations should be dispersed around the fishing pier so that anyone fishing at these locations has the same variety of options as anyone else fishing on the same pier.

1105.3 Edge Protection. Where railings, guards, or handrails complying with Section 1105.2 are provided, edge protection complying with Section 1105.3.1 or 1105.3.2 shall be provided.

❖ At accessible fishing locations with a barrier, designers have a choice of two different ways to provide edge protection. The intent is to protect a person from possibly slipping forward over the edge of the pier. If a railing or barrier is not provided, edge protection is not required. Without having to reach over the railing, it is assumed a person could sit far enough back from the edge to be safe. A designer could provide a curb at the edge if desired.

FIGURE C1105.2
EXAMPLE OF FISHING PIER WITHOUT GUARDS

1105.3.1 Curb or Barrier. Curbs or barriers shall extend 2 inches (51 mm) minimum in height above the surface of the fishing pier or platform.

❖ One option of edge protection is a curb that is at least 2 inches (51 mm) high that runs at least the length of the accessible fishing location. There is no minimum width for this curb, so it literally could be a plate along the edge of the pier. This curb could extend along the entire edge of the pier if the designer chooses.

The edge protection could be part of the barrier [see Commentary Figures C1105.3.1(a), (b) and (c)]. The intent is to not allow for the front wheel of a wheelchair to slip below the barrier and over the edge of the pier.

Note that this is different from the edge protection option along piers for boat embarking and disembarking addressed in Sections 1103.3.1 and 1103.3.2.

1105.3.2 Extended Ground or Deck Surface. The ground or deck surface shall extend 12 inches (305 mm) minimum beyond the inside face of the railing. Toe clearance shall be provided and shall be 30 inches (760 mm) minimum in width and 9 inches (230 mm) minimum in height above the ground or deck surface beyond the railing.

❖ Another option for edge protection is the extension of the pier edge in front of the rail or barrier. The edge must be at least 12 inches (305 mm) in front of the rail or barrier. This can be either an extension of the edge in front of the barrier at the accessible fishing location, or the barrier can be held back 12 inches (305 mm) from the edge of the pier. In order for a person to move forward as much as possible, the barrier has a top edge of 34 inches (865 mm) maximum and a bottom edge of 9 inches (230 mm) minimum. This toe clearance has to be at least 30 inches (760 mm) wide, but should extend the full width of the accessible fishing location (see Figure 1105.3.2 and Commentary Figure C1105.3.2).

1105.4 Clear Floor Space. At each location where there are railings, guards, or handrails complying with Section 1105.2.1, a clear floor space complying with Section 305 shall be provided. Where there are no railings, guards, or handrails, at least one clear floor space complying with Section 305 shall be provided on the fishing pier or platform.

❖ At each location where accessible railing and edge protection are provided, there must be at least one 30-inch by 48-inch (760 by 1220 mm) space for the person fishing to sit in their mobility device. Where there are no rails along the fishing pier, at least one clear floor space is still required. Good design would allow for an accessible route to be available past the spaces where wheelchairs will sit so someone does not have to move to let another person past.

1105.5 Turning Space. At least one turning space complying with Section 304.3 shall be provided on fishing piers and platforms.

❖ At least one 60-inch (1525 mm) turning circle or a T-turn must be provided on the fishing pier to allow a person to turn around. This space can overlap the accessible route and any accessible fishing locations.

(a)

(B)

(c)

FIGURE C1105.3.1(a), (b) and (c)
EXAMPLE OF RAILING AND EDGE PROTECTION AT ACCESSIBLE FISHING LOCATIONS

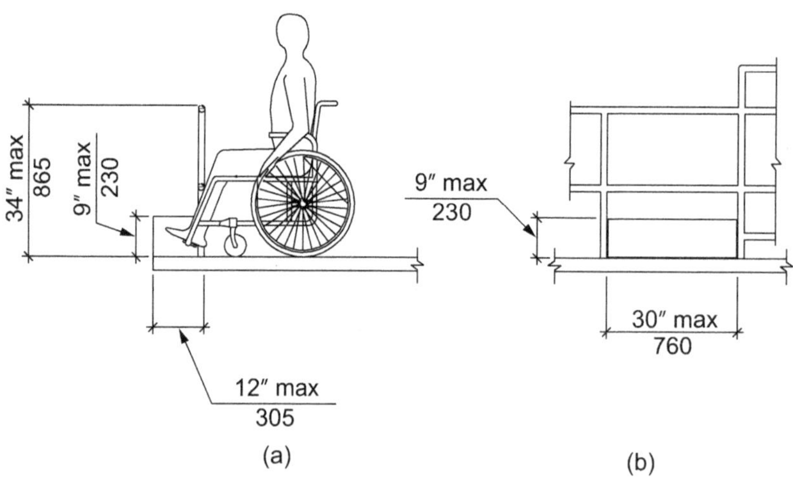

FIGURE 1105.3.2
EXTENDED GROUND OR DECK SURFACE AT FISHING PIERS AND PLATFORMS

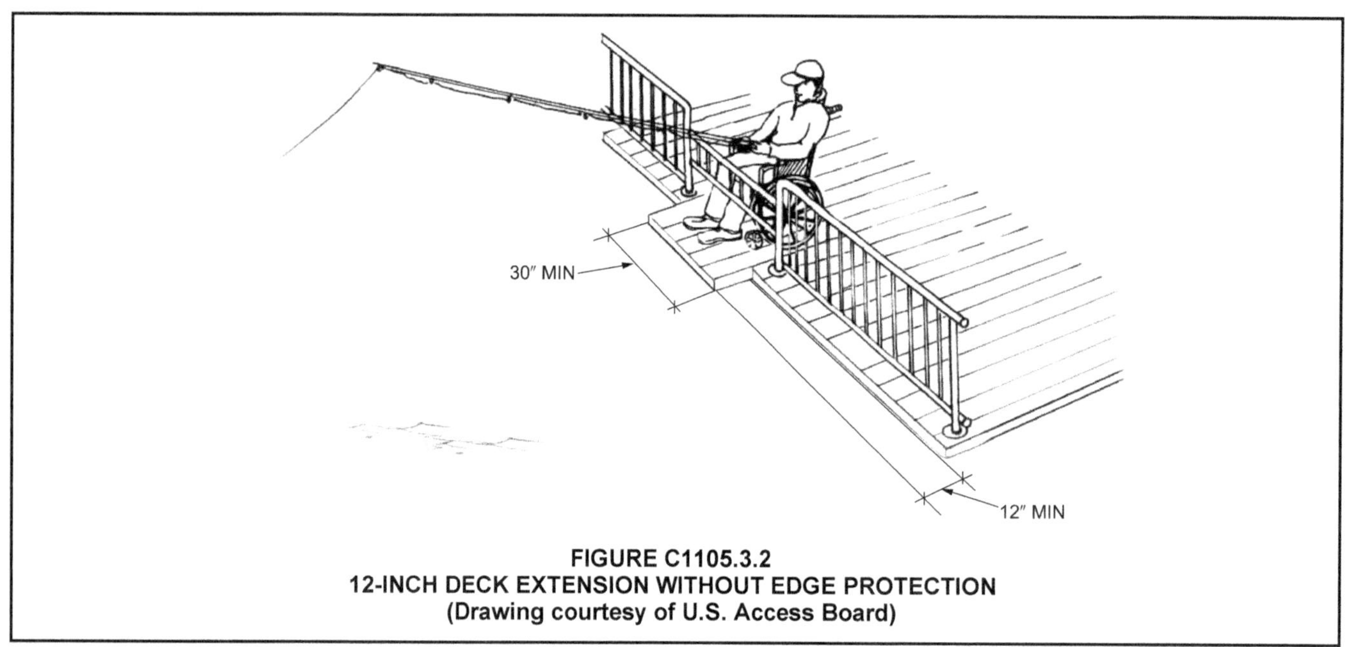

FIGURE C1105.3.2
12-INCH DECK EXTENSION WITHOUT EDGE PROTECTION
(Drawing courtesy of U.S. Access Board)

1106 Golf Facilities

❖ Golf courses are required to be accessible. This includes access from parking to the clubhouse (including the restaurant, locker rooms and bathrooms, and pro shop), driving range, golf car rental, practice putting greens as well as the greens and tees on the golf course [see Commentary Figure C1106(a)]. Because making the entire course accessible for wheelchairs would change the effective nature of the game, portions of the accessible route can be accessed by using a golf car.

The authority having jurisdiction may provide allowances for some of the elements in the scoping requirements. For example, where multiple tees are provided on the same hole, only the forward tee is required to be accessible. Another allowance example would be the percentage of teeing stations at the driving range—typically 5 percent.

Defined terms that are relevant to this section are "golf car passage" and "teeing ground" (see Section 106).

While facilities are not required to provide separate types of golf cars to provide better accessibility, the club may choose to provide them due to concerns both for its members' comfort and maintenance issues associated with standard golf cars driving on practice putting greens and the tees and green for the holes on the course [see Commentary Figure C1106(b)] for an example of one of the types available.

1106.1 General. Golf facilities shall comply with Section 1106.

❖ The provisions addressed for golf courses include an accessible route throughout the facility, including locations where a golf car can serve as the mobility device instead of the wheelchair or scooter. Where there are weather shelters out on the golf course, those shelters must accommodate the golf car.

FIGURE C1106(a)
EXAMPLE OF A GOLF COURSE

FIGURE C1106(b)
EXAMPLE OF AN ACCESSIBLE GOLF CART

1106.2 Accessible Routes. Accessible routes serving teeing grounds, practice teeing grounds, putting greens, practice putting greens, teeing stations at driving ranges, course weather shelters, golf car rental areas, bag drop areas, and course toilet rooms shall comply with Chapter 4 and shall be 48 inches (1220 mm) minimum in width. Where handrails are provided, accessible routes shall be 60 inches (1525 mm) minimum in width.

EXCEPTION: Handrails shall not be required on golf courses. Where handrails are provided on golf courses, the handrails shall not be required to comply with Section 505.

❖ The route of play for a golfer is dependent on where the ball lands, so the exact direction of large portions of the route is unpredictable. Therefore, it is assumed that most of the exterior route will be by use of a golf car. An accessible route is required to connect all elements on the site of the golf course [see Commentary Figures C1106.2(a) through (f)].

While interior routes are permitted to provide 36-inch (915 mm) clear width, any exterior routes are required to be a minimum of 48 inches (1220 mm) wide. This will allow for the golf course passage required by Section 1106.3. The exterior accessible route connects areas outside of the boundary of the course, such as the golf car rental areas, bag drop-off areas, practice putting greens and driving ranges, These are areas where an adaptable golf car may be used. Where there are handrails along the accessible route, to allow for the passage of the car, the width must increase to 60 inches (1525 mm). While this section specifically says handrails, good design would follow this same guideline wherever barriers or walls were present. The intent of the exception is to emphasize that any rails provided along exterior paths are not required to meet the handrail provisions in Section 505. However, if handrails were provided along a ramp or stairway where people may be walking, the specific criteria for handrails would apply.

1106.3 Golf Car Passages. Golf car passages shall comply with Section 1106.3.

❖ Golf car passage is a continuous passage on which a motorized golf car can operate (see Section 106). While there are no requirements for special golf cars to be provided, many courses typically do not allow standard golf cars to drive up onto the tees or greens, so they will want to provide them. Where a design uses the option of golf car passage to meet the accessible route requirements, they must provide adequate clearance.

1106.3.1 Clear Width. The clear width of golf car passages shall be 48 inches (1220 mm) minimum.

❖ Where golf cars are utilized to provide the accessible route, the width of the route must be a minimum of 48 inches (1220 mm) wide.

FIGURE C1106.2(a)
GOLF CART RENTAL

FIGURE C1106.2(b)
PRACTICE PUTTING GREEN

FIGURE C1106.2(c)
GOLF TEE

FIGURE C1106.2(d)
GOLF GREEN

FIGURE C1106.2(e)
DRIVING RANGE

FIGURE C1106.2(f)
BAG DROP AREAS

1106.3.2 Barriers. Where curbs or other constructed barriers prevent golf cars from entering a fairway, openings 60 inches (1525 mm) minimum in width shall be provided at intervals not to exceed 75 yards (69 m).

❖ The main golf car paths are often paved. If this route has some type of edge barrier, there must be a gap in the edge barrier for a minimum width of 60 inches (1525 mm) to allow for golf car access onto the course. These gaps must be provided at least once every 75 yards (68.6 m) (see Commentary Figure C1106.3.2).

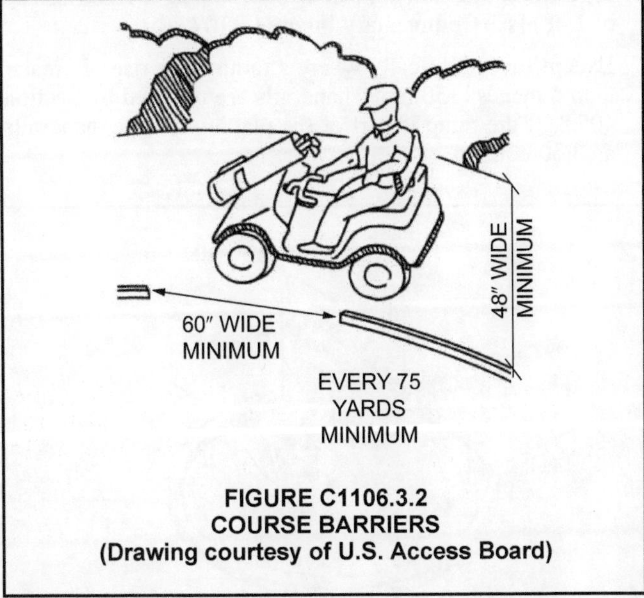

FIGURE C1106.3.2 COURSE BARRIERS (Drawing courtesy of U.S. Access Board)

1106.4 Weather Shelters. A clear floor space 60 inches (1525 mm) minimum by 96 inches (2440 mm) minimum shall be provided within weather shelters.

❖ Where weather shelters are provided along the course, in addition to be reachable by a golf car, they should have a clear space for the car inside. This will help when there are adverse weather conditions while people are out on the course (see Commentary Figure C1106.4).

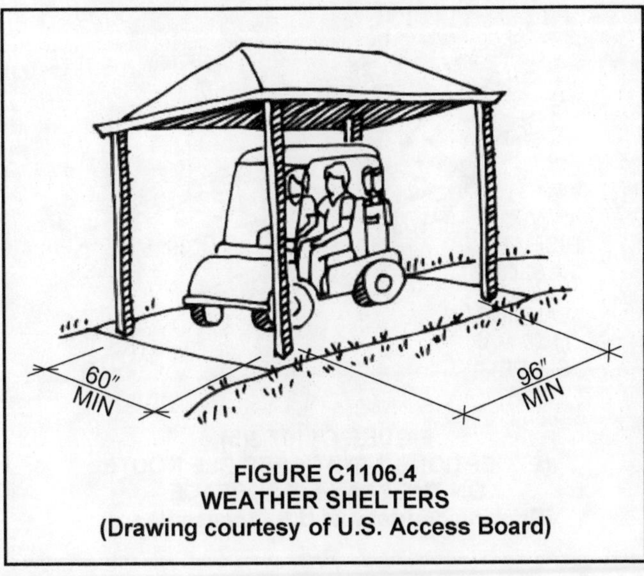

FIGURE C1106.4 WEATHER SHELTERS (Drawing courtesy of U.S. Access Board)

1107 Miniature Golf Facilities

❖ Miniature golf is a miniature version of the sport of golf. There are many other names for the game: mini golf, pee-wee golf and crazy golf. Miniature golf courses typically are 18 holes. They can be constructed inside or outside. Many have a theme for the course, and include trick holes that spill the ball out in a different area or other obstructions (see Commentary Figure C1107). The number of holes required to be accessible comes from the authority having jurisdiction. Typically this is 50 percent of the holes. The accessible holes are expected to be contiguous. For example, the accessible holes could be 1 through 5 and then 15 through 18, however, the route to the accessible holes should not require the person using the accessible route to travel through other parts of the course to play the game.

FIGURE C1107(a) and (b) EXAMPLES OF MINIATURE GOLF

1107.1 General. Miniature golf facilities shall comply with Section 1107.

❖ Accessible routes are required to the accessible holes. There are different criteria based on whether the route is located on the holes, or adjacent to the holes. When the route is adjacent, you must be able to reach the golf ball with the club from the accessible route. Each accessible hole must have an appropriate teeing area.

1107.2 Accessible Routes. Accessible routes serving holes on miniature golf courses shall comply with Chapter 4.

EXCEPTION: Accessible routes located on playing surfaces of miniature golf holes shall be permitted to comply with the following:

1. Playing surfaces shall not be required to comply with Section 302.2.
2. Where accessible routes intersect playing surfaces of holes, a curb that is 1 inch (25 mm) maximum in height and 32 inches (815 mm) minimum in width shall be permitted.
3. A slope of 1:4 maximum shall be permitted for a rise of 4 inches (100 mm) maximum.
4. Ramp landing slopes specified by Section 405.7.1 shall be permitted to be 1:20 maximum.
5. Ramp landing length specified by Section 405.7.3 shall be permitted to be 48 inches (1220 mm) minimum.
6. Ramp landing size at a change in direction specified by Section 405.7.4 shall be permitted to be 48 inches (1220 mm) minimum by 60 inches (1525 mm) minimum.
7. Handrails shall not be required on holes. Where handrails are provided on holes, the handrails shall not be required to comply with Section 505.

❖ The accessible route through the course can be either on the playing surface or adjacent to the playing surface. The accessible route must meet the same provisions as a typical accessible route for clear width, surface and slope. The accessible route must be within 36 inches (915 mm) of any area where the ball can come to rest (see Section 1107.3.2). There are exceptions for when the accessible route is along the playing surface.

Exception 1: The playing surface must be stable and firm, however, if carpet is used for the playing surface, the pile height requirements are not applicable.

Exception 2: Typically in a miniature golf course the hole is surrounded by a curb to keep the ball within the playing surface. Where the accessible route leaves one hole to move to the next, a 32-inch (815 mm) clear width opening is required, however, a 1-inch (25 mm) curb is permitted at this location versus the typical $^1/_2$-inch (13 mm) maximum threshold height. The intent is to allow the accessible route to move through the hole without doubling back, and at the same time contain the ball within the hole [see Commentary Figure C1107.2(a)].

Exception 3: Rises of less than 4 inches (100 mm) can be sloped up to 1:4 instead of the standard 1:12 [see Commentary Figure C1107.2(b)].

Exceptions 4, 5 and 6: Landings must still be provided at the top and bottom of ramp slopes. However, the ramp landing size is permitted to be reduced. Where the landing does not require a change in direction, the landing can be 36 inches (915 mm) wide and 48 inches (1220 mm) long (instead of 60 inches). Where the landing is at a change in direction, the landing can be 48 inches by 60 inches (1220 by 1525 mm) (instead of 60 inches by 60 inches) (1525 by 1525 mm). The landing can also be sloped at 1:20 (instead of 1:48) [see Commentary Figure C1107.2(b)].

Exception 7: Typically where a ramp has a rise of greater than 6 inches (150 mm), handrails are required by Section 405.8. If the ramp is part of the playing surface, handrails are not required.

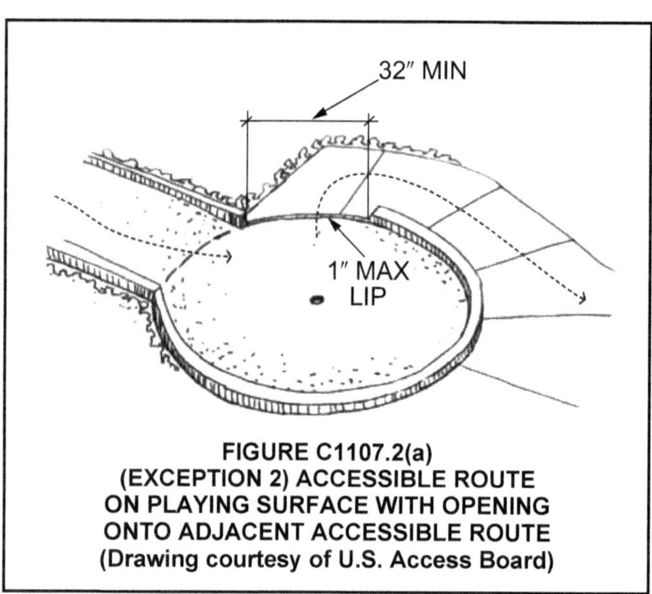

FIGURE C1107.2(a)
(EXCEPTION 2) ACCESSIBLE ROUTE ON PLAYING SURFACE WITH OPENING ONTO ADJACENT ACCESSIBLE ROUTE
(Drawing courtesy of U.S. Access Board)

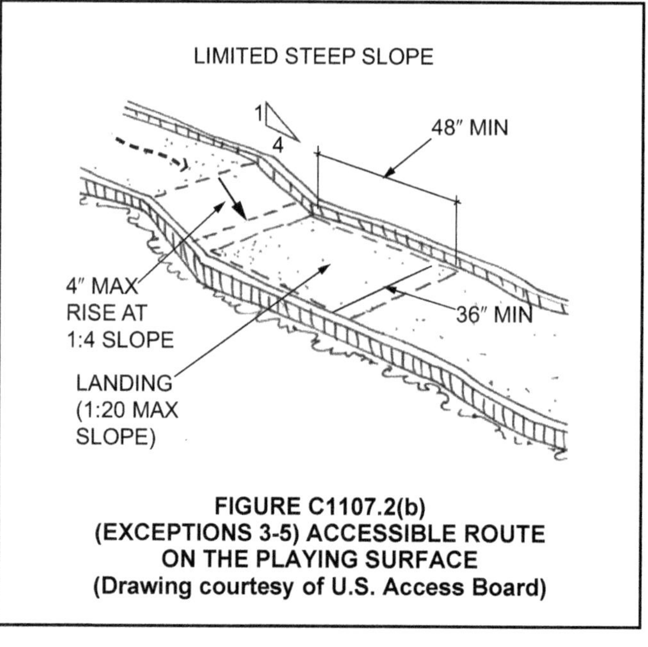

FIGURE C1107.2(b)
(EXCEPTIONS 3-5) ACCESSIBLE ROUTE ON THE PLAYING SURFACE
(Drawing courtesy of U.S. Access Board)

1107.3 Miniature Golf Holes. Miniature golf holes shall comply with Section 1107.3.

❖ For a person to be able to effectively play each hole, in addition to the route requirements, there are special concerns for the start of the hole (see Section 1107.3.1) and that wherever the ball may stop, it should be within reach of the accessible route (see Section 1107.3.1).

1107.3.1 Start of Play. A clear floor space 48 inches (1220 mm) minimum by 60 inches (1525 mm) minimum with slopes not steeper than 1:48 shall be provided at the start of play.

❖ A level playing surface is required at the start of each hole. The minimum size is 48 inches by 60 inches (1220 by 1525 mm). The orientation in relation to the start of the hole can be either direction. The idea is that a person would not have to start the hole on a sloped surface [see Commentary Figures C1107.3.1(a) and C1107.3.1(b)].

1107.3.2 Golf Club Reach Range Area. All areas within holes where golf balls rest shall be within 36 inches (915 mm) maximum of a clear floor space 36 inches (915 mm) minimum in width and 48 inches (1220 mm) minimum in length having a running slope not steeper than 1:20. The clear floor space shall be served by an accessible route.

❖ With the club in hand, a person's maximum reach would be 36 inches (915 mm) away from the accessible route. A level 36-inch by 48-inch (915 by 1220 mm) clear floor space must be provided adjacent to any location where the ball may come to rest on the hole [see Figure 1107.3.2 and Commentary Figures C1107.3.2(a) and C1107.3.2(b)].

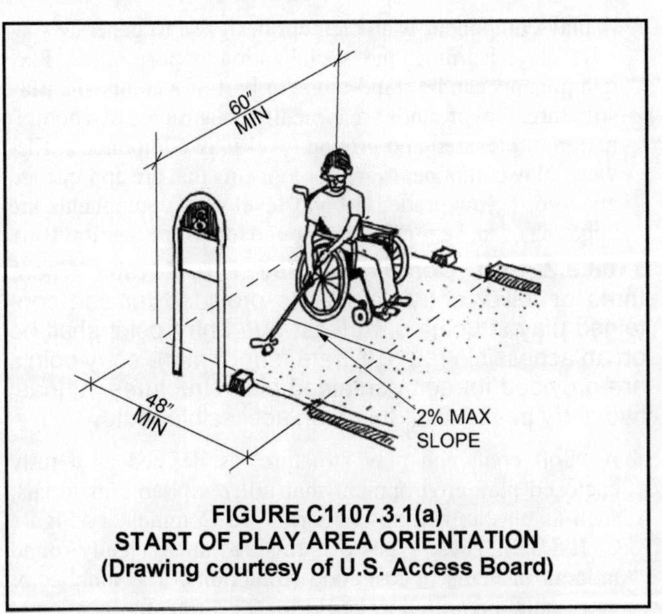

FIGURE C1107.3.1(a)
START OF PLAY AREA ORIENTATION
(Drawing courtesy of U.S. Access Board)

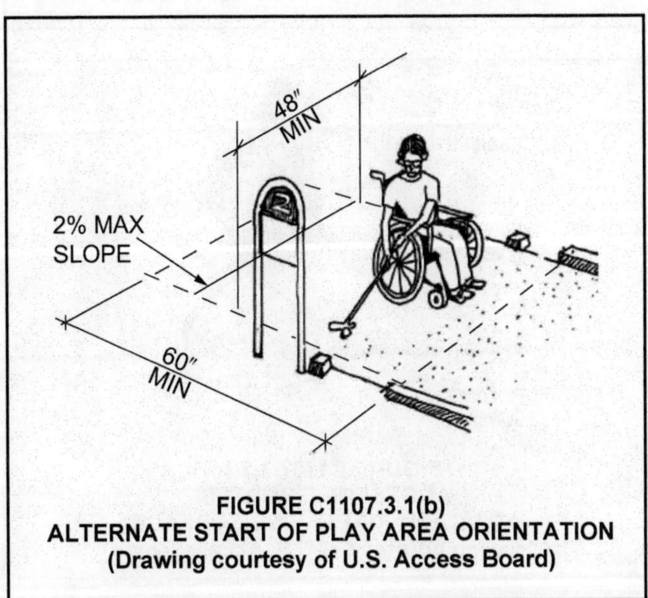

FIGURE C1107.3.1(b)
ALTERNATE START OF PLAY AREA ORIENTATION
(Drawing courtesy of U.S. Access Board)

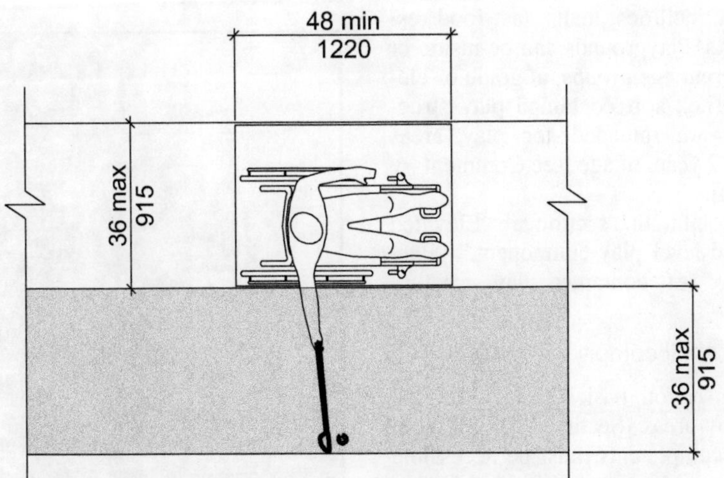

Note: Running Slope of Clear Floor or Ground Space Not Steeper Than 1:20

FIGURE 1107.3.2
GOLF CLUB REACH RANGE AREA

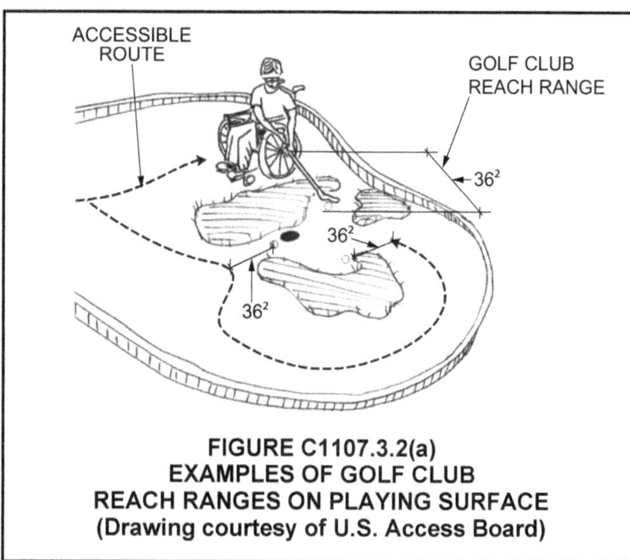

FIGURE C1107.3.2(a)
EXAMPLES OF GOLF CLUB
REACH RANGES ON PLAYING SURFACE
(Drawing courtesy of U.S. Access Board)

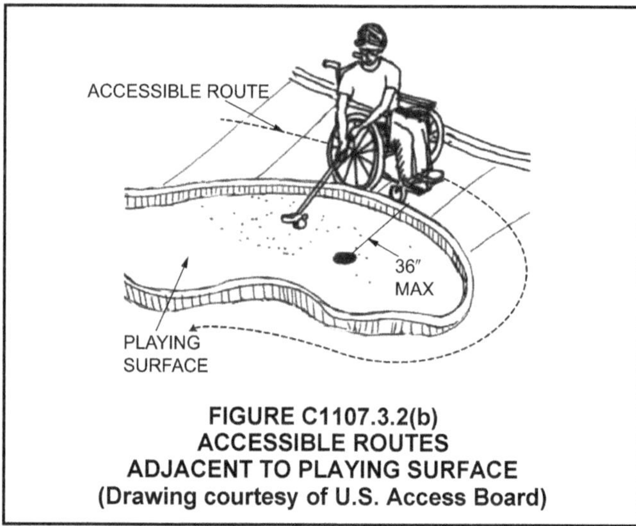

FIGURE C1107.3.2(b)
ACCESSIBLE ROUTES
ADJACENT TO PLAYING SURFACE
(Drawing courtesy of U.S. Access Board)

1108 Play Areas

❖ Playgrounds are provided in a variety of locations, such as at parks, schools, day care facilities, malls, fast food restaurants, hotels and airports. Playgrounds can be inside or outside; designed for different age groups; at grade or elevated; or different types (i.e., soft contained play structures). These provisions are intended for play areas designed for children over 2 years of age [see Commentary Figure 1108(a) through (d)].

Definitions that are relevant to this section are "Elevated play component," "Ground level play component," "Play area," "Play component," "Soft contained play structure and use zone."

1108.1 Scope. Play areas shall comply with 1108.

❖ The organization of this section basically includes the accessible route to the play areas (Section 1108.2); what number and type of play components must be accessible (Section 1108.3) and accessible routes within the play areas (Section 1108.4).

1108.2 Accessible Routes for Play Areas. Play areas shall provide accessible routes in accordance with Section 1108.2. Accessible routes serving play areas shall comply with Chapter 4 except as modified by Section 1108.4.

❖ A "Play area" is defined as the portion of a site containing play components designed for children (see Section 106). An accessible route is required to connect the arrival points to the playground, and then to provide access to a variety of play options.

For purposes of these requirements, ramps, transfer systems, steps, decks and roofs are not play components.

1108.2.1 Ground Level and Elevated Play Components. At least one accessible route shall be provided within the play area. The accessible route shall connect ground level play components required to comply with Section 1108.3.2.1 and elevated play components required to comply with Section 1108.3.2.2, including entry and exit points of the play components.

❖ A play component is an element designed to generate specific play, learning and socialization opportunities. Play components can be stand-alone or part of a composite play structure. Playgrounds are typically constructed of a combination of elevated and ground level play components. Elevated play components are components that are approached above or below grade. Ground level play components are approached and exited at the ground level (see Section 106).

1108.2.2 Soft Contained Play Structures. Where three or fewer entry points are provided for soft contained play structures, at least one entry point shall be on an accessible route. Where four or more entry points are provided for soft contained play structures, at least two entry points shall be on an accessible route.

❖ A "Soft contained play structure" is defined as a fully enclosed play environment that utilizes pliable materials, such as plastic, netting or fabric (see Commentary Figure C1108.2.2). These types of structures are typically found indoors in malls or fast food restaurants. The number of entry points required to be set up for a transfer location is based on the number of entrances provided to the play structure itself.

FIGURE C1108.2.2
SOFT CONTAINED PLAY STRUCTURES

1108.3 Age Groups. Play areas for children ages 2 and over shall comply with Section 1108.3. Where separate play areas are provided within a site for specific age groups, each play area shall comply with Section 1108.3.

EXCEPTIONS:

1. Play areas located in family child care facilities where the proprietor actually resides shall not be required to comply with Section 1108.3.
2. In existing play areas, where play components are relocated for the purposes of creating safe use zones and the ground surface is not altered or extended for more than one use zone, the play area shall not be required to comply with Section 1108.3.
3. Amusement attractions shall not be required to comply with Section 1108.3.
4. Where play components are altered and the ground surface is not altered, the ground surface shall not be required to comply with Section 1108.4.1.6 unless required by the authority having jurisdiction.

❖ Play areas specifically designed for infants and toddlers are not required to comply with these provisions. Sometimes separate play areas are provided for different age groups in an attempt to reduce the risk of injury. Where there are play areas specifically designed for different age groups, each play area shall be accessible.

Exception 1: These provisions are not applicable to day care facilities provided within someone's private home.

Exceptions 2 and 4: When a playground has limited movement of equipment, these provisions for an accessible route and ground surfaces are not applicable.

Exception 3: Amusement attractions are found in amusement or theme parks and include items such as fun houses, barrels and other attractions without seats (see Section 1106). These elements are not required to comply with the playground equipment provisions.

1108.3.1 Additions. Where play areas are designed and constructed in phases, the requirements of Section 1108.3 shall apply to each successive addition so that when the addition is completed, the entire play area complies with all the applicable requirements of Section 1108.3.

❖ When play areas are constructed in phases, they must continue to meet the accessibility provisions throughout construction.

(a) (b) (c) (d)

FIGURE C1108
EXAMPLES OF PLAYGROUNDS

1108.3.2 Play Components. Where provided, play components shall comply with Section 1108.3.2.

❖ The number of ground level and elevated play components required to be accessible are indicated in Sections 1108.3.2.1 and 1108.3.2.2.

1108.3.2.1 Ground Level Play Components. Ground level play components shall be provided in the number and types required by Section 1108.3.2.1. Ground level play components that are provided to comply with Section 1108.3.2.1.1 shall be permitted to satisfy the additional number required by Section 1108.3.2.1.2 if the minimum required types of play components are satisfied. Where two or more required ground level play components are provided, they shall be dispersed throughout the play area and integrated with other play components.

❖ Ground level play components are approached and exited at ground levels. Examples are swings, spring riders, basketball hoops, and water/sand tables (see Commentary Figure C1108.3.2.1). There are two requirements addressing how many ground level play components must be on an accessible route: one of each type and based on the number of elevated play components required. The accessible elements must be integrated with the other play components; there should not be a separate accessible playground.

If more than one child can play on a component at one time, that element is still considered one play component. For example, a set of swings is one play component.

1108.3.2.1.1 Minimum Number and Types. Where ground level play components are provided, at least one of each type shall be on an accessible route and shall comply with Section 1108.4.3.

❖ At least one of each type of ground level play component must be accessible. A different type is based on the general experience provided by the component. Examples are rocking, swinging, climbing, spinning or sliding. For example, while a straight slide provides a different experience from a spiral slide, the primary experience of sliding is the same, so the two slides would be considered one type.

1108.3.2.1.2 Additional Number and Types. Where elevated play components are provided, ground level play components shall be provided in accordance with Table 1108.3.2.1.2 and shall comply with Section 1108.4.3.

EXCEPTION: If at least 50 percent of the elevated play components are connected by a ramp and at least 3 of the elevated play components connected by the ramp are different types of play components, the play area shall not be required to comply with Section 1108.3.2.1.2.

❖ Where a combination of ground level and elevated play components is provided in accordance with Table 1108.3.2.1.2, the number of ground level play components must comply with both the type of (Section 1108.3.2.1.1) and the number of components in the table. The intent is to provide a variety of play options for children who choose to stay with their mobility devices and not transfer to the elevated play areas.

If ramps provide access to at least 50 percent of the elevated play components and the elevated play components include at least three different types, the additional ground level play components are not required. This is due to the fact that a person using a mobility device can participate in the elevated areas without transferring out of their mobility device.

1108.3.2.2 Elevated Play Components. Where elevated play components are provided, at least 50 percent shall be on an accessible route and shall comply with Section 1108.4.3.

❖ Elevated play components are play components that are approached above or below grade and are part of a composite play structure. An item that is attached to a composite play structure and can be accessed from either the play structure or the ground is considered an elevated play component (see Commentary Figure C1108.3.2.2). The climbers attached to the elevated structure are considered an elevated play component since they can be approached from ground level or above grade from a platform on the play structure.

TABLE 1108.3.2.1.2—NUMBER AND TYPES OF GROUND LEVEL PLAY COMPONENTS REQUIRED TO BE ON ACCESSIBLE ROUTES

Number of Elevated Play Components Provided	Minimum Number of Ground Level Play Components Required to be on an Accessible Route	Minimum Number of Different Types of Ground Level Play Components Required to be on an Accessible Route
1	Not applicable	Not applicable
2 to 4	1	1
5 to 7	2	2
8 to 10	3	3
11 to 13	4	3
14 to 16	5	3
17 to 19	6	3
22 to 22	7	4
23 to 25	8	4
26 and over	8, plus 1 for each additional 3, or fraction thereof, over 25	5

(a) (b) (c) (d) (e) (f) (g) (h)

FIGURE C1108.3.2.1
EXAMPLES OF GROUND LEVEL PLAY COMPONENTS

(a) (b) (c) (d)

FIGURE C1108.3.2.2
EXAMPLES OF ELEVATED PLAY COMPONENTS

1108.4 Accessible Routes Within Play areas. Play areas shall comply with Section 1108.4.

❖ Once the number of accessible play components is identified (see Section 1108.3.2), those elements must be connected by an accessible route. Routes can be on the ground or elevated. Sections 1108.4.1.1 through 1108.4.1.3 address where transfer devices can be used along accessible routes. Sections 1108.4.1.4 through 1108.4.1.6 address clear width, ramps and ground surfaces along the accessible route. Transfer systems are addressed in Section 1108.4.2 and access to individual play components is covered in Section 1108.4.3.

1108.4.1 Accessible Routes. Accessible routes serving play areas shall comply with Chapter 4 and Section 1108.4.1 and shall be permitted to use the exceptions in Sections 1108.4.1.1 through 1108.4.1.3. Where accessible routes serve ground level play components, the vertical clearance shall be 80 inches (2030 mm) minimum in height.

❖ The general requirements for accessible routes in Chapter 4 must be followed for the accessible routes that connect accessible play components. The 80-inch (2030 mm) headroom height is consistent with protruding object limitations in Section 307.4.

1108.4.1.1 Ground Level and Elevated Play Components. Accessible routes serving ground level play components and elevated play components shall be permitted to use the exceptions in Section 1108.4.1.1.

EXCEPTIONS:

1. Transfer systems complying with Section 1108.4.2 shall be permitted to connect elevated play components except where 20 or more elevated play components are provided no more

than 25 percent of the elevated play components shall be permitted to be connected by transfer systems.

2. Where transfer systems are provided, an elevated play component shall be permitted to connect to another elevated play component as part of an accessible route.

❖ In accordance with Section 1108.3.2.2, at least 50 percent of the elevated play components must be accessible and on an accessible route.

Where play areas have 20 or more elevated components, at least 75 percent of the elevated play components must be accessed by a ramp. A transfer system or ramps may connect the other elevated components. Where play areas have less than 20 components, transfer systems are permitted to provide the accessible route to all the play components.

Transfer systems may be utilized to provide access to more than one play component. Providing variety through elevated play structures benefits all children. For example, providing a crawling tube makes getting there part of the fun and provides an innovative accessible route.

1108.4.1.2 Soft Contained Play Structures. Accessible routes serving soft contained play structures shall be permitted to use the exception in Section 1108.4.1.2.

EXCEPTION: Transfer systems complying with Section 1108.4.2 shall be permitted to be used as part of an accessible route.

❖ Section 1108.2.2 requires a minimum number of accessible entry points for a soft contained play structure. Access into and through the play components can be by either a standard accessible route or via a transfer system.

1108.4.1.3 Water Play Components. Accessible routes serving water play components shall be permitted to use the exceptions in Section 1108.4.1.3.

EXCEPTIONS:

1. Where the surface of the accessible route, clear floor spaces, or turning spaces serving water play components is submerged, complying with Sections 302, 403.3, 405.2, 405.3, and 1108.4.1.6 shall not be required.
2. Transfer systems complying with Section 1108.4.2 shall be permitted to connect elevated play components in water.

❖ Play components that are part of a water park or playground are required to be accessible in the same way as a regular playground. This would include play components within a pool or a sprinkler park (see Commentary Figure C1108.4.1.3). A transfer system can be used as part of the accessible route.

Where access to the accessible play components is under water, that portion of the route is exempted from the standard accessible route requirements for floor surface and slope.

1108.4.1.4 Clear Width. Accessible routes connecting play components shall provide a clear width complying with Section 1108.4.1.4.

❖ The clear width of the accessible route is different for the ground level and elevated portions of the route within the play area. Ground level requirements are greater than the typical width requirements in Section 403.5.

1108.4.1.4.1 Ground Level. At ground level, the clear width of accessible routes shall be 60 inches (1525 mm) minimum.

EXCEPTIONS:

1. In play areas less than 1000 square feet (93 m^2), the clear width of accessible routes shall be permitted to be 44 inches (1120 mm) minimum, if at least one turning space complying with Section 304.3 is provided where the restricted accessible route exceeds 30 feet (9145 mm) in length.
2. The clear width of accessible routes shall be permitted to be 36 inches (915 mm) minimum for a distance of 60 inches (1525 mm) maxi-

(a)

(b)

FIGURE C1108.4.1.3
EXAMPLES OF WATER PLAY COMPONENTS

mum provided that multiple reduced width segments are separated by segments that are 60 inches (1525 mm) minimum in width and 60 inches (1525 mm) minimum in length.

❖ A ground level accessible route must be at least 60 inches (1525 mm) wide. In accordance with Exception 2, this can be reduced to 36 inches (915 mm) wide for a distance of 60 inches (1525 mm). The narrow areas must be at least 60 inches (1525 mm) apart [see Commentary Figure C1108.4.1.4.1(b)].

Exception 1 allows for a reduction in smaller play areas—those with less than 1000 square feet (93 m^2) in area. The accessible route can be 44 inches (1120 mm) wide, provided that there is space for either a turning circle or T-turn at least once every 30 feet (760 mm) [see Commentary Figure C1108.4.1.4.1(a)].

1108.4.1.4.2 Elevated. The clear width of accessible routes connecting elevated play components shall be 36 inches (915 mm) minimum.

EXCEPTIONS:

1. The clear width of accessible routes connecting elevated play components shall be permitted to be reduced to 32 inches (815 mm) minimum for a distance of 24 inches (610 mm) maximum provided that reduced width segments are separated by segments that are 48 inches (1220 mm) minimum in length and 36 inches (915 mm) minimum in width.
2. The clear width of transfer systems connecting elevated play components shall be permitted to be 24 inches (610 mm) minimum.

❖ Where the accessible route is elevated, the minimum width is 36 inches (915 mm). The allowance in Exception 1 for narrowing down to 32 inches (815 mm) is the same as that covered in Section 403.5 (see Commentary Figure C1108.4.1.4.2). Remember that the 80-inch (2030 mm) head clearance is not required for elevated accessible routes (Section 1108.4.1). The intent is to allow for climbing tubes or roofs for sun shelter.

Exception 2 allows transfer steps of platforms to provide a maximum width of 24 inches (610 mm). This is consistent with the specific criteria for transfer systems in Section 1108.4.2.

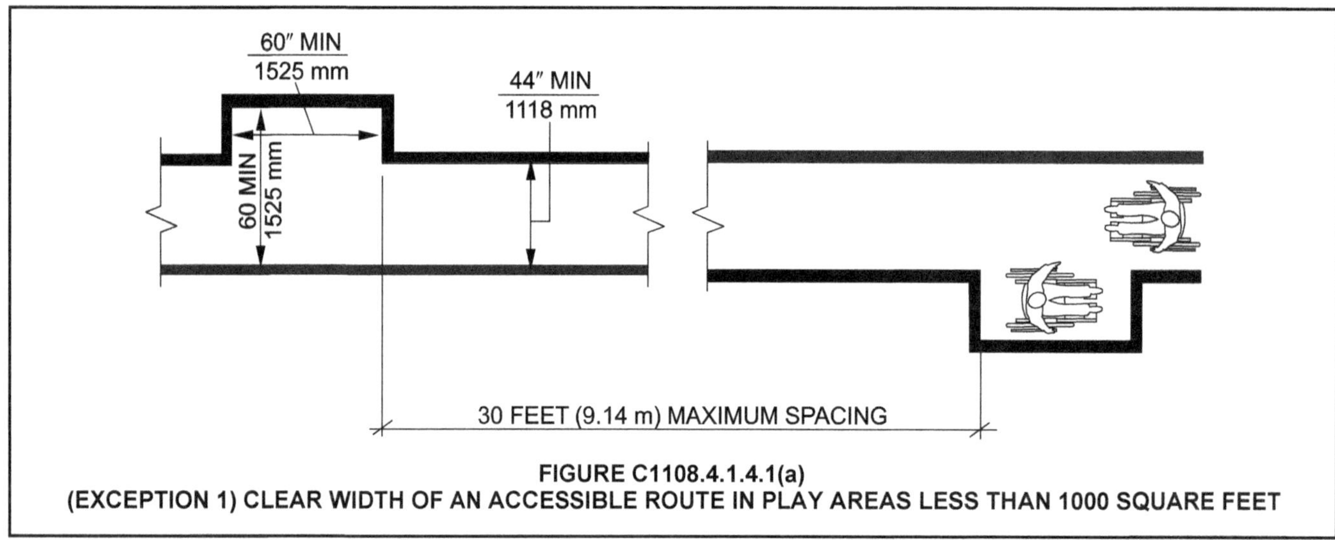

FIGURE C1108.4.1.4.1(a)
(EXCEPTION 1) CLEAR WIDTH OF AN ACCESSIBLE ROUTE IN PLAY AREAS LESS THAN 1000 SQUARE FEET

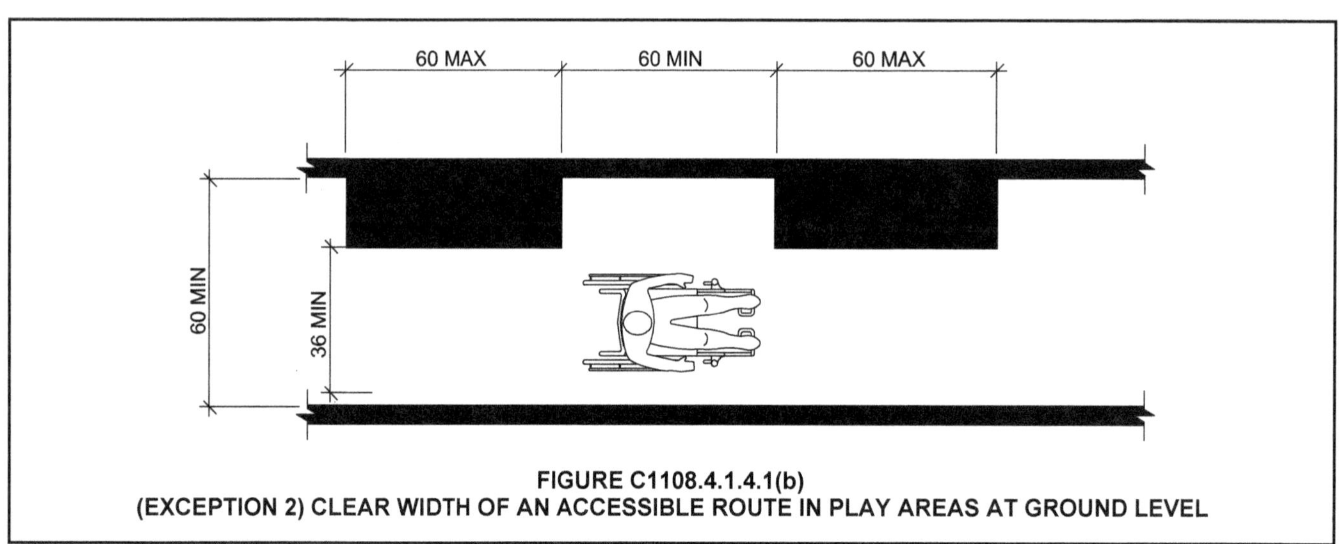

FIGURE C1108.4.1.4.1(b)
(EXCEPTION 2) CLEAR WIDTH OF AN ACCESSIBLE ROUTE IN PLAY AREAS AT GROUND LEVEL

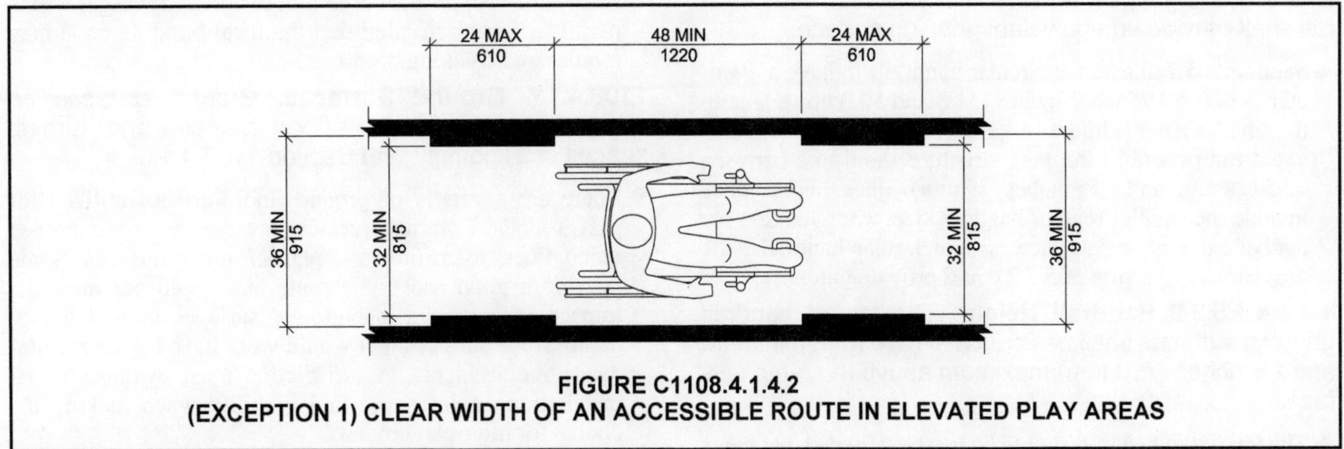

FIGURE C1108.4.1.4.2
(EXCEPTION 1) CLEAR WIDTH OF AN ACCESSIBLE ROUTE IN ELEVATED PLAY AREAS

1108.4.1.5 Ramps. Within play areas, ramps connecting ground level play components and ramps connecting elevated play components shall comply with Section 1108.4.1.5.

❖ Section 1108.4.1.1 requires play structures with 20 or more components to have at least 25 percent of components accessible via a ramp instead of a transfer system. Ramps that are part of that elevated route through a play structure and any ramps within the play area must comply with slope, rise and handrails requirements in this section. Where ramps are utilized on the ground level that provide access to the playground area, they should comply with the provisions in Sections 405. See Commentary Figure C1108.4.1.5 for examples of ramps providing access to and within play structures.

Since some children either prefer to remain in their transport devices or are unable to transfer from their devices easily, ramp access is preferred over the transfer system.

1108.4.1.5.1 Ground Level. Ramp runs connecting ground level play components shall have a running slope not steeper than 1:16.

❖ Ramps are defined as having a slope of greater than 1:20. Where they are part of an accessible route connecting ground level components, the maximum running slope is 1:16. This is less than the standard 1:12 maximum in Section 405.2. Ramps connecting elevated play components can use 1:12 maximum slope, but good design would suggest following the 1:16 maximum within the play structure as well.

1108.4.1.5.2 Elevated. The rise for any ramp run connecting elevated play components shall be 12 inches (305 mm) maximum.

❖ Standard ramp runs allow for a 30-inch (760 mm) maximum rise between landings (Section 405.6). Where elevated ramps are used within a play structure, the maximum rise between landings is 12 inches (305 mm) maximum. Remember that all ramps are required to have landings at the top and bottom in accordance with Section 405.7. Clear floor spaces required at accessible play components (see Section 1108.4.3.2) are permitted to overlap ramp landings.

1108.4.1.5.3 Handrails. Where required on ramps serving play components, the handrails shall comply with Section 505 except as modified by Section 1108.4.1.5.3.

EXCEPTIONS:

1. Handrails shall not be required on ramps located within ground level use zones.
2. Handrail extensions shall not be required.

❖ Handrails are typically required on both sides of ramps where there is a rise of more than 6 inches (150 mm) (Sections 405.8 and 505.2). To allow children to pull themselves around within the play structure, good design would provide handrails on both sides of all elevated ramps. The continuity, clearance, gripping surface, surface and fitting requirements in Section 505 are all applicable. There are special allowances for the handrail cross section and height due to the area being designed for children. The local building code may also require guards for safety reasons. Typically guards are required where there is more than a 30-inch (760 mm) drop-off adjacent to a walking surface. Safety concerns would also dictate edge protection by either a curb or bottom rail.

Use zones are defined as the ground level area beneath and immediately adjacent to the play structure or equipment. There are areas where there is free circulation around the equipment, and the areas where a child might land when falling from or exiting the play equipment. In accordance with Exception 1, if there are ramps on the ground level within this area, handrails are not required. There is a concern that someone could fall and land on the handrails and possibly cause themselves further injury.

Handrail extensions are not required on the ramps within the elevated play structure. Exception 2 is intended to recognize that extensions may obstruct access to the attached play components. To allow children to pull themselves off the sloped surface of the ramp and onto the level landings, providing handrail extensions where there is room would be permitted.

1108.4.1.5.3.1 Handrail Gripping Surfaces. Handrail gripping surfaces with a circular cross section shall have an outside diameter of 0.95 inch (24 mm) minimum and 1.55 inches (39 mm) maximum. Where the

shape of the gripping surface is noncircular, the handrail shall provide an equivalent gripping surface.

❖ Section 505.7 allows for circular handrails to have a diameter between $1^1/_4$ and 2 inches (31.8 and 50.8 mm). Due to the smaller size of children's hands, the handrails on the elevated ramps within the play structure should be between 0.95 (24 mm) and 1.55 inches (39 mm). Since this size does include the smaller regular handrail size, when looking for equivalent gripping surface on noncircular handrails, the provisions in Section 505.7.2 could provide guidance.

1108.4.1.5.3.2 Handrail Height. The top of handrail gripping surfaces shall be 20 inches (510 mm) minimum and 28 inches (710 mm) maximum above the ramp surface.

❖ The top of the handrail should be between 20 and 28 inches (510 and 710 mm) above the ramp surface. If adults may also be using the ramps, providing a second handrail at the standard 34- to 38-inch (865 mm to 965 mm) height is also permitted. Keep in mind that the local building code may require guards along drop-offs.

1108.4.1.6 Ground Surfaces. Ground surfaces on accessible routes, clear floor spaces, and turning spaces shall comply with Section 1108.4.1.6.

❖ There are a variety of ground floor surfaces utilized for playgrounds. Common surfaces are concrete, compressed wood fiber, foam tiles and plastic/rubber surfaces. Some provide a good accessible route but would not meet the impact concerns for playground surfaces around equipment. Some surfaces that would work have higher maintenance requirements. A jurisdiction must evaluate initial installation, maintenance and usability when making the choice for their playgrounds.

Accessible and nonaccessible surfaces can be combined to provide a variety of textures and experiences in the play area.

(a) (b) (c) (d)

FIGURE C1108.4.1.5
EXAMPLES OF RAMPS TO AND WITHIN PLAY STRUCTURES

1108.4.1.6.1 Surface Condition. Ground surfaces shall be stable, firm and slip resistant. Ground surfaces shall be inspected and maintained regularly and frequently to ensure continued compliance with this requirement.

❖ When choosing a playground surface, the work that an individual would exert to propel a wheelchair across the surface is part of the consideration. This must be evaluated for both straight-ahead and turning movement. Ideally, the force required to move across the surface is the same amount of energy as it would require a person using a wheelchair to propel up a slope of 1:14. Another evaluation is if the chosen surface will be stable and firm. Once chosen, regular inspection and maintenance of the surface are necessary to maintain the accessible route.

1108.4.1.6.2 Use Zones. Ground surfaces located within use zones shall comply with ASTM F 1292 listed in Sections 105.2.8 or 105.2.9.

❖ The surface within the use zone, where children could fall, must also meet the impact attenuation requirements in ASTM F 1292. This standard specifies impact performance requirements for surfaces and provides a means of determining impact performance. This standard is referenced inside a play area use zone where a fall attenuation surcease is required in the same areas where an accessible route is required. Either the 1999 or 2004 edition of the ASTM standard can be used.

1108.4.2 Transfer Systems. Where transfer systems are provided to connect to elevated play components, the transfer systems shall comply with Section 1108.4.2.

❖ A transfer system provides an accessible route to elevated play components within a composite system by connecting different levels with transfer platforms (Section 1108.4.2.1) and steps (Section 1108.4.2.2). If a play structure has less than 20 play components, at least 50 percent of the play components must be connected by a transfer system (Section 1108.3.2.2). If a play structure has 20 or more play components, at least 75 percent of that 50 percent (i.e., 37.5 percent of the total) must be accessed by a ramp, and the remaining (i.e., 12.5 percent of the total) components can be accessed by transfer systems (see Commentary Figure C1108.4.2).

1108.4.2.1 Transfer Platforms. Transfer platforms shall be provided where transfer is intended from wheelchairs or other mobility aids. Transfer platforms shall comply with Section 1108.4.2.1.

❖ Transfer platforms are permitted as part of an accessible route into elevated play structures. A combination of transfer platforms and transfer steps makes up the system, with the transfer platform being located closest to the ground level. Consideration of the distance someone must travel to reach play components via a transfer system is important. Integration and minimizing how far someone would have to travel after transfer should be considered together.

The purpose of the transfer platform is to have a location where someone can transfer from their wheelchair and leave the wheelchair behind. Consideration of the traffic patterns for other children using the play structure should be considered so that the wheelchair will not be pushed out of the transfer space by other children entering or leaving the play structure.

1108.4.2.1.1 Size. Transfer platforms shall have level surfaces 14 inches (355 mm) minimum in depth and 24 inches (610 mm) minimum in width.

❖ The transfer platform and transfer steps are the same size (see Section 1108.4.2.2.1 and Figures 1108.4.2.1 and 1108.4.2.2).

1108.4.2.1.2 Height. The top of the transfer platforms shall be 11 inches (280 mm) minimum and 18 inches (455 mm) maximum in height above the floor.

❖ The height of the transfer platform is intended to be consistent with the height of the wheelchair seat so that a child does not have to transfer up from their seat. Adding a transfer step that leads to the ground as well as up allows for children to exit and play on the ground if desired (see Figure 1108.4.2.1).

1108.4.2.1.3 Transfer Space. A transfer space complying with Sections 305.2 and 305.3 shall be provided adjacent to the transfer platform. The 48-inch (1220 mm) minimum length dimension of the transfer space shall be centered on and parallel to the 24-inch (610 mm) minimum length side of the transfer platform. The side of the transfer platform serving the transfer space shall be unobstructed.

❖ A level wheelchair parking space should be located parallel and centered on the 24-inch (610 mm) side of the transfer platform. There should be no lip, curb or rail on that side of the transfer platform that could obstruct the transfer to or from the wheelchair to the platform (see Figure 1108.4.2.1).

1108.4.2.1.4 Transfer Supports. At least one means of support for transferring shall be provided.

❖ Transfer supports are provided at transfer platforms and steps to work as a handhold or support to aid in transfer. The support location, shape and material used can vary and should be chosen based on what would work best for each unique situation.

1108.4.2.2 Transfer Steps. Transfer steps shall be provided where movement is intended from transfer platforms to levels with elevated play components required to be on accessible routes. Transfer steps shall comply with Section 1108.4.2.2.

❖ Transfer steps are permitted as part of an accessible route into elevated play structures. A combination of transfer platforms and transfer steps makes up the system, with the transfer platform being located closest to the ground level. Consideration of the distance someone must travel to reach play components via a transfer system is important. Integration and minimizing how far someone would have to travel after transfer should be considered together.

The purpose of the transfer steps is to allow for children to continue up into the play structure or down to the ground from the transfer platform.

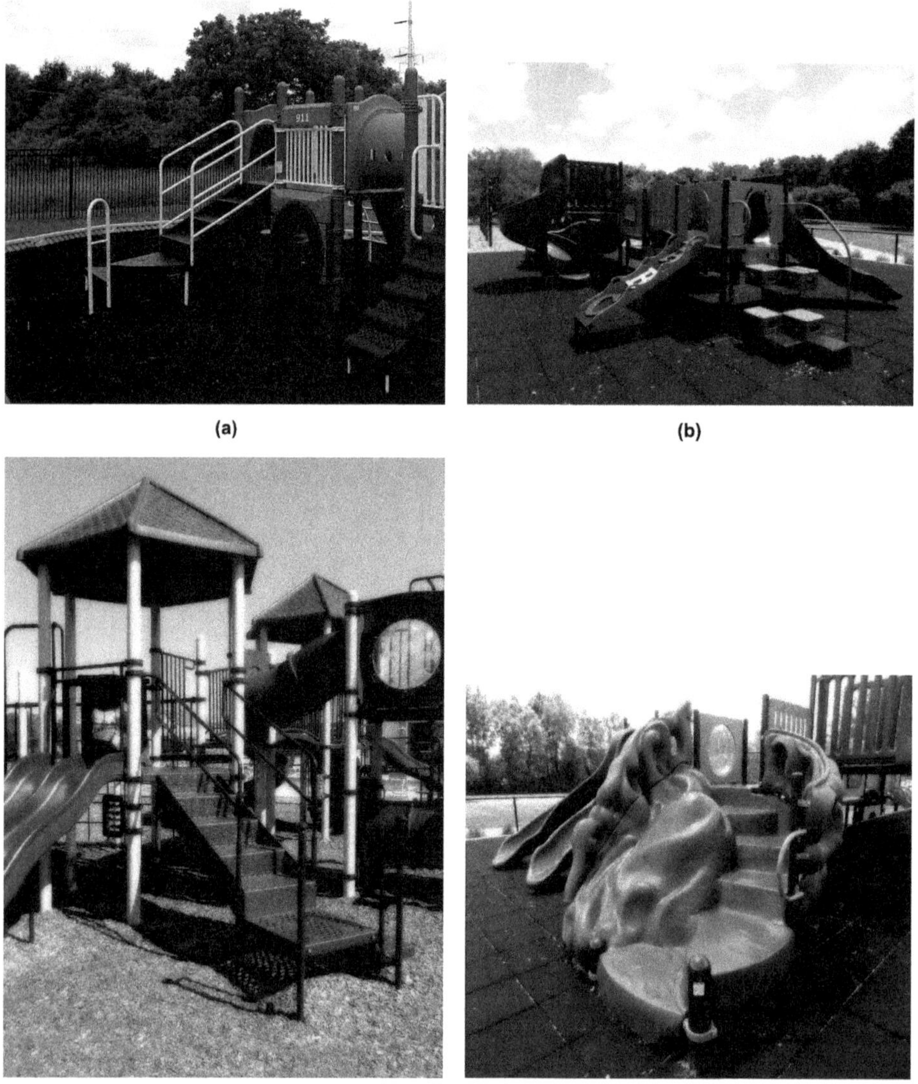

(a) (b) (c) (d)

FIGURE C1108.4.2
EXAMPLES OF TRANSFER SYSTEMS
(Photo courtesy of U.S. Access Board)

(a) elevation (b) plan

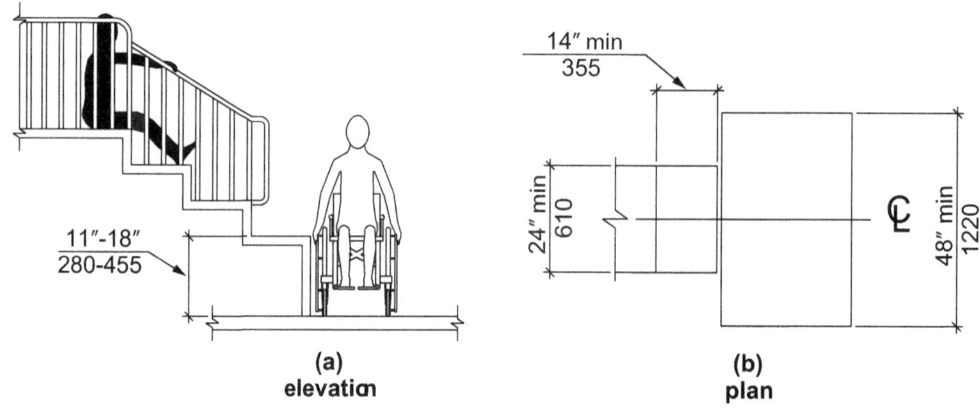

FIGURE 1108.4.2.1
TRANSFER PLATFORMS

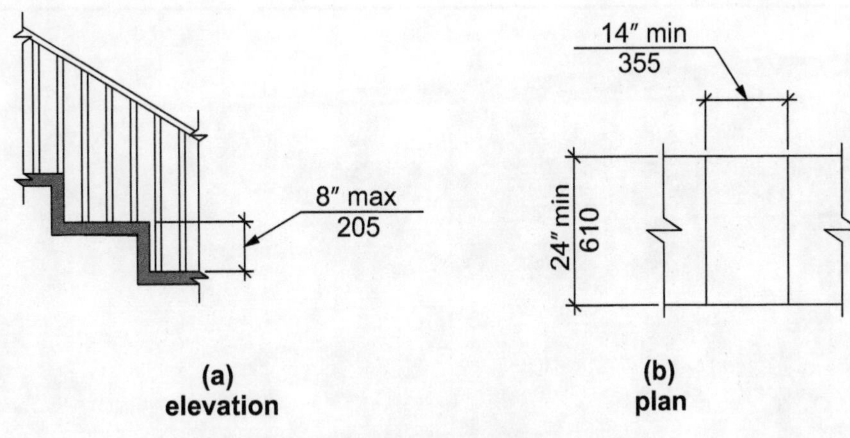

FIGURE 1108.4.2.2
TRANSFER STEPS

1108.4.2.2.1 Size. Transfer steps shall have level surfaces 14 inches (355 mm) minimum in depth and 24 inches (610 mm) minimum in width.

❖ The transfer platform and transfer steps are the same size (see Section 1108.4.2.1.1 and Figures 1108.4.2.1 and 1108.4.2.2).

1108.4.2.2.2 Height. Each transfer step shall be 8 inches (205 mm) maximum in height.

❖ The height of the steps is limited to allow for a child to "bump" up each step. Where play areas are intended for smaller children, it would be advisable to provide steps with lesser elevation.

1108.4.2.2.3 Transfer Supports. At least one means of support for transferring shall be provided.

❖ Transfer supports are provided at transfer platforms and steps to work as a handhold or support to aid in transfer. The support location, shape and material used can vary and should be chosen based on what would work best for each unique situation. Handrails or guards also can serve as transfer supports along the transfer steps (see Commentary Figure C1108.4.2).

1108.4.3 Play Components. Ground level play components on accessible routes and elevated play components connected by ramps shall comply with Section 1108.4.3.

❖ Each play component must be located on an accessible route along with certain spaces that are crucial to making the play area usable by children with disabilities. Each accessible play component must comply with the following five features, as applicable: turning space, clear floor space, knee and toe clearance, transfer systems and supports.

1108.4.3.1 Turning Space. At least one turning space complying with Section 304 shall be provided on the same level as play components. Where swings are provided, the turning space shall be located immediately adjacent to the swing.

❖ A turning circle or T-turn that will allow a child to turn around shall be provided on the same level as each play component. One turning space can serve multiple play components. The turning space can overlap clear floor space at components, the accessible route and any landings for ramps.

Where swings are provided, a turning space must be located adjacent to the swing. The requirements do not specify which side the turning space is located (see Commentary Figure C1108.4.3.1) for a suggested configuration.

1108.4.3.2 Clear Floor Space. Clear floor space complying with Sections 305.2 and 305.3 shall be provided at play components.

❖ Play components come in a variety of sizes and shapes and provide a wide variety of experiences. A specific location for each clear floor space is not indicated because what is best is dependent on the component. Clear floor spaces required at accessible play components are permitted to overlap the accessible route, turning spaces and ramp landings.

1108.4.3.3 Play Tables. Where play tables are provided, knee clearance 24 inches (610 mm) minimum in height, 17 inches (430 mm) minimum in depth, and 30 inches (760 mm) minimum in width shall be provided. The tops of rims, curbs, or other obstructions shall be 31 inches (785 mm) maximum in height.

EXCEPTION: Play tables designed and constructed primarily for children 5 years and younger shall not be required to provide knee clearance where the clear floor space required by Section 1108.4.3.2 is arranged for a parallel approach.

❖ Play tables are table tops, counters or boxes that are created for play surfaces. This includes sand and water tables or other activity tables. Where play tables serve as accessible play components, they should have knee and toe clearances appropriate for children. This is a knee clearance of 24 inches (610 mm) high and 30 inches (760 mm) wide. The knee space shall extend at least 17 inches (430 mm) under the surface. The top edge of the counter or box should be a maximum of 31 inches (785 mm) high (see Commentary Figure C1108.4.3.3).

Where play tables are designed for toddlers and preschoolers, a parallel approach is permitted.

FIGURE C1108.4.3.1
ACCESS TO SWINGS

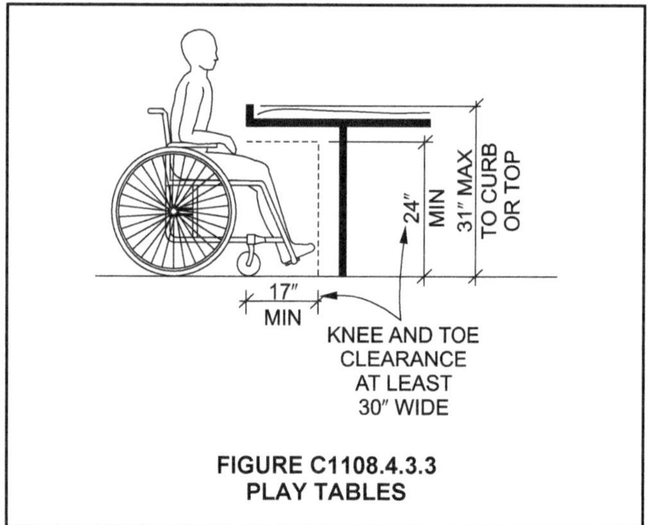

FIGURE C1108.4.3.3
PLAY TABLES

1108.4.3.4 Entry Points and Seats. Where play components require transfer to entry points or seats, the entry points or seats shall be 11 inches (280 mm) minimum and 24 inches (610 mm) maximum from the clear floor space.

EXCEPTION: Entry points of slides shall not be required to comply with Section 1108.4.3.4.

❖ Entry points or seats are where children sit or transfer, in order to gain access to or use play components. This is different from transfer seats or platforms because the child transfers directly to the component. Examples are swing seats, spring rocker seats and crawl tubes (see Commentary Figure C1108.4.3.4). The height limits vary from the transfer platform height (see Section 1108.4.2.1). The higher height allows for items such as swings. However, the middle height of 18 inches (455 mm) is recommended where possible. An entry point for a slide does not have a transfer height requirement.

FIGURE C1108.4.3.4
EXAMPLE OF ENTRY POINTS

1108.4.3.5 Transfer Supports. Where play components require transfer to entry points or seats, at least one means of support for transferring shall be provided.

❖ Transfer supports are required similar to transfer platforms and steps. This will help facilitate support and movement.

1109 Swimming Pools, Wading Pools, Hot tubs and Spas

❖ Swimming pools, wading pools, hot tubs and spas are often provided as part of a larger recreation facility (see Commentary Figure C1109). An accessible route should be provided from parking areas into the arrival points for the site, and then throughout the facilities provided. This would include items such as ticket/admission windows, gates, concessions, storage lockers, locker rooms, bathing and toilet facilities, the pool deck and associated play areas. This section addresses access from the pool deck into the water itself.

The organization of this section includes the number of entry points (Section 1109.1) required, and then the specifics for the types of entry permitted, including pool lifts (Section 1109.2), sloped entry (Section 1109.3), transfer walls (Section 1109.4), transfer systems (Section 1109.5), and pool stairs (Section 1109.6).

1109.1 General. Swimming pools, wading pools, hot tubs and spas shall comply with Section 1109.

❖ Means of entry for swimming pools, wading pools, hot tubs and spas are addressed in this section. Due to the different sizes and depths, different options work for different pools.

1109.1.1 Swimming pools. At least two accessible means of entry shall be provided for swimming pools. Accessible means of entry shall be swimming pool lifts complying with Section 1109.2; sloped entries complying with Section 1109.3; transfer walls complying with Section 1109.4, transfer systems complying with Section 1109.5; and pool stairs complying with Section 1109.6. At least one accessible means of entry provided shall comply with Section 1109.2 or 1109.3

EXCEPTIONS:

1. Where a swimming pool has less than 300 linear feet (91 m) of swimming pool wall, no more than one accessible means of entry shall be required.
2. Wave action pools, leisure rivers, sand bottom pools, and other pools where user access is limited to one area shall not be required to provide more than one accessible means of entry provided that the accessible means of entry is a swimming pool lift complying with Section 1109.2, a sloped entry complying with Section 1109.3, or a transfer system complying with Section 1109.5.
3. Catch pools shall not be required to provide an accessible means of entry provided that the catch pool edge is on an accessible route.

❖ The number of entry points required for a typical swimming pool is based on the perimeter size. If a pool has a perimeter of 300 feet (91 m) or more, two means of entry are required. At least one must be a sloped entry or a pool lift. The second entry can be by any of the five options described in this section. Any side of a pool that cannot be entered due to landscaping or adjacent structures still counts as part of the pool perimeter.

If a pool has a perimeter of less than 300 feet (91 m), then it only needs one means of entry, but it must be either a sloped entry or a pool lift. The only means of entry to smaller pools cannot be transfer walls, transfer systems or pool stairs.

FIGURE C1109
SWIMMING POOL

Aquatic recreation facilities provide a variety of action pools, such as lazy rivers or wave pools, where access to the water is limited to one area where everyone gets in and out of the water. These types of pools are only required to provide one accessible means of entry [see Commentary Figure C1109.1.1(a)]. In these types of pools the entry can be by sloped entry, pool lifts or transfer devices.

Catch pools are defined in Section 106.5 as a pool or area of a pool where water slide flumes drop people into the water at the end of the slide [see Commentary Figure C1109.1.1(b)]. For safety reasons, no other swimmers are allowed in the water, therefore, no accessible means of entry is required into a catch pool. There must still be an accessible route to the edge of the pool so people can watch.

FIGURE C1109.1.1(a)
(EXCEPTION 2) LAZY RIVER

1109.1.2 Wading pools. At least one sloped entry complying with Section 1109.3 shall be provided in wading pools.

❖ Wading pools are designed for wading, mostly for toddlers and infants (see Commentary Figure C1109.1.2). While not specifically defined, the depth is expected to be below 24 inches (610 mm). This depth would not allow for a pool lift to be used due to the water depth needed and supporting construction for the seat of the pool lift. Therefore, the only option available for wading pools is sloped entry. The sloped entry at wading pools is not required to have handrails (see Section 1109.3.3, Exception 3).

FIGURE C1109.1.1(b)
(EXCEPTION 3) CATCH POOLS

FIGURE C1109.1.2
WADING POOL

1109.1.3 Hot tubs and Spas. At least one accessible means of entry shall be provided for hot tubs and spas. Accessible means of entry shall comply with swimming pool lifts complying with Section 1109.2; transfer walls complying with Section 1109.4; or transfer systems complying with Section 1109.5.

EXCEPTION: Where hot tubs or spas are provided in a cluster, no more than 5 percent, but not less than one hot tub or spa in each cluster shall be required to comply with Section 1109.1.3.

❖ Hot tubs or spas can be constructed so the edge is at grade or elevated to the height of the pool (see Commentary Figure C1109.1.3). Options for providing entry are by pool lifts, transfer walls or transfer systems. If there is a group of hot tubs, then only one in each location is required to have an entry point.

The text does not address when there may be different types of spas, such as a cold tub and a hot tub. This is sometimes provided associated with saunas. Good design would provide an entry point to both.

Note that Section 1109.2.6 states that where pool lifts are provided for hot tub or spa access, footrests are not required. Basically there is not enough depth for footrests and the submersion requirements for the seat unless the water is at least 34 inches (864 mm) deep.

1109.2 Pool Lifts. Pool lifts shall comply with Section 1109.2.

❖ Pool lifts have requirements in this section for where they should be located along the edge of the pool, access to the pool lift by a person using a mobility device, how the seat of the pool lift should be located both in the raised and lowered positions and criteria for the seat itself, including armrests, footrests, operation and load capacity (see Commentary Figure C1109.2).

FIGURE C1109.1.3
HOT TUB OR SPA

1109.2.1 Pool Lift Location. Pool lifts shall be located where the water level does not exceed 48 inches (1220 mm).

EXCEPTIONS:

1. Where the entire pool depth is greater than 48 inches (1220 mm), compliance with Section 1109.2.1 shall not be required.
2. Where multiple pool lift locations are provided, no more than one pool lift shall be required to be located in an area where the water level is 48 inches (1220 mm) maximum.

❖ Ideally pool lifts will be located where the adjacent water depth is between 34 inches (865 mm) and 48 inches (1220 mm) deep. This allows the seat to submerge for buoyancy with the additional depth needed for the footrests, but at the same time allows for someone to stand in the water to offer assistance for the person using the pool lift.

For pools with two required entry points and the designer has chosen to do both entry points with pool lifts, or where the entire pool is greater than 48 inches (1220 mm) deep, the pool lift can be located adjacent to deeper water.

FIGURE C1109.2
POOL LIFT

1109.2.2 Seat Location. In the raised position, the centerline of the seat shall be located over the deck and 16 inches (405 mm) minimum from the edge of the pool. The deck surface between the centerline of the seat and the pool edge shall have a slope not steeper than 1:48.

❖ When the pool lift is in the upper or loading position, the pool lift should be located so that the centerline of the seat is at least 16 inches (405 mm) from the edge of the pool (see Figure 1109.2.2). Adjacent to the seat, on the side away from the pool, is a wheelchair parking space oriented for transfer. The back of the pool lift seat should line up with the back of the wheelchair. There must be no obstructions between the clear floor space and the chair of the pool lift. The entire location needs to be level (see Figure 1109.2.3 and Commentary Figure C1109.2.2). The intent of the 1:48 slope is to keep the space level enough for safe and easy transfer, but still allow enough of a slope for water to drain from the area.

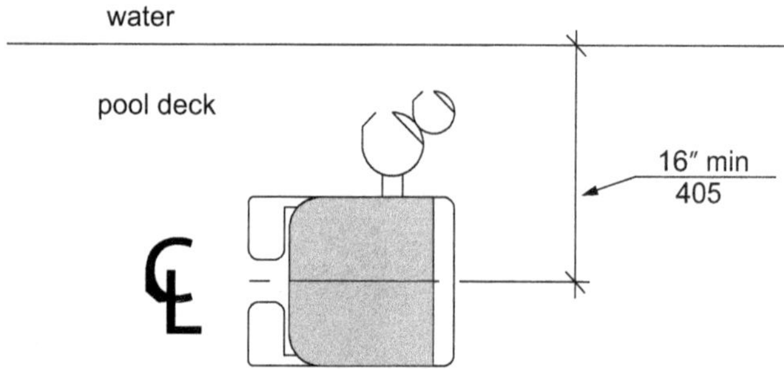

FIGURE 1109.2.2
POOL LIFT SEAT LOCATION

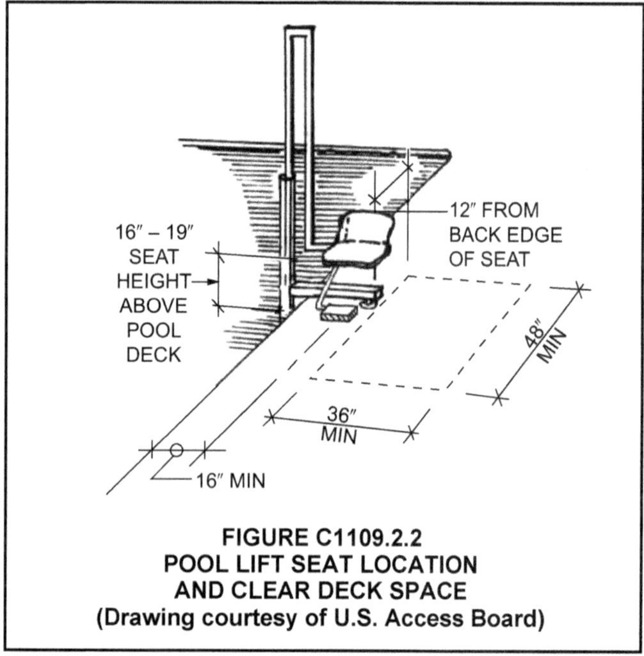

FIGURE C1109.2.2
POOL LIFT SEAT LOCATION AND CLEAR DECK SPACE
(Drawing courtesy of U.S. Access Board)

1109.2.3 Clear Deck Space. On the side of the seat opposite the water, a clear deck space shall be provided parallel with the seat. The space shall be 36 inches (915 mm) minimum in width and shall extend forward 48 inches (1220 mm) minimum from a line located 12 inches (305 mm) behind the rear edge of the seat. The clear deck space shall have a slope not steeper than 1:48.

❖ See the commentary to Section 1109.2.2.

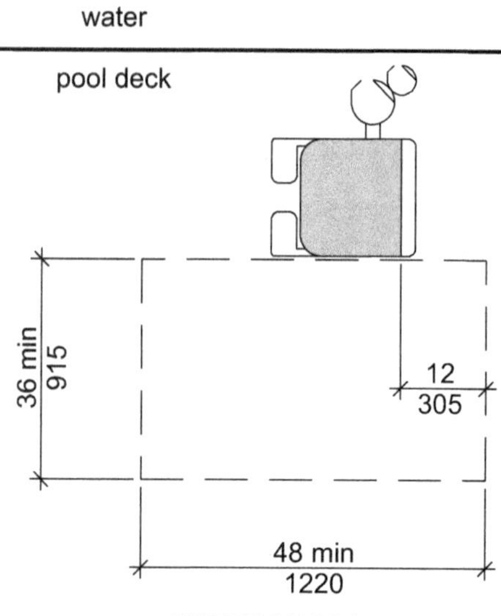

FIGURE 1109.2.3
CLEAR DECK SPACE AT POOL LIFTS

1109.2.4 Seat Height. The height of the lift seat shall be designed to allow a stop at 16 inches (405 mm) minimum and 19 inches (485 mm) maximum measured from the deck to the top of the seat surface when in the raised (load) position.

❖ There are a variety of pool lift seats available. For ease of transfer, the height of the seat should line up with the typical wheelchair seat height between 16 inches (405 mm) and 19 inches (485 mm). For good support, the seat must be at least 16 inches (405 mm) wide and have a backrest and footrests. There is not a depth indicated for the seat, but most designs are typically 15 to 16 inches (380 to 405 mm) deep (i.e., similar to transfer shower seats).

If a seat with armrests is chosen to offer additional stability, the armrest on the side away from the pool must either be fold up or removable to allow for a side transfer.

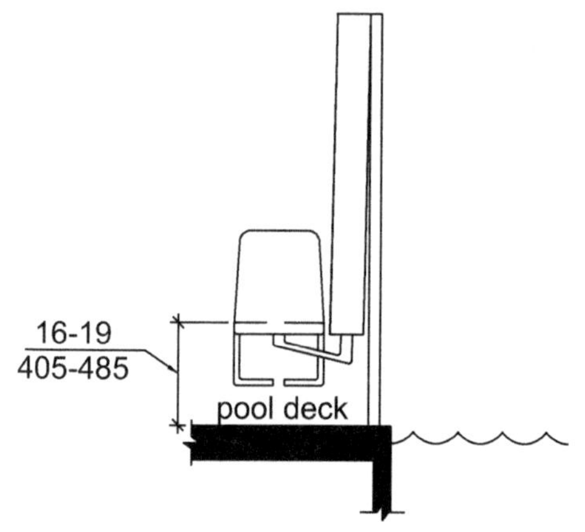

FIGURE 1109.2.4
POOL LIFT SEAT HEIGHT

1109.2.5 Seat. The seat shall be 16 inches (405 mm) minimum in width, provide a back rest, and be of a firm and stable design.

❖ See the commentary to Section 1109.2.4.

1109.2.6 Footrests and Armrests. Footrests shall be provided and shall move with the seat. If provided, the armrest positioned opposite the water shall be removable or shall fold clear of the seat when the seat is in the raised (load) position.

EXCEPTION: Footrests shall not be required on pool lifts provided in spas.

❖ See the commentary to Section 1109.2.4. As described in the commentary to Section 1109.1.3, footrests are not required for hot tubs or spas that chose the option of pool lifts because there may not be enough depth (see commentary Section 1109.2.4).

1109.2.7 Operation. The lift shall be capable of unassisted operation from both the deck and water levels. Controls and operating mechanisms shall be unobstructed when the lift is in use and shall comply with Section 309.4.

❖ Controls to operate the lift must be reachable from both the water and the deck. This allows for a person swimming to be able to get themselves out of the pool unassisted, even if someone else has used the lift to exit the pool and left it in the load position. There is a safety concern that someone would possibly get stuck in the water for an extended period of time. While the controls don't have to meet the typical clear floor space and reach range requirements, they are required to be operable with no tight pinching or grasping, and must not require more than 5 pounds force to operate.

1109.2.8 Submerged Depth. The lift shall be designed so that the seat will submerge to a water depth of 18 inches (455 mm) minimum below the stationary water level.

❖ The seat of the lift must submerge at least 18 inches (455 mm) to allow for a person to achieve some buoyancy so they can dismount and mount easily (see Figure 1109.2.8).

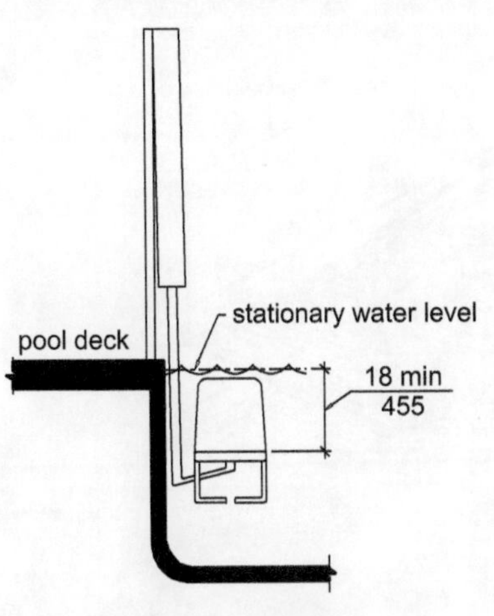

FIGURE 1109.2.8
POOL LIFT SUBMERGED DEPTH

1109.2.9 Lifting Capacity. Single person pool lifts shall have a weight capacity of 300 pounds (136 kg) minimum and be capable of sustaining a static load of at least one and a half times the rated load.

❖ For safety reasons, the static load on the pool lift must be a minimum of 450 pounds (204 kg). The lift itself must work with a capacity of at least 300 pounds (136 kg).

1109.3 Sloped Entries. Sloped entries shall comply with Section 1109.3.

❖ Sloped entries can look like a traditional ramp, can be as wide as the entire entry such as at a lazy river, or can be the entire width of the pool, which is common for wading pools or wave pools [see Commentary Figures C1109.3(a) and (b)]. Swimming pools must have either a sloped entry or a pool lift as their first choice of entry.

If a pool has a sloped entry option, a wheelchair should be considered that can be used to move into the water since a person's typical wheelchair or scooter is not waterproof. These chairs are typically made of plastic tubing with mesh seats [see Commentary Figure C1109.3(c)].

FIGURE C1109.3(a)
SLOPED ENTRY IN A SWIMMING POOL

FIGURE C1109.3(b)
SLOPED ENTRY AT A LAZY RIVER

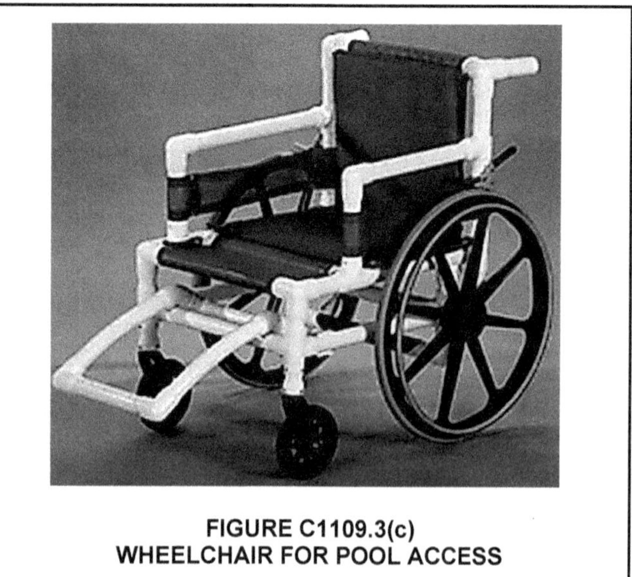

FIGURE C1109.3(c)
WHEELCHAIR FOR POOL ACCESS

1109.3.1 Sloped Entry Route. Sloped entries shall comply with Chapter 4 except as modified by Sections 1109.3.1 through 1109.3.3.

EXCEPTION: Where sloped entries are provided, the surfaces shall not be required to be slip resistant.

❖ With the reference to Chapter 4, this is basically stating that sloped entries must meet provisions for sloped walks or ramps (see Commentary Figure C1109.3.1). Along ramps, this would include providing handrails and edge protection. Because the walking surface is submerged, the issue of slip resistance is no longer present. The bottom of the pool can be the same surface everywhere.

1109.3.2 Submerged Depth. Sloped entries for swimming pools shall comply with Section 1109.3.2.1. Sloped entries for wading pools shall comply with Section 1109.3.2.2.

❖ Since the depth of pools can vary greatly, the depth that the sloped entry must reach depends on the type of pool. Remember that wading pools are typically less than 24 inches (610 mm) in depth.

1109.3.2.1 Swimming Pools. Sloped entries for swimming pools shall extend to a depth of 24 inches (610 mm) minimum and 30 inches (760 mm) maximum below the stationary water level. Where landings are required by Section 405.7, at least one landing shall be located 24 inches (610 mm) minimum and 30 inches (760 mm) maximum below the stationary water level.

❖ If a swimming pool uses the sloped entry option, the entry must comply with the same minimum requirements as sloped walks and ramps. The sloped surface must extend to a depth between 24 inches (610 mm) and 30 inches (760 mm) deep to allow for a person to achieve some buoyancy. If the slope is between 1:20 and 1:12, there should be a minimum 60-inch-deep (1525 mm) landing at the bottom of the sloped surface (see Figure 1109.3.2).

1109.3.2.2 Wading Pools. In wading pools, the sloped entry shall extend to the deepest part of the wading pool.

❖ Since wading pools are typically less than 24 inches (610 mm) deep, this requirement is addressed by sloping the entire pool from zero at one end to the full depth of the pool at the other. Slopes can be anywhere between 0 and 1:12. However, handrails are not required (Section 1109.3, Exception 3).

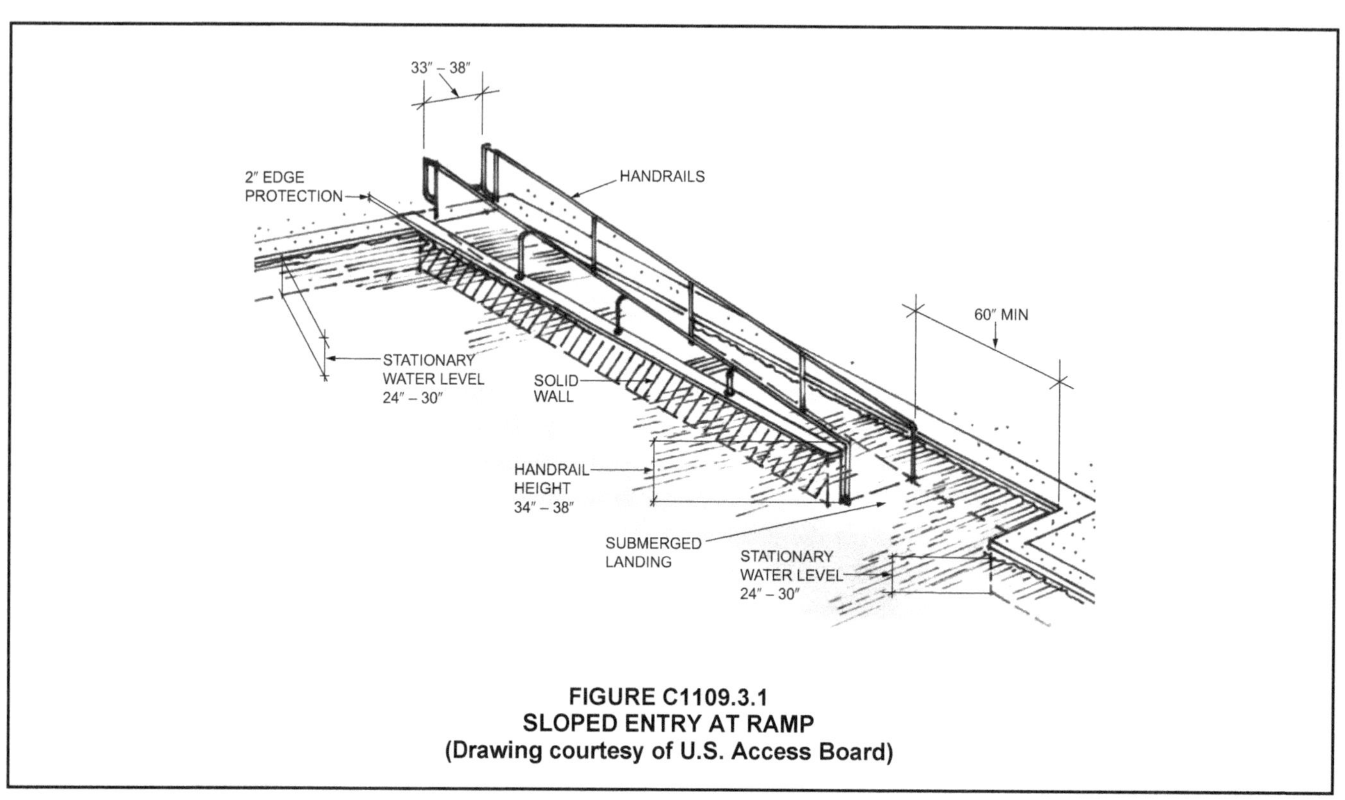

FIGURE C1109.3.1
SLOPED ENTRY AT RAMP
(Drawing courtesy of U.S. Access Board)

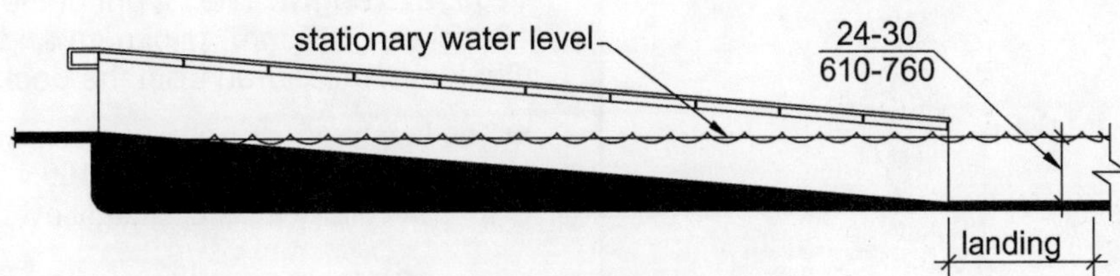

FIGURE 1109.3.2
SLOPED ENTRY SUBMERGED DEPTH

1109.3.3 Handrails. At least two handrails complying with Section 505 shall be provided on the sloped entry. The clear width between required handrails shall be 33 inches (840 mm) minimum and 38 inches (965 mm) maximum.

EXCEPTIONS:

1. Handrail extensions specified by Section 505.10.1 shall not be required at the bottom landing serving a sloped entry.
2. Where a sloped entry is provided for wave action pools, leisure rivers, sand bottom pools, and other pools where user access is limited to one area, the handrails shall not be required to comply with the clear width requirements of Section 1109.3.3.
3. Sloped entries in wading pools shall not be required to provide handrails complying with Section 1109.3.3. If provided, handrails on sloped entries in wading pools shall not be required to comply with Section 505.

❖ Handrails are required at sloped entries, even where the slope is less than 1:20. When an entry to a swimming pool is similar to a standard ramp, the handrails must be located between 33 inches (840 mm) and 38 inches (965 mm) apart (see Figure 1109.3.3). This will allow someone with mobility impairments to use the handrails for support as they move into the water. Because this width may be an issue for the types of pools where everyone enters at the same point, the handrails can be located at the far sides of the sloped entry at lazy rivers, action pools, etc. (Exception 2).

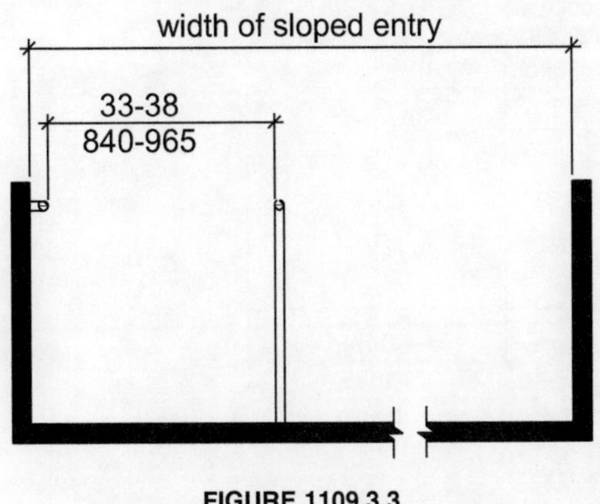

FIGURE 1109.3.3
HANDRAIL FOR SLOPED ENTRY

There are issues of possible entrapment with handrails for others swimming in the pool. The requirement for the ramp only extending to a maximum depth of 30 inches (760 mm) will keep the handrail (at a height of 34 inches to 38 inches (865 mm to 965 mm) out of the water. This is also one of the reasons to not require handrail extensions at the bottom of the ramp (Exception 1).

Wading pools are most commonly designed with a low sloped entry. Regardless of the slope, they are not required to have handrails to provide access into the pool. If a designer wishes to provide some sort of rail for assistance, it is not required to meet the handrail requirements in Section 505. For example, a designer may want to provide a rail with the top surface at the height appropriate for 2- or 3-year-old children.

1109.4 Transfer Walls. Transfer walls shall comply with Section 1109.4.

❖ Transfer walls are a second option for pools, but are one of the primary options for hot tubs or spas. This system works when the edge of the pool is constructed above the deck surface. The idea is that someone transfers from their wheelchair or scooter to the top of the wall, and then down into the water [see Commentary Figures C1109.4(a) and C1109.4(b)].

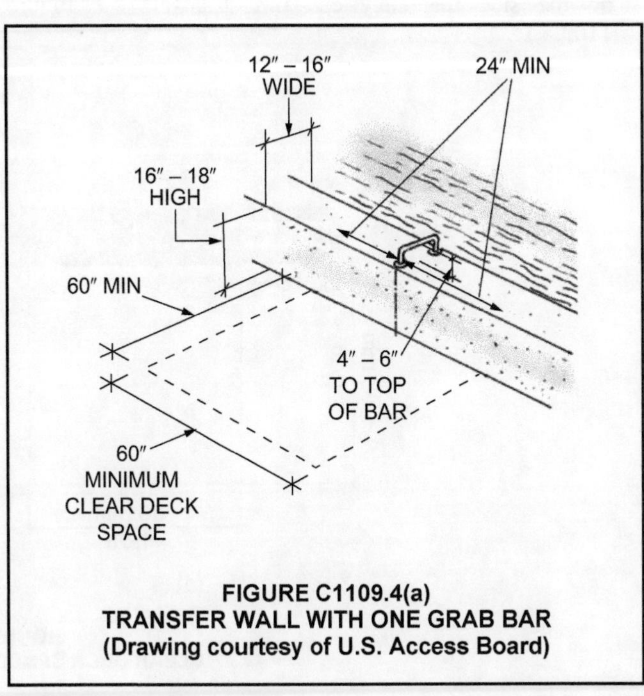

FIGURE C1109.4(a)
TRANSFER WALL WITH ONE GRAB BAR
(Drawing courtesy of U.S. Access Board)

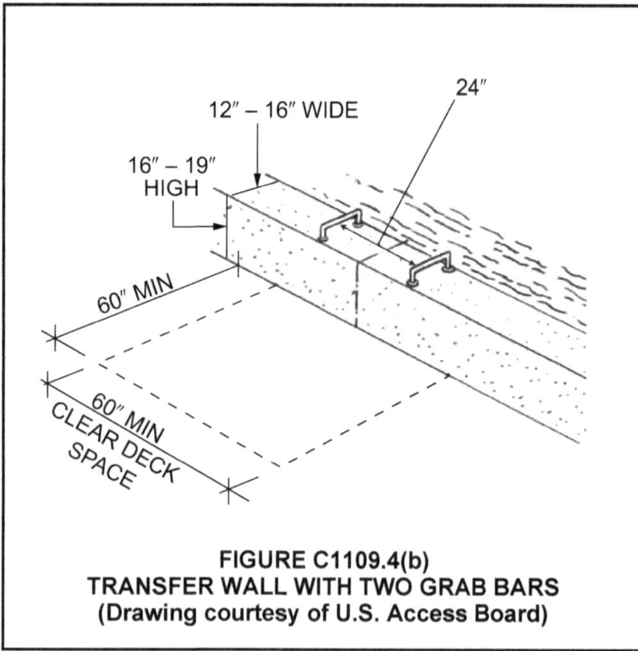

FIGURE C1109.4(b)
TRANSFER WALL WITH TWO GRAB BARS
(Drawing courtesy of U.S. Access Board)

1109.4.1 Clear Deck Space. A clear deck space of 60 inches (1525 mm) minimum by 60 inches (1525 mm) minimum with a slope not steeper than 1:48 shall be provided at the base of the transfer wall. Where one grab bar is provided, the clear deck space shall be centered on the grab bar. Where two grab bars are provided, the clear deck space shall be centered on the clearance between the grab bars.

❖ Basically a level clear floor space large enough for a turning space must be provided next to the wall of the tub. The adjustment left or right is dependent on the number and locations of handholds provided on the top of the wall. This will allow a person to turn around and access the wall on the side that they can best transfer (see Figure 1109.4.1).

1109.4.2 Height. The height of the transfer wall shall be 16 inches (405 mm) minimum and 19 inches (485 mm) maximum measured from the deck.

❖ The height of the wall is consistent with the height of the wheelchair seat (see Figure 1109.4.2). It requires less effort for someone to transfer straight over rather than up or down.

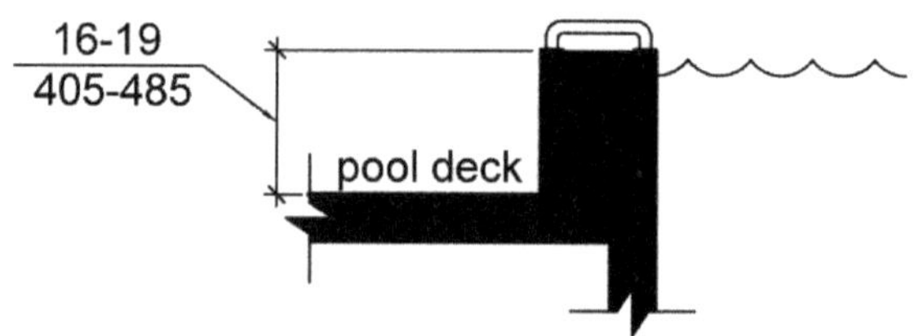

FIGURE 1109.4.2
TRANSFER WALL HEIGHT

1109.4.3 Wall Depth and Length. The transfer wall shall be 12 inches (305 mm) minimum and 16 inches (405 mm) maximum in depth. The transfer wall shall be 60 inches (1525 mm) minimum in length and shall be centered on the clear deck space.

❖ In order for someone to sit comfortably on the top of the wall, the thickness of the wall must be in the range of 12 inches (405 mm) to 16 inches (405 mm). This wall must match up with the entire length of the adjacent clear deck space required by Section 1109.4.1 (see Figure 1109.4.3).

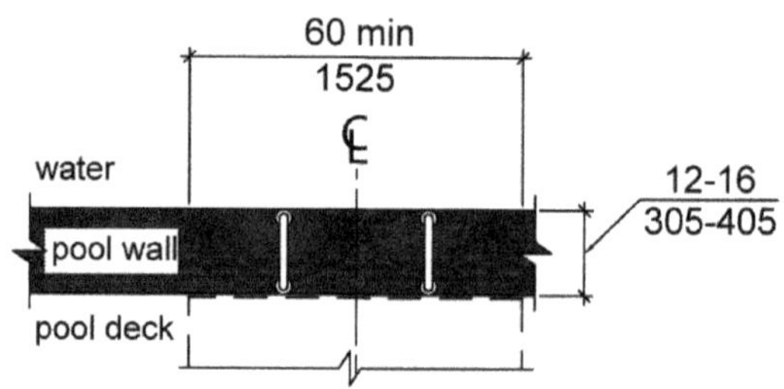

FIGURE 1109.4.3
DEPTH AND LENGTH OF TRANSFER WALL

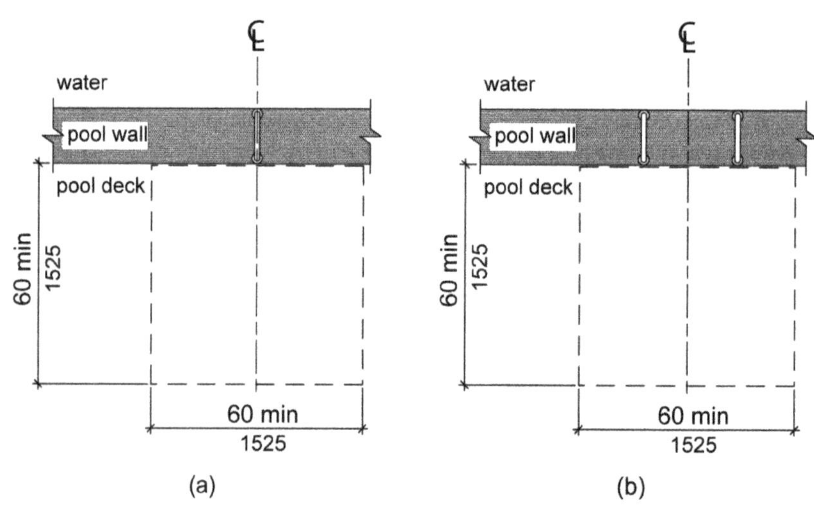

FIGURE 1109.4.1
CLEAR DECK SPACE AT TRANSFER WALLS

1109.4.4 Surface. Surfaces of transfer walls shall not be sharp and shall have rounded edges.

❖ The top of the wall can be any surface, however, since people are transferring in swimsuits, the top of the wall is exposed to wet, bare skin. A smooth surface with curved edges will be considerably more comfortable to use. Good design would pick a surface that was slip resistant to some degree since the surface could also be wet.

1109.4.5 Grab Bars. At least one grab bar complying with Sections 609.1 through 609.3 and 609.5 through 609.8 shall be provided on the transfer wall. Grab bars shall be perpendicular to the pool wall and shall extend the full depth of the transfer wall. The top of the gripping surface shall be 4 inches (100 mm) minimum and 6 inches (150 mm) maximum above the transfer wall. Where one grab bar is provided, clearance shall be 24 inches (610 mm) minimum on both sides of the grab bar. Where two grab bars are provided, clearance between grab bars shall be 24 inches (610 mm) minimum.

❖ The references provide requirements for grab bar cross section, clearance, stability and strength. Section 609.4 is not referenced because the locations are provided in this section. The requirement for the grab bars to extend the full depth of the wall is intended to allow for curvature at the ends of the horizontal bar and gusset plates where the bars attach to the wall. When two grab bars are provided, they should be a minimum of 24 inches (610 mm) apart to allow for a person to fit between the grab bars when they transfer (see Figure 1109.4.5). While the clearances associated with the grab bars are 24 inches (610 mm), the transfer wall is required to be 60 inches (1525 mm) wide.

The height of the grab bars over the wall is between 4 and 6 inches (100 and 150 mm) measured from the top of the bar to the top of the wall.

1109.5 Transfer Systems. Transfer systems shall comply with Section 1109.5.

❖ A transfer system is made up of a transfer platform and steps. This system allows for someone to transfer from their wheelchair to the platform and then move down step by step into the water (see Commentary Figure C1109.5). This system is a second option for entry into pools.

1109.5.1 Transfer Platform. A transfer platform shall be provided at the head of each transfer system. Transfer platforms shall provide a clear depth of 19 inches (485 mm) minimum and a clear width of 24 inches (610 mm) minimum.

❖ The transfer system must be 24 inches (610 mm) minimum wide at both the platform and steps. The top platform must be at least 19 inches (485 mm) deep. This platform is accessed from the transfer space in Section 1109.5.2. This platform is where a person transfers from their wheelchair in order to maneuver via the transfer steps into the water.

1109.5.2 Transfer Space. A transfer space of 60 inches (1525 mm) minimum by 60 inches (1525 mm) minimum with a slope not steeper than 1:48 shall be provided at the base of the transfer platform surface. The transfer space shall be centered along a 24-inch (610 mm) minimum side of the transfer platform. The side of the transfer platform serving the transfer space shall be unobstructed.

❖ A level clear floor space large enough for a turning space must be provided next to and centered on the platform of the transfer system and centered on that platform (see Commentary Figure C1109.5.2). This will allow for a person to turn around and access the platform on the side that they can do the best transfer.

1109.5.3 Height. The height of the transfer platform shall comply with Section 1109.4.2.

❖ The height of the platform is consistent with the height of the wheelchair seat [i.e., 16 inches (405 mm) to 19 inches (485 mm)]. It requires less effort for someone to transfer straight over rather than up or down.

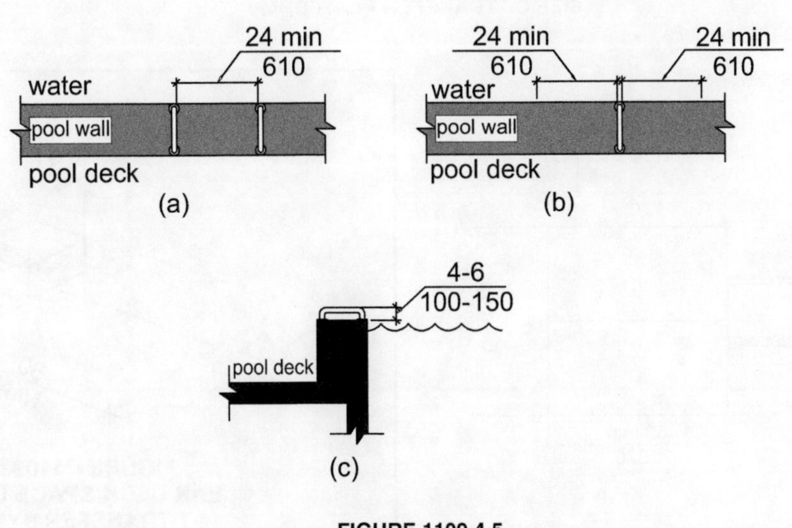

FIGURE 1109.4.5
GRAB BARS FOR TRANSFER WALLS

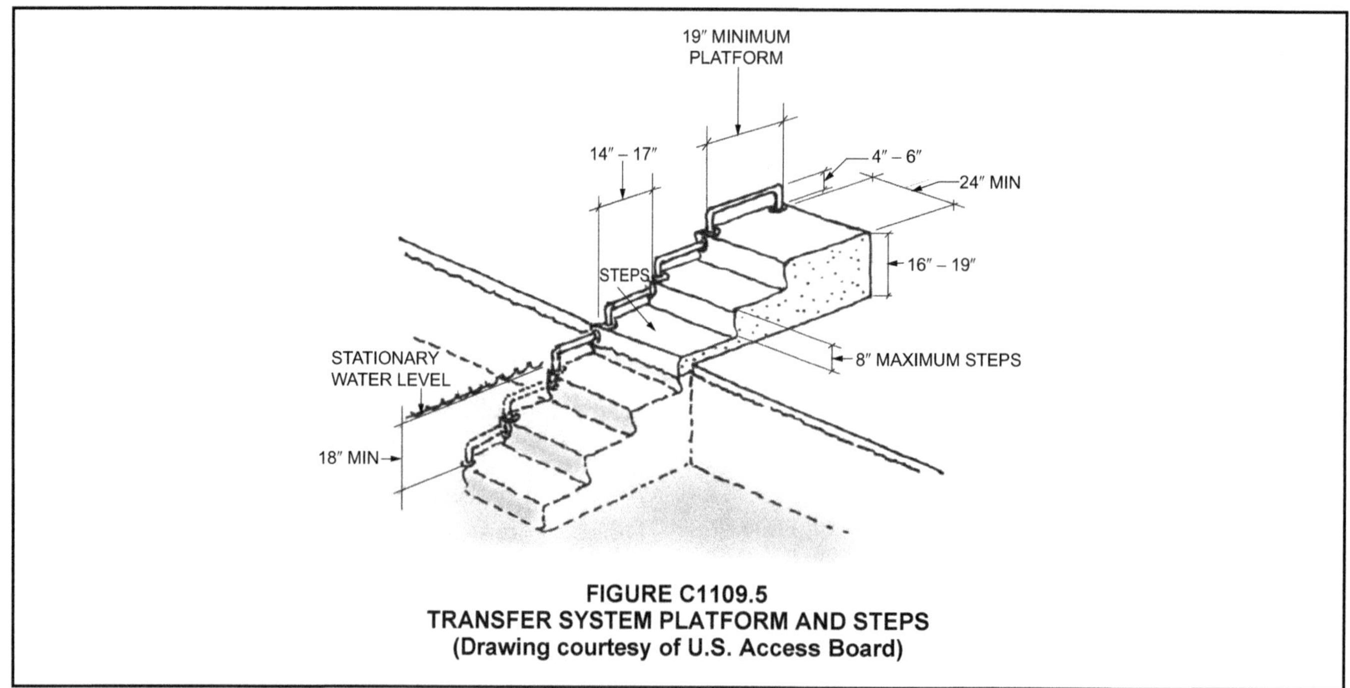

FIGURE C1109.5
TRANSFER SYSTEM PLATFORM AND STEPS
(Drawing courtesy of U.S. Access Board)

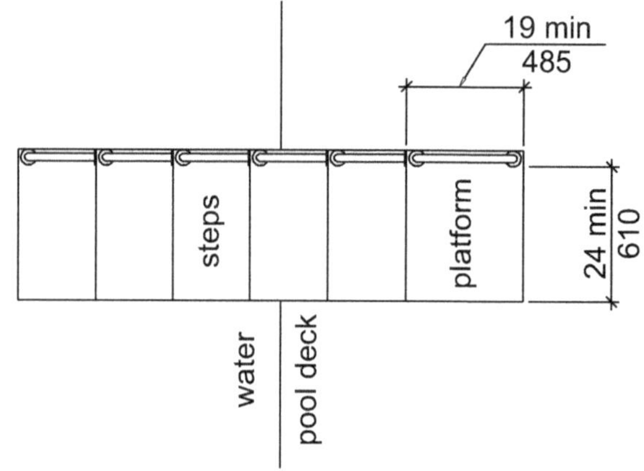

FIGURE 1109.5.1
SIZE OF TRANSFER PLATFORM

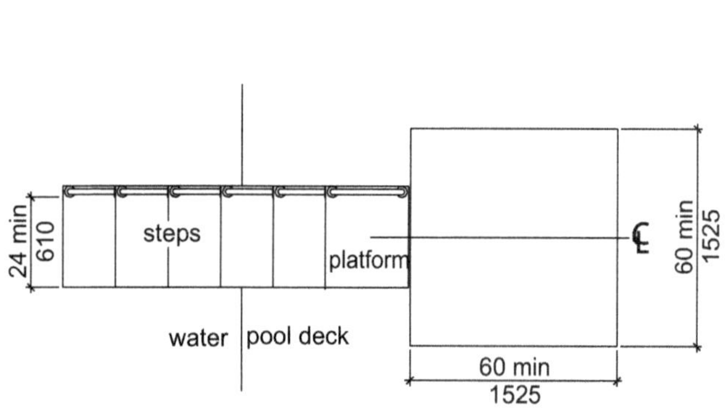

FIGURE 1109.5.2
CLEAR DECK SPACE AT TRANSFER PLATFORM

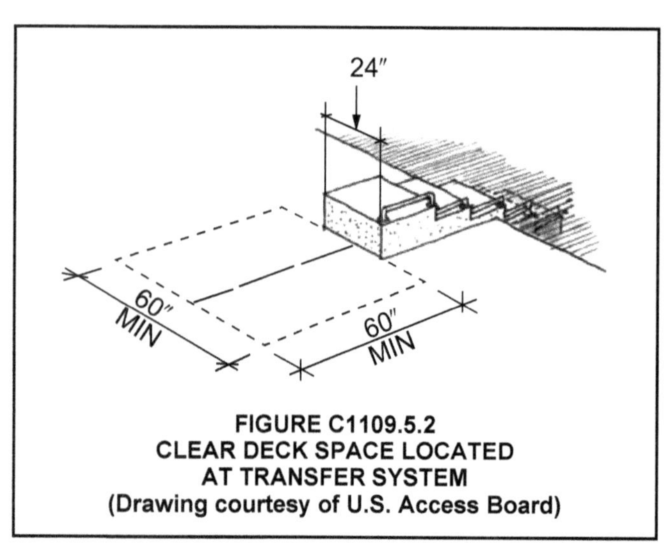

FIGURE C1109.5.2
CLEAR DECK SPACE LOCATED AT TRANSFER SYSTEM
(Drawing courtesy of U.S. Access Board)

1109.5.4 Transfer Steps. Transfer steps shall be 8 inches (205 mm) maximum in height. The surface of the bottom tread shall extend to a water depth of 18 inches (455 mm) minimum below the stationary water level.

❖ Transfer steps must be a minimum of 24 inches (610 mm) wide, 14 to 17 inches (355 to 430 mm) deep and a maximum of 8 inches (205 mm) high (Sections 1009.5.4 and 1109.5.6). The transfer system must allow for a person to move from the transfer platform [at 16 inches (405 mm) to 19 inches (485 mm) above the deck], into the water to a depth of at least 18 inches (485 mm) (see Figure 1109.5.4). This will allow for a person to achieve a level of buoyancy before leaving the transfer system for the pool.

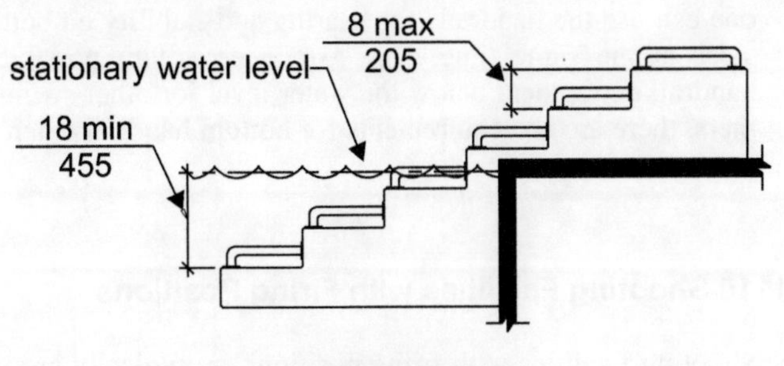

FIGURE 1109.5.4
TRANSFER STEPS

1109.5.5 Surface. The surface of the transfer system shall not be sharp and shall have rounded edges.

❖ The transfer system can be any surface, however, since people are transferring in swimsuits, the surface of the platform and steps is exposed to wet, bare skin. A smooth surface with curved edges will be considerably more comfortable to use. Good design would pick a surface that was slip resistant to some degree since the surface could also be wet.

1109.5.6 Size. Each transfer step shall have a tread clear depth of 14 inches (355 mm) minimum and 17 inches (430 mm) maximum and shall have a tread clear width of 24 inches (610 mm) minimum.

❖ See the commentary to Section 1109.5.4 and Figure 1109.5.6.

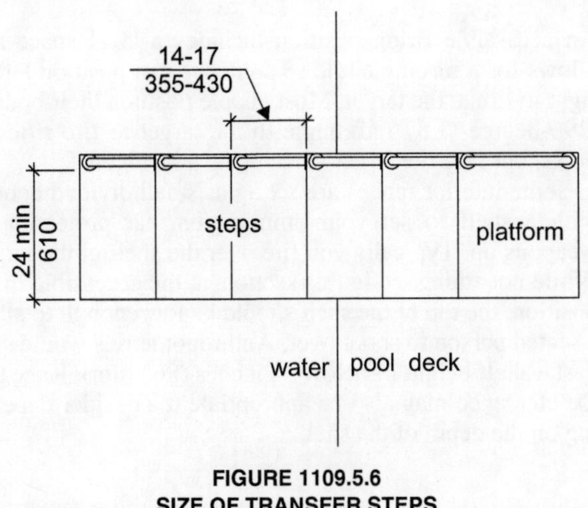

FIGURE 1109.5.6
SIZE OF TRANSFER STEPS

1109.5.7 Grab Bars. At least one grab bar on each transfer step and the transfer platform or a continuous grab bar serving each transfer step and the transfer platform shall be provided. Where a grab bar is provided on each step, the tops of gripping surfaces shall be 4 inches (100 mm) minimum and 6 inches (150 mm) maximum above each step and transfer platform. Where a continuous grab bar is provided, the top of the gripping surface shall be 4 inches (100 mm) minimum and 6 inches (150 mm) maximum above the step nosing and transfer platform. Grab bars shall comply with Sections 609.1 through 609.3 and 609.5 through 609.8 and be located on at least one side of the transfer system. The grab bar located at the transfer platform shall not obstruct transfer.

❖ The references provide requirements for grab bar cross section, clearance, stability and strength. Section 609.4 is not referenced because the locations are provided in this section. The grab bar must be on at least one side of the platform and steps. The grab bars can be on each step, or there can be one continuous grab bar (see Commentary Figures C1109.5 and C1109.5.7). Good design may add a second grab bar along the steps, especially where the steps move under the water, to assist in mounting and dismounting of the transfer system in the water. There should not be any extra grab bars along the platform and some of the top steps, because they could obstruct transfer.

When the bar is horizontal, the height of the grab bar is between 4 and 6 inches (100 and 150 mm) measured from the top of the bar to the top of the step. When the bar is continuous, the height of the bar is measured at the nosing of the step (see Figure 1109.5.7).

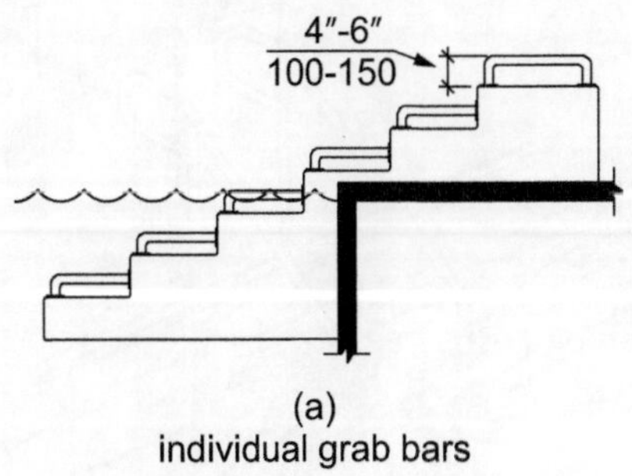

(a)
individual grab bars

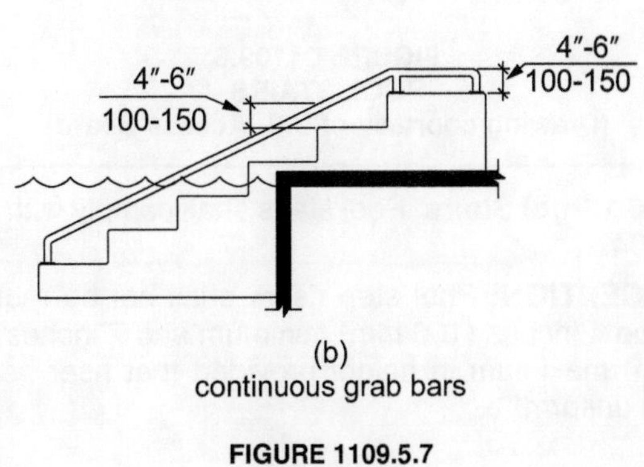

(b)
continuous grab bars

FIGURE 1109.5.7
GRAB BARS

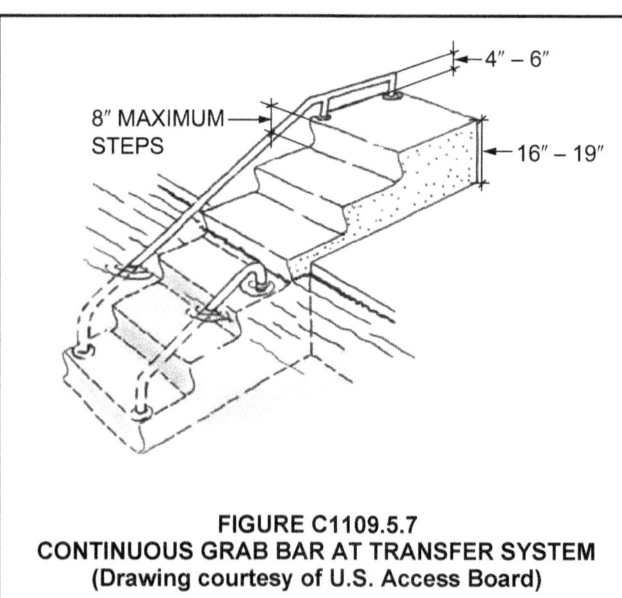

FIGURE C1109.5.7
CONTINUOUS GRAB BAR AT TRANSFER SYSTEM
(Drawing courtesy of U.S. Access Board)

1109.6 Pool Stairs. Pool stairs shall comply with Section 1109.6.

❖ Pool stairs are designed to provide assistance with balance and support from a standing position when moving from the pool deck into and out of the water (see Commentary Figure C1109.6). This system is a second option for entry into pools. Other steps provided in the pool are not required to meet these guidelines.

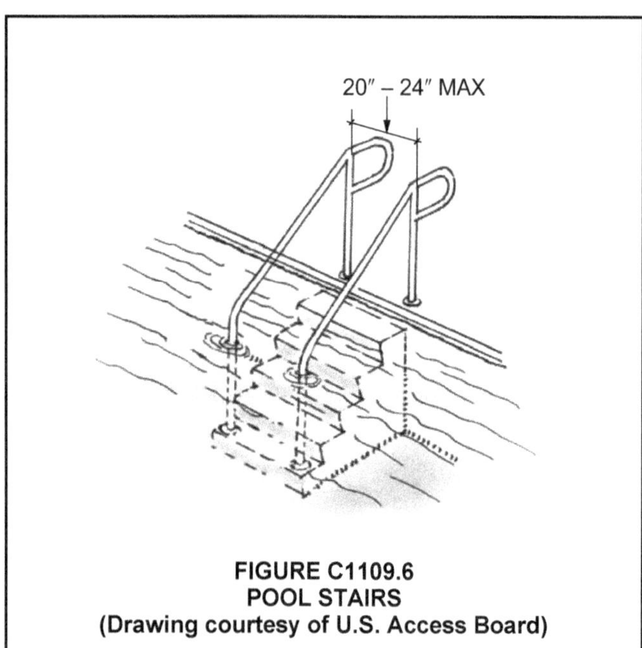

FIGURE C1109.6
POOL STAIRS
(Drawing courtesy of U.S. Access Board)

1109.6.1 Pool Stairs. Pool stairs shall comply with Section 504.

EXCEPTION: Pool step risers shall not be required to be 4 inches (100 mm) minimum and 7 inches (180 mm) maximum in height provided that riser heights are uniform.

❖ The reference to Section 504 includes stairway provisions for tread and riser size, solid risers, level treads and nosing. There is no limitation for riser height, high or low, provided the risers are uniform. Treads must be a minimum of 11 inches (279 mm) deep (see Commentary Figure C1109.6).

1109.6.2 Handrails. The width between handrails shall be 20 inches (510 mm) minimum and 24 inches (610 mm) maximum. Handrail extensions required by 505.10.3 shall not be required on pool stairs.

❖ The reference to Section 504 in Section 1109.6.1 effectively requires two handrails along the pool stair (see Section 504.6). There must be a clear width between the handrails of 20 to 24 inches (510 to 610 mm) so that someone can use the handrails for bearing and stability on both sides at the same time. Due to concerns with possible handrail entrapment below the water level for other swimmers, there are no requirements for bottom handrail extensions.

1110 Shooting Facilities with Firing Positions

❖ Shooting facilities with firing positions are typically practice ranges. Where such facilities are provided, they can be inside or outside a building. Outside ranges can be open to the sky and surrounded by berms, or covered to provide protection from the sun and weather. They are typically separated by the type of equipment: rifles and shotguns; handguns or bows and arrows. They can be for shooting at stationary targets or moving targets, such as clay pigeons. The scoping provisions for firing positions are provided by the authority having jurisdiction. Typical requirements are 5 percent of each type provided (see Commentary Figure C1110 for examples).|

These provisions are not intended to address practice ranges where a person moves through a course, such as at a police or army training facility.

1110.1 Turning Space. A circular turning space complying with Section 304.3.1 with slopes not steeper than 1:48 shall be provided at shooting facility firing positions.

❖ An accessible firing position includes a level space that allows for a turning circle so someone can position left or right to fire at the target. Most people position their body at a 90-degree (1.57 rad) angle to the target to fire rifles or bows, but face the target when using a handgun.

Some interior ranges are set up as small divided booths, with a shelf to set your ammunition, ear protection or weapons on. Typically you fire over the shelf at the target. While not addressed in this section, at the accessible firing position, the top of the shelf should be low enough to allow a seated person to shoot over. Anthropometrics would suggest a shelf height of below 34 inches (865 mm). Knee and toe clearance may also be appropriate to consider depending on the depth of the shelf.

FIGURE C1110(a)
ARCHERY RANGE

FIGURE C1110(c)
RIFLE RANGE WITH CLAY PIGEONS

FIGURE C1110(b)
COVERED PISTOL RANGE

FIGURE C1110(d)
INDOOR PISTOL RANGE

Index

(continued)

(continued)

(continued)

(continued)

(continued)

(continued)

(continued)

(continued)

(continued)

(continued)

(continued)

(continued)